Praise for *J2EE™ Web Services*

"*J2EE™ Web Services* is written in the tradition [illegible] from author Richard Monson-Haefel. More than [illegible] ence, this essential guide is the way for J2EE deve[illegible] tecture and development."

—Floyd Marinescu
Author, *EJB Design Patterns*
Director, TheServerSide.com

"Written in a straightforward and approachable style, Monson-Haefel's latest book is a must-read for any Java developer who is serious about understanding and applying the J2EE APIs in support of Web services. By concentrating on the core technologies endorsed by the WS-I, it clearly explains why Web services will succeed in realizing the interoperability promise where previous attempts have failed."

—James McCabe
Software IT Architect
IBM

"This is the best—and most complete—description of J2EE Web services that I've seen. If you're a Java developer, you need this book."

—David Chappell
Chappell & Associates

"For Java Web service developers, this book is going to be there on their desk next to their PC for easy reference. The book has it all, clear guides as to what WSDL, SAAJ, UDDI are, and how they are used in a variety of examples. Monson-Haefel has created another classic with this volume."

—Dr. Bruce Scharlau
Department of Computing Science
University of Aberdeen, Scotland

"Richard Monson-Haefel provides the most comprehensive analysis of J2EE Web services that I've seen so far to date. This book covers the core Web services technologies (XML, SOAP, WSDL, and UDDI), as well as the Java APIs for Web services (JAX-RPC, SAAJ, JAXR, JAXP, and Web Services for J2EE, version 1.1). Richard also goes into detail on issues such as fault handling, type mapping, and JAX-RPC handlers. Developers will find this book to be a very valuable reference."

—Anne Thomas Manes
Research Director, Burton Group
Author, *Web Services: A Manager's Guide*

"*J2EE™ Web Services* is an excellent reference and tutorial for both beginning and seasoned Web services architects and developers. This book is the first to fully cover the WS-I 1.0 Web services standards and their integration with J2EE 1.4 components. Spend time with this book, and you'll soon master J2EE Web Services and be able to successfully use this technology to solve key business integration problems in your enterprise."

—Tom Marrs
Senior J2EE/XML/Web Services Architect
Distributed Computing Solutions, Inc.

J2EE™ Web Services

J2EE™ Web Services

Richard Monson-Haefel

Addison-Wesley

Boston • San Francisco • New York • Toronto • Montreal
London • Munich • Paris • Madrid • Capetown
Sydney • Tokyo • Singapore • Mexico City

The publisher offers discounts on this book when ordered in quantity for bulk purchases and special sales. For more information, please contact:

U.S. Corporate and Government Sales
(800) 382-3419
corpsales@pearsontechgroup.com

For sales outside of the U.S., please contact:

International Sales
(317) 581-3793
international@pearsontechgroup.com

Visit Addison-Wesley on the Web: www.awprofessional.com

Library of Congress Cataloging-in-Publication Data
Monson-Haefel, Richard.
J2EE Web services / Richard Monson-Haefel.
p. cm.
Includes bibliographical references and index.
ISBN 0-321-14618-2 (alk. paper)
1. Web services. 2. Internet programming. 3. Java (Computer program language) I. Title.

TK5105.88813.M66 2004
005.2'762—dc22

2003014346

ISBN: 0-321-14618-2
Text printed on recycled paper
1 2 3 4 5 6 7 8 9 10—CRS—0706050403
First printing, October 2003

Reproductions of woodblock prints by Katsushika Hokusai (1760–1849) courtesy of The Minneapolis Institute of Arts, Bequest of Richard P. Gale. Individual credits appear on page 841.

To my children, Henry and Olivia. I love you.

—Papa

Brief Contents

Contents

Chapter 18 The JAXR Technical Objects 545

Preface

This book is sharply focused. It concentrates on only those Web services standards that are sanctioned by the Web Services Interoperability Organization's Basic Profile 1.0, because these are the only standards that have been proven in production and are explicitly required by the J2EE Web Services platform. This book also covers only those J2EE APIs and components that are specific to Web services. The truth is, the primary Web service standards (XML, SOAP, WSDL, and UDDI), as well as the J2EE Web Services APIs (JAX-RPC, SAAJ, JAXR, and JAXP), are pretty complicated, and you are going to need to spend time studying this book in order to master them. That said, I think you will find this book to be a pretty easy read and an excellent desk-side reference.

Are Web Services Important?

Revolutionary technologies tend to take the media by storm and then eventually become ubiquitous. The World Wide Web, Java technology, and XML seem to be everywhere, don't they? Each of these technologies saw rapid adoption and today are considered essential ingredients of enterprise-level computing.

First introduced in 2000, Web services is also a revolutionary technology. It was introduced with a great deal of media hyperbole, but has since settled down to business and is just beginning to enjoy rapid adoption by the developer community. If you did not get involved in Web services before 2003, don't worry; you didn't miss much. The first two years should be considered experimental, the beta period of Web services. It was a time when the Web services community defined a cornucopia of specifications and discovered numerous real-world problems when attempting to make those specifications work in production. The year 2003, however, marks the beginning of hyperactive growth in Web services. If you are just jumping on board the Web services bandwagon, your timing couldn't be better. Consider yourself a pioneer of a revolutionary technology, and prepare to immerse yourself in one of the most important innovations in the history of distributed computing.

What Do I Need to Know to Read This Book?

This book is written for Java developers who want to learn about Web services and related APIs defined by J2EE 1.4. It is more of a reference than a tutorial, but many of the chapters have a tutorial-like style. This book is designed to *teach* J2EE Web Services and is more than a reference.

You must have experience in the Java programming language to read this book. If you don't, you'll find all the material after Chapter 9 difficult to understand. In addition, you should have some basic understanding of the J2EE platform. This book covers only the Web services functionality of J2EE, not other J2EE APIs or technologies.

To read this book, you do not need to know anything about XML, SOAP, WSDL, UDDI, or any of the J2EE Web Services APIs (JAX-RPC, SAAJ, JAXR, or JAXP). I've covered these topics in enough detail that I'm confident even a complete novice will be able to understand them.

What Does This Book Cover?

This book focuses only on the Web services standards and the J2EE 1.4 Web Services APIs and components—all other topics are deferred to other specialized books or to more general books. Specifically this book covers the following Web service standards:

- XML 1.0
- SOAP 1.1
- SOAP Messages with Attachments
- WSDL 1.1
- UDDI 2.0
- WS-I Basic Profile 1.0

The Web services standards take up the first third of the book, Chapters 1–8, while the rest of the book focuses on the J2EE Web Services APIs:

- JAX-RPC 1.1
- SAAJ 1.2
- JAXR 1.0
- JAXP 1.2

This book covers the use of the Web Services APIs as specified in J2EE 1.4 because version 1.4 is the first Java platform that fully embraces the Web service paradigm.

How Is This Book Organized?

The book is designed as a reference and a tutorial about J2EE Web Services. The chapters tend to build on one another. Once you read Part I on XML, you are prepared to read Part II on SOAP and WSDL. Similarly, before you read Part IV on JAX-RPC (Java API for XML-based RPC) you should understand XML, SOAP, and WSDL. Once you have read this book and understand J2EE Web services, it should continue to be very helpful as a reference. You can use it in your everyday work to look up information about Web service standards and the J2EE 1.4 Web Services APIs.

The book is divided into seven parts, each of which is made up of two or more chapters about a specific Web service standard or J2EE API, plus one introductory chapter. Each part begins with an introduction page that tells you how to read the chapters, and specifically which parts you really must read and which parts are optional reference material.

Every chapter is organized into four to five levels of headings labeled with a hierarchical dot notation. This labeling scheme is used in many specifications today, and is particularly useful for a reference book because it makes it much easier to discuss certain portions of the book with your colleagues. The book also includes appendices that cover important topics like XML regular expressions, Base64 encoding, DTDs, SOAP Messages with Attachments, and RPC/Encoded messaging.

The following outline of the book includes a short description of each chapter.

- **Chapter 1** summarizes the topics covered by this book, presents a brief architectural overview of J2EE 1.4, and provides abstracts about XML, SOAP, WSDL, UDDI, WS-I, JAX-RPC, SAAJ, JAXR, and JAXP.

Part I: XML

Chapters 2 and 3 cover in detail XML 1.0 and the XML Schema standard defined by the World Wide Web Consortium (W3C). This part assumes you have no prior knowledge of XML and explains the topic from the ground up.

- **Chapter 2** covers XML and XML namespaces.
- **Chapter 3** provides both basic and advanced coverage of the W3C's XML Schema standard.

Part II: SOAP and WSDL

Chapters 4 and 5 gently introduce SOAP 1.1 and WSDL 1.1. This part assumes you are already familiar with XML, XML namespaces, and XML schema as described in Part I.

- **Chapter 4** explains the structure of SOAP messages, terminology, and processing rules.
- **Chapter 5** covers WSDL 1.1.

Part III: UDDI

Chapters 6 through 8 provide a reference to the UDDI 2.0 data types, and to query and publishing methods. This part of the book assumes you are already familiar with XML, XML schema, SOAP, and WSDL as covered in Parts I and II.

- **Chapter 6** provides a gentle introduction to the UDDI data types.
- **Chapters 7 and 8** are pure reference material; they provide schema information about the UDDI Inquiry and Publishing APIs.

Part IV: JAX-RPC

Chapters 9 through 15 provide very detailed coverage of the entire Java API for XML-based RPC (JAX-RPC), version 1.1. This part assumes you already know XML, XML schema, SOAP, and WSDL.

- **Chapter 9** introduces various features of JAX-RPC.
- **Chapter 10** covers JAX-RPC service endpoints (JSEs) and their relationship to the servlet container system.
- **Chapter 11** covers EJB endpoints, EJB stateless session beans that act as Web services.
- **Chapter 12** studies in detail the JAX-RPC client APIs you will use to communicate with other Web services.
- **Chapter 13** covers the use of SAAJ 1.2.
- **Chapter 14** describes the use and configuration of message handlers, which are used to pre- and post-process SOAP messages.
- **Chapter 15** covers Java-to-WSDL and Java-to-XML mapping, which describes how XML and WSDL types are translated into Java code.

Part V: JAXR

Chapters 16 through 19 cover in detail the Java API for XML Registries (JAXR), version 1.0. Specifically they explain how to use the JAXR API to publish and query information in a UDDI registry.

- **Chapter 16** gives you an overview of JAXR and helps you prepare for subsequent chapters.
- **Chapter 17 and 18** present a detailed study of the JAXR domain objects that are mapped to UDDI data types.
- **Chapter 19** covers the JAXR Inquiry and Publishing APIs, which can be used to query, add, and update information in a UDDI registry.

Part VI: JAXP

Chapters 20 and 21 serve as a primer on the Java API for XML Processing, version 1.2. Specifically they cover the use of SAX2 and DOM 2.

- **Chapter 20** covers SAX2, the event-driven XML parser API.
- **Chapter 21** covers the DOM 2 XML parser API.

Part VII: Deployment

Chapters 22 through 24 provide a detailed study of the XML deployment descriptors used in J2EE Web Services, as well as an overview of JAR packaging and deployment.

- **Chapter 22** covers general J2EE deployment descriptors used for deploying JSEs and EJB endpoints.
- **Chapter 23** covers the Web service-specific deployment descriptors as defined by the Web Services for J2EE (WS-J2EE) specification.
- **Chapter 24** covers the JAX-RPC mapping file, which determines how WSDL and XML types are mapped to Java interfaces and Java beans.

What Doesn't This Book Cover?

As I said at the start of this preface, this book focuses only on standard Web service technologies and the core J2EE 1.4 Web Services APIs. There is simply too much material in this book to allow for coverage of other topics.

Non-Web Service Aspects of the J2EE Platform

Although this book provides detailed coverage of the J2EE 1.4 Web Services APIs, as well as an overview of servlets and EJBs, J2EE is too large a topic to cover comprehensively. It's expected that you have some general knowledge about J2EE or that you will seek to learn more about the J2EE platform and APIs unrelated to Web services from other resources.

> *The author of this book has written two other J2EE books:* Enterprise JavaBeans *(Fourth Edition, O'Reilly 2004) and* Java Message Service *(with David A. Chappell, O'Reilly, 2000).*

Vendor-Specific Configuration and Administration

There is a wide variety of J2EE platforms for you to choose from: BEA's WebLogic, IBM's WebSphere, Sun Microsystems' Sun ONE, Oracle9*i* Application Server, IONA's Application Server Platform, Apple WebObjects, Borland Enterprise Server, Pramati's Pramati Server, the Apache J2EE, jBoss and ObjectWeb open source projects, and many others. While each of these platforms adheres to the J2EE specification, they all specify very different procedures and interfaces for installing, configuring, and deploying applications. Because the administration of each J2EE platform is different, this book doesn't attempt to cover installation, configuration, or deployment except in terms of standard J2EE requirements. To learn about vendor-specific administration and configuration requirements, please consult the vendor's documentation.

Other Web Service "Standards"

There are a number of new Web service standards that have been proposed by various organizations (W3C, OASIS, ebXML, and IBM/Microsoft) including things like DISCO, WSCI, BTP, WS-Security, DIME, etc. Many of these proposed standards actually conflict or compete with each other. It's unclear which of them will become Web service standards and which of them will die on the vine, so this book covers only the core, WS-I Approved Web service protocols.

Acknowledgments

It takes a village to produce a book, and this one is no exception. While my name is on the cover, there are many other people without whose help this book would not have been published.

First and foremost, I would like to thank Mary O'Brien of Addison-Wesley for convincing me to join the AW family and providing guidance while I was writing this book. Mary's merry band of professionals at AW were also very helpful, including Amy Fleischer, Brenda Mulligan, Jim Markham, Debby VanDijk, Laurie McGuire, Jerry Votta, John Fuller, Julie Nahil, Kelli Brooks, Stephanie Hiebert, and Kathy Glidden. In addition, I would like to thank Vicki Hochstedler for the beautiful typesetting, Dick Hannus for his work on the book's cover, Janis Owens for the striking interior design, Altova for the free copy of xmlspy, the Minneapolis Institute of Art for the use of the beautiful Japanese woodblock prints, and Brian Christeson, the best content editor in the business.

While working on this book I was very fortunate to have the help of some of the world's foremost experts on J2EE and Web services. I owe a special debt of gratitude to Don Box, Anne Thomas Manes, Roberto Chinnici, David Chappell, Elliotte Rusty Harold, Scott Seeley, Mike Champion, Pete Hendry, James McCabe, Bruce Scharlau, Jean-Jacques Moreau, Duncan Donald Davidson, Farrukh Najmi, Kathy Walsh, Tom Marrs, Iyad Elayyan, Mike Hendrickson, Anthony Robie, and Douglas Barry. All of these individuals volunteered to review some or all of this book before it was published. Without their help, this book would not have been possible.

I'm also thankful for the many people who answered technical questions for me while I was writing this book, among them Jim Knutson, Bill Shannon, Rahul Sharma, Russell Butek, Simon Fell, Tim Ewald, Zdenek Svoboda, Bill Venners, John D. Mitchell, Kyle Brown, Scott Ziegler, Seth White, Mark Hapner, Ping Wang, and Paul Garvie.

Finally, I would like to thank my wife, Hollie, who gave me love and support and managed to take care of everything else in my life while I focused on this book.

Chapter 1

An Overview of J2EE 1.4 Web Services

In a nutshell, J2EE Web Services is about interoperability. That goal is perhaps the most important thing to remember while reading this book. Not just interoperability between different brands of J2EE application servers, but between J2EE servers and any other Web services platform, including the .NET Framework, Perl, Apache Axis, Python, and C++, to name a few. Web service technologies provide J2EE with an opportunity to become truly interoperable with any other system. That's because Web service technologies are platform-agnostic; in other words, the medium used to communicate is not specific to any combination of programming language, operating system, and hardware.

At the heart of J2EE Web Services interoperability, and of Web services interoperability in general, is the **Basic Profile 1.0** (**BP**), published by the **Web Services Interoperability Organization** (**WS-I**). The BP provides a set of rules that govern how applications make use of common Web service technologies so that everyone is speaking the same language. The BP makes Web service interoperability practical, and coverage of it is a critical aspect of this book.

Although this book assumes you will want to develop Web services that comply with WS-I, only J2EE 1.4 vendors are required to support the BP. It's not mandatory that you use it. In fact, J2EE 1.4 Web Services APIs are also required to support technologies that don't conform to the BP, like SOAP Messages with Attachments and RPC/Encoded messaging. These two non-BP-conformant technologies are covered in appendices.

The purpose of this chapter is to provide an architectural overview of the J2EE 1.4 platform, Web service technologies, and the J2EE 1.4 Web Services APIs. Before you read any further, you should read the Preface if you haven't already, because it provides important information on the scope and organization of this book.

1.1 The J2EE Platform

The **J2EE (Java 2 Platform, Enterprise Edition)** specification describes how a variety of enterprise Java APIs are integrated into a complete platform. Specifically, the J2EE 1.4 specification tells us how an application server configures and deploys Enterprise JavaBeans (EJB) 2.1, Java Servlets 2.4, and JavaServer Pages (JSP) 2.0 components, and manages them at runtime. The J2EE specification also tells us how these server-side components interact with each other, the application server, and resource APIs like Java Database Connectivity (JDBC) and Java Message Service (JMS). Figure 1–1 shows the various components and APIs supported by the J2EE specification.

Figure 1–1 doesn't show a lot of detail, but it does give you an overview of the J2EE architecture. The EJB and servlet/JSP components reside in their own containers, which manage their life cycles, incoming and outgoing messages, transactions, security, and other qualities of service. EJB and Servlet/JSP components have access to all of the resource APIs, such as Web Services, J2EE Connectors (including JDBC), JMS, JavaMail, Security, Transactions, and J2EE Management APIs. The entire platform is built on the Java 2 Platform, Standard Edition (J2SE) 1.4, and runs in one or more Java Virtual Machines.

The J2EE specification depends on several other specifications. For example, the programming model and behavior of the EJB components are described in a separate EJB specification; the same is true of the servlet and JSP components as well as the J2EE Connector, JDBC, JMS, JavaMail, JMX, and other resource APIs. It's the job

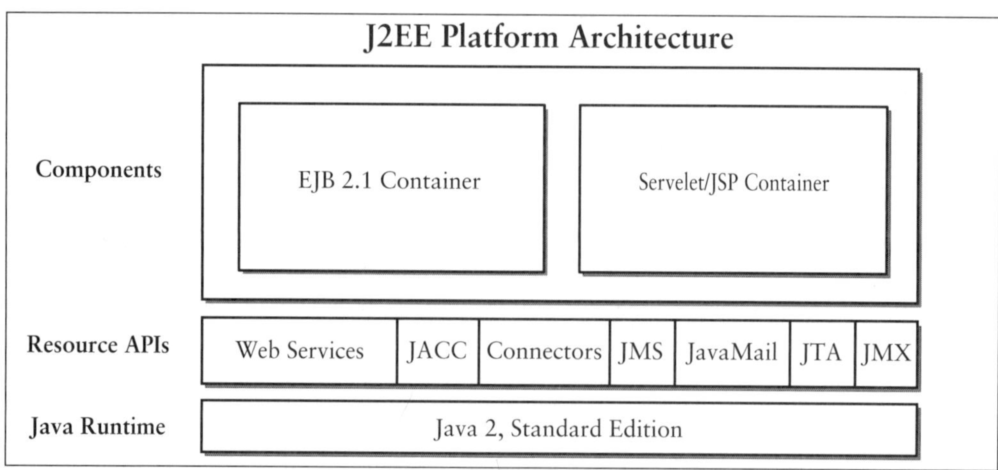

Figure 1–1 The J2EE Platform

of the J2EE specification to glue all of these specifications together. As I mentioned in the Preface, this book doesn't go into detail about J2EE components or APIs other than those related to Web services—the J2EE platform is simply too big. That said, this book does cover the J2EE Web Services components and APIs in detail.

The Web services components and APIs are actually described by the Web Services for J2EE 1.1 specification. WS-J2EE 1.1 requires compliance with the WS-I Basic Profile 1.0. The BP is discussed later in this chapter.

The primary goal of J2EE is portability of components and developer skills. Because every J2EE vendor must support exactly the same server-side component models (EJBs, servlets, and JSPs) you can expect the components that you developed for J2EE brand A to run on J2EE brand B—with a little bit of work. Unfortunately, component portability in J2EE is not as simple as originally envisioned because each J2EE vendor provides very different configuration and deployment facilities. That said, portability in J2EE is far simpler than in any of J2EE's predecessors, including CORBA and DCE components.

In addition to component portability, J2EE offers developer portability. A developer who learns to develop components on one vendor's J2EE platform can easily transfer those skills to another vendor's. Of course, the developer may have to learn new procedures for deployment and server administration, but otherwise the J2EE developer's skills are applicable to any brand of J2EE.

While portability has been the main focus of J2EE, interoperability, specifically the ability of one brand of J2EE application server to talk to another, has recently become an important focus as well. In the past interoperability was based on the CORBA IIOP protocol, which is fine in theory but in practice is difficult to get working properly. CORBA interoperability has never been easy with pure CORBA products, and that trend continues with J2EE products.

As of J2EE 1.4, however, interoperability takes a new shape in the form of Web services, the topic of this book. Specifically, this book covers the four primary Web service standards (XML, SOAP, WSDL, and UDDI) and the J2EE 1.4 Web Services APIs (JAX-RPC, SAAJ, JAXR, and JAXP). The next two sections provide an overview of Web services, the Web service standards, and the J2EE Web Services APIs.

1.2 The Technologies of Web Services

The term **Web services** has many different definitions, depending on your perspective. Some definitions that have been proposed by the media and Web services experts are so ambiguous as to be almost useless. This is not the fault of the people who have tried to define the term. They are simply attempting to verbalize something that has, until recently, been a somewhat sketchy idea.

In the J2EE 1.4 environment, however, the term "Web services" has a very specific meaning, which is based on a standard adopted by Sun Microsystems, Microsoft,

IBM, BEA, Software AG, and just about every other major enterprise vendor. In a nutshell, Web services can be defined as follows:

> ***A Web service is a software application that conforms to the Web Service Interoperability Organization's Basic Profile 1.0.***

That's a bit of a mouthful, but it's probably the most exact definition of the term you will encounter today. Before the WS-I defined the Basic Profile 1.0, the term "Web service" was simply too general to fulfill the technology's main purpose, interoperability. In other words, the main purpose of Web service technologies is to allow applications on different platforms to exchange business data. Web service technologies are used for **Application-to-Application (A2A)** integration or **Business-to-Business (B2B)** communication. A2A refers to disparate applications within a single organization communicating and exchanging data—A2A is also known as **Enterprise Application Integration (EAI)**. B2B refers to multiple organizations, typically business partners, exchanging data. Web service technologies today are used mostly in A2A/EAI settings, but they are also seeing growth in the B2B arena.

For a computer programmer, interoperability is the capability of two different software applications to communicate. For example, the ability to access an application written in C++ running on Windows from a Java application running on Linux is a matter of interoperability. In order for a Java application on a Linux platform to access a C++ application on a Windows platform, you have to use network technologies that are independent of both the operating system and the hardware. This capability is already met by TCP/IP, DNS, and HTTP, and the Web service standards: XML, SOAP, WSDL, and UDDI.

XML (eXtensible Markup Language), SOAP (Simple Object Access Protocol), WSDL (Web Services Description Language), and **UDDI (Universal Description, Discovery, and Integration)** are used in concert to provide Web service applications with a type system (XML), a messaging protocol (SOAP), an interface definition language (WSDL), and a registry for publishing Web services (UDDI). XML documents contain the information being exchanged between two parties, while SOAP provides a packaging and routing standard for exchanging XML documents over a network. WSDL allows an organization to describe the types of XML documents and SOAP messages that must be used to interact with their Web services. Finally, UDDI allows organizations to register their Web services in a uniform manner within a common directory, so clients can locate their Web services and learn how to access them. Figure 1–2 shows how these pieces fit together in a Web service interaction between two parties.

The first three parts of this book cover XML, SOAP, WSDL, and UDDI. These core Web services technologies are also the basis of J2EE 1.4 Web Services. Each of the J2EE Web Services APIs (JAX-RPC, SAAJ, JAXR, JAXP) conforms with one or more of the Web services technologies, so developing a fundamental understanding of XML, SOAP, WSDL, and UDDI is crucial to understanding how J2EE 1.4 Web Services works. In addition to the specifications of XML, SOAP, WSDL, and UDDI,

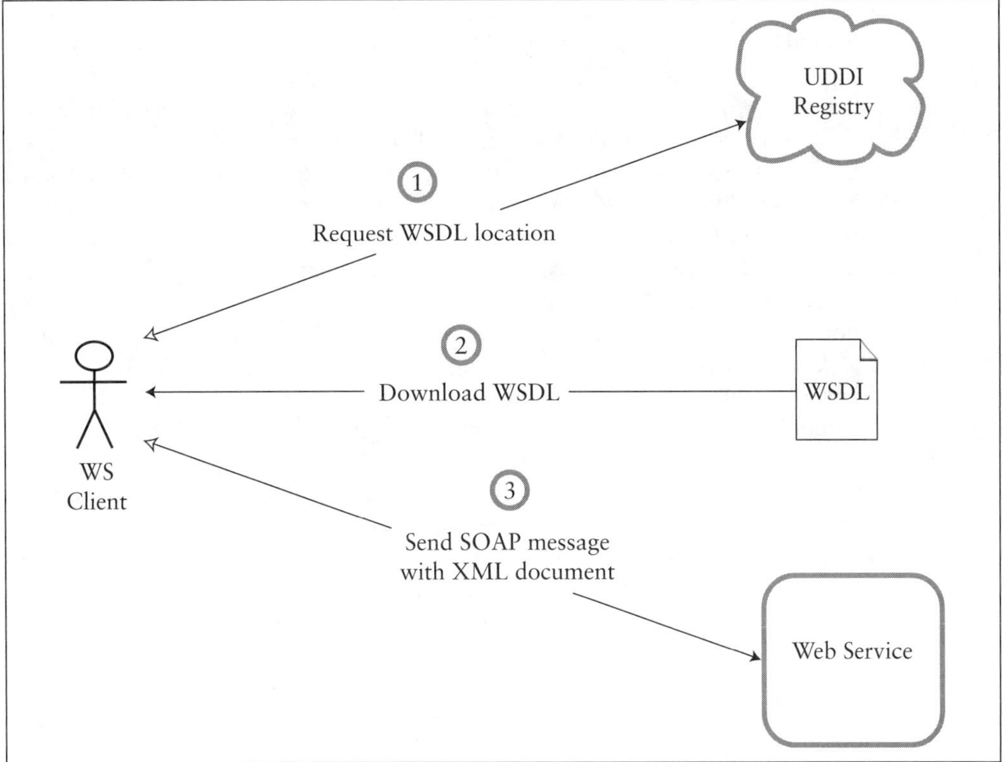

Figure 1–2 Web Services Interaction Diagram

this book covers the WS-I Basic Profile 1.0, which is necessary to ensure interoperability across a broad range of platforms. The rest of this section provides an overview of the WS-I Basic Profile 1.0, XML 1.0, SOAP 1.1, WSDL 1.1, and UDDI 2.0. These topics are covered in more detail in Parts I through III.

1.2.1 WS-I Basic Profile 1.0

The Web Services Interoperability Organization is an organization of Web services vendors that are committed to defining a standard for Web services interoperability. The first deliverable of the WS-I was the Basic Profile 1.0, which details how to use the four primary Web services specifications together in Web services. The BP defines a set of conformance rules that clear up ambiguities in the specifications of XML, WSDL, SOAP, and UDDI, and defines in concrete terms how to use these technologies in concert to register, describe, and communicate with Web services.

The BP is necessary because the primary specifications are too broad and open to interpretation to make interoperability a given. For example, WSDL is a very generalized technology, which allows you to describe any kind of Web service. Unfortunately, WSDL is so general that it's difficult in some circumstances to determine exactly how, for example, a SOAP message exchanged with the Web service should be formatted. In addition, WSDL defines features that have, in practice, made interoperability more difficult, such as the SMTP and MIME bindings. The BP fixes these interoperability problems by telling us exactly how WSDL should describe SOAP-based Web services, and by restricting the use of WSDL.

No one is required to adhere to the BP, but doing so makes interoperability a lot easier. When you encounter a Web service that conforms with the BP, you have a much easier time locating and communicating with that Web service than you have with a non-conformant Web service. To be perfectly honest, interoperability without the BP is pretty difficult to achieve. While XML, SOAP, WSDL, and UDDI have important roles, their use together is not well coordinated because each specification was developed independently. The BP defines the glue that binds these technologies together into one coherent specification.

Microsoft, IBM, Sun Microsystems, BEA, and many others have agreed to support the BP, which means you should be able to communicate with WS-I-conformant Web services hosted by products from any of these vendors with little or no interoperability problems. The BP makes reality of what was basically a pipe dream in the past; it makes it possible to define applications that are interoperable across most application platforms.

The BP is the specification around which this book revolves, because J2EE 1.4 vendors are required to support it. This book assumes you will want to develop applications that conform to the BP because, if they don't, general interoperability simply isn't practical. Unless you have complete control over all the parties involved in a B2B or A2A system, defining a Web service that is interoperable with arbitrary systems is very difficult, if not impossible. The BP makes it possible to define Web services that are easily understood and operated on by any application written in any programming language (Java, C++, C#, Perl, et al.), on any operating system (Unix, Microsoft, Linux, Mac, et al.), using any development platform (the .NET Framework, WebLogic Application Server, WebSphere Application Server, et al.)

Although the BP is important, there is no chapter dedicated to the subject. Instead, this book addresses the requirements of the BP on Web service technologies and J2EE 1.4 Web Service APIs as they come up—directly in the text of each chapter. You'll know when you are seeing a BP-conformance rule because I will explicitly call it out, or will append the superscript [BP] to the end of a sentence that states a BP-conformance rule.

1.2.2 XML

XML (**eXtensible Markup Language**) is used to organize documents and business data. XML files can be stored or transmitted between two applications on a network. Basically, they are just plain text documents that contain special tags that label different parts of a document or fields of data. For example, the XML document in Listing 1–1 contains Amazon.com's mailing address.

Listing 1–1

Sample XML Document

```
<?xml version="1.0" encoding="UTF-8"?>
<address>
   <name>Amazon.com</name>
   <street>1516 2nd Ave</street>
   <city>Seattle</city>
   <state>WA</state>
   <zip>90952</zip>
</address>
```

Notice how each piece of data (name, street, city, state, and zip) is demarcated by a pair of tags, such as `<name>` and `</name>`. This syntax makes it very easy to tell where a field of data begins and ends, and what it represents. The address information in Listing 1–1 might be stored in a text file or sent across the network to another application, perhaps to synchronize mailing information in a database.

XML is the foundation for all the other Web services technologies, so having a good understanding of XML is critical. Part I (Chapters 2 and 3) of this book provides a detailed overview of XML and XML schema, which is the typing system used to validate the contents of XML documents.

Currently there is only one version, XML 1.0, which is managed by the World Wide Web Consortium (W3C).[1] XML is dialect of SGML, which the publishing industry and the U.S. military among others have used for years to provide structure to written documents. Although XML has its roots in SGML, it has greatly surpassed its parent in popularity and usefulness.

1.2.3 SOAP

When we think of Web services, we are basically discussing the exchange of XML documents, or data that is organized into an XML format. Although XML is an excellent technology for exchanging business data, until SOAP came along there was no widely accepted standard for routing and packaging XML data exchanged between two applications on a network. If you wanted to build an EAI or B2B system based on XML, you had to define your own networking, addressing, and routing protocols, or use a proprietary system provided by a vendor. No two vendors were using the same protocols for exchanging data, so interoperability was

[1] XML 1.1 is currently a W3C candidate recommendation.

difficult, to say the least. Before SOAP, interoperability usually required tedious custom-built solutions to get any two XML-based systems to communicate.

SOAP (from **Simple Object Access Protocol**) defines a standard packaging format for transmitting XML data between applications on a network. It is not specific to any programming language, product, or hardware platform, so it can be used by just about any kind of application (C++, Java, .NET, Perl, legacy systems, and others). A SOAP message is just an XML document. SOAP is specially designed, however, to contain and transmit other XML documents as well as information related to routing, processing, security, transactions, and other qualities of service. For example, Listing 1–2 shows a SOAP message that contains XML address information. This message might be sent from one application to another to synchronize contact information on two different systems.

Listing 1–2

A SOAP Message That Contains Address Information

```
<?xml version="1.0" encoding="UTF-8"?>
<soap:Envelope
 xmlns:soap="http://schemas.xmlsoap.org/soap/envelope/"
 xmlns:addr="http://www.Monson-Haefel.com/jwsbook/ADDR" >
  <soap:Body>
    <addr:address>
      <addr:name>Amazon.com</addr:name>
      <addr:street>1516 2nd Ave</addr:street>
      <addr:city>Seattle</addr:city>
      <addr:state>WA</addr:state>
      <addr:zip>90952</addr:zip>
    </addr:address>
  </soap:Body>
</soap:Envelope>
```

SOAP takes advantage of advanced XML features like **XML namespaces** (similar to Java package names) and **XML schemas** (used to type data), all of which are covered in detail in Part I of this book. The important thing to understand at this point is that SOAP messages serve as a network envelope for exchanging XML documents and data. Having a single industry standard for packaging and exchanging XML data makes Web service applications more interoperable, more understandable, and easier to implement. Part II (Chapters 4 and 5) provides a very detailed discussion of the SOAP messaging protocol and processing requirements, as described by the SOAP 1.1 and WS-I Basic Profile 1.0 standards.

There are actually two versions of SOAP today, versions 1.1 and 1.2. SOAP 1.1 was defined as a Note by the W3C in 2000 and has been the basis for most Web services development since that time. The BP requires the use of SOAP 1.1 and provides a number of clarifications and restrictions that largely eliminate interoperability problems associated with this sometimes poorly specified standard. SOAP 1.2 wasn't finalized until 2003 and, while it represents a significant improvement over SOAP 1.1, adoption of SOAP 1.2 by vendors may take a while because they are currently focused on providing solutions based on SOAP 1.1 and the BP. This book covers only SOAP 1.1—SOAP 1.2 was only in draft form when this book was written, and it's not supported by J2EE 1.4 Web Services.

There is an ancillary specification called **SOAP Messages with Attachments** (**SwA**) that is covered in Appendix E. SwA defines a message format for attaching binary data (images, sound files, documents, and so on) to SOAP messages. Although SwA is not sanctioned by the BP, support for it is required by the J2EE 1.4 Web Services specifications—SwA will also be supported in the next version of the BP, version 1.1, which is still in development.

1.2.4 WSDL

WSDL (**Web Services Description Language**) is a standard for describing the structure of the XML data exchanged between two systems using SOAP. When you create a new Web service, you can also create a WSDL document that describes the type of data you're exchanging. WSDL is complicated and unless you're already familiar with it an example WSDL document will make no sense at all. Suffice it to say that WSDL is based on XML. It's used to describe the SOAP messages that can be transmitted between Web service clients and servers. WSDL is covered in detail in Part II of this book.

There are two versions of WSDL today, versions 1.1 and 1.2. Like SOAP 1.1, WSDL 1.1 was defined as a Note by the W3C (February 2001) and has been used a lot in Web services development. WSDL 1.1 is a good specification, but its flexibility creates interoperability problems. The BP requires the use of WSDL 1.1, but also provides strict rules on how it's used, to improve interoperability. WSDL 1.2 wasn't completed when this book was being written, and is not supported by J2EE 1.4 Web Services, so it's not covered by this book.

1.2.5 UDDI

Although WSDL provides an excellent format for describing the types of SOAP messages used by a Web service, it provides no guidance on where to store the WSDL documents or how to find them. In other words, WSDL doesn't describe where the WSDL documents should be kept so that others can find them easily and use them to communicate with your Web services.

UDDI (**Universal Description, Discovery, and Integration**) defines a standard set of Web service operations (methods) that are used to store and look up information about other Web service applications. In other words, UDDI defines a standard SOAP-based interface for a Web services registry. You can use a UDDI registry to find a particular type of Web service, or to find out about the Web services hosted by a specific organization. A UDDI registry is often referred to as a "Yellow Pages" for Web services. When you look up information about a Web service in a UDDI registry, you can narrow your search using various categories (technologies used, business types, industry, and so on). Each entry in a UDDI registry provides information on where the Web service is located and how to communicate with it.[2] The UDDI registry also provides information about the organization that hosts a particular Web service.

The UDDI specification is now maintained by the **Organization for the Advancement of Structured Information Standards** (**OASIS**), but was originally created by Microsoft and IBM, which led a multi-vendor organization called UDDI.org. The UDDI.org has set up a free UDDI registry open to everyone—something like a Yahoo! for Web services. Most UDDI registries, however, are private systems deployed by individual companies or trade organizations. For example, a very large organization like General Electric might set up a private UDDI registry that contains information about all the Web service applications offered within the corporation. Another example is a trade organization, like the Association of American Manufacturers, which might set up a UDDI registry that contains information about all its members and their Web service applications.

Of the four principal Web services technologies, UDDI is the only one the BP says is optional. You don't have to use UDDI, but if you need a Web service registry, UDDI is the preferred technology. UDDI is covered in detail in Part III (Chapters 6–8).

There are three versions of UDDI at this time, versions 1.0, 2.0, and 3.0. The BP specifies the use of UDDI version 2.0, the one covered by this book. While version 3.0 is more recent, it was only newly completed when the BP was finalized and so wasn't supported by enough vendors for the WS-I to consider it.

1.3 The J2EE Web Service APIs

Parts IV through VI of this book cover the four **J2EE Web Service APIs:** JAX-RPC, SAAJ, JAXR, and JAXP. These are the APIs you will need to understand if you want to implement Web service applications using the J2EE platform. Perhaps the most important Web service API is JAX-RPC, which is used to implement J2EE Web service clients and endpoints (services). A substantial portion of this book (seven chapters) covers JAX-RPC.

1.3.1 JAX-RPC

You can think of **JAX-RPC** (**Java API for XML-based RPC**) as Java RMI over SOAP. While this characterization provides a good vantage point for learning about JAX-RPC, it's not the complete story. You can obtain a good understanding of JAX-RPC only by studying it in detail. Part IV (Chapters 9–15) provides detailed coverage of JAX-RPC.

[2] UDDI can also store data about other types of services, such as a Web site or a phone service. This book, however, is concerned only with UDDI's role in Web services.

JAX-RPC is divided into two parts: a set of client-side APIs, and a set of server-side components, called **endpoints.** The client-side APIs allow you to communicate with Web service endpoints hosted on some other platform. For example, you can use one of the client-side APIs to send SOAP messages to a VB.NET or an Apache Axis Web service. The client-side APIs can be used from standalone Java applications or from J2EE components like servlets, JSPs, or EJBs. There are three client-side APIs: **generated stub, dynamic proxy,** and **DII** (**Dynamic Invocation Interface**). The generated stub is the one you will use the most, and its semantics closely resemble those of Java RMI. The dynamic proxy API also follows many of the Java RMI semantics, but is used less often. The DII is a very low-level API used primarily by vendor tools, but can also be employed by Web services developers if necessary.

The server-side components include the **JAX-RPC service endpoint** (**JSE**) and the **EJB endpoint.** The JSE component is actually a type of servlet that has been adapted for use as a Web services component. It's very easy to implement, yet it has access to the full array of services and interfaces common to servlets. The EJB endpoint is simply a type of stateless session EJB that has been adapted for use as a Web service endpoint. The EJB endpoint provides all the transactional and security features of a normal stateless session bean, but it's specifically designed to process SOAP requests.

There are currently two versions of JAX-RPC, 1.0 and 1.1. Version 1.0 is used with J2EE 1.3, while version 1.1 is used with J2EE 1.4. The primary difference between 1.0 and 1.1 is that 1.1 is required to conform with the BP. Because this book focuses on BP-conformant applications, version 1.0 is not covered in this book.

1.3.2 SAAJ

SAAJ (**SOAP with Attachments API for Java**) is a low-level SOAP API that complies with SOAP 1.1 and the SOAP Messages with Attachments specification. SAAJ allows you to build SOAP messages from scratch as well as read and manipulate SOAP messages. You can use it alone to create, transmit, and process SOAP messages, but you're more likely to use it in conjunction with JAX-RPC. In JAX-RPC, SAAJ is used primarily to process SOAP header blocks (the SOAP message meta-data). Chapter 13 covers the SAAJ API in detail.

Although the BP does not support SOAP Messages with Attachments, J2EE 1.4 requires SwA, so it's covered in Appendix F: SAAJ Attachments.

1.3.3 JAXR

JAXR (**Java API for XML Registries**) provides an API for accessing UDDI registries. It simplifies the process of publishing and searching for Web service endpoints. JAXR was originally intended for ebXML registries, a standard that competes with UDDI, but was adapted for UDDI and works pretty well in most cases.

JAXR has a set of business-domain types like `Organization`, `PostalAddress`, and `Contact` as well as technical-domain types like `ServiceBinding`, `ExternalLink`, and `Classification`. These domain models map nicely to UDDI data types. JAXR also defines APIs for publishing and searching for information in a UDDI registry. There is only one version of JAXR, version 1.0, which is the subject of Part V (Chapters 16–19) of this book.

1.3.4 JAXP

JAXP (Java API for XML Processing) provides a framework for using DOM 2 and SAX2, standard Java APIs that read, write, and modify XML documents.

DOM 2 (Document Object Model, Level 2) is a Java API that models XML documents as trees of objects. It contains objects that represent elements, attributes, values, and so on. DOM 2 is used a lot in situations where speed and memory are *not* factors, but complex manipulation of XML documents is required. DOM 2 is also the basis of SAAJ 1.1.

SAX2 (Simple API for XML, version 2) is very different in functionality from DOM 2. When a SAX parser reads an XML document, it fires events as it encounters start and end tags, attributes, values, etc. You can register listeners for these events, and they will be notified as the SAX2 parser detects changes in the XML document it is reading.

JAXP comes in several versions including 1.1, 1.2, and 1.3. Version 1.3 is very new and is not supported by J2EE 1.4 Web Services. Instead, J2EE 1.4 requires support for JAXP 1.2, which is the subject of Part VI (Chapters 20 and 21) in this book.

1.4 Wrapping Up

The Web service standards and J2EE 1.4 APIs covered in this book do not represent the full complement of Web service technologies available today. Web services is a fast-growing field, and it seems like a new messaging standard or API is released every week. The Web services technologies this book covers, however, are the ones that are absolutely fundamental to understanding the others. Before you can learn about Web services security, orchestration, transactions, and the like, you must first have a complete and clear understanding of XML, SOAP, WSDL, and to a lesser extent UDDI. This book provides you with an in-depth study of these fundamentals so that you will be prepared to implement interoperable Web service clients and services using the J2EE 1.4 platform. This book also provides you with a solid foundation for learning about new and future standards that have recently been introduced, but have yet to prove themselves in production.

Throughout this book, particular care is given to framing most discussions in the context of the Web Services Interoperability Organization's Basic Profile 1.0. If you have worked with Web service technologies in the past and have had a chance to study the BP, then you will probably appreciate why it's so important. To be completely blunt: I do not believe general Web service interoperability with anonymous parties is actually feasible without the guidance of the WS-I Basic Profile 1.0. Experienced Web service developers can tell you numerous interoperability horror stories related to the loose language and broad visions defined by standards like SOAP, WSDL, and UDDI. The WS-I Basic Profile eliminates many, if not all, of the ambiguities inherent in these primary standards, finally making interoperability among disparate Web service platforms (.NET, J2EE, Apache Axis, Perl, etc.) possible.

Part I

XML

It's important that you have a good understanding of XML, XML namespaces, and the W3C XML Schema Language before proceeding, because these technologies are fundamental to understanding SOAP and WSDL, which are the foundation of Web Services as defined by J2EE and the WS-I Basic Profile 1.0.

While most developers understand and have used basic XML, many have not used XML namespaces or the W3C XML Schema Language, so the emphasis of this first part of the book is on these two topics. Chapter 2 includes two major sections: Section 2.1: XML Primer, which you can skip if you are already familiar with basic XML concepts, and Section 2.2: XML Namespaces, which you should read if XML is new to you.

Chapter 3 covers the W3C XML Schema Language, which you need to understand before you can understand SOAP, WSDL, and UDDI. If you've never worked with the W3C XML Schema Language before, you should read at least the first section of Chapter 3, Section 3.1: XML Schema Basics. The second section in Chapter 3, Section 3.2: Advanced XML Schema, covers more advanced and somewhat trickier features.

The XML schema is very rich and includes a lot of features not covered by Chapter 3—it actually requires an entire book to cover all the features of the W3C XML Schema Language. The bibliography includes a book recommendation for this topic, but the material in Chapter 3 should satisfy most of your needs.

As a supplement to this part of the book, Appendix A covers XML DTDs (document type definitions). The use of DTDs is very common, which is why it's covered in this book. The W3C XML Schema Language is the preferred mechanism for describing and validating the structure of XML documents in Web services, however, so DTDs are not given much attention other than in Appendix A.

In This Part

Related Appendices

Chapter 2
XML Basics

XML is the basic building block of Web services. All the Web services technologies specified by the WS-I Basic Profile 1.0 are built on XML and the W3C XML Schema Language. This chapter covers the XML fundamentals you'll need to understand before learning about W3C XML Schema Language. Section 2.1 covers the basic XML syntax, including elements, attributes, and CDATA sections. If you've never worked with XML before, then this first section will give you a jump-start. Section 2.2 covers XML namespaces, which you must understand in order to learn about the W3C XML Schema Language. If you have not used XML namespaces before, even if you're already conversant with XML generally, you should read Section 2.2.

2.1 XML Primer

The **eXtensible Markup Language** (**XML**) is a meta-language—a language for defining other languages—defined by a specification. It's not a product you can buy—although there are lots of products for sale that work with XML. As a specification, XML defines the rules for creating **XML markup languages.** An XML markup language defines a set of **tags** that are used to organize and describe text. Tags are usually paired; together, a **start tag,** an **end tag,** and everything between them are called an **element.** For example, you could save the addresses of your friends, family members, and business associates in a text file using XML as in Listing 2–1. Note the nesting of some elements inside others.

Listing 2–1

XML Address Document

```
<?xml version="1.0" encoding="UTF-8" ?>
<addresses>
   <address category="friend">
       <name>Bill Frankenfiller</name>
       <street>3243 West 1st Ave.</street>
       <city>Madison</city>
       <state>WI</state>
       <zip>53591</zip>
   </address>
   <address category="business">
       <name>Amazon.com</name>
       <street>1516 2nd Ave</street>
       <city>Seattle</city>
       <state>WA</state>
       <zip>90952</zip>
   </address>
</addresses>
```

Even if you don't know anything about XML, Listing 2–1 is pretty self-explanatory. It's easy to figure out which data is the street information and which is the city, and where each address begins and ends. That the organization of the information is so obvious is XML's greatest strength. It's self-describing; that is, not only does XML organize text into a hierarchy, it describes its organization directly in the text. Compare this to other text formats like comma-delimited or tab-delimited data. To understand the contents of the text you are reading, you need to look at a separate document that describes the organization of the data. With XML referring to an extra document is not necessary; the organization and description are immediately apparent.

Each of the elements in Listing 2–1 contains other elements or text. These elements can be identified by the label used in their start and end tags. The elements in Listing 2–1 are `addresses`, `address`, `name`, `street`, `city`, `state`, and `zip`. Elements are discussed in more detail a little later, in Section 2.1.2.2.

XML documents are composed of Unicode text (usually UTF-8), so people as well as software can understand them. In other words, you can open an XML document and read it in any text editor (vi, Emacs, MS Word, and others). Because XML's syntactical rules are strict, however, you can also parse and manipulate it with a variety of software tools, many of which are open source or otherwise free. Compare XML's transparency to non-text formats such as PDF and most relational database file formats, which contain binary data in opaque proprietary formats. Non-text documents cannot be understood by a person using a common text editor—you must have special software to parse and manipulate them. The fact that XML is in plain text makes it more accessible and therefore more desirable.

XML describes the syntax used to create other markup languages. In other words, it dictates how elements must start and end, the kinds of characters that can be used for element names, how elements can be nested, which attributes they contain, and so on—but XML itself does not dictate which names are used for elements. For example, XML doesn't define the element names I used in Listing 2–1, like `street` and `city`—I made up these names on the spot! A specific **XML markup language** (also known as an **XML application**[1]) describes which element names are used and how they are organized. Because anyone can make up a new markup language at any time, the number of them is potentially infinite. Some XML markup languages are de facto standards within their industries: CML (chemistry), MathML (mathematics), DocBook (publishing), SVG (multimedia), XHTML (Web pages), among others. Even the XML shown in Listing 2–1, which is used only in this book, is a markup language—call it the **Address Book Markup Language.** The ability to create an infinite number of new markup languages is why XML is called *eXtensible.*

The relationship of XML to a specific XML markup language, like the Address Book Markup Language or MathML, is analogous to the relationship of the Java programming language to a program or code library (package) written in that language. The Java language specification defines the legal syntax of the programming language, but developers can create any Java program or package they want as long as it adheres to the Java language syntax. The XML specification defines the legal syntax of every XML markup language, but developers can create any XML markup language they want as long as it adheres to XML syntax. While useful, this analogy should not be misunderstood: XML is *not* a programming language like Java, C++, or VisualBasic.NET. XML only defines the syntax of elements used in text—it is not software and isn't compiled, interpreted, or executed. It's just plain text[2].

XML is used for two different purposes: **document-oriented** and **data-oriented** applications. Document-oriented markup languages like XHTML and DocBook are focused on the format and presentation of literature. They describe how books, magazines, and business and scientific papers are organized, and how they look. Data-oriented markup languages focus on how data is organized and typed; they define a **schema** for storing and exchanging data between software applications. Some XML markup languages are industry standards, like SOAP and XHTML, while most are designed to serve a single application, organization, or individual.

[1] In proper XML-speak, the term **XML application** means the use of XML; it doesn't mean "computer program." The term **XML application** is synonymous with **XML markup language**. That said, the term is often misused to refer to a software application that processes XML documents.

[2] While XML itself is not a programming language, there are XML markup languages that can be compiled and interpreted. For example, XSLT (eXtensible Stylesheet Language Transformation) is a programming language based on XML.

The XML markup languages used in this book, both custom and standard, are decidedly data-oriented.

Regardless of the source of a markup language, if it's based on XML it must follow the same syntax and rules defined by the XML specification, which makes XML documents portable. Portability means you can use any standard XML parsers, editors, and other utilities to process most, if not all, of the XML documents you will encounter.

> ***An XML parser is a utility that can read and analyze an XML document. In most cases an XML parser is combined with a parser API (such as SAX2 or DOM 2) that allows a developer to interact with the XML document while it's being parsed, or after. This subject is covered in more depth in Section 2.1.3.***

2.1.1 XML Document Instance

An XML document can be saved or transferred over a network. A Web page written in XHTML (a variant of HTML), which is a text file, is an XML document. Similarly, a SOAP message, which is generated and exchanged over a network, is an XML document.

A business might choose to store address information as an XML document. In this case the text file might look like Listing 2–2:

Listing 2–2

An XML Address Document Instance

```
<?xml version="1.0" encoding="UTF-8" ?>
<address>
   <name>Amazon.com</name>
   <street>1516 2nd Ave</street>
   <city>Seattle</city>
   <state>WA</state>
   <zip>90952</zip>
</address>
```

The above example is called an **XML document instance,** which means it represents one possible set of data for a particular markup language. It might be saved as a file or sent over the Internet as the payload of a SOAP message. If you were to create another XML document with the same tags but different contents (like a different street or Zip code) it would be considered a different XML document instance. In this book, I use the terms "XML document" and "XML instance" interchangeably to mean "XML document instance."

2.1.2 Anatomy of an XML Document

An XML document is made up of declarations, elements, attributes, text data, comments, and other components. This section examines an XML document instance in detail and explains its most important components.

2.1.2.1 XML Declaration

An XML document may start with an XML declaration, but it's not required. An XML declaration declares the version of XML used to define the document (there is only one version at this time, version 1.0). It may also indicate the character encoding used to store or transfer the document, and whether the document is standalone or not (the `standalone` attribute is not used in this book). The following snippet from Listing 2–2 shows the XML declaration in bold.

```
<?xml version="1.0" encoding="UTF-8" ?>
<address>
   <name>Amazon.com</name>
   <street>1516 2nd Ave</street>
   <city>Seattle</city>
   <state>WA</state>
   <zip>90952</zip>
</address>
```

2.1.2.2 Elements

XML markup languages organize data hierarchically, in a tree structure, where each branch of the tree is called an **element** and is delimited by a pair of **tags.** All elements are named and have a **start tag** and an **end tag.** A start tag looks like <*tagname*> and an end tag looks like </*tagname*>. The *tagname* is a label that usually describes the information contained by the element. Between the start and end tags, an element may contain text or other elements, which themselves may contain text or more elements. The following is an example, based on Listing 2–2, of an XML instance of the Address Markup Language, which I'll call Address Markup for short.

```
<?xml version="1.0" encoding="UTF-8" ?>
<address>
   <name>Amazon.com</name>
   <street>1516 2nd Ave</street>
   <city>Seattle</city>
   <state>WA</state>
   <zip>90952</zip>
</address>
```

There are six elements in this example (`address`, `name`, `street`, `city`, `state`, and `zip`). The `address` element uses the start tag `<address>` and the end tag `</address>`, and contains the other five elements. The `address` element, because it contains all the other elements, is referred to as the **root element.** Each XML document must have one root element, and that element must contain all the other elements and text, except the XML declaration, comments, and certain processing instructions.

The other elements (name, street, city, state, zip) all contain text. According to the WS-I Basic Profile 1.0, XML documents used in Web services must use either UTF-8 or UTF-16 encoding. This limitation simplifies things for Web service vendors and makes interoperability easier, because there is only one character encoding standard to worry about, Unicode. UTF-8 and UTF-16 encoding allows you to use characters from English, Chinese, French, German, Japanese, and many other languages.

An element name must always begin with a letter or underscore, but can contain pretty much any Unicode character you like, including underscores, letters, digits, hyphens, and periods. Some characters may not be used: /, <, >, ?, ", @, &, and others. Also, an element name must never start with the string xml, as this is reserved by the XML 1.0 specification. As long as you follow XML's rules you may name elements anything and your elements may contain any combination of valid text and other elements.

Elements do not have to contain any data at all. It's perfectly acceptable to use an **empty-element tag,** a single tag of the form *<tagname/>*, which is interpreted as a pair of start and end tags with no content (*<tagname></tagname>*). Empty-element tags are typically used when an element has no data, when it acts like flag, or when its pertinent data is contained in its attributes (attributes are described in the next section).

2.1.2.3 *Attributes*

An element may have one or more **attributes.** You use an attribute to supplement the data contained by an element, to provide information about it not captured by its contents. For example, we could describe the *kind* of address in an XML address document by declaring a category attribute as in Listing 2–3.

Listing 2–3

Using Attributes in XML

```
<?xml version="1.0" encoding="UTF-8" ?>
<address category="business" >
   <name>Amazon.com</name>
   <street>1516 2nd Ave</street>
   <city>Seattle</city>
   <state>WA</state>
   <zip>90952</zip>
</address>
```

Each attribute is a name-value pair. The value must be in single or double quotes. You can define any number of attributes for an element, but a particular attribute may occur only once in a single element. Attributes *cannot* be nested like elements. Attribute names have the same restrictions as element names. Attributes must be declared in the start tag and never the end tag of an element.

In many cases, empty-element tags (discussed in previous section) are used when the attributes contain all the data. For example, we could add an empty `phone` element to the XML address document as in Listing 2–4.

Listing 2–4

Using the Empty-Element Tag in XML

```
<?xml version="1.0" encoding="UTF-8" ?>
<address category="business" >
  <name>Amazon.com</name>
  <street>1516 2nd Ave</street>
  <city>Seattle</city>
  <state>WA</state>
  <zip>90952</zip>
  <phone countrycode="01" areacode="715" number="55529482" ext="341" />
</address>
```

Using attributes instead of nested elements is considered a matter of style, rather than convention. There are no "standard" design conventions for using attributes or elements.

2.1.2.4 Comments

You can add comments to an XML document just as you can add comments to a Java program. A comment is considered documentation about the XML document and is not part of the data it describes. Comments are placed between a `<!--` designator and a `-->` designator, as in HTML: `<!-- comment goes here -->`. As an example we can comment our XML address document as shown in Listing 2–5.

Listing 2–5

Using Comments in XML

```
<?xml version="1.0" encoding="UTF-8" ?>
<!-- This document contains address information -->
<address category="business" >
   <name>Amazon.com</name>
   <street>1516 2nd Ave</street>
   <city>Seattle</city>
   <state>WA</state>
   <zip>90952</zip>
</address>
```

2.1.2.5 CDATA Section

An element may contain other elements, text, or a mixture of both. When an element contains text, you have to be careful about which characters you use because certain characters have special meaning in XML. Using quotes (single or double), less-than and greater-than signs (< and >), the ampersand (&), and other special characters in the contents of an element will confuse parsers, which consider these characters to be special parsing symbols. To avoid parsing problems you can use escape characters like `>` for greater-than or `&` for ampersand, but this technique can become cumbersome.

A **CDATA section** allows you to mark a section of text as **literal** so that it will not be parsed for tags and symbols, but will instead be considered just a string of characters. For example, if you want to put HTML in an XML document, but you don't want it parsed, you can embed it in a CDATA section. In Listing 2–6 the address document contains a note in HTML format.

Listing 2–6

Using a CDATA Section in XML

```
<?xml version="1.0" encoding="UTF-8" ?>
<!-- This document contains address information -->
<address category="business" >
   <name>Amazon.com</name>
   <street>1516 2nd Ave</street>
   <city>Seattle</city>
   <state>WA</state>
   <zip>90952</zip>
   <note>
   <![CDATA[
     <html>
       <body>
            <p>
            Last time I contacted <b>Amazon.com</b> I spoke to ...
       </body>
     </html>
   ]]>
  </note>
</address>
```

CDATA Sections take the form `<![CDATA[ text goes here ]]>`. If we include the HTML in the `note` element without embedding it in a CDATA section, XML processors will parse it as Address Markup, instead of treating it as ordinary text, causing two kinds of problems: First, HTML's syntax isn't as strict as XML's so parsing problems are likely. Second, the HTML is not actually part of Address

Markup; it's simply a part of the text contained by the `note` element, and we want it treated as literal text.

2.1.3 Processing XML Documents

Although XML is just plain text, and can be accessed using a common text editor, it's usually read and manipulated by software applications and not by people using text editors. A software application that reads and manipulates XML documents will use an XML parser. In general, parsers read a stream of data (usually a file or network stream) and break it down into functional units that can then be processed by a software application. An XML parser can read an XML document and parse its contents according to the XML syntax. Parsers usually provide a programming API that allows developers to access elements, attributes, text, and other constructs in XML documents. There are basically two standard kinds of XML parser APIs: SAX and DOM.

SAX (**Simple API for XML**) was the first standard XML parser API and is very popular. Although several individuals created it, David Brownell currently maintains SAX2, the latest version, as an open development project at SourceForge.org. SAX2 parsers are available in many programming languages including Java. SAX2 is based on an event model. As the SAX2 parser reads an XML document, starting at the beginning, it fires off events every time it encounters a new element, attribute, piece of text, or other component. SAX2 parsers are generally very fast because they read an XML document sequentially and report on the markup as it's encountered.

DOM (Document Object Model) was developed after SAX2 and maintained by the W3C. DOM level 2 (DOM 2) is the current version, but there is a DOM level 3 in the works. DOM 2 parsers are also available for many programming languages, including Java. DOM 2 presents the programmer with a generic, object-oriented model of an XML document. Elements, attributes, and text values are represented as objects organized into a hierarchical tree structure that reflects the hierarchy of the XML document being processed. DOM 2 allows an application to navigate the tree structure, modify elements and attributes, and generate new XML documents in memory. It's a very powerful and flexible programming model, but it's also slow compared to SAX2, and consumes a lot more memory.

In addition to providing a programming model for reading and manipulating XML documents, the parser's primary responsibility is checking that documents are **well formed;** that is, that their elements, attributes, and other constructs conform to the syntax prescribed by the XML 1.0 specification. For example, an element without an end tag, or with an attribute name that contains invalid characters, will result in a syntax error. A parser may also, optionally, enforce **validity** of an XML document. An XML document may be well formed, but invalid because it is not organized according to its schema. This will make more sense when you read about schemas in Chapter 3.

Two popular Java parser libraries, Crimson and Xerces-J, include both SAX2 and DOM 2, so you can pick the API that better meets your needs. Crimson is a part of the Java 2 platform (JDK 1.4), which means it's available to you automatically. Xerces, which some people feel is better, is maintained by the Apache Software

Foundation. You must download it as a JAR file and place it in your classpath (or `ext` directory) before you can use it. Either parser library is fine for most cases, but Xerces supports W3C XML Schema validation while Crimson doesn't.

JAXP (Java API for XML Processing), which is part of the J2EE platform, is not a parser. It's a set of factory classes and wrappers for DOM 2 and SAX2 parsers. Java-based DOM 2 and SAX2 parsers, while conforming to standard DOM 2 or SAX2 programming models, are instantiated and configured differently, which inhibits their portability. JAXP eliminates this portability problem by providing a consistent programming model for instantiating and configuring DOM 2 and SAX2 parsers. JAXP can be used with Crimson or Xerces-J. JAXP is a standard Java extension library, so using it will help keep your J2EE applications portable.

Other non-standard XML APIs are also available to Java developers, including JDOM, dom4j, and XOM. These APIs are tree-based like DOM 2, and although they are non-standard, they tend to provide simpler programming models than DOM 2. JDOM and dom4j are actually built on top of DOM 2 implementations, wrapping DOM 2 with their own object-oriented programming model. JDOM and dom4j can both be used with either Xerces-J or Crimson. If ease of use is important, you may want to use one of these non-standard parser libraries, but if J2EE portability is more important, stick with JAXP, DOM 2, and SAX2.

2.2 XML Namespaces

An **XML namespace** provides a qualified name for an XML element or attribute, the same way that a Java package provides a qualified name for a Java class. In most Java programs, classes are imported from other packages (`java.io`, `javax.xml`, and the rest). When the Java program is compiled, every operation performed on every object or class is validated against the class definition in the appropriate package. If Java didn't have package names, the classes in the Java core libraries (I/O, AWT, JDBC, etc.) would all be lumped together with developer-defined classes. Java package names allow us to separate Java classes into distinct namespaces, which improves organization and access control, and helps us avoid name conflicts (collisions). XML namespaces are similar to Java packages, and serve the same purposes; an XML namespace provides a kind of package name for individual elements and attributes.

2.2.1 An Example of Using Namespaces

Creating XML documents based on multiple markup languages is often desirable. For example, suppose we are building a billing and inventory control system for a company called Monson-Haefel Books. We can define a standard markup language for address information, the Address Markup Language, to be used whenever an XML document needs to contain address information. An instance of Address Markup is shown in Listing 2–7.

Listing 2–7

An Instance of the Address Markup Language

```
<?xml version="1.0" encoding="UTF-8" ?>
<address category="business" >
   <name>Amazon.com</name>
   <street>1516 2nd Ave</street>
   <city>Seattle</city>
   <state>WA</state>
   <zip>90952</zip>
</address>
```

Address Markup is used in Address Book Markup (nested in the `addresses` element) defined in Listing 2–1 at the start of this chapter, but it will also be reused in about half of Monson-Haefel Books' other XML markup languages (types of XML documents): Invoice, Purchase Order, Shipping, Marketing, and others.

Address Markup has its own schema, defined using either **DTD** (**Document Type Definition**) or the **W3C XML Schema Language,** which dictates how its elements are organized. Every time we use address information in an XML document, it should be validated against Address Markup's schema. For example, in Listing 2–8 the address information is included in the `PurchaseOrder` XML document.

Listing 2–8

The PurchaseOrder Document Using the Address Markup Langauge

```
<?xml version="1.0" encoding="UTF-8" ?>
<purchaseOrder orderDate="2003-09-22" >
   <accountName>Amazon.com</accountName>
   <accountNumber>923</accountNumber>
   <address>
      <name>AMAZON.COM</name>
      <street>1850 Mercer Drive</street>
      <city>Lexington</city>
      <state>KY</state>
      <zip>40511</zip>
   </address>
   <book>
      <title>J2EE Web Services</title>
      <quantity>300</quantity>
      <wholesale-price>29.99</wholesale-price>
   </book>
   <total>8997.00</total>
</purchaseOrder>
```

If the purchase-order document has its own schema (defined by the Purchase Order Markup Language) and the address information has its own schema (defined by the Address Markup Language), how do we indicate that the `address` element should conform to the Address Markup Language, while the rest of the elements conform to the Purchase Order Markup Language? We use **namespaces.**

We can state that the address elements conform to Address Markup by declaring the namespace of Address Markup in the `address` element. We can do the same thing for the purchase order elements by declaring, in the `purchaseOrder` element, that they conform to the Purchase Order Markup. Listing 2–9 illustrates.

Listing 2–9

Declaring Namespaces in XML

```
<?xml version="1.0" encoding="UTF-8" ?>
<purchaseOrder orderDate="2003-09-22"
 xmlns="http://www.Monson-Haefel.com/jwsbook/PO">
   <accountName>Amazon.com</accountName>
   <accountNumber>923</accountNumber>

   <address xmlns="http://www.Monson-Haefel.com/jwsbook/ADDR">
      <name>AMAZON.COM</name>
      <street>1850 Mercer Drive</street>
      <city>Lexington</city>
      <state>KY</state>
      <zip>40511</zip>
   </address>

   <book>
      <title>J2EE Web Services</title>
      <quantity>300</quantity>
      <wholesale-price>29.99</wholesale-price>
   </book>
   <total>8997.00</total>
</purchaseOrder>
```

The `xmlns` attribute declares a specific **XML namespace** in the form `xmlns="`*`someURI`*`"`. The value of an `xmlns` attribute is a URI reference, which must conform to the URI specification (RFC2396) defined by the **IETF** (**Internet Engineering Task Force**). **URIs** (**Uniform Resource Identifiers**) can take many different forms; the most common is the **URL** (**Universal Resource Locator**) . For example, in Listing 2–9 the URLs for both namespaces start with `http://www.Monson-Haefel.com/jwsbook`, which is the namespace used for examples throughout this book—it's the namespace of our fictitious wholesaler, Monson-Haefel Books. The final part of the URL (/PO or /ADDR in the example) completes the URL to create a unique identifier for each namespace.

In Listing 2–9, standard HTTP URLs are used, which may or may not point to an actual document or resource. It's important to remember that the URI used for the XML namespace should be unique to that markup language, but it doesn't have to point to an actual resource or document.

2.2.2 Default Namespaces, Prefixes, and Qualified Names

The xmlns declarations made in Listing 2-9 defined the **default namespace** for the element and all its descendants. The scope of a default namespace applies only to the element and its descendants, so the xmlns used in the address element applies only to the address, name, street, city, state, and zip elements. The default xmlns declared in the purchaseOrder element applies to all the elements except the address elements, because the address element overrides the default namespace of the purchaseOrder element to define its own default namespace.

Using default XML namespaces can get tricky, especially when elements are interleaved or when a lot of markup languages are used in the same document. To simplify things, XML Namespaces defines a shorthand notation for associating elements and attributes with namespaces. You can assign an XML namespace to a **prefix,** then use that prefix to fully qualify each element name. The code in Listing 2–10 assigns the prefix "addr:" to the http://www.Monson-Haefel.com/jwsbook/ADDR namespace and the prefix "po:" to the http://www.Monson-Haefel.com/jwsbook/PO namespace, then uses one prefix or the other to qualify each element.

Listing 2–10

Declaring and Using Namespaces Prefixes in XML

```
<?xml version="1.0" encoding="UTF-8" ?>
<po:purchaseOrder orderDate="2003-09-22"
   xmlns:po="http://www.Monson-Haefel.com/jwsbook/PO"
   xmlns:addr="http://www.Monson-Haefel.com/jwsbook/ADDR">

   <po:accountName>Amazon.com</po:accountName>
   <po:accountNumber>923</po:accountNumber>

   <addr:address>
      <addr:name>AMAZON.COM</addr:name>
      <addr:street>1850 Mercer Drive</addr:street>
      <addr:city>Lexington</addr:city>
      <addr:state>KY</addr:state>
      <addr:zip>40511</addr:zip>
   </addr:address>
```

```
    <po:book>
        <po:title>J2EE Web Services</po:title>
        <po:quantity>300</po:quantity>
        <po:wholesale-price>29.99</po:wholesale-price>
    </po:book>
    <po:total>8997.00</po:total>
</po:purchaseOrder>
```

The elements prefixed with `addr:` belong to the `http://www.Monson-Haefel.com/jwsbook/ADDR` namespace and the elements prefixed with `po:` belong to the `http://www.Monson-Haefel.com/jwsbook/PurchaseOrder` namespace.

It's not necessary to qualify every element with a namespace prefix. You can rely on default namespaces to determine the namespaces of all elements not explicitly prefixed, as in listing 2–11.

Listing 2–11

Combining Default Namespaces and Namespaces Prefixes in XML

```
<?xml version="1.0" encoding="UTF-8" ?>
<purchaseOrder orderDate="2003-09-22"
    xmlns="http://www.Monson-Haefel.com/jwsbook/PO"
    xmlns:addr="http://www.Monson-Haefel.com/jwsbook/ADDR">

    <accountName>Amazon.com</accountName>
    <accountNumber>923</accountNumber>

    <addr:address>
        <addr:name>AMAZON.COM</addr:name>
        <addr:street>1850 Mercer Drive</addr:street>
        <addr:city>Lexington</addr:city>
        <addr:state>KY</addr:state>
        <addr:zip>40511</addr:zip>
    </addr:address>

    <book>
        <title>J2EE Web Services</title>
        <quantity>300</quantity>
        <wholesale-price>29.99</wholesale-price>
    </book>
    <total>8997.00</total>
</purchaseOrder>
```

In this example the namespace for the entire document is declared to be `http://www.Monson-Haefel.com/jwsbook/PO`—it's the default for all of the children of the root element, `purchaseOrder`. Any element that doesn't have a prefix is, by default, a member of `http://www.Monson-Haefel.com/jwsbook/PO`.

When a namespace prefix is applied to an element, however, it overrides the default namespace. In Listing 2-11, the `"addr:"` prefix is assigned to the address elements, which makes `http://www.Monson-Haefel.com/jwsbook/ADDR` the namespace of the `address`, `name`, `street`, `city`, `state`, and `zip` elements.

The way you use prefixes with namespaces can depend on how the document is defined by its schema. The schema may determine whether you need to prefix all the elements, or just the parent elements, and whether default namespace declarations apply to unprefixed elements. The next chapter covers XML schemas in detail.

In XML-speak, a prefix combined with an element name is called a **QName**, which stands for "qualified name." Conceptually, a QName like `addr:address` can be dereferenced to `http://www.Monson-Haefel.com/jwsbook/ADDR:address`—but this is not done in practice.

A QName has two parts, the XML namespace and the local name. For example, the QName of the `street` element declared in Listing 2–10 is composed of the `http://www.Monson-Haefel.com/jwsbook/ADDR` XML namespace and the `street` local name.

XML namespaces based on URLs tend to be universally unique, which makes it easy for parsers and software applications to distinguish between instances of different markup languages within the same document. Namespaces help avoid name collisions, where two elements from different markups share a common local name. For example, a WSDL document can use Monson-Haefel's postal `address` element as well as the SOAP-binding `address` element in the same document. Although both elements are named `address`, they belong to different namespaces with different QNames, so there is no name conflict. Listing 2–12 illustrates.

Listing 2–12

Avoiding Element Name Collisions by Using XML Namespaces

```
<?xml version="1.0" encoding="UTF-8" ?>
<definitions name="Address-Update"
   targetNamespace="http://www.monson-haefel.org/jwsbook/Address-
Update"
   xmlns:tns="http://www.monson-haefel.org/jwsbook/Address-Update"
   xmlns:addr="http://www.Monson-Haefel.com/jwsbook/ADDR"
   xmlns:soap="http://schemas.xmlsoap.org/wsdl/soap/"
   xmlns:xsd="http://www.w3.org/2001/XMLSchema"
   xmlns="http://schemas.xmlsoap.org/wsdl/">
...

<!-- message elements describe the paramters and return values -->
```

```
<message name="AddressMessage">
   <part name="address" element="addr:address" />
</message>

...

<!-- service tells us the Internet address of a Web service -->
<service name="AddressUpdateService">
  <documentation>Update a customers mailing address</documentation>
  <port name="AddressUpdate_Port" binding="tns:AddressUpdate_Binding">
     <soap:address
      location="http://www.monson-haefel.org/jwsbook/BookPrice" />
  </port>
</service>

</definitions>
```

XML parsers and other tools can use XML namespaces to process, sort, and search XML elements in a document according to their QNames. This allows reusable code modules to be invoked for specific namespaces. For example, you can create a custom Java tool to map an instance of Address Markup to a relational database. It will be invoked only for `address` elements that belong to the Address Markup namespace, `http://www.Monson-Haefel.org/addr`, and not for `address` elements of any other namespace.

XML namespaces also allow for a great versioning system. If the Address Markup changes, we can assign the new version its own namespace, such as `http://www.Monson-Haefel.org/ADDR-2`, so it can be distinguished from its predecessor. We can support both the old and new versions of the Address Markup Language simultaneously, because the parser can uniquely identify each version by its namespace. Each version has its own markup for validation and perhaps its own code modules.

2.3 Wrapping Up

This chapter has provided you with a basic understanding of XML syntax and XML namespaces. XML is the very foundation on which the entire Web services platform is based. SOAP, WSDL, and UDDI are defined in XML, but they are also based on The W3C XML Schema Language, so in order to understand them you have to understand The W3C XML Schema Language. That's the topic of the next chapter.

Chapter 3

The W3C XML Schema Language

SOAP, WSDL, and UDDI are markup languages defined using the W3C XML Schema Language, so understanding the latter is critical to understanding J2EE Web Services. This chapter will provide you with a good understanding of both W3C XML Schema Language basics and, optionally, advanced concepts, so that you are ready to learn about SOAP, WSDL, and the UDDI standards covered later.

Throughout this chapter the term **XML schema** will be used to refer to the W3C XML Schema Language as a technology, while the word **schema** by itself will refer to a specific XML schema document.

3.1 XML Schema Basics

The XML specification includes the **Document Type Definition** (**DTD**), which can be used to describe XML markup languages and to validate instances of them (XML documents). While DTDs have proven very useful over the years, they are also limited. To address limitations of DTDs, the W3C (World Wide Web Consortium), which manages the fundamental XML standards, created a new way to describe markup languages called **XML schema.**

3.1.1 Why XML Schema Is Preferred to DTDs in Web Services

DTDs have done an adequate job of telling us how elements and attributes are organized in a markup language, but they fail to address data typing.

For example, the DTD in Listing 3–1 describes the valid organization of the Address Markup Language we created earlier. The DTD declares that an `address` element may contain one or more `street` elements and must contain exactly one of each of the `city`, `state`, and `zip` elements. It also declares that the `address` element must have a `category` attribute.

Listing 3–1

A DTD

```
<?xml version="1.0" encoding="UTF-8"?>
<!ELEMENT address (street+, city, state, zip)>
<!ELEMENT street (#PCDATA) >
<!ELEMENT city (#PCDATA) >
<!ELEMENT state (#PCDATA) >
<!ELEMENT zip (#PCDATA) >
<!ATTLIST address category CDATA #REQUIRED >
```

A parser reading an XML instance determines whether it's valid by comparing it to its DTD—if it declares that it uses a DTD. To be valid, an XML instance must conform to its DTD, which means it must use the elements specified by the DTD in the correct order and multiplicity (zero, one, or many times).

While constraints provided by DTDs are useful for validating XML instances, the probability that an XML instance will have a valid organization but contain invalid data is pretty high. DTDs have a very weak typing system that restricts elements to four broad types of data: EMPTY, ANY, element content, or mixed element-and-text content. In other words, DTDs can only restrict elements to containing nothing, other elements, or text—not a very granular typing system. DTDs don't support types like `integer`, `decimal`, `boolean`, and `enumeration`. For example, the Address Markup DTD cannot restrict the contents of the `zip` element to an integer value or the `state` element to a set of valid state codes.

XML schema, by contrast, provides a much stronger type system. Many believe that XML schema is superior to DTD because it defines a richer type system, which includes simple primitives (`integer`, `double`, `boolean`, among others) as well as facilities for more complex types. XML schema facilitates type inheritance, which allows simple or complex types to be extended or restricted to create new types. In addition, XML schema supports the use of XML namespaces to create compound documents composed of multiple markup languages.

Appendix A explains XML DTDs, but understanding the DTD schema language is not necessary for this book.

3.1.2 The XML Schema Document

A schema describes an XML markup language. Specifically it defines which elements and attributes are used in a markup language, how they are ordered and nested, and what their data types are.

A schema describes the structure of an XML document in terms of **complex types** and **simple types.** Complex types describe how elements are organized and nested. Simple types are the primitive data types contained by elements and attributes. For example, Listing 3–2 shows a portion of a schema that describes the Monson-Haefel Markup Language. Monson-Haefel Markup defines a set of XML schema types used by Monson-Haefel Books: `USAddress`, `PurchaseOrder`, `Invoice`, `Shipping`, and the like. At this point all the different types used by Monson-Haefel Books are combined into one schema; later you'll learn how to separate them into their own schemas and independent markup languages.

Listing 3–2

The Address Definition in a Schema

```
<?xml version="1.0" encoding="UTF-8"?>
<schema xmlns="http://www.w3.org/2001/XMLSchema"
 xmlns:mh="http://www.Monson-Haefel.com/jwsbook"
 targetNamespace="http://www.Monson-Haefel.com/jwsbook">

    <element name="address" type="mh:USAddress" />

    <complexType name="USAddress">
      <sequence>
        <element name="name"    type="string" />
        <element name="street"  type="string" />
        <element name="city"    type="string" />
        <element name="state"   type="string" />
        <element name="zip"     type="string" />
      </sequence>
    </complexType>
    ...
</schema>
```

The first thing you may have noticed is that Listing 3–2 is actually an XML document. That schemas are XML documents is a critical point: It makes the development of validating parsers and other software tools easier, because the operations that manipulate schemas can be based on XML parsers, which are already widely available. DTDs, the predecessor to schemas, were not based on XML, so processing them required special parsing.

The root element of a schema document is always the schema element. Nested within the schema element are element and type declarations. Listing 3–2 declares a complex type named USAddress, and an element of that type named address.

The schema element assigns the XML schema namespace ("http://www.w3.org/2001/XMLSchema") as the default namespace. This namespace is the standard namespace defined by the XML schema specification—all the XML schema elements must belong to this namespace. The schema element also defines the targetNamespace attribute, which declares the XML namespace of all new types explicitly created within the schema. For example, the USAddress type is automatically assigned to targetNamespace, "http://www.Monson-Haefel.com/jwsbook".

The schema element also uses an XML namespace declaration to assign the prefix mh to the targetNamespace. Subsequently, newly created types in the schema can be referred to as "mh:*Typename*". For example, the type attribute in the element declaration in Listing 3–2 refers to the USAddress as "mh:USAddress":

```
<element name="address" type="mh:USAddress" />
```

An instance document based on this schema would use the address element directly or refer to the USAddress type. When a parser that supports XML schema reads the document, it can validate the contents of the XML document against the USAddress type definition in Listing 3–2. Listing 3–3 shows a conforming XML instance.

Listing 3–3

An Instance of the Address Markup Language

```
<?xml version="1.0" encoding="UTF-8"?>
<addr:address xmlns:addr="http://www.Monson-Haefel.com/jwsbook">
   <name>Amazon.com</name>
   <street>1516 2nd Ave</street>
   <city>Seattle</city>
   <state>WA</state>
   <zip>90952</zip>
</addr:address>
```

Using XML schema, we can state exactly how an instance of the address element should be organized and the types of data its elements and attributes should contain.

3.1.3 Simple Types

A **simple type** resembles a Java primitive type in that both are atomic; they cannot be broken down into constituent parts. In other words, a simple element type will not contain other elements; it will contain only data. The XML schema specification defines many standard simple types, called **built-in types.** The built-in types are the

Table 3–1 Comparing the Use of XML Schema Simple Types and Java Primitive Types

XML Schema Built-in Simple Types (shown in bold)	Java Primitive Types (shown in bold)
<?xml version="1.0" encoding="UTF-8"?>	
<schema xmlns="http://www.w3.org/2001/XMLSchema"	
xmlns:mh="http://www.Monson-Haefel.com/jwsbook"	
targetNamespace="http://www.Monson-Haefel.com/jwsbook">	package com.monsonhaefel.jwsbook;
...	
<complexType name="PurchaseOrder">	public class PurchaseOrder {
<sequence>	
<element name="accountName" **type="string"** />	**String** accountName;
<element name="accountNumber" **type="integer"** />	**int** accountNumber;
<element name="total" **type="float"** />	**float** total;
<!-- More stuff follows -->	// more stuff follows
</sequence>	
</complexType>	}
...	
</schema>	

standard building blocks of an XML schema document. They are members of the XML schema namespace, "`http://www.w3.org/2001/XMLSchema`".

The `PurchaseOrder` complex type declares three of its elements and an attribute using the XML schema built-in types: `string`, `integer`, and `float`. These simple types are similar to familiar types in the Java programming language and others. In a schema, simple types are used to construct complex types, much as Java primitives are used as fields of Java class definitions. Table 3–1 provides a comparison. The next section explains complex types in more detail.

The XML schema specification describes its 44 built-in simple types in precise detail. This precision enables XML parsers to process the built-in types predictably and consistently, for the most part, and provides a solid foundation for creating your own complex and custom simple types.

For example, the XML schema specification tells us that a `string` is defined as an unlimited length of characters based on the Universal Character Set;[1] an `unsignedShort` is a non-decimal number between 0 and 65,535; a `float` is a 32-bit floating-point type; and a `date` is represented as YYYY-MM-DD.

You can find complete and concise definitions of all the built-in types in *XML Schema Part 2: Datatypes*.[2] Table 3–2 provides a partial list, with brief definitions in plain English.

[1] The Universal Character Set (ISO/IEC 10646-1993) is a superset of all other character codes, including UTF-8 and UTF-16.

[2] World Wide Web Consortium, *XML Schema Part 2: Datatypes*, W3C Recommendation, May 2, 2001. Available at http://www.w3.org/TR/xmlschema-2/.

Table 3–2 A Subset of the XML Schema Built-in Simple Types

Simple Type	Definition
`string`	A sequence of characters conforming to UCS
`normalizedString`	A string without carriage returns, line feeds, or tabs
`token`	A string without spaces, line feeds, or tabs
`NMTOKEN`	A token used in attributes
`byte`	A non-decimal number between –128 and 127
`unsignedByte`	A non-decimal number between 0 and 255
`base64Binary`	Base64-encoded binary data (RFC 2045)[a]
`hexBinary`	Hex-encoded binary data[b]
`integer`	A base-10-integer number of any size (...)[c]
`positiveInteger`	A base-10 integer greater then zero (1, 2, ...)
`negativeInteger`	A base-10 integer less then zero (..., –2, –1)
`int`	A base-10 integer between –2,147,483,648 and 2,147,483,647 (–2 billion and 2 billion)
`unsignedInt`	A base-10 integer between 0 and 4,294,967,295 (zero and 4 billion)
`long`	A base-10 integer between –9,223,372,036,854,775,808 and 9,223,372,036,854,775,807 (–9 quintillion and 9 quintillion)
`unsignedLong`	A base-10 integer between 0 and 18,446,744,073,709,551,615 (zero and 18 quintillion)
`short`	A base-10 integer between –32,767 and 32,767
`unsignedShort`	A base-10 integer between 0 and 65,535
`decimal`	A decimal number of any precision and size
`float`	A decimal number conforming to the IEEE single-precision 32-bit floating-point type[d]
`double`	A decimal number conforming to the IEEE double-precision 64-bit floating-point type[d]
`boolean`	A boolean value of `"true"` or `"false"` You can also use the values of `"0"` (false) or `"1"` (true); either convention is fine.
`time`	A time in hours, minutes, seconds, and milliseconds formatted as hh:mm:ss.sss (e.g., 1:20 PM is 13:20:00) You may include the optional Coordinated Universal Time (UTC) designator (e.g., 1:20 PM Eastern Standard Time (EST) is 13:20:00-05:00)[e]

Table 3–2 Continued

Simple Type	Definition
`date`	A Gregorian date in centuries, years, months, and days (e.g., December 31, 2004 is 2004-12-31)[e]
`dateTime`	A Gregorian date measured in centuries, years, months, and days, with a time field set off by a T (e.g., 1:20 PM EST on December 31, 2004 would be 2004-12-31T13:20:00-05:00)[e]
`duration`	A span of time measured in years, months, days, and seconds (e.g., 1 year, 2 months, 3 days, 10 hours, and 30 minutes would be P1Y2M3DT10H30M) Duration may be negative, and zero values can be left off (e.g., 120 days earlier is P120D). The value must always start with the letter P.[f]

[a] N. Freed and N. Borenstein, *RFC 2045: Multipurpose Internet Mail Extensions (MIME) Part One: Format of Internet Message Bodies* (1996). Available at http://www.ietf.org/rfc/rfc2045.txt.
[b] A very good explanation of the hexadecimal numbering system can be found at http://webster.cs.ucr.edu/Page_asm/ArtofAssembly/ch01/CH01-2.html#HEADING2-1.
[c] Computers can't actually support infinite numbers, so the XML schema specification requires that the parser must support at least 18 digits, which is a pretty huge number.
[d] Institute of Electrical and Electronics Engineers, *IEEE Standard for Binary Floating-Point Arithmetic*. See http://standards.ieee.org/reading/ieee/std_public/description/busarch/754-1985_desc.html.
[e] International Organization for Standardization (ISO). *Representations of dates and times* (1988).
[f] The duration type is defined in the XML schema specification and is not based on ISO's *Representations of dates and times*.

All built-in simple and complex types are ultimately derived from `anyType`, which is the ultimate base type, like the `Object` class in Java. The *XML Schema Part 2: Datatypes* specification offers a diagram of the data type hierarchy; see Figure 3–1 on the next page.

3.1.4 Complex Types

A schema may declare **complex types,** which define how elements that contain other elements are organized. The `USAddress` schema type in Listing 3–2, for example, is a complex type definition for a United States postal address. It tells us that an element based on this type will contain five other elements called `name`, `street`, `city`, `state`, and `zip`.

A complex type is analogous to a Java class definition with fields but no methods. The fields in a Java class declare the names and types of variables that an instance of that class will contain. Similarly, a complex type declares the names and types of elements and attributes that an XML instance of that type may contain. An instance of a complex type is an element in an XML document. Table 3–3 compares an XML schema type and a Java class definition for a U.S. address.

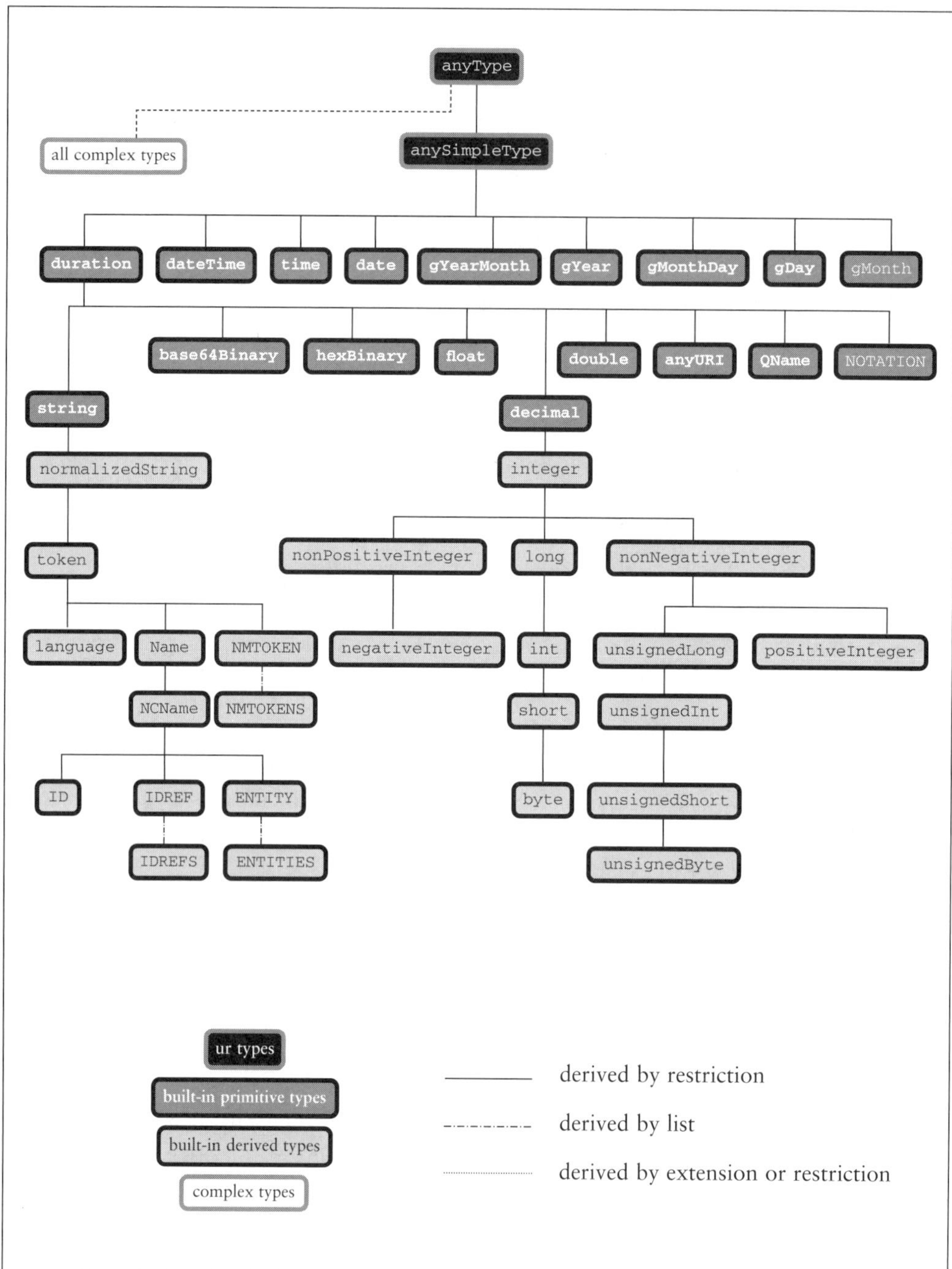

Figure 3–1 XML Schema Type Hierarchy

Table 3–3 Comparing XML Schema Complex Types to Java Class Definitions

XML Schema: Complex Type	Java Class Definition
`<complexType name="USAddress">`	
`<sequence>`	`public class USAddress {`
`<element name="name" type="string" />`	`public String name;`
`<element name="street" type="string" />`	`public String street;`
`<element name="city" type="string" />`	`public String city;`
`<element name="state" type="string" />`	`public String state;`
`<element name="zip" type="string" />`	`public String zip;`
`</sequence>`	`}`
`</complexType>`	

While this analogy between XML schema complex types and Java class definitions is helpful, take care not to confuse them. A schema is used to define elements and attributes in a markup language and verify the correctness of an XML instance; it's not a computer program.

3.1.4.1 Sequences of Elements

Most `complexType` declarations in schemas will contain a `sequence` element that lists one or more `element` definitions. The `element` definitions tell you which elements are nested in the type, the order in which they appear, and the kind of data each element contains.

The `USAddress` type clearly defines the proper structure of a U.S. postal address and can be used to verify the proper contents of any element based on that type. For example, the `address` element used throughout Chapter 2 could be an instance of the type `USAddress`, and we could use that type to verify the contents of the address element when it was used in an XML instance. Table 3–4 shows the `USAddress` type alongside the `address` element so you can see how a complex type definition maps to an XML instance.

A complex type may contain a sequence of elements that are simple types or other complex types. For example, we can define an element for a purchase-order document by adding a `PurchaseOrder` type to the Monson-Haefel Markup Language you saw in Listing 3–2. In Listing 3–4, the new `PurchaseOrder` type has two nested elements, `billAddress` and `shipAddress`, both of type `USAddress`.

Listing 3–4

The `PurchaseOrder` *Type in a Schema*

```
<?xml version="1.0" encoding="UTF-8"?>
<schema xmlns="http://www.w3.org/2001/XMLSchema"
```

```
    xmlns:mh="http://www.Monson-Haefel.com/jwsbook"
    targetNamespace="http://www.Monson-Haefel.com/jwsbook" >

  <element name="purchaseOrder" type="mh:PurchaseOrder" />
  <element name="address" type="mh:USAddress" />

  <complexType name="PurchaseOrder">
    <sequence>
      <element name="accountName"    type="string" />
      <element name="accountNumber" type="unsignedShort" />
      <element name="shipAddress"    type="mh:USAddress" />
      <element name="billAddress"    type="mh:USAddress" />
      <element name="book"           type="mh:Book" />
      <element name="total"          type="float" />
    </sequence>
  </complexType>

  <complexType name="USAddress">
    <sequence>
      <element name="name"    type="string" />
      <element name="street"  type="string" />
      <element name="city"    type="string" />
      <element name="state"   type="string" />
      <element name="zip"     type="string" />
    </sequence>
  </complexType>
```

Table 3–4 Mapping a Schema Complex Type to an XML Element

<table>
<tr><th>XML Schema: USAddress</th><th>XML Document: address</th></tr>
<tr><td><pre>
<complexType name="USAddress">
  <sequence>
    <element name="name" type="string" />
    <element name="street" type="string" />
    <element name="city" type="string" />
    <element name="state" type="string" />
    <element name="zip" type="string" />
  </sequence>
</complexType>
</pre></td><td><pre>
<address>
  <name>Amazon.com</name>
  <street>1516 2nd Ave</street>
  <city>Seattle</city>
  <state>WA</state>
  <zip>90952</zip>
</address>
</pre></td></tr>
</table>

```
<complexType name="Book">
  <sequence>
    <element name="title"            type="string" />
    <element name="quantity"         type="unsignedShort" />
    <element name="wholesale-price"  type="float" />
  </sequence>
</complexType>

</schema>
```

The schema makes use of both complex types (`PurchaseOrder`, `USAddress`, and `Book`) and simple types (`string`, `unsignedShort`, and `float`).

The `USAddress` type is a member of the `targetNamespace`, so we refer to it by its fully qualified name, `"mh:USAddress"`. (Recall that `targetNamespace` is assigned the namespace prefix `mh` in the `schema` element.)

As you can see, the `PurchaseOrder` type takes full advantage of `USAddress` by using it to define both its `billAddress` and `shipAddress` elements. In this way, complex type declarations can build on other complex type definitions to create rich types that easily describe very complex XML structures. The `PurchaseOrder` type also uses `Book`, another complex type that describes the book being ordered.

The names of XML schema types are case-sensitive. When an element declares that it is of a particular type, it must specify both the namespace and the name of that type exactly as the type declares them.

3.1.4.2 Attributes

In addition to sequences of elements, a complex type may also define its own attributes. For example, Listing 3–5 shows a new version of the `PurchaseOrder` type that includes the definition of an `orderDate` attribute.

Listing 3–5

Adding an Attribute to a Complex Type

```
<?xml version="1.0" encoding="UTF-8" standalone="yes"?>
<schema
    xmlns="http://www.w3.org/2001/XMLSchema"
    xmlns:mh="http://www.Monson-Haefel.com/jwsbook"
    targetNamespace="http://www.Monson-Haefel.com/jwsbook">

  <element name="purchaseOrder" type="mh:PurchaseOrder"/>
  <complexType name="PurchaseOrder">
    <sequence>
      <element name="accountName" type="string"/>
      <element name="accountNumber" type="unsignedShort"/>
```

```
      <element name="shipAddress" type="mh:USAddress"/>
      <element name="billAddress" type="mh:USAddress"/>
      <element name="book" type="mh:Book"/>
      <element name="total" type="float"/>
    </sequence>
    <attribute name="orderDate" type="date"/>
  </complexType>
  <complexType name="USAddress">
    <sequence>
      <element name="name" type="string"/>
      <element name="street" type="string"/>
      <element name="city" type="string"/>
      <element name="state" type="string"/>
      <element name="zip" type="string"/>
    </sequence>
  </complexType>
  <complexType name="Book">
    <sequence>
      <element name="title" type="string"/>
      <element name="quantity" type="unsignedShort"/>
      <element name="wholesale-price" type="float"/>
    </sequence>
  </complexType>
</schema>
```

The next code sample, Listing 3–6, shows a valid XML document based on the `PurchaseOrder` type defined by the schema you saw in Listing 3–5. The XML document in Listing 3–6 would contain all the elements and the `orderDate` attribute as described by the `PurchaseOrder` complex type—and would be verifiable against that type.

Listing 3–6

An Instance of the Schema in Listing 3–5

```
<?xml version="1.0" encoding="UTF-8"?>
<po:purchaseOrder orderDate="2003-09-22"
 xmlns:po="http://www.Monson-Haefel.com/jwsbook">
                 <accountName>Amazon.com</accountName>
                 <accountNumber>923</accountNumber>
                 <shipAddress>
                        <name>AMAZON.COM</name>
                        <street>1850 Mercer Drive</street>
                        <city>Lexington</city>
                        <state>KY</state>
```

```
                <zip>40511</zip>
            </shipAddress>
            <billAddress>
                <name>Amazon.com</name>
                <street>1516 2nd Ave</street>
                <city>Seattle</city>
                <state>WA</state>
                <zip>90952</zip>
             </billAddress>
             <book>
                <title>J2EE Web Services</title>
                <quantity>300</quantity>
                <wholesale-price>24.99</wholesale-price>
             </book>
 <total>8997.00</total>
</po:purchaseOrder>
```

3.1.4.3 Occurrence Constraints

The **multiplicity** of an element, the number of times it occurs in an instance document, is controlled by **occurrence constraints,** which are declared by the `maxOccurs` and `minOccurs` attributes. For example, we can enhance the `USAddress` complex type by placing occurrence constraints on the `street` element as shown in Listing 3–7.

Listing 3–7

Using Occurrence Constraints

```
<complexType name="USAddress">
   <sequence>
      <element name="name"    type="string" />
      <element name="street"  type="string"
                              minOccurs="1" maxOccurs="2" />
      <element name="city"    type="string" />
      <element name="state"   type="string" />
      <element name="zip"     type="string" />
   </sequence>
</complexType>
```

The occurrence constraints specify that in any instance of `USAddress` the `street` element must be present at least once and at most twice. In other words, a `USAddress` can contain either one or two `street` elements. The default value for both `maxOccurs` and `minOccurs` is `"1"`, so if these attributes are not specified the element must be present exactly once. Thus, by default, each `USAddress` must have exactly one `name`, `city`, `state`, and `zip`.

The `minOccurs` attribute may be `"0"`, indicating that an element is optional, or any positive integer value that is less than or equal to the `maxOccurs` value. The `maxOccurs` value may be any positive integer greater than or equal to the `min Occurs` value.

```
minOccurs ≥ 0
maxOccurs ≥ minOccurs
```

You may also define a `maxOccurs` value to be `"unbounded"` to specify that the element may occur an unlimited number of times.

For example, suppose Monson-Haefel Books wants to avoid storing a billing address that is identical to the shipping address, and to allow customers to buy an unlimited number of books on a single order. We can redefine the `PurchaseOrder` type, setting the occurrence constraints on the `billAddress` and the `book` elements as highlighted in Listing 3–8.

Listing 3–8

Using the `"unbounded"` *Occurrence Value*

```
<complexType name="PurchaseOrder">
   <sequence>
      <element name="accountName"   type="string" />
      <element name="accountNumber" type="unsignedShort" />
      <element name="shipAddress"   type="mh:USAddress" />
      <element name="billAddress"   type="mh:USAddress"
                                       minOccurs="0" />
      <element name="book"          type="mh:Book"
                                       maxOccurs="unbounded" />
      <element name="total"         type="float" />
   </sequence>
   <attribute name="orderDate" type="date" />
</complexType>
```

The `billAddress` element is now optional. It may occur at most once, because its `maxOccurs` value is `"1"` by default, but it may also be omitted because its `minOccurs` value is `"0"`. The `book` element must be present at least once because the default value of `minOccurs` is `"1"`, but it may be repeated many times because its `maxOccurs` is `"unbounded"`.

Attributes also have occurrence constraints, but they are different from those of elements. Instead of `maxOccurs` and `minOccurs`, attribute types declare the `use` occurrence constraint, which may be `"required"`, `"optional"`, or `"prohibited"`, indicating that the attribute must, may, or may not be used, respectively. The default is `"optional"`. An attribute might be `"prohibited"` if you want to stop the use of a particular attribute, perhaps one that is inappropriate or no longer in use.

In `PurchaseOrder` we want to make the `orderDate` attribute mandatory, so Listing 3–9 sets its `use` occurrence constraint to `"required"`.

Listing 3–9

Declaring the `use` *Value of an Attribute*

```
<complexType name="PurchaseOrder">
   <sequence>
      <element name="accountName"    type="string" />
      <element name="accountNumber" type="unsignedShort" />
      <element name="shipAddress"    type="mh:USAddress" />
      <element name="billAddress"    type="mh:USAddress"
                                         minOccurs="0" />
      <element name="book"           type="mh:Book"
                                         maxOccurs="unbounded" />
      <element name="total"          type="float" />
   </sequence>
   <attribute name="orderDate" type="date" use="required" />
</complexType>
```

An attribute may also have a default value, to be assigned if no value is explicitly declared in the instance document. For example, the `USAddress` type may include an attribute called `category` that can have the value `"business"`, `"private"`, or `"government"`. Almost all addresses used by Monson-Haefel Books are business addresses, so we set the `default` for the `category` attribute to `"business"` in Listing 3–10.

Listing 3–10

Declaring the Default Value of an Attribute

```
<complexType name="USAddress">
   <sequence>
      <element name="name"    type="string" />
      <element name="street"  type="string" />
      <element name="city"    type="string" />
      <element name="state"   type="string" />
      <element name="zip"     type="string" />
   </sequence>
   <attribute name="category" type="string" default="business" />
</complexType>
```

The default attribute can be used only when the use attribute is "optional" (recall that "optional" is the default value for the use attribute). It wouldn't make sense to declare a default when the use is "required" or "prohibited". If the use attribute is "required", there is no need for a default because the attribute must appear in the instance document. If the use is "prohibited", the attribute's not allowed so there is no sense having a default value.

An attribute may also be declared fixed: A fixed value is assigned to the attribute no matter what value appears in the XML instance document. This feature is useful in rare situations where you want to force a particular attribute always to have the same value. For example, if a particular schema is assigned a version number, then that version number should be fixed for that schema (UDDI does this).

3.1.4.4 The all *Element*

Most of the time you'll base complex types on sequence elements, but occasionally you may want to use the all element. Unlike sequence, which defines the exact order of child elements, the XML schema all element allows the elements in it to appear in any order. Each element in an all group may occur once or not at all; no other multiplicity is allowed. In other words, minOccurs is always "0" and maxOccurs is always "1". Finally, only single elements may be used in an all group; it can't include other groupings like sequence or all. Listing 3–11 shows the schema for the address element using the all element grouping instead of sequence.

Listing 3–11

Using the XML Schema all *Element*

```
<?xml version="1.0" encoding="UTF-8"?>
<schema xmlns="http://www.w3.org/2001/XMLSchema"
        xmlns:mh="http://www.Monson-Haefel.com/jwsbook"
        targetNamespace="http://www.Monson-Haefel.com/jwsbook" >
  ...
  <complexType name="USAddress">
    <all>
      <element name="name"    type="string" />
      <element name="street"  type="string" />
      <element name="city"    type="string" minOccurs="0"/>
      <element name="state"   type="string" minOccurs="0"/>
      <element name="zip"     type="string" />
    </all>
  </complexType>
  ...
</schema>
```

In Listing 3–11 the name, street, and zip elements must be present in the instance document, but the city and state elements may be absent. The elements can be in any order, but none of the elements may occur more than once. Listing 3–12 shows a valid instance of the USAddress type as defined using the all element in Listing 3–11.

Listing 3–12

An Instance of the Schema in Listing 3–11

```
<?xml version="1.0" encoding="UTF-8"?>
<addr:address xmlns:addr="http://www.Monson-Haefel.com/jwsbook" >
   <zip>90952</zip>
   <street>1516 2nd Ave</street>
   <name>Amazon.com</name>
</addr:address>
```

Notice the missing city and state elements and that the order of the elements is different from that in the type definition.

3.1.5 Declaring Global Elements in a Schema

In addition to declaring simple and complex types, a schema may also declare **global elements,** which XML instance documents can refer to directly. Global elements are declared as direct children of the schema element, rather than children of a complex type. For example, the following shows a portion of the schema defined in Listing 3–5, which declared the purchaseOrder element (shown in bold) to be global.

```
<?xml version="1.0" encoding="UTF-8"?>
<schema
    xmlns="http://www.w3.org/2001/XMLSchema"
    xmlns:mh="http://www.Monson-Haefel.com/jwsbook"
    targetNamespace="http://www.Monson-Haefel.com/jwsbook">

  <element name="purchaseOrder" type="mh:PurchaseOrder"/>
  <complexType name="PurchaseOrder">
    <sequence>
      <element name="accountName" type="string"/>
      <element name="accountNumber" type="unsignedShort"/>
      <element name="shipAddress" type="mh:USAddress"/>
      <element name="billAddress" type="mh:USAddress"/>
      <element name="book" type="mh:Book"/>
      <element name="total" type="float"/>
    </sequence>
    <attribute name="orderDate" type="date"/>
```

```
  </complexType>
  ...
</schema>
```

An XML document based on Listing 3–5 can use the `purchaseOrder` element as in Listing 3–6.

```
<?xml version="1.0" encoding="UTF-8"?>
<po:purchaseOrder orderDate="2003-09-22"
 xmlns:addr="http://www.Monson-Haefel.com/jwsbook">

   <accountName>Amazon.com</accountName>
   <accountNumber>923</accountNumber>
   <shipAddress>
   ...

</po:purchaseOrder>
```

The root element of a valid XML document must have a corresponding global element declaration in the schema. A schema may define more than one global element. For example, we can modify the schema for Monson-Haefel Books so that it declares two global elements: `purchaseOrder` and `address`. Listing 3–13 illustrates.

Listing 3–13

Defining Multiple Element Declarations

```
<?xml version="1.0" encoding="UTF-8" standalone="yes"?>
<schema
    xmlns="http://www.w3.org/2001/XMLSchema"
    xmlns:mh="http://www.Monson-Haefel.com/jwsbook"
    targetNamespace="http://www.Monson-Haefel.com/jwsbook">

  <element name="address" type="mh:USAddress"/>
  <element name="purchaseOrder" type="mh:PurchaseOrder"/>
  <complexType name="PurchaseOrder">
    <sequence>
      <element name="accountName" type="string"/>
      <element name="accountNumber" type="unsignedShort"/>
      <element name="shipAddress" type="mh:USAddress"/>
      <element name="billAddress" type="mh:USAddress"/>
      <element name="book" type="mh:Book"/>
      <element name="total" type="float"/>
```

```
    </sequence>
    <attribute name="orderDate" type="date"/>
  </complexType>
  <complexType name="USAddress">
    <sequence>
      <element name="name" type="string"/>
      <element name="street" type="string"/>
      <element name="city" type="string"/>
      <element name="state" type="string"/>
      <element name="zip" type="string"/>
    </sequence>
  </complexType>
  ...
</schema>
```

The schema in Listing 3–13 allows you to create XML documents in which the purchaseOrder element is the root, but it also allows you to create XML documents in which the address element is the root. Listing 3–14 is an XML document that defines the address element as its root element and conforms to the schema in Listing 3–13.

Listing 3–14

An Address Document Based on the Monson-Haefel Books Schema

```
<?xml version="1.0" encoding="UTF-8"?>
<addr:address
    xmlns:addr="http://www.Monson-Haefel.com/jwsbook">

  <name>AMAZON.COM</name>
  <street>1850 Mercer Drive</street>
  <city>Lexington</city>
  <state>KY</state>
  <zip>40511</zip>
</addr:address>
```

By declaring two different global elements in the Monson-Haefel Books schema (Listing 3–13), you effectively create two schema-verifiable markup languages, a Purchase Order Markup Language and a U.S. Address Markup Language. The implication here is that a single schema can be used to validate two—indeed many—different kinds of documents. XML schema also supports **global attributes** that can be referred to anywhere in the schema, and that provide a consistent attribute name and type across elements. An example of a standard global attribute is xml:lang, which any element can use to indicate the language used in an element's value (`"es"` for Spanish, `"en"` for English, and so on).

Local elements are those declared within the scope of a complex type. In Listing 3–13 all the elements, *except* for `purchaseOrder` and `address`, are local elements, because they are declared within one complex type or another. Similarly, `orderDate` is a **local attribute.** Table 3–5 illustrates.

Table 3–5 Global and Local Elements in Listing 3–13

Global Elements	Local Elements
`purchaseOrder`	`accountName`
`address`	`accountNumber`
	`shipAddress`
	`billAddress`
	`book`
	`total`
	`name`
	`street`
	`city`
	`state`
	`zip`

In a nutshell, global elements and attributes are declared as direct children of the `schema` element, while local elements and attributes are not; they are the children of complex types.

3.1.6 Qualified and Unqualified Elements

In Section 2.2.2 you learned that elements can be **qualified** by a namespace, or **unqualified;** that is, that elements in an XML document may or may not require QName prefixes. Global elements and attributes must always be qualified, which means that in an XML instance you must prefix them to form a QName. The exception is when a global element is a member of the default namespace, in which case it does not have to be qualified with a prefix—all unqualified elements are assumed to be part of the default namespace. The default namespace does not apply to global attributes; global attributes must always be prefixed.

While global elements and attributes must always be qualified, local elements may not need to be qualified. XML schema defines two attributes, `elementsFormDefault` and `attributesFormDefault`, that determine whether local elements in an XML instance need to be qualified with a prefix or not. For example, the schema for the Address Markup Language can be modified to require namespace prefixes on all local elements in an XML instance, as in Listing 3–15.

Listing 3–15

Declaring That Elements Must Be Namespace-Qualified

```
<?xml version="1.0" encoding="UTF-8"?>
<schema xmlns="http://www.w3.org/2001/XMLSchema"
 xmlns:mh="http://www.Monson-Haefel.com/jwsbook"
 targetNamespace="http://www.Monson-Haefel.com/jwsbook"
 elementFormDefault="qualified" >

    <element name="address" type="mh:USAddress" />

    <complexType name="USAddress">
      <sequence>
        <element name="name"    type="string" />
        <element name="street"  type="string" />
        <element name="city"    type="string" />
        <element name="state"   type="string" />
        <element name="zip"     type="string" />
      </sequence>
    </complexType>
    ...
</schema>
```

When the `elementFormDefault` attribute is set to `"qualified"`, in any XML instance all the local elements in the `targetNamespace` must be qualified with a prefix. For example, Listing 3–16 shows an XML instance that conforms to the schema in Listing 3–15.

Listing 3–16

Qualified Local Elements in an XML Document

```
<?xml version="1.0" encoding="UTF-8"?>
<addr:address
 xmlns:addr="http://www.Monson-Haefel.com/jwsbook" >

  <addr:name>AMAZON.COM</addr:name>
  <addr:street>1850 Mercer Drive</addr:street>
  <addr:city>Lexington</addr:city>
  <addr:state>KY</addr:state>
  <addr:zip>40511</addr:zip>
</addr:address>
```

If, on the other hand, the value for `formElementDefault` is `"unqualified"`, only the global elements must be qualified. Listing 3–17 represents a valid XML instance when `formElementDefault` is `"unqualified"`. Notice that the `address` element is qualified with the `addr` prefix, but the local elements (`name`, `street`, `city`, `state`, and `zip`) are not.

Listing 3–17

Unqualified Local Elements in an XML Document

```
<?xml version="1.0" encoding="UTF-8"?>
<addr:address
 xmlns:addr="http://www.Monson-Haefel.com/jwsbook" >

  <name>AMAZON.COM</name>
  <street>1850 Mercer Drive</street>
  <city>Lexington</city>
  <state>KY</state>
  <zip>40511</zip>
</addr:address>
```

The `attributeFormDefault` attribute works in exactly the same way. If the value is `"qualified"`, then the attributes for `targetNamespace` must be qualified with a prefix. If `attributeFormDefault` is `"unqualified"`, they do not.

The default value of the `fromElementDefault` and the `attributeElement Default` attributes is `"unqualified"`, so if they're not used then the local attributes and elements of `targetNamespace` do not need to be qualified. All of the XML documents before Listing 3–14 were unqualified by default, which is why the global elements (`address` and `purchaseOrder`) had prefixes but the other elements did not.

If the XML document declares a default namespace, then all elements without prefixes are assigned to that namespace. This rule makes things tricky because unqualified elements are not supposed to be qualified, yet if there is a default namespace, then they are assigned to that namespace and are effectively qualified. As an exercise can you explain why the XML document in Listing 3–18 is valid for the XML schema in Listing 3–15?

Listing 3–15 requires that all elements be qualified. Listing 3–18 declares the default namespace, which is the namespace automatically assigned any element that is not prefixed, so even though the elements in Listing 3–18 are not prefixed, they are qualified and are therefore valid when checked against the XML schema in Listing 3–15.

You are free to configure your schemas any way you want, but I've found that it's generally less confusing if you require that all elements be namespace-qualified by setting `elementFormDefault` equal to `"qualified"`. That said, this book uses both qualified and unqualified local elements with abandon. You'll see this kind of inconsistency in your real-world development efforts, and it's best if you get used to thinking about local-element qualification early in your work with XML.

3.1.7 Assigning and Locating Schemas

The whole point of schemas is that they define the grammar by which XML documents can be validated. In other words, schemas are used by parsers to verify that an XML document conforms to a specific markup language.

To validate an XML document against one or more schemas, you need to specify which schemas to use. You do so by identifying the schemas' locations, using the `schemaLocation` attribute, which is an **XML schema-instance attribute.**

The XML document in Listing 3–18 uses this attribute to declare the location of the one schema it's based on.

Listing 3–18

Using `schemaLocation` *with XML documents*

```
<?xml version="1.0" encoding="UTF-8"?>
<purchaseOrder orderDate="2003-09-22"
   xmlns="http://www.Monson-Haefel.com/jwsbook"
   xmlns:xsi="http://www.w3.org/2001/XMLSchema-instance"
   xsi:schemaLocation="http://www.Monson-Haefel.com/jwsbook
       http://www.Monson-Haefel.com/jwsbook/po.xsd">
  <accountName>Amazon.com</accountName>
  <accountNumber>923</accountNumber>
  <shipAddress>
    <name>AMAZON.COM</name>
    <street>1850 Mercer Drive</street>
    <city>Lexington</city>
    <state>KY</state>
    <zip>40511</zip>
  </shipAddress>
  <billAddress>
    <name>Amazon.com</name>
    <street>1516 2nd Ave</street>
    <city>Seattle</city>
    <state>WA</state>
    <zip>90952</zip>
  </billAddress>
  <book>
    <title>J2EE Web Services</title>
    <quantity>300</quantity>
    <wholesale-price>24.99</wholesale-price>
```

```
  </book>
  <total>8997.00</total>
</purchaseOrder>
```

The second namespace declared in Listing 3–18, `xmlns:xsi="http://www.w3.org/2001/XMLSchema-instance"` is the **XML schema-instance namespace,** which is defined by the XML schema specification. The XML schema specification explicitly defines a few attributes belonging to this namespace, which can be used in XML documents, including the `xsi:schemaLocation` attribute. Another important attribute from the XML schema-instance namespace is `xsi:type`, which is addressed in Section 3.2.

The `xsi:schemaLocation` attribute helps an XML processor locate the actual physical schema document used by the XML instance. Each schema is listed in an `xsi:schemaLocation` attribute as a namespace-location pair, which associates a namespace with a physical URL. In Listing 3–18, the Monson-Haefel namespace, `"http://www.Monson-Haefel.com/jwsbook"`, is associated with a schema file located at Monson-Haefel Books' Web site. You can use `xsi:schemaLocation` to point at several schemas if you need to. For example, we can add the schema location for the XML schema-instance, as in Listing 3–19.

Listing 3–19

Declaring Multiple Schema Locations

```
<?xml version="1.0" encoding="UTF-8"?>
<purchaseOrder orderDate="2003-09-22"
  xmlns="http://www.Monson-Haefel.com/jwsbook"
  xmlns:xsi="http://www.w3.org/2001/XMLSchema-instance"
  xsi:schemaLocation="http://www.Monson-Haefel.com/jwsbook
                      http://www.Monson-Haefel.com/jwsbook/po.xsd

                      http://www.w3.org/2001/XMLSchema-instance
                      http://www.w3.org/2001/XMLSchema.xsd">
```

You use white space to separate the namespace and the location URL in each namespace-location set—and to separate namespace-location pairs from each other. For readability, it's a good idea to use more white space to separate sets than to separate each namespace from its location.

You don't actually need to specify the XML schema-instance schema location,[3] because it must be supported natively by any XML schema validating parser, but you should list any other schemas used in an XML document.

[3] Whether you *should* is open to interpretation. For example, declaring the location of the XML Schema-Instance works with the Apache Xerces-J's SAX parser but not with Altova's XMLSpy (version 5, release 3).

For the schemas identified by `xsi:schemaLocation` to be useful, they must explicitly define themselves as belonging to one of the namespaces identified in the XML instance document. In this case the schema, Listing 3–12, belongs to the Monson-Haefel Books namespace, `"http://www.Monson-Haefel.com/jwsbook"`, the same namespace specified by the instance document.

A schema can be located on the Internet, as the Monson-Haefel Books schema in Listing 3–18 is, or on a local hard drive. When using a local schema, specify the location relative to the directory in which the XML document is located. For example, Listing 3–20 shows a schema that's in the same local directory as the XML instance.

Listing 3–20

Pointing to a Schema on a Local File System

```
<?xml version="1.0" encoding="UTF-8"?>
<purchaseOrder orderDate="2003-09-22"
   xmlns="http://www.Monson-Haefel.com/jwsbook"
   xmlns:xsi="http://www.w3.org/2001/XMLSchema-instance"
   xsi:schemaLocation="http://www.Monson-Haefel.com/jwsbook
                       po.xsd">
  <accountName>Amazon.com</accountName>
  <accountNumber>923</accountNumber>
```

It's important to note that the `xsi:schemaLocation` attribute is considered a "hint" by the XML schema specification, which means that XML parsers are not required to use the schema identified by `xsi:schemaLocation`, but a good parser will, and some, like Xerces-J, allow you to override the location identified by the `xsi:schemaLocation` attribute programmatically—useful if you want to avoid downloading the schema every time an XML document based on it is parsed; you can use a cached copy instead of the original.

The `xsi:schemaLocation` attribute is usually declared in the root element of an XML document, but it doesn't have to be. You can declare it later in the document, as long as it's in the scope of the elements it applies to.

3.2 Advanced XML Schema

The key goal of Web services is interoperability, so choosing technologies and standards like XML, SOAP, and WSDL, which are supported by the majority of platforms, is critical. XML is the foundation of Web service interoperability, but even XML can trip you up if you're not careful, particularly the more advanced XML schema types. The painful truth is that XML schema is still new, and some Web service platforms do not support all of its features. That said, according to the WS-I

Basic Profile 1.0, Web services must support all of the XML schema features, including those covered in this "Advanced" section.

3.2.1 Inheritance of Complex Types

XML schema supports type inheritance much as object-oriented programming languages do, but XML schema inheritance is actually more comprehensive than in most object-oriented languages. Unfortunately, the richness of XML schema inheritance can cause interoperability headaches.

Many Web service platforms map XML schema types to native primitive types, structures, and objects so that developers can manipulate XML data using constructs native to their programming environment. For example, JAX-RPC maps some of the XML schema built-in types to Java primitives, and basic complex types to Java beans. JAX-RPC can map most derived complex types to Java beans, but not all. Similar limitations are found in other platforms like .NET and SOAP::Lite for Perl. Most object-oriented languages do not support the full scope of inheritance defined by the XML schema specification. For this reason, you should use type inheritance in schemas with care.

Complex types can use two types of inheritance: **extension** and **restriction**. Both allow you to derive new complex types from existing complex types. Extension *broadens* a derived type by adding elements or attributes not present in the base type, while restriction *narrows* a derived type by omitting or constraining elements and attributes defined by the base type.

3.2.1.1 Extension

An **extension** type inherits the elements and attributes of its base type, and adds new ones. For example, we could redefine the `USAddress` type to be an extension of a base type called `Address` as shown in Listing 3–21.

Listing 3–21

Using XML Schema Inheritance

```
<?xml version="1.0" encoding="UTF-8" standalone="yes"?>
<schema
  targetNamespace="http://www.Monson-Haefel.com/jwsbook"
  xmlns:mh="http://www.Monson-Haefel.com/jwsbook"
  xmlns="http://www.w3.org/2001/XMLSchema"
  elementFormDefault="qualified">

<element name="address" type="mh:Address"/>

<complexType name="Address">
    <sequence>
```

```
    <element name="name" type="string"/>
    <element name="street" type="string" maxOccurs="unbounded"/>
    <element name="city" type="string"/>
    <element name="country" type="string"/>
   </sequence>
   <attribute name="category" type="string" default="business"/>
  </complexType>

  <complexType name="USAddress">
   <complexContent>
    <extension base="mh:Address">
     <sequence>
      <element name="state" type="string"/>
      <element name="zip" type="string"/>
     </sequence>
    </extension>
   </complexContent>
  </complexType>
  …
</schema>
```

The complexType and extension elements in Listing 3–21 tell us that USAddress extends Address. It adds the state and zip elements, so that the USAddress type has a total of six elements (name, street, city, state, zip, and country).

The base type Address defined in Listing 3–21 can be used to create other derived types as well. For example, we could extend it to define a United Kingdom address type, UKAddress, as in Listing 3–22.

Listing 3–22

A UK Address Type Extends the Address Type in Listing 3–21

```
<complexType name="UKAddress" >
   <complexContent>
      <extension base="mh:Address">
         <sequence>
            <element name="postcode" type="string"/>
         </sequence>
      </extension>
   </complexContent>
</complexType>
```

We now have two types derived from the `Address` type, `USAddress` and `UKAddress`, which capture the addressing proper to their respective postal systems.[4]

3.2.1.2 Restriction

Restriction is very easy to understand. You simply redefine or omit those elements and attributes that change, and list all the other elements and attributes exactly as they were in the base type. For example, we can create a `USAddress` type that omits the `city` and `state` elements, as shown in Listing 3–23. (If you have a zip code you don't need a city and state, because any zip code can be cross-referenced to a specific city and state.)

Listing 3–23

An Extension of the `USAddress` *Type Defined in Listing 3–21*

```
<complexType name="BriefUSAddress">
  <complexContent>
    <restriction base="mh:USAddress">
      <sequence>
        <element name="name" type="string"/>
        <element name="street" type="string"/>
        <element name="zip" type="string"/>
      </sequence>
      <attribute name="category" type="string" default="business"/>
    </restriction>
  </complexContent>
</complexType>
```

In this example, the derived type, `BriefUSAddress`, contains the `name`, `street`, and `zip` elements, but not the `city`, `state`, and `country` elements, because the schema simply omits them. In addition we have redefined the occurrence constraints on the `street` element so that it may occur only once (recall that the default values of `maxOccurs` and `minOccurs` are both `"1"`). Compare `BriefUSAddress` to the `Address` base type in Listing 3–21, which defined the `street` element with a `maxOccurs` equal to `"unbounded"`.

While the above paragraph is correct, there are some important limits on what you can do: You cannot omit an element from a restriction unless the parent type declared it to be `optional(minOccurs="0")`. In addition, the derived type's occurrence constraints cannot be less strict than those of its base type. For example, you cannot constrain an element to `minOccurs="0"` and `maxOccurs="4"` in the child if the parent's element is defined as `minOccurs="1"` and `maxOccurs="2"`. The restricted occurrence attributes must fall within the boundaries defined by the

[4] Actually, many UK addresses may not have a city, but we will ignore that detail in this example.

parent type. For the BriefUSAddress in Listing 3–23 to work, we will need to redefine the USAddress type in Listing 3–21 to make the city and state elements optional (set minOccurs="0"); if we don't, the parser will report an error.

The necessity of repeating all the elements and attributes, even if they don't change, makes restriction a bit cumbersome, but it's the only logical way of indicating which elements and attributes are omitted or constrained.

While restriction is useful, it's used less than extension because it doesn't map as well to programming languages. For this reason, it's risky to use restriction when defining complex types in your XML documents.

3.2.1.3 Polymorphism and Abstract Base Types

The real power of extension, and of restriction for that matter, is that derived types can be used polymorphically with elements of the base type. In other words, you can use a derived type in an instance document in place of the base type specified in the schema.

For example, suppose we redefine the PurchaseOrder type to use the base Address type for its billAddress and shipAddress elements, instead of the USAddress type, as shown in Listing 3–24.

Listing 3–24

Setting Up Polymorphism in a Schema

```
<?xml version="1.0" encoding="UTF-8" standalone="yes"?>
<schema
    xmlns="http://www.w3.org/2001/XMLSchema"
    xmlns:mh="http://www.Monson-Haefel.com/jwsbook"
    targetNamespace="http://www.Monson-Haefel.com/jwsbook"
    elementFormDefault="qualified">

  <element name="address" type="mh:Address"/>
  <element name="purchaseOrder" type="mh:PurchaseOrder"/>
  <complexType name="PurchaseOrder">
    <sequence>
      <element name="accountName" type="string"/>
      <element name="accountNumber" type="unsignedShort"/>
      <element name="shipAddress" type="mh:Address"/>
      <element name="billAddress" type="mh:Address"/>
      <element name="book" type="mh:Book"/>
      <element name="total" type="float"/>
    </sequence>
    <attribute name="orderDate" type="date"/>
  </complexType>
  ...
</schema>
```

Because XML schema supports polymorphism, an instance document can now use any type derived from `Address` for the `shipAddress` and `billAddress` elements. For example, in Listing 3–25 the XML instance of `PurchaseOrder` uses `BriefUSAddress` for the `billAddress` element and `UKAddress` for the `shipAddress` element.

Listing 3–25

Using Polymorphism in an XML Instance

```
<?xml version="1.0" encoding="UTF-8"?>
<purchaseOrder orderDate="2003-09-22"
  xmlns="http://www.Monson-Haefel.com/jwsbook"
  xmlns:mh="http://www.Monson-Haefel.com/jwsbook"
  xmlns:xsi="http://www.w3.org/2001/XMLSchema-instance"
  xsi:schemaLocation="http://www.Monson-Haefel.com/jwsbook
                      http://www.Monson-Haefel.com/jwsbook/po2.xsd">

   <accountName>Amazon.com</accountName>
   <accountNumber>923</accountNumber>
   <shipAddress xsi:type="mh:UKAddress">
       <name>Amazon.co.uk</name>
       <street>Ridgmont Road</street>
       <city>Bedford</city>
       <country>United Kingdom</country>
       <postcode>MK43 0ZA</postcode>
   </shipAddress>
   <billAddress xsi:type="mh:BriefUSAddress">
      <name>Amazon.com</name>
      <street>1516 2nd Ave</street>
      <zip>90952</zip>
   </billAddress>
   <book>
      <title>Java Web Services</title>
      <quantity>300</quantity>
      <wholesale-price>24.99</wholesale-price>
   </book>
   <total>8997.00</total>
</purchaseOrder>
```

The `xsi:type` attribute explicitly declares the type of the element in the instance document. Explicitly declaring an element's type with `xsi:type` tells the parser to validate the element against the derived type instead of the type declared in the schema. You can think of this as "casting" an element, similar to casting a value in

Java. The `xsi:type` must be a type derived from the element's type declared in the schema.

The `xsi:type` belongs to the XML schema-instance namespace, which is defined by the XML schema specification for use in instance documents. It's the same namespace that's used for the `schemaLocation` attribute.

3.2.1.4 Abstract and Final Complex Types

You can declare complex types to be abstract much as you do Java classes. For example, although the `Address` type is a good base type for `USAddress`, `UKAddress`, and `BriefUSAddress`, it's too vague to be used directly in an instance document. To prevent such use, you can declare the type to be **abstract.** For example, if we add `abstract="true"` to the earlier definition of `Address`, as in the following snippet, it cannot be used directly in an instance document. A member of its **substitution group** (the types derived from it) must be used instead.

```
<complexType name="Address" abstract="true">
  <sequence>
    <element name="name" type="string"/>
    <element name="street" type="string" maxOccurs="unbounded"/>
    <element name="city" type="string"/>
    <element name="country" type="string"/>
  </sequence>
  <attribute name="category" type="string" default="business"/>
</complexType>
```

You can also declare complex types to be **final,** just as Java classes can be final, to prevent a complex type from being used as a base type for restriction or extension. The possible values for the `final` attribute are `"restriction"`, `"extension"`, and `"#all"`.

For example, we can declare the `USAddress` type defined in Listing 3–21 to be "final by extension," which prevents it from being extended but allows restriction.

```
<complexType name="USAddress" final="extension">
  <complexContent>
    <extension base="mh:Address">
      <sequence>
        <element name="state" type="string"/>
        <element name="zip" type="string"/>
      </sequence>
    </extension>
  </complexContent>
</complexType>
```

If a type is declared `final="restriction"`, it can be extended but not restricted. If the final attribute equals `"#all"`, the type cannot used as a base type at all.

3.2.2 Inheritance of Simple Types

The built-in simple types are atomic and very restrictive, so they are an excellent foundation for validating data. For example, an `unsignedShort` type cannot contain letters (only digits), it cannot contain a decimal point, and its value must be between 0 and 65,535. That's pretty restrictive, but what if it's not restrictive enough? XML schema allows us to create new simple types that are derived from existing simple types in order to constrain further the range of possible values that a simple type may represent.

For example, `PurchaseOrder` declares the `total` element as an XML schema `float` type, which means it can contain any decimal value that can be represented with 32 bits of precision. That's a huge range of values, which includes very large negative and positive numbers. For example, both 2,093,020.99 and –24.9941 are valid `float` values. Monson-Haefel Books wants to limit the value of the `total` element to a much smaller range: any dollar amount between $0.00 and $100,000.00, a normal range of values used in purchase orders.

To constrain data in the `total` element to this range, we restrict the built-in `float` type to create a new type called `Total`, as shown in Listing 3–26.

Listing 3–26

Defining a Simple Type

```
<simpleType name="Total">
  <restriction base="float">
    <minInclusive value="0"/>
    <maxExclusive value="100000"/>
  </restriction>
</simpleType>
```

We declare the new `Total` simple type with the `simpleType` schema element. The `restriction` element enables us to limit the range of an existing type, as well as determine its format.

The `restriction` element for simple types contains one or more **facet** elements. A facet is an element that represents an aspect or characteristic of the built-in type that can be modified. For example, the `Total` simple type declares that its `minInclusive` facet is `"0"` and its `maxExclusive` facet is `"100000"`, thereby specifying that values held by elements of this type must be at least zero and less then 100,000.

The XML schema specification defines several facets you may use when restricting a `float` type. The modifiable facets for `float` are shown in Table 3–6.[5]

[5] Missing from this table is the `whiteSpace` facet, not shown because its value cannot be modified for a `float` type, which must always be `"constrain"`.

Table 3–6 Float Facets

Float Facet	Meaning
`maxInclusive`	The inclusive upper bound. The value may not exceed this amount.
`maxExclusive`	The exclusive upper bound. The value must be less than this amount.
`minInclusive`	The inclusive lower bound. The value must be at least this amount.
`minExclusive`	The exclusive lower bound. The value must be greater than this amount.
`pattern`	The format of the value, defined using a regular expression.
`enumeration`	The set of allowed values.

You can use the `Total` type in `PurchaseOrder` or elsewhere, just as you can a built-in type. Listing 3–27 shows the `PurchaseOrder` type using the new `Total` simple type.

Listing 3–27

Using Derived Simple Types in a Schema

```
<schema
  xmlns="http://www.w3.org/2001/XMLSchema"
  xmlns:mh="http://www.Monson-Haefel.com/jwsbook"
  targetNamespace="http://www.Monson-Haefel.com/jwsbook"
  elementFormDefault="qualified" >
  ...
  <simpleType name="Total">
    <restriction base="float">
      <minInclusive value="0.00"/>
      <maxExclusive value="100000.00"/>
    </restriction>
  </simpleType>
  <complexType name="PurchaseOrder">
    <sequence>
      <element name="accountName" type="string"/>
      <element name="accountNumber" type="unsignedShort"/>
      <element name="shipAddress" type="mh:Address"/>
      <element name="billAddress" type="mh:Address"/>
      <element name="book" type="mh:Book"/>
      <element name="total" type="mh:Total"/>
    </sequence>
    <attribute name="orderDate" type="date"/>
  </complexType>
  ...
</schema>
```

There are many kinds of facets, and each built-in type is assigned a subset of facets, which can be used to create new simple types. A complete list of facets for each data type can be found in *XML Schema Part 2: Data Types*.[6]

3.2.2.1 The `pattern` *Facet*

Most built-in types support the `pattern` facet, which is very powerful. While other facets are pretty self-explanatory, the `pattern` facet will look strange if you've never worked with regular expressions before. In XML schema, a **regular expression** is used to verify that the contents of an element or attribute adhere to a predefined character pattern.

For example, in addition to restricting the range of the `Total` type defined in Listing 3–27 to values between 0 and 100,000, we can declare a `pattern` facet to limit fractional amounts to two digits after the decimal point, as is conventional for dollar amounts.

```
<simpleType name="Total">
   <restriction base="float">
      <pattern value="[0-9]+\.[0-9]{2}" />
      <minInclusive value="0"/>
      <maxExclusive value="100000" />
   </restriction>
</simpleType>
```

The regular expression `"[0-9]+\.[0-9]{2}"` specifies that there must be at least one digit before the decimal point and exactly two digits following the decimal point. The following table shows valid and invalid values for the `Total` type.

Valid Values	Invalid Values
0.00	.00
0.10	0.1
1.01	–1.00
99,999.99	100,001.00

The `pattern` facet is commonly applied to `string` types. For example, we can define a `USZipCode` type that restricts a `string` value either to five digits, or to nine digits with the last four set off by a hyphen. Listing 3–28 illustrates.

[6] World Wide Web Consortium, *XML Schema Part 2: Datatypes,* W3C Recommendation, May 2, 2001. Available at http://www.w3.org/TR/xmlschema-2/.

Listing 3–28

Using the `pattern` *Facet*

```
<simpleType name="USZipCode">
   <restriction base="string">
      <pattern value="[0-9]{5}(-[0-9]{4})?" />
   </restriction>
</simpleType>
```

We could modify Listing 3–21 as in the following snippet to use the `USZipCode` simple type for the `USAddress` and `BriefUSAddress` types, to provide stronger validation of U.S. addresses.

```
<complexType name="USAddress" final="extension">
  <complexContent>
    <extension base="mh:Address">
      <sequence>
        <element name="state" type="string"/>
        <element name="zip" type="mh:USZipCode"/>
      </sequence>
    </extension>
  </complexContent>
</complexType>
...
<complexType name="BriefUSAddress">
  <complexContent>
    <restriction base="mh:USAddress">
      <sequence>
        <element name="name" type="string"/>
        <element name="street" type="string"/>
        <element name="zip" type="mh:USZipCode"/>
      </sequence>
      <attribute name="category" type="string"
                 default="business"/>
    </restriction>
  </complexContent>
</complexType>
```

Appendix B provides an overview of schema regular expressions. Readers already familiar with regular expressions may also find this appendix valuable because XML schema's regular-expression syntax has some small but important differences from that of other languages or tools (Perl, for example).

3.2.2.2 The `enumeration` *Facet*

The `enumeration` facet restricts the value of any simple type (except `boolean`) to a set of distinct values. For example, we can create a new `USState` type, which restricts the value of a `string` type to two-letter state abbreviations as shown in Listing 3–29.[7]

Listing 3–29

Defining an Enumeration

```
<simpleType name="USState">
   <restriction base="string">
      <enumeration value="AK"/> <!-- Alaska   -->
      <enumeration value="AL"/> <!-- Alabama  -->
      <enumeration value="AR"/> <!-- Arkansas -->
      <!-- and so on -->
   </restriction>
</simpleType>
```

We can then modify Listing 3–21 to use the `USState` enumeration type in the `state` element of the `USAddress` type, in order to constrain its value to valid U.S. state abbreviations.

```
<complexType name="USAddress" final="extension">
  <complexContent>
    <extension base="mh:Address">
      <sequence>
        <element name="state" type="mh:USState"/>
        <element name="zip" type="mh:USZipCode"/>
      </sequence>
    </extension>
  </complexContent>
</complexType>
```

3.2.3 List and Union Types

The simple types we have examined thus far are all atomic, which means that each one represents a single piece of data. For example, although the `name` element of `Address` may contain spaces (e.g., `<name>Richard W. Monson-Haefel</name>`), the

[7] The `USState` type would also include the District of Columbia (D.C.), commonwealths (e.g., Puerto Rico), territories (e.g., Virgin Islands), as well as special codes for the U.S. armed services abroad (e.g., Armed Forces Europe).

string value is still considered one piece of data. List and union types, however, allow us to define elements or attributes that contain multiple pieces of data separated by spaces.

While list types are supported by many Web service platforms, union types are not. Union and list types should be used with care, especially when interoperability across programming environments is important.

3.2.3.1 List Types

A **list** is a sequence of simple-type values separated by white space. For example, you can define a USStateList type to contain several USState type values, as shown in Listing 3–30.

Listing 3–30

Defining a List Type

```
<simpleType name="USStateList">
    <list itemType="mh:USState"/>
</simpleType>
```

In an instance document, an element of the USStateList type could contain zero or more state abbreviations separated by spaces.

```
<list-of-states>CA  NY  FL  AR  NH</list-of-states>
```

A list type may have length, minLength, maxLength, and enumeration facets. The length facets control the number of tokens contained by the element or attribute, while the enumeration facet defines a strict set of valid values.

A list type can be based on any simple type, built-in or derived, but not on other list types or on complex types. XML schema defines a built-in list type called NMTOKENS. NMTOKENS is a list of the NMTOKEN simple type, which is a string without spaces, line feeds, or tabs (see Table 3–2). NMTOKENS can be used *only* with attributes.

List types should be based on simple types that do not have spaces because the parser assumes that spaces separate values in the list. NMTOKENS is recommended for lists of attributes. For elements, a list type based on the token type (see Table 3–2) or simple types with no spaces, such as USState and USZipCode, is strongly recommended.

3.2.3.2 Union Types

A **union** is a set of valid simple types. It's a lot like a list type, except it can accommodate more than one kind of simple type. For example, the union type USStateOrZipUnion allows the value to be either a USStateList type or a USZipCode type, as shown in Listing 3–31.

Listing 3–31

Defining a Union Type

```
<simpleType name="USStateOrZipUnion">
   <union memberTypes="mh:USStateList mh:USZipCode"/>
</simpleType>
```

An element or attribute based on this type can hold either a `USStateList` or a `USZipCode`. It cannot, however, contain a mix of values. In other words, a `USState OrZipUnion` can contain a list of state codes or a single zip code, but not a mix of states and zip codes or more than one zip code. In the following example, valid and invalid values are shown for the hypothetical `location` element of type `USStateOrZipUnion`.

```
<!-- valid use of union type -->
<location>CA NJ AK</location>
<location>94108</location>

<!-- invalid use of union type -->
<location>94108 CA 554011 MN</location>
```

3.2.4 Anonymous Types

You can combine an element declaration with a complex or simple type declaration to create an anonymous type. An anonymous type is not named and cannot be referred to outside the element that declares it. For example, throughout this chapter the Purchase Order schema has defined a `PurchaseOrder` type and a `purchase Order` element separately, as shown in the following snippet from Listing 3–13.

```
<element name="purchaseOrder" type="mh:PurchaseOrder"/>

<complexType name="PurchaseOrder">
  <sequence>
    <element name="accountName" type="string"/>
    <element name="accountNumber" type="unsignedShort"/>
    <element name="shipAddress" type="mh:Address"/>
    <element name="billAddress" type="mh:Address"/>
    <element name="book" type="mh:Book"/>
    <element name="total" type="mh:Total"/>
  </sequence>
  <attribute name="orderDate" type="date"/>
</complexType>
```

The PurchaseOrder type is not very useful outside the purchaseOrder element, so we can combine the two declarations into one as in Listing 3–32.

Listing 3–32

Defining an Anonymous Type

```
<element name="purchaseOrder">
  <complexType>
    <sequence>
      <element name="accountName" type="string"/>
      <element name="accountNumber" type="unsignedShort"/>
      <element name="shipAddress" type="mh:Address"/>
      <element name="billAddress" type="mh:Address"/>
      <element name="book" type="mh:Book"/>
      <element name="total" type="mh:Total"/>
    </sequence>
    <attribute name="orderDate" type="date"/>
  </complexType>
</element>
```

We've combined definition of the PurchaseOrder type with declaration of the purhaseOrder element. Notice that the element declaration doesn't need a type attribute because it defines its own type, and that the complexType declaration doesn't declare a name attribute; it's **anonymous.**

Anonymous types can simplify schemas, but they can also be abused if nested too deeply or applied indiscriminately. A balanced approach is better, using a combination of anonymous types and named types. For example, the purchaseOrder anonymous type can contain other anonymous types as well as named types. In Listing 3–33 the book and total elements are nested anonymous types, while USAddress remains a named type that is defined elsewhere.

Listing 3–33

Nesting Anonymous Types

```
<element name="purchaseOrder">
  <complexType>
    <sequence>
      <element name="accountName" type="string"/>
      <element name="accountNumber" type="unsignedShort"/>
      <element name="shipAddress" type="mh:Address"/>
      <element name="billAddress" type="mh:Address"/>
      <element name="book">
```

```
        <complexType>
          <sequence>
            <element name="title" type="string"/>
            <element name="quantity" type="unsignedShort"/>
            <element name="wholesale-price" type="float"/>
          </sequence>
        </complexType>
      </element>
      <element name="total">
        <simpleType>
          <restriction base='float'>
            <minInclusive value="0"/>
            <maxExclusive value="100000"/>
            <pattern value="[0-9]+\.[0-9]{2}"/>
          </restriction>
        </simpleType>
      </element>
    </sequence>
    <attribute name="orderDate" type="date"/>
  </complexType>
</element>
```

Anonymous types can be based on complex or simple types. In this example, the `total` element is defined with an anonymous simple type, using simple type inheritance.

Because anonymous types have no names, they cannot be referred to outside the element that defines them. Anonymous types are not reusable, and you should employ them only when you know that the type won't be useful in other schemas. For example, the `book` and `total` elements are based on anonymous types that might well be useful in other circumstances; you might benefit from defining them separately as named types. In the end it's a judgment call.

3.2.5 Importing and Including Schemas

You can combine schemas using two different elements, `include` and `import`. An `import` allows you to combine schemas from different namespaces, while an `include` lets you combine schemas from the same namespace.

3.2.5.1 Importing

A schema may **import** types from other schemas, allowing more modular schema design and type reuse. For example, we can define a separate schema and namespace for all the types related to mailing addresses: `Address`, `USAddress`, `UKAddress`, `BriefUSAddress`, `USZipCode`, and `USState`. This schema would define the complete Address Markup Language for Monson-Haefel Books. Listing 3–34 shows an abridged version of this schema.

Listing 3–34

The Address Markup Schema

```
<?xml version="1.0" encoding="UTF-8" ?>
<schema
   targetNamespace="http://www.Monson-Haefel.com/addr"
   xmlns:addr="http://www.Monson-Haefel.com/addr"
   xmlns="http://www.w3.org/2001/XMLSchema">

  <element name="address" type="addr:Address"/>

  <simpleType name="USZipCode">
    <restriction base="string">
      <pattern value="[0-9]{5}(-[0-9]{4})?"/>
    </restriction>
  </simpleType>

  <simpleType name="USState">
    <restriction base="string">
      <enumeration value="AK"/> <!-- Alaska   -->
      <enumeration value="AL"/> <!-- Alabama  -->
      <enumeration value="AR"/> <!-- Arkansas -->
      <!-- and so on -->
    </restriction>
  </simpleType>

  <complexType name="Address" abstract="true">
    <sequence>
      <element name="name" type="string"/>
      <element name="street" type="string" maxOccurs="unbounded"/>
      <element name="city" type="string"/>
      <element name="country" type="string"/>
    </sequence>
    <attribute name="category" type="string" default="business"/>
  </complexType>

  <complexType name="USAddress" final="extension">
    <complexContent>
      <extension base="addr:Address">
        <sequence>
```

```
          <element name="state" type="addr:USState"/>
          <element name="zip" type="addr:USZipCode"/>
        </sequence>
      </extension>
    </complexContent>
  </complexType>

  <complexType name="UKAddress">
    <complexContent>
      <extension base="addr:Address">
        <sequence>
          <element name="postcode" type="string"/>
        </sequence>
      </extension>
    </complexContent>
  </complexType>

  <complexType name="BriefUSAddress">
    <complexContent>
      <restriction base="addr:USAddress">
        <sequence>
          <element name="name" type="string"/>
          <element name="street" type="string"/>
          <element name="zip" type="addr:USZipCode"/>
        </sequence>
        <attribute name="category" type="string" default="business"/>
      </restriction>
    </complexContent>
  </complexType>

</schema>
```

The `targetNamespace` of the Address Markup schema is `"http://www.Monson-Haefel.com/jwsbook/ADDR"`, which is a separate namespace from that of the purchase-order elements. Because the `PurchaseOrder` type depends on the `Address` type, we'll need to import the Address Markup schema into the Purchase Order schema as in Listing 3–35.

Listing 3–35

Importing a Schema

```
<?xml version="1.0" encoding="UTF-8" ?>
<schema
  targetNamespace="http://www.Monson-Haefel.com/jwsbook/PO"
```

```
  xmlns:po="http://www.Monson-Haefel.com/jwsbook/PO"
  xmlns:addr="http://www.Monson-Haefel.com/jwsbook/ADDR"
  xmlns="http://www.w3.org/2001/XMLSchema">

 <import namespace="http://www.Monson-Haefel.com/jwsbook/ADDR"
  schemaLocation="http://www.Monson-Haefel.com/jwsbook/addr.xsd" />
  <element name="purchaseOrder" type="po:PurchaseOrder"/>
  <simpleType name="Total">
    <restriction base="float">
      <minInclusive value="0.00"/>
      <maxExclusive value="100000.00"/>
      <pattern value="[0-9]+\.[0-9]{2}"/>
    </restriction>
  </simpleType>
  <complexType name="PurchaseOrder">
    <sequence>
      <element name="accountName" type="string"/>
      <element name="accountNumber" type="unsignedShort"/>
      <element name="shipAddress" type="addr:Address"/>
      <element name="billAddress" type="addr:Address"/>
      <element name="book" type="po:Book"/>
      <element name="total" type="po:Total"/>
    </sequence>
    <attribute name="orderDate" type="date"/>
  </complexType>
  <complexType name="Book">
    <sequence>
      <element name="title" type="string"/>
      <element name="quantity" type="unsignedShort"/>
      <element name="wholesale-price" type="float"/>
    </sequence>
  </complexType>
</schema>
```

The import mechanism enables you to combine schemas to create larger, more complex schemas. It's very useful when you see that some aspects of a schema, such as the address types, are reusable and need their own namespace and schema. The imported namespace needs to be assigned a prefix before we can use it. In this case, it's assigned the prefix `addr` in the root schema element.

3.2.5.2 Including

In addition to the `import` element, there is another way of combining schemas called **include**, which can be used only to combine schemas with exactly the same `targetNamespace`. Including is useful when a schema becomes large and difficult to maintain. The Purchase Order schema has not become that unwieldy, but just as an example, we could place the definitions of the `Total` and `Book` types into a separate schema, then use an `include` element to combine them with the Purchase Order schema. Listing 3–36 shows a schema document for the `Total` and `Book` elements, which we'll soon include in the Purchase Order schema.

Listing 3–36

The Book and Total Schema

```
<?xml version="1.0" encoding="UTF-8" ?>
<schema
  targetNamespace="http://www.Monson-Haefel.com/jwsbook/PO"
  xmlns:po="http://www.Monson-Haefel.com/jwsbook/PO"
  xmlns="http://www.w3.org/2001/XMLSchema">

  <simpleType name="Total">
    <restriction base="float">
      <minInclusive value="0.00"/>
      <maxExclusive value="100000.00"/>
      <pattern value="[0-9]+\.[0-9]{2}"/>
    </restriction>
  </simpleType>

  <complexType name="Book">
    <sequence>
      <element name="title" type="string"/>
      <element name="quantity" type="unsignedShort"/>
      <element name="wholesale-price" type="float"/>
    </sequence>
  </complexType>
</schema>
```

Here the `Book` and `Total` types have been placed in their own schema document—but notice that the `targetNamespace` is the same as in the Purchase Order schema in Listing 3–35. We can combine these two schemas using an `include` statement. Listing 3–37 shows the use of both `import` and `include`.

Listing 3–37

Using `Import` *and* `Include` *Together*

```
<?xml version="1.0" encoding="UTF-8" ?>
<schema
```

```
  targetNamespace="http://www.Monson-Haefel.com/jwsbook/PO"
  xmlns:po="http://www.Monson-Haefel.com/jwsbook/PO"
  xmlns:addr="http://www.Monson-Haefel.com/jwsbook/ADDR"
  xmlns="http://www.w3.org/2001/XMLSchema">

 <include
  schemaLocation="http://www.Monson-Haefel.com/jwsbook/po.xsd" />

 <import namespace="http://www.Monson-Haefel.com/jwsbook/ADDR"
  schemaLocation="http://www.Monson-Haefel.com/jwsbook/addr.xsd" />

  <element name="purchaseOrder" type="po:PurchaseOrder"/>
  <complexType name="PurchaseOrder">
    <sequence>
      <element name="accountName" type="string"/>
      <element name="accountNumber" type="unsignedShort"/>
      <element name="shipAddress" type="addr:Address"/>
      <element name="billAddress" type="addr:Address"/>
      <element name="book" type="po:Book"/>
      <element name="total" type="po:Total"/>
    </sequence>
    <attribute name="orderDate" type="date"/>
  </complexType>
</schema>
```

Notice that we don't specify the namespace of the included schema, because it's expected to match the `targetNamespace` of the schema, doing the including.

3.3 Wrapping Up

XML schema provides a standard typing system for defining markup languages and validating XML documents. SOAP, WSDL, and UDDI data structures are all defined in XML schema, so a good understanding of this technology is essential. There is a lot more to XML schema than this chapter covers; it would require an entire book to do the topic justice, but with this primer under your belt you are prepared to investigate new concepts by reading the W3C recommendation entitled *XML Schema* directly.

The W3C's XML schema recommendation is the last word on the topic, but it's not always an easy read. It's divided into three parts. The Primer, Part 0, is usually the best place to start when you need to learn about new features. It's a non-normative overview with examples. Part 1 covers the structure of schemas, and Part 2 defines concisely the XML schema data types. You can find these three documents at

```
http://www.w3.org/TR/xmlschema-0/
http://www.w3.org/TR/xmlschema-1/
http://www.w3.org/TR/xmlschema-2/
```

Although XML schema is the basis of Web services in J2EE, it's not the only XML schema language available today. In fact there are a couple of other schema languages, including DTDs (see Appendix A), Schematron, RELAX-NG, and a few others. Of these, Schematron appears to be the best complement to XML schema, or at least to offer validation checks that XML schema cannot duplicate.

Schematron is based on Xpath and XSLT and is used for defining context-dependent rules for validating XML documents. For example, in the purchase-order document you could use Schematron to ensure that the value of the `total` element equals the value of the `quantity` element multiplied by the value of the `wholesale-price` element, as shown in Listing 3–38.

Listing 3–38

`PurchaseOrder` *Instance Document*

```
<?xml version="1.0" encoding="UTF-8"?>
<purchaseOrder orderDate="2003-09-22"
     xmlns:mh="http://www.Monson-Haefel.com/jwsbook">
                   ...
                   <book>
                        <title>J2EE Web Services</title>
                        <quantity>300</quantity>
                        <wholesale-price>24.99</wholesale-price>
                   </book>
 <total>7485.00</total>
</purchaseOrder>
```

XML schema does not provide this type of business-rule support, so you may well want to use Schematron in combination with XML schema to provide more robust validation. You can find out more about Schematron at Rick Jelliffe's Web site, http://www.ascc.net/xml/schematron/.

Part II

SOAP and WSDL

At the heart of Web services today are SOAP and WSDL, so it's important that you have a good understanding of them and how they're used. That said, memorizing the details of SOAP and WSDL is not critical. While these technologies are central to Web services, in many cases you may not deal with them directly, as they will be hidden in the communication and deployment layer of the J2EE Web Services platform.

This part of the book covers SOAP 1.1 and WSDL 1.1. Although support for SOAP 1.1 and WSDL 1.1 is required by the WS-I Basic Profile 1.0, support for

SOAP Messages with Attachments is not. SwA is a significant feature of Web services practice today, however, and it's supported by J2EE Web Services, as well as a future version of the BP, version 1.1, so it's covered in Appendix E.

Once you have read Part II, you should have a pretty decent understanding of SOAP 1.1 and WSDL 1.1. If you desire more detailed knowledge, I suggest you read the Notes describing these technologies, published by the World Wide Web Consortium. You must complement that reading with study of the Basic Profile, however, because the BP imposes lots of restrictions and provides many clarifications that make SOAP 1.1 more interoperable and WSDL 1.1 more portable. Still, for most developers the level of coverage in this part of the book will be more than sufficient.

In This Part

Related Appendices

Chapter 4
SOAP

SOAP was originally an acronym for Simple Object Access Protocol. (Now it's just a name.) SOAP 1.1 is the standard messaging protocol used by J2EE Web Services, and is the de facto standard for Web services in general. SOAP's primary application is Application-to-Application (A2A) communication. Specifically, it's used in Business-to-Business (B2B) and Enterprise Application Integration (EAI), which are two sides of the same coin: Both focus on integrating software applications and sharing data. To be truly effective in B2B and EAI, a protocol must be platform-independent, flexible, and based on standard, ubiquitous technologies. Unlike earlier B2B and EAI technologies, such as CORBA and EDI, SOAP meets these requirements, enjoys widespread use, and has been endorsed by most enterprise software vendors and major standards organizations (W3C, WS-I, OASIS, etc.).

Despite all the hoopla, however, SOAP is just another XML markup language accompanied by rules that dictate its use. SOAP has a clear purpose: exchanging data over networks. Specifically, it concerns itself with encapsulating and encoding XML data and defining the rules for transmitting and receiving that data. In a nutshell, SOAP is a network application protocol.

A SOAP XML document instance, which is called a **SOAP message,**[1] is usually carried as the payload of some other network protocol. For example, the most common way to exchange SOAP messages is via HTTP (HyperText Transfer Protocol), used by Web browsers to access HTML Web pages. The big difference is that you don't view SOAP messages with a browser as you do HTML. SOAP messages are exchanged between applications on a network and are not meant for human

[1] The SOAP XML document is also called the *SOAP envelope*.

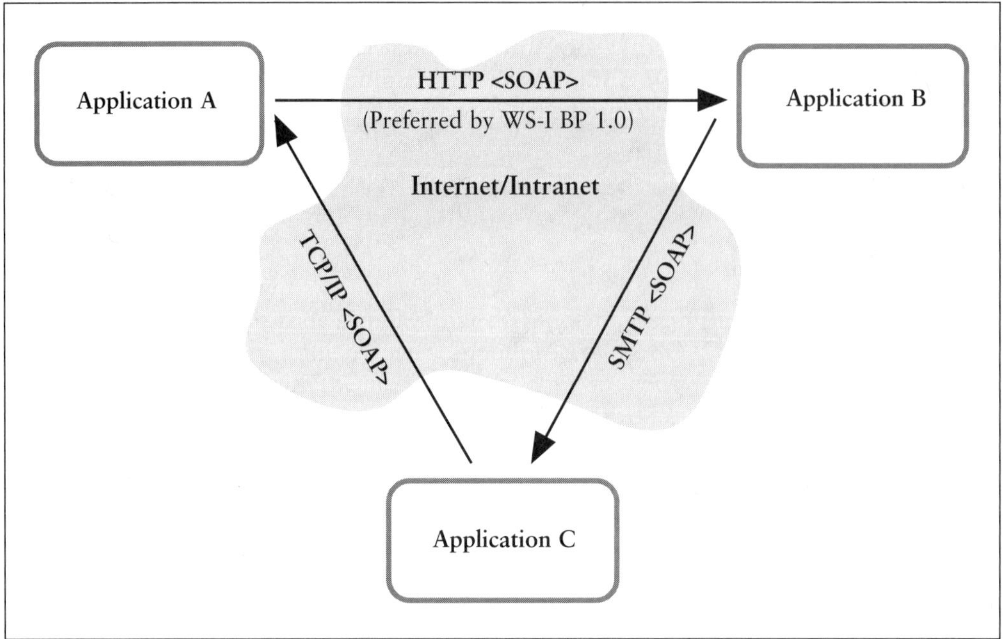

Figure 4–1 SOAP over HTTP, SMTP, and Raw TCP/IP

consumption. HTTP is just a convenient way of sending and receiving SOAP messages.

SOAP messages can also be carried by e-mail using SMTP (Simple Mail Transfer Protocol) and by other network protocols, such as FTP (File Transfer Protocol) and raw TCP/IP (Transmission Control Protocol/Internet Protocol). At this time, however, the WS-I Basic Profile 1.0 sanctions the use of SOAP only over HTTP. Figure 4–1 illustrates how SOAP can be carried by various protocols between software applications on a network.

Web services can use **One-Way messaging** or **Request/Response messaging.** In the former, SOAP messages travel in only one direction, from a sender to a receiver. In the latter, a SOAP message travels from the sender to the receiver, which is expected to send a reply back to the sender. Figure 4–2 illustrates these two forms of messaging.

SOAP defines how messages can be structured and processed by software in a way that is independent of any programming language or platform, and thus facilitates interoperability between applications written in different programming languages and running on different operating systems. Of course, this is nothing new: CORBA IIOP and DCE RPC also focused on cross-platform interoperability. These legacy protocols were never embraced by the software industry as a whole, however, so they never became pervasive technologies. SOAP, on the other hand, has enjoyed

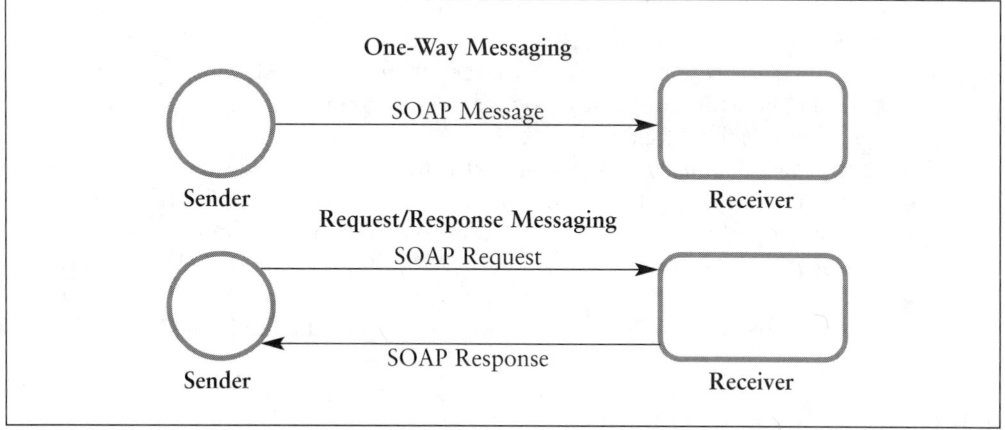

Figure 4–2 One-Way versus Request/Response Messaging

unprecedented acceptance, and adoption by virtually all the players in distributed computing, including Microsoft, IBM, Sun Microsystems, BEA, HP, Oracle, and SAP, to name a few.

The tidal wave of support behind SOAP is interesting. One of the main reasons is probably its grounding in XML. The SOAP message format is defined by an XML schema, which exploits XML namespaces to make SOAP very extensible. Another advantage of SOAP is its explicit definition of an HTTP binding, a standard method for **HTTP tunneling.** HTTP tunneling is the process of hiding another protocol inside HTTP messages in order to pass through a firewall unimpeded. Firewalls will usually allow HTTP traffic through port 80, but will restrict or prohibit the use of other protocols and ports.

A port is a communication address on a computer that complements the Internet address. Each network application on a computer uses a different port to communicate. By convention, Web servers use port 80 for HTTP requests, but application servers can use any one of thousands of other ports.

The power that comes from XML's extensibility and the convenience of using the ubiquitous, firewall-immune HTTP protocol partly explain SOAP's success. It's difficult to justify SOAP's success purely on its technical merits, which are good but less than perfect. Another factor in SOAP's success is the stature of its patrons. SOAP is the brainchild of Dave Winner, Don Box, and Bob Atkinson. Microsoft and IBM supported it early, which sent a strong signal to everyone else in the industry: "If you want to compete in this arena, you better jump aboard SOAP." The event that secured industry-wide support for SOAP was its publication by the World Wide Web

Consortium as a Note[2] in May of 2000, making it the de facto standard protocol for A2A messaging. Overnight, SOAP became the darling of distributed computing and started the biggest technology shift since the introduction of Java in 1995 and XML in 1998. SOAP is the cornerstone of what most people think of as Web services today, and will be for a long time to come.

Recently, the W3C has defined a successor to SOAP 1.1. SOAP 1.2 does a decent job of tightening up the SOAP processing rules and makes a number of changes that will improve interoperability. SOAP 1.2 is very new and has not yet been widely adopted, however, so it's not included in the WS-I Basic Profile 1.0. This exclusion is bound to end when the BP is updated, but for now J2EE 1.4 Web Services, which adheres to the WS-I Basic Profile 1.0, does not support the use of SOAP 1.2.

4.1 The Basic Structure of SOAP

As you now know, a SOAP message is a kind of XML document. SOAP has its own XML schema, namespaces, and processing rules. This section focuses on the structure of SOAP messages and the rules for creating and processing them.

A SOAP message is analogous to an envelope used in traditional postal service. Just as a paper envelope contains a letter, a SOAP message contains XML data. For example, a SOAP message could enclose a `purchaseOrder` element, as in Listing 4–1. Notice that XML namespaces are used to keep SOAP-specific elements separate from `purchaseOrder` elements—the SOAP elements are shown in bold.

Listing 4–1

A SOAP Message That Contains an Instance of Purchase Order Markup

```
<?xml version="1.0" encoding="UTF-8"?>
<soap:Envelope
 xmlns:soap="http://schemas.xmlsoap.org/soap/envelope/" >
  <soap:Body>
    <po:purchaseOrder orderDate="2003-09-22"
     xmlns:po="http://www.Monson-Haefel.com/jwsbook/PO">
      <po:accountName>Amazon.com</po:accountName>
      <po:accountNumber>923</po:accountNumber>
      <po:address>
        <po:name>AMAZON.COM</po:name>
        <po:street>1850 Mercer Drive</po:street>
        <po:city>Lexington</po:city>
```

[2] In the W3C standardization process, a Note does not represent commitment by the W3C to pursue work related to the technology it describes, but the W3C has taken responsibility for SOAP 1.2 and is working to make it an official recommendation, which is the highest level of endorsement offered by the W3C.

```
        <po:state>KY</po:state>
        <po:zip>40511</po:zip>
      </po:address>
      <po:book>
        <po:title>J2EE Web Services</po:title>
        <po:quantity>300</po:quantity>
        <po:wholesale-price>24.99</po:wholesale-price>
      </po:book>
    </po:purchaseOrder>
  </soap:Body>
</soap:Envelope>
```

This message is an example of a SOAP message that contains an arbitrary XML element, the `purchaseOrder` element. In this case, the SOAP message will be One-Way; it will be sent from the initial sender to the ultimate receiver with no expectation of a reply. Monson-Haefel Books' retail customers will use this SOAP message to submit a purchase order, a request for a shipment of books. In this example, Amazon.com is ordering 300 copies of this book for sale on its Web site.

A SOAP message may have an XML declaration, which states the version of XML used and the encoding format, as shown in this snippet from Listing 4–1.

```
<?xml version="1.0" encoding="UTF-8"?>
```

If an `xml` declaration is used, the version of XML must be 1.0 and the encoding must be either UTF-8 or UTF-16. If `encoding` is absent, the assumption is that the SOAP message is based on XML 1.0 and UTF-8. An XML declaration isn't mandatory. Web services are required to accept messages with or without them.[BP] (Remember that I said I'd use a superscript [BP] to signal a BP-conformance rule.)

Every XML document must have a root element, and in SOAP it's the `Envelope` element. `Envelope` may contain an optional `Header` element, and must contain a `Body` element. If you use a `Header` element, it must be the immediate child of the `Envelope` element, and precede the `Body` element. The `Body` element contains, in XML format, the actual application data being exchanged between applications. The `Body` element delimits the application-specific data. Listing 4–2 shows the structure of a SOAP message.

Listing 4–2

The Structure of a SOAP Message

```
<?xml version="1.0" encoding="UTF-8"?>
<soap:Envelope xmlns:soap="http://schemas.xmlsoap.org/soap/envelope/">
  <soap:Header>
    <!-- Header blocks go here -->
```

```
  </soap:Header>
  <soap:Body>
    <!-- Application data goes here -->
  </soap:Body>
</soap:Envelope>
```

A SOAP message adheres to the SOAP 1.1 XML schema, which requires that elements and attributes be fully qualified (use prefixes or default namespaces). A SOAP message may have a single `Body` element preceded, optionally, by one `Header` element. The `Envelope` element cannot contain any other children.

Because SOAP doesn't limit the type of XML data carried in the SOAP `Body`, SOAP messages are extremely flexible; they can exchange a wide spectrum of data. For example, the application data could be an arbitrary XML element like a `purchaseOrder`, or an element that maps to the arguments of a procedure call.

The `Header` element contains information about the message, in the form of one or more distinct XML elements, each of which describes some aspect or quality of service associated with the message. Figure 4–3 illustrates the structure of a basic SOAP message.

The `Header` element can contain XML elements that describe security credentials, transaction IDs, routing instructions, debugging information, payment tokens, or any other information about the message that is important in processing the data in the `Body` element.

For example, we may want to attach a unique identifier to every SOAP message, to be used for debugging and logging. Although unique identifiers are not an integral

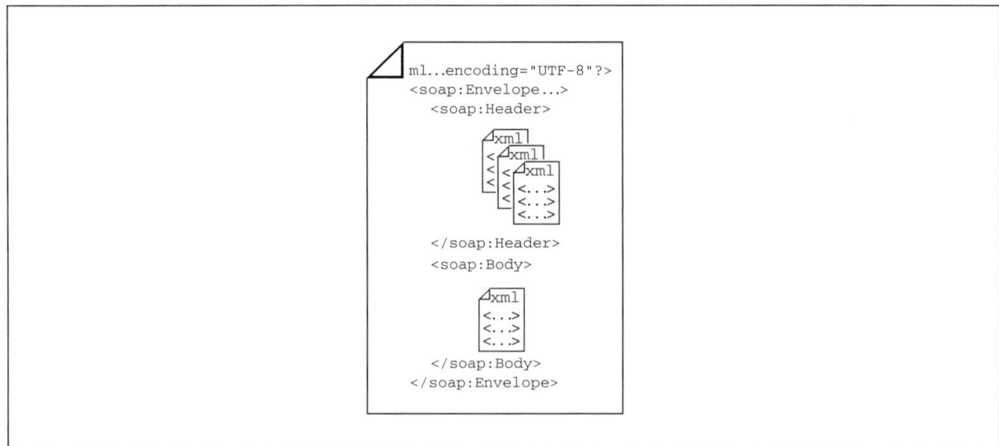

Figure 4–3 The Structure of a Basic SOAP Message

part of the SOAP protocol itself, we can easily add an identifier to the `Header` element as in Listing 4–3.

Listing 4–3

A SOAP Message with a Unique Identifier

```
<?xml version="1.0" encoding="UTF-8"?>
<soap:Envelope
 xmlns:soap="http://schemas.xmlsoap.org/soap/envelope/"
 xmlns:mi="http://www.Monson-Haefel.com/jwsbook/message-id" >
  <soap:Header>
    <mi:message-id>11d1def534ea:b1c5fa:f3bfb4dcd7:-8000</mi:message-id>
  </soap:Header>
  <soap:Body>
    <!-- Application-specific data goes here -->
  </soap:Body>
</soap:Envelope>
```

The `message-id` element is called a **header block,** and is an arbitrary XML element identified by its own namespace. A header block can be of any size and can be very extensive. For example, the header for an XML digital signature, shown in bold in Listing 4–4, is relatively complicated.

Listing 4–4

A SOAP Message with an XML Digital-Signature Header Block

```
<?xml version="1.0" encoding="UTF-8"?>
<soap:Envelope
 xmlns:soap="http://schemas.xmlsoap.org/soap/envelope/"
 xmlns:sec="http://schemas.xmlsoap.org/soap/security/2000-12"
 xmlns:ds="http://www.w3.org/2000/09/xmldsig#"
 xmlns:mi="http://www.Monson-Haefel.com/jwsbook/message-id">
  <soap:Header>
    <mi:message-id>11d1def534ea:b1c5fa:f3bfb4dcd7:-8000</mi:message-id>
    <sec:Signature >
      <ds:Signature>
        <ds:SignedInfo>
          <ds:CanonicalizationMethod Algorithm=
           "http://www.w3.org/TR/2000/CR-xml-c14n-20001026"/>
          <ds:SignatureMethod Algorithm=
           "http://www.w3.org/2000/09/xmldsig#dsa-sha1"/>
```

```
          <ds:Reference URI="#Body">
            <ds:Transforms>
              <ds:Transform Algorithm=
               "http://www.w3.org/TR/2000/CR-xml-c14n-20001026"/>
            </ds:Transforms>
            <ds:DigestMethod Algorithm=
             "http://www.w3.org/2000/09/xmldsig#sha1"/>
            <ds:DigestValue>u29dj93nnfksu937w93u8sjd9=
            </ds:DigestValue>
          </ds:Reference>
        </ds:SignedInfo>
        <ds:SignatureValue>CFFOMFCtVLrklR…</ds:SignatureValue>
      </ds:Signature>
    </sec:Signature>
  </soap:Header>
  <soap:Body sec:id="Body">
    <!-- Application-specific data goes here -->
  </soap:Body>
</soap:Envelope>
```

You can place any number of header blocks in the `Header` element. The example above contains both the `message-id` and XML digital signature header blocks, each of which would be processed by appropriate functions. Header blocks are discussed in more detail in Section 4.3.

4.2 SOAP Namespaces

XML namespaces play an important role in SOAP messages. A SOAP message may include several different XML elements in the `Header` and `Body` elements, and to avoid name collisions each of these elements should be identified by a unique namespace. For example, a SOAP message that contains the `purchaseOrder` element as well as `message-id` and XML digital-signature header blocks would include no fewer than six different namespaces, as shown in bold in Listing 4–5.

Listing 4–5

Using XML Namespaces in a SOAP Message

```
<?xml version="1.0" encoding="UTF-8"?>
<soap:Envelope
 xmlns:soap="http://schemas.xmlsoap.org/soap/envelope/"
 xmlns:sec="http://schemas.xmlsoap.org/soap/security/2000-12"
 xmlns:ds="http://www.w3.org/2000/09/xmldsig#"
```

```
 xmlns:mi="http://www.Monson-Haefel.com/jwsbook/message-id">
  <soap:Header>
    <mi:message-id>11d1def534ea:b1c5fa:f3bfb4dcd7:-8000</mi:message-id>
    <sec:Signature>
      ...
    </sec:Signature>
  </soap:Header>
  <soap:Body sec:id="Body">
    <po:purchaseOrder orderDate="2003-09-22"
     xmlns:po="http://www.Monson-Haefel.com/jwsbook/PO"
     xmlns:xsi="http://www.w3.org/2001/XMLSchema-instance">
     ...
    </po:purchaseOrder>
  </soap:Body>
</soap:Envelope>
```

The use of XML namespaces is what makes SOAP such a flexible and extensible protocol. An XML namespace fully qualifies an element or attribute name, as you learned in Section 2.2. Because their use was discussed in detail there, the basic mechanics of XML namespaces aren't covered here.

Of the six namespaces declared in Listing 4–5, the first, declared in the `Envelope` element, defines the namespace of the standard SOAP elements—`Envelope`, `Header`, and `Body`—as shown in bold in the following snippet from Listing 4–5.

```
<?xml version="1.0" encoding="UTF-8"?>
<soap:Envelope
 xmlns:soap="http://schemas.xmlsoap.org/soap/envelope/"
 xmlns:sec="http://schemas.xmlsoap.org/soap/security/2000-12"
 xmlns:ds="http://www.w3.org/2000/09/xmldsig#"
 xmlns:mi="http://www.Monson-Haefel.com/jwsbook/message-id">
 ...
</soap:Envelope>
```

This namespace determines the version of SOAP used (1.1 at this point). SOAP messages must declare the namespace of the `Envelope` element to be the standard SOAP 1.1 envelope namespace, `"http://schemas.xmlsoap.org/soap/envelope/"`. If a SOAP application receives a message based on some other namespace, it must generate a fault. This rule ensures that all conforming messages are using exactly the same namespace and XML schema, and therefore the same processing rules.[BP]

The second, third, and fourth namespaces declared in the `Envelope` element are associated with XML elements in the header blocks:

```
<?xml version="1.0" encoding="UTF-8"?>
<soap:Envelope
 xmlns:soap="http://schemas.xmlsoap.org/soap/envelope/"
 xmlns:sec="http://schemas.xmlsoap.org/soap/security/2000-12"
 xmlns:ds="http://www.w3.org/2000/09/xmldsig#"
 xmlns:mi="http://www.Monson-Haefel.com/jwsbook/message-id">
  <soap:Header>
    <mi:message-id>11d1def534ea:b1c5fa:f3bfb4dcd7:-8000</mi:message-id>
    <sec:Signature>
      <ds:Signature>
        ...
      </ds:Signature>
    </sec:Signature>
  </soap:Header>
  <soap:Body>
    <!-- Application-specific data goes here -->
  </soap:Body>
</soap:Envelope>
```

Each header block in the `Header` element should have its own namespace. This is particularly important because namespaces help SOAP applications identify header blocks and process them separately. A variety of "standard" header blocks that address topics such as security, transactions, and other qualities of service are in development by several organizations, including W3C, OASIS, IETF, Microsoft, BEA, and IBM. All of the proposed standards define their own namespaces and XML schemas, as well as processing requirements—but none of these "standard" header blocks is addressed by J2EE 1.4 Web Services yet.

In Listing 4–5, two other namespaces are declared in the immediate child of the `Body` element, as shown in the following snippet. The first namespace declaration belongs to the Purchase Order Markup Language defined by Monson-Haefel Books (see Part I: XML).

```
<?xml version="1.0" encoding="UTF-8"?>
<soap:Envelope
 xmlns:soap="http://schemas.xmlsoap.org/soap/envelope/"
 xmlns:sec="http://schemas.xmlsoap.org/soap/security/2000-12"
 xmlns:ds="http://www.w3.org/2000/09/xmldsig#"
 xmlns:mi="http://www.Monson-Haefel.com/jwsbook/message-id" >
  <soap:Header>
    <!-- Header blocks go here -->
  </soap:Header>
  <soap:Body sec:id="Body">
    <po:purchaseOrder orderDate="2003-09-22"
     xmlns:po="http://www.Monson-Haefel.com/jwsbook/PO"
```

```
    xmlns:xsi="http://www.w3.org/2001/XMLSchema-instance">
      ...
    </po:purchaseOrder>
  </soap:Body>
</soap:Envelope>
```

All of the local elements of a SOAP message must be namespace-qualified (prefixed with the SOAP 1.1 namespace), because the XML schema for SOAP 1.1 specifies the `elementFormDefault` attribute as `"qualified"`. In addition, the Basic Profile 1.0 requires that all the application-specific elements contained by the `Body` element must be qualified.[BP] Unqualified elements in a SOAP `Body` element create too much ambiguity as to the meaning and proper structure of elements. (See Section 3.1.6 for details about qualified and unqualified local elements.)

The `xsi:schemaLocation` attribute (the attribute that provides the URL of the schema) may be declared for validation, but in most cases the **SOAP stack** will have handled this matter at design time, so that explicit declaration of the `xsi:schemaLocation` in a SOAP message is not necessary.

A SOAP stack is a library of code designed to process and transmit SOAP messages. For example, Apache Axis, J2EE 1.4, Perl::Lite, and Microsoft .NET all have their own SOAP stacks, their own libraries of code for processing SOAP messages.

Some SOAP stacks make extensive use of the XML schema-instance namespace to indicate the data types of elements (for example, `xsi:type = "xsd:float"`). Other SOAP stacks do not, though, which causes problems when the receiver expects elements to be typed but the sender doesn't type them. According to the BP, the `xsi:type` attribute must be used only to indicate that a derived XML type is being used in place of its base type—for example, a `USAddress` in place of an `Address`.[BP]

As you learned in Section 2.2, the real power of XML namespaces goes beyond simply avoiding name collisions, to proper versioning and processing. Using fully qualified names for the SOAP and application-specific data tells the SOAP receiver how to process the message, and which XML schemas to apply in order to validate its contents. Differences in a particular version of a header block, for example, can affect how a receiver processes messages, so identifying the header-block version by its namespace enables a receiver to switch processing models, or to reject messages if it doesn't support the specified version. Similarly, properly identifying the types of XML elements contained in the `Body` element enables a SOAP receiver either to process those elements using the appropriate code modules or possibly to reject the message if it doesn't support the specified namespace.

The term "code module" is used to express an aspect of computer code that performs some function. A code module may be a separate code library, a service, or simply a branch of logic within a larger set of code.

For example, if a new algorithm is used to generate the message-id header block, then the namespace of the message-id header could change to reflect the use of the new algorithm. The SOAP message in Listing 4–6 contains a message-id header block with a new namespace, which indicates that it's different from the message-id header block used in previous examples.

Listing 4–6

Changing the Namespace of a Header Block

```
<?xml version="1.0" encoding="UTF-8"?>
<soap:Envelope
 xmlns:soap="http://schemas.xmlsoap.org/soap/envelope/"
 xmlns:sec="http://schemas.xmlsoap.org/soap/security/2000-12"
 xmlns:ds="http://www.w3.org/2000/09/xmldsig#"
 xmlns:mi2="http://www.Monson-Haefel.com/jwsbook/message-id_version2/">
  <soap:Header>
    <mi2:message-id>1-203950-3485-30503453098</mi2:message-id>
    <sec:Signature>
      ...
    </sec:Signature>
  </soap:Header>
  <soap:Body>
    <!-- Application-specific data goes here -->
  <soap:Body>
</soap:Envelope>
```

Namespaces enable a SOAP receiver to handle different versions of a SOAP message, without impairing backward compatibility or requiring different Web service endpoints for each version of a particular SOAP message.

As you can see from the previous examples, a SOAP message may contain many different namespaces, which makes SOAP messaging very modular. This modularity enables different parts of a SOAP message to be processed independently of other parts and to evolve separately. The version of the SOAP Envelope or header blocks may change over time, while the structure of the application-specific contents in the Body element remains the same. Similarly, the application-specific contents may change while the version of the SOAP message and the header blocks do not.

The modularity of SOAP messaging permits the code that processes the SOAP messages to be modular as well. The code that processes the element Envelope is independent of the code that processes the header blocks, which is independent of the code that processes application-specific data in the SOAP Body element. Modularity enables you to use different code libraries to process different parts of a SOAP message. Figure 4–4 shows the structure of a SOAP message and the code modules used to process each of its parts. The code modules in gray boxes are associated with

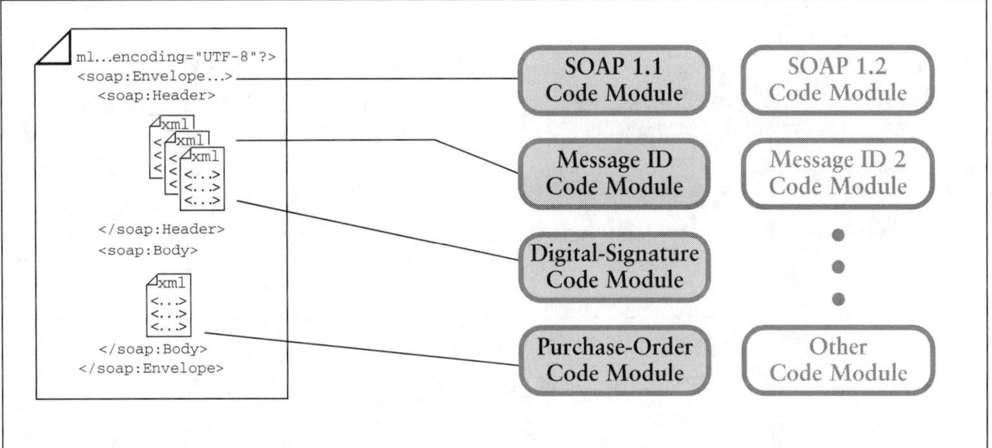

Figure 4–4 Using the Appropriate Code Modules with SOAP Namespaces

namespaces used in this SOAP message. The code modules in white boxes represent alternatives; they are associated with different namespaces, used to process alternative versions of the SOAP message.

In all the examples so far, the namespaces of the header blocks have been declared in the `Envelope` element. Doing so is not required; we could just as easily declare those namespaces in the `Header` element or the header blocks. As you learned in Section 2.2, namespaces are always locally scoped and can be declared at any level as long as the elements in question are within that scope (the element the namespace is declared in, and its subelements). For example, we could declare the header-block namespaces in the `Header` element, as shown in the boldface code lines in Listing 4–7.

Listing 4–7

Declaring XML Namespaces in a `Header` *Element*

```
<?xml version="1.0" encoding="UTF-8"?>
<soap:Envelope
 xmlns:soap="http://schemas.xmlsoap.org/soap/envelope/" >
  <soap:Header
   xmlns:sec="http://schemas.xmlsoap.org/soap/security/2000-12"
   xmlns:ds="http://www.w3.org/2000/09/xmldsig#"
   xmlns:mi="http://www.Monson-Haefel.com/jwsbook/message-id" >
    <mi:message-id>11d1def534:b1c5fa:f3bfb4dcd7:-8000</mi:message-id>
    <sec:Signature>
      ...
```

```
    </sec:Signature>
  </soap:Header>
  <soap:Body>
    <!-- Application-specific data goes here -->
  </soap:Body>
</soap:Envelope>
```

We could also declare each namespace in its own header block as in Listing 4–8.

Listing 4–8

Declaring XML Namespaces in Header Blocks

```
<?xml version="1.0" encoding="UTF-8"?>
<soap:Envelope
 xmlns:soap="http://schemas.xmlsoap.org/soap/envelope/" >
  <soap:Header>
    <mi:message-id
      xmlns:mi="http://www.Monson-Haefel.com/jwsbook/message-id" >
      11d1def534ea:b1c5fa:f3bfb4dcd7:-8000
    </mi:message-id>
    <sec:Signature
      xmlns:sec="http://schemas.xmlsoap.org/soap/security/2000-12"
      xmlns:ds="http://www.w3.org/2000/09/xmldsig#">
      ...
    </sec:Signature>
  </soap:Header>
  <soap:Body>
    <!-- Application-specific data goes here -->
  </soap:Body>
</soap:Envelope>
```

Although application-specific elements in the `Body` element must be qualified by prefixes, there is no such requirement for the elements contained within a `Header` element. Local elements of header blocks may be qualified or unqualified.

The way to declare namespaces is really a matter of style. As long as you adhere to the conventions and limitations of namespace declarations as they're described in the W3C *Namespaces in XML* recommendation,[3] you can use any style you wish. Table 4–1 shows the namespace prefixes used in this book and in the WS-I Basic Profile 1.0.

[3] World Wide Web Consortium, *Namespaces in XML*, W3C Recommendation, 1999. Available at http://www.w3.org/TR/REC-xml-names/.

Table 4–1 Namespace Prefixes

Prefix	Namespace
soap	"http://schemas.xmlsoap.org/soap/envelope/"
xsi	"http://www.w3.org/2001/XMLSchema-instance"
xsd	"http://www.w3.org/2001/XMLSchema"
soapenc	"http://schemas.xmlsoap.org/soap/encoding/"
wsdl	"http://schemas.xmlsoap.org/wsdl/"
soapbind	"http://schemas.xmlsoap.org/wsdl/soap/"
wsi	"http://ws-i.org/schemas/conformanceClaim/"

4.3 SOAP Headers

The SOAP specification defines rules by which header blocks must be processed in the **message path.** The message path is simply the route that a SOAP message takes from the initial sender to the ultimate receiver. It includes processing by any intermediaries. The SOAP rules specify which nodes must process particular header blocks and what should be done with header blocks after they've been processed.

The SOAP specifications and the Web services community in general use a lot of terminology that may seem a little confusing at first, because, unlike other application protocols, SOAP is not limited to a single messaging paradigm. SOAP can be used with a variety of messaging systems (asynchronous, synchronous, RPC, One-Way, and others), which can be combined in non-traditional ways. In order to describe all the parties that participate in SOAP messaging, new terminology was invented to avoid restrictive and preconceived notions associated with more traditional terms, such as "client" and "server." Although this new terminology wasn't introduced until early drafts of SOAP 1.2 were published, it applies equally well to SOAP 1.1.

SOAP is a protocol used to exchange messages between **SOAP applications** on a network, usually an intranet or the Internet. A SOAP application is simply any piece of software that generates or processes SOAP messages. For example, any Java application or J2EE component that uses JAX-RPC (covered in Part IV) would be considered a SOAP application, because JAX-RPC is used to generate and process SOAP messages. The application sending a SOAP message is called the **sender,** and the application receiving it is called the **receiver.** As a J2EE Web services developer you will be creating SOAP applications using JAX-RPC-enabled applications and components, which will act as receivers or senders or both.

A SOAP message travels along the message path from a sender to a receiver (see Figure 4–5). All SOAP messages start with the **initial sender,** which creates the SOAP

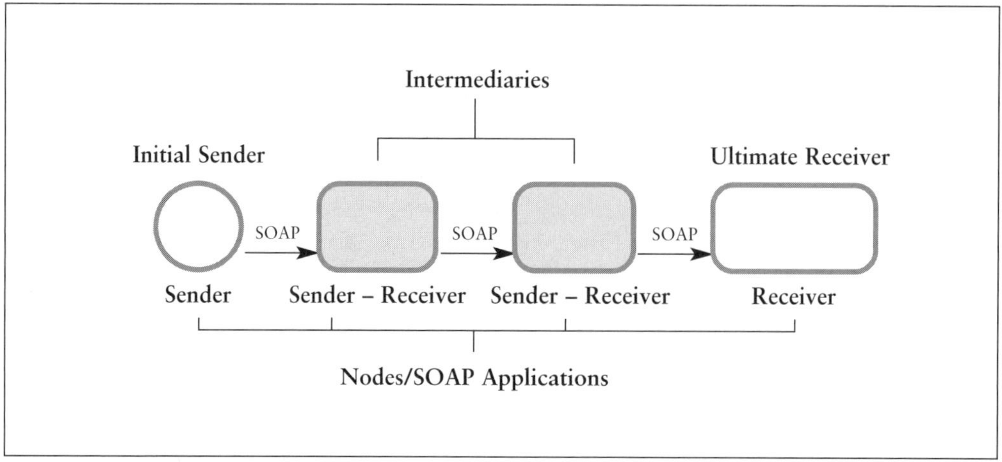

Figure 4–5 The SOAP Message Path

message, and end with the **ultimate receiver.** The term **client** is sometimes associated with the initial sender of a request message, and the term **Web service** with the ultimate receiver of a request message.

As a SOAP message travels along the message path, its header blocks may be intercepted and processed by any number of **SOAP intermediaries** along the way. A SOAP intermediary is both a receiver and a sender. It receives a SOAP message, processes one or more of the header blocks, and sends it on to another SOAP application. The applications along the message path (the initial sender, intermediaries, and ultimate receiver) are also called **SOAP nodes.**

To illustrate how nodes in a message path process header blocks, I'll use an example with two relatively simple header blocks: `message-id` and `processed-by`. The `processed-by` header block keeps a record of the SOAP applications (nodes) that process a SOAP message on its way from the initial sender to the ultimate receiver. Like the `message-id` header, the `processed-by` header block is useful in debugging and logging.

In this example, a SOAP message passes through several intermediaries before reaching the ultimate receiver. Figure 4–6 depicts the message path of a purchase-order SOAP message that is generated by a customer and processed by sales, accounts-receivable, inventory, and shipping systems.

Intermediaries in a SOAP message path must not modify the application-specific contents of the SOAP `Body` element, but they may, and often do, manipulate the SOAP header blocks.

In the present example, each SOAP intermediary is required to add a `node` element to the `processed-by` header block, identifying itself and the time it

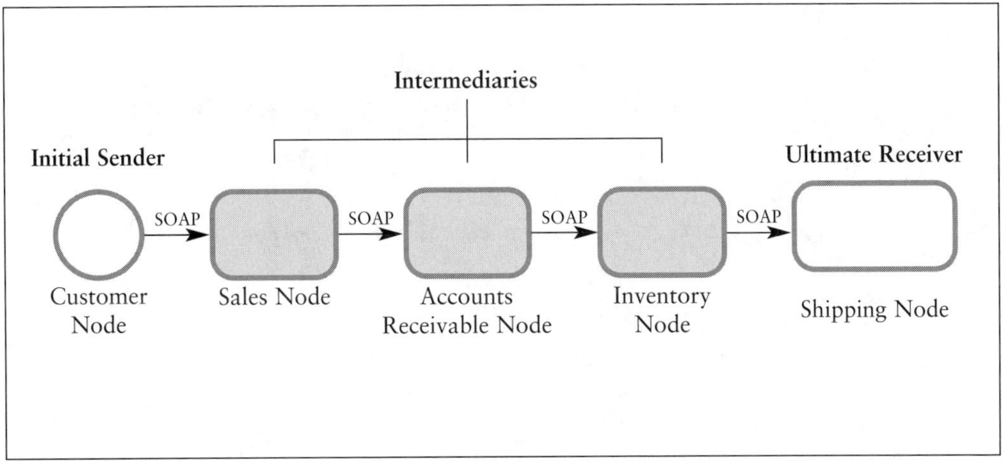

Figure 4–6 The Message Path of the Purchase-Order SOAP Message

processed the message. Listing 4–9 shows a message after each of five applications has added a `node` element to the `processed-by` header block.

Listing 4–9

The `processed-by` *Header Block*

```
<?xml version="1.0" encoding="UTF-8"?>
<soap:Envelope
 xmlns:soap="http://schemas.xmlsoap.org/soap/envelope/"
 xmlns:mi="http://www.Monson-Haefel.com/jwsbook/message-id"
 xmlns:proc="http://www.Monson-Haefel.com/jwsbook/processed-by">
  <soap:Header>
    <mi:message-id>11d1def534ea:b1c5fa:f3bfb4dcd7:-8000</mi:message-id>
    <proc:processed-by>
      <node>
        <time-in-millis>1013694680000</time-in-millis>
        <identity>http://www.customer.com</identity>
      </node>
      <node>
        <time-in-millis>1013694680010</time-in-millis>
        <identity>http://www.Monson-Haefel.com/sales</identity>
      </node>
      <node>
        <time-in-millis>1013694680020</time-in-millis>
        <identity>http://www.Monson-Haefel.com/AR</identity>
```

```
        </node>
        <node>
          <time-in-millis>1013694680030</time-in-millis>
          <identity>http://www.Monson-Haefel.com/inventory</identity>
        </node>
        <node>
          <time-in-millis>1013694680040</time-in-millis>
          <identity>http://www.Monson-Haefel.com/shipping</identity>
        </node>
      </proc:processed-by>
   </soap:Header>
   <soap:Body>
      <!-- Application-specific data goes here -->
   </soap:Body>
</soap:Envelope>
```

When processing a header block, each node reads, acts on, and removes the header block from the SOAP message before sending it along to the next receiver. Any node in a message path may also add a new header block to a SOAP message. But how does a node in the message path know which headers it's supposed to process?

SOAP 1.1 applications use the `actor` attribute to identify the nodes that should process a specific header block. SOAP also employs the `mustUnderstand` attribute to indicate whether a node processing the block needs to recognize the header block and know how to process it.

4.3.1 The `actor` Attribute

The `actor` attribute is defined by the SOAP Note and is a part of the same namespace as the SOAP `Envelope`, `Body`, and `Header` elements; that is, `"http://schemas.xmlsoap.org/soap/envelope/"`.

You use an `actor` attribute to identify a function to be performed by a particular node.

> *Just as a person can perform one or more roles in a stage play, a node can play one or more roles in a SOAP message path. Unfortunately, the designers of SOAP 1.1 confused the words "actor" and "role"; they specified that you must identify the* roles *a node will play by declaring an* `actor` *attribute. They've recognized their mistake, and in SOAP 1.2 this attribute has been renamed* `role`*. Because this book focuses on SOAP 1.1, you and I will have to work with the earlier terminology: An* `actor` *attribute specifies a* role *a node must play. I'll try to minimize the confusion as much as I can as we go along.*

The actor attribute uses a URI (Uniform Resource Identifier) to identify the role that a node must perform in order to process that header block. When a node receives a SOAP message, it examines each of the header blocks to determine which ones are targeted to roles supported by that node. For example, every SOAP message processed by a Monson-Haefel Books Web service might pass through a **logging intermediary,** a code module that records information about incoming messages in a log, to be used for debugging.

The logging module represents a particular role played by a node. A node may have many modules that operate on a message, and therefore many roles, so every node in a message path may identify itself with several different roles. For example, our company's Sales node (see Figure 4–6) may have a logging module, a security authentication module, and a transaction module. Each of these modules will read and process incoming SOAP messages in some way, and each module may represent a different role played by the Sales node.

The actor attribute is used in combination with the XML namespaces to determine which code module will process a particular header block. Conceptually, the receiving node will first determine whether it plays the role designated by the actor attribute, and then choose the correct code module to process the header block, based on the XML namespace of the header block. Therefore, the receiving node must recognize the role designated by the actor attribute assigned to a header block, as well as the XML namespace associated with the header block.

For example, the actor attribute identifies the logger role with the URL "http://www.Monson-Haefel.com/logger". A node that's intended to perform the logger role will look for header blocks where that URL is the value of the actor attribute. The message-id header block in the purchase-order SOAP message might be assigned the actor attribute value "http://www.Monson-Haefel.com/logger" as shown in Listing 4–10.

Listing 4–10

The actor *Attribute*

```
<?xml version="1.0" encoding="UTF-8"?>
<soap:Envelope
 xmlns:soap="http://schemas.xmlsoap.org/soap/envelope/"
 xmlns:mi="http://www.Monson-Haefel.com/jwsbook/message-id"
 xmlns:proc="http://www.Monson-Haefel.com/jwsbook/processed-by">
  <soap:Header>
    <mi:message-id soap:actor="http://www.Monson-Haefel.com/logger" >
      11d1def534ea:b1c5fa:f3bfb4dcd7:-8000
    </mi:message-id>
    <proc:processed-by>
      <node>
        <time-in-millis>1013694680000</time-in-millis>
```

```
        <identity>http://www.customer.com</identity>
      </node>
    </proc:processed-by>
  </soap:Header>
  <soap:Body>
      <!-- Application-specific data goes here -->
  </soap:Body>
</soap:Envelope>
```

Only those nodes in the message path that identify themselves with the `actor` value `"http://www.Monson-Haefel.com/logger"` will process the `message-id` header block; all other nodes will ignore it.

In addition to custom URIs like `"http://www.Monson-Haefel.com/logger"`, SOAP identifies two standard roles for the `actor` attribute: `next` and `ultimate receiver`. (These phrases don't actually appear by themselves in SOAP message documents. Nevertheless this chapter will show `next` and `ultimate receiver` in code font when they represent role names, to signal we're not referring to their more general meanings.) These standard roles indicate which nodes should process the header block, and they are relatively self-explanatory.

The `next` role indicates that the next node in the message path must process the header. The `next` role has a designated URI, which must be used as the value of the `actor` attribute: `"http://schemas.xmlsoap.org/soap/actor/next"`.

The `ultimate receiver` role indicates that only the ultimate receiver of the message should process the header block. The protocol doesn't specify an explicit URI for this purpose; it's the *absence* of an `actor` attribute in the header block that signals that the role is `ultimate receiver`.

We can use the `next` role in the `processed-by` header block of the purchase-order SOAP message, as shown in Listing 4–11.

Listing 4–11

A Header Block Uses the `actor` *Attribute*

```
<?xml version="1.0" encoding="UTF-8"?>
<soap:Envelope
 xmlns:soap="http://schemas.xmlsoap.org/soap/envelope/"
 xmlns:mi="http://www.Monson-Haefel.com/jwsbook/message-id"
 xmlns:proc="http://www.Monson-Haefel.com/jwsbook/processed-by">
  <soap:Header>
    <mi:message-id soap:actor="http://www.Monson-Haefel.com/logger" >
      11d1def534ea:b1c5fa:f3bfb4dcd7:-8000
    </mi:message-id>
    <proc:processed-by
     soap:actor=" http://schemas.xmlsoap.org/soap/actor/next">
```

```
      <node>
        <time-in-millis>1013694680000</time-in-millis>
        <identity>http://www.customer.com</identity>
      </node>
    </proc:processed-by>
  </soap:Header>
  <soap:Body>
      <!-- Application-specific data goes here -->
  </soap:Body>
</soap:Envelope>
```

In this case, the next receiver in the message path, no matter what other purpose it may serve, should process the `processed-by` header block. If an intermediary node in the message path supports the logger role, then it should process the `processed-by` header block in addition to the `message-id` header block. In this scenario, the intermediary node fulfills two roles: it's both a logger and the `next` receiver.

When a node processes a header block, it must remove it from the SOAP message. The node may also add new header blocks to the SOAP message. SOAP nodes frequently feign removal of a header block by simply modifying it, which is logically the same as removing it, modifying it, and then adding it back to the SOAP message—a little trick that allows a node to adhere to the SOAP specifications while propagating header blocks without losing any data. For example, the logger node may remove the `message-id` header block, but we don't want it to remove the `processed-by` header block, because we want all the nodes in the message path to add information to it. Therefore, the logger node will simply add its own data to the `processed-by` header block, then pass the SOAP message to the next node in the message path. Listing 4–12 shows the SOAP message after the logger node has processed it. Notice that the `message-id` header block has been removed and the `processed-by` header block has been modified.

Listing 4–12

The SOAP Message After the Header Blocks Are Processed

```
<?xml version="1.0" encoding="UTF-8"?>
<soap:Envelope
 xmlns:soap="http://schemas.xmlsoap.org/soap/envelope/"
 xmlns:mi="http://www.Monson-Haefel.com/jwsbook/message-id"
 xmlns:proc="http://www.Monson-Haefel.com/jwsbook/processed-by">
  <soap:Header>
    <proc:processed-by
     soap:actor="http://schemas.xmlsoap.org/soap/actor/next">
      <node>
        <time-in-millis>1013694680000</time-in-millis>
```

```
      <identity>http://www.customer.com</identity>
    </node>
    <node>
      <time-in-millis>1013694680010</time-in-millis>
      <identity>http://www.Monson-Haefel.com/sales</identity>
    </node>
  </proc:processed-by>
</soap:Header>
<soap:Body>
    <!-- Application-specific data goes here -->
</soap:Body>
</soap:Envelope>
```

4.3.2 The `mustUnderstand` Attribute

The use of standard role types, especially the `next` type, raises some interesting issues. In many cases we may not know the exact message path or the capabilities of all the nodes in a message path, which means we don't always know whether nodes can process header blocks correctly. For example, the `processed-by` header block is targeted at the `next` role, which means the next node to receive it should process it. But what if the next node doesn't recognize that kind of header block?

Header blocks may indicate whether processing is mandatory or not by using the `mustUnderstand` attribute, which is defined by the standard SOAP 1.1 namespace `"http://schemas.xmlsoap.org/soap/envelope/"`. The `mustUnderstand` attribute can have the value of either `"1"` or `"0"`, to represent true and false, respectively.

> ***The SOAP 1.1 XML Schema actually defines the*** `mustUnderstand` ***attribute as an*** `xsd:boolean` ***type, which allows any of*** **four** ***lexical literals:*** `"1", "true", "0", or "false"`***. This flexibility has caused interoperability problems in the past, when a receiver expected a value of*** `"1"` ***or*** `"0"`***, but the sender supplied*** `"true"` ***or*** `"false"`***. According to the BP, SOAP applications must set the*** `mustUnderstand` ***attribute to*** `"1"` ***or*** `"0"`—`"true"` ***and*** `"false"` ***are*** **not** ***allowed.***[BP]

If the `mustUnderstand` attribute is omitted, then its default value is `"0"` (false). Explicitly declaring the `"0"` value is considered a waste of bandwidth.

When a header block has a `mustUnderstand` attribute equal to `"1"`, it's called a **mandatory header block.** SOAP nodes must be able to process any header block that is marked as mandatory *if* they play the role specified by the `actor` attribute of the header block.

The "understand" in `mustUnderstand` means that the node must recognize the header block by its XML structure and namespace, and know how to process it. In other words, if the node plays the role indicated by the `actor` attribute of a header block, but it's not programmed to process that header block, then that header block is *not* understood. This problem can arise very easily if you add an intermediate node but fail to account for all possible header blocks targeted to it, or more likely, fail to consider the `next` role.

If a node doesn't understand a mandatory header block, it must generate a **SOAP fault** (similar to a remote exception in Java) and discard the message; it must not forward the message to the next node in the message path.[BP]

> ***The SOAP 1.1 Note didn't explain what should be done after a SOAP fault is generated. It didn't say whether the message should continue to be processed, which made it hard to predict what a receiver would do after generating a fault. The Basic Profile requires that the receiver discontinue normal processing of the message and generate a fault message.***[BP]

In Listing 4–13, the SOAP message declares the `mustUnderstand` attribute in the `processed-by` header to be true.

Listing 4–13

Using the `mustUnderstand` *Attribute to Make Processing of a Header Block Mandatory*

```
<?xml version="1.0" encoding="UTF-8"?>
<soap:Envelope
 xmlns:soap="http://schemas.xmlsoap.org/soap/envelope/"
 xmlns:proc="http://www.Monson-Haefel.com/jwsbook/processed-by">
  <soap:Header>
    <proc:processed-by
     soap:actor="http://schemas.xmlsoap.org/soap/actor/next"
     soap:mustUnderstand="1" >
      <node>
        <time-in-millis>1013694684723</time-in-millis>
        <identity>http://local/SOAPClient2</identity>
      </node>
      <node>
        <time-in-millis>1013694685023</time-in-millis>
        <identity>http://www.Monson-Haefel.com/logger</identity>
      </node>
    </proc:processed-by>
  </soap:Header>
  <soap:Body>
    <!-- Application-specific data goes here -->
  </soap:Body>
</soap:Envelope>
```

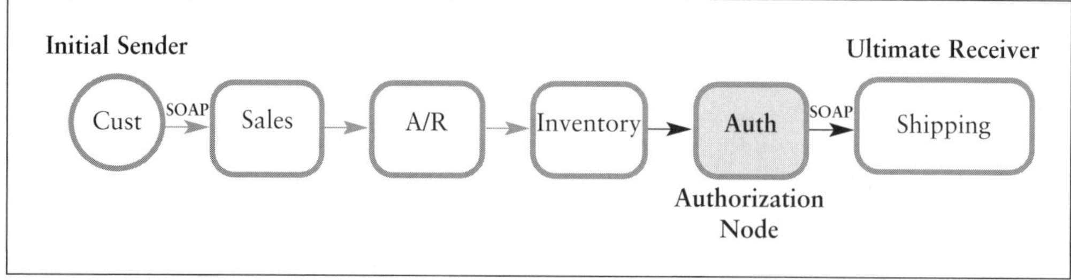

Figure 4–7 The Purchase-Order Message Path with Logger and Authentication-Filter Nodes

Let's say that Monson-Haefel adds a new Authentication node to the purchase-order message path. A SOAP message will be processed by the Authentication node before it's processed by the ultimate receiver, as illustrated in Figure 4–7.

Now suppose that when the Authentication node is added, the programmer neglects to include logic to handle the `processed-by` header block. As a result, the authentication node will not recognize the `processed-by` header block and will have no idea how to process it. Because the header block's `mustUnderstand` attribute has a value of `"1"`, the authentication node will have to discard the SOAP message, generate a SOAP fault, and send it back to the sender.

A SOAP receiver is required to generate a fault with the fault code `MustUnderstand` if it fails to understand a mandatory header block.[BP] This issue is covered in more detail in Section 4.6: SOAP Faults.

Whether or not a fault is sent back to the sender depends on whether the **messaging exchange pattern** (**MEP**) is One-Way or Request/Response. If a SOAP application uses Request/Response messaging, it's required to send a SOAP fault back to the sender; if it uses One-Way messaging, it's not.[BP]

If the `mustUnderstand` attribute is `"0"`, the processing requirements specified by SOAP are very different. If a node performs the role declared by a non-mandatory header block, and an application fails to understand the header (it doesn't recognize the XML structure or the namespace), it must remove the header block. It's not obliged, however, to try and process it, or to discard the message; it's free to remove the header and pass the message on to the next node in the message path.

Receivers should not reject a message simply because a header block targeted at some other node has not been processed (and removed). In other words, receivers should not attempt to determine whether a message was successfully processed by previous nodes in the path based on which header blocks are present. This rule applies especially to the ultimate receiver, which shouldn't reject a message because a header block intended for some unknown role was never processed. If receivers started analyzing and rejecting messages based on the status of header blocks for which they are not targeted, it would be impossible to make changes to the message path without worrying about the ripple effect of those changes downstream. Because nodes are required to "mind their own business," message paths can evolve and are very dynamic. Adding new intermediaries (or removing them) doesn't require adjustments to every other node in a message path.

> ***Although this processing rule is not mentioned in SOAP 1.1 or the BP, it's an explicit requirement in SOAP 1.2 and should be applied when developing receivers for SOAP 1.1.***

4.3.3 The WS-I Conformance Header Block

Although the BP doesn't endorse any particular type of header block, it does specify an optional conformance header block that indicates that the SOAP message complies with the BP. Listing 4–14 shows how the conformance header block may appear in a SOAP message.

Listing 4–14

Including a `Claim` *Header Block in a SOAP Message*

```
<?xml version="1.0" encoding="UTF-8"?>
<soap:Envelope
 xmlns:soap="http://schemas.xmlsoap.org/soap/envelope/"
  <soap:Header>
    <wsi:Claim conformsTo="http://ws-i.org/profiles/basic/1.0"
     xmlns:wsi="http://ws-i.org/schemas/conformanceClaim/" />
  </soap:Header>
  <soap:Body sec:id="Body">
    <!-- Application-specific data goes here -->
  </soap:Body>
</soap:Envelope>
```

The WS-I Basic Profile states that the `Claim` header block is not required. It also states that "absence of a conformance claim in a message must not be construed as inferring that the message does or does not conform to one or more profiles."

A SOAP message can declare a separate `Claim` header for each profile it adheres to. At the time of this writing the WS-I has defined only the Basic Profile 1.0, but it's expected to release other profiles. In the future, it's possible that a SOAP message will conform to both the Basic Profile 1.0 and other, as yet undefined, profiles.

A `Claim` element may be declared only as an immediate child of the `Header` element; it cannot appear in any other part of a SOAP message. In addition, the `Claim` header block is always considered optional, so its `mustUnderstand` attribute must not be `"1"`. You cannot require receivers to process a `Claim` header block.[BP]

4.3.4 Final Words about Headers

SOAP headers are a very powerful way of extending the SOAP protocol. As a construct for meta-data, a SOAP header is far more flexible and easier for developers and vendors to take advantage of than similar mechanisms in other protocols (such as the "service context" in CORBA IIOP). The extensibility of the SOAP headers is another reason why SOAP has become so popular and is likely to succeed where other protocols have not.

The `message-id` and `processed-by` headers are only custom header blocks I created for use in this book. Standards bodies frequently drive the definition of general-purpose SOAP header blocks. These organizations are primarily concerned with header blocks that address **qualities of service,** such as security, transactions, message persistence, and routing. OASIS, for example, is defining the WS-Security SOAP headers used with XML digital signatures—an XML security mechanism. Another example is the ebXML-specific header blocks defined by OASIS for such qualities of service as routing, reliable messaging, and security. Microsoft and IBM are also defining "standard" header blocks for these same qualities of service. The BP does not address any of these potential standards, but WS-I will eventually create more advanced profiles that incorporate many of the proposals evolving at OASIS, W3C, Microsoft, IBM, and other organizations—in fact, at the time of this writing, WS-I has started defining the WS-I Security Profile based on the OASIS WS-Security standard.

4.4 The SOAP Body

Although the `Header` element is optional, all SOAP messages must contain exactly one `Body` element.[BP] The `Body` element contains either the application-specific data or a fault message. Application-specific data is the information that we want to exchange with a Web service. It can be arbitrary XML data or parameters to a procedure call. Either way, the `Body` element contains the application data being exchanged. A fault message is used only when an error occurs. The receiving node that discovers a problem, such as a processing error or a message that's improperly structured, sends it back to the sender just before it in the message path. A SOAP message may carry either application-specific data or a fault, but not both.

Whether the `Body` element contains application-specific data or a fault, most SOAP experts agree that only the ultimate receiver of the SOAP message should process the contents of the `Body`. Intermediary nodes in the message path may view the `Body` element, but they should not alter its contents in any way. This is very different from header blocks, which may be processed by any number of intermediaries along the message path. This is a critical point: Only the ultimate receiver should alter the contents of the `Body` element.

Neither SOAP 1.1 nor the BP explicitly prohibits intermediaries from modifying the contents of the `Body` ***element. As a result, the ultimate***

receiver has no way of knowing if the application-specific data has changed somewhere along the message path. SOAP 1.2 reduces this uncertainty by explicitly prohibiting certain intermediaries, called forwarding intermediaries, *from changing the contents of the* `Body` *element and recommending that all other intermediaries, called* active intermediaries, *use a header block to document any changes to the* `Body` *element.*

4.5 SOAP Messaging Modes

Except in the case of fault messages, SOAP does not specify the contents of the `Body` element (although it does specify the general structure of RPC-type messages). As long as the `Body` contains well-formed XML, the application-specific data can be anything. The `Body` element may contain any XML element or it can be empty.

Although SOAP supports four modes of messaging (RPC/Literal, Document/Literal, RPC/Encoded, and Document/Encoded) the BP permits the use of RPC/Literal or Document/Literal only. The RPC/Encoded and Document/Encoded modes are explicitly prohibited.[BP]

A messaging mode is defined by its messaging style (RPC or Document) and its encoding style. There are two common types of encoding used in SOAP messaging: SOAP encoding as described in Section 5 of the SOAP 1.1 specification, and Literal encoding. SOAP encoding is not supported by WS-I-conformant Web services because it causes significant interoperability problems.[BP] The term "Literal" means that the XML document fragment can be validated against its XML schema.

4.5.1 Document/Literal

In the **Document/Literal mode** of messaging, a SOAP `Body` element contains an **XML document fragment,** a well-formed XML element that contains arbitrary application data (text and other elements) that belongs to an XML schema and namespace separate from the SOAP message's.

For example, a set of XML elements that describes a purchase order, embedded within a SOAP message, is considered an XML document fragment. The purchase-order SOAP message, which is used as an example throughout this chapter, is a Document/Literal message. Listing 4–15 shows the complete purchase-order SOAP message, which contains the `purchaseOrder` XML document fragment.

Listing 4–15

A Document-Style SOAP Message

```
<?xml version="1.0" encoding="UTF-8"?>
<soap:Envelope
```

```
    xmlns:soap="http://schemas.xmlsoap.org/soap/envelope/"
    xmlns:mi="http://www.Monson-Haefel.com/jwsbook/message-id"
    xmlns:proc="http://www.Monson-Haefel.com/jwsbook/processed-by">
     <soap:Header>
       <!-- Header blocks go here -->
     </soap:Header>
     <soap:Body>
       <po:purchaseOrder orderDate="2003-09-22"
        xmlns:po="http://www.Monson-Haefel.com/jwsbook/PO">

         <po:accountName>Amazon.com</po:accountName>
         <po:accountNumber>923</po:accountNumber>
         ...
         <po:book>
           <po:title>J2EE Web Services</po:title>
           <po:quantity>300</po:quantity>
           <po:wholesale-price>24.99</po:wholesale-price>
         </po:book>
       </po:purchaseOrder>
     </soap:Body>
  </soap:Envelope>
```

4.5.2 RPC/Literal

The **RPC/Literal mode** of messaging enables SOAP messages to model calls to procedures or method calls with parameters and return values. In RPC/Literal messaging, the contents of the `Body` are always formatted as a `struct`. An RPC request message contains the method name and the input parameters of the call. An RPC response message contains the return value and any output parameters (or a fault). In many cases, RPC/Literal messaging is used to expose traditional components as Web services. A traditional component might be a servlet, stateless session bean, Java RMI object, CORBA object, or DCOM component. These components do not explicitly exchange XML data; rather, they have methods with parameters and return values.

For example, Monson-Haefel Books has a JAX-RPC service endpoint (a J2EE Web Service endpoint) called BookQuote that Monson-Haefel's sales force uses. The remote interface to the BookQuote looks like this:

```
package com.jwsbook.soap;
import java.rmi.RemoteException;

public interface BookQuote extends java.rmi.Remote {
    // Get the wholesale price of a book
    public float getBookPrice(String ISBN)
```

```
        throws RemoteException, InvalidISBNException;
}
```

The `getBookPrice()` method declares a parameter in the form of an ISBN (International Standard Book Number), a unique string of characters assigned to every retail book. When you invoke this method with a proper ISBN, the Web service will return the wholesale price of the book identified.

This JAX-RPC service endpoint can use the RPC/Literal mode of messaging. The Web service uses two SOAP messages: a request message and a reply message. The request message is sent from an initial sender to the Web service and contains the method name, `getBookPrice`, and the ISBN string parameter. The reply message is sent back to the initial sender and contains the price of the book as a `float` value. Listing 4–16 shows the SOAP request message for the BookQuote Web service.

Listing 4–16

An RPC/Literal SOAP Request Message

```
<?xml version="1.0" encoding="UTF-8"?>
<soap:Envelope
 xmlns:soap="http://schemas.xmlsoap.org/soap/envelope/"
 xmlns:mh="http://www.Monson-Haefel.com/jwsbook/BookQuote">
   <soap:Body>
      <mh:getBookPrice>
          <isbn>0321146182</isbn>
      </mh:getBookPrice>
   </soap:Body>
</soap:Envelope>
```

Listing 4–17 shows the corresponding response.

Listing 4–17

An RPC/Literal SOAP Response Message

```
<?xml version="1.0" encoding="UTF-8"?>
<soap:Envelope
 xmlns:soap="http://schemas.xmlsoap.org/soap/envelope/"
 xmlns:mh="http://www.Monson-Haefel.com/jwsbook/BookQuote" >
   <soap:Body>
      <mh:getBookPriceResponse>
          <result>24.99</result>
      </mh:getBookPriceResponse>
   </soap:Body>
</soap:Envelope>
```

Unlike Document/Literal messaging, which makes no assumptions about the type and structure of elements contained in the `Body` of the message—except that the document fragment adheres to some XML schema—RPC/Literal messages carry a simple set of arguments. RPC-style messaging is a common idiom in distributed technologies, including EJB, CORBA, DCOM, and others, so SOAP defines a standard XML format for RPC-style messaging, called RPC/Literal. The RPC/Literal mode of messaging specifies how methods and their arguments (parameters and return values) are represented within the `Body` element of a SOAP message.

It's important to understand that RPC/Literal and Document/Literal may be indistinguishable from the perspective of a developer using tools like JAX-RPC, because JAX-RPC can present procedure-call semantics for both RPC/Literal and Document/Literal. A few people question the usefulness of RPC/Literal in the first place. Why use it when you can use Document/Literal, which is arguably simpler to implement in some respects, and can exploit XML schema validation? This book covers both models without taking sides on this issue.

4.5.3 Messaging Modes versus Messaging Exchange Patterns

It's easy to confuse Document/Literal and RPC/Literal modes of messaging with the One-Way and Request/Response message exchange patterns (MEPs), but the concepts are distinctly different. When you say a messaging mode is Document/Literal or RPC/Literal, you are usually describing the *payload* of the SOAP message: an XML document fragment or an XML representation of the parameters and return values associated with a remote procedure call. In contrast, One-Way and Request/Response MEPs refer to the *flow* of messages, not their contents. One-Way messaging is unidirectional, Request/Response is bi-directional. You can use the

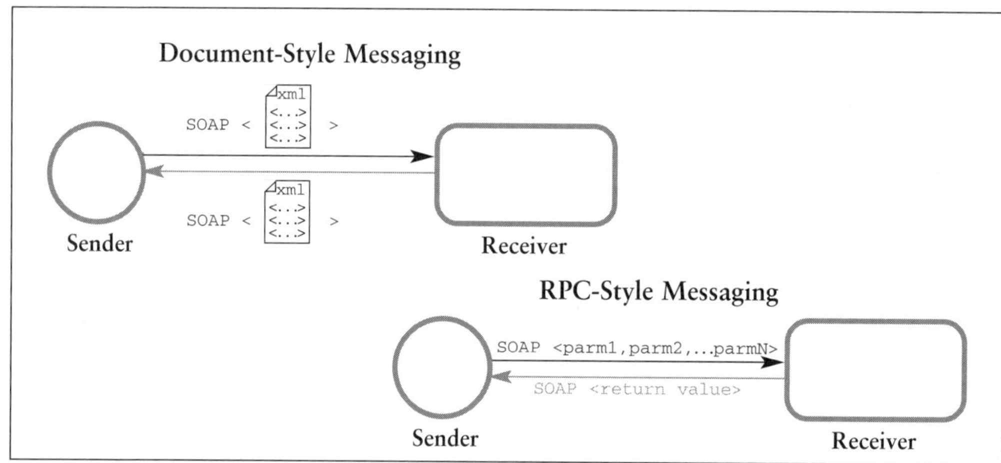

Figure 4–8 Using Document/Literal and RPC/Literal with One-Way and Request/Response Messaging

Document/Literal mode of messaging with either One-Way or Request/Response messaging. The RPC/Literal mode of messaging can also be used with either MEP, although it's usually used with Request/Response messaging.

Figure 4–8 shows the response message flows (the gray arrows) as optional in both document-style and RPC-style messaging.

4.5.4 Other Messaging Modes

Two other modes of messaging can be used with SOAP, **RPC/Encoded** and **Document/Encoded,** but the BP frowns on them, for two reasons: XML schema makes them obsolete, and they introduce a number of difficult interoperability problems.[BP]

RPC/Encoded actually receives more attention from SOAP than any other messaging mode. It attempts to define a mapping between common RPC semantics and programmatic types on one hand and XML on the other. An entire section of the SOAP 1.1 Note (the infamous Section 5) is devoted to explaining SOAP encoding. RPC/Encoded relies on built-in XML schema types, but it is designed to represent a graph of objects. XML schema organizes data into a tree, which is not nearly as flexible as an object graph. Although RPC/Encoded messaging was popular at first, its overall complexity and the interoperability problems it has caused have convinced most SOAP specialists to avoid it. You can accomplish pretty much the same results using the RPC/Literal or Document/Literal modes of messaging, with the added bonuses of better interoperability and conformance with the XML schema. It's likely, however, that you will encounter legacy Web service implementations that continue to use RPC/Encoded messaging despite its lack of support from the WS-I. To help you understand and work with these services, Appendix D: SOAP RPC/Encoded provides detailed coverage of this messaging mode.

Document/Encoded messaging applies SOAP encoding as defined in Section 5 of the SOAP 1.1 Note to document-style messaging. This mode of messaging is rarely, if ever, used in practice because Document/Literal messaging is much simpler, and interoperable. Document/Encoded messaging is not supported in J2EE Web services, so it's given no more consideration in this book.

4.6 SOAP Faults

SOAP fault messages are the mechanism by which SOAP applications report errors "upstream," to nodes earlier in the message path. It's the mission of this section to provide a full and detailed explanation of SOAP faults so that you can handle them appropriately in your own Web services.

SOAP faults are generated by receivers, either an intermediary or the ultimate receiver of a message. The receiver is required to send a SOAP fault back to the sender only if the Request/Response messaging mode is used. In One-Way mode, the receiver should generate a fault and may store it somewhere, but it must not attempt to transmit it to the sender.

SOAP faults are returned to the receiver's immediate sender. For example, if the third node in a message path generates a fault, that fault message is sent to the second node in the message path and nowhere else. In other words, you don't send the fault to the original sender unless it's also the immediate sender. When that sender receives the fault message, it may take some action, such as undoing operations, and may send another fault further upstream to the next sender if there is one.

Most developers see error handling as a pretty dull subject, so it's often ignored or poorly implemented. The tendency to ignore error handling is natural, but it's not wise. As the saying goes, "Stuff happens": Things can, and often do, go wrong; it's inevitable that errors will occur in the normal course of events. Because errors are fairly common, it's logical that some time should be dedicated to error handling. The SOAP Note recognizes the importance of error handling and dedicates a considerable amount of verbiage to addressing the issue. Even so, SOAP is not strict enough to avoid interoperability problems, so the BP provides a lot more guidance on the generation and processing of SOAP fault messages.

A SOAP message that contains a `Fault` element in the `Body` is called a **fault message.** A fault message is analogous to a Java exception; it's generated when an error occurs. Fault messages are used in Request/Response messaging. Nodes in the message path generate them when processing a request message. When an error occurs, the receiving node sends a fault message back to the sender just upstream, instead of the anticipated reply message. Faults are caused by improper message formatting, version mismatches, trouble processing a header, and application-specific errors.

When a fault message is generated, the `Body` of the SOAP message must contain only a single `Fault` element and nothing else. The `Fault` element itself must contain a `faultcode` element and a `faultstring` element, and optionally `faultactor` and `detail` elements. Listing 4–18 is an example of a SOAP fault message.

Listing 4–18

A SOAP Fault Message

```
<?xml version="1.0" encoding="UTF-8"?>
<soap:Envelope
 xmlns:soap="http://schemas.xmlsoap.org/soap/envelope/"
 xmlns:mh="http://www.Monson-Haefel.com/jwsbook/BookQuote" >
  <soap:Body>
    <soap:Fault>
      <faultcode>soap:Client</faultcode>
      <faultstring>
        The ISBN value contains invalid characters
      </faultstring>
      <faultactor>http://www.xyzcorp.com</faultactor>
```

```
        <detail>
          <mh:InvalidIsbnFaultDetail>
            <offending-value>19318224-D</offending-value>
            <conformance-rules>
              The first nine characters must be digits. The last
              character may be a digit or the letter 'X'. Case is
              not important.
            </conformance-rules>
          </mh:InvalidIsbnFaultDetail>
        </detail>
      </soap:Fault>
    </soap:Body>
</soap:Envelope>
```

Note that the `Fault` element and its children are part of the SOAP namespace, just as the SOAP `Envelope` and `Body` elements are.

Did you notice in Listing 4–18 that the children of the `Fault` element weren't qualified with the `soap` prefix? The children of the `Fault` element may be unqualified.[BP] In other words, they need *not* be prefixed with the SOAP 1.1 namespace. Note as well that it's forbidden for the `Fault` element to contain any immediate child elements other than `faultcode`, `faultstring`, `faultactor`, and `detail`.[BP]

4.6.1 The `faultcode` Element

The `faultcode` element may use any of four standard SOAP fault codes to identify an error.

SOAP Standard Fault Codes

`Client`
`Server`
`VersionMismatch`
`MustUnderstand`

Although you're allowed to use arbitrary fault codes, you should use only the four standard codes listed.[BP]

The `faultcode` element should contain one of the standard codes listed above, with the appropriate SOAP namespace prefix. Prefixing the code, as in **`soap:`**`Client`, allows for easy versioning of standard fault codes. As SOAP evolves, it's possible that new fault codes will be added. New fault codes can easily be distinguished from legacy fault codes by their namespace prefix. The meaning of a fault code will always correlate to both the code (the local name) and the namespace (the prefix).

The SOAP Note recommends the use of the dot separator between names to discriminate general standard fault codes from specific application subcodes. This convention is not used in J2EE Web services, which prefers the use of XML namespace-based prefixes for SOAP fault codes. If you use one of the standard SOAP fault codes, the namespace prefix must map to the SOAP namespace `"http://schemas.xmlsoap.org/soap/envelope/"`.[BP]

4.6.1.1 *The* `Client` *Fault*

The `Client` fault code signifies that the node that sent the SOAP message caused the error. Basically, if the receiver cannot process the SOAP message because there is something wrong with the message or its data, it's considered the fault of the client, the sender. The receiving node generates a `Client` fault if the message is not well formed, or contains invalid data, or lacks information that was expected, like a specific header. For example, in Listing 4–19, the SOAP fault indicates that the sender provided invalid information.

Listing 4–19

An Example of a SOAP Fault with a `Client` *Fault Code*

```
<?xml version="1.0" encoding="UTF-8"?>
<soap:Envelope
 xmlns:soap="http://schemas.xmlsoap.org/soap/envelope/" >
  <soap:Body>
    <soap:Fault>
      <faultcode>soap:Client</faultcode>
      <faultstring>The ISBN contains invalid characters</faultstring>
      <detail/>
    </soap:Fault>
  </soap:Body>
</soap:Envelope>
```

When a node receives a fault message with a `Client` code, it should not attempt to resend the same message. It should take some action to correct the problem or abort completely.

4.6.1.2 *The* `Server` *Fault*

The `Server` fault code indicates that the node that received the SOAP message malfunctioned or was otherwise unable to process the SOAP message. This fault is a reflection of an error by the receiving node (either an intermediary or the ultimate receiver) and doesn't point to any problems with the SOAP message itself. In this case the sender can assume the SOAP message to be correct, and can redeliver it after pausing some period of time to give the receiver time to recover.

If, for example, the receiving node is unable to connect to a resource such as a database while processing a SOAP message, it might generate a `Server` fault. The following is an example of a `Server` fault, generated when the BookPrice Web service could not access the database to retrieve price information in response to a SOAP message.

```
<?xml version="1.0" encoding="UTF-8"?>
<soap:Envelope
 xmlns:soap="http://schemas.xmlsoap.org/soap/envelope/" >
  <soap:Body>
    <soap:Fault>
      <faultcode>soap:Server</faultcode>
      <faultstring> Database is unavailable.</faultstring>
      <detail/>
    </soap:Fault>
  </soap:Body>
</soap:Envelope>
```

4.6.1.3 The `VersionMismatch` *Fault*

A receiving node generates a `VersionMismatch` fault when it doesn't recognize the namespace of a SOAP message's `Envelope` element. For example, a SOAP 1.1 node will generate a fault with a `VersionMismatch` code if it receives a SOAP 1.2 message, because it finds an unexpected namespace in the `Envelope`. This scenario is illustrated by the fault message in Listing 4–20.

Listing 4–20

An Example of a `VersionMismatch` *Fault*

```
<?xml version="1.0" encoding="UTF-8"?>
<soap:Envelope
 xmlns:soap="http://schemas.xmlsoap.org/soap/envelope/" >
  <soap:Body>
    <soap:Fault>
      <faultcode>soap:VersionMismatch</faultcode>
      <faultstring>Message was not SOAP 1.1-conformant</faultstring>
      <detail/>
    </soap:Fault>
  </soap:Body>
</soap:Envelope>
```

The `VersionMismatch` fault applies only to the namespace assigned to the `Envelope`, `Header`, `Body`, and `Fault` elements. It does not apply to other parts of the SOAP message, like the header blocks, XML document version, or application-specific elements in the `Body`.

The `VersionMismatch` fault is also used in the unlikely event that the root element of a message is not `Envelope`, but something else. Sending a `VersionMismatch` fault message back to the sender in this case may not be helpful, however: The sender may be designed to handle a different protocol and doesn't understand SOAP faults.

4.6.1.4 *The* `MustUnderstand` *Fault*

When a node receives a SOAP message, it must examine the `Header` element to determine which header blocks, if any, are targeted at that node. If a header block is targeted at the current node (via the `actor` attribute) and sets the `mustUnderstand` attribute equal to `"1"`, then the node is required to know how to process the header block. If the node doesn't recognize the header block, it must generate a fault with the `MustUnderstand` code. Listing 4–21 shows an example.

Listing 4–21

A `MustUnderstand` *Fault*

```
<?xml version="1.0" encoding="UTF-8"?>
<soap:Envelope
 xmlns:soap="http://schemas.xmlsoap.org/soap/envelope/" >
  <soap:Body>
    <soap:Fault>
      <faultcode>soap:MustUnderstand</faultcode>
      <faultstring>Mandatory header block not understood.</faultstring>
      <detail/>
    </soap:Fault>
  </soap:Body>
</soap:Envelope>
```

4.6.1.5 *Non-standard SOAP Fault Codes*

It is also possible to use non-standard SOAP fault codes that are prescribed by other organizations and belong to a separate namespace. For example, Listing 4–22 uses a fault code specified by the WS-Security specification.

Listing 4–22

Using Non-standard Fault Codes

```
<?xml version="1.0" encoding="UTF-8"?>
<soap:Envelope
 xmlns:soap="http://schemas.xmlsoap.org/soap/envelope/"
 xmlns:wsse="http://schemas.xmlsoap.org/ws/2002/06/secext">
  <soap:Body>
    <soap:Fault>
```

```
      <faultcode>wsse:InvalidSecurityToken</faultcode>
      <faultstring>An invalid security token was provided</faultstring>
      <detail/>
    </soap:Fault>
  </soap:Body>
</soap:Envelope>
```

4.6.2 The faultstring Element

The `faultstring` element is mandatory. It should provide a human-readable description of the fault. Although the `faultstring` element is required, the text used to describe the fault is not standardized.

Optionally, the `faultstring` element can indicate the language of the text message using a special attribute, `xml:lang`.[BP] The set of valid codes is defined by IETF RFC 1766.[4] For example, a `Client` fault could be generated with a Spanish-language text as shown in Listing 4–23.

Listing 4–23

Using the `xml:lang` Attribute in the `faultstring` Element

```
<?xml version="1.0" encoding="UTF-8"?>
<soap:Envelope
 xmlns:soap="http://schemas.xmlsoap.org/soap/envelope/" >
  <soap:Body>
    <soap:Fault>
      <faultcode>soap:Client</faultcode>
      <faultstring xml:lang="es" >
        El ISBN tiene letras invalidas
      </faultstring>
     <detail/>
   </soap:Fault>
  </soap:Body>
</soap:Envelope>
```

Although it's not specified, it's assumed that, in the absence of the `xml:lang` attribute, the default is English (`xml:lang="en"`). The `xml:lang` attribute is part of the XML 1.0 namespace, which does not need to be declared in an XML document.

[4] Internet Engineering Task Force, *RFC 1766: Tags for the Identification of Languages* (1995). Available at http://www.ietf.org/rfc/rfc1766.txt. The codes themselves are derived from ISO 639, and can be found at http://www.w3.org/WAI/ER/IG/ert/iso639.htm.

4.6.3 The `faultactor` Element

The `faultactor` element indicates which node encountered the error and generated the fault (the **faulting node**). This element is required if the faulting node is an intermediary, but optional if it's the ultimate receiver. For example, let's assume that an intermediary node in the message path, the authentication node, did not recognize the mandatory (`mustUnderstand="1"`) `processed-by` header block, so it generated a `MustUnderstand` fault. In this case the authentication node must identify itself using the `faultactor` element, as in Listing 4–24.

Listing 4–24

Locating the Source of the Fault Using the `faultactor` *Element*

```
<?xml version="1.0" encoding="UTF-8"?>
<soap:Envelope
 xmlns:soap="http://schemas.xmlsoap.org/soap/envelope/">
  <soap:Body>
    <soap:Fault>
      <faultcode>soap:MustUnderstand</faultcode>
      <faultstring>Mandatory header block not understood. </faultstring>
      <faultactor>
        http://www.Monson-Haefel.com/jwsbook/authenticator
      </faultactor>
      <detail/>
    </soap:Fault>
  </soap:Body>
</soap:Envelope>
```

The `faultactor` element may contain any URI, but is usually the Internet address of the faulting node, or the URI used by the `actor` attribute if a header block was the source of the error.

SOAP 1.1 doesn't recognize the concept of a *role* as distinct from a *node*. In fact, it lumps these two concepts together into the single concept *actor*. Thus you can see the `faultactor` as identifying both the node that generated the fault and the role that it was manifesting when it generated the fault.

4.6.4 The `detail` Element

The `detail` element of a fault message must be included if the fault was caused by the contents of the `Body` element, but it must *not* be included if the error occurred while processing a header block. The SOAP message in Listing 4–25 provides further details about the invalid ISBN reported in the `faultstring` element.

Listing 4–25

A SOAP Fault `detail` *Element*

```
<?xml version="1.0" encoding="UTF-8"?>
<soap:Envelope
 xmlns:soap="http://schemas.xmlsoap.org/soap/envelope/"
 xmlns:mh="http://www.Monson-Haefel.com/jwsbook/BookQuote" >
  <soap:Body>
    <soap:Fault>
      <faultcode>soap:Client</faultcode>
      <faultstring>
        The ISBN value contains invalid characters
      </faultstring>
      <detail>
        <mh:InvalidIsbnFaultDetail>
          <offending-value>19318224-D</offending-value>
          <conformance-rules>
            The first nine characters must be digits. The last
            character may be a digit or the letter 'X'. Case is
            not important.
          </conformance-rules>
        </mh:InvalidIsbnFaultDetail>
      </detail>
    </soap:Fault>
  </soap:Body>
</soap:Envelope>
```

> ***The*** `detail` ***element may contain any number of application-specific elements, which may be qualified or unqualified, according to their XML schema. In addition, the*** `detail` ***element itself may contain any number of qualified attributes, as long as they do not belong to the SOAP 1.1 namespace,*** `"http://schemas.xmlsoap.org/soap/envelope"`.[BP]

It's perfectly legal to use an empty `detail` element, but you must *not* omit the `detail` element entirely if the fault resulted while processing the contents of the original message's `Body` element.

4.6.4.1 *Processing Header Faults: Omitting the* `detail` *Element*

SOAP provides little guidance on how details about header faults should be provided. It says only that detailed information must be included in the `Header` element. Some SOAP toolkits place a SOAP `Fault` element inside the `Header` element, or nested within a header block, while other toolkits may use a different strategy.

4.6.5 Final Words about Faults

As a developer, it's your responsibility to be aware of the various circumstances under which faults must be generated, and to ensure that your code properly implements the processing of those faults.

This is probably a good time to recap. Faults result from one of several conditions:

1. The message received by the receiver is improperly structured or contains invalid data.
2. The incoming message is properly structured, but it uses elements and namespaces in the `Body` element that the receiver doesn't recognize.
3. The incoming message contains a mandatory header block that the receiver doesn't recognize.
4. The incoming message specifies an XML namespace for the SOAP `Envelope` and its children (`Body`, `Fault`, `Header`) that is not the SOAP 1.1 namespace.
5. The SOAP receiver has encountered an abnormal condition that prevents it from processing an otherwise valid SOAP message.

The first two conditions generate what are considered `Client` faults, faults that relate to the contents of the message: The client has sent an invalid or unfamiliar SOAP message to the receiver. The third condition results in a `MustUnderstand` fault, and the fourth results in a `VersionMismatch` fault. The fifth condition is considered a `Server` fault, which means the error was unrelated to the contents of the SOAP message. A server fault is generated when the receiver cannot process a SOAP message because of an abnormal condition.

4.7 SOAP over HTTP

The vast majority of all Internet traffic today is data transferred using HTTP (HyperText Transfer Protocol), mostly by people browsing the World Wide Web. HTTP is ubiquitous because it is supported by an extensive, long-established infrastructure of servers and browsers. The inventors of SOAP took note of this infrastructure and shrewdly designed SOAP so that every message can be carried as the payload of an HTTP message. This "tunneling" has been fundamental to SOAP's rapid adoption and unprecedented success.

It's possible to deliver SOAP messages using other protocols, such as SMTP and FTP as well, but details of these non-HTTP bindings are not specified by SOAP and are not supported by the BP, so this book discusses SOAP over HTTP only.

SOAP messages sent over HTTP are placed in the payload of an HTTP request or response, an area that is normally occupied by form data and HTML. HTTP is a Request/Response protocol, which means that the sender expects a response (either an error code or data) from the receiver. HTTP requests are typified by the messages that your browser sends to a Web server to request a Web page or submit a form. A request for a Web page is usually made in an HTTP GET message, while submission of a form is done with an HTTP POST message.

There is nothing intrinsic to HTTP that limits it to requesting Web pages, but that's been its primary occupation for the past decade. Most HTTP traffic is composed of HTTP GET requests and HTTP replies. The HTTP GET request identifies the Web page requested and may include some parameters. An HTTP reply message returns the Web page to the requester as its payload.

While the HTTP GET request is perfectly suited for requesting Web pages, it doesn't have a payload area and therefore cannot be used to carry SOAP messages. The HTTP POST request, on the other hand, does have a payload area and is perfectly suited to carrying a SOAP message. HTTP reply messages, whether they are replies to GET or POST messages, follow the same format and carry a payload. Web services that use SOAP 1.1 with HTTP always use HTTP POST and not HTTP GET messages.

4.7.1 Transmitting SOAP with HTTP POST Messages

Sending a SOAP message as the payload of an HTTP POST message is very simple. Listing 4–26 shows the BookQuote SOAP message embedded in an HTTP POST message.

Listing 4–26

A SOAP Request over HTTP

```
POST /jwsbook/BookQuote HTTP/1.1
Host: www.Monson-Haefel.com
Content-Type: text/xml; charset="utf-8"
Content-Length: 295
SOAPAction=""

<?xml version="1.0" encoding="UTF-8"?>
<soap:Envelope
 xmlns:soap="http://schemas.xmlsoap.org/soap/envelope/"
 xmlns:mh="http://www.Monson-Haefel.com/jwsbook/BookQuote">
   <soap:Body>
      <mh:getBookPrice>
          <isbn>0321146182</isbn>
      </mh:getBookPrice>
   </soap:Body>
</soap:Envelope>
```

The HTTP POST message must contain a `SOAPAction` header field, but the value of this header field is not specified. The `SOAPAction` header field can improve throughput by providing routing information outside the SOAP payload. A node can then do some of the routing work using the `SOAPAction`, rather than having to parse the SOAP XML payload.

While the `SOAPAction` header field can improve efficiency, it's also the source of a lot of debate in the Web services industry. SOAP purists don't like the use of the `SOAPAction` HTTP header field because it expands the SOAP processing model to include the carrier protocol (in this case HTTP). They believe that all of the routing and payload should be contained in the SOAP document, so that SOAP messages are not dependent on the protocol over which they are delivered. This is a creditable argument, so the `SOAPAction` header field may contain an empty string, as indicated by an empty pair of double quotes. The decision to use a value for the `SOAPAction` header field is up to the person who develops the Web service. SOAP 1.2 will replace the `SOAPAction` header with the protocol-independent **action media type** (a parameter to the `"application/soap+xml"` MIME type) , so dependency on this feature may result in forward-compatibility problems. The BP requires that the `SOAPAction` header field be present and that its value be a quoted string that matches the value of the `soapAction` attribute declared by the corresponding WSDL document. If that document declares no `soapAction` attribute, the `SOAPAction` header field can be an empty string. Details are provided in Chapter 5: WSDL.

You may have noticed that the `Content-Type` is `text/xml`, which indicates that the payload is an XML document. The WS-I Basic Profile 1.0 prefers that the `text/xml Content-Type` be used with SOAP over HTTP. It's possible to use others (for example, SOAP with Attachments would specify `multipart/related`) but it's not recommended.

The reply to the SOAP message is placed in an HTTP reply message that is similar in structure to the request message, but contains no `SOAPAction` header. Listing 4–27 illustrates.

Listing 4–27

A SOAP Reply over HTTP

```
HTTP/1.1 200 OK
Content-Type: text/xml; charset='utf-8'
Content-Length: 311

<?xml version="1.0" encoding="UTF-8"?>
<soap:Envelope
 xmlns:soap="http://schemas.xmlsoap.org/soap/envelope/"
 xmlns:mh="http://www.Monson-Haefel.com/jwsbook/BookQuote" >
   <soap:Body>
      <mh:getBookPriceResponse>
          <result>24.99</result>
      </mh:getBookPriceResponse>
```

```
    </soap:Body>
</soap:Envelope>
```


4.7.2 HTTP Response Codes

Although SOAP faults provide an error-handling system in the SOAP context, you must also understand HTTP response codes, which indicate the success or failure of an HTTP request. In Listing 4–27 you'll notice that the first line of text is `HTTP/1.1 200 OK`. The `HTTP/1.1` portion indicates the version of HTTP used. Although HTTP 1.1 is the preferred protocol, you may also use HTTP 1.0.[BP] The rest of the line, `200 OK`, is the HTTP response code.

HTTP defines a number of success and failure codes that can be included in an HTTP reply message, but the BP takes special care to specify exactly which codes can be used by conformant SOAP applications. The types of response codes used depend on the success or failure of the SOAP request and the type of messaging exchange pattern used, Request/Response or One-Way.

4.7.2.1 Success Codes

The 200-level HTTP success codes are used to indicate that a SOAP request was received or successfully processed. The `200 OK` and `202 Accepted` HTTP success codes are used in Web services.

`200 OK` When a SOAP operation generates a response SOAP message, the HTTP response code for successful processing is `200 OK`. This response code indicates that the reply message is not a fault, that it does contain a normal SOAP response message.

`202 Accepted` This response code means that the request was processed successfully but that there is no SOAP response data. This type of SOAP operation is similar to a Java method that has a return type of `void`.

Although a One-Way SOAP message is conceptually unidirectional, when it's sent over HTTP some type of HTTP reply will be transmitted back to the receiver. One-Way SOAP messages do not return SOAP faults or results of any kind, so the HTTP `202 Accepted` response code indicates only that the message made it to the receiver—it doesn't indicate whether the message was successfully processed.[BP]

4.7.2.2 Error Codes

In general, HTTP uses the 400-level response codes to indicate that the client made some kind of error when transmitting the message. For example, you have undoubtedly encountered the infamous `404 Resource Not Found` error when using a Web browser. The `404` error code signifies that the client attempted to access a Web page or some other resource that doesn't exist. Web services uses a specific set of

400-level codes when the error is related to the contents of the SOAP message itself, rather than the HTTP request. HTTP also uses the 500-level response codes to indicate that the server suffered some type of failure that is not the client's fault.

`400 Bad Request` This error code is used to indicate that either the HTTP request or the XML in the SOAP message was not well formed.

`405 Method Not Allowed` If a Web service receives a SOAP message via any HTTP method other than HTTP POST, the service should return a `405 Method Not Allowed` error to the sender.

`415 Unsupported Media Type` HTTP POST messages must include a `Content-Type` header with a value of `text/xml`. If it's any other value, the server must return a `415 Unsupported Media Type` error.

`500 Internal Server Error` This code must be used when the response message in a Request/Response MEP is a SOAP fault.

4.7.3 Final Words about HTTP

HTTP provides a solid bedrock on which to base SOAP messaging. HTTP is ubiquitous, well understood, and widely supported. That said, HTTP has its detractors. For example, Don Box has characterized HTTP as the "cockroach of the Internet," to convey his view that it's an undesirable protocol that can't easily be done away with. The fact that modern firewalls do not restrict HTTP traffic on port 80 makes HTTP convenient for accessing servers and clients behind firewalls—which are a major impediment to distributed computing. Of course this introduces security issues because we are effectively circumventing the firewalls that help keep organizations safe from malicious hackers. It seems likely that firewall vendors will not permit "tunneling" to go on forever. Eventually they will feel compelled to enhance firewall products so that they will filter for, and block, HTTP communications that carry SOAP messages.

Blocking SOAP messages at the firewall is not necessary, however. Because SOAP is a transparent protocol (it's simple text rather than opaque data), a firewall can easily inspect the contents and route the message to a SOAP-specific security processor.

HTTP is not the only protocol over which you can send SOAP messages. You can also use SMTP (e-mail) and raw TCP/IP. The WS-I may one day extend the BP to include these other protocols—but for now HTTP is the only protocol endorsed by the WS-I.

4.8 Wrapping Up

SOAP 1.1, the focus of this chapter, is the XML protocol used in J2EE 1.4 Web Services because it's well supported and fairly well understood. The BP has done a lot to clear up ambiguities in SOAP 1.1, and the SOAP 1.2 protocol also includes these clarifications. It seems likely that SOAP 1.2 will supplant SOAP 1.1, but I wouldn't expect that development to occur for a while yet. Usually it takes a new version of a protocol a couple of years to replace the earlier version—in some cases longer.

I'm pretty sure that the WS-I will have updated the BP to support SOAP 1.2 by the time the next version of J2EE, tentatively labeled J2EE 1.5, is released, and thus that J2EE 1.5 Web Services will support SOAP 1.2. Until that day, though, jumping on the SOAP 1.2 bandwagon is a risk. Interoperability depends on common understanding of the protocol and a lack of ambiguity. It will be a while before we know where SOAP 1.2's bugs lie and have a BP to address them. For now, save yourself some headaches and stick with SOAP 1.1 and the BP.

Chapter 5

WSDL

To use SOAP with a particular Web service, you need to know in advance how the SOAP messages are structured, which protocol will be employed (HTTP or SMTP, for example), and the Internet address of the Web service. In a word, you need *documentation*. For example, the BookQuote SOAP message is pretty simple, but how did you learn about it? You read about it in the preceding chapter; it's documented in this book. Listing 5–1 shows the BookQuote SOAP 1.1 request message.

Listing 5–1

A BookQuote RPC/Literal SOAP Request Message

```
<?xml version="1.0" encoding="UTF-8"?>
<soap:Envelope
 xmlns:soap="http://schemas.xmlsoap.org/soap/envelope/"
 xmlns:mh="http://www.Monson-Haefel.com/jwsbook/BookQuote">
   <soap:Body>
      <mh:getBookPrice>
          <isbn>0321146182</isbn>
      </mh:getBookPrice>
   </soap:Body>
</soap:Envelope>
```

While the description of the BookQuote Web service presented in Chapter 4 is easy to understand, it's not well documented. Imagine that all Web services were described this way. You would have to read an informal document—a chapter in a book, a Web page, or an owner's manual perhaps—every time you wanted to use a new Web service. To avoid problems associated with informal documentation, the Web services community has adopted the **Web Services Description Language (WSDL)**, which is a document format for precisely describing Web services.

WSDL (routinely pronounced "whiz-dul") is used to specify the exact message format, Internet protocol, and address that a client must use to communicate with a particular Web service. In other words, a WSDL document tells us how to use a Web service. WSDL is another de facto standard for Web services and, like SOAP, it enjoys widespread adoption; it has been endorsed by most enterprise software vendors and major standard organizations, including W3C, WS-I, and OASIS.

WSDL is well suited for code generators, which can read a WSDL document and generate a programmatic interface for accessing a Web service. For example, a JAX-RPC provider uses WSDL 1.1 to generate Java RMI interfaces and network stubs, which can be used to exchange SOAP messages with a Web service.

> ***A JAX-RPC provider is a vendor implementation of the JAX-RPC API. For example, BEA WebLogic is a JAX-RPC provider. All J2EE 1.4 application servers are JAX-RPC providers, because they all provide their own implementations of the JAX-RPC API.***

JAX-RPC is not the only technology that can generate interfaces and network stubs from WSDL documents. There are many other code generators, including tools in IBM WebSphere, Microsoft .NET, and Apache Axis, to name a few. Figure 5–1 illustrates how a JAX-RPC toolkit would use a WSDL document to generate a Java

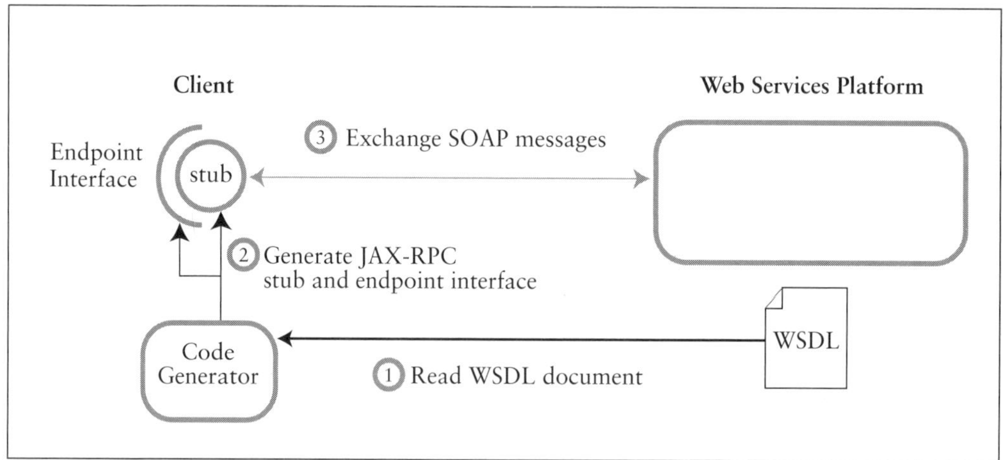

Figure 5–1 A WSDL Code Generator

RMI interface (an **endpoint interface**) and a networking stub that implements that interface.

While WSDL is especially useful for code generators, it's also an asset when using other Web services tools and APIs. Many Web service clients, for example, use SOAP APIs instead of generated call interfaces and stubs. These APIs usually model the structure of the SOAP message using objects like `Envelope`, `Header`, `Body`, and `Fault`. Examples of SOAP APIs include SAAJ (SOAP with Attachments API for Java), Perl::Lite, Apache SOAP, and others. When you use a SOAP API, you can use a Web service's WSDL as a guide for exchanging SOAP messages with that Web service.

Although WSDL is considered a Web services standard,[1] it's not very simple, which is perhaps its greatest handicap. Its complexity results from its designers' intention to create an IDL (interface definition language) for Web services that is not tied to any specific protocol, programming language, or operating system. Note that WSDL 1.1 is not specific to SOAP; it can be used to describe non-SOAP-based Web services as well.

Modularity was another design goal. Because WSDL is very modular, you can reuse its artifacts to describe more than one Web service. Unfortunately, modularity makes WSDL documents difficult to understand at first. This chapter's purpose is to enable you to make sense of WSDL so that you can write WSDL documents that describe your Web services, and read WSDL documents that describe others' Web services. That said, in many cases you may never need to read or write WSDL documents yourself because your J2EE platform will usually create and process them automatically.

5.1 The Basic Structure of WSDL

A WSDL document is an XML document that adheres to the WSDL XML schema. As an XML document instance, a WSDL document must use the correct elements in the correct fashion if it is to be valid and well formed. The rest of this chapter explains the structure of a WSDL document and how to construct one that describes a Web service properly. While WSDL can, in theory, be used to describe any kind of Web service, this chapter focuses on WSDL documents that describe Web services that are SOAP-based and compliant with the WS-I Basic Profile 1.0 (BP).

A WSDL document contains seven important elements: `types`, `import`, `message`, `portType`, `operations`, `binding`, and `service`, which are nested in the `definitions` element, the root element of a WSDL document. Figure 5–2 illustrates the basic structure of a WSDL document.

[1] WSDL 1.1 was submitted as a "note" to the W3C by IBM and Microsoft in March of 2001. The next version of WSDL, WSDL 1.2, is being developed under the auspices of the W3C and will become a full recommendation.

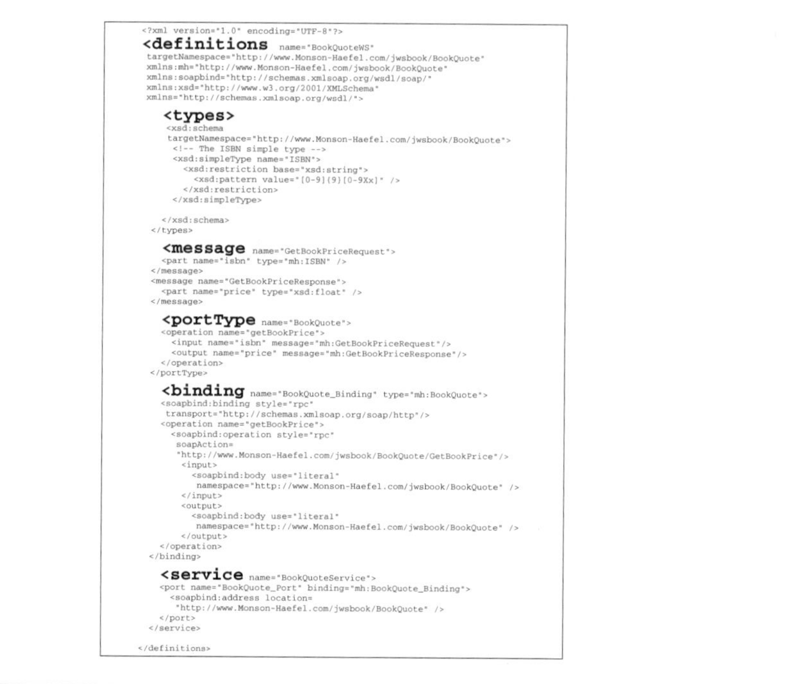

```
<?xml version="1.0" encoding="UTF-8"?>
<definitions name="BookQuoteWS"
 targetNamespace="http://www.Monson-Haefel.com/jwsbook/BookQuote"
 xmlns:mh="http://www.Monson-Haefel.com/jwsbook/BookQuote"
 xmlns:soapbind="http://schemas.xmlsoap.org/wsdl/soap/"
 xmlns:xsd="http://www.w3.org/2001/XMLSchema"
 xmlns="http://schemas.xmlsoap.org/wsdl/">

   <types>
    <xsd:schema
    targetNamespace="http://www.Monson-Haefel.com/jwsbook/BookQuote">
     <!-- The ISBN simple type -->
     <xsd:simpleType name="ISBN">
       <xsd:restriction base="xsd:string">
         <xsd:pattern value="[0-9]{9}[0-9Xx]" />
       </xsd:restriction>
     </xsd:simpleType>

   </xsd:schema>
  </types>

   <message name="GetBookPriceRequest">
   <part name="isbn" type="mh:ISBN" />
  </message>
  <message name="GetBookPriceResponse">
   <part name="price" type="xsd:float" />
  </message>

   <portType name="BookQuote">
   <operation name="getBookPrice">
     <input name="isbn" message="mh:GetBookPriceRequest"/>
     <output name="price" message="mh:GetBookPriceResponse"/>
   </operation>
  </portType>

   <binding name="BookQuote_Binding" type="mh:BookQuote">
   <soapbind:binding style="rpc"
    transport="http://schemas.xmlsoap.org/soap/http"/>
   <operation name="getBookPrice">
     <soapbind:operation style="rpc"
      soapAction=
      "http://www.Monson-Haefel.com/jwsbook/BookQuote/GetBookPrice"/>
       <input>
         <soapbind:body use="literal"
          namespace="http://www.Monson-Haefel.com/jwsbook/BookQuote" />
       </input>
       <output>
         <soapbind:body use="literal"
          namespace="http://www.Monson-Haefel.com/jwsbook/BookQuote" />
       </output>
   </operation>
  </binding>

   <service name="BookQuoteService">
   <port name="BookQuote_Port" binding="mh:BookQuote_Binding">
     <soapbind:address location=
      "http://www.Monson-Haefel.com/jwsbook/BookQuote" />
   </port>
  </service>

</definitions>
```

Figure 5–2 The Basic Structure of a WSDL Document

The **`types`** **element** uses the XML schema language to declare complex data types and elements that are used elsewhere in the WSDL document.

The **`import`** **element** is similar to an `import` element in an XML schema document; it's used to import WSDL definitions from other WSDL documents.

The **`message`** **element** describes the message's payload using XML schema built-in types, complex types, or elements that are defined in the WSDL document's `types` element, or defined in an external WSDL document the `import` element refers to.

The **`portType`** **and** **`operation`** **elements** describe a Web service's interface and define its methods. A `portType` and its `operation` elements are analogous to a Java interface and its method declarations. An `operation` element uses one or more `message` types to define its input and output payloads.

The **`binding`** **element** assigns a `portType` and its `operation` elements to a particular protocol (for instance, SOAP 1.1) and encoding style.

The **`service`** **element** is responsible for assigning an Internet address to a specific binding.

The **`documentation`** **element** explains some aspect of the WSDL document to human readers. Any of the other WSDL elements may contain `documentation elements.`

The documentation element is not critical, so it will not be mentioned again in this chapter.

Listing 5–2 is an example of a very simple WSDL document, which describes the BookQuote Web service discussed in Chapter 4. When you look at the WSDL definition, keep in mind that it's supposed to describe a Web service and the types of SOAP messages, protocols, and Internet addresses used to access that Web service.

Listing 5–2

The WSDL Definition for the BookQuote Web Service

```
<?xml version="1.0" encoding="UTF-8"?>
<definitions name="BookQuoteWS"
 targetNamespace="http://www.Monson-Haefel.com/jwsbook/BookQuote"
 xmlns:mh="http://www.Monson-Haefel.com/jwsbook/BookQuote"
 xmlns:soapbind="http://schemas.xmlsoap.org/wsdl/soap/"
 xmlns:xsd="http://www.w3.org/2001/XMLSchema"
 xmlns="http://schemas.xmlsoap.org/wsdl/">

  <!-- message elements describe the input and output parameters -->
  <message name="GetBookPriceRequest">
    <part name="isbn" type="xsd:string" />
  </message>
  <message name="GetBookPriceResponse">
    <part name="price" type="xsd:float" />
  </message>

  <!-- portType element describes the abstract interface of a Web service -->
  <portType name="BookQuote">
    <operation name="getBookPrice">
      <input name="isbn" message="mh:GetBookPriceRequest"/>
      <output name="price" message="mh:GetBookPriceResponse"/>
    </operation>
  </portType>

  <!-- binding tells us which protocols and encoding styles are used -->
  <binding name="BookPrice_Binding" type="mh:BookQuote">
    <soapbind:binding style="rpc"
     transport="http://schemas.xmlsoap.org/soap/http"/>
    <operation name="getBookPrice">
      <soapbind:operation style="rpc"
       soapAction=
       "http://www.Monson-Haefel.com/jwsbook/BookQuote/GetBookPrice"/>
```

```
        <input>
          <soapbind:body use="literal"
           namespace="http://www.Monson-Haefel.com/jwsbook/BookQuote" />
        </input>
        <output>
          <soapbind:body use="literal"
           namespace="http://www.Monson-Haefel.com/jwsbook/BookQuote" />
        </output>
    </operation>
  </binding>

  <!-- service tells us the Internet address of a Web service -->
  <service name="BookPriceService">
    <port name="BookPrice_Port" binding="mh:BookPrice_Binding">
      <soapbind:address location=
       "http://www.Monson-Haefel.com/jwsbook/BookQuote" />
    </port>
  </service>

</definitions>
```

You're not expected to understand this document at this point. If you're confused by its structure, don't despair—that's the normal reaction for developers just learning WSDL. The rest of this chapter explains in detail how a WSDL document is organized and what all its elements and attributes do—and explains Listing 5–2 piece by piece.

5.2 WSDL Declarations: The `definitions`, `types`, and `import` Elements

This section focuses on the first two child elements of the `definitions` element (the root element), `types` and `import`, which define the data types and other artifacts used by the WSDL document. Before we examine these crucial elements, though, we need to look at the beginning of the document.

5.2.1 The XML Declaration

The XML declaration in Listing 5–2 specified a character encoding of UTF-8.

```
<?xml version="1.0" encoding="UTF-8"?>
```

A WSDL document must use either UTF-8 or UTF-16 encoding; other encoding systems are not allowed.[BP]

5.2.2 The definitions Element

The root element of all WSDL documents is the definitions element, which encapsulates the entire document and also provides a WSDL document with its name.

```
<definitions name="BookQuoteWS"
 targetNamespace="http://www.Monson-Haefel.com/jwsbook/BookQuote"
 xmlns:mh="http://www.Monson-Haefel.com/jwsbook/BookQuote"
 xmlns:soapbind="http://schemas.xmlsoap.org/wsdl/soap/"
 xmlns:xsd="http://www.w3.org/2001/XMLSchema"
 xmlns="http://schemas.xmlsoap.org/wsdl/">
```

The definitions element usually contains several XML namespace declarations, which is normal for a root element. Among these declarations is one for the namespace of the WSDL 1.1 XML schema "http://schemas.xmlsoap.org/wsdl/". Declaring the WSDL namespace as the default namespace avoids having to qualify every WSDL element explicitly, with a prefix.

The first attribute you see in the definitions element is name, which is used to name the entire WSDL document. In practice the WSDL name is not all that important. Nothing refers to it, and it's optional.

The definitions element also declares a targetNamespace attribute, which identifies the namespace of elements defined in the WSDL document—much as it does in XML schema documents.

The message, portType, and binding elements are assigned labels using their name attributes; these labels automatically take on the namespace specified by the targetNamespace attribute. (In this book the URL of the targetNamespace is also assigned a prefix of mh.) Labeled message, portType, and binding elements are commonly called **definitions.** These definitions assume the namespace specified by targetNamespace.

Other elements in the document refer to the definitions using their label and namespace prefix. A prefixed label is considered a fully qualified name (QName) for a definition. For example, in the following snippet from Listing 5–2, input and output elements refer to the message definitions using their QNames.

```
<!-- message elements describe the input and output parameters -->
<message name="GetBookPriceRequest">
  <part name="isbn" type="xsd:string" />
</message>
<message name="GetBookPriceResponse">
  <part name="price" type="xsd:float" />
</message>
```

```
<!-- portType element describes the abstract interface of a Web service -->
<portType name="BookQuote">
  <operation name="getBookPrice">
    <input name="isbn" message="mh:GetBookPriceRequest"/>
    <output name="price" message="mh:GetBookPriceResponse"/>
  </operation>
</portType>
```

5.2.3 The types Element

WSDL adopts, as its basic type system, the W3C XML schema built-in types. The `types` element serves as a container for defining any data types that are not described by the XML schema built-in types: complex types and custom simple types. The data types and elements defined in the `types` element are used by message definitions when declaring the parts (payloads) of messages.

The `types` element is not used in Listing 5–2, because it's unnecessary—the message definitions, `GetBookPriceRequest` and `GetBookPriceResponse`, refer to simple built-in types.

If we wanted to, we could define a custom simple type for ISBN number and use that in the `GetBookPriceRequest` message instead of the built-in `string` type, as in Listing 5–3.

Listing 5–3

Using XML Schema Types Defined in the WSDL `types` *Element*

```
<?xml version="1.0" encoding="UTF-8"?>
<definitions name="BookQuoteWS"
 targetNamespace="http://www.Monson-Haefel.com/jwsbook/BookQuote"
 xmlns:mh="http://www.Monson-Haefel.com/jwsbook/BookQuote"
 xmlns:soapbind="http://schemas.xmlsoap.org/wsdl/soap/"
 xmlns:xsd="http://www.w3.org/2001/XMLSchema"
 xmlns="http://schemas.xmlsoap.org/wsdl/">

  <types>

    <xsd:schema
     targetNamespace="http://www.Monson-Haefel.com/jwsbook/BookQuote">
      <!-- The ISBN simple type -->
      <xsd:simpleType name="ISBN">
        <xsd:restriction base="xsd:string">
          <xsd:pattern value="[0-9]{9}[0-9Xx]" />
        </xsd:restriction>
      </xsd:simpleType>
```

```
    </xsd:schema>

  </types>

  <!-- message elements describe the input and output parameters -->
  <message name="GetBookPriceRequest">
    <part name="isbn" type="mh:ISBN" />
  </message>
  <message name="GetBookPriceResponse">
    <part name="price" type="xsd:float" />
  </message>
  ...
</definitions>
```

In Listing 5–3 a complete W3C XML schema document is nested directly in the `types` element. The custom simple type, labeled `ISBN`, is defined and assigned to the `mh` namespace by the XML schema `targetNamespace` attribute. The `mh:ISBN` type is then used to define the `isbn` part of the `GetBookPriceRequest` message definition.

The `targetNamespace` attribute of the XML schema must be a valid non-null value, otherwise the types and element will not belong to a valid namespace. In addition, the XML schema defined in the `types` element must belong to a namespace specified by the WSDL document (usually in the `definitions` element) or to a namespace of an imported WSDL document.[BP] In other words, the WSDL document must be aware of any and all namespaces used in the document. The mechanism for importing WSDL documents is discussed in the next section.

SOAP and WSDL both define attributes and encoding types you can use to define array data types. Such array types and attributes have created a lot of confusion and interoperability problems, however, so the BP strictly prohibits their use. In a nutshell, you are not allowed to use the `Array` type, or the `arrayType` attribute defined for SOAP 1.1 Encoding (SOAP 1.1 Note, Section 5), or the WSDL `arrayType` attribute defined by WSDL. In addition you should not label array types as "ArrayOfXXX" as suggested by the WSDL 1.1 Note.[BP] These requirements are not a handicap at all, because XML schema provides a much simpler way to define arrays. All you need to do is define a complex type with a `maxOccurs` value greater than 0 (for example, `"10"`, `"32000"`, or `"unbounded"`) and you have yourself a basic array. The following snippet defines an array-like type in this way.

```
<?xml version="1.0" encoding="UTF-8"?>
<definitions name="BookQuoteWS"
 targetNamespace="http://www.Monson-Haefel.com/jwsbook/BookQuote"
 xmlns:mh="http://www.Monson-Haefel.com/jwsbook/BookQuote"
 xmlns:soapbind="http://schemas.xmlsoap.org/wsdl/soap/"
```

```
xmlns:xsd="http://www.w3.org/2001/XMLSchema"
xmlns="http://schemas.xmlsoap.org/wsdl/">

 <types>

   <xsd:schema
    targetNamespace="http://www.Monson-Haefel.com/jwsbook/BookQuote">
     <!--A simple array-like type -->
     <xsd:complexType name="IntArray">
       <xsd:sequence>
          <xsd:element name="arg" type="xsd:int" maxOccurs="unbounded"/>
       </xsd:sequence>
     </xsd:complexType>

   </xsd:schema>
 </types>
```

5.2.4 The `import` Element

The `import` element makes available in the present WSDL document the definitions from a specified namespace in another WSDL document. This feature can be useful if you want to modularize WSDL documents—for example, to separate the abstract definitions (the `types`, `message`, and `portType` elements) from the concrete definitions (the `binding`, `service`, and `port` elements). Another reason to use `import` is to consolidate into one WSDL document several definitions you want to maintain separately. For example, your organization may want to maintain WSDL documents for shipping and order processing separately, but present a complete definition of all Web services in a public directory accessible by business partners. The following snippet illustrates.

```
<definitions name="AllMhWebServices"
 xmlns="http://schemas.xmlsoap.org/wsdl/">

    <import namespace="http://www.Monson-Haefel.com/jwsbook/BookQuote"
     location="http://www.Monson-Haefel.com/jwsbook/BookPrice.wsdl"/>
    <import namespace="http://www.Monson-Haefel.com/jwsbook/po"
     location="http://www.Monson-Haefel.com/jwsbook/wsdl/PurchaseOrder.wsdl"/>
    <import namespace="http://www.Monson-Haefel.com/jwsbook/Shipping"
     location="http://www.Monson-Haefel.com/jwsbook/wsdl/Shipping.wsdl"/>

</definitions >
```

The WSDL `import` element must declare two attributes: `namespace` and `location`. The value of the `namespace` attribute must match the `target`

Namespace declared by the WSDL document being imported. The location attribute must point to an actual WSDL document; it cannot be empty or null. That said, the location is considered a hint. If the application reading the WSDL document has cached or stored copies of the imported WSDL document locally, it may use those instead.[BP]

Use of the* import *element is convenient, but it can also create versioning headaches. If WSDL documents are maintained separately, the risk of an imported document being changed without regard to the WSDL documents that import it is pretty high. Take care to ensure that imported WSDL documents are not changed without considering versioning.

You can use import and types together, but you should list the import elements before the types element in a WSDL document.

There has been a lot of confusion about the purpose of the WSDL import element. Some believed it could be used to import either WSDL documents or XML schema documents, while others believed it was only for importing WSDL documents. Varying interpretations have created interoperability problems, so the Basic Profile specifies that a WSDL import element may refer only to WSDL documents. If you need to import an XML schema element, you should do so in the XML schema definition contained in the WSDL types element, using the standard XML schema import statement as described in Section 3.2.5. It's important to note that you cannot use the XML schema import statement to import an XML schema directly from the types element of some other WSDL document.[BP]

5.3 The WSDL Abstract Interface: The message, portType, and operation Elements

The message, portType, and operation elements describe the abstract interface of the Web service. The portType combines the operation and message definitions into an abstract interface that is analogous to a Java interface definition. The portType describes the kinds of operations that a Web service supports—the messaging mode and payloads—without specifying the Internet protocol or address used.

5.3.1 The message Element

The message element describes the payload of a message used by a Web service. A message element can describe the payloads of outgoing or incoming messages—that is, messages that are directly sent to or received from a Web service. In addition, the message element can describe the contents of SOAP header blocks and fault detail elements. The way to define a message element depends on whether you use RPC-style or document-style messaging.

5.3.1.1 The `message` *Element for RPC-Style Web Services*

When RPC-style messaging is used, `message` elements describe the payloads of the SOAP request and reply messages. They may describe call parameters, call return values, header blocks, or faults. For example, the BookQuote Web service uses two `message` elements to describe the parameters and return value of that service. (Messages describing faults and header blocks are discussed later.) This snippet from Listing 5–2 illustrates.

```
<!-- message elements describe the input and output parameters -->
<message name="GetBookPriceRequest">
  <part name="isbn" type="xsd:string" />
</message>
<message name="GetBookPriceResponse">
  <part name="price" type="xsd:float" />
</message>
```

The `GetBookPriceRequest` message represents the parameters (the input), while `GetBookPriceResponse` represents the reply (the output). In other words, the `GetBookPriceRequest` message definition describes the payload of the message transmitted from a SOAP client to the BookQuote Web service, while the `GetBookPriceResponse` message definition describes the payload of the message transmitted by the BookQuote Web service back to the client.

There is no prescribed convention for naming messages. In this book, messages transmitted from the SOAP client to the server are suffixed with `Request`, and messages transmitted back to the client are suffixed with `Response`. You aren't required to use this convention; use any naming system you like. Message names are arbitrary and only serve to qualify a message definition. A message element cannot declare itself to be input or output—that distinction can be made only by the `operation` elements discussed in the next section—so naming a message `Request` or `Output` or whatever won't determine how it's used.

In RPC-style messaging, messages commonly have more than one part. For example, you can define a message called `GetBulkBookPriceRequest` with multiple `part` elements, each of which represents a different parameter.

```
<definitions name="BookPrice" ...>
  ...
  <message name="GetBulkBookPriceRequest">
    <part name="isbn" type="xsd:string"/>
    <part name="quantity" type="xsd:int"/>
  </message>
  <message name="GetBulkBookPriceResponse">
    <part name="price" type="mh:prices" />
  </message>
```

```
...
</definitions>
```

Both input and output messages in Web services can have multiple parts, which is a departure from Java method-call semantics, which recognize multiple inputs (parameters) but only one output (the return value). It's common, however, for programming languages like C++, C#, and Perl to declare parameters that are either input or output arguments. WSDL is intended to be programming-language neutral, so it must be flexible enough to accommodate all programming languages, not just Java. Both SAAJ and JAX-RPC, covered in Part IV, have facilities to support output messages with multiple parts.

5.3.1.2 The `message` *Element for Document-Style Web Services*

When you use document-style messaging, the `message` definition refers to a top-level element in the `types` definition.[BP] For example, Listing 5–4 is a WSDL document that describes a SubmitPurchaseOrder Web Service. The Purchase Order schema defined in Part II of this book is imported into the `types` element of the WSDL document. In this case, the Web service uses One-Way messaging, so there is no reply message, which is common in document-style messaging.

Listing 5–4

Using the XML Schema `import` *Element*

```
<?xml version="1.0" encoding="UTF-8"?>
<definitions name="PurchaseOrderWS"
 targetNamespace="http://www.Monson-Haefel.com/jwsbook/PO"
 xmlns:mh="http://www.Monson-Haefel.com/jwsbook/PO"
 xmlns:soapbind="http://schemas.xmlsoap.org/wsdl/soap/"
 xmlns:xsd="http://www.w3.org/2001/XMLSchema"
 xmlns="http://schemas.xmlsoap.org/wsdl/">

  <types>
    <xsd:schema targetNamespace="http://www.Monson-Haefel.com/jwsbook/PO">
      <!-- Import the PurchaseOrder XML schema document -->
      <xsd:import namespace="http://www.Monson-Haefel.com/jwsbook/PO"
       schemaLocation="http://www.Monson-Haefel.com/jwsbook/po.xsd" />
    </xsd:schema>
  </types>
  <!-- message elements describe the input and output parameters -->
  <message name="SubmitPurchaseOrderMessage">
    <part name="order" element="mh:purchaseOrder" />
  </message>
```

```
...
</definitions>
```

A message part may declare either a `type` attribute or an `element` attribute, but not both. Which to use depends on the kind of messaging you're doing. If you're using RPC-style messaging, the `part` elements must use the `type` attribute; if you're using document-style messaging, the `part` elements must use the `element` attribute.[BP] RPC-style messaging uses types to define procedure calls, where each element represents a type of parameter. Document-style messaging, on the other hand, exchanges XML document fragments and refers to their top-level (global) elements.

5.3.1.3 Declaring Fault Messages

You can use message definitions to declare faults in the same way you use them to declare input and output messages. For example, Listing 5–5 defines a fault message that is sent back if a BookQuote request message contains an invalid ISBN. It includes a single part, an error message.

Listing 5–5

Declaring a Fault Message

```
<definitions name="BookQuote" ...>

  <types>
    <xsd:schema targetNamespace="http://www.Monson-Haefel.com/jwsbook/PO">
      <!-- Import the PurchaseOrder XML schema document -->
      <xsd:element name="InvalidIsbnFaultDetail" >
        <xsd:complexType>
          <xsd:sequence>
            <xsd:element name="offending-value" type="xsd:string"/>
            <xsd:element name="conformance-rules" type="xsd:string" />
          </xsd:sequence>
        </xsd:complexType>
      </xsd:element>
    </xsd:schema>
  </types>

  <!-- message elements describe the input and output parameters -->
  <message name="GetBookPriceRequest">
    <part name="isbn" type="xsd:string" />
  </message>
  <message name="GetBookPriceResponse">
    <part name="price" type="xsd:float" />
  </message>
```

```
  <message name="InvalidArgumentFault">
    <part name="error_message" element="mh:InvalidIsbnFaultDetail" />
  </message>
</definitions>
```

Fault messages used by SOAP-based Web services can have only one part because, as you learned in Chapter 4, SOAP faults must adhere to a specified schema. In the case of a SOAP fault, the `part` definition refers to the contents of the detail section of the fault message. While there is no industry convention for naming fault messages, it's the convention of this book to suffix the name with the word `Fault`.

The message definitions used by faults use Document/Literal encoding style and therefore must be based on a top-level element defined in the `types` element or imported in a WSDL or XML schema document.[BP] In Listing 5–5 the `types` element defines the `InvalidIsbnFaultDetail` top-level element as an anonymous type (see Section 3.2.4 for details about anonymous types). A SOAP fault message that adhered to this definition would look something like the SOAP message in Listing 5–6.

Listing 5–6

A SOAP Message That Conforms to the WSDL Document Definition in Listing 5–5

```
<?xml version="1.0" encoding="UTF-8"?>
<soap:Envelope
 xmlns:soap="http://schemas.xmlsoap.org/soap/envelope/"
 xmlns:mh="http://www.Monson-Haefel.com/jwsbook/BookQuote" >
  <soap:Body>
    <soap:Fault>
      <faultcode>soap:Sender</faultcode>
      <faultstring>
        The ISBN value contains invalid characters
      </faultstring>
      <faultactor>http://www.xyzcorp.com</faultactor>
      <detail>
        <mh:InvalidIsbnFaultDetail>
          <offending-value>19318224-D</offending-value>
          <conformance-rules>
            The first nine characters must be digits. The last
            character may be a digit or the letter 'X'. Case is
            not important.
          </conformance-rules>
        </mh:InvalidIsbnFaultDetail>
      </detail>
    </soap:Fault>
  </soap:Body>
</soap:Envelope>
```

Message definitions can also be used to describe SOAP header blocks and fault header blocks. This SOAP-specific feature is discussed at the end of this chapter.

5.3.2 The `portType` Element

A `portType` defines the abstract interface of a Web service. Conceptually, it's a lot like a Java interface because it defines an abstract type and its methods, but not an implementation. In WSDL the `portType` is implemented by the `binding` and `service` elements, which dictate the Internet protocols, encoding schemes, and an Internet address used by a Web service implementation. The "methods" of the `portType` are its `operation` elements. A `portType` may have one or more `operation` elements, each of which defines an RPC- or document-style Web service method. Each `operation` is composed of at most one `input` or `output` element and any number of `fault` elements. In Table 5–1, a single `portType` named `"BookQuote"`, (shown in the left column) declares three operations named `GetBookPrice`, `GetBulkBookPrice`, and `GetBookIsbn`. Although the comparison is only illustrative, a corresponding Java interface is shown in the right column.

Table 5–1 Comparing a WSDL `portType` Definition to a Java Interface Definition

WSDL `portType`	**Java Interface**
`<portType name="BookQuote">`	`public interface BookQuote {`
`  <operation name="GetBookPrice">`	`    public float getBookPrice`
`    <input`	`        (String isbn);`
`     name="isbn"`	
`     message="mh:GetBookPriceRequest"/>`	
`    <output`	
`     name="price"`	
`     message="mh:GetBookPriceResponse"/>`	
`  </operation>`	
`  <operation name="GetBulkBookPrice">`	`    public float getBulkBookPrice`
`    <input`	`        (String isbn, int quantity);`
`     name="request"`	
`     message="mh:GetBulkBookPriceRequest"/>`	
`    <output name="prices"`	
`     message="mh:GetBulkBookPriceResponse"/>`	
`  </operation>`	
`  <operation name="GetBookIsbn">`	`    public String getBookIsbn`
`    <input`	`        (String bookTitle);`
`     name="title"`	`}`
`     message="mh:GetBookIsbnRequest"/>`	

Table 5–1 Continued

WSDL portType	Java Interface

`<output`
`name="isbn"`
`message="mh:GetBookIsbnResponse"/>`
`</operation>`
`</portType>`	

The analogy between a WSDL portType and a Java interface is not perfect, but it's very close. In fact, most Java-based Web service code generators create mappings between Java interfaces and WSDL portType elements. They actually generate Java interfaces from WSDL portType elements—and can also generate WSDL portType, operation, and message elements from simple Java interfaces.

A WSDL document can have one or more portType elements, each of which describes the abstract interface to a different Web service. For example, a WSDL Web service might define one portType named "BookQuote" and another named "SubmitPurchaseOrder".

5.3.3 The operation Element

Each operation element declared by a portType uses one or more message definitions to define its input, output, and faults. In Listing 5–7 the "BookQuote" portType declares the GetBookPriceRequest as its input, GetBookPrice Response as its output, and InvalidArgumentFault as its fault.

Listing 5–7

Declaring input, output, *and* fault *Messages in a* portType

```
<portType name="BookQuote">
  <operation name="getBookPrice">
    <input name="isbn" message="mh:GetBookPriceRequest"/>
    <output name="price" message="mh:GetBookPriceResponse"/>
    <fault name="InvalidArgumentFault" message="mh:InvalidArgumentFault"/>
  </operation>
</portType>
```

An input message represents the payload sent to the Web service, and the output message represents the payload sent to the client. In RPC-style messaging the input is the request, and the output is the response. In document-style messaging the input is the XML document fragment sent to the Web service, and the output is the XML document fragment sent back to the client. In addition to input and output messages an operation may include zero or more fault messages, each of which describes a different kind of error.

5.3.3.1 Parameter Order within an Operation

In WSDL, when RPC-style messaging is used, it's assumed that the client uses procedure-call semantics. For example, JAX-RPC uses Java RMI interfaces with method calls to model RPC-style SOAP-based Web services. In many cases the parameters of the input and output messages must be transferred in a specific order, the same order as the parameters of the procedure call. To enforce proper ordering of input or output message parameters, the operation element may declare a parameterOrder attribute. For example, in Listing 5–8 the operation named "GetBulkBookPrice" uses the parameterOrder attribute to specify the order of its input parameters.

Listing 5–8

Using the parameterOrder *Attribute*

```
<message name="GetBulkBookPriceRequest">
  <part name="isbn" type="xsd:string"/>
  <part name="quantity" type="xsd:int"/>
</message>
<message name="GetBulkBookPriceResponse">
  <part name="prices" type="mh:prices" />
</message>
<portType name="GetBulkBookPrice" >
  <operation name="getBulkBookPrice" parameterOrder="isbn quantity">
     <input name="request" message="mh:GetBulkBookPriceRequest"/>
     <output name="prices" message="mh:GetBulkBookPriceResponse"/>
  </operation>
</portType>
```

When a parameterOrder attribute is used, it must include all the input parts and only the output parts that are not the return type. So if an output has only one part, as in the preceding example, it's assumed to be the return value and should not be listed by the parameterOrder attribute. If an output part is listed by the parameterOrder attribute, it's treated as an OUT parameter. When the input and output elements in a portType declare a part with the same name, it's an INOUT parameter, and the type must be the same in the input and output elements. OUT and INOUT type parameters are alien to most Java developers, but they are familiar features in C++, C#, and other languages. Section 15.3 provides a detailed explanation of OUT and INOUT parameters and how they are handled in Java.

Different interpretations of the meaning of the `parameterOrder` attribute have caused some interoperability problems. The Basic Profile fixes these by providing a single interpretation of the `parameterOrder` attribute. The order of parameters transmitted from sender to receiver must follow the order of `part` declarations made in `input` and `output` message definitions. The parameter order in Listing 5–8, for example, would be `isbn` followed by `quantity` because this is the order (from top to bottom) that these parts are declared in the input message definition named `"GetBulkBookPrice"`. The purpose of the `parameterOrder` attribute is to indicate which part, if any, is the return type. Any part that is omitted from the list provided by the `parameterOrder` attribute is assumed to be the return type of the operation. A procedure call can have only one return type, so only a single output part may be omitted from the `parameterOrder` attribute.[BP]

5.3.3.2 Operation Overloading

WSDL supports operation overloading that is very similar to Java method overloading. In WSDL, two operations may have the same name, provided their input or output messages differ. Unfortunately, this feature has caused enough interoperability problems that the Basic Profile prohibits operation overloading. Every operation defined by a particular `portType` must have a unique name. That said, it's perfectly acceptable for two or more `portType` elements to declare operation elements with the same name, because each `portType` is considered a separate definition.[BP]

5.4 WSDL Messaging Exchange Patterns

There are four basic message exchange patterns (MEPs) used in Web services: Request/Response, One-Way, Notification, and Solicit/Response. Although Notification and Solicit/Response messaging are supported by WSDL, they are not supported by the Basic Profile,[BP] and are rarely used in practice. Most WSDL-based Web services today use either Request/Response or One-Way messaging,[2] and they're the only MEPs that can be used with J2EE Web Services.

A WSDL document can dictate the MEP for a specific operation by the way it declares its input and output elements. Figure 5–3 illustrates the chief difference between Request/Response and One-Way messaging: In the former, the sender expects a reply; in the latter it doesn't.

5.4.1 Request/Response Messaging

In Request/Response messaging the client initiates the communication by sending the Web service a request message, and the Web service replies with a response message.

[2] This may change with the introduction of WSDL 1.2, which supports a larger set of messaging patterns.

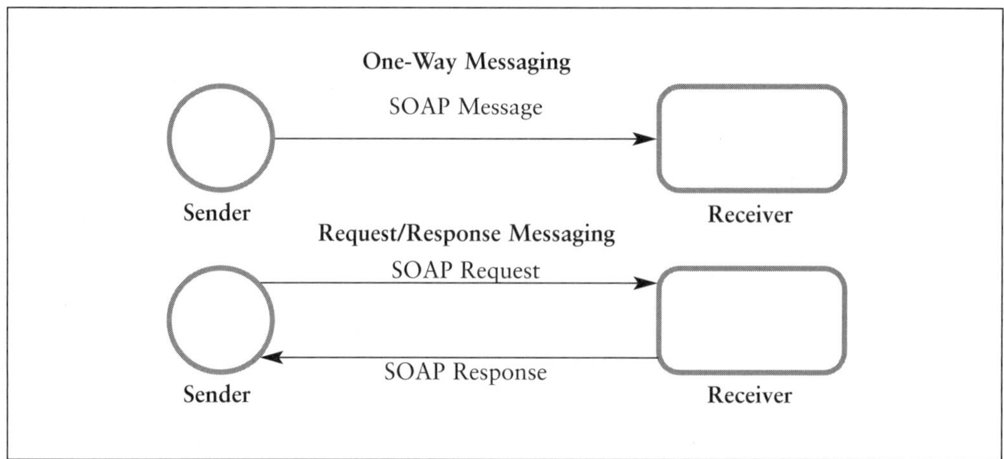

Figure 5–3 Comparing Messaging Modes: Request/Response versus One-Way

If an `operation` is declared with a single `input` element followed by a single `output` element, it defines a Request/Response operation. By listing the `input` first, the `operation` indicates that the Web service receives a message that is initially sent by the client. Listing the `output` second indicates that the Web service should respond to the message. The following snippet from Listing 5–2 represents a classic Request/Response operation, with exactly one `input` and one `output`.

```
<!-- portType element describes the abstract interface of a Web service -->
<portType name="BookQuote">
  <operation name="getBookPrice">
    <input name="isbn" message="mh:GetBookPriceRequest"/>
    <output name="price" message="mh:GetBookPriceResponse"/>
  </operation>
</portType>
```

In addition to its one `input` and one `output`, a Request/Response operation may also include `fault` elements, which are returned to the client in the event of an error. A Request/Response operation can have zero or more faults. The following snippet illustrates.

```
<portType name="BookQuote">
  <operation name="getBookPrice">
     <input name="isbn" message="mh:GetBookPriceRequest"/>
     <output name="price" message="mh:GetBookPriceResponse"/>
```

```
    <fault name="InvalidArgumentFault" message="mh:InvalidArgumentFault"/>
    <fault name="SecurityFault" message="mh:SecurityFault"/>
  </operation>
</portType>
```

5.4.2 One-Way Messaging

In One-Way messaging, the client sends a message to a Web service, but doesn't expect a reply message. This MEP is typically thought of as asynchronous messaging. Next to Request/Response, it is the most popular MEP employed today.

If an operation is declared with a single `input` but *no* `output`, it defines a One-Way operation. By listing only an `input` message, the `operation` indicates that clients will send messages to the Web service without expecting a response. The following snippet shows the `SubmitPurchaseOrder` `portType` that defines a One-Way operation.

```
<portType name="SubmitPurchaseOrder_PortType">
  <operation name="SubmitPurchaseOrder">
    <input name="order" message="mh:SubmitPurchaseOrderMessage"/>
  </operation>
</portType>
```

Unlike Request/Response operations, One-Way operations may not specify fault elements and do not generate fault messages. The messaging model is strictly unidirectional—faults cannot be sent back to the client.

5.4.3 Notification and Solicit/Response Messaging

Neither the Notification nor the Solicit/Response MEP can be used in J2EE Web Services. The unwillingness to support these styles is practical because they are poorly specified by the WSDL 1.1 specification and tend to introduce more problems than they solve. On the other hand, it's probably a good idea for you to understand the basic mechanics of these MEPs just for general purposes.

In Notification messaging the Web service sends a message to a client, but doesn't expect a reply message. A Web service that uses the Notification MEP follows the **push model** of distributed computing. The assumption is that the client has registered with the Web service to receive messages (notifications) about an event. The clients that register to receive notifications are called **subscribers.** In Notification messaging, the `portType` contains an `output` element but *no* `input` message definitions.

Solicit/Response is similar to Notification, except that the client is expected to respond to the Web service. As with Notification messaging, clients of Solicit/Response Web services must subscribe to the service in order to receive messages. In this MEP the `portType` first declares an `output` message, then an `input` message—exactly the reverse of a Request/Response operation.

5.5 WSDL Implementation: The `binding` Element

The `binding` element maps an abstract `portType` to a set of concrete protocols such as SOAP and HTTP, messaging styles (RPC or document), and encoding styles (Literal or SOAP Encoding). The `binding` element, and its subelements, are used in combination with protocol-specific elements. The `binding` elements identify which `portType` and `operation` elements are being bound, while the protocol-specific elements declare the protocol and encoding style to be associated with the `portType`. Each type of protocol (SOAP, MIME, and HTTP) has its own set of protocol-specific elements and its own namespace. For example, the following snippet from Listing 5–2 declares that the `"BookQuote"` `portType` is bound to the SOAP 1.1 protocol using SOAP-specific protocol elements.

```
<?xml version="1.0" encoding="UTF-8"?>
<definitions name="BookQuoteWS"
 targetNamespace="http://www.Monson-Haefel.com/jwsbook/BookQuote"
 xmlns:mh="http://www.Monson-Haefel.com/jwsbook/BookQuote"
 xmlns:soapbind="http://schemas.xmlsoap.org/wsdl/soap/"
 xmlns:xsd="http://www.w3.org/2001/XMLSchema"
 xmlns="http://schemas.xmlsoap.org/wsdl/">
  ...
  <!-- binding tells us which protocols and encoding styles are used -->
  <binding name="BookPrice_Binding" type="mh:BookQuote">
    <soapbind:binding style="rpc"
     transport="http://schemas.xmlsoap.org/soap/http"/>
    <operation name="getBookPrice">
      <soapbind:operation style="rpc"
       soapAction=
       "http://www.Monson-Haefel.com/jwsbook/BookQuote/GetBookPrice"/>
        <input>
          <soapbind:body use="literal"
           namespace="http://www.Monson-Haefel.com/jwsbook/BookQuote" />
        </input>
        <output>
          <soapbind:body use="literal"
           namespace="http://www.Monson-Haefel.com/jwsbook/BookQuote" />
        </output>
    </operation>
```

```
  </binding>
  ...
</definitions>
```

The first thing you should notice is that the binding element declared in Listing 5–2 is actually composed of two different namespaces. The elements without a namespace prefix (shown in bold) are members of the WSDL 1.1 namespace "http://schemas.xmlsoap.org/wsdl/", which is the default namespace of the WSDL document. The WSDL 1.1-generic binding elements are binding, operation, input, and output. The soapbind:binding, soapbind:operation, and soapbind:body elements, on the other hand, are protocol-specific. They are members of the namespace for the SOAP-WSDL binding, "http://schemas.xmlsoap.org/wsdl/soap/". Here's the same snippet from Listing 5–2 again, this time with the SOAP-specific elements in bold:

```
<definitions name="BookQuoteWS"
 targetNamespace="http://www.Monson-Haefel.com/jwsbook/BookQuote"
 xmlns:mh="http://www.Monson-Haefel.com/jwsbook/BookQuote"
 xmlns:soapbind="http://schemas.xmlsoap.org/wsdl/soap/"
 xmlns:xsd="http://www.w3.org/2001/XMLSchema"
 xmlns="http://schemas.xmlsoap.org/wsdl/">
  ...
  <!-- binding tells us which protocols and encoding styles are used -->
  <binding name="BookPrice_Binding" type="mh:BookQuote">
    <soapbind:binding style="rpc"
     transport="http://schemas.xmlsoap.org/soap/http"/>
    <operation name="getBookPrice">
      <soapbind:operation style="rpc"
       soapAction=
       "http://www.Monson-Haefel.com/jwsbook/BookQuote/GetBookPrice"/>
        <input>
          <soapbind:body use="literal"
           namespace="http://www.Monson-Haefel.com/jwsbook/BookQuote" />
        </input>
        <output>
          <soapbind:body use="literal"
           namespace="http://www.Monson-Haefel.com/jwsbook/BookQuote" />
        </output>
    </operation>
  </binding>
  ...
</definitions>
```

The soapbind:binding and soapbind:body elements are responsible for expressing the SOAP-specific details of the Web service. For example, soapbind :binding tells us that the messaging style is RPC and that the network application protocol is HTTP. The soapbind:body element tells us that both the input and output messages use literal encoding. The SOAP-specific binding elements are discussed in more detail later in this chapter. The children of the binding element (operation, input, and output) map directly to the corresponding children of the portType element. Figure 5–4 shows the relationship between the "BookQuote" portType and the "BookQuote_Binding" binding element.

Although the binding example given thus far uses SOAP-binding elements, the WSDL specification actually defines two other protocol-specific bindings, for HTTP and MIME. Listing 5–9 shows an example of an HTTP/URL encoding and a MIME payload binding.

Listing 5–9

Using the HTTP and MIME bindings

```
<!--HTTP/MIME-binding of BookQuote -->
<binding name="BookPrice_HttpMimeBinding" type="mh:BookQuote">
  <http:binding verb="GET"/>
  <operation name="getBookPrice">
    <http:operation location="alt.http.service"/>
    <input>
      <http:urlEncoded/>
```

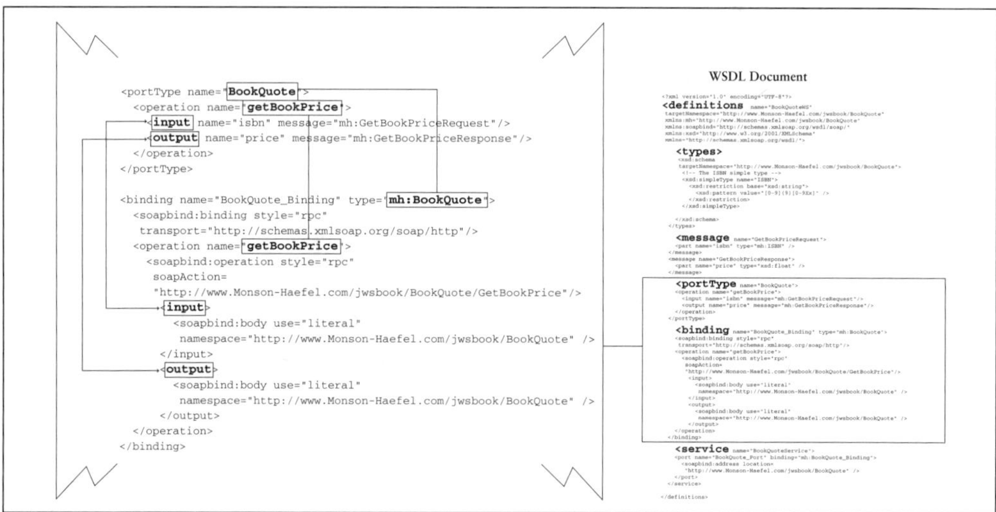

Figure 5–4 Binding to portType Mapping

```
        </input>
        <output>
            <mime:content type="text/html"/>
        </output>
    </operation>
</binding>
```

Although WSDL 1.1 allows the use of MIME and HTTP bindings as shown in Listing 5–9, the Basic Profile does not because they're poorly documented. Web services are required to use SOAP 1.1 binding, as illustrated in Listing 5–2.[BP]

This restriction will only be enforced by the Basic Profile 1.0. The WS-I has announced that it will explicitly extend support for SwA, including the WSDL MIME bindings in the next version of the Basic Profile, version 1.1. SwA is covered in Appendix E. SwA is still a subject of debate, however. Some leading SOAP authorities believe that SwA is the wrong solution to a rather simple problem. SwA relies on the MIME standard, which introduces a second packaging standard on top of the SOAP envelope. SwA critics argue that binary data can simply be encoded, using W3C's Hexadecimal or Base-64 built in types. It seems likely however, that SwA will remain the de facto standard for attaching binary data to SOAP messages.

5.5.1 SOAP Binding

Several SOAP 1.1-specific binding elements are used in combination with the WSDL binding elements. These include `soapbind:binding`, `soapbind:operation`, `soapbind:body`, `soapbind:fault`, `soapbind:header`, and `soapbind:headerfault`. The `soapbind:binding` and `soapbind:body` elements are required, but the other elements are optional. Using the `soapbind` prefix with the SOAP-binding namespace is a convention used in this book, but it's not required; you can use any prefix, just as with any XML namespace. The namespace assigned to that prefix must, however, be associated with the namespace defined by WSDL 1.1 for SOAP 1.1 bindings, `"http://schemas.xmlsoap.org/wsdl/soap/"`.

5.5.1.1 The `soapbind:binding` *Element*

The `soapbind:binding` element identifies the Internet protocol used to transport SOAP messages and the default messaging style (RPC or document) of its operations. The following snippet from Listing 5–2 shows the proper declaration of a `soapbind:binding` element.

```
<!-- binding tells us which protocols and encoding styles are used -->
<binding name="BookPrice_Binding" type="mh:BookQuote">
  <soapbind:binding style="rpc"
   transport="http://schemas.xmlsoap.org/soap/http"/>
  <operation name="getBookPrice">
```

```
    <soapbind:operation style="rpc"
     soapAction=
     "http://www.Monson-Haefel.com/jwsbook/BookQuote/GetBookPrice"/>
      <input>
        <soapbind:body use="literal"
         namespace="http://www.Monson-Haefel.com/jwsbook/BookQuote" />
      </input>
      <output>
        <soapbind:body use="literal"
         namespace="http://www.Monson-Haefel.com/jwsbook/BookQuote" />
      </output>
  </operation>
</binding>
```

Because J2EE Web Services supports only SOAP bindings, the `soapbind:binding` element must be declared in the WSDL `binding` element.[BP] In addition, the `style` attribute must be declared as either `"rpc"` or `"document"`; no other values are acceptable.[BP]

Because HTTP is the only transport protocol allowed by J2EE Web Services, the `transport` attribute must be declared to be HTTP, which means its value must be `"http://schemas.xmlsoap.org/soap/http/"`.[BP] This is the transport that corresponds to the SOAP-HTTP binding defined by SOAP 1.1. The `transport` attribute *must* be declared with an explicit value; there is no default.

The requirement that you use the HTTP protocol does not prohibit use of HTTPS—HTTP 1.1 over SSL (Secure Sockets Layer). In WSDL, HTTPS is actually a part of the HTTP namespace. Whether vanilla HTTP or HTTPS is used depends on the schema declared by the `location` attribute of the `port` element, which is discussed later in Section 5.6.[BP]

It's possible that the Basic Profile will support other standard SOAP transports besides HTTP eventually, including SMTP and TCP/IP.

5.5.1.2 The `soapbind:operation` *Element*

The `soapbind:operation` element is required. It specifies the messaging style (RPC or document) for a specific operation and the value of the `SOAPAction` header field. The following snippet from Listing 5–2 highlights the proper declaration of `soapbind:operation`.

```
<!-- binding tells us which protocols and encoding styles are used  -->
<binding name="BookPrice_Binding" type="mh:BookQuote">
  <soapbind:binding style="rpc"
   transport="http://schemas.xmlsoap.org/soap/http"/>
  <operation name="getBookPrice">
```

```
    <soapbind:operation style="rpc"
     soapAction=
     "http://www.Monson-Haefel.com/jwsbook/BookQuote/GetBookPrice"/>
      <input>
        <soapbind:body use="literal"
         namespace="http://www.Monson-Haefel.com/jwsbook/BookQuote" />
      </input>
      <output>
        <soapbind:body use="literal"
         namespace="http://www.Monson-Haefel.com/jwsbook/BookQuote" />
      </output>
  </operation>
</binding>
```

In WSDL 1.1 the `style` attribute is optional. It can be used to override the default messaging style declared by the `soapbind:binding` element—a capability that has been a source of interoperability problems. Accordingly, the Basic Profile requires that `style` attributes declared by `soapbind:operation` elements have the same value as the `style` attribute of their `soapbind:binding` element.[BP]

The `soapAction` attribute dictates the value that must be placed in the `SOAPAction` header field of the HTTP request message. You aren't required to declare the WSDL `soapAction` attribute; it can be omitted. You can also declare the `soapAction` attribute's value to be empty (indicated by two quotes), which is the same as omitting it.[BP] If this attribute is omitted or empty, then the `SOAPAction` HTTP header field must be present and must contain an empty string.[BP] The value of the `SOAPAction` HTTP header field must match, exactly, the value of the corresponding `soapAction` attribute in the `soapbind:operation` element. Listing 5–10 shows an HTTP SOAP request message whose `SOAPAction` header field matches the `soapAction` attribute declared in Listing 5–2.

Listing 5–10

An HTTP SOAP Message Declaring a `SOAPAction` *Header Field*

```
POST 1ed/BookQuote HTTP/1.1
Host: www.Monson-Haefel.com
Content-Type: text/xml; charset="utf-8"
Content-Length: nnnn
SOAPAction="http://www.Monson-Haefel.com/jwsbook/BookQuote/GetBookPrice"

<?xml version="1.0" encoding="UTF-8"?>
<soap:Envelope
 xmlns:soap="http://schemas.xmlsoap.org/soap/envelope/"
 xmlns:mh="http://www.Monson-Haefel.com/jwsbook/BookQuote">
```

```
    <soap:Body>
      <mh:getBookPrice>
          <isbn>0321146182</isbn>
      </mh:getBookPrice>
    </soap:Body>
</soap:Envelope>
```

You can find an example of an HTTP SOAP message that declares the `SOAPAction` header field to be empty in Chapter 4, Listing 4–26.

The style of messaging has a direct impact on how the body of the SOAP message is constructed, so declaring the correct `style`, `"rpc"` or `"document"`, is important. When you use RPC-style messaging, the `Body` of the SOAP message will contain an element that represents the operation to be performed. This element gets its name from the `operation` defined in the `portType`. The `operation` element will contain zero or more parameter elements, which are derived from the `input` message's parts—each parameter element maps directly to a message part. An output message works exactly the same way. Figure 5–5 illustrates.

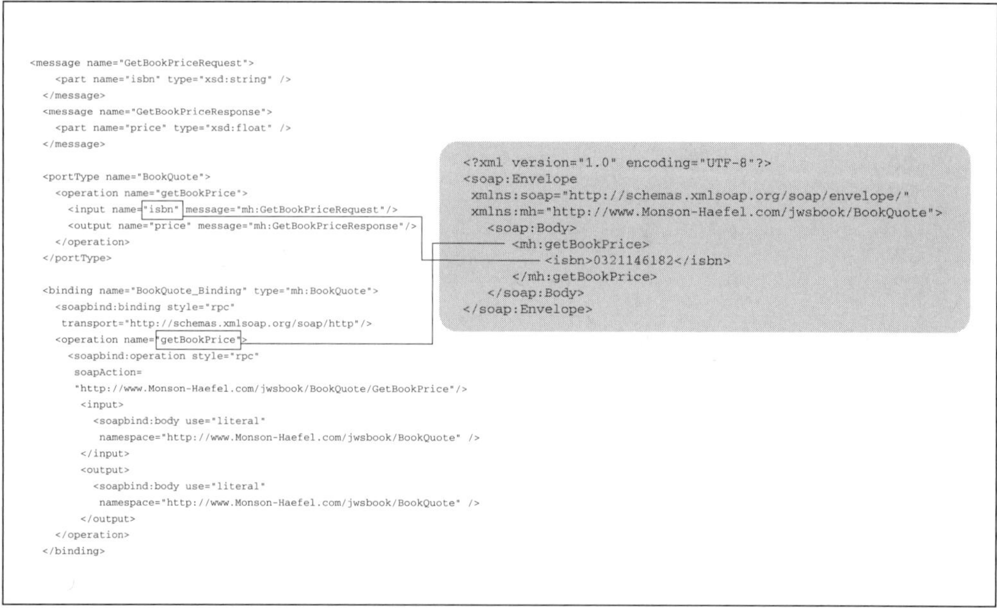
<message name="GetBookPriceRequest">
<part name="isbn" type="xsd:string" />
</message>
<message name="GetBookPriceResponse">
<part name="price" type="xsd:float" />
</message>
<portType name="BookQuote">
<operation name="getBookPrice">
<input name="isbn" message="mh:GetBookPriceRequest"/>
<output name="price" message="mh:GetBookPriceResponse"/>
</operation>
</portType>
<binding name="BookQuote_Binding" type="mh:BookQuote">
<soapbind:binding style="rpc"
transport="http://schemas.xmlsoap.org/soap/http"/>
<operation name="getBookPrice">
<soapbind:operation style="rpc"
soapAction=
"http://www.Monson-Haefel.com/jwsbook/BookQuote/GetBookPrice"/>
<input>
<soapbind:body use="literal"
namespace="http://www.Monson-Haefel.com/jwsbook/BookQuote" />
</input>
<output>
<soapbind:body use="literal"
namespace="http://www.Monson-Haefel.com/jwsbook/BookQuote" />
</output>
</operation>
</binding>
<?xml version="1.0" encoding="UTF-8"?>
<soap:Envelope
xmlns:soap="http://schemas.xmlsoap.org/soap/envelope/"
xmlns:mh="http://www.Monson-Haefel.com/jwsbook/BookQuote">
<soap:Body>
<mh:getBookPrice>
<isbn>0321146182</isbn>
</mh:getBookPrice>
</soap:Body>
</soap:Envelope>

Figure 5–5 Mapping the `portType` Operation and Message Parts to an RPC-Style SOAP Message

When you use document-style messaging, the XML document fragment will be the direct child of the Body element of the SOAP message.[BP] The operation is not identified.

5.5.1.3 The soapbind:body *Element*

You may have noticed that attributes of the soapbind:body element change depending on whether you use RPC- or document-style messaging. The soapbind:body element has four kinds of attributes: use, namespace, part, and encodingStyle.

The use attribute is required to be "literal"—and that value is assumed if the soapbind:body element fails to declare the use attribute.[BP] The encodingStyle attribute is never used at all, because WS-I-conformant Web services are based on the W3C XML schema, which is implied by the use="literal" declaration. Other encoding styles, like SOAP 1.1 Encoding, are not used. The part attribute specifies which part elements in the message definition are being used. The part attribute is necessary only if you are using a subset of the part elements declared by a message.

In "rpc"-style messages, the namespace attribute must be specified with a valid URI.[BP] The URI can be the same as the targetNamespace of the WSDL document, as in the following snippet from Listing 5–2.

```
<?xml version="1.0" encoding="UTF-8"?>
<definitions name="BookQuoteWS"
 targetNamespace="http://www.Monson-Haefel.com/jwsbook/BookQuote"
 xmlns:mh="http://www.Monson-Haefel.com/jwsbook/BookQuote"
 xmlns:soapbind="http://schemas.xmlsoap.org/wsdl/soap/"
 xmlns:xsd="http://www.w3.org/2001/XMLSchema"
 xmlns="http://schemas.xmlsoap.org/wsdl/">
  ...
  <!-- binding tells us which protocols and encoding styles are used -->
  <binding name="BookPrice_Binding" type="mh:BookQuote">
    <soapbind:binding style="rpc"
     transport="http://schemas.xmlsoap.org/soap/http"/>
    <operation name="getBookPrice">
      <soapbind:operation style="rpc"
       soapAction=
       "http://www.Monson-Haefel.com/jwsbook/BookQuote/GetBookPrice"/>
        <input>
          <soapbind:body use="literal"
           namespace="http://www.Monson-Haefel.com/jwsbook/BookQuote" />
        </input>
        <output>
          <soapbind:body use="literal"
           namespace="http://www.Monson-Haefel.com/jwsbook/BookQuote" />
        </output>
```

```
    </operation>
  </binding>
  ...
</definitions>
```

In contrast, document-style messages must *not* specify the namespace attribute in the soapbind:body element. The namespace of the XML document fragment is derived from its XML schema.[BP] Listing 5–11 shows the binding element of a document-style WSDL definition—notice that the soap:body element does not specify a namespace attribute.

Listing 5–11

A Document-Style Binding Doesn't Declare the namespace *Attribute*

```
<!-- binding tells us which protocols and encoding styles are used -->
<binding name="SubmitPurchaseOrder_Binding" type="mh:SubmitPurchaseOrder">
  <soapbind:binding style="document"
   transport="http://schemas.xmlsoap.org/soap/http"/>
  <operation name="submit">
    <soapbind:operation style="document"/>
      <input>
        <soapbind:body use="literal" />
      </input>
      <output>
        <soapbind:body use="literal" />
      </output>
  </operation>
</binding>
```

5.5.1.4 The soapbind:fault *Element*

In addition to the soapbind:body element, a binding operation may also declare fault elements. The fault message elements are on a par with the input and output message elements. Listing 5–12 shows an example of a binding with fault and soapbind:fault elements.

Listing 5–12

Using the soapbind:fault *Element*

```
<binding name="BookPrice_Binding" type="mh:BookQuote">
  <soapbind:binding style="rpc"
   transport="http://schemas.xmlsoap.org/soap/http"/>
  <operation name="getBookPrice">
```

```
    <soapbind:operation style="rpc"
     soapAction=
     "http://www.Monson-Haefel.com/jwsbook/BookQuote/GetBookPrice"/>
    <input>
      <soapbind:body use="literal"
       namespace="http://www.Monson-Haefel.com/jwsbook/BookQuote" />
    </input>
    <output>
      <soapbind:body use="literal"
       namespace="http://www.Monson-Haefel.com/jwsbook/BookQuote" />
    </output>
   <fault name="InvalidArgumentFault">
     <soapbind:fault name="InvalidArgumentFault" use="literal" />
    </fault>
  </operation>
</binding>
```

The WSDL fault and soapbind:fault elements include a mandatory name attribute,[BP] which refers to a specific fault message declared in the associated portType. In Listing 5–12, the fault and soapbind:fault elements refer to the InvalidArgumentFault, which was defined in the BookQuote port and soapbind:fault element, as shown in the following snippet from Listing 5–7.

```
<portType name="BookQuote">
  <operation name="getBookPrice">
     <input name="isbn" message="mh:GetBookPriceRequest"/>
     <output name="price" message="mh:GetBookPriceResponse"/>
     <fault name="InvalidArgumentFault" message="mh:InvalidArgumentFault"/>
  </operation>
</portType>
```

An operation may have zero or more fault elements, each with its own soapbind:fault element. Each soapbind:fault element may declare a use attribute. If it does, the value must be "literal". If it doesn't, the value is "literal" by default.[BP]

5.5.1.5 *The* soapbind:header *Element*

In Chapter 4 you learned that a SOAP message may have header blocks. WSDL explicitly identifies a SOAP header block by using the soapbind:header element in the binding's input element, its output element, or both. As an example we can create a binding that describes the message-id header block as in Listing 5–13.

Listing 5–13

Declaring a SOAP Header Block

```
<types>
  <xsd:schema targetNamespace=
   "http://www.Monson-Haefel.com/jwsbook/BookQuote"
   xmlns="http://www.w3.org/2001/XMLSchema">
    <xsd:element name="message-id" type="string" />
  </xsd:schema>
</types>

<!-- message elements describe the input and output parameters -->
<message name="Headers">
  <part name="message-id" element="mh:message-id" />
</message>
<message name="GetBookPriceRequest">
  <part name="isbn" type="xsd:string" />
</message>
<message name="GetBookPriceResponse">
  <part name="price" type="xsd:float" />
</message>

<!-- portType element describes the abstract interface of a Web service -->
<portType name="BookQuote">
  <operation name="getBookPrice">
    <input name="isbn" message="mh:GetBookPriceRequest"/>
    <output name="price" message="mh:GetBookPriceResponse"/>
  </operation>
</portType>

<!-- binding tells us which protocols and encoding styles are used -->
<binding name="BookPrice_Binding" type="mh:BookQuote">
  <soapbind:binding style="rpc"
   transport="http://schemas.xmlsoap.org/soap/http"/>
  <operation name="getBookPrice">
    <soapbind:operation style="rpc"
     soapAction=
     "http://www.Monson-Haefel.com/jwsbook/BookQuote/GetBookPrice"/>
      <input>
        <soapbind:header message="mh:Headers" part="message-id"
         use="literal" />
```

```
        <soapbind:body use="literal"
          namespace="http://www.Monson-Haefel.com/jwsbook/BookQuote" />
      </input>
      <output>
        <soapbind:body use="literal"
          namespace="http://www.Monson-Haefel.com/jwsbook/BookQuote" />
      </output>
    </operation>
  </binding>
```

The `message` and `part` attributes used by the `soapbind:header` element refer to the specific message `part` used for the fault. The `part` referred to must use an `element` attribute.[BP] In other words, you can't base a header block on a type definition, it must be based on a top-level element defined in the `types` element, or imported in some other XML schema document or WSDL document. The `use` attribute is always equal to `"literal"`, whether it's explicitly declared or not.[BP]

5.5.1.6 *The* `soapbind:headerfault` *Element*

The `soapbind:headerfault` element describes a header block-specific fault message. As you learned in Chapter 4, if there is a response message, any header block-specific faults must be returned in its `Header` element. WSDL maintains this scoping by requiring that `soapbind:headerfault` elements be nested in their associated headers. For example, a fault message specific to the `message-id` header block would be declared as in Listing 5–14, which adds a `soapbind:headerfault` to the WSDL document defined in Listing 5–13.

Listing 5–14

Declaring a `soapbind:headerfault` *Element*

```
<!-- message elements describe the input and output parameters -->
 <message name="HeaderFault">
  <part name="faultDetail" element="mh:detailMessage" />
</message>
...
<!-- binding tells us which protocols and encoding styles are used  -->
<binding name="BookPrice_Binding" type="mh:BookQuote">
  <soapbind:binding style="rpc"
   transport="http://schemas.xmlsoap.org/soap/http"/>
  <operation name="getBookPrice">
    <soapbind:operation style="rpc"
     soapAction=
     "http://www.Monson-Haefel.com/jwsbook/BookQuote/GetBookPrice"/>
```

```
        <input>
          <soapbind:header message="mh:Header" use="literal">
            <soapbind:headerfault message="mh:Headers" use="literal" />
          </soapbind:header>
          <soapbind:body use="literal"
           namespace="http://www.Monson-Haefel.com/jwsbook/BookQuote" />
        </input>
        <output>
          <soapbind:body use="literal"
           namespace="http://www.Monson-Haefel.com/jwsbook/BookQuote" />
        </output>
    </operation>
  </binding>
```

The `soapbind:headerfault` element has the same requirements as the `soapbind:header`. It must declare a `message` attribute that points to the appropriate `message` definition, and its `use` attribute must be equal to `"literal"`, whether explicitly declared or by default.[BP]

5.6 WSDL Implementation: The `service` and `port` Elements

The `service` element contains one or more `port` elements, each of which represents a different Web service. The `port` element assigns the URL to a specific `binding`. The following snippet shows a complete service definition from Listing 5–2 and Listing 5–13.

```
<service name="BookPriceService">
  <port name="BookPrice_Port" binding="mh:BookPrice_Binding">
    <soapbind:address location=
     "http://www.Monson-Haefel.com/jwsbook/BookQuote" />
  </port>
</service>
```

A `service` may have more than one `port` element, each of which assigns a URL to a specific binding. It's even possible for two or more `port` elements to assign different URLs to the same `binding`, which might be useful for load balancing or failover. Listing 5–15 shows a `service` element that contains three `port` elements, two of which refer to the same `binding`.

Listing 5–15

Defining a `service` *with Multiple* `port` *Elements*

```
<service name="BookPriceService">
  <port name="BookPrice_Port" binding="mh:BookPrice_Binding">
    <soapbind:address location=
     "http://www.Monson-Haefel.com/jwsbook/BookQuote" />
  </port>
  <port name="BookPrice_Failover_Port" binding="mh:BookPrice_Binding">
    <soapbind:address location=
     "http://www.monson-haefel.org/jwsbook/BookPrice" />
  </port>
  <port name="SubmitPurchaseOrder_Port"
   binding="mh:SubmitPurchaseOrder_Binding">
    <soapbind:address location=
     "https://www.monson-haefel.org/jwsbook/po" />
  </port>
</service>
```

5.6.1 The `soapbind:address` Element

The `soapbind:address` element is pretty straightforward; it simply assigns an Internet address to a SOAP binding via its `location` attribute (its only attribute). Although WSDL allows any type of address (HTTP, FTP, SMTP, and so on), the Basic Profile allows only those URLs that use the HTTP or HTTPS schema.[BP] For example, in Listing 5–15 the first two `port` elements declare an HTTP address for the `location` attribute, while the third `port` declares an HTTPS address.

Two or more `port` elements within the same WSDL document must not specify exactly the same URL value for the `location` attribute of the `soapbind:address`.[BP]

5.7 WS-I Conformance Claims

A WS-I **conformance claim** can be assigned to any WSDL definition, asserting adherence to the WS-I Basic Profile 1.0 specification. Child elements inherit their parents' conformance claims; for example, a `portType`'s claim that it conforms to the BP also applies to all the `operation` and `message` definitions associated with that `portType`. The best place to put a conformance claim is inside the `port` definition, because it applies to all the other definitions associated with that `port` (`binding`, `portType`, `operation`, and `message`).

5.8 Wrapping Up

The most important thing to remember about WSDL is that it provides a precise, structured, and standard format for describing Web services. This is advantageous for both vendors creating code generators and developers using SOAP APIs. The precision and strict structure of WSDL allows vendors to offer tools that automatically generate callable interfaces to a specific Web service, and enables developers using SOAP APIs to construct, deliver, and process SOAP messages correctly when using lower-level APIs like SAAJ.

In many cases you will not deal directly with WSDL documents, because code generators such as JAX-RPC providers will create convenient language-specific call interfaces for invoking Web services. In addition, existing interfaces can be used with tools to generate WSDL documents, so in many cases you may not be exposed to the contents of WSDL documents at all. While a detailed knowledge of WSDL document structure isn't necessary when using code generators, it is important for you to understand the organization and purpose of WSDL documents if you wish to truly master Web services. You have to understand WSDL to construct and exchange SOAP messages properly when using SOAP APIs, and these tools are often important when code generators are not available or are not robust enough to support your messaging requirements.

WSDL 1.1 is a lot more flexible than the WS-I Basic Profile allows, but the requirements of the Basic Profile make WSDL documents more portable and the SOAP messages they describe interoperable. Although the WS-I does a great job of constraining WSDL and therefore increasing interoperability, it doesn't state where the WSDL documents may be stored. In some cases the location of the WSDL document might be relative to the access URL of the Web service itself, in other cases it may not. The Basic Profile does, however, tell us how to refer to WSDL documents from a UDDI registry. Use of UDDI is optional, but if it is used, it must be implemented according to a strict set of guidelines. UDDI is the subject of the next part of this book.

Part III

UDDI

The basic goal of UDDI is to provide a standard data model for storing information about organizations and their Web services. UDDI defines a SOAP-based API that allows remote clients to access, update, and search the information in a UDDI registry.

UDDI's standard data model makes it easier to identify and categorize information about business and their Web services, but it also makes UDDI more complicated, because you have to learn the data model and how to implement it. It's the complexity of UDDI that turns some people off—and that makes this part of the book fairly large.

I prefer to think of Part III as a reference that you can use as needed, rather than something you should read in full right now. Chapter 6 provides a detailed explanation of the various UDDI data structures, which is helpful to understanding the underlying schema of UDDI. Chapters 7 and 8 provide WSDL and XML schema definitions for all of the standard SOAP operations used to search, access, update, and delete information in a UDDI registry. These chapters also provide plain-English explanations of concepts like authentication, search elements, and fault messages, among others. In addition, the WS-I Basic Profile 1.0 rules for UDDI are applied throughout these chapters. The Basic Profile requires that WSDL Web services be registered in the way described by the UDDI's Best Practices for *Using WSDL in a UDDI Registry, Version 1.08*.[1] These chapters stick to these guidelines, providing you with a single consolidated reference for UDDI version 2.0, the Basic Profile, and the UDDI Best Practices for using WSDL with UDDI.

The truth is you will probably use JAXR (the Java API for XML Registries) to access a UDDI registry and won't need to know much about the underlying UDDI data structures and SOAP messages. JAXR has a slightly different data model from UDDI's, and it hides the SOAP messaging behind an API, so if you want to reduce the amount of information you need to process, you can just read Part V: JAXR and skip most of Part III. I do, however, suggest you read the first couple of pages of Chapter 6, which provide an overview of UDDI.

That said, I have no doubt that many people reading this book will want to learn everything about UDDI, to round out their Web services skills. If you're one of those people, than dive in and have fun!

In This Part

[1] Organization for the Advancement of Structured Information Standards, *Using WSDL in a UDDI Registry, Version 1.08* (2002). Available at http://www.oasis-open.org/committees/uddi-spec/doc/bp/uddi-spec-tc-bp-using-wsdl-v108-20021110.htm.

Chapter 6

The UDDI Data Structures

UDDI (Universal Description, Discovery, and Integration) is a specification for creating a registry service that catalogs organizations and their Web services. An implementation of the UDDI specification is called a UDDI **registry.** A UDDI registry is a database that supports a set of standard data structures defined by the UDDI specification. The data structures model information about organizations (corporations, business units, government agencies, etc.) and the technical requirements for access to Web services hosted by those organizations. You can search a UDDI registry for specific kinds of companies or Web services. You can also register your own business and Web services in a UDDI registry. The usual analogy is that a UDDI registry is like an electronic "Yellow Pages" that businesses can search to find other organizations, and specific types of Web services. You can access the data in a UDDI directory using SOAP, which makes a UDDI registry a Web service.

Microsoft, IBM, and Ariba originally developed the UDDI specification, first published in September of 2000. Shortly thereafter they formed UDDI.org and invited 12 other companies to participate in the development of versions 2.0 and 3.0. UDDI.org was responsible for managing the specification and ancillary documents. In the summer of 2002, UDDI.org turned over management of the UDDI specifications to OASIS (Organization for the Advancement of Structured Information Standards). UDDI products based on the UDDI specification are offered by a number of vendors, including IBM, Microsoft, Sun, Oracle, Fujitsu, Systinet, and others. Although most UDDI products today run on a relational database management system, they can be implemented using other technologies, including LDAP servers and XML databases.

A UDDI registry must provide access to its data by way of a set of SOAP-based Web services. The UDDI specification describes about thirty different SOAP operations that allow you to add, update, delete, and find information contained in a UDDI registry. Most UDDI products also provide a Web interface for access to information in the registry.

Anyone can set up a UDDI registry for private use within an organization or marketplace. For example, the U.S. Navy is establishing a UDDI registry that provides centralized management for tens of thousands of applications. The navy's UDDI registry is being used to help reduce duplication across the entire organization. ISEC (the Integrated Shipbuilding Environment Consortium) is using UDDI to build a trading partner network for U.S. shipbuilders, which is hosted by NIIIP (the National Industrial Infrastructure Protocols Consortium). ISEC's registry will be used to manage an organization-wide supply-chain system for shipbuilders. Private and marketplace UDDI directories are not usually accessible to the general public; they are used by one organization, which might be a single company, a consortium of companies, or a government entity.[1]

In addition to private UDDI registries, which are the main focus of UDDI development today, there is a massive public UDDI registry called the **UDDI Business Registry (UBR)**, which is run jointly by IBM, Microsoft, NTT, and SAP, under an umbrella organization called the UBR Operators Council. This registry allows any organization to register its business and Web services, or peruse the registry, for free. The UDDI Business Registry is currently running on four main **operator sites** hosted by IBM, Microsoft, SAP, and NTT. These sites are synchronized, so that if you register your business and Web services with one of them, the information is copied to the others. Anyone can look up your organization and learn about your Web services using any of the four registries, but you can modify data only through the operator site where you originally submitted it.

Many people think of UDDI as a good way of cataloging a corporation's software applications, in order to provide a centralized source for documentation and discovery. UDDI is getting attention in electronic marketplaces, where companies of a common ilk organize and share data in the pursuit of commerce. The UBR has not, however, gained as much momentum as originally hoped. Although the UBR is free (all you need to do is register with the operator site), organizations have yet to see value in the idea of registering with a global UDDI registry. David A. Chappell, author of *Understanding .NET,*[2] summed up the degree of success of the UBR with the quip "There are literally *dozens* of corporations registered with the UBR worldwide!"

[1] Anne Thomas Manes, *Web Services: A Manager's Guide*. Boston: Addison-Wesley, 2003.

[2] David A. Chappell, *Understanding .NET.* Boston: Addison-Wesley, 2002.

UDDI defines five **primary data structures,** which are used to represent an organization, its services, implementation technologies, and relationships to other businesses:

1. A `businessEntity` represents the business or organization that provides the Web service.
2. A `businessService` represents a Web service or some other electronic service.
3. A `bindingTemplate` represents the technical binding of a Web service to its access point (its URL), and to `tModels`.
4. A `tModel` represents a specific kind of technology, such as SOAP or WSDL, or a type of categorization system, such as U.S. Federal Tax ID numbers or D-U-N-S numbers. The `tModels` that a `bindingTemplate` refers to reveal the type of technologies used by a Web service. Most of the data structures also use `tModels` to indicate the categorization system of an identifier assigned to the structure.
5. A `publisherAssertion` represents a relationship between two business entities.

Figure 6–1 shows how these data structures are related.

The Self-Organizing Myth

When UDDI was first introduced, the concept of self-organizing systems was high on the list of motivations for creating the registry standard. The idea was that software applications could look up Web services and integrate with them automatically, without any human intervention. In other words, your software would choose which services you used and create B2B partnerships on the fly. Sounded pretty good, but in reality it doesn't work.

When you decide to integrate with some other organization's Web service, you need to define the terms of that integration in a contract, or at least a general set of guidelines. You need to establish some form of business partnership with the other organization before they use your service or you use theirs. Another possibility is that you are using Web services to integrate stovepipe applications within a single organization.

In either case, you are going to choose these integration points purposefully and with deliberation—no one is going to trust software to choose business partners and integrate with foreign systems dynamically. The myth of self-organizing systems that automatically choose business partners and integrate on the fly is one that has been around for a while. Similar motivations were behind the CORBA Trading Service. The truth is that integration is an up-front design decision that is made by management and executed by developers; it's not something that software can do effectively at this point. The level of artificial intelligence required to make the heuristic decisions involved in choosing new business partners and integrating with foreign systems simply doesn't exist yet.

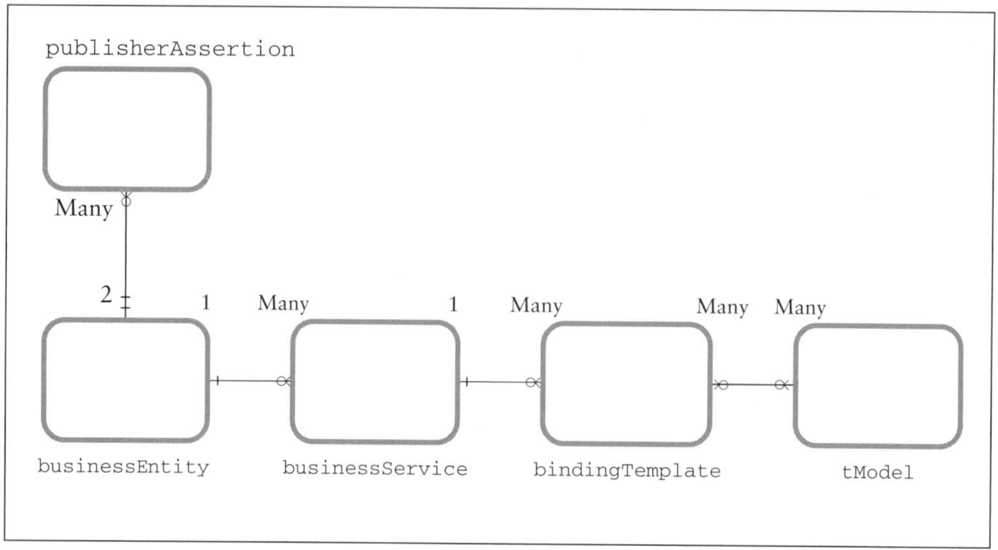

Figure 6–1 Entity Relationship Diagram of the Primary UDDI Data Structures

Actually, Figure 6–1 oversimplifies the relationship between the `tModel` and the other data structures. The `tModel` data structure and its relationship to all the other data structures are addressed in more detail later in the chapter. The five primary data structures are not the only data types defined by UDDI, but they are the most important ones, and the only ones assigned unique keys that allow them to be stored separately, yet still refer to each other. There are also data structures that represent address information, categories, contact information, URLs, and other common business data. All the standard data structures in UDDI are defined as XML schema complex types in a single XML schema document.

Currently there are three versions of UDDI, versions 1.0, 2.0, and 3.0. Version 2.0 is the one that is supported by J2EE Web Services and sanctioned by the Basic Profile, so it's the topic of this part of the book. The rest of this chapter provides you with a detailed understanding of the standard data structures used to store information about organizations and their Web services. Chapters 7 and 8 describe precisely the structures and purposes of the SOAP messages that can be sent and received from a UDDI registry.

6.1 The `businessEntity` Structure

A `businessEntity` is a data structure that represents any individual or enterprise that is publishing one or more Web services to a UDDI registry. It could be a company, a corporate division, a non-profit, a government agency—almost any kind of organization. The `businessEntity` provides very general information: names used by the organization, descriptions, contact information, Web services offered, and identity and categorization information. Listing 6–1 shows the definition of the `businessEntity` data structure.

Listing 6–1

The Definition of the `businessEntity` *Structure*

```
<schema targetNamespace="urn:uddi-org:api_v2"
            xmlns="http://www.w3.org/2001/XMLSchema"
            xmlns:uddi="urn:uddi-org:api_v2"
            version="2.03" id="uddi">
...
<element name="businessEntity" type="uddi:businessEntity"/>
<complexType name="businessEntity">
   <sequence>
      <element ref="uddi:discoveryURLs" minOccurs="0"/>
      <element ref="uddi:name" maxOccurs="unbounded"/>
      <element ref="uddi:description" minOccurs="0"
                                      maxOccurs="unbounded"/>
      <element ref="uddi:contacts" minOccurs="0"/>
      <element ref="uddi:businessServices" minOccurs="0"/>
      <element ref="uddi:identifierBag" minOccurs="0"/>
      <element ref="uddi:categoryBag" minOccurs="0"/>
   </sequence>
   <attribute name="businessKey" type="uddi:businessKey"
                  use="required"/>
   <attribute name="operator" type="string" use="optional"/>
   <attribute name="authorizedName" type="string" use="optional"/>
</complexType>
 ...
</schema>
```

Based on the definition of this complex type, the `businessEntity` instance data for Monson-Haefel Books would look like Listing 6–2.

Listing 6–2

A `businessEntity` *Structure*

```
<?xml version='1.0' encoding='UTF-8'?>
<businessEntity businessKey="01B1FA80-2A15-11D6-9B59-000629DC0A53"
                 xmlns="urn:uddi-org:api_v2">
```

```
  <discoveryURLs>
    <discoveryURL useType="buinessEntity">
      http://uddi.ibm.com/registry/uddiget?businessKey=01B1FA80…000629DC0A53
    </discoveryURL>
  </discoveryURLs>
  <name>Monson-Haefel Books, Inc.</name>
  <description xml:lang="en">Technical Book Wholesaler</description>
  <contacts>
    <contact>
      <description xml:lang="en">Web Service Tech. Support</description>
      <personName>Stanley Kubrick</personName>
      <phone useType="Voice">01-555-222-4000</phone>
    </contact>
  </contacts>
  <businessServices>
    <!-- businessService data goes here -->
  </businessServices>
  <identifierBag>
    <!-- D-U-N-S Number Identifier System -->
    <keyedReference
        keyName="D-U-N-S"
        keyValue="03-892-4499"
        tModelKey="uuid:8609C81E-EE1F-4D5A-B202-3EB13AD01823"/>
  </identifierBag>
  <categoryBag>
    <!-- North American Industry Classification System (NAICS) 1997 -->
    <keyedReference
        keyName="Book, Periodical, and Newspaper Wholesalers"
        keyValue="42292"
        tModelKey="uuid:C0B9FE13-179F-413D-8A5B-5004DB8E5BB2"/>
    <!-- Universal Standard Products and Services Classification (UNSPSC)
         Version 6.3 -->
    <keyedReference
        keyName="Educational or vocational textbooks"
        keyValue="55.10.15.09.00"
        tModelKey="uuid:CD153256-086A-4236-B336-6BDCBDCC6634"/>
    <!-- ISO 3166 Geographic Taxonomy -->
    <keyedReference
        keyName="Minnesota, USA"
        keyValue="US-MN"
        tModelKey="uuid:4E49A8D6-D5A2-4FC2-93A0-0411D8D19E88"/>
  </categoryBag>
</businessEntity>
```

There's a lot of information here, so we'll take it in pieces, and address the structure and purpose of each element individually.

6.1.1 The businessEntity Element and the businessKey Attribute

The businessEntity element is the root element of the businessEntity data structure. All the other elements related to the organization that the structure represents are contained in or referred to by elements nested within this element.

If you look closely at the businessEntity element, you'll notice it has an attribute called businessKey. The value of this attribute is a **UUID** (Universally Unique Identifier) key that is automatically generated from the data structure by the UDDI registry when it's first created. The businessService, bindingTemplate, and tModel data structures also have UUID keys. UUID keys are discussed in more detail in Section 6.5.

6.1.2 The discoveryURL Element

The discoveryURL element contains the Web address where the raw businessEntity can be accessed using an HTTP GET message. A discoveryURL can refer to two types of documents: a required businessEntity type and zero or more businessEntityExt types.

The data the businessEntity type URL refers to should be in XML format, but it may vary depending on the UDDI product. In most cases it will be an XML document but it might be something else, like a simple text file. The businessEntity's discoveryURL is generated by the UDDI registry automatically when the businessEntity data is added or modified. The businessEntity's discoveryURL is useful when perusing a UDDI registry with an HTML browser, which doesn't normally show the raw XML data. Instead, data is prettied up for HTML viewing. The following snippet shows the discoveryURL from Listing 6–2. Note that you can nest one or more discoveryURL (singular) elements in a discoveryURLs (plural) element.

```
<?xml version='1.0' encoding='UTF-8' ?>
<businessEntity businessKey="01B1FA80-2A15-11D6-9B59-000629DC0A53"
                xmlns="urn:uddi-org:api_v2">
  ...
  <discoveryURLs>
    <discoveryURL useType="businessEntity">
      http://uddi.ibm.com/registry/uddiget?businessKey=01B1FA80…000629DC0A53
    </discoveryURL>
  </discoveryURLs>
```

When the discoveryURL declares a useType attribute value to be "businessEntity", then it was generated by the UDDI registry and contains the raw businessEntity data. If, however, the discoveryURL's useType attribute value is "businessEntityExt", then the URL refers to non-UDDI data provided by the publisher. This might include technical specifications, or financial documents, or a Web site, or something else that the publisher feels is important. A publisher may define zero or more businessEntityExt-type discoveryURL elements, but usually there is only one or none.

6.1.3 The name Element

The name element holds the common name of the organization that the businessEntity represents. If there is only one name element, then the company has only one name, which is used internationally. If the company uses more than one name, perhaps one in the U.S. and another in Europe, then each can be listed within its own name element. For example, Monson-Haefel Books has two legal names, "Monson-Haefel Books, Inc." used in English-speaking countries and "Livres de Monson-Haefel, S.A." used in French-speaking countries. In this case both company names might be listed, as in the following snippet.

```
<?xml version='1.0' encoding='UTF-8' ?>
<businessEntity businessKey="01B1FA80-2A15-11D6-9B59-000629DC0A53"
                xmlns="urn:uddi-org:api_v2">
  ...
  <name xml:lang="en" >Monson-Haefel Books, Inc.</name>
  <name xml:lang="fr" >Livres de Monson-Haefel, S.A.</name>
```

The xml:lang attribute, which is defined by the XML specification, indicates the language to which the name applies. If your company has more than one name, use xml:lang to indicate the language of each. You may omit the attribute if the company uses only one name—for example, if it's a made-up brand name.

The XML specification says that the legal values for the xml:lang attribute are specified in the IETF standard RFC 1766 and its successors (RFC 3066, currently), which are based in part on ISO 639:1988. Language values begin with a primary two-character language identifier, optionally followed by a series of hyphen-delimited sub-identifiers for country or dialect. Examples include "en-us" for United States English and "fr-ca" for Canadian French. You don't have to use the sub-ids if they don't meet a business need; just "en" and "fr" are fine. The identifiers are not case-sensitive.

6.1.4 The description Element

As the element's name suggests, description presents a description of the organization. Unlike the name attribute, the description element *must* include an `xml:lang` attribute, which indicates the language in which the description is given. It's possible for a company to include descriptions in several languages, but not very common. Usually, the `description` element is in English, but in the spirit of internationalization the following example shows the description for Monson-Haefel Books in English, French, and Spanish.

```
<?xml version='1.0' encoding='UTF-8' ?>
<businessEntity businessKey="01B1FA80-2A15-11D6-9B59-000629DC0A53"
                xmlns="urn:uddi-org:api_v2">
  ...
  <description xml:lang="en">Technical Book Wholesaler</description>
  <description xml:lang="fr">Le Livre technique plus en gros</description>
  <description xml:lang="es">El Mayorista técnico del Libro</description>
  ...
```

6.1.5 The `contacts` Element

The `contacts` element contains contact information for people at the organization who maintain the UDDI information or fulfill some other function. The `contacts` element is optional. If it's present, it contains one or more `contact` elements, which are based on the XML schema in Listing 6–3.

Listing 6–3

The Definition of the `contact` *Type*

```
<schema targetNamespace="urn:uddi-org:api_v2"
        xmlns="http://www.w3.org/2001/XMLSchema"
        xmlns:uddi="urn:uddi-org:api_v2"
        version="2.03" id="uddi">
  ...
  <xsd:element name="contact" type="uddi:contact"/>
  <xsd:complexType name="contact">
    <xsd:sequence>
      <xsd:element ref="uddi:description" minOccurs="0" maxOccurs="unbounded"/>
      <xsd:element ref="uddi:personName"/>
      <xsd:element ref="uddi:phone" minOccurs="0" maxOccurs="unbounded"/>
      <xsd:element ref="uddi:email" minOccurs="0" maxOccurs="unbounded"/>
      <xsd:element ref="uddi:address" minOccurs="0" maxOccurs="unbounded"/>
    </xsd:sequence>
    <xsd:attribute name="useType" type="string" use="optional"/>
  </xsd:complexType>
  ...
</schema>
```

The following snippet shows a `contact` element that might be used in a `businessEntity`. It includes a description of the contact, his name, phone number, e-mail address, and postal address.

```
<?xml version='1.0' encoding='UTF-8' ?>
<businessEntity businessKey="01B1FA80-2A15-11D6-9B59-000629DC0A53"
                xmlns="urn:uddi-org:api_v2">
  ...
  <contacts>
    <contact useType="TechSupport" >
      <description xml:lang="en">Web Service Tech. Support</description>
      <personName>Stanley Kubrick</personName>
      <phone useType="Voice">01-555-222-4000</phone>
      <email>skubrick@Monson-Haefel.com</email>
      <address>
        <addressLine>2001 Odyssey Ave.</addressLine>
        <addressLine>Galaxy, CA 91223</addressLine>
      </address>
    </contact>
  </contacts>
  ...
```

The `address` element can get pretty complicated because it can work with varying address formats, like the `USAddress` and `UKAddress` types we developed in Section 3.2. These formats can be referred to by the `address` element, each `addressLine` element, or both. In the example above, the `address` element is free-form, with each `addressLine` containing unstructured data. In practice this free-form style is the most common use of the `address` element.

6.1.6 The `businessServices` Element

The `businessServices` element contains one or more `businessService` data structures, each of which represents a Web service implementation. The `businessService` data structure is covered in more detail in a little bit.

6.1.7 The `identifierBag` Element

The `identifierBag` element is optional and may contain one or more `keyedReference` elements. When used with a `businessEntity`, a `keyedReference` element contains a name-value pair that declares some type of identifier for the organization: a D-U-N-S number (from an identification system created by Dun & Bradstreet), a tax identification number, or some other form of identification. As an example, the following `identifierBag` contains two `keyedReference` elements: a D-U-N-S number and a U.S. Federal Tax ID number.

```
<?xml version='1.0' encoding='UTF-8' ?>
<businessEntity businessKey="01B1FA80-2A15-11D6-9B59-000629DC0A53"
                xmlns="urn:uddi-org:api_v2">
  ...
  <identifierBag>
    <!-- D-U-N-S Number Identifier System -->
    <keyedReference keyName="D-U-N-S"
                    keyValue="03-892-4499"
                    tModelKey="uuid:8609C81E-EE1F-4D5A-B202-3EB13AD01823" />
    <!-- U.S. Federal Tax Identifier -->
    <keyedReference keyName="TaxID"
                    keyValue="42-993029502"
                    tModelKey="uuid:9594A23D-CC1F-3A7A-B456-1CF13ED0045943" />
  </identifierBag>
  ...
```

The UDDI specification requires that UDDI products support several identifier systems, including two industry standards, the D-U-N-S Number Identification System and the Thomas Register Supplier Identifier Code System. These systems are useful for looking up companies in a UDDI registry. You are not required to use these types of identifiers, but be sure that the UDDI registry you are using supports them.

UDDI also defines fixed `tModels` and keys for the D-U-N-S and Thomas Register identification systems. You are free to use other identification systems and to provide `tModel` data structures that describe them.

A `tModel` is a data structure that identifies the specifications for a specific taxonomy or classification system. Every `tModel` has a unique `tModelKey`, which can be used to look up the `tModel` in a UDDI registry. In the case of both D-U-N-S and Thomas Register, the `tModel` referred to by the `tModelKey` points to the organization's Web site. The `tModel` data type is covered in more detail later in this chapter.

The `keyedReference` elements include a description attribute called `keyName`, which you can use to describe the `keyValue`. For example, the `keyName` for D-U-N-S numbers is `"D-U-N-S"`, and the `keyName` for the Federal Tax ID is `"TaxID"`. You can omit the `keyName` or give it any value you want; it's not standardized for most uses. The `tModelKey` and `keyValue` attributes are always required.[3]

The XML comments in the listings are added for your benefit; in a real-world registry they wouldn't be available. The next two sections explain how the D-U-N-S and Thomas Register identifier systems work.

[3] The `keyName` attribute is only required for the `general_keyword` taxonomy.

6.1.7.1 *The D-U-N-S Identification System*

Dun & Bradstreet (D&B) created the D-U-N-S identification system circa 1962, and continues to maintain it. D&B keeps track of the credit histories of many companies, and organizations use their services to check out the stability of potential suppliers, clients, and business partners. You can get a D-U-N-S number for free, but D&B charges fees for credit information. The identification system itself has become a de facto standard; D-U-N-S numbers are widely accepted as unique identifiers for businesses. The following is an example of a `keyedReference` element for a D-U-N-S identifier.

```
<identifierBag>
  <keyedReference keyName="D-U-N-S"
                  keyValue="03-892-4499"
                  tModelKey="uuid:8609C81E-EE1F-4D5A-B202-3EB13AD01823" />
</identifierBag>
```

6.1.7.2 *The Thomas Register Identification System*

The Thomas Register Supplier Identifier Code System is used in an on-line registry for products produced by over 189,000 U.S. and Canadian manufacturing companies. It contains product information (including CAD drawings), Web site URLs, and other information about products and their suppliers. Although searching the registry is free, companies pay a fee to have themselves and their products listed in the Thomas Register. Every company in the register is assigned a unique identifier code. The following is an example of a `keyedReference` for a Thomas Register identifier.

```
<identifierBag>
  <keyedReference keyName="ThomasRegister Supplier ID"
                  keyValue="749659325"
                  tModelKey="uuid:B1B1BAF5-2329-43E6-AE13-BA8E97195039" />
</identifierBag>
```

6.1.8 The `categoryBag` Element

A `categoryBag` element has the same structure as an `identifierBag` element, but its `keyedReference` elements refer to categorization codes rather than unique identifiers. For example, a `businessEntity` might be categorized as a manufacturer, or as providing a specific kind of product, or by its geographic location. The UDDI specification requires that all UDDI registries support three industry-standard categorization code sets: NAICS, UNSPSC, and ISO 3166, explained in the next three sections.

6.1.8.1 *The NAICS Category System*

NAICS (North American Industry Classification System) provides classifications for businesses across Canada, Mexico, and the United States—the participants in the

North American Free Trade Agreement. There are currently two versions: NAICS 1997 replaced the earlier SIC (U.S. Standard Industrial Classification) system, and NAICS 2002 was just released. UDDI repositories are only required to support NAICS 1997. A `categoryBag` that contained a NAICS 1997 `keyedReference` element would look like this snippet from Listing 6–2.

```
<?xml version='1.0' encoding='UTF-8' ?>
<businessEntity businessKey="01B1FA80-2A15-11D6-9B59-000629DC0A53"
                xmlns="urn:uddi-org:api_v2">
  ...
  <categoryBag>
    <!-- North American Industry Classification System (NAICS) 1997  -->
    <keyedReference keyName="Book, Periodical, and Newspaper Wholesalers"
                    keyValue="42292"
                    tModelKey="uuid:C0B9FE13-179F-413D-8A5B-5004DB8E5BB2" />
  </categoryBag>
...
```

The value of the `keyName` attribute for a NAICS code is usually a descriptive element, while the value of the `keyValue` attribute is a five- or six-digit number. A NAICS `keyedReference` element always refers to the standard UDDI NAICS `tModel`, using exactly the same `tModel` key in all registries. A complete listing of the NAICS codes can be found at the UDDI operator's Web site or at the U.S. Census Bureau's Web site, http://www.census.gov/epcd/www/naics.html.

6.1.8.2 The UNSPSC Category System

UNSPSC (Universal Standard Products and Services Classification) provides a classification system for over 12,000 products and services in 56 industries. It's an open source standard created by the United Nations and maintained by volunteer organizations. UNSPSC version 6.3 supersedes version 3.1, which is maintained for backward-compatibility. The UNSPSC code uses a dot notation, which allows products and services to be categorized into a hierarchy of four two-digit codes. The hierarchy begins with a very general two-digit industry code (Healthcare Services, Published Products, and so on) and drills down to a specific service or product code (Midwifery, Textbooks, and so on) The following shows the UNSPSC `keyedReference` element from Listing 6–2.

```
<?xml version='1.0' encoding='UTF-8' ?>
<businessEntity businessKey="01B1FA80-2A15-11D6-9B59-000629DC0A53"
                xmlns="urn:uddi-org:api_v2">
  ...
  <categoryBag>
    <!-- Universal Standard Products and Services Classification v. 6.3 -->
```

```
    <keyedReference keyName="Educational or vocational textbooks"
                    keyValue="55.10.15.09"
                    tModelKey="uuid:CD153256-086A-4236-B336-6BDCBDCC6634" />
  </categoryBag>
  ...
```

The value of the keyName attribute for a UNSPSC code is a description, while the value of the keyValue attribute is an eight-digit, dot-separated code. A UNSPSC version 6.3 keyedReference always refers to the standard UDDI UNSPSC tModel, using exactly the same tModel key in all registries. A complete listing of the UNSPSC codes can be found at the ECCMA (Electronic Commerce Code Management Association) Web site, http://eccma.org/unspsc/.

6.1.8.3 *The ISO 3166 Geographic Locator System*

Created in 1997 by the International Standards Organization, this code set identifies both the country and the region (city, state, province, and so on) in which a business is located. A categoryBag that contained an ISO 3166 keyedReference element for the state of Minnesota in the United States would look like the following snippet from Listing 6–2.

```
<?xml version='1.0' encoding='UTF-8' ?>
<businessEntity businessKey="01B1FA80-2A15-11D6-9B59-000629DC0A53"
                xmlns="urn:uddi-org:api_v2">
  ...
  <categoryBag>
    <!-- ISO 3166 Geographic Taxonomy -->
    <keyedReference keyName="Minnesota, USA"
                    keyValue="US-MN"
                    tModelKey="uuid:4E49A8D6-D5A2-4FC2-93A0-0411D8D19E88" />
  </categoryBag>
  ...
```

The value of the keyName attribute for an ISO 3166 code is the name of the region and country. The value of the keyValue attribute is a location code comprising a two-character country code and a two-character region code, separated by a hyphen. An ISO 3166 keyedReference always refers to the standard UDDI ISO 3166 tModel, using exactly the same tModel key in all registries. The ISO charges a fee to access the 3166 standard, but you can usually discover the codes for your location using your UDDI operator's Web site inquiry service—which is free.

6.1.8.4 *Other Categorizations*

While the UDDI standard categories (NAICS, UNSPSC, and ISO 3166) are useful across a broad spectrum, other taxonomies are often useful for categorizing organizations, especially in private or marketplace UDDI directories. There are basically two types of non-standard categorizations: `tModel`-Based, and General Keyword.

6.1.8.4.1 `tModel`-Based Categorizations

Anyone can add a new categorization system to a UDDI registry by creating a `tModel` that defines the system. This `tModel` can then be referred to by `keyedReference` elements with appropriate `keyName` and `keyValue` attributes. In most cases these custom `tModel`-based categorization systems will be created by industry-specific organizations for categorizing their own members. In addition, the operators of the UBR (the free global UDDI registry) are allowed to define their own categorizations in addition to the standard UDDI categories. For example, the IBM UBR supports the WAND (World Access Network of Directories) categorization system, an on-line product and service classification system with over 65,000 (and growing) codes for different products and services. The following snippet shows an example of a WAND categorization for Monson-Haefel Books.

```
<?xml version='1.0' encoding='UTF-8' ?>
<businessEntity businessKey="01B1FA80-2A15-11D6-9B59-000629DC0A53"
                xmlns="urn:uddi-org:api_v2">
  ...
  <categoryBag>
    <!-- WAND Classification System -->
    <keyedReference keyName="Technical Books"
                    keyValue="3283989"
                    tModelKey="uuid:61388A00-2495-11D5-9EB0-832611502FD0" />
  </categoryBag>
  ...
```

Microsoft also supports a custom categorization system called GeoWeb 2000, a geographic locator system that is similar to ISO 3166 but more specific. The following is an example of a GeoWeb 2000 categorization.

```
<?xml version='1.0' encoding='UTF-8' ?>
<businessEntity businessKey="01B1FA80-2A15-11D6-9B59-000629DC0A53"
                xmlns="urn:uddi-org:api_v2">
  ...
  <categoryBag>
    <!-- GeoWeb 2000 Classification System -->
    <keyedReference keyName="Minneapolis"
                    keyValue="516765"
                    tModelKey="uuid:297AAA46-2dE3-4454-A04A-CF38E889D0C4" />
  </categoryBag>
  ...
```

6.1.8.4.2 General Keyword Categorizations

A General Keyword taxonomy is not based on a custom tModel. Instead, it's applied to a UDDI data structure, and its context is provided by the keyName attribute. For example, a UDDI registry for book printers might categorize companies by the quantities of books they can print, or the types (soft cover, hard cover, oversized). A General Keyword taxonomy is different from the standard UDDI taxonomies in that the keyName is significant, rather than descriptive. In some cases, the keyName will be a URI provided by the organization that maintains the non-standard taxonomy. Think of this URI as an XML namespace, because it serves the same purpose (identifying a scope for names), and can be based on an actual XML namespace. The following shows an example of a General Keyword taxonomy defined by the fictitious IPA (International Printers Association) to categorize printers.

```
<?xml version='1.0' encoding='UTF-8' ?>
<businessEntity businessKey="01B1FA80-2A15-11D6-9B59-000629DC0A53"
                xmlns="urn:uddi-org:api_v2">
  ...
  <categoryBag>
    <!-- International Printers Association Category Code -->
    <keyedReference keyName="ipa-org:BookPrinter"
                    keyValue="B"
                    tModelKey="uuid:A035A07C-F362-44dd-8F95-E2B134BF43B4" />
  </categoryBag>
  ...
```

The tModelKey refers to a general-purpose tModel with the qualified name of uddi-org:general_keywords. This tModel can be used as an ad hoc, informal taxonomy.

6.2 The businessService and bindingTemplate Structures

The businessEntity complex type declares an element called businessServices (plural), which may contain one or more businessService (singular) primary data structures. Each businessService contains one or more bindingTemplate entries. The relationship between a businessService data structure and the binding Template data structure is similar to the relationship between a WSDL service and the WSDL port elements: A businessService represents a grouping of related bindingTemplate data entries. A bindingTemplate describes a Web service endpoint and represents the "technical fingerprint" of a Web service. In other words, it lists all the tModel types that describe a Web service, which uniquely identify the Web service's technical specifications.

6.2.1 The businessService Structure

Like other structures in UDDI, the businessService data structure is described by an XML schema complex type in the UDDI XML schema document. Listing 6–4 shows its definition.

Listing 6–4

The Definition of the businessService *Structure*

```
<schema targetNamespace="urn:uddi-org:api_v2"
            xmlns="http://www.w3.org/2001/XMLSchema"
            xmlns:uddi="urn:uddi-org:api_v2"
            version="2.03" id="uddi">
  ...
  <element name="businessService" type="uddi:businessService"/>
  <complexType name="businessService">
    <sequence>
      <element ref="uddi:name" minOccurs="0" maxOccurs="unbounded"/>
      <element ref="uddi:description" minOccurs="0"
                                      maxOccurs="unbounded"/>
      <element ref="uddi:bindingTemplates" minOccurs="0"/>
      <element ref="uddi:categoryBag" minOccurs="0"/>
    </sequence>
    <attribute name="serviceKey" type="uddi:serviceKey" use="required"/>
    <attribute name="businessKey" type="uddi:businessKey" use="optional"/>
  </complexType>
  ...
</schema>
```

Listing 6–5 shows the businessService instance defined by Monson-Haefel Books for its BookQuote Web service—this information was not shown in Listing 6–2.

Listing 6–5

A businessService *Structure*

```
<?xml version='1.0' encoding='UTF-8' ?>
<businessEntity businessKey="01B1FA80-2A15-11D6-9B59-000629DC0A53"
                operator="uddi:ibm"
                xmlns="urn:uddi-org:api_v2">
  ...
  <businessServices>
    <businessService serviceKey="3902AEE0-3301-11D6-9F18-000629DC0A53">
```

```
<name>BookQuoteService</name>
<description xml:lang="en">
  Given an ISBN number, this service returns the wholesale price
</description>
<bindingTemplates>
  <bindingTemplate bindingKey="391E2620-3301-11D6-9F18-000629DC0A53">
    <description xml:lang="en">
      This service uses a SOAP RPC/Literal Endpoint
    </description>
    <accessPoint URLType="http">
      http://www.Monson-Haefel.com/jwsed1/BookQuote
    </accessPoint>
    <tModelInstanceDetails>
      <tModelInstanceInfo
        tModelKey="uddi:4C9D3FE0-2A16-11D6-9B59-000629DC0A53"/>
    </tModelInstanceDetails>
  </bindingTemplate>
</bindingTemplates>
</businessService>
</businessServices>
```

The `name` and `description` elements may appear multiple times for different languages—qualified by the `xml:lang` attribute—as was the case in the `businessEntity` structure (see Sections 6.1.3 and 6.1.4).

6.2.1.1 *The* `categoryBag` *Element*

The `categoryBag` element used in a `businessService` structure is the same type that is used in the `businessEntity` structure (see Section 6.1.8). The difference is in the types of categories used to describe the `businessService`. In private UDDI registries, the `categoryBag` of the `businessService` is used to indicate things like department number, version number, and such.

6.2.1.2 *The* `bindingTemplates` *Element*

The `bindingTemplates` element will contain one or more `bindingTemplate` entries, each of which represents a different Web service port or binding. The structure and use of the `bindingTemplate` entries are covered next.

6.2.2 The `bindingTemplate` Structure

Like the WSDL `port` element, a `bindingTemplate` declares the Internet address of a Web service, and a reference to the implementation details. Its definition is shown in Listing 6–6.

Listing 6–6

The Definition of the `bindingTemplate` *Structure*

```
<schema targetNamespace="urn:uddi-org:api_v2"
            xmlns="http://www.w3.org/2001/XMLSchema"
            xmlns:uddi="urn:uddi-org:api_v2"
            version="2.03" id="uddi">
  ...
  <element name="bindingTemplate" type="uddi:bindingTemplate"/>
  <complexType name="bindingTemplate">
    <sequence>
      <element ref="uddi:description" minOccurs="0" maxOccurs="unbounded"/>
      <choice>
        <element ref="uddi:accessPoint"/>
        <element ref="uddi:hostingRedirector"/>
      </choice>
      <element ref="uddi:tModelInstanceDetails"/>
    </sequence>
    <attribute name="serviceKey" type="uddi:serviceKey" use="optional"/>
    <attribute name="bindingKey" type="uddi:bindingKey" use="required"/>
  </complexType>
```

6.2.2.1 *The* `accessPoint` *Element*

When you define a `bindingTemplate`, the UDDI specification gives you a choice: You can declare an `accessPoint` element, or a `hostingRedirector` element (but not both). The Basic Profile, however, mandates use of the `accessPoint` element in `bindingTemplates` that represent Web services; using the `hostingRedirector` is not permitted.[BP]

The `accessPoint` element provides the exact electronic address of the service. This address may be one of several standard types, including `"mailto"` (e-mail), `"http"`, `"https"`, `"ftp"`, `"phone"`, or `"other"`. The type of address is indicated by the `URLType` attribute of the `accessPoint` element. For example, the following snippet from Listing 6–5 shows the HTTP `accessPoint` for the BookQuote Web service.

```
<bindingTemplates>
  <bindingTemplate bindingKey="391E2620-3301-11D6-9F18-000629DC0A53">
    <description xml:lang="en">
       This service uses a SOAP RPC/Encoded Endpoint
    </description>
    <accessPoint URLType="http">
       http://www.Monson-Haefel.com/jwsed1/BookQuote
```

```
      </accessPoint>
      <tModelInstanceDetails>
        <tModelInstanceInfo
           tModelKey="uddi:4C9D3FE0-2A16-11D6-9B59-000629DC0A53"/>
      </tModelInstanceDetails>
    </bindingTemplate>
  </bindingTemplates>
```

A `bindingTemplate` may have only one `accessPoint` element. If a Web service is accessible via more than one URL, you must define a different `bindingTemplate` for each URL.

6.2.2.2 *The* `hostingRedirector` *Element*

As I noted in the previous section, WS-I does not permit use of the `hostingRedirector` services, so I don't cover it. As a practical point, this element doesn't appear to be used by anyone in production UDDI registries anyway.

6.2.2.3 *The* `tModelInstanceDetails` *and* `tModelInstanceInfo` *Elements*

The `tModelInstanceDetails` element contains one or more `tModelInstanceInfo` elements, each of which refers to a `tModel` that describes some technical aspect of the Web service. For example, when using a WSDL-based Web service with UDDI, the convention is to refer to a single `tModel` that refers to a specific `port` of a particular WSDL document. In this case the `tModelInstanceDetails` element would be very simple, containing one empty `tModelInstanceInfo` element, with a `tModelKey` attribute that refers to the WSDL `tModel` in the UDDI directory. In the following snippet from Listing 6–5 these elements are shown in bold.

```
<bindingTemplates>
  <bindingTemplate bindingKey="391E2620-3301-11D6-9F18-000629DC0A53">
    <description xml:lang="en">
       This service uses a SOAP RPC/Encoded Endpoint
    </description>
    <accessPoint URLType="http">
       http://www.Monson-Haefel.com/jwsed1/BookQuote
    </accessPoint>
    <tModelInstanceDetails>
      <tModelInstanceInfo
         tModelKey="uddi:4C9D3FE0-2A16-11D6-9B59-000629DC0A53"/>
    </tModelInstanceDetails>
  </bindingTemplate>
</bindingTemplates>
```

A `tModelInstanceInfo` element may contain zero or more `description` elements, but it must contain a `tModelKey` attribute that points to a `tModel` data structure representing the WSDL binding for the Web service.

The `tModelInstanceInfo` element may also contain zero or more `instanceDetails` elements, which provide ancillary data that clients need when using the referenced `tModel`. It's unclear whether WS-I approves use of the `instanceDetail` element, so you probably should avoid it if you want your Web services to conform to the Basic Profile.

6.3 The `tModel` Structure

The `t` in `tModel` resulted from a debate among the authors that created the first UDDI specification. Some wanted to call the data structure a "type model," while others preferred to call it a "technical model." `tModel` reflects their compromise; the `t` stands for both "type" and "technical."[4]

A `tModel` is essentially a namespace with meta-data. It represents a single specification, taxonomy, model, category, identity system, or any other technical concept. For example, UDDI specifies a standard `tModel` that represents the entire D-U-N-S Business Identifier System. The D-U-N-S `tModel` provides the following information:

Name: dnb-com:D-U-N-S

Description: Dun & Bradstreet D-U-N-S Number

UUID: uuid:8609C81E-EE1F-4D5A-B202-3EB13AD01823

Overview URL: http://www.uddi.org/taxonomies/UDDI_Taxonomy_tModels.htm#D-U-N-S

Categorization: identifier

Because the D-U-N-S `tModel` is a UDDI-standard `tModel`, it's exactly the same in every UDDI registry. There are many standard `tModels`, and you can specify your own custom `tModels` that identify just about anything that can be named. For example, the following is an example of the kind of information required for a WSDL `tModel`:

Name: Monson-Haefel:BookQuote

Description: Given an ISBN, this Web service returns the wholesale price of the book.

UUID: uuid:4C9D3FE0-2A16-11D6-9B59-000629DC0A53

[4] E-mail conversation with Anne Thomas Manes, March 9, 2003.

Overview URL: http://www.Monson-Haefel.com/jwsed1/BookQuote.wsdl#xmlns (wsdl=http://schemas.xmlsoap.org/wsdl/) xpointer(/wsdl:definitions/wsdl:portType [@name="BookQuoteBinding"])

Categorization: wsdlSpec

The BookQuote WSDL `tModel` includes a name (it's common to prefix a name with a domain identifier), a description, a unique identifier, the URL of the WSDL document (which uses XPointer—more about that later), and a categorization.

At this point you may be asking yourself: Why use a `tModel` to represent a WSDL document? Good question. For one thing, UDDI is very generalized and is not specifically aligned with WSDL, so there is no way to store a WSDL document directly in a UDDI registry. A WSDL document can be stored somewhere else and *referred to* by a UDDI entry, however. The WSDL `tModel` provides that reference. More importantly, the WSDL `tModel` allows us to attach meta-data to a WSDL reference in the form of categorizations. The BookQuote `tModel` is identified with a categorization of `wsdlSpec`, which indicates that this `tModel` refers to a WSDL document. The D-U-N-S `tModel`, in contrast, declares the categorization of `identifier`, which means it refers to some type of identification system. `tModels` make it easy to search for different types of organizations and Web services by categorization or identifiers.

A `tModel` may be assigned any number of categorizations, but every `tModel` must be assigned one of 16 standard categorizations, called the **UDDI types**, or a subtype thereof. These are a predefined set of types that allow us to categorize all `tModels` using a single system of categorization. A few of the UDDI types are shown in the following listing (a complete list of UDDI types is provided later, in Section 6.3.3):

`tModel`: The root type of all UDDI types. Every `tModel` is based on this type, or a subtype of it.

`identifier`: A type of identification system, like the D-U-N-S or Thomas Registry `tModel`.

`categorization`: A type of taxonomy, like NAICS, UNSPSC, or WAND.

`specification`: A type of `tModel` that represents some kind of specification for a Web service, like a WSDL document, a RosettaNet PIP document, or a CORBA IDL file.

`wsdlSpec`: A type of `tModel` that represents a WSDL document.

The `tModel` UDDI type is analogous to the `java.lang.Object` type in Java; it's the type from which all other types are derived. Each of the 16 UDDI types is itself categorized as some type of `tModel` data structure, and most of them are categorized using the `tModel` UDDI type.

The `wsdlSpec` UDDI type is applied to a `tModel` when the `tModel` refers to a WSDL document. The BookQuote `tModel` is a good example. `wsdlSpec`, like all

UDDI types, is itself categorized by a `tModel` called `specification`, and the `specification` `tModel` is in turn categorized as a `tModel` UDDI type.

The `tModel` is a very versatile data structure you can use to identify or categorize many other UDDI structures. It represents the core purpose of UDDI, which is to categorize or identify Web services and their organization so they can be located using queries. `tModel` is probably the most important data structure in UDDI.

6.3.1 `tModels` for WSDL Documents

When publishing a Web service in UDDI, the `bindingTemplate` must refer to a WSDL `tModel`.[BP] In addition, the `tModel` must be categorized as a `wsdlSpec` UDDI type (it may have other categorizations as well) and it must provide an XPointer to a specific WSDL binding element in an accessible WSDL document. Listing 6–7 shows an example of the BookQuote `tModel` in its XML format (the schema for the `tModel` data structure is discussed in more detail later, in Section 6.3.5).

Listing 6–7

A WS-I-Conformant WSDL `tModel`

```
<tModel tModelKey="UUID:4C9D3FE0-2A16-11D6-9B59-000629DC0A53">
  <name>Monson-Haefel:BookQuote</name>
  <description xml:lang="en">
     Provides a wholesale price given for a ISBN number.
  </description>
  <overviewDoc>
    <description xml:lang="en">
       This URL points to the BookQuote WSDL document.
    </description>
    <overviewURL>http://www.Monson-Haefel.com/jwsed1/BookQuote.wsdl
#xmlns(wsdl=http://schemas.xmlsoap.org/wsdl/)
xpointer(/wsdl:definitions/wsdl:portType[ @name="BookQuoteBinding"])
    </overviewURL>
  </overviewDoc>
  <categoryBag>
    <keyedReference
      tModelKey="uuid:C1ACF26D-9672-4404-9D70-39B756E62AB4"
      keyName="types"
      keyValue="wsdlSpec"/>
  </categoryBag>
</tModel>
```

Of particular importance is the `overviewURL` element, which points to the actual WSDL binding represented by the `tModel`. A WSDL `tModel` follows the recommendations of version 1.08 of the UDDI Best Practices for *Using WSDL in a UDDI Registry.*[BP] This document defines the use of the XPointer reference system to identify a specific `binding` in a specific WSDL document. XPointer is a powerful XML reference technology.[5] XPointer is outside the scope of this book, but you don't need to understand it to use it in your WSDL `tModels`. You just have to insert into a small template the proper URL and the name of the WSDL `binding` element you are referring to. Listing 6–8 shows an XPointer template you can use in your WSDL `tModel`'s `overviewURL` element.

Listing 6–8

An XPointer WSDL `tModel` *Template*

```
url-goes-here#xmlns(wsdl=http://schemas.xmlsoap.org/wsdl/) xpointer(/wsdl:
definitions/wsdl:portType[ @name="binding-name-goes-here"])
```

All you need to do is replace the bold portions in this template with the correct values and you have a valid XPointer. For example, if your WSDL document is located at `http://www.xyxcorp.com/my_wsdl.wsdl` and the WSDL `binding` element is named `FooBinding`, you create an XPointer that looks like this:

```
http://www.xyxcorp.com/my_wsdl.wsdl#xmlns(wsdl=http://schemas.xmlsoap.org/
wsdl/) xpointer(/wsdl:definitions/wsdl:portType[ @name="FooBinding"])
```

You must assign the `wsdlSpec` UDDI type to the WSDL `tModel` in the `category Bag` element. You can also assign other UDDI types or custom types to your WSDL `tModel`, but at the very least it must have the `wsdlSpec` UDDI type, as shown in Listing 6–7.[BP]

The `bindingTemplate` that refers to a WSDL `tModel` will provide the correct URL for the actual Web service, which means that the `bindingTemplate` fulfills the same role as the WSDL `port` element: It assigns a URL to a Web service. When accessing a WSDL binding from a UDDI registry, the `port` elements in the WSDL document are ignored, because the `bindingTemplate` should provide the correct URL for the Web service. This arrangement allows you to change the access point dynamically in UDDI, without having to modify the WSDL document. If you access a WSDL document via UDDI, use the `accessPoint` specified by the UDDI `bindingTemplate`, but if you access a WSDL document without UDDI, use the URL specified by the WSDL `port` element.

[5] World Wide Web Consortium, *XPointer xpointer() Scheme,* July 10, 2002. Available at `http://www.w3.org/TR/2002/WD-xptr-xpointer-20020710/`

6.3.2 `tModel`s as Taxonomy Identifiers

When a `tModel` is used as a taxonomy identifier, it is basically providing context for `keyedReference` elements in `identifierBag` and `categoryBag` elements (and in `publisherAssertion` entries, described later in the chapter). Without an associated `tModel`, the meaning of the name-value pair in a `keyedReference` is impossible to discern. For example, consider the following `keyedReference` element:

```
<keyedReference keyName="Book, Periodical, and Newspaper Wholesalers"
                keyValue="42292"/>
```

Obviously, it's some kind of categorization, but is it NAICS, UNSPSC, WAND, some private corporate categorization, or something else? Without the `tModelkey` there's no way to tell. Adding a reference to a specific `tModel`, using a `tModelKey` attribute, gives the `keyedReference` context. For example, if the `keyedReference` refers to a NAICS 1997 number, then we know it refers to the UDDI standard `tModel` for NAICS 1997, as shown in bold in this snippet:

```
<keyedReference keyName="Book, Periodical, and Newspaper Wholesalers"
                keyValue="42292"
                tModelKey="uuid:C0B9FE13-179F-413D-8A5B-5004DB8E5BB2"/>
```

By looking up the `tModel` associated with the `keyedReference` we can determine the type of system to which the name-value pair belongs. The `tModel` for NAICS 1997 is shown in Listing 6–9.

Listing 6–9

The NAICS 1997 `tModel`

```
<tModel tModelKey="uuid:C0B9FE13-179F-413D-8A5B-5004DB8E5BB2">
  <name>ntis-gov:naics:1997</name>
  <description xml:lang="en">
     Business Taxonomy: NAICS (1997 Release)
  </description>
  <overviewDoc>
    <description xml:lang="en">
      This tModel defines the NAICS industry taxonomy.
    </description>
    <overviewURL>
      http://www.uddi.org/taxonomies/UDDI_Taxonomy_tModels.htm#NAICS
    </overviewURL>
  </overviewDoc>
  <categoryBag>
```

```
      <keyedReference
        tModelKey="uuid:C1ACF26D-9672-4404-9D70-39B756E62AB4"
        keyName="types"
        keyValue="categorization"/>
      <keyedReference
        tModelKey="uuid:C1ACF26D-9672-4404-9D70-39B756E62AB4"
        keyName="types"
        keyValue="checked"/>
    </categoryBag>
</tModel>
```

The real power of `tModels`, when used as taxonomies, is that they allow for more concise searching of UDDI registries. For example, you can conduct a search for a specific business by its D-U-N-S number, or you can search for businesses that fall under a specific NAICS category or are located in a specific ISO 3166 region.

The seven `tModels` that represent industry-standard identification and classification systems are listed in Table 6–1, and most of them are described in detail in Sections 6.1.7 and 6.1.8. A complete description of the standard UDDI taxonomies can be found at UDDI.org, at

http://uddi.org/taxonomies/UDDI_Taxonomy_tModels.htm

Table 6–1 UDDI Standard `tModels`

Name	Description
`uddi-org:types`	UDDI categorization codes for `tModels`
`ntis-gov:naics:1997`	North American Industry Classification System (NAICS), 1997 release
`unspsc-org:unspsc`	Universal Standard Products and Services Classification (UNSPSC), version 6.3
`uddi-org:iso-ch:3166-1999`	ISO 3166 Geographic Taxonomy
`dnb-com:D-U-N-S`	D-U-N-S Number Identifier System
`thomasregister-com:supplierID`	Thomas Register Supplier Identifier Code System
`uddi-org:general-keywords`	UDDI "other" taxonomy

6.3.3 The `uddi-org:types tModel`

As I noted earlier, the UDDI type `tModel` provides a taxonomy for categorizing all other `tModels`. It's kind of a super `tModel`, that all other `tModels` can refer to from their `categoryBag` elements. For example, the `tModel` for NAICS 1997 shown in Listing 6–9 is associated with the UDDI type `categorization`, thus identifying itself as a categorization `tModel`.

The uddi-org:types tModel includes 16 categories to which a tModel can belong. These categories are listed in Table 6–2 (the descriptions are taken from UDDI.org's taxonomy overview).[6]

Table 6–2 uddi-org:types Categories for tModels

Key Value	Description
tModel	The UDDI type taxonomy is structured to allow for categorization of registry entries other than tModels. This key is the root of the branch of the taxonomy that is intended for use in categorization of tModels within the UDDI registry. Categorization is not allowed with this key.
identifier	An identifier tModel represents a specific set of values used to uniquely identify information. identifier tModels are intended to be used in keyedReferences inside of identifierBags. For example, a Dun & Bradstreet D-U-N-S number uniquely identifies companies globally. The D-U-N-S number taxonomy is an identifier taxonomy.
namespace	A namespace tModel represents a scoping constraint or domain for a set of information. In contrast to an identifier, a namespace does not have a predefined set of values within the domain, but acts to avoid collisions. It is similar to the namespace functionality used for XML. For example, the uddi-org:relationship tModel, which is used to assert relationships between business entities, is a namespace tModel.
categorization	A categorization tModel is used for information taxonomies within the UDDI registry. NAICS and UNSPSC are examples of categorization tModels.
relationship	A relationship tModel is used for relationship categorizations within the UDDI registry; relationship tModels are typically used in connection with publisher-relationship assertions.
postalAddress	A postalAddress tModel is used to identify different forms of postal address within the UDDI registry; postalAddress tModels may be used with the address element to distinguish different forms of postal address.
specification	A specification tModel is used for tModels that define interactions with a Web service. These interactions typically include the definition of the set of requests and responses, or other types of interaction, that are prescribed by the service. tModels describing XML, COM, CORBA, or any other service are specification tModels.

[6] UDDI.org, *UDDI Core tModels: Taxonomy and Identifier Systems* (2001). Available at http:// www.uddi.org/taxonomies/Core_Taxonomy_OverviewDoc.htm. Copyright © 2000–2002 by Accenture, Ariba, Inc., Commerce One, Inc. Fujitsu Limited, Hewlett-Packard Company, i2 Technologies, Inc., Intel Corporation, International Business Machines Corporation, Microsoft Corporation, Oracle Corporation, SAP AG, Sun Microsystems, Inc., and VeriSign, Inc. All rights reserved.

Table 6–2 uddi-org:types Categories for tModels (Continued)

Key Value	Description
xmlSpec	An xmlSpec tModel is a refinement of the specification tModel type. It is used to indicate that the interaction with the service is via XML. The UDDI API tModels are xmlSpec tModels.
soapSpec	Further refining the xmlSpec tModel type, a soapSpec is used to indicate that the interaction with the service is via SOAP. The UDDI API tModels are soapSpec tModels, in addition to xmlSpec tModels.
wsdlSpec	A tModel for a Web Service described using WSDL is categorized as a wsdlSpec.
protocol	A tModel describing a protocol of any sort.
transport	A transport tModel is a specific type of protocol. HTTP, FTP, and SMTP are types of transport tModels.
signatureComponent	A signatureComponent is used in cases where a single tModel cannot represent a complete specification for a Web service. This is the case for specifications like RosettaNet, where implementation requires the composition of three tModels to be complete—a general tModel indicating RNIF, one for the specific PIP, and one for the error-handling services. Each of these tModels would be of type signatureComponent, in addition to any others as appropriate.
unvalidatable	Used to mark a categorization or identifier tModel as unavailable for use. tModels representing checked value sets are marked unvalidatable as they are brought on-line, and to retire them.
checked	Marking a tModel with this classification asserts that it represents a categorization, identifier, or namespace tModel that has a properly registered validation service per the UDDI Version 2.0 Operators Specification Appendix A.
unchecked	Marking a tModel with this classification asserts that it represents a categorization, identifier, or namespace tModel that does not have a validation service.

The UDDI types are also handy for searches. If, for example, you wanted a list of all the organizations that had WSDL-based Web services, you could get it by searching for organizations whose technology tModel was categorized with a keyValue of "wsdlSpec". If you go back to Listing 6–7, you can see a WSDL tModel with this categorization.

6.3.4 Checked and Unchecked `tModels`

A taxonomy `tModel` (one which can be referred to by a `keyedReference` in a `categoryBag` or `identifierBag` element) may be **checked** or **unchecked.** A checked `tModel` is a categorization or identification system that requires validation to ensure that values added in a `keyedReference` element are correct.

Except for General Keyword, all of the UDDI-standard `tModels` listed in Table 6–1 are checked `tModels`. When you submit a `keyedReference` for an `identifierBag` or `categoryBag` that refers to UDDI types, NAICS, UNSPSC v7, or ISO 3166, the UDDI registry will validate the `keyValues` before saving them to the database. In many cases, the UDDI will maintain a cache of the taxonomies in the UDDI registry so that submitted data can be validated very quickly.

It's possible for external organizations to validate `keyedReference` values that refer to checked `tModels`. For example, the WAND categorization service offered by the IBM operator site uses an external service to validate `keyedReferences` that refer to the WAND taxonomy. The UDDI specification defines a standard SOAP messaging API that an external service must support in order to provide validation of checked `tModels`.[7] When you submit a WAND `keyedReference` element in a `categoryBag`, the IBM UBR will send a SOAP message containing the `keyedReference` values to the validating service hosted by WAND, Inc. WAND's validating service determines whether the `keyedReference` values are correct, and sends a response to the IBM UBR confirming or rejecting them. If the values are confirmed, they're stored in the UDDI registry. If the values are rejected, the registry sends the publisher a fault message indicating that the `keyedReference` values are invalid.

In many cases, the UDDI registry caches categorization codes so that it doesn't need to consult the external validation service every time a `keyedReference` is submitted—in accordance with terms already agreed to by the validating service, including rules for refreshing the cache. It's not all that easy to add a new checked `tModel` to a UDDI registry, especially the UBR. You must follow a multi-step process, which is set forth in the UDDI Operator Site specification. Adding new checked and unchecked taxonomies to your UDDI registry is one of things that makes UDDI so powerful, though—it's the ability to define new taxonomies that allows you to customize UDDI to your specific needs.

If a `tModel` is checked, it will contain a `uddi-org:type` categorization of `checked`. A `tModel` not categorized as `checked` is assumed to be unchecked, but you can also explicitly categorize it as such.

[7] OASIS provides a useful technical note: Organization for the Advancement of Structured Information Standards, *Providing a Taxonomy for Use in UDDI version 2* (2002). Available at http://www.oasis-open.org/committees/uddi-spec/doc/tn/uddi-spec-tc-tn-taxonomy-provider-v100-20010716.htm.

6.3.5 The tModel XML Schema

Although the use of tModels varies, their structures are all the same. They include name, description, overviewDoc, identifierBag, and categoryBag elements, as shown in Listing 6–10.

Listing 6–10

The Definition of the tModel *Structure*

```
<schema targetNamespace="urn:uddi-org:api_v2"
           xmlns="http://www.w3.org/2001/XMLSchema"
           xmlns:uddi="urn:uddi-org:api_v2"
           version="2.03" id="uddi">
  ...
  <element name="tModel" type="uddi:tModel"/>
  <complexType name="tModel">
    <sequence>
      <element ref="uddi:name"/>
      <element ref="uddi:description" minOccurs="0" maxOccurs="unbounded"/>
      <element ref="uddi:overviewDoc" minOccurs="0"/>
      <element ref="uddi:identifierBag" minOccurs="0"/>
      <element ref="uddi:categoryBag" minOccurs="0"/>
    </sequence>
    <attribute name="tModelKey" type="uddi:tModelKey" use="required"/>
    <attribute name="operator" type="string" use="optional"/>
    <attribute name="authorizedName" type="string" use="optional"/>
  </complexType>
```

The rest of this section examines each of these elements in detail.

6.3.5.1 *The* name *and* description *Elements*

The name element is, by convention, based on a URI and is used to identify the tModel succinctly. The name doesn't have to be unique within a particular UDDI registry, however; the tModel's UUID is its unique identifier. A tModel may have only one name element, and it must not be blank; it should contain a meaningful URI. For example, the tModel used for the NAICS codes discussed in Section 6.1.8.1 is named ntis-gov:naics:1997, while the tModel for the D-U-N-S identifier system described in Section 6.1.7.1 is named dnb-com:D-U-N-S. Both are valid URIs that identify the agency that manages the taxonomy, the taxonomy's name, and in the case of NAICS, the version.

Non-standard examples include the names of the tModels used by RosettaNet to describe Web services, such as

```
Rosettanet-org:PIP2A2:QueryProductInformation:v1.0
```

and

`Rosettanet-org:PIP1A1:RequestAccountSetup:vB01.00.00A.`

You can choose the name value that is most appropriate to the Web service you're listing. For example, Monson-Haefel Books might name the `tModel` for its BookQuote Web service `Monson-Haefel:BookQuote` as shown in this snippet:

```
<tModel tModelKey="UUID:4C9D3FE0-2A16-11D6-9B59-000629DC0A53">
  <name>Monson-Haefel:BookQuote</name>
  <description xml:lang="en">The WSDL document for BookQuote</description>
  ...
</tModel>
```

The `description` element may appear multiple times for different languages—qualified by the `xml:lang` attribute, as in the `businessEntity` structure (see Section 6.1.4).

6.3.5.2 *The* `overviewDoc` *Element*

The `overviewDoc` may contain an optional `description` element (`xml:lang`-qualified) and an `overviewURL` element. The complex type definition for the `overviewDoc` element is shown in Listing 6–11.

Listing 6–11

The Definition of the `overviewDoc` *Type*

```
<schema targetNamespace="urn:uddi-org:api_v2"
        xmlns="http://www.w3.org/2001/XMLSchema"
        xmlns:uddi="urn:uddi-org:api_v2"
        version="2.03" id="uddi">
  ...
  <element name="overviewDoc" type="uddi:overviewDoc"/>
  <complexType name="overviewDoc">
    <sequence>
      <element ref="uddi:description" minOccurs="0" maxOccurs="unbounded"/>
      <element ref="uddi:overviewURL" minOccurs="0"/>
    </sequence>
  </complexType>
  <element name="overviewURL" type="string"/>
```

The `overviewURL` element can be any valid URL, but the convention is to use a URL that points to a file you can obtain with a standard HTTP GET operation, or download using a common Web browser. For example, the `overviewURL` for the

D-U-N-S `tModel` points to a document that describes all of the standard UDDI taxonomies. The following is the `tModel` definition for D-U-N-S.

```
<tModel tModelKey="UUID:8609C81E-EE1F-4D5A-B202-3EB13AD01823">
  <name>dnb-com:D-U-N-S</name>
  <description xml:lang="en">
      Dun & Bradstreet D-U-N-S Number
  </description>
  <overviewDoc>
    <description xml:lang="en">
        This tModel is used for the Dun & Bradstreet D-U-N-S Number
        identifier.
    </description>
    <overviewURL>
        http://www.uddi.org/taxonomies/Core_Taxonomy_OverviewDoc.htm#D-U-N-S
    </overviewURL>
  </overviewDoc>
  <categoryBag>
    <keyedReference keyName="uddi-org:types"
                    keyValue="identity"
                    tModelKey="uuid:C1ACF26D-9672-4404-9D70-39B756E62AB4" />
  </categoryBag>
</tModel>
```

Similarly, the `tModel` used for a WSDL-based Web service will usually point to a WSDL document, which can be accessed with an HTTP GET operation. The following shows the `tModel` used for Monson-Haefel's BookQuote Web service from Listing 6–7 earlier in this chapter. In this case the URL uses XPointer to specify a specific `binding` element in a specific WSDL document.

```
<tModel tModelKey="UUID:4C9D3FE0-2A16-11D6-9B59-000629DC0A53">
  <name>Monson-Haefel:BookQuote</name>
  <description xml:lang="en">
     Provides a wholesale price given for an ISBN number.
  </description>
  <overviewDoc>
    <description xml:lang="en">
       This URL points to the BookQuote WSDL document.
    </description>
    <overviewURL> http://www.Monson-Haefel.com/jwsed1/BookQuote.wsdl
#xmlns(wsdl=http://schemas.xmlsoap.org/wsdl/)
xpointer(/wsdl:definitions/wsdl:portType[ @name="BookQuoteBinding"])
    </overviewURL>
  </overviewDoc>
```

```
    <categoryBag>
      <keyedReference
        tModelKey="uuid:C1ACF26D-9672-4404-9D70-39B756E62AB4"
        keyName="types"
        keyValue="wsdlSpec"/>
    </categoryBag>
  </tModel>
```

6.3.5.3 *The* identifierBag *and* categoryBag *Elements*

The identifierBag element is not used much with tModels except for a special UDDI identifier called isReplacedBy. The isReplacedBy identifier indicates that one tModel has been replaced by another—this might occur if a new version of the technology represented by the tModel is used. Listing 6–12 illustrates.

Listing 6-12

Using identifierBag *and* categoryBag *with a WSDL* tModel

```
<tModel tModelKey="UUID:4C9D3FE0-2A16-11D6-9B59-000629DC0A53">
  <name>Monson-Haefel:BookQuote</name>
  <description xml:lang="en">
     Provides a wholesale price given for an ISBN number.
  </description>
  <overviewDoc>
    <description xml:lang="en">
       This URL points to the BookQuote WSDL document.
    </description>
    <overviewURL> http://www.Monson-Haefel.com/jwsed1/BookQuote.wsdl
#xmlns{wsdl=http://www.Monson-Haefel.com/BookQuote}
xpointer{//wsdl:binding[@name='BookQuoteBinding']}
    </overviewURL>
  </overviewDoc>
  <identifierBag>
    <keyedReference keyName="uddi-org:isReplacedBy"
                    keyValue= "uuid:A84ED203-33D5-04A2-C262-49C293E82DE2"
                    tModelKey="uuid:E59AE320-77A5-11D5-B898-0004AC49CC1E" />
  </identifierBag>
  <categoryBag>
    <keyedReference
         tModelKey="uuid:65719168-72c6-3f29-8c20-62defb0961c0"
         keyName="ws-I_conformance:BasicProfile1.0"
         keyValue="http://ws-i.org/profiles/basic/1.0" />
    <keyedReference
         tModelKey="uuid:C1ACF26D-9672-4404-9D70-39B756E62AB4"
         keyName="uddi-org:types"
```

```
        keyValue="wsdlSpec"/>

  </categoryBag>
</tModel>
```

The `categoryBag`, on the other hand, is used with `tModels` quite a bit. For example, Listing 6–12 shows (in bold) the `tModel` for Monson-Haefel Books' BookQuote Web service, which is categorized as both a `wsdlSpec tModel` and a `ws-I_conformance:BasicProfile1.0 tModel`. The WS-I-conformant `tModel` is covered in more detail in Section 6.6.

6.4 The `publisherAssertion` Structure

In a large organization like GE, IBM, or AOL Time Warner, it's likely that some of the many divisions and departments will want to create their own UDDI entries for Web services they offer, but still want to be recognized as belonging to the larger organization. This objective can be accomplished using a `publisherAssertion`.

A `publisherAssertion` structure defines relationships between two business entities. The data structure identifies both participants, as well as a `keyedReference` to a `tModel` that defines the relationship. Listing 6–13 shows the structure of the `publisherAssertion`.

Listing 6–13

The Definition of the `publisherAssertion` *Structure*

```
<schema targetNamespace="urn:uddi-org:api_v2"
        xmlns="http://www.w3.org/2001/XMLSchema"
        xmlns:uddi="urn:uddi-org:api_v2"
        version="2.03" id="uddi">
  ...
  <element name="publisherAssertion" type="uddi:publisherAssertion"/>
  <complexType name="publisherAssertion">
    <sequence>
      <element ref="uddi:fromKey"/>
      <element ref="uddi:toKey"/>
      <element ref="uddi:keyedReference"/>
    </sequence>
  </complexType>
```

In an instance of this structure, the `fromKey` and `toKey` elements will contain the unique UDDI `businessEntity` identifiers of the entities involved in the relationship. For example, the `fromKey` might contain the UUID of the IBM Corporation, while the `toKey` contains the UUID of IBM's Professional Services division. The keyedReference element will point to a tModel that represents the relationship between these organizations. This tModel must be categorized using the relationship UDDI type (see Table 6–2). Listing 6–14 shows a publisher Assertion expressing the relationship between a fictitious corporation and one of its divisions.

Listing 6–14

A publisherAssertion *Structure*

```
<publisherAssertion>
    <fromKey>0207DE98-9C61-4138-A121-4B9E636B7649</fromKey>
    <toKey>1EE48BF0-9356-11D5-8838-002035229C64</toKey>
    <keyedReference keyName="subsidiary"
                    keyValue="parent-child"
                    tModelKey="uuid:807A2C62-EE22-470D-ADC6-E0424A337C03"/>
</publisherAssertion>
```

In order for the publisherAssertion to be valid and therefore visible in the UDDI registry, both entities must submit complementary publisherAssertion entries. If only one of them does, that assertion will not be visible to anyone but the publisher, and will not be considered valid. This requirement prevents misrepresentation. An organization cannot feign a relationship that the other organization does not recognize—for example, that it's a division of another company, a member of a consortium, or a preferred vendor.

6.5 UUID Keys

Most of the primary UDDI data structures (businessEntity, business Service, bindingTemplate, and tModel) are automatically assigned a Universally Unique Identifier (UUID) key when they are added to the UDDI registry. The UUID is a hexadecimal-encoded number that is about 30 characters long and is generated using the DCE UUID-generation algorithm.[8] The UUID is globally unique—there will not be duplicates even in other registries. The following is an example of a UUID generated for a businessEntity:

```
01B1FA80-2A15-11D6-9B59-000629DC0A53
```

The UUIDs for the primary data structures all take the same form, except for the tModel, which prefixes its UUID value with "uuid:". The tModel is the only data structure that does this, because the tModelKey is supposed to be a valid URI (Uniform Resource Identifier)—hence the uuid prefix. In version 3.0 of UDDI, the

[8] The specification for the DCE UUID-generating algorithm can be found at http://www.ics.uci.edu/pub/ietf/webdav/uuid-guid/draft-leach-uuids-guids-01.txt.

specification of `tModelKey` has been broadened so that you can use values that are understandable to humans, instead of always using UUID values.

6.6 WS-I Conformance Claims

A `tModel` that represents a Web service may claim that it adheres to the WS-I Basic Profile 1.0 by including a WS-I **conformance claim** categorization, as shown in Listing 6–15.

Listing 6–15

Including a Conformance Claim in a WSDL `tModel`

```
<tModel tModelKey="UUID:4C9D3FE0-2A16-11D6-9B59-000629DC0A53">
  <name>Monson-Haefel:BookQuote</name>
  <description xml:lang="en">
     Provides a wholesale price given for a ISBN number.
  </description>
  <overviewDoc>
    ...
  </overviewDoc>
  <categoryBag>
    <keyedReference
         tModelKey="uuid:65719168-72c6-3f29-8c20-62defb0961c0"
         keyName="ws-I_conformance:BasicProfile1.0"
         keyValue="http://ws-i.org/profiles/basic/1.0" />
  </categoryBag>
</tModel>
```

The only data structure in UDDI that may contain this type of conformance claim is a `tModel` that represents a WSDL binding. If a conformance claim is used in UDDI, there must be a corresponding WS-I conformance claim in the WSDL `binding` element, as discussed in Section 5.7.

6.7 Wrapping Up

The UDDI data model is a bit complicated because it attempts to be open to any type of service, not just WSDL-based Web services. There is some indication that this strategy is paying off, as some of the major Web service standards organizations, including RosettaNet, WS-I, ebXML, and the Open Application Group, have recognized UDDI and are creating taxonomies and standards for integrating their offerings with it. These developments are slow-going, but encouraging to UDDI advocates.

Chapter 7

The UDDI Inquiry API

One of the things that makes UDDI interesting is that it requires support for SOAP 1.1 over HTTP. In fact, the UDDI specification requires that UDDI registries support a specific set of SOAP-based Web service operations called the UDDI Programming API. These SOAP messages use the Document/Literal mode of messaging and are described in detail by WSDL documents located at the UDDI.org Web site. This makes UDDI a Web service, just like any other WSDL/SOAP-based Web service. UDDI's standard Web services are divided into two WSDL/SOAP-based APIs: The Inquiry API and the Publishing API. The Inquiry API is used to search and read data in a UDDI registry, while the Publishing API is used to add, modify, and delete data in a UDDI registry. This chapter will cover the Inquiry API; specifically we'll be examining the WSDL operations and their corresponding SOAP message structures. Chapter 8 covers the Publisher API.

7.1 General Information about UDDI SOAP Messaging

All UDDI Inquiry and Publishing operations use Document/Literal SOAP messages and all of them are Request/Response; meaning that the UDDI registry always replies with either a SOAP message or a SOAP fault. It's interesting to note that UDDI requires the use of UTF-8, but not UTF-16. This means that UDDI is not exactly conformant with the WS-I Basic Profile 1.0, which requires Web services to support both UTF-8 and UTF-16. WS-I recognizes this irregularity, but chooses to overlook it because UDDI 2.0 was specified before the WS-I Basic Profile 1.0. The basic structure of a UDDI SOAP message and its HTTP header is shown in Listing 7–1.

Listing 7–1

The General Structure of a UDDI SOAP Message

```
POST /someVerbHere HTTP/1.1
Host: www.someoperator.org
Content-Type: text/xml; charset="utf-8"
Content-Length: nnnn
SOAPAction: ""

<?xml version="1.0" encoding="UTF-8" ?>
<Envelope xmlns="http://schemas.xmlsoap.org/soap/envelope/">
  <Body>
    <some-uddi-element generic="2.0" xmlns="urn:uddi-org:api_v2">
      ...
    </some-uddi-element>
  </Body>
</Envelope>
```

Because UDDI doesn't support the use of the `Header` element and all messages are Document/Literal, all you need to know is the structure of the XML document fragment in the `Body` element. Just replace `some-uddi-element` with the proper UDDI data structure and you have a UDDI SOAP message. The reply message follows the same conventions.

All UDDI XML types are part of the `"urn:uddi-org:api_v2"` namespace for UDDI 2.0, the subject of this part of the book. In addition to specifying the proper namespace, you also have to include the `generic` attribute with a value of `"2.0"`, to signify that the SOAP message conforms to the UDDI 2.0 Programming API. Why you need a version identifier as well as a namespace identifier is puzzling, but that's the requirement. All SOAP messages in UDDI are carried in HTTP POST and reply messages. An HTTP POST request message must declare a `SOAPAction` header, but the value can be an empty string or any value.

Any UDDI registry will provide URLs for calling Inquiry and Publishing operations. In the case of private UDDI registries, the URLs are not generally made public, but in the case of the Universal Business Registry (UBR) the Inquiry and Publishing URLs are public and free for anyone's access. Following are the URLs for all the operator sites in the UBR.

IBM

UBR Node

Home page = http://uddi.ibm.com/
Inquiry API = http://uddi.ibm.com/ubr/inquiryapi
Publishing API = https://uddi.ibm.com/ubr/publishapi

Test Node
Home page = http://uddi.ibm.com/testregistry/registry.html
Inquiry API = http://uddi.ibm.com/testregistry/inquiryapi
Publishing API = https://uddi.ibm.com/testregistry/publishapi

Microsoft

UBR Node
Home page = http://uddi.microsoft.com/
Inquiry API = http://uddi.microsoft.com/inquire
Publishing API = https://uddi.microsoft.com/publish

Test Node
Home page = http://test.uddi.microsoft.com/
Inquiry API = http://test.uddi.microsoft.com/inquire
Publishing API = https://test.uddi.microsoft.com/publish

SAP

UBR Node
Home page = http://uddi.sap.com/
Inquiry API = http://uddi.sap.com/uddi/api/inquiry
Publishing API = https://uddi.sap.com/uddi/api/publish

Test Node
Home page = http://udditest.sap.com/
Inquiry API = http://udditest.sap.com/UDDI/api/inquiry
Publishing API = https://udditest.sap.com/UDDI/api/publish

NTT

UBR Node
Home page = http://www.ntt.com/uddi/
Inquiry API = http://www.uddi.ne.jp/ubr/inquiryapi
Publishing API = https://www.uddi.ne.jp/ubr/publishapi

Except for NTT, all the operator sites offer a test node as well as a production node. You should use the test node until you are confident in your abilities to query and publish data to UDDI properly.

You can access a UDDI Inquiry or Publishing API using any SOAP 1.1 toolkit. Generating interfaces from UDDI's WSDL documents can result in a convenient Java API for UDDI. You can do so using JAX-RPC, covered in Part IV of this book, or using JAXR, covered in Part V. I recommend you use JAXR, because it's easier to work with. There are also a couple of other APIs you can use to access a UDDI registry, including the very popular UDDI4J (UDDI for Java), which is an open source project under the auspices of IBM—but remember that only JAXR and JAX-RPC are parts of the J2EE Web Services platform.

7.2 The Inquiry Operations

You use the Inquiry API for querying the UDDI registry and fetching specific UDDI data structures. When you want to search the registry, you use a SOAP **find operation.** When you want to get the data associated with a specific entry, such as a `businessEntity`, `businessService`, or `tModel`, you use a SOAP **get operation.** The rest of this chapter provides detailed explanations for each of the Inquiry operations.

7.2.1 Find Operations

The find operations allow you to search the UDDI registry for data structures that match some criteria. There are five find operations:

1. `find_business` finds matching `businessEntity` entries.
2. `find_relatedBusiness` finds matching `publisherAssertion` entries.
3. `find_service` finds matching `businessService` entries.
4. `find_binding` finds matching `bindingTemplate` entries.
5. `find_tModel` finds matching `tModel` entries.

The criteria used in these find operations are based on `tModel` values (both WSDL and taxonomy `tModels`), data fields, and modifiers of the default searching rules used by UDDI. As an example, the SOAP message in Listing 7–2 is designed to find all of the `businessEntity` entries that fall into the categories specified.

Listing 7–2

Finding `businessEntity` *Entries by Category*

```
POST /someVerbHere HTTP/1.1
Host: www.someoperator.org
Content-Type: text/xml; charset="utf-8"
Content-Length: nnnn
SOAPAction: ""

<?xml version="1.0" encoding="UTF-8" ?>
<Envelope xmlns="http://schemas.xmlsoap.org/soap/envelope/">
  <Body>
    <find_business generic="2.0" xmlns="urn:uddi-org:api_v2">
      <categoryBag>
        <!-- ISO 3166 -->
        <keyedReference
                    keyName="Minnesota, USA"
                    keyValue="US-MN"
```

```
                    tModelKey="uuid:4E49A8D6-D5A2-4FC2-93A0-0411D8D19E88" />
      <!-- NAICS -->
      <keyedReference
                    keyName="Book, Periodical, and Newspaper Wholesalers"
                    keyValue="42292"
                    tModelKey="uuid:C0B9FE13-179F-413D-8A5B-5004DB8E5BB2" />
    </categoryBag>
  </find_business>
 </Body>
</Envelope>
```

This query will return a list of businesses with matching `keyedReference` values. Only those `businessEntity` entries that declare both of these `keyedReference` values in their `categoryBag` will be a match. For `categoryBag`, the default behavior is an AND condition: Both `keyedReference` values must match. In this case the client is searching for all book wholesalers that are also located in the state of Minnesota (United States).

7.2.1.1 *Using Search Elements*

A variety of search elements can be used in the find operations, including `identifierBag`, `categoryBag`, `name`, `tModelBag`, and `findQualifiers`. These search elements are covered in the next three sections.

7.2.1.1.1 The `identifierBag` and `categoryBag` Search Elements

As Listing 7–2 illustrated, you can use `keyedReference` values in a `categoryBag` element when performing a `find_business` operation. You can also use the same technique with the `find_service` and `find_tModel` operations. For example, the query message defined in Listing 7–2 would find a positive match with Monson-Haefel's business because its `businessEntity` structure contains matching `keyedReference` values in its `categoryBag` element. Listing 7–3 highlights the matching elements.

Listing 7–3

Monson-Haefel's `businessEntity` *Entry*

```
<?xml version='1.0' encoding='UTF-8'?>
<businessEntity businessKey="01B1FA80-2A15-11D7-9B59-000629DC0A53"
                xmlns="urn:uddi-org:api_v2">
  ...
  <identifierBag>
    <!-- D-U-N-S® Number Identifier System -->
    <keyedReference keyName="Monson-Haefel Books, Inc."
        keyValue="038924499"
```

```
        tModelKey="uuid:8609C81E-EE1F-4D5A-B202-3EB13AD01823"/>
  </identifierBag>
  <categoryBag>
    <!-- North American Industry Classification System (NAICS) 1997 -->
    <keyedReference keyName="Book, Periodical, and Newspaper Wholesalers"
        keyValue="42292"
        tModelKey="uuid:C0B9FE13-179F-413D-8A5B-5004DB8E5BB2"/>
    <!-- Universal Standard Products and Services Classification (UNSPSC)
        Version 7.3 -->
    <keyedReference keyName="Educational or vocational textbooks"
        keyValue="55.10.15.09.00"
        tModelKey="uuid:CD153257-086A-4237-B336-6BDCBDCC6634"/>
    <!-- ISO 3166 Geographic Taxonomy -->
    <keyedReference keyName="Minnesota, USA"
        keyValue="US-MN"
        tModelKey="uuid:4E49A8D6-D5A2-4FC2-93A0-0411D8D19E88"/>
  </categoryBag>
</businessEntity>
```

If Monson-Haefel's businessEntity didn't have both NAICS and ISO 3166 keyedReference values equal to the ones in the query, there would be no match. Notice that Monson-Haefel's categoryBag contains an extra keyedReference that does not match those in the find operation. Such non-matching values in the target entity's categoryBag are not a problem as long as it does contain keyedReference values that do match.

You can use the identifierBag in the same way. You can search for entries that have matching keyedReference values in their identifierBag elements, using the find_business and find_tModel operations. The default behavior for identifierBag searches is an OR match: Any entity that contains at least one matching value is considered a match. Listing 7–4 shows a SOAP message that uses the identifierBag to search for a businessEntity with a specified D-U-N-S number.

Listing 7–4

Finding businessEntity *Entries by Identifier*

```
<?xml version="1.0" encoding="UTF-8" ?>
<Envelope xmlns="http://schemas.xmlsoap.org/soap/envelope/">
  <Body>
    <find_business generic="2.0" xmlns="urn:uddi-org:api_v2">
      <identifierBag>
        <!-- D-U-N-S -->
        <keyedReference keyName="Monson-Haefel Books, Inc."
                keyValue="038924499"
```

```
                    tModelKey="uuid:8609C81E-EE1F-4D5A-B202-3EB13AD01823" />
      </identifierBag>
    </find_business>
  </Body>
</Envelope>
```

The query defined in Listing 7–4 would be a match for Monson-Haefel Books, because the `keyedReference` element in the query matches the `keyedReference` value in the `identifierBag` of the Monson-Haefel `businessEntity` entry you saw in Listing 7–3.

You can search for matching values in both `categoryBag` and `identifierBag` in a single search operation (`find_business` and `find_tModel` only), but you'll get more matches if you modify the default behavior to use OR search criteria—otherwise the `categoryBag` is likely to force an exact match. To override the default search behavior you use the `findQualifiers` element, which you'll see in Section 7.2.1.1.4.

The `identifierBag` and `categoryBag` search elements follow the XML schema shown in Sections 6.1.7 and 6.1.8 respectively.

7.2.1.1.2 The `name` Search Element

You can also search for UDDI entries by name, with the `find_business`, `find_service`, and `find_tModel` operations. For example, the SOAP message in Listing 7–5 will initiate a search for `businessEntity` entries whose name begins with "Monson-Haefel" or "Addison."

Listing 7–5

Finding `businessEntity` *Entries by Name*

```
<?xml version="1.0" encoding="UTF-8" ?>
<Envelope xmlns="http://schemas.xmlsoap.org/soap/envelope/">
  <Body>
    <find_business generic="2.0" xmlns="urn:uddi-org:api_v2">
      <name>Monson-Haefel</name>
      <name xml:lang="en">Addison</name>
    </find_business>
  </Body>
</Envelope>
```

You can specify multiple `name` elements to perform, by default, an ORed search. In the above example the reply message will contain all the business whose name starts with either "Monson-Haefel" or "Addison."

You can use a wild-card character (`%`) in `name` searches. By default, a wild card is assumed to be at the end of each name, so a search on `"Monson-Haefel"`, for example, might return entries named Monson-Haefel Books and Monson-Haefel Industries, Inc. You can explicitly specify one or more wild-card characters, overriding the default behavior. For example, a `name` search on the value `"Am%com"` might return entries for Amazon.com and American Qualicom.

You can also adorn a `name` search with the `xml:lang` attribute in order to restrict results to only those entries with matching names in the same language. In Listing 7–5, the second `name` element specifies the English language. Name searches are, by default, case-insensitive.

The structure of the `name` element was described in Section 6.1.3—it's just an XML schema `string` type with an optional `xml:lang` attribute.

7.2.1.1.3 The `tModelBag` Search Element

The `find_business`, `find_service`, and `find_binding` operations can all use the `tModelBag` search element in their request messages. The `tModelBag` search element contains one or more `tModelKey` elements, each of which specifics a unique identifier for a technical `tModel`. The search is actually applied to the `tModels` that describe the Web service. These `tModels` are listed in the `tModelInstanceDetails` element shown in Listing 7–6.

Listing 7–6

A `tModelInstanceDetails` *Element*

```
<?xml version="1.0" encoding="UTF-8"?>
<businessEntity businessKey="01B1FA80-2A15-11D7-9B59-000629DC0A53"
 xmlns="urn:uddi-org:api_v2">
  ...
  <name>Monson-Haefel Books, Inc.</name>
  <description xml:lang="en">Technical Book Wholesaler</description>
  <businessServices>
    <businessService serviceKey="3902AEE0-3301-11D7-9F17-000629DC0A53">
      <name>BookQuote</name>
      <bindingTemplates>
        <bindingTemplate bindingKey="391E2620-3301-11D7-9F17-000629DC0A53">
          <accessPoint URLType="http">
            http://www.Monson-Haefel.com/jwsed1/BookQuote
          </accessPoint>
          <tModelInstanceDetails>
            <tModelInstanceInfo tModelKey="uddi:4C9D3FE0…9B59-000629DC0A53"/>
            <tModelInstanceInfo tModelKey="uddi:2B4C3DE0…7B22-000438FE0C22"/>
          </tModelInstanceDetails>
        </bindingTemplate>
      </bindingTemplates>
    </businessService>
```

```
  </businessServices>
</businessEntity>
```

As you can see from Listing 7–6, the two tModel keys referred to by the tModel InstanceDetails element are owned by the bindingTemplate, business Service, and businessEntity data structures, which are its ancestors in the UDDI hierarchy. A tModelBag search element will list only those data structures that contain all the tModelKeys specified—in other words it's an AND search. For example, Listing 7–7 defines a UDDI find_service message that would match the businessService in Listing 7–6.

Listing 7–7

Finding businessService *Entries by* tModel

```
<?xml version="1.0" encoding="UTF-8" ?>
<Envelope xmlns="http://schemas.xmlsoap.org/soap/envelope/">
  <Body>
    <find_service generic="2.0" xmlns="urn:uddi-org:api_v2">
      <tModelBag>
          <tModelKey>uddi:4C9D3FE0-2A16-11D7-9B59-000629DC0A53</tModelKey>
          <tModelKey>uddi:2B4C3DE0-23B4-84FE-7B22-000438FE0C22</tModelKey>
      </tModelBag>
    </find_service>
  </Body>
</Envelope>
```

Because the find_service message contains two tModel keys that are also listed in the Monson-Haefel Books tModelInstanceInfo shown in Listing 7–6, Monson-Haefel's businessService matches—so would a find_business or find_binding call that used the same criteria.

The tModelBag element is defined by UDDI as shown in Listing 7–8. It simply holds one or more tModelKey elements.

Listing 7–8

Definition of the tModelBag *Type*

```
<schema targetNamespace="urn:uddi-org:api_v2"
            xmlns="http://www.w3.org/2001/XMLSchema"
            xmlns:uddi="urn:uddi-org:api_v2"
            version="2.03" id="uddi">
  ...
  <element name="tModelKey" type="uddi:tModelKey"/>
```

```
  <simpleType name="tModelKey">
    <restriction base="string"/>
  </simpleType>

  <element name="tModelBag" type="uddi:tModelBag"/>
  <complexType name="tModelBag">
    <sequence>
      <element ref="uddi:tModelKey" maxOccurs="unbounded"/>
    </sequence>
  </complexType>
  ...
</schema>
```

7.2.1.1.4 The findQualifiers Search Element

By default, when searching a UDDI registry the find operations all follow the same set of matching rules. The default rules can be limiting, so UDDI enables you to modify the default matching behavior using the findQualifiers element.

The findQualifiers element (plural) may contain one or more findQualifier elements (singular), each of which may specify a different qualifier for modifying the default matching behavior of the find operation. For example, the SOAP message in Listing 7–9 uses findQualifiers to change the default behavior of the find operation from an AND match of keyedReference values to an OR match.

Listing 7–9

Using the findQualifiers *Element in a Query*

```
<?xml version="1.0" encoding="UTF-8" ?>
<Envelope xmlns="http://schemas.xmlsoap.org/soap/envelope/">
  <Body>
    <find_business generic="2.0" xmlns="urn:uddi-org:api_v2">
      <findQualifiers>
        <findQualifier>orAllKeys</findQualifier>
      </findQualifiers>
      <categoryBag>
        <keyedReference keyName="Minnesota, USA"
                     keyValue="US-MN"
                     tModelKey="uuid:4E49A8D6-D5A2-4FC2-93A0-0411D8D19E88" />
        <keyedReference keyName="Book, Periodical, and Newspaper Wholesalers"
                     keyValue="42292"
                     tModelKey="uuid:C0B9FE13-179F-413D-8A5B-5004DB8E5BB2" />
      </categoryBag>
    </find_business>
```

```
  </Body>
</Envelope>
```

This find operation will return a list of all businesses that have at least one matching `keyedReference` element: all the companies located in the state of Minnesota, regardless of their industry, as well as all the wholesale book companies, regardless of their location. As you can imagine, the result set for this query will be substantially larger and less specific than the default AND behavior.

UDDI defines the structure of the `findQualifiers` element as in Listing 7–10. It simply holds one or more `findQualifier` elements, each of which is a string.

Listing 7–10

Definition of the `findQualifiers` *Type*

```
<schema targetNamespace="urn:uddi-org:api_v2"
        xmlns="http://www.w3.org/2001/XMLSchema"
        xmlns:uddi="urn:uddi-org:api_v2"
        version="2.03" id="uddi">
  ...
  <element name="findQualifier" type="string"/>
  <element name="findQualifiers" type="uddi:findQualifiers"/>
  <complexType name="findQualifiers">
    <sequence>
      <element ref="uddi:findQualifier" minOccurs="0" maxOccurs="unbounded"/>
    </sequence>
  </complexType>
  ...
</schema>
```

There are 11 qualifier values you can use with find operations, some of which apply only to certain find operations. Others apply to all of them. Table 7–1 provides a list of the qualifiers, a description, and the find operations you can use them with (the descriptions are taken from the Programming API specification[1] and only lightly edited).

[1] Organization for the Advancement of Structured Information Standards, *UDDI Version 2.04 API Specification* (2002). Available at http://uddi.org/pubs/ProgrammersAPI-V2.04-Published-20020719.htm.

Table 7–1 The Find Operation Qualifiers

Qualifier	Description	Applicable Find Operations
exactNameMatch	Signifies that lexical-order—i.e., leftmost in left-to-right languages—name match behavior should be overridden. When this behavior is specified, only entries that exactly match the entry passed in the name argument will be returned.	find_business find_service find_tModel
caseSensitiveMatch	Signifies that the default case-insensitive behavior of a name match should be overridden. When this behavior is specified, case is relevant in the search results, and only entries that match the case of the value passed in the name argument will be returned.	find_business find_service find_tModel
sortByNameAsc	Signifies that the result returned by a find_xx inquiry should be sorted on the name field in ascending alphabetic sort order. When there is more than one name field, the sort uses the first of them. This sort is applied prior to any truncation of result sets. Only applicable on queries that return a name element in the topmost detail level of the result set. If no conflicting sort qualifier is specified, this is the default sort order for inquiries that return name values at this topmost detail level.	find_business find_relatedBusinesses find_service find_tModel
sortByNameDesc	Signifies that the result returned by a find_xx inquiry call should be sorted on the name field in descending alphabetic sort order. When there is more than one name field, the sort uses the first of them. This sort is applied prior to any truncation of result sets. Only applicable on queries that return a name element in the topmost detail level of the result set. This is the reverse of the default sort order for this kind of result.	find_business find_relatedBusinesses find_service find_tModel
sortByDateAsc	Signifies that the result returned by a find_xx inquiry call should be sorted based on the date last updated in ascending chronological sort order (earliest returns first). If no conflicting sort qualifier is specified, this is the default sort order for all result sets.	find_binding find_business find_relatedBusinesses find_service find_tModel

Table 7–1 Continued

Qualifier	Description	Applicable Find Operations
sortByDateDesc	Signifies that the result returned by a find_xx inquiry call should be sorted based on the date last updated in descending chronological sort order (most recent change returns first). Sort qualifiers involving date are secondary in precedence to the sortBy Name qualifiers. This causes sortByName elements to be sorted within name by date, newest to oldest.	find_binding find_business find_relatedBusinesses find_service find_tModel
orLikeKeys	When a bag container contains multiple keyedReference elements (i.e., in a categoryBag or identifierBag), any keyedReference filters that come from the same namespace (e.g., have the same tModelKey value) are ORed together rather than ANDed. This qualifier allows one to request "any of these four values from this namespace, and any of these two values from this namespace."	find_business find_service find_tModel
orAllKeys	This qualifier changes the behavior for tModelBag and categoryBag to OR keys rather than ANDing them. This qualifier negates any AND treatment, as well as the effect of orLikeKeys.	find_binding find_business find_service find_tModel
combineCategoryBags	This is used only in the find_business message. This qualifier makes the categoryBag entries for the full business Entity element behave as though all categoryBag elements found at the businessEntity level and in all contained or referenced businessService elements were combined. Searching for a category will yield a positive match on a registered business if any of the categoryBag elements contained within the full businessEntity element (including the categoryBag elements within contained or referenced businessService elements) contains the filter criteria.	find_business
serviceSubset	This qualifier is used only in the find _business message. It is used only in conjunction with a passed categoryBag argument, causes the component of the search that involves categorization to use	find_business

Table 7–1 The Find Operation Qualifiers (Continued)

Qualifier	Description	Applicable Find Operations
serviceSubset (continued)	categoryBag elements from contained or referenced businessService elements within the registered data, and ignores any entries found in the categoryBag direct-descendant element of registered businessEntity elements. The resulting businessList message will return those businesses that matched based on this modified behavior, in conjunction with any other search arguments provided. Additionally, the contained serviceInfos elements will reflect summary data (in a serviceInfo element) only for those services (contained or referenced) that matched on one of the supplied categoryBag arguments.	find_business
andAllKeys	This qualifier changes the behavior for identifierBag to AND keys rather than ORing them.	find_business find_tModel

7.2.1.2 Operation Definitions and Payloads

Every find operation takes exactly the same form, because they are all Document/Literal SOAP messages. The data structure, which contains the criteria of the search, is nested directly in the SOAP Body element:

```
<?xml version="1.0" encoding="UTF-8" ?>
<Envelope xmlns="http://schemas.xmlsoap.org/soap/envelope/">
  <Body>
    <!-- the find data structure goes here -->
  </Body>
</Envelope>
```

Similarly, the response messages are Document/Literal SOAP messages that carry a result set as an XML structure. There is also a standard way for handling faults. This section provides you with an opportunity to try out your knowledge of XML schema and WSDL, because operations are defined in terms of XML schema complex type definitions of message payloads, as well as the WSDL definition for each find operation.

A find request message may specify a maxRows attribute that allows the UDDI registry to limit the number of results returned. Response messages will include the operator attribute, which provides the URI of the UDDI operator you are querying, and possibly a `truncation` attribute, which indicates that the data returned was too large and was truncated.

The XML schema definitions of the `findQualifiers`, `name`, `identifierBag`, `categoryBag`, and `tModelBag` search elements were shown in previous sections and will not be redefined here.

7.2.1.2.1 `xxxInfos` Response Structures

Many of the response messages for find operations (as well as some operations in the Publishing API) make use of elements whose names fit the patterns `xxxInfo` and `xxxInfos`. For example, the `serviceInfos` element contains `serviceInfo` elements as in the following:

```
<serviceInfos>
  <serviceInfo serviceKey="23ED3F90-B44D-11D5-A0D9-002035229C64"
               businessKey="01B1FA80-2A15-11D7-9B59-000629DC0A53">
    <name>BookQuote</name>
  </serviceInfo>
  <serviceInfo serviceKey="B6996940-4827-11D6-BC3E-000C0E00ACDD"
               businessKey="01B1FA80-2A15-11D7-9B59-000629DC0A53">
    <name>SubmitBook</name>
  </serviceInfo>
</serviceInfos>
```

There are several `xxxInfos` elements, and they are hierarchical: One may contain others. Their type definitions are shown in Listing 7–11, so you can refer to them at one location while studying the data structure of the request and response messages in the following sections. Skip this listing for now and come back to it whenever you need to know the structure of an `xxxInfos` element.

Listing 7–11

Definitions of the `xxxInfos` *Types*

```
<schema targetNamespace="urn:uddi-org:api_v2"
           xmlns="http://www.w3.org/2001/XMLSchema"
           xmlns:uddi="urn:uddi-org:api_v2"
           version="2.03" id="uddi">
  ...
  <element name="businessInfo" type="uddi:businessInfo"/>
  <complexType name="businessInfo">
    <sequence>
      <element ref="uddi:name" maxOccurs="unbounded"/>
      <element ref="uddi:description" minOccurs="0" maxOccurs="unbounded"/>
      <element ref="uddi:serviceInfos"/>
```

```
    </sequence>
    <attribute name="businessKey" type="uddi:businessKey" use="required"/>
  </complexType>
  <element name="businessInfos" type="uddi:businessInfos"/>
  <complexType name="businessInfos">
    <sequence>
      <element ref="uddi:businessInfo" minOccurs="0" maxOccurs="unbounded"/>
    </sequence>
  </complexType>
  <element name="relatedBusinessInfo" type="uddi:relatedBusinessInfo"/>
  <complexType name="relatedBusinessInfo">
    <sequence>
      <element ref="uddi:businessKey"/>
      <element ref="uddi:name" maxOccurs="unbounded"/>
      <element ref="uddi:description" minOccurs="0" maxOccurs="unbounded"/>
      <element ref="uddi:sharedRelationships" maxOccurs="2"/>
    </sequence>
  </complexType>
  <element name="relatedBusinessInfos" type="uddi:relatedBusinessInfos"/>
  <complexType name="relatedBusinessInfos">
    <sequence>
      <element ref="uddi:relatedBusinessInfo"
               minOccurs="0" maxOccurs="unbounded"/>
    </sequence>
  </complexType>
  <element name="serviceInfo" type="uddi:serviceInfo"/>
  <complexType name="serviceInfo">
    <sequence>
      <element ref="uddi:name" minOccurs="0" maxOccurs="unbounded"/>
    </sequence>
    <attribute name="serviceKey" type="uddi:serviceKey" use="required"/>
    <attribute name="businessKey" type="uddi:businessKey" use="required"/>
  </complexType>
  <element name="serviceInfos" type="uddi:serviceInfos"/>
  <complexType name="serviceInfos">
    <sequence>
      <element ref="uddi:serviceInfo" minOccurs="0" maxOccurs="unbounded"/>
    </sequence>
  </complexType>
  <element name="tModelInfo" type="uddi:tModelInfo"/>
  <complexType name="tModelInfo">
    <sequence>
      <element ref="uddi:name"/>
```

```
    </sequence>
    <attribute name="tModelKey" type="uddi:tModelKey" use="required"/>
  </complexType>
  <element name="tModelInfos" type="uddi:tModelInfos"/>
  <complexType name="tModelInfos">
    <sequence>
      <element ref="uddi:tModelInfo" minOccurs="0" maxOccurs="unbounded"/>
    </sequence>
  </complexType>
  ...
</schema>
```

The request and response structures shown in the following listings refer to many other types of elements, far too many to list in this chapter. You may want to go to UDDI.org and view the Version 2.0 UDDI XML Schema (2001) while examining this section. This document can be found at http://uddi.org/schema/uddi_v2.xsd.

7.2.1.2.2 The `find_business` Operation

Given a set of criteria (categories, identifiers, `tModels`, or `discoveryURLs`), the `find_business` operation will return a lightweight list of `businessEntity` listings, including their keys, names, descriptions, and `businessService` names and keys. You are most likely to use this operation to browse for businesses.

Type Definitions

```
<schema targetNamespace="urn:uddi-org:api_v2"
          xmlns="http://www.w3.org/2001/XMLSchema"
          xmlns:uddi="urn:uddi-org:api_v2"
          version="2.03" id="uddi">
  ...
  <!-- Request Structure -->
  <element name="find_business" type="uddi:find_business"/>
  <complexType name="find_business">
    <sequence>
      <element ref="uddi:findQualifiers" minOccurs="0"/>
      <element ref="uddi:name" minOccurs="0" maxOccurs="unbounded"/>
      <element ref="uddi:identifierBag" minOccurs="0"/>
      <element ref="uddi:categoryBag" minOccurs="0"/>
      <element ref="uddi:tModelBag" minOccurs="0"/>
      <element ref="uddi:discoveryURLs" minOccurs="0"/>
    </sequence>
    <attribute name="generic" type="string" use="required"/>
    <attribute name="maxRows" type="int" use="optional"/>
  </complexType>
  <!-- Response Structure -->
```

```
    <xsd:element name="businessList" type="uddi:businessList"/>
    <complexType name="businessList">
      <sequence>
        <element ref="uddi:businessInfos"/>
      </sequence>
      <attribute name="generic" type="string" use="required"/>
      <attribute name="operator" type="string" use="required"/>
      <attribute name="truncated" type="uddi:truncated" use="optional"/>
    </complexType>
  …
  </schema>
```

WSDL `message` and `portType` Definitions

```
  <definitions …
    xmlns="http://schemas.xmlsoap.org/wsdl/"
    xmlns:uddi="urn:uddi-org:api_v2">
    …
    <message name="find_business">
      <part name="body" element="uddi:find_business"/>
    </message>
    <message name="businessList">
      <part name="body" element="uddi:businessList"/>
    </message>
    …
    <portType name="Inquire">
      …
      <operation name="find_business">
        <input message="tns:find_business"/>
        <output message="tns:businessList"/>
        <fault name="error" message="tns:dispositionReport"/>
      </operation>
      …
    </portType>
    …
  </definitions>
```

7.2.1.2.3 The `find_relatedBusinesses` Operation

The `find_relatedBusinesses` operation returns a lightweight list of all the businesses that have visible `publisherAssertion` relationships with a specified organization. The search can be modified to list a subset of all related business, according to `keyedReference` elements.

Type Definitions

```
<schema targetNamespace="urn:uddi-org:api_v2"
            xmlns="http://www.w3.org/2001/XMLSchema"
            xmlns:uddi="urn:uddi-org:api_v2"
            version="2.03" id="uddi">
  ...
  <!-- Request Structure -->
  <element name="find_relatedBusinesses" type="uddi:find_relatedBusinesses"/>
  <complexType name="find_relatedBusinesses">
    <sequence>
      <element ref="uddi:findQualifiers" minOccurs="0"/>
      <element ref="uddi:businessKey"/>
      <element ref="uddi:keyedReference" minOccurs="0"/>
    </sequence>
    <attribute name="generic" type="string" use="required"/>
    <attribute name="maxRows" type="int" use="optional"/>
  </complexType>

 <!-- Response Structure -->
  <xsd:element name="relatedBusinessesList"
            type="uddi:relatedBusinessesList"/>
  <xsd:complexType name="relatedBusinessesList">
    <xsd:sequence>
      <xsd:element ref="uddi:businessKey"/>
      <xsd:element ref="uddi:relatedBusinessInfos"/>
    </xsd:sequence>
    <xsd:attribute name="generic" type="string" use="required"/>
    <xsd:attribute name="operator" type="string" use="required"/>
    <xsd:attribute name="truncated" type="uddi:truncated" use="optional"/>
  </xsd:complexType>
  ...
</schema>
```

WSDL message and portType Definitions

```
<definitions ...
  xmlns="http://schemas.xmlsoap.org/wsdl/"
  xmlns:uddi="urn:uddi-org:api_v2">
  ...
  <message name="find_relatedBusinesses">
    <part name="body" element="uddi:find_relatedBusinesses"/>
  </message>
  <message name="relatedBusinessesList">
    <part name="body" element="uddi:relatedBusinessesList"/>
```

```
  </message>
  ...
  <portType name="Inquire">
    ...
    <operation name="find_relatedBusinesses">
      <input message="tns:find_relatedBusinesses"/>
      <output message="tns:relatedBusinessesList"/>
      <fault name="error" message="tns:dispositionReport"/>
    </operation>
    ...
  </portType>
  ...
</definitions>
```

7.2.1.2.4 The find_service Operation

The find_service operation will return a lightweight list of all the businessService entries that match the given categories, tModel keys, or both.

Type Definitions

```
<schema targetNamespace="urn:uddi-org:api_v2"
        xmlns="http://www.w3.org/2001/XMLSchema"
        xmlns:uddi="urn:uddi-org:api_v2"
        version="2.03" id="uddi">
  ...
  <!-- Request Structure -->
  <element name="find_service" type="uddi:find_service"/>
  <complexType name="find_service">
    <sequence>
      <element ref="uddi:findQualifiers" minOccurs="0"/>
      <element ref="uddi:name" minOccurs="0" maxOccurs="unbounded"/>
      <element ref="uddi:categoryBag" minOccurs="0"/>
      <element ref="uddi:tModelBag" minOccurs="0"/>
    </sequence>
    <attribute name="generic" type="string" use="required"/>
    <attribute name="maxRows" type="int" use="optional"/>
    <attribute name="businessKey" type="uddi:businessKey" use="optional"/>
  </complexType>

  <!-- Response Structure -->
  <element name="serviceList" type="uddi:serviceList"/>
  <complexType name="serviceList">
    <sequence>
      <element ref="uddi:serviceInfos"/>
```

```
      </sequence>
      <attribute name="generic" type="string" use="required"/>
      <attribute name="operator" type="string" use="required"/>
      <attribute name="truncated" type="uddi:truncated" use="optional"/>
    </complexType>
…
</schema>
```

WSDL message and portType Definitions

```
<definitions …
  xmlns="http://schemas.xmlsoap.org/wsdl/"
  xmlns:uddi="urn:uddi-org:api_v2">
  …
  <message name="find_service">
    <part name="body" element="uddi:find_service"/>
  </message>
  <message name="serviceList">
    <part name="body" element="uddi:serviceList"/>
  </message>
  …
  <portType name="Inquire">
    …
    <operation name="find_service">
      <input message="tns:find_service"/>
      <output message="tns:serviceList"/>
      <fault name="error" message="tns:dispositionReport"/>
    </operation>
    …
  </portType>
  …
</definitions>
```

7.2.1.2.5 The find_binding Operation

The find_binding operation returns a set of zero or more bindingTemplate entries whose tModels match those specified in the query.

Type Definitions

```
<schema targetNamespace="urn:uddi-org:api_v2"
          xmlns="http://www.w3.org/2001/XMLSchema"
          xmlns:uddi="urn:uddi-org:api_v2"
          version="2.03" id="uddi">
  …
  <!-- Request Structure -->
```

```
    <element name="find_binding" type="uddi:find_binding"/>
    <complexType name="find_binding">
      <sequence>
        <element ref="uddi:findQualifiers" minOccurs="0"/>
        <element ref="uddi:tModelBag"/>
      </sequence>
      <attribute name="generic" type="string" use="required"/>
      <attribute name="maxRows" type="int" use="optional"/>
      <attribute name="serviceKey" type="uddi:serviceKey" use="required"/>
    </complexType>

    <!-- Response Structure -->
    <element name="bindingDetail" type="uddi:bindingDetail"/>
    <complexType name="bindingDetail">
      <sequence>
        <element ref="uddi:bindingTemplate" minOccurs="0"
                 maxOccurs="unbounded"/>
      </sequence>
      <attribute name="generic" type="string" use="required"/>
      <attribute name="operator" type="string" use="required"/>
      <attribute name="truncated" type="uddi:truncated" use="optional"/>
    </complexType>
  …
  </schema>
```

WSDL message and portType Definitions

```
<definitions …
  xmlns="http://schemas.xmlsoap.org/wsdl/"
  xmlns:uddi="urn:uddi-org:api_v2">
  …
  <message name="find_binding">
    <part name="body" element="uddi:find_binding"/>
  </message>
  <message name="bindingDetail">
    <part name="body" element="uddi:bindingDetail"/>
  </message>
  …
  <portType name="Inquire">
    …
    <operation name="find_binding">
      <input message="tns:find_binding"/>
      <output message="tns:bindingDetail"/>
      <fault name="error" message="tns:dispositionReport"/>
    </operation>
```

```
    ...
  </portType>
  ...
</definitions>
```

7.2.1.2.6 The find_tModel Operation

The find_tModel operation finds all the tModels that match the names, identifiers, or categories listed in the request message. It returns a lightweight list of tModel keys.

Type Definitions

```
<schema targetNamespace="urn:uddi-org:api_v2"
          xmlns="http://www.w3.org/2001/XMLSchema"
          xmlns:uddi="urn:uddi-org:api_v2"
          version="2.03" id="uddi">
  ...
  <!-- Request Structure -->
  <element name="find_tModel" type="uddi:find_tModel"/>
  <complexType name="find_tModel">
    <sequence>
      <element ref="uddi:findQualifiers" minOccurs="0"/>
      <element ref="uddi:name" minOccurs="0"/>
      <element ref="uddi:identifierBag" minOccurs="0"/>
      <element ref="uddi:categoryBag" minOccurs="0"/>
    </sequence>
    <attribute name="generic" type="string" use="required"/>
    <attribute name="maxRows" type="int" use="optional"/>
  </complexType>

  <!-- Response Structure -->
  <element name="tModelList" type="uddi:tModelList"/>
  <complexType name="tModelList">
    <sequence>
      <element ref="uddi:tModelInfos"/>
    </sequence>
    <attribute name="generic" type="string" use="required"/>
    <attribute name="operator" type="string" use="required"/>
    <attribute name="truncated" type="uddi:truncated" use="optional"/>
  </complexType>
...
</schema>
```

WSDL message and portType Definitions

```
<definitions ...
  xmlns="http://schemas.xmlsoap.org/wsdl/"
```

```
    xmlns:uddi="urn:uddi-org:api_v2">
  ...
  <message name="find_tModel">
    <part name="body" element="uddi:find_tModel"/>
  </message>
  <message name="tModelList">
    <part name="body" element="uddi:tModelList"/>
  </message>
  ...
  <portType name="Inquire">
    ...
    <operation name="find_tModel">
      <input message="tns:find_tModel"/>
      <output message="tns:tModelList"/>
      <fault name="error" message="tns:dispositionReport"/>
    </operation>
    ...
  </portType>
  ...
</definitions>
```

7.2.2 Get Operations

The get operations allow you to request specific data structures by their unique identifiers. A get operation can return one or many of the same type of data structure, depending on how many unique identifiers you supply in the request message. There are five get operations:

1. `get_businessDetail` gets `businessEntity` entries.
2. `get_businessDetailExt` gets `businessEntityExt` entries.
3. `get_serviceDetail` gets `businessService` entries.
4. `get_bindingDetail` gets `bindingTemplate` entries.
5. `get_tModelDetail` gets `tModel` entries.

The SOAP request messages used by the get operations all have the same basic form. In the request message the XML fragment in the SOAP `Body` element contains a list of UUID keys:

```
<?xml version="1.0" encoding="UTF-8" ?>
<Envelope xmlns="http://schemas.xmlsoap.org/soap/envelope/">
  <Body>
    <get_something generic="2.0" operator="operatorURL"
                   xmlns="urn:uddi-org:api_v2">
      <somethingKey>4C9D3FE0-2A16-11D7-9B59-000629DC0A53</somethingKey>
```

```
      <somethingKey>2B4C3DE0-23B4-84FE-7B22-000438FE0C22</somethingKey>
      ...
    </get_something>
  </Body>
</Envelope>
```

All the response messages are structured alike as well. They simply return a list of data structures appropriate to the get operation.

```
<?xml version="1.0" encoding="UTF-8" ?>
<Envelope xmlns="http://schemas.xmlsoap.org/soap/envelope/">
  <Body>
    <somethingDetail generic="2.0" xmlns="urn:uddi-org:api_v2">
      <some-data-structure>...<some-data-structure>
      <some-data-structure>...<some-data-structure>
      ...
    </somethingDetail>
  </Body>
</Envelope>
```

For example, the `get_businessDetail` operation returns a list of `business Entity` data structures. The `get_bindingDetail` returns a list of `binding Template` data structures, and so on.

The following sections define the XML schema complex type definitions of message payloads, as well as the WSDL definition for each get operation. The payloads refer to the primary data structures that were discussed in detail in Chapter 6: `businessEntity`, `businessEntityExt`, `businessService`, `binding Template`, and `tModel`. If you have difficulty understanding the XML schema or WSDL definitions, you can go back and review Chapter 3: The W3C XML Schema Language, Chapter 5: WSDL, or both. They will provide you with the background you need.

Response messages will include the `operator` attribute, which provides the URI of the UDDI operator you are querying, and possibly a `truncation` attribute, which indicates that the data requested was too large and had to be truncated.

7.2.2.1 *The* `get_businessDetail` *Operation*

The `get_businessDetail` operation requests one or more `businessEntity` data structures by their unique business keys.

Type Definitions

```
<schema targetNamespace="urn:uddi-org:api_v2"
        xmlns="http://www.w3.org/2001/XMLSchema"
        xmlns:uddi="urn:uddi-org:api_v2"
        version="2.03" id="uddi">
```

```
...
<!-- Request Structure -->
<xsd:element name="get_businessDetail" type="uddi:get_businessDetail"/>
<xsd:complexType name="get_businessDetail">
  <xsd:sequence>
    <xsd:element ref="uddi:businessKey" maxOccurs="unbounded"/>
  </xsd:sequence>
  <xsd:attribute name="generic" type="string" use="required"/>
</xsd:complexType>

<!-- Response Structure -->
<xsd:element name="businessDetail" type="uddi:businessDetail"/>
<xsd:complexType name="businessDetail">
  <xsd:sequence>
    <xsd:element ref="uddi:businessEntity" minOccurs="0"
                 maxOccurs="unbounded"/>
  </xsd:sequence>
  <xsd:attribute name="generic" type="string" use="required"/>
  <xsd:attribute name="operator" type="string" use="required"/>
  <xsd:attribute name="truncated" type="uddi:truncated" use="optional"/>
</xsd:complexType>
...
</schema>
```

WSDL message and portType Definitions

```
<definitions ...
  xmlns="http://schemas.xmlsoap.org/wsdl/"
  xmlns:uddi="urn:uddi-org:api_v2">
  ...
  <message name="get_businessDetail">
    <part name="body" element="uddi:get_businessDetail"/>
  </message>
  <message name="businessDetail">
    <part name="body" element="uddi:businessDetail"/>
  </message>
  ...
  <portType name="Inquire">
    ...
    <operation name="get_businessDetail">
    <input message="tns:get_businessDetail"/>
      <output message="tns:businessDetail"/>
      <fault name="error" message="tns:dispositionReport"/>
    </operation>
    ...
```

```
  </portType>
  …
</definitions>
```

7.2.2.2 *The* `get_businessDetailExt` *Operation*

The `get_businessDetailExt` operation requests one or more `businessEntityExt` data structures by the unique business keys assigned to the `businessEntitys`.

Type Definitions

```
<schema targetNamespace="urn:uddi-org:api_v2"
        xmlns="http://www.w3.org/2001/XMLSchema"
        xmlns:uddi="urn:uddi-org:api_v2"
        version="2.03" id="uddi">
  …

  <!-- Request Structure -->
  <xsd:element name="get_businessDetailExt"
               type="uddi:get_businessDetailExt"/>
  <xsd:complexType name="get_businessDetailExt">
    <xsd:sequence>
      <xsd:element ref="uddi:businessKey" maxOccurs="unbounded"/>
    </xsd:sequence>
    <xsd:attribute name="generic" type="string" use="required"/>
  </xsd:complexType>

  <!-- Response Structure -->
  <xsd:element name="businessDetailExt" type="uddi:businessDetailExt"/>
  <xsd:complexType name="businessDetailExt">
    <xsd:sequence>
      <xsd:element ref="uddi:businessEntityExt" maxOccurs="unbounded"/>
    </xsd:sequence>
    <xsd:attribute name="generic" type="string" use="required"/>
    <xsd:attribute name="operator" type="string" use="required"/>
    <xsd:attribute name="truncated" type="uddi:truncated" use="optional"/>
  </xsd:complexType>
  …
</schema>
```

WSDL `message` and `portType` Definitions

```
<definitions …
  xmlns="http://schemas.xmlsoap.org/wsdl/"
  xmlns:uddi="urn:uddi-org:api_v2">
```

```
...
<message name="get_businessDetailExt">
  <part name="body" element="uddi:get_businessDetailExt"/>
</message>
<message name="businessDetailExt">
  <part name="body" element="uddi:businessDetailExt"/>
</message>
...
<portType name="Inquire">
  ...
  <operation name="get_businessDetailExt">
    <input message="tns:get_businessDetailExt"/>
    <output message="tns:businessDetailExt"/>
    <fault name="error" message="tns:dispositionReport"/>
  </operation>
  ...
</portType>
...
</definitions>
```

7.2.2.3 The `get_serviceDetail` *Operation*

The `get_serviceDetail` operation requests one or more `businessService` data structures by their unique service keys.

Type Definitions

```
<schema targetNamespace="urn:uddi-org:api_v2"
            xmlns="http://www.w3.org/2001/XMLSchema"
            xmlns:uddi="urn:uddi-org:api_v2"
            version="2.03" id="uddi">
  ...

  <!-- Request Structure -->
  <xsd:element name="get_serviceDetail" type="uddi:get_serviceDetail"/>
  <xsd:complexType name="get_serviceDetail">
    <xsd:sequence>
      <xsd:element ref="uddi:serviceKey" maxOccurs="unbounded"/>
    </xsd:sequence>
    <xsd:attribute name="generic" type="string" use="required"/>
  </xsd:complexType>

  <!-- Response Structure -->
  <xsd:element name="serviceDetail" type="uddi:serviceDetail"/>
  <xsd:complexType name="serviceDetail">
```

```
    <xsd:sequence>
      <xsd:element ref="uddi:businessService" minOccurs="0"
                   maxOccurs="unbounded"/>
    </xsd:sequence>
    <xsd:attribute name="generic" type="string" use="required"/>
    <xsd:attribute name="operator" type="string" use="required"/>
    <xsd:attribute name="truncated" type="uddi:truncated" use="optional"/>
  </xsd:complexType>
…
</schema>
```

WSDL `message` and `portType` Definitions

```
<definitions …
  xmlns="http://schemas.xmlsoap.org/wsdl/"
  xmlns:uddi="urn:uddi-org:api_v2">
  …
  <message name="get_serviceDetail">
    <part name="body" element="uddi:get_serviceDetail"/>
  </message>
  <message name="serviceDetail">
    <part name="body" element="uddi:serviceDetail"/>
  </message>
  …
  <portType name="Inquire">
    …
    <operation name="get_serviceDetail">
      <input message="tns:get_serviceDetail"/>
      <output message="tns:serviceDetail"/>
      <fault name="error" message="tns:dispositionReport"/>
    </operation>
    …
  </portType>
  …
</definitions>
```

7.2.2.4 The `get_bindingDetail` *Operation*

The `get_bindingDetail` operation requests one or more `bindingTemplate` data structures by their unique binding keys.

Type Definitions

```
<schema targetNamespace="urn:uddi-org:api_v2"
          xmlns="http://www.w3.org/2001/XMLSchema"
          xmlns:uddi="urn:uddi-org:api_v2"
```

```
            version="2.03" id="uddi">
  ...

  <!-- Request Structure -->
  <xsd:element name="get_bindingDetail" type="uddi:get_bindingDetail"/>
  <xsd:complexType name="get_bindingDetail">
    <xsd:sequence>
      <xsd:element ref="uddi:bindingKey" maxOccurs="unbounded"/>
    </xsd:sequence>
    <xsd:attribute name="generic" type="string" use="required"/>
  </xsd:complexType>

  <!-- Response Structure -->
  <xsd:complexType name="bindingDetail">
    <xsd:sequence>
      <xsd:element ref="uddi:bindingTemplate" minOccurs="0"
                   maxOccurs="unbounded"/>
    </xsd:sequence>
    <xsd:attribute name="generic" type="string" use="required"/>
    <xsd:attribute name="operator" type="string" use="required"/>
    <xsd:attribute name="truncated" type="uddi:truncated" use="optional"/>
  </xsd:complexType>
...
</schema>
```

WSDL `message` and `portType` Definitions

```
<definitions ...
  xmlns="http://schemas.xmlsoap.org/wsdl/"
  xmlns:uddi="urn:uddi-org:api_v2">
  ...
  <message name="get_bindingDetail">
    <part name="body" element="uddi:get_bindingDetail"/>
  </message>
  <message name="bindingDetail">
    <part name="body" element="uddi:bindingDetail"/>
  </message>
  ...
  <portType name="Inquire">
    ...
    <operation name="get_bindingDetail">
      <input message="tns:get_bindingDetail"/>
      <output message="tns:bindingDetail"/>
      <fault name="error" message="tns:dispositionReport"/>
```

```
    </operation>
    ...
  </portType>
  ...
</definitions>
```

7.2.2.5 *The* get_tModelDetail *Operation*

The get_tModelDetail operation requests one or more tModel data structures by their unique tModel keys.

Type Definitions

```
<schema targetNamespace="urn:uddi-org:api_v2"
        xmlns="http://www.w3.org/2001/XMLSchema"
        xmlns:uddi="urn:uddi-org:api_v2"
        version="2.03" id="uddi">
  ...

  <!-- Request Structure -->
  <xsd:element name="get_tModelDetail" type="uddi:get_tModelDetail"/>
  <xsd:complexType name="get_tModelDetail">
    <xsd:sequence>
      <xsd:element ref="uddi:tModelKey" maxOccurs="unbounded"/>
    </xsd:sequence>
    <xsd:attribute name="generic" type="string" use="required"/>
  </xsd:complexType>

  <!-- Response Structure -->
  <xsd:element name="tModelDetail" type="uddi:tModelDetail"/>
  <xsd:complexType name="tModelDetail">
    <xsd:sequence>
      <xsd:element ref="uddi:tModel" maxOccurs="unbounded"/>
    </xsd:sequence>
    <xsd:attribute name="generic" type="string" use="required"/>
    <xsd:attribute name="operator" type="string" use="required"/>
    <xsd:attribute name="truncated" type="uddi:truncated" use="optional"/>
  </xsd:complexType>
...
</schema>
```

WSDL message and portType Definitions

```
<definitions ...
  xmlns="http://schemas.xmlsoap.org/wsdl/"
  xmlns:uddi="urn:uddi-org:api_v2">
  ...
```

```
    <message name="get_tModelDetail">
      <part name="body" element="uddi:get_tModelDetail"/>
    </message>
    <message name="tModelDetail">
      <part name="body" element="uddi:tModelDetail"/>
    </message>
    ...
    <portType name="Inquire">
      ...
      <operation name="get_tModelDetail">
        <input message="tns:get_tModelDetail"/>
        <output message="tns:tModelDetail"/>
        <fault name="error" message="tns:dispositionReport"/>
      </operation>
      ...
    </portType>
    ...
</definitions>
```

7.3 Wrapping Up

Personally, I have mixed feelings about UDDI Inquiry as a SOAP API. It looks good on the surface, until you actually attempt to search a UDDI registry—that's when you discover the weakness of UDDI. In order to execute a search effectively you have to know the names (at least some of the names) of the things you're seeking, or the proper categories to search by. This is more difficult than it sounds because organizations are not using categorizations consistently, as you would expect them to. In addition, some organizations are simply entering the data improperly. Amazon.com, for example, has an entry in IBM's UDDI operation site, in which they have placed their WSDL document URL in the `accessPoint` element of the `businessService`, rather than in a `tModel` where it's supposed to be. Access any UDDI public directory and try to find organizations by a specific category and you'll quickly discover that searching is difficult.

One solution to this problem would be for Web service standards organizations to define strict requirements on how organizations list and categorize their `businessEntitys`, `bindingTemplates`, and `tModels`. More predictability would reduce the difficulty of searching a UDDI directory. The WS-I organization defines such requirements in its WS-I Basic Profile 1.0—we can hope other standards organizations follow suit.

Another problem with the UDDI Inquiry API is that you cannot search description elements for key words, such as "book" or "wholesale." When I brought this problem to the attention of a UDDI expert, I was assured that it would be addressed in UDDI version 4.0, which probably won't be available for a while.

Chapter 8

The UDDI Publishing API

Organizations use the Publishing API to add, change, and delete information in a UDDI registry. This API allows organizations to save their own `businessEntity`, `businessService`, `bindingTemplate`, `tModel`, and `publisherAssertion` data structures in a UDDI registry, and to remove them when necessary.

Like the Inquiry API, the Publishing API is a full-fledged Web service based on SOAP's Document/Literal mode of messaging, and is described by a WSDL document. Unlike the Inquiry API, the Publishing API requires that UDDI operators use HTTPS (HTTP with SSL 3.0) for confidentiality and some form of authentication. In addition, every message—except for the login—must include an authorization token that is automatically issued by the UDDI registry at the start of a session. Each session will have a unique authentication token, which is good only for the life of the session.

The SOAP messages used in the Publishing API are not complicated and are defined in detail in the following sections. The API supports four kinds of operations: authorization operations, save operations, delete operations, and get operations. The authorization operations allow you to authenticate yourself, obtain an authorization token, and terminate a session and its authentication token. The save operations let you add or update the primary data structures. The delete operations let you remove primary data structures. The get operations let you view `publisherAssertions` and a summary of registered information.

8.1 Operation Definitions and Payloads

This section defines all the operations in the Publishing API in terms of their WSDL `portType` and `message` definitions and SOAP payloads (the XML schema document complex types referred to by the `message` definitions.)

Listings in this section show the complex types of most payloads, but a few types were defined in Chapters 6 and 7 and are not redefined here. These include the five primary data structures (`businessEntity`, `bindingTemplate`, and so on) defined in Chapter 6, as well as the `xxxInfos` types addressed in Section 7.2.1.3.1. You'll also see definitions of three element types that are reused in many of the messages: `dispositionReport`, `result`, and `authInfo`.[1] The `dispositionReport` and `result` types are used for response messages to delete operations as well as for error messages. The `authInfo` type, which contains the authentication token, is included in every publisher request message except `get_authToken`. These elements and their corresponding complex types are defined in Listing 8–1. You don't need to examine this listing now; just refer to it as needed.

Listing 8–1

Common XML Schema Elements and Complex Types

```
<schema targetNamespace="urn:uddi-org:api_v2"
        xmlns="http://www.w3.org/2001/XMLSchema"
        xmlns:uddi="urn:uddi-org:api_v2"
        version="2.03" id="uddi">
  ...
  <xsd:element name="authInfo" type="string"/>

  <xsd:element name="dispositionReport" type="uddi:dispositionReport"/>
  <xsd:complexType name="dispositionReport">
    <xsd:sequence>
      <xsd:element ref="uddi:result" maxOccurs="unbounded"/>
    </xsd:sequence>
    <xsd:attribute name="generic" type="string" use="required"/>
    <xsd:attribute name="operator" type="string" use="required"/>
    <xsd:attribute name="truncated" type="uddi:truncated" use="optional"/>
  </xsd:complexType>

  <xsd:element name="result" type="uddi:result"/>
```

[1] There is also an element called `uploadRegister`, but this isn't used in UDDI version 2.0 or its successors.

```
    <xsd:complexType name="result">
      <xsd:sequence>
        <xsd:element ref="uddi:errInfo" minOccurs="0"/>
      </xsd:sequence>
      <xsd:attribute name="keyType" type="uddi:keyType" use="optional"/>
      <xsd:attribute name="errno" type="int" use="required"/>
    </xsd:complexType>
    ...
  </schema>
```

8.1.1 Authorization Operations

Before you can publish anything to a UDDI registry, you have to enroll with a specific UDDI operator. Enrolling with a private UDDI registry may involve some red tape within the organization that runs it. Enrolling with one of the Universal Business Registry (UBR) operators (IBM, Microsoft, SAP, or NTT) requires that you go to one of the operators' Web sites, fill out a form about your organization, and choose a user-id and password.

Once you've enrolled, you can use your user-id and password to log in, then use the Publishing APIs to add, modify, and delete data in the UDDI registry. Actually, the type of credential used may not be a user-id and password; it could be based on a public-key certificate or Kerberos ticket or whatever the operator prefers. All four of the UBR operators are currently using user-ids and passwords to authenticate—when combined with Secure Sockets Layer it's a pretty secure way to authenticate a client. There are two authorization operations:

1. `get_authToken` logs you into the registry.
2. `discard_authToken` logs you out of the registry.

Response messages will include the `operator` attribute, which provides the URI of the UDDI operator you are querying.

Only the authenticated party that created a data structure in a UDDI registry is permitted to modify or delete that data structure using the Publishing API.

8.1.1.1 The `get_authToken` *Operation*

UDDI operators are not required to support the `get_authToken` operation; a token or certificate can be issued using other mechanisms. Where operators do support `get_authToken`, as the UBR operators do, the client must invoke it before starting a publishing session. To start a publishing session with a UDDI operator, you first establish an HTTPS connection with the UDDI registry and then send it a `get_authToken` SOAP message containing your login credentials (usually user-id and password). If your credentials pass authentication, then the reply message will contain an authorization token, which you must send back to the UDDI registry in all subsequent SOAP messages for the duration of your connection.

Type Definitions

```
<schema targetNamespace="urn:uddi-org:api_v2"
            xmlns="http://www.w3.org/2001/XMLSchema"
            xmlns:uddi="urn:uddi-org:api_v2"
            version="2.03" id="uddi">
  …

  <!-- Request Structure -->
  <xsd:element name="get_authToken" type="uddi:get_authToken"/>
  <xsd:complexType name="get_authToken">
    <xsd:attribute name="generic" type="string" use="required"/>
    <xsd:attribute name="userID" type="string" use="required"/>
    <xsd:attribute name="cred" type="string" use="required"/>
  </xsd:complexType>

  <!-- Response Structure -->
  <xsd:element name="authToken" type="uddi:authToken"/>
  <xsd:complexType name="authToken">
    <xsd:sequence>
      <xsd:element ref="uddi:authInfo"/>
    </xsd:sequence>
    <xsd:attribute name="generic" type="string" use="required"/>
    <xsd:attribute name="operator" type="string" use="required"/>
  </xsd:complexType>
…
</schema>
```

WSDL message and portType Definitions

```
<definitions …
  xmlns="http://schemas.xmlsoap.org/wsdl/"
  xmlns:uddi="urn:uddi-org:api_v2">
  …
  <message name="get_authToken">
    <part name="body" element="uddi:get_authToken"/>
  </message>
  <message name="authToken">
    <part name="body" element="uddi:authToken"/>
  </message>

  …
  <portType name="Publish">
    …
```

```
    <operation name="get_authToken">
      <input message="tns:get_authToken" />
      <output message="tns:authToken" />
      <fault name="error" message="tns:dispositionReport" />
    </operation>
    ...
  </portType>
  ...
</definitions>
```

8.1.1.2 *The* discard_authToken *Operation*

When you are finished accessing the UDDI Publishing endpoint, you can terminate your session by sending a discard_authToken message. The registry will then invalidate your authorization token. Further access with that token will cause an error, so your session is effectively ended. If the discard_authToken is never sent, the session will simply time out, which also invalidates the authorization token.

Type Definitions

```
<schema targetNamespace="urn:uddi-org:api_v2"
          xmlns="http://www.w3.org/2001/XMLSchema"
          xmlns:uddi="urn:uddi-org:api_v2"
          version="2.03" id="uddi">
  ...

  <!-- Request Structure -->
  <xsd:element name="discard_authToken" type="uddi:discard_authToken"/>
  <xsd:complexType name="discard_authToken">
    <xsd:sequence>
      <xsd:element ref="uddi:authInfo"/>
    </xsd:sequence>
    <xsd:attribute name="generic" type="string" use="required"/>
  </xsd:complexType>
...
</schema>
```

WSDL message and portType Definitions

```
<definitions ...
  xmlns="http://schemas.xmlsoap.org/wsdl/"
  xmlns:uddi="urn:uddi-org:api_v2">
  ...
  <message name="discard_authToken">
    <part name="body" element="uddi:discard_authToken"/>
  </message>
  <message name="dispositionReport">
```

```
    <part name="body" element="uddi:dispositionReport"/>
  </message>

  ...
  <portType name="Publish">
    ...
    <operation name="discard_authToken">
      <input message="tns:discard_authToken" />
      <output message="tns:dispositionReport" />
      <fault name="error" message="tns:dispositionReport" />
    </operation>
    ...
  </portType>
  ...
</definitions>
```

8.1.2 Save Operations

The save operations allow you to add or update information in the UDDI registry. Each of the five primary data structures has a corresponding save operation except `publisherAssertion`, which has special add and set operations:

- `save_business` adds or updates one or more `businessEntity` entries.
- `save_service` adds or updates one or more `businessService` entries.
- `save_binding` adds or updates one or more `bindingTemplate` entries.
- `save_tModel` adds or updates one or more `tModel` entries.
- `add_publisherAssertions` adds one or more `publisherAssertion` entries.
- `set_publisherAssertions` updates one or more `publisherAssertion` entries.

The SOAP request and response messages used for the save operations all take the same basic form: The request message carries one or more primary data structures to be added or updated, while the response returns the data structures that were successfully updated or added. To update any part of a data structure, you have to submit the whole thing; you cannot update a single field. SOAP request messages for save operations all look much the same:

```
<?xml version="1.0" encoding="UTF-8" ?>
<Envelope xmlns="http://schemas.xmlsoap.org/soap/envelope/">
  <Body>
    <save_something generic="2.0" xmlns="urn:uddi-org:api_v2">
      <authInfo>...</authInfo>
      <some-data-structure>...<some-data-structure>
      <some-data-structure>...<some-data-structure>
      ...
```

```
    </save_something>
  </Body>
</Envelope>
```

The response message, provided it's not a SOAP fault, returns the data structures that were updated, as shown in the following listing.

```
<?xml version="1.0" encoding="UTF-8" ?>
<Envelope xmlns="http://schemas.xmlsoap.org/soap/envelope/">
  <Body>
    <somethingDetail generic="2.0" operator="operatorURI"
                     xmlns="urn:uddi-org:api_v2">
      <some-data-structure>…<some-data-structure>
      <some-data-structure>…<some-data-structure>
      …
    </somethingDetail>
  </Body>
</Envelope>
```

Response messages include the `operator` attribute, which provides the URI of the UDDI operator you are querying, and possibly a `truncation` attribute, which indicates that the data returned was too large and was truncated.

The rest of this section provides more details on each of the save operations, and on the `add_publisherAssertions` and `set_publisherAssertions` operations. For each, you'll see the schema of the operation's XML payload and the relevant WSDL definitions. The schemas have been edited to remove the `uploadRegister` element, because it's no longer used.

8.1.2.1 The `save_business` *Operation*

The `save_business` operation adds or updates one or more `businessEntity` data structures in a UDDI registry.

Type Definitions

```
<schema targetNamespace="urn:uddi-org:api_v2"
            xmlns="http://www.w3.org/2001/XMLSchema"
            xmlns:uddi="urn:uddi-org:api_v2"
            version="2.03" id="uddi">
  …

  <!-- Request Structure -->
  <xsd:element name="save_business" type="uddi:save_business"/>
  <xsd:complexType name="save_business">
    <xsd:sequence>
```

```
      <xsd:element ref="uddi:authInfo"/>
      <xsd:element ref="uddi:businessEntity" minOccurs="0"
                   maxOccurs="unbounded"/>
    </xsd:sequence>
    <xsd:attribute name="generic" type="string" use="required"/>
  </xsd:complexType>

  <!-- Response Structure -->
  <xsd:element name="businessDetail" type="uddi:businessDetail"/>
  <xsd:complexType name="businessDetail">
    <xsd:sequence>
      <xsd:element ref="uddi:businessEntity" minOccurs="0"
                   maxOccurs="unbounded"/>
    </xsd:sequence>
    <xsd:attribute name="generic" type="string" use="required"/>
    <xsd:attribute name="operator" type="string" use="required"/>
    <xsd:attribute name="truncated" type="uddi:truncated" use="optional"/>
  </xsd:complexType>
…
</schema>
```

WSDL `message` and `portType` Definitions

```
<definitions …
  xmlns="http://schemas.xmlsoap.org/wsdl/"
  xmlns:uddi="urn:uddi-org:api_v2">
  …
  <message name="save_business">
    <part name="body" element="uddi:save_business"/>
  </message>
  <message name="">
    <part name="body" element="uddi:businessDetail"/>
  </message>

  …
  <portType name="Publish">
    …
     <operation name="save_business">
      <input message="tns:save_business" />
      <output message="tns:businessDetail" />
      <fault name="error" message="tns:dispositionReport" />
    </operation>
    …
  </portType>
```

```
  ...
</definitions>
```

8.1.2.2 *The* save_service *Operation*

The save_service operation adds or updates one or more businessService data structures in a UDDI registry.

Type Definitions

```
<schema targetNamespace="urn:uddi-org:api_v2"
            xmlns="http://www.w3.org/2001/XMLSchema"
            xmlns:uddi="urn:uddi-org:api_v2"
            version="2.03" id="uddi">
  ...

  <!-- Request Structure -->
  <xsd:element name="save_service" type="uddi:save_service"/>
  <xsd:complexType name="save_service">
    <xsd:sequence>
      <xsd:element ref="uddi:authInfo"/>
      <xsd:element ref="uddi:businessService" maxOccurs="unbounded"/>
    </xsd:sequence>
    <xsd:attribute name="generic" type="string" use="required"/>
  </xsd:complexType>

  <!-- Response Structure -->
  <xsd:element name="serviceDetail" type="uddi:serviceDetail"/>
  <xsd:complexType name="serviceDetail">
    <xsd:sequence>
      <xsd:element ref="uddi:businessService" minOccurs="0"
                   maxOccurs="unbounded"/>
    </xsd:sequence>
    <xsd:attribute name="generic" type="string" use="required"/>
    <xsd:attribute name="operator" type="string" use="required"/>
    <xsd:attribute name="truncated" type="uddi:truncated" use="optional"/>
  </xsd:complexType>
...
</schema>
```

WSDL message and portType Definitions

```
<definitions ...
  xmlns="http://schemas.xmlsoap.org/wsdl/"
  xmlns:uddi="urn:uddi-org:api_v2">
  ...
  <message name="save_service">
```

```
    <part name="body" element="uddi:save_service"/>
  </message>
  <message name="serviceDetail">
    <part name="body" element="uddi:serviceDetail"/>
  </message>

  …
  <portType name="Publish">
    …
    <operation name="save_service">
      <input message="tns:save_service" />
      <output message="tns:serviceDetail" />
      <fault name="error" message="tns:dispositionReport" />
    </operation>
    …
  </portType>
  …
</definitions>
```

8.1.2.3 *The* save_binding *Operation*

The save_binding operation adds or updates one or more bindingTemplate data structures in a UDDI registry.

Type Definitions

```
<schema targetNamespace="urn:uddi-org:api_v2"
          xmlns="http://www.w3.org/2001/XMLSchema"
          xmlns:uddi="urn:uddi-org:api_v2"
          version="2.03" id="uddi">
  …

  <!-- Request Structure -->
  <xsd:element name="save_binding" type="uddi:save_binding"/>
  <xsd:complexType name="save_binding">
    <xsd:sequence>
      <xsd:element ref="uddi:authInfo"/>
      <xsd:element ref="uddi:bindingTemplate" maxOccurs="unbounded"/>
    </xsd:sequence>
    <xsd:attribute name="generic" type="string" use="required"/>
  </xsd:complexType>

  <!-- Response Structure -->
  <xsd:element name="bindingDetail" type="uddi:bindingDetail"/>
  <xsd:complexType name="bindingDetail">
    <xsd:sequence>
```

```
      <xsd:element ref="uddi:bindingTemplate" minOccurs="0"
                   maxOccurs="unbounded"/>
    </xsd:sequence>
    <xsd:attribute name="generic" type="string" use="required"/>
    <xsd:attribute name="operator" type="string" use="required"/>
    <xsd:attribute name="truncated" type="uddi:truncated" use="optional"/>
  </xsd:complexType>
…
</schema>
```

WSDL `message` and `portType` Definitions

```
<definitions …
  xmlns="http://schemas.xmlsoap.org/wsdl/"
  xmlns:uddi="urn:uddi-org:api_v2">
  …
  <message name="save_binding">
    <part name="body" element="uddi:save_binding"/>
  </message>
  <message name="bindingDetail">
    <part name="body" element="uddi:bindingDetail"/>
  </message>

  …
  <portType name="Publish">
    …
    <operation name="save_binding">
      <input message="tns:save_binding" />
      <output message="tns:bindingDetail" />
      <fault name="error" message="tns:dispositionReport" />
    </operation>
    …
  </portType>
  …
</definitions>
```

8.1.2.4 The `save_tModel` *Operation*

The `save_tModel` operation adds or updates one or more `tModel` data structures in a UDDI registry.

Type Definitions

```
<schema targetNamespace="urn:uddi-org:api_v2"
          xmlns="http://www.w3.org/2001/XMLSchema"
          xmlns:uddi="urn:uddi-org:api_v2"
```

```
            version="2.03" id="uddi">
  …

  <!-- Request Structure -->
  <xsd:element name="save_tModel" type="uddi:save_tModel"/>
  <xsd:complexType name="save_tModel">
    <xsd:sequence>
      <xsd:element ref="uddi:authInfo"/>
      <xsd:element ref="uddi:tModel" minOccurs="0" maxOccurs="unbounded"/>
    </xsd:sequence>
    <xsd:attribute name="generic" type="string" use="required"/>
  </xsd:complexType>

  <!-- Response Structure -->
  <xsd:element name="tModelDetail" type="uddi:tModelDetail"/>
  <xsd:complexType name="tModelDetail">
    <xsd:sequence>
      <xsd:element ref="uddi:tModel" maxOccurs="unbounded"/>
    </xsd:sequence>
    <xsd:attribute name="generic" type="string" use="required"/>
    <xsd:attribute name="operator" type="string" use="required"/>
    <xsd:attribute name="truncated" type="uddi:truncated" use="optional"/>
  </xsd:complexType>
…
</schema>
```

WSDL `message` and `portType` Definitions

```
<definitions …
  xmlns="http://schemas.xmlsoap.org/wsdl/"
  xmlns:uddi="urn:uddi-org:api_v2">
  …
  <message name="save_tModel">
    <part name="body" element="uddi:save_tModel"/>
  </message>
  <message name="tModelDetail">
    <part name="body" element="uddi:tModelDetail"/>
  </message>

  …
  <portType name="Publish">
    …
    <operation name="save_tModel">
      <input message="tns:save_tModel" />
      <output message="tns:tModelDetail" />
```

```
      <fault name="error" message="tns:dispositionReport" />
    </operation>
    ...
  </portType>
  ...
</definitions>
```

8.1.2.5 *The* add_publisherAssertions *Operation*

The add_publisherAssertions operation adds one or more publisherAssertion data structures to a UDDI registry. Recall from Section 6.4 that a publisherAssertion is not valid and visible until both parties submit assertions with the same data.

Type Definitions

```
<schema targetNamespace="urn:uddi-org:api_v2"
            xmlns="http://www.w3.org/2001/XMLSchema"
            xmlns:uddi="urn:uddi-org:api_v2"
            version="2.03" id="uddi">
  ...

  <!-- Request Structure -->
  <xsd:element name="add_publisherAssertions"
               type="uddi:add_publisherAssertions"/>
  <xsd:complexType name="add_publisherAssertions">
    <xsd:sequence>
      <xsd:element ref="uddi:authInfo"/>
      <xsd:element ref="uddi:publisherAssertion" maxOccurs="unbounded"/>
    </xsd:sequence>
    <xsd:attribute name="generic" type="string" use="required"/>
  </xsd:complexType>

...
</schema>
```

WSDL message and portType Definitions

```
<definitions ...
  xmlns="http://schemas.xmlsoap.org/wsdl/"
  xmlns:uddi="urn:uddi-org:api_v2">
  ...
  <message name="add_publisherAssertions">
    <part name="body" element="uddi:add_publisherAssertions"/>
  </message>
  <message name="dispositionReport">
    <part name="body" element="uddi:dispositionReport"/>
```

```
  </message>
  …
  <portType name="Publish">
    …
    <operation name="add_publisherAssertions">
      <input message="tns:add_publisherAssertions" />
      <output message="tns:dispositionReport" />
      <fault name="error" message="tns:dispositionReport" />
    </operation>
    …
  </portType>
  …
</definitions>
```

8.1.2.6 *The* `set_publisherAssertions` *Operation*

The `set_publisherAssertions` operation updates one or more existing `publisher Assertion` data structures to a UDDI registry. Because a `publisher Assertion` is not valid unless both parties assert the same relationship, they must perform complementary updates in order to keep the `publisherAssertion` visible.

Type Definitions

```
<schema targetNamespace="urn:uddi-org:api_v2"
        xmlns="http://www.w3.org/2001/XMLSchema"
        xmlns:uddi="urn:uddi-org:api_v2"
        version="2.03" id="uddi">
  …

  <!-- Request Structure -->
  <xsd:element name="set_publisherAssertions"
               type="uddi:set_publisherAssertions"/>
  <xsd:complexType name="set_publisherAssertions">
    <xsd:sequence>
      <xsd:element ref="uddi:authInfo"/>
      <xsd:element ref="uddi:publisherAssertion" minOccurs="0"
                   maxOccurs="unbounded"/>
    </xsd:sequence>
    <xsd:attribute name="generic" type="string" use="required"/>
  </xsd:complexType>

  <!-- Response Structure -->
  <xsd:element name="publisherAssertions" type="uddi:publisherAssertions"/>
  <xsd:complexType name="publisherAssertions">
    <xsd:sequence>
```

```
      <xsd:element ref="uddi:publisherAssertion" minOccurs="0"
                   maxOccurs="unbounded"/>
    </xsd:sequence>
    <xsd:attribute name="generic" type="string" use="required"/>
    <xsd:attribute name="operator" type="string" use="required"/>
    <xsd:attribute name="authorizedName" type="string" use="required"/>
  </xsd:complexType>
…
</schema>
```

WSDL message and portType Definitions

```
<definitions …
  xmlns="http://schemas.xmlsoap.org/wsdl/"
  xmlns:uddi="urn:uddi-org:api_v2">
  …
  <message name="set_publisherAssertions">
    <part name="body" element="uddi:set_publisherAssertions"/>
  </message>
  <message name="publisherAssertions">
    <part name="body" element="uddi:publisherAssertions"/>
  </message>

  …
  <portType name="Publish">
    …
    <operation name="set_publisherAssertions">
      <input message="tns:set_publisherAssertions" />
      <output message="tns:publisherAssertions" />
      <fault name="error" message="tns:dispositionReport" />
    </operation>
    …
  </portType>
  …
</definitions>
```

8.1.3 Delete Operations

The delete operations allow you to remove information from the UDDI registry. Each delete operation corresponds with a primary data structure:

- delete_business deletes one or more businessEntity entries.
- delete_service deletes one or more businessService entries.
- delete_binding deletes one or more bindingTemplate entries.

- `delete_tModel` deletes (or rather, hides) one or more `tModel` entries.
- `delete_publisherAssertions` deletes one or more `publisherAssertion` entries.

The SOAP request and response messages used for the delete operations all take the same basic form: The request message carries keys to one or more primary data structures to be deleted, as shown in the following example.

```
<?xml version="1.0" encoding="UTF-8" ?>
<Envelope xmlns="http://schemas.xmlsoap.org/soap/envelope/">
  <Body>
    <delete_something generic="2.0" xmlns="urn:uddi-org:api_v2">
      <authInfo>…</authInfo>
      <data-structure-Key>…<data-structure-Key>
      <data-structure-Key>…<data-structure-Key>
      …
    </delete_something>
  </Body>
</Envelope>
```

Unlike the response message of a save operation, the delete operation's response doesn't contain the data in question. Unless it's reporting a fault, the response message contains a `dispositionReport` element. Listing 8–2 shows a standard `dispositionReport` reply message.

Listing 8–2

Standard `dispositionReport` *for Successful Delete Operations*

```
<?xml version="1.0" encoding="UTF-8" ?>
<Envelope xmlns="http://schemas.xmlsoap.org/soap/envelope/">
  <Body>
    <dispositionReport generic="2.0" operator="operatorURI"
                    xmlns="urn:uddi-org:api_v2">
      <result errno="0" >
         <errInfo errCode="E_success" />
      </result>
    </dispositionReport>
  </Body>
</Envelope>
```

If the operation is a success, the reply message for all delete operations will look exactly like the one in Listing 8–2, with an `errCode` equal to `"E_success"`. The `dispositionReport` element is also used to report errors, as you'll see in Section

8.2: Fault Messages. The rest of this section provides a detailed definition of each of the delete operations.

8.1.3.1 The `delete_business` *Operation*

The `delete_business` operation deletes one or more `businessEntity` entries from a UDDI registry. In addition, all `businessServices`, `bindingTemplates`, and `publisherAssertions` owned by any deleted `businessEntity` will be permanently removed from the UDDI registry. The only exceptions are

- `bindingTemplates` that other `bindingTemplates` refer to as **hosting redirectors** (see Section 6.2.2.2)
- **projected references,** data types referred to by the `businessEntity` being deleted, but owned by some other `businessEntity`
- `tModels`, which must be deleted explicitly using the `delete_tModel` operation

Type Definitions

```
<schema targetNamespace="urn:uddi-org:api_v2"
            xmlns="http://www.w3.org/2001/XMLSchema"
            xmlns:uddi="urn:uddi-org:api_v2"
            version="2.03" id="uddi">
  ...

  <!-- Request Structure -->
  <xsd:element name="delete_business" type="uddi:delete_business"/>
  <xsd:complexType name="delete_business">
    <xsd:sequence>
      <xsd:element ref="uddi:authInfo"/>
      <xsd:element ref="uddi:businessKey" maxOccurs="unbounded"/>
    </xsd:sequence>
    <xsd:attribute name="generic" type="string" use="required"/>
  </xsd:complexType>
...
</schema>
```

WSDL `message` **and** `portType` **Definitions**

```
<definitions ...
  xmlns="http://schemas.xmlsoap.org/wsdl/"
  xmlns:uddi="urn:uddi-org:api_v2">
  ...
  <message name="delete_business">
    <part name="body" element="uddi:delete_business"/>
  </message>
  <message name="dispositionReport">
```

```
    <part name="body" element="uddi:dispositionReport"/>
  </message>

  ...
  <portType name="Publish">
    ...
    <operation name="delete_business">
      <input message="tns:delete_business" />
      <output message="tns:dispositionReport" />
      <fault name="error" message="tns:dispositionReport" />
    </operation>
    ...
  </portType>
  ...
</definitions>
```

8.1.3.2 The `delete_service` *Operation*

The `delete_service` operation deletes one or more `businessService` data structures from a UDDI registry. All `bindingTemplates` owned by the deleted `businessService` will also be permanently removed from the UDDI registry. The exceptions are the same as for `delete_business`: projected references, hosting redirectors, and `tModels`.

Type Definitions

```
<schema targetNamespace="urn:uddi-org:api_v2"
            xmlns="http://www.w3.org/2001/XMLSchema"
            xmlns:uddi="urn:uddi-org:api_v2"
            version="2.03" id="uddi">
  ...

  <!-- Request Structure -->
  <xsd:element name="delete_service" type="uddi:delete_service"/>
  <xsd:complexType name="delete_service">
    <xsd:sequence>
      <xsd:element ref="uddi:authInfo"/>
      <xsd:element ref="uddi:serviceKey" maxOccurs="unbounded"/>
    </xsd:sequence>
    <xsd:attribute name="generic" type="string" use="required"/>
  </xsd:complexType>
...
</schema>
```

WSDL `message` **and** `portType` **Definitions**

```
<definitions ...
  xmlns="http://schemas.xmlsoap.org/wsdl/"
```

```
  xmlns:uddi="urn:uddi-org:api_v2">
  …
  <message name="delete_service">
    <part name="body" element="uddi:delete_service"/>
  </message>
  <message name="dispositionReport">
    <part name="body" element="uddi:dispositionReport"/>
  </message>

  …
  <portType name="Publish">
    …
    <operation name="delete_service">
      <input message="tns:delete_service" />
      <output message="tns:dispositionReport" />
      <fault name="error" message="tns:dispositionReport" />
    </operation>
    …
  </portType>
  …
</definitions>
```

8.1.3.3 The delete_binding *Operation*

The delete_binding operation deletes one or more bindingTemplate data structures from a UDDI registry. tModels referred to by bindingTemplates being deleted are not affected. They must be deleted explicitly using the delete_tModel operation.

Type Definitions

```
<schema targetNamespace="urn:uddi-org:api_v2"
          xmlns="http://www.w3.org/2001/XMLSchema"
          xmlns:uddi="urn:uddi-org:api_v2"
          version="2.03" id="uddi">
  …

  <!-- Request Structure -->
  <xsd:element name="delete_binding" type="uddi:delete_binding"/>
  <xsd:complexType name="delete_binding">
    <xsd:sequence>
      <xsd:element ref="uddi:authInfo"/>
      <xsd:element ref="uddi:bindingKey" maxOccurs="unbounded"/>
    </xsd:sequence>
    <xsd:attribute name="generic" type="string" use="required"/>
  </xsd:complexType>
```

```
…
</schema>
```

WSDL message and portType Definitions

```
<definitions …
  xmlns="http://schemas.xmlsoap.org/wsdl/"
  xmlns:uddi="urn:uddi-org:api_v2">
  …
  <message name="delete_binding">
    <part name="body" element="uddi:delete_binding"/>
  </message>
  <message name="dispositionReport">
    <part name="body" element="uddi:dispositionReport"/>
  </message>

  …
  <portType name="Publish">
    …
    <operation name="delete_binding">
      <input message="tns:delete_binding" />
      <output message="tns:dispositionReport" />
      <fault name="error" message="tns:dispositionReport" />
    </operation>
    …
  </portType>
  …
</definitions>
```

8.1.3.4 The delete_tModel *Operation*

The delete_tModel operation does not actually delete tModel data structures from a UDDI registry. Instead the tModels are made invisible to find operations—although you can still retrieve them using a get_tModelDetail message. To remove a tModel from a UDDI registry permanently, you must petition the UDDI operator to delete it.

Type Definitions

```
<schema targetNamespace="urn:uddi-org:api_v2"
            xmlns="http://www.w3.org/2001/XMLSchema"
            xmlns:uddi="urn:uddi-org:api_v2"
            version="2.03" id="uddi">
  …

  <!-- Request Structure -->
  <xsd:element name="delete_tModel" type="uddi:delete_tModel"/>
  <xsd:complexType name="delete_tModel">
```

```
      <xsd:sequence>
        <xsd:element ref="uddi:authInfo"/>
        <xsd:element ref="uddi:tModelKey" maxOccurs="unbounded"/>
      </xsd:sequence>
      <xsd:attribute name="generic" type="string" use="required"/>
    </xsd:complexType>
  …
</schema>
```

WSDL message and portType Definitions

```
<definitions …
  xmlns="http://schemas.xmlsoap.org/wsdl/"
  xmlns:uddi="urn:uddi-org:api_v2">
  …
  <message name="delete_tModel">
    <part name="body" element="uddi:delete_tModel"/>
  </message>
  <message name="dispositionReport">
    <part name="body" element="uddi:dispositionReport"/>
  </message>

  …
  <portType name="Publish">
    …
    <operation name="delete_tModel">
      <input message="tns:delete_tModel" />
      <output message="tns:dispositionReport" />
      <fault name="error" message="tns:dispositionReport" />
    </operation>
    …
  </portType>
  …
</definitions>
```

8.1.3.5 The delete_publisherAssertions *Operation*

The delete_publisherAssertions operation deletes one or more publisherAssertion data structures from a UDDI registry. This delete operation is different from others because a publisherAssociation doesn't have a UUID key; you delete a publisherAssociation using its to and from keys as a compound key.

Type Definitions

```
<schema targetNamespace="urn:uddi-org:api_v2"
          xmlns="http://www.w3.org/2001/XMLSchema"
          xmlns:uddi="urn:uddi-org:api_v2"
```

```
            version="2.03" id="uddi">
  ...

  <!-- Request Structure -->
  <xsd:element name="delete_publisherAssertions"
               type="uddi:delete_publisherAssertions"/>
  <xsd:complexType name="delete_publisherAssertions">
    <xsd:sequence>
      <xsd:element ref="uddi:authInfo"/>
      <xsd:element ref="uddi:publisherAssertion" maxOccurs="unbounded"/>
    </xsd:sequence>
    <xsd:attribute name="generic" type="string" use="required"/>
  </xsd:complexType>
...
</schema>
```

WSDL `message` and `portType` Definitions

```
<definitions ...
  xmlns="http://schemas.xmlsoap.org/wsdl/"
  xmlns:uddi="urn:uddi-org:api_v2">
  ...
  <message name="delete_publisherAssertions">
    <part name="body" element="uddi:delete_publisherAssertions"/>
  </message>
  <message name="dispositionReport">
    <part name="body" element="uddi:dispositionReport"/>
  </message>

  ...
  <portType name="Publish">
    ...
    <operation name="delete_publisherAssertions">
      <input message="tns:delete_publisherAssertions" />
      <output message="tns:dispositionReport" />
      <fault name="error" message="tns:dispositionReport" />
    </operation>
    ...
  </portType>
  ...
</definitions>
```

8.1.4 Get Operations

The get operations are used to obtain summary data about data structures published by the client. There are two `publisherAssertion` operations and one general operation for getting all businessEntity and tModel data structures controlled by an authenticated user:

1. get_assertionStatusReport gets a summary of publisherAssertion entries.
2. get_publisherAssertions gets a list of publisherAssertion entries.
3. get_registeredInfo gets an abbreviated list of businessEntity and tModel entries.

8.1.4.1 *The* get_assertionStatusReport *Operation*

The get_assertionStatusReport operation allows you to see the status of any assertions that you have made, or that have been made about businessEntity entries that you control. You specify the assertion status you want to view using a code in the request message. For example, the SOAP message in Listing 8–3 requests a list of all publisherAssertion entries that are complete—that is, visible.

Listing 8–3

The get_assertionStatusReport *Request Message*

```
<?xml version="1.0" encoding="UTF-8" ?>
<Envelope xmlns="http://schemas.xmlsoap.org/soap/envelope/">
  <Body>
    <get_assertionStatusReport generic="2.0" xmlns="urn:uddi-org:api_v2">
      <authInfo>…</authInfo>
      <completionStatus>status:complete</completionStatus>
    </get_assertionStatusReport>
  </Body>
</Envelope>
```

The three completionStatus codes you can use are summarized in Table 8–1.

Table 8–1 Completion Status Codes for the get_assertionStatusReport Operation[2]

completionStatus **Value**	**Description**
status:complete	This value indicates that you want to see a list of all the publisherAssertions that refer to any businessEntity that you have added (that you are authorized to update and delete). In order to be considered "complete," or visible, both parties must have submitted equivalent publisherAssertions.

[2] Organization for the Advancement of Structured Information Standards, *UDDI Version 2.04 API Specification* (2002). The descriptions are based on those in the UDDI specification, available at http://uddi.org/ pubs /ProgrammersAPI-V2.04-Published-20020719.htm.

Table 8–1 Completion Status Codes for the `get_assertionStatusReport` Operation (Continued)

`completionStatus` **Value**	Description
`status:toKey_incomplete`	This value indicates that you want to see all `publisherAssertions` in which a `businessEntity` you control is referred to by the `publisherAssertion toKey` element. These can be assertions that you added, but have not been confirmed by the other party, or assertions that someone else has added, but you have not confirmed.
`status:fromKey_incomplete`	This value indicates that you want to see all `publisherAssertions` in which a `businessEntity` you control is referred to by the `publisherAssertion fromKey` element. These can be assertions that you added, but have not been confirmed by the other party, or assertions that someone else has added, but you have not confirmed.

The reply SOAP message will contain a list of zero or more `assertionStatusItem` elements. Each of these provides the same data as a `publisherAssertion` entry but also includes a `keysOwned` element. The `keysOwned` element indicates which of the keys (`toKey` or `fromKey`) is owned by the person making the request—which makes it a little easier to figure out who is making the assertion, you or the other party. Listing 8–4 shows a `get_assertionStatusReport` reply message.

Listing 8–4

The `get_assertionStatusReport` *Response Message*

```
<?xml version="1.0" encoding="UTF-8" ?>
<Envelope xmlns="http://schemas.xmlsoap.org/soap/envelope/">
  <Body>
    <assertionStatusReport generic="2.0" operator="operatorURI"
                           xmlns="urn:uddi-org:api_v2" >

      <assertionStatusItem completionStatus="status:complete" >
        <fromKey>0207DE98-9C61-4138-A121-4B9E636B7649</fromKey>
        <toKey>1EE40DF0-9357-11D5-8838-002035229C64</toKey>
        <keyedReference
           keyName="corporate division"
           keyValue="parent-child"
           tModelKey="uuid:807A2C6A-EE22-470D-ADC7-E0424A337C03"  />
        <keysOwned>
           <toKey>1EE48BF0-9357-11D5-8838-002035229C64</toKey>
```

```
        </keysOwned>
      </assertionStatusItem>
    </assertionStatusReport>
  </Body>
</Envelope>
```

Response messages will include the operator attribute, which provides the URI of the UDDI operator you are querying.

Type Definitions

```
<schema targetNamespace="urn:uddi-org:api_v2"
            xmlns="http://www.w3.org/2001/XMLSchema"
            xmlns:uddi="urn:uddi-org:api_v2"
            version="2.03" id="uddi">
  ...

  <!-- Request Structure -->
  <xsd:element name="get_assertionStatusReport"
               type="uddi:get_assertionStatusReport"/>
  <xsd:complexType name="get_assertionStatusReport">
    <xsd:sequence>
      <xsd:element ref="uddi:authInfo"/>
      <xsd:element ref="uddi:completionStatus" minOccurs="0"/>
    </xsd:sequence>
    <xsd:attribute name="generic" type="string" use="required"/>
  </xsd:complexType>

  <xsd:element name="completionStatus" type="string"/>

  <!-- Response Structures -->
  <xsd:element name="assertionStatusReport"
               type="uddi:assertionStatusReport"/>
  <xsd:complexType name="assertionStatusReport">
    <xsd:sequence>
      <xsd:element ref="uddi:assertionStatusItem" minOccurs="0"
                   maxOccurs="unbounded"/>
    </xsd:sequence>
    <xsd:attribute name="generic" type="string" use="required"/>
    <xsd:attribute name="operator" type="string" use="required"/>
  </xsd:complexType>

  <xsd:element name="assertionStatusItem" type="uddi:assertionStatusItem"/>
  <xsd:complexType name="assertionStatusItem">
    <xsd:sequence>
```

```
      <xsd:element ref="uddi:fromKey"/>
      <xsd:element ref="uddi:toKey"/>
      <xsd:element ref="uddi:keyedReference"/>
      <xsd:element ref="uddi:keysOwned"/>
    </xsd:sequence>
    <xsd:attribute name="completionStatus" type="string" use="required"/>
  </xsd:complexType>

  <xsd:element name="keysOwned" type="uddi:keysOwned"/>
  <xsd:complexType name="keysOwned">
    <xsd:sequence>
      <xsd:element ref="uddi:fromKey" minOccurs="0"/>
      <xsd:element ref="uddi:toKey" minOccurs="0"/>
    </xsd:sequence>
  </xsd:complexType>
…
</schema>
```

WSDL message and portType Definitions

```
<definitions …
  xmlns="http://schemas.xmlsoap.org/wsdl/"
  xmlns:uddi="urn:uddi-org:api_v2">
  …
  <message name="get_assertionStatusReport">
    <part name="body" element="uddi:get_assertionStatusReport"/>
  </message>
  <message name="assertionStatusReport">
    <part name="body" element="uddi:assertionStatusReport"/>
  </message>

  …
  <portType name="Publish">
    …
    <operation name="get_assertionStatusReport">
      <input message="tns:get_assertionStatusReport" />
      <output message="tns:assertionStatusReport" />
      <fault name="error" message="tns:dispositionReport" />
    </operation>
    …
  </portType>
  …
</definitions>
```

8.1.4.2 *The* `get_publisherAssertions` *Operation*

The `get_publisherAssertions` operation returns all the `publisherAssertion` entries you have submitted to the UDDI registry, both visible and invisible. The SOAP request message is very simple: It contains only the `authInfo` element. The UDDI registry will look up all the `publisherAssertion` entries made by the party associated with the `authInfo` value. Listing 8–5 shows an example of the `get_publisherAssertions` SOAP request message.

Listing 8–5

The `get_publisherAssertions` *Request Message*

```
<?xml version="1.0" encoding="UTF-8" ?>
<Envelope xmlns="http://schemas.xmlsoap.org/soap/envelope/">
  <Body>
    <get_publisherAssertions generic="2.0" xmlns="urn:uddi-org:api_v2">
      <authInfo>…</authInfo>
    </get_publisherAssertions>
  </Body>
</Envelope>
```

The SOAP response message will contain zero or more `publisherAssertion` data structures that you have submitted in the past, both visible (confirmed by the other party) and invisible (not confirmed by the other party). Listing 8–6 illustrates.

Listing 8–6

The `get_publisherAssertions` *Response Message*

```
<?xml version="1.0" encoding="UTF-8" ?>
<Envelope xmlns="http://schemas.xmlsoap.org/soap/envelope/">
  <Body>
    <publisherAssertions generic="2.0" authorName="yourName"
        operator="OperatorURL" xmlns="urn:uddi-org:api_v2" >

      <publisherAssertion>
        <fromKey>0207DE98-9C61-4138-A121-4B9E636B7649</fromKey>
        <toKey>1EE48BF0-9357-11D5-8838-002035229C64</toKey>
        <keyedReference
           keyName="Corporation"
           keyValue="corporation-has-division"
           tModelKey="uuid:807A2C6A-EE22-470D-ADC7-E0424A337C03"  />
      </publisherAssertion>
      ...
```

```
    </publisherAssertions>
  </Body>
</Envelope>
```

Response messages will include the `operator` attribute, which provides the URI of the UDDI operator you are querying, and the `authorizedName` attribute, which is the name of the authorized party.

Type Definitions

```
<schema targetNamespace="urn:uddi-org:api_v2"
          xmlns="http://www.w3.org/2001/XMLSchema"
          xmlns:uddi="urn:uddi-org:api_v2"
          version="2.03" id="uddi">
  ...

  <!-- Request Structure -->
  <xsd:element name="get_publisherAssertions"
               type="uddi:get_publisherAssertions"/>
  <xsd:complexType name="get_publisherAssertions">
    <xsd:sequence>
      <xsd:element ref="uddi:authInfo"/>
    </xsd:sequence>
    <xsd:attribute name="generic" type="string" use="required"/>
  </xsd:complexType>

  <!-- Response Structure -->
  <xsd:element name="publisherAssertions" type="uddi:publisherAssertions"/>
  <xsd:complexType name="publisherAssertions">
    <xsd:sequence>
      <xsd:element ref="uddi:publisherAssertion" minOccurs="0"
                   maxOccurs="unbounded"/>
    </xsd:sequence>
    <xsd:attribute name="generic" type="string" use="required"/>
    <xsd:attribute name="operator" type="string" use="required"/>
    <xsd:attribute name="authorizedName" type="string" use="required"/>
  </xsd:complexType>
...
</schema>
```

WSDL `message` and `portType` Definitions

```
<definitions ...
  xmlns="http://schemas.xmlsoap.org/wsdl/"
  xmlns:uddi="urn:uddi-org:api_v2">
```

```
...
<message name="get_publisherAssertions">
  <part name="body" element="uddi:get_publisherAssertions"/>
</message>
<message name="publisherAssertions">
  <part name="body" element="uddi:publisherAssertions"/>
</message>

...
<portType name="Publish">
  ...
  <operation name="get_publisherAssertions">
    <input message="tns:get_publisherAssertions" />
    <output message="tns:publisherAssertions" />
    <fault name="error" message="tns:dispositionReport" />
  </operation>
  ...
</portType>
...
</definitions>
```

8.1.4.3 The `get_registeredInfo` *Operation*

The `get_registeredInfo` operation returns an abbreviated list of all the `businessEntity` and `tModel` structures controlled by the individual who made the request. Listing 8–7 shows an example of the SOAP request message, which contains only the `authInfo` element.

Listing 8–7

The `get_registeredInfo` *Request Message*

```
<?xml version="1.0" encoding="UTF-8" ?>
<Envelope xmlns="http://schemas.xmlsoap.org/soap/envelope/">
  <Body>
    <get_registeredInfo generic="2.0" xmlns="urn:uddi-org:api_v2">
      <authInfo>...</authInfo>
    </get_registeredInfo >
  </Body>
</Envelope>
```

The response SOAP message contains a summary of the data controlled by the requester in the form of `businessInfos` and `tModelInfos` elements, which are described in Section 7.2.1.3.1. Listing 8–8 shows a typical SOAP response message.

Listing 8–8

The `get_registeredInfo` *Response Message*

```
<?xml version="1.0" encoding="UTF-8" ?>
<Envelope xmlns="http://schemas.xmlsoap.org/soap/envelope/">
  <Body>
    <registeredInfo generic="2.0" xmlns="urn:uddi-org:api_v2"
                    operator="OperatorURL">
      <businessInfos>
         <businessInfo businessKey="01B1FA80-2A15-11D7-9B58-000629DC0A53">
           <name>Monson-Haefel, Inc.</name>
           <serviceInfos>
             <serviceInfo businessKey="01B1FA80-2A15-11D7-9B58-000629DC0A53"
                          serviceKey="807A2C6A-EE22-470D-ADC7-E0424A337C03">
              <name>BookQuoteService</name>
             </serviceInfo>
           </serviceInfos>
         </businessInfo>
         ...
      </businessInfos>
      <tModelInfos>
        <tModelInfo tModelKey="UUID:4C9D3FE0-2A16-11D7-9B58-000629DC0A53">
           <name>Monson-Haefel:BookQuote</name>
        </tModelInfo>
        ...
      </tModelInfos>
    </registeredInfo>
  </Body>
</Envelope>
```

Response messages will include the `operator` attribute, which provides the URI of the UDDI operator you are querying, and possibly a `truncation` attribute, which indicates that the data returned was too large and was truncated.

Type Definitions

```
<schema targetNamespace="urn:uddi-org:api_v2"
            xmlns="http://www.w3.org/2001/XMLSchema"
            xmlns:uddi="urn:uddi-org:api_v2"
            version="2.03" id="uddi">
  ...

  <!-- Request Structure -->
  <xsd:element name="get_registeredInfo" type="uddi:get_registeredInfo"/>
  <xsd:complexType name="get_registeredInfo">
```

```
    <xsd:sequence>
      <xsd:element ref="uddi:authInfo"/>
    </xsd:sequence>
    <xsd:attribute name="generic" type="string" use="required"/>
  </xsd:complexType>

  <!-- Response Structure -->
  <xsd:element name="registeredInfo" type="uddi:registeredInfo"/>
  <xsd:complexType name="registeredInfo">
    <xsd:sequence>
      <xsd:element ref="uddi:businessInfos"/>
      <xsd:element ref="uddi:tModelInfos"/>
    </xsd:sequence>
    <xsd:attribute name="generic" type="string" use="required"/>
    <xsd:attribute name="operator" type="string" use="required"/>
    <xsd:attribute name="truncated" type="uddi:truncated" use="optional"/>
  </xsd:complexType>
…
</schema>
```

WSDL message and portType Definitions

```
<definitions …
  xmlns="http://schemas.xmlsoap.org/wsdl/"
  xmlns:uddi="urn:uddi-org:api_v2">
  …
  <message name="get_registeredInfo">
    <part name="body" element="uddi:get_registeredInfo"/>
  </message>
  <message name="registeredInfo">
    <part name="body" element="uddi:registeredInfo"/>
  </message>

  …
  <portType name="Publish">
    …
    <operation name="get_registeredInfo">
      <input message="tns:get_registeredInfo" />
      <output message="tns:registeredInfo" />
      <fault name="error" message="tns:dispositionReport" />
    </operation>
    …
  </portType>
  …
</definitions>
```

8.2 Fault Messages

A UDDI registry is a SOAP-based Web service, and just like any other Web service it can generate standard SOAP faults when something goes amiss: when the SOAP message sent by the client is malformed, contains unknown elements, or requires understanding of a header block, or when the UDDI registry is having trouble processing the message because of some server-side malfunction. For example, if you send a SOAP 1.2 message to a UDDI version 2 registry, which is based on SOAP 1.1, you will receive a `VersionMismatch` fault message, as shown in Listing 8–9.

Listing 8–9

A Standard SOAP Fault Generated by a UDDI Registry

```
<Envelope xmlns="http://schemas.xmlsoap.org/soap/envolope/" >
  <Body>
    <Fault>
      <faultcode>VersionMismatch</faultcode>
      <faultstring>Message was not SOAP 1.1 conformant</faultstring>
      <detail/>
    </Fault>
  </Body>
</Envelope>
```

The types of fault codes used for standard SOAP fault messages and their causes are detailed in Table 8–2.

Table 8–2 Standard SOAP Fault Codes Used by UDDI[3]

Fault Code	Fault Condition
`VersionMismatch`	An invalid namespace reference for the SOAP envelope element was passed. The valid namespace value is `"http://www.xmlsoap.org/soap/envelope/"`.
`MustUnderstand`	A SOAP header element was passed to an operator site. Operator sites do not support SOAP headers, and will return this error whenever a SOAP request is received that contains a `Header` element.
`Client`	A message was incorrectly formed or did not contain enough information to perform more exhaustive error reporting.

[3] Organization for the Advancement of Structured Information Standards, *UDDI Version 2.04 API Specification* (2002), Appendix B.4. The descriptions are based on those in the UDDI specification, available at http://uddi.org/pubs/ProgrammersAPI-V2.04-Published-20020719.htm.

Table 8–2 Continued

Fault Code	Fault Condition
Server	The message could not be processed for reasons not directly attributable to the contents of the message itself but rather to the processing of the message. For example, faulty processing could include communicating with a back-end processor that didn't respond. The message may succeed at a later time.

Complete coverage of SOAP fault messages and fault codes can be found in Chapter 4: SOAP.

UDDI also specifies how UDDI-specific errors are reported using SOAP fault messages. If there is some inconsistency in the data (an unknown key value or an oversized message, for example), then the error will be reported using a SOAP fault that carries a `dispositionReport` element. If you examine the WSDL `portType` definitions for the UDDI operations (the Publishing and Inquiry APIs), you'll see that they all define each fault message to refer to a single part, a `dispositionReport` element. The `dispositionReport` element is carried in the `detail` element of the fault message and contains an error number, an error code, and a description. Listing 8–10 shows an example.

Listing 8–10

A UDDI Fault Message with a `dispositionReport` *Element*

```
<?xml version="1.0" encoding="UTF-8" ?>
<Envelope xmlns="http://schemas.xmlsoaporg.org/soap/envelope/">
  <Body>
    <Fault>
      <faultcode>Client</faultcode>
      <faultstring>Client Error</faultstring>
      <detail>
        <dispositionReport generic="2.0" operator="OperatorURI"
                           xmlns="urn:uddi-org:api_v2" >
          <result errno="10210" >
            <errInfo errCode="E_invalidKeyPassed">
              The businesskey passed did not match with any known key values:
              InvalidKey=01B1FA80-2A15-11D7-9B58-000629DC0A43
            </errInfo>
          </result>
        </dispositionReport>
      </detail>
    </Fault>
```

```
  </Body>
</Envelope>
```

UDDI 2.0 uses 24 standard error codes (and a few more are deprecated). A list of error codes used and their descriptions is provided in Table 8–3.

Table 8–3 Standard UDDI Error Codes[4]

Error Code	Error Number	Description
`E_assertionNotFound`	30000	Signifies that a particular publisher assertion (consisting of two `businessKey` values, and a keyed reference with three components) cannot be identified in a save or delete operation.
`E_authTokenExpired`	10110	Signifies that the authentication token information has timed out.
`E_authTokenRequired`	10120	Signifies that an invalid authentication token was passed to an API call that requires authentication.
`E_accountLimitExceeded`	10160	Signifies that a save request exceeded the quantity limits for a given data type. See "Structure Limits" in Appendix D [of the UDDI specification] for details.
`E_busy`	10400	Signifies that the request cannot be processed at the current time.
`E_fatalError`	10500	Signifies that a serious technical error has occurred while processing the request.
`E_invalidKeyPassed`	10210	Signifies that the `uuid_key` value passed did not match with any known key values. The details on the invalid key will be included in the `dispositionReport` element.
`E_invalidProjection`	20230	Signifies that an attempt was made to save a `businessEntity` containing a service projection that does not match the `businessService` being projected. The `serviceKey` of at least one such `businessService` will be included in the `dispositionReport`.
`E_invalidCompletionStatus`	30100	Signifies that one of the assertion status values passed is unrecognized. The completion status that caused the problem will be clearly indicated in the error text.

[4] Organization for the Advancement of Structured Information Standards, *UDDI Version 2.04 API Specification* (2002), Appendix A.1. The descriptions are based on those in the UDDI specification, available at http://uddi.org/pubs/ProgrammersAPI-V2.04-Published-20020719.htm.

Table 8–3 Continued

Error Code	Error Number	Description
E_invalidValue	20200	A value that was passed in a keyValue attribute did not pass validation. This applies to checked categorizations, identifiers, and other validated code lists. The error text will clearly indicate the key-and-value combination that failed validation.
E_languageError	10060	Signifies that an error was detected while processing elements that were annotated with xml:lang qualifiers. Presently, only the description and name elements support xml:lang qualification.
E_messageTooLarge	30110	Signifies that the message is too large. The upper limit will be clearly indicated in the error text.
E_publisherCancelled	30220	The target publisher cancelled the custody-transfer operation.
E_requestDenied	30210	A custody-transfer request has been refused.
E_requestTimeout	20240	Signifies that the request could not be carried out because a needed Web service, such as validate_values, did not respond in a reasonable amount of time. Details identifying the failing service will be included in the dispositionReport element.
E_secretUnknown	30230	The target publisher was unable to match the shared secret and the five-attempt limit was exhausted. The target operator automatically cancelled the transfer operation.
E_tooManyOptions	10030	Signifies that too many or incompatible arguments were passed. The error text will clearly indicate the nature of the problem.
E_transferAborted	30200	Signifies that a custody-transfer request will not succeed.
E_unrecognizedVersion	10040	Signifies that the value of the generic attribute passed is unsupported by the operator instance being queried.
E_unknownUser	10150	Signifies that the user-ID-and-password pair passed in a get_authToken message is not known to the operator site or is not valid.
E_unsupported	10050	Signifies that the implementer does not support a feature or API.
E_userMismatch	10140	Signifies that an attempt was made to use the publishing API to change data that is controlled by another party.

Table 8–3 Standard UDDI Error Codes (Continued)

Error Code	Error Number	Description
E_valueNotAllowed	20210	Signifies that a value did not pass validation because of contextual problems. The value may be valid in some contexts, but not in the context used. The error text may contain information about the contextual problem.
E_unvalidatable	20220	Signifies that an attempt was made to refer to a taxonomy or identifier system in a keyedReference whose tModel is categorized with the unvalidatable categorization.

A UDDI registry is required to report only the first error it encounters, so if a message has multiple errors it might take several attempts before you know about all of them. Some UDDI implementations may report all of the errors in a single message, but this behavior is not required.

In addition to being used for fault messages the dispositionReport element is also used as the return data structure for a successful delete operation, in which case the error code is "E_success". This topic is covered in more detail in Section 8.1.3: Delete Operations.

8.3 Wrapping Up

The UDDI Inquiry and Publishing APIs provide a nice interface for perusing and modifying data in the database, but the amount of use you'll get out of these interfaces is pretty limited. That's because searching and publishing information in a UDDI registry is not something you'll do very often. When you create a new Web service, you may choose to list it in a public or private UDDI registry, at which time you'll use the Publishing API. You may need to update entries from time to time, but for the most part they'll be static.

When you need to peruse a public or private UDDI registry to find out more about a business partner or some freely available Web service, you'll use the Inquiry API—but those occasions will come along pretty seldom as well. Finding out the details about another Web service is pretty much a one-time deal (unless the interface or endpoint changes). You look it up once, save the tModel, and build or generate your interface to the Web service.

It's likely that these APIs will be used by tools and not directly by Web services developers. UDDI browsers seem the most likely type of software to use the UDDI

SOAP operations. A UDDI browser might provide you with a GUI interface that allows you to navigate a UDDI registry easily. The UBR UDDI operator sites are already required to provide a Web interface, but these are a bit difficult to use and tend to be slow. Many of the UDDI registry products offer graphical user interfaces that allow you to query and publish information to a UDDI registry.

Part IV

JAX-RPC

Everything you have learned so far in this book has led to this part, on JAX-RPC. To master JAX-RPC you'll need to build on what you learned about XML, WSDL, and SOAP. If, however, you're just trying to get started by learning as little as possible, then you're in luck. You can develop very basic Web services using JAX-RPC with little or no knowledge about underlying Web services technologies.

The quickest way to get started with JAX-RPC is to read Chapter 9, which is an overview of the entire JAX-RPC platform. It will help you decide which chapters you should read from this part of the book. You don't need to read all of Part IV to start developing Web services. After reading Chapter 9, you'll probably want to read Chapter 10 and Section 12.1, which cover JAX-RPC service endpoints and generated stubs respectively. These are the programming models that you are most likely to use to develop basic Web service clients and services. The rest of the material in this part of the book covers intermediate and advanced topics that are important to developing a well-rounded understanding of JAX-RPC.

While Part IV provides extensive coverage of the JAX-RPC programming APIs, it doesn't cover deployment descriptors and packaging, which are essential to J2EE development. Deployment considerations are pretty complex in their own right and are covered in detail in Part VII: Deployment. You'll need to read and understand at least some of Part VII to be able to deploy J2EE Web Services clients and services.

There is one JAX-RPC topic not covered by this book: extensible type mappings. An extensible type mapping is a mechanism for defining custom translations between XML and Java. The supporting mechanism is not clearly defined and is always implemented in a vendor-specific manner. It's simply not possible to cover this topic without covering all vendors, and that isn't practical. For more information on implementing extensible type mappings, see your J2EE product documentation, as it will usually be the best guide to vendor-specific features.

In This Part

Related Appendices

Chapter 9

JAX-RPC Overview

The fundamental purpose of JAX-RPC is to make communications between Java and non-Java platforms easier, first by using BP-conformant Web service technologies like XML, SOAP, and WSDL, and then by providing a simple object-oriented API that Java developers can use to communicate using those technologies. You can use JAX-RPC to access Web services that run in non-Java environments. For example, you might use JAX-RPC to access a Web service that another department or organization has written in C++. You can also use JAX-RPC to host your own Web service endpoints on a J2EE application server, so that non-Java client applications can access your services. JAX-RPC is designed as a Java API for Web services, so that J2EE applications can interoperate with non-Java applications.

JAX-RPC is the very soul of J2EE Web Services. It defines the standard programming model for both Web service clients and endpoints in J2EE. There are essentially two sides to the JAX-RPC model: client-side and server-side. The **client-side programming model** allows you to access a remote Web service as if it were a local object, using methods that represent SOAP operations. The **server-side programming model** allows you to develop Web service endpoints as Java objects or Enterprise JavaBeans, which run on the J2EE platform.

JAX-RPC 1.1 vendors must support SOAP 1.1 clients and endpoints and the WS-I Basic Profile 1.0. They are required to support RPC/Literal and Document/Literal messaging modes, and both One-Way and Request/Response operation styles, using HTTP. These are the messaging styles and modes that conform to the Basic Profile.

In addition to the BP-conformant Web services technologies, JAX-RPC vendors are required to support RPC/Encoded messaging and SOAP with Attachments. RPC/

Encoded messaging is covered in Appendix D, and SwA is covered in Appendices E, F, and G. Vendors have the option to support protocols other than HTTP, such as SMTP, but this book doesn't cover other protocols because they are not clearly specified, or even supported by most products at this time.

JAX-RPC covers a lot of territory, which is why Part IV is the largest part of this book. The purpose of this chapter is to provide you with a 10,000-foot view of JAX-RPC to help decide which of its many features you should study now, and which ones you can learn about later.

9.1 The Server-Side Programming Models

JAX-RPC defines two server-side programming models for creating J2EE Web service endpoints: **JAX-RPC service endpoints** and **EJB endpoints.** A JAX-RPC service endpoint is the simplest type of endpoint to develop and will be the one you use the most. EJB endpoints allow stateless EJBs to act as endpoints. EJB endpoints are valuable if you want to expose existing EJBs to Web service clients, or need to exploit the transactional qualities of Enterprise JavaBeans.

9.1.1 JAX-RPC Service Endpoint

A JAX-RPC service endpoint (JSE) is easy to develop because it's just a plain old Java object—sort of. In fact, it's a lot more than that, but on the surface it seems that simple. In reality, a JSE is a full-fledged J2EE component, which runs inside the J2EE Servlets container system. It has access to the same resources and contexts as a standard servlet, but instead of exposing HTTP streams, it marshals SOAP messages into method invocations defined by a remote interface.

As an example, we can implement the BookQuote Web service as a JSE very easily. The following code shows a static version that always returns the same price—we'll beef it up with database access later, in Chapter 10. A JSE is composed of two parts: an implementation class that does all the work, and a `java.rmi.Remote` interface, called the **endpoint interface,** that declares the Web service's publicly accessible methods. Listing 9–1 shows the endpoint interface, and Listing 9–2 shows the implementation class.

Listing 9–1

An Endpoint Interface

```
public interface BookQuote extends java.rmi.Remote {
    public float getBookPrice(String isbn)
     throws java.rmi.RemoteException;
}
```

Listing 9–2

The Implementation Object

```
public class BookQuote_Impl_1 implements BookQuote {

    // Given the ISBN of a book, get its wholesale price.
    public float getBookPrice(String isbn){
        return 24.99f;
    }
}
```

Once you have defined the endpoint interface and implementation objects, you can use them, along with other deployment files, to generate a WSDL document that provides a platform-independent description of the JSE. JSEs are covered in depth in Chapter 10.

9.1.2 Enterprise JavaBeans Endpoints

Because JAX-RPC is used to invoke methods on remote services, it seems natural to use it to access EJBs, which are already accessible via Java RMI-IIOP and proprietary flavors of Java RMI. Using JAX-RPC to talk to EJBs implies that EJBs can act as Web service endpoints, and they can—at least, stateless session beans can. Because SOAP is a stateless messaging protocol, only stateless session beans can act as EJB endpoints. SOAP has no notion of object identity, so it can't be used with stateful session beans or entity beans.

The J2EE Web service specification defines a new Web service endpoint interface for stateless session beans that is on a par with the remote and local interfaces already used by enterprise beans. Unlike the remote and local interfaces already familiar to EJB developers, though, the endpoint interface does not extend an EJB object type—that is, an `EJBObject` or `EJBLocalObject`. Instead, the endpoint interface extends the `javax.ejb.Remote` interface directly. The EJB endpoint interface follows basically the same rules as the JSE endpoint interface. In fact, an EJB endpoint could easily implement the `BookQuote` interface to a JSE that you saw in Listing 9–1:

```
public interface BookQuote extends java.rmi.Remote {
    public float getBookPrice(String isbn)
     throws java.rmi.RemoteException;
}
```

In addition to the endpoint interface, you'll need to define the stateless session bean that implements the interface, as in Listing 9–3.

Listing 9–3

An EJB Endpoint's Stateless Session Bean

```
public class BookPriceWS implements javax.ejb.SessionBean, BookQuote  {
     public void setSessionContext(javax.ejb.SessionContext ctx){}
     public void ejbCreate(){}

     public float getBookPrice(String isbn){
        return 24.99f;
     }

     public void ejbRemove(){}
     public void ejbActivate(){}
     public void ejbPassivate(){}
}
```

For now, the `getBookPrice()` method returns a literal value. This example is expanded in Chapter 11 to use JDBC to get the price from a database.

EJB endpoints do not require a corresponding home interface. SOAP doesn't specify support for pass-by-reference, so you can't ask one Web service interface (a home interface) to pass you a reference to another (a remote interface). Furthermore, you can't create or remove a Web service. For these reasons a home interface is unnecessary.

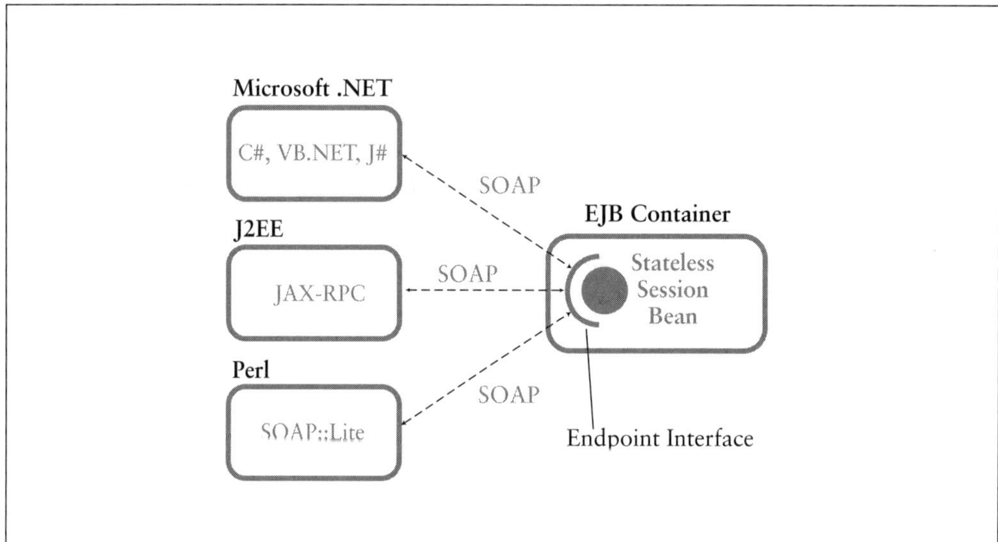

Figure 9–1 Using SOAP to Access a Stateless Session Bean

When developing a Web service as a stateless session bean, you'll define the endpoint interface first, then use it along with other deployment descriptors to generate the WSDL document. The WSDL document can be read and used by other Web service platforms to access the EJB endpoint (see Figure 9–1). EJB endpoints are covered in detail in Chapter 11.

9.2 The Client-Side Programming Models

The JAX-RPC client-side programming models can be used by Java applications, servlets, JSPs, JAX-RPC service endpoints (JSEs), and EJBs to exchange SOAP messages with remote Web service endpoints on any platform. JAX-RPC defines three client-programming models: **generated stub, dynamic proxy,** and **DII** (Dynamic Invocation Interface). While all three are available for you to use, you're most likely to use generated stubs in your work.

9.2.1 Generated Stubs

For a client to use JAX-RPC to access a Web service endpoint, the endpoint must publish a WSDL document. The JAX-RPC compiler, which is provided by your J2EE vendor, generates Java remote interfaces and stubs that implement the endpoint operations described by the WSDL document. Once the stubs and interfaces are generated, you can bind them to the JNDI ENC (Environment Naming Context) of any J2EE component and use them to communicate with the endpoint. In this model, the stubs are generated at deployment time (see Figure 9–2).

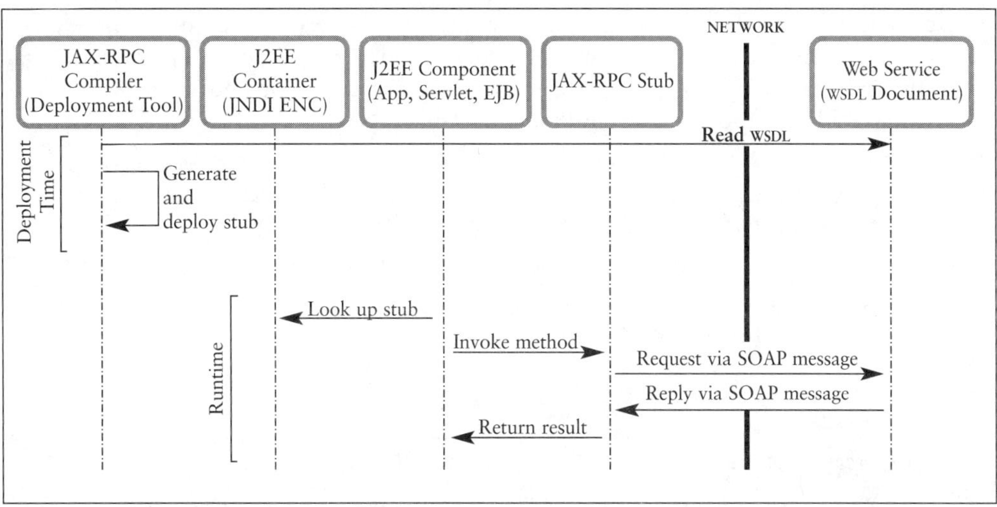

Figure 9–2 JAX-RPC Stub Generation Sequence Diagram

WSDL describes the interfaces to Web service endpoints using `portType` definitions; each `portType` may have one or more `operation` elements. WSDL `portType` and `operation` elements are analogous to Java interfaces and methods, respectively. In fact, JAX-RPC defines a mapping between WSDL and Java that generates remote interfaces from ports, with methods that correspond to port operations. For example, a WSDL document might describe a port called `BookQuote` with a single operation called `getBookPrice` as shown in Listing 9–4.

Listing 9–4

WSDL `portType` *and* `message` *Definitions*

```
<message name="getBookPrice">
  <part name="string" type="xsd:string"/>
</message>
<message name="getBookPriceResponse">
  <part name="result" type="xsd:float"/>
</message>
<portType name="BookQuote">
  <operation name="getBookPrice">
    <input name="isbn" message="mh:getBookPrice"/>
    <output message="mh:getBookPriceResponse"/>
  </operation>
</portType>
```

At deployment time a JAX-RPC compiler converts the WSDL `portType` into a corresponding remote interface—the endpoint interface. The JAX-RPC compiler also generates a stub that implements the endpoint interface according to the `port` and `binding` definitions. It can also create a factory for accessing the stub that conforms to the WSDL `service` definition. The endpoint and service interfaces would look like those in Listings 9–5 and 9–6.

Listing 9–5

An Endpoint Interface Generated by the JAX-RPC Compiler

```
public interface BookQuote extends java.rmi.Remote {
    public float getBookPrice(String isbn)
     throws java.rmi.RemoteException;
}
```

Listing 9–6

A Service Interface Generated by the JAX-RPC Compiler

```
public interface BookQuoteService extends javax.xml.rpc.Service{
    public BookQuote getBookQuotePort( ) throws java.rmi.RemoteException;
}
```

Once the endpoint interface and stub have been generated, they can be used at runtime to invoke operations on the Web service endpoint. The code fragment shown in Listing 9–7 demonstrates how a J2EE component such as a servlet, application client, or EJB uses a JAX-RPC generated stub to get the wholesale price of a book from a .NET Web service.

Listing 9–7

Using a Generated Stub in a J2EE Component

```
InitialContext jndiContext = new InitialContext ( );

BookQuoteService service = (BookQuoteService)
              jndiContext.lookup("java:comp/env/service/BookQuoteService");
BookQuote bookQuote = service.getBookQuotePort();

float price = bookQuote.getBookPrice( isbn );
```

When the `getBookPrice()` method is invoked, the JAX-RPC stub sends a SOAP message to the Web service endpoint, in this case a .NET program. The .NET endpoint then processes the SOAP message and sends a response back to the stub. The stub extracts the result from the SOAP message and returns it to the client (see Figure 9–3).

The generated stubs can include methods with primitive argument types like `int` and `long`, primitive wrappers like `java.lang.Integer` and `java.lang.Long`, arrays, a few standard Java types such as `String` and `Date`, custom object types,

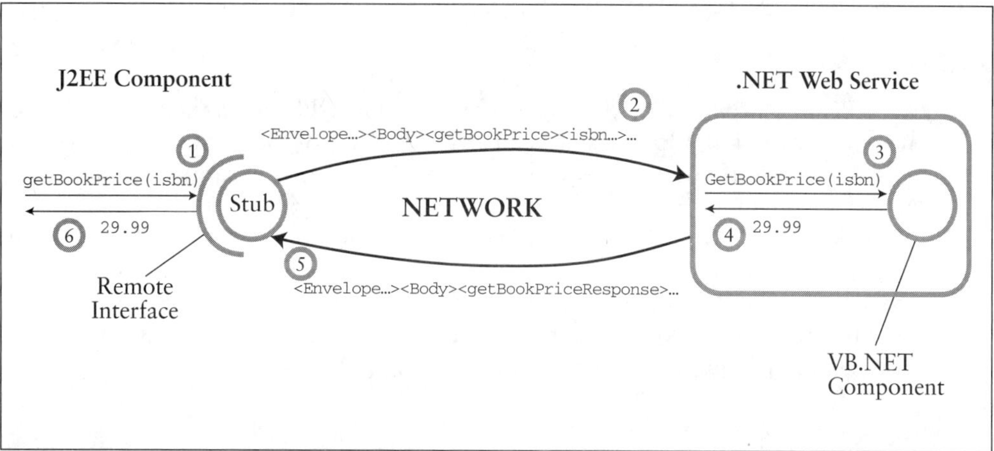

Figure 9–3 JAX-RPC Invocation Loop

and special **holder types.** Holder types allow the JAX-RPC stubs to model INOUT and OUT parameter modes. Generated stubs are addressed in detail in Section 12.1.

9.2.2 Dynamic Proxies

In addition to generated stubs, JAX-RPC also supports **dynamic proxies.** A dynamic proxy is used in the same way as a generated stub, except the remote interface's stub implementation is generated dynamically, at runtime. If you're familiar with the Proxy architecture of the Java Reflection API, then dynamic JAX-RPC will make sense to you. The code fragment shown in Listing 9–8 demonstrates how a J2EE component such as a servlet, application client, or EJB uses a JAX-RPC dynamic proxy to get the wholesale price of a book from some Web service.

Listing 9–8

Using a Dynamic Proxy in a J2EE Component

```
InitialContext jndiContext = new InitialContext ( );

BookQuoteService service = (BookQuoteService)
                 jndiContext.lookup("java:comp/env/service/DynamicService");
BookQuote BookQuote_port = (BookQuote)service.getPort(BookQuote.class);

float price = BookQuote_port.getBookPrice( isbn );
```

At runtime the `getPort()` method automatically maps the `BookQuote` interface to a corresponding `port` definition in the WSDL document, then generates a stub for the interface that implements the protocol defined by the associated `binding`. Dynamic proxies are covered in Section 12.2: Dynamic Proxies.

9.2.3 DII

JAX-RPC also provides another, even more dynamic API, called the Dynamic Invocation Interface. DII allows the developer to assemble SOAP method calls dynamically at runtime. If you have used the CORBA Dynamic Invocation Interface, then JAX-RPC DII will be a familiar concept.

JAX-RPC DII is kind of like Java Reflection. It enables you to get a reference to an object that represents a Web service operation, in the form of a method, and to invoke that method without having to use a stub or a remote interface. For example, the following fragment of code demonstrates how a J2EE component uses JAX-RPC DII to get the wholesale price of a book from some Web service.

```
InitialContext jndiContext = new InitialContext ( );
javax.xml.rpc.Service service =  (javax.xml.rpc.Service)
```

```
        jndiContext.lookup("java:comp/env/service/DynamicService");

QName port = new QName("http://www.xyz.com/BookQuote ","BookQuote");
QName operation = new QName("http://www.xyz.com/BookQuote","getBookPrice");

Call callObject = service.createCall(port, operation);

Object []  parameters = new Object[1];
parameters[0] = isbn;

Float price = (Float) callObject.invoke( parameters );
```

You can actually configure—at runtime—the parameters, invocation style, encoding, and so on. Everything you can configure statically with WSDL you can configure dynamically with DII.

DII is covered in detail in Section 12.3. While it is certainly useful for self-organizing systems and IDEs, the majority of J2EE developers will use generated stubs for access to Web services. In most cases, you will know in advance the Web service endpoints and specific operations you will be accessing, so the DII will not be necessary.

9.3 Other JAX-RPC Topics Covered

Message handlers are an important extension of JAX-RPC. They allow you to manipulate SOAP header blocks as they flow in and out of JAX-RPC endpoint and client applications. Handlers are covered in detail in Chapter 14: Message Handlers.

One of the primary goals of the JAX-RPC specification is to define **mappings** from WSDL and XML to Java. Specifically, it details how Java endpoint interfaces used by JAX-RPC Web services are converted into WSDL and how WSDL documents are converted into JAX-RPC generated stubs and dynamic proxies. It also details how method calls to JAX-RPC client APIs—generated stubs, dynamic proxies, and DII—are converted into SOAP messages, and how SOAP messages are mapped to JAX-RPC service endpoint and EJB endpoint methods. The client and Web service programming models hide most of these mapping details, but there are caveats to these mappings that you will need to know about. Chapter 15 provides a detailed explanation of all these mappings.

JAX-RPC vendors must also support **SOAP Messaging with Attachments**. Actually, using JAX-RPC to send and receive SwA messages can be extremely simple, provided the vendor provides decent support for the Java Activation Framework. SwA messaging with JAX-RPC is covered in detail in Appendix G: JAX-RPC and SwA.

9.4 SAAJ

SAAJ (SOAP with Attachments API for Java) is used for constructing and manipulating SOAP messages. It's especially important for you to have a good working knowledge of SAAJ because it plays an important role in JAX-RPC—and can be used independently of JAX-RPC as well. Chapter 13 covers the basics of parsing and constructing SOAP messages using SAAJ 1.2. You should understand the basic structure of a SOAP message, covered in Chapter 4, before reading Chapter 13.

SAAJ is based on the W3C Note *SOAP Messages with Attachments*, which is covered in Appendix E: SOAP Messages with Attachments. SAAJ support for SwA is covered in Appendix F. Appendices E, F, and G are considered optional, because SwA is not sanctioned by the BP.

9.5 Wrapping Up

This overview has provided you with a 10,000-foot view of JAX-RPC so that you can get a handle on what it is, and on the different programming models it defines. The next six chapters will go into detail about the programming models, message handlers, SAAJ, and the mappings from WSDL and XML to Java. You don't need to read every chapter in this part of the book unless you want to understand all the capabilities of JAX-RPC. Simply pick a topic that's of interest and go from there. I do recommend, though, that you read Chapter 10: JAX-RPC Service Endpoints and Section 12.1: Generated Stubs, because these are the programming models you are most likely to use when you first start developing JAX-RPC solutions.

Chapter 10

JAX-RPC Service Endpoints

A JAX-RPC service endpoint (JSE) is the simplest way to create a Web service in J2EE. In fact, it's so simple to create basic endpoints with JSEs that you will probably be reluctant to try anything else. Of course, there is a lot more to JAX-RPC than JSEs, but this chapter will give you enough information to get up and running with your first Web service.

10.1 A Simple JSE Example

Writing the code for a JSE is extremely simple. To create a JSE all you do is define an **endpoint interface** and an **implementation class.** An endpoint interface defines each of the Web service operations that your JSE will support in the form of a Java method. The implementation class implements these **endpoint methods.** For example, Listing 10–1 shows an endpoint interface for the BookQuote Web service. It defines a single method, `getBookPrice()`, and thus a single Web service operation.

Listing 10–1

An Endpoint Interface

```
package com.jwsbook.jaxrpc;

public interface BookQuote extends java.rmi.Remote {
  public float getBookPrice(String isbn) throws java.rmi.RemoteException;
}
```

The endpoint interface defines the Web service operations that will be publicly accessible—in other words, the operations that Web service clients can access using SOAP. The endpoint interface is required to extend (directly or indirectly) the `java.rmi.Remote` interface and to throw the `java.rmi.RemoteException` type from all of its methods.

In addition to the endpoint interface you must define the class that implements the endpoint methods. The implementation class will be instantiated and run inside the J2EE server. For example, the `BookQuote_Impl_1` class in Listing 10–2 implements the `BookQuote` endpoint interface, and will serve as the Web service at runtime.

Listing 10–2

An Implementation Class

```
package com.jwsbook.jaxrpc;

public class BookQuote_Impl_1 implements BookQuote {
  // Given the ISBN of a book, get its wholesale price.
  public float getBookPrice(String isbn){
      return 24.99f;
  }
}
```

In this example, `BookQuote_Impl_1` is a very simple class, which always returns the same value. Later in this chapter we will add JDBC logic that will dynamically access a relational database to fetch the correct wholesale price for a specific ISBN number.

Once you have defined the endpoint interface and its implementation class, you are ready to deploy the JSE into your J2EE server. Most J2EE servers will provide you with GUIs or command-line utilities for doing this work; some will require you to create your own deployment descriptor files.

To run the `BookQuote` example and the rest of the examples in this book, you'll need to have a J2EE platform installed, the proper classpaths set up, and supporting services. Creating WAR files and deployment descriptors for JSEs is a lot more involved than defining the endpoint interface and the implementation class. Although general packaging and deployment descriptors are covered in Part VII, you will need to consult your vendor's documentation on setup, configuration, and administration.

10.2 The JSE Runtime Environment

JSEs are deployed into a J2EE servlet container, and have access to the same resources and context information a servlet has. When a JSE is deployed, it is embedded in a special JAX-RPC servlet provided by the vendor, which is responsible for responding to HTTP-based SOAP requests, parsing the SOAP messages, and invoking the corresponding methods of the JSE implementation object. When the JSE returns a value from the method invocation, the JAX-RPC servlet creates a SOAP message to hold the return value (or a SOAP fault if an exception is thrown) and sends that SOAP message back to the requesting client via an HTTP reply message. Figure 10–1 illustrates how a JAX-RPC servlet receives and delegates SOAP calls to a JSE.

Invoking a JSE Web service as illustrated in Figure 10–1 proceeds as follows:

1. A Web services client sends a SOAP 1.1 request message over HTTP 1.1 to an endpoint URL that is hosted by the J2EE application server.
2. A JAX-RPC servlet receives the SOAP message and marshals it into a method call on the JSE object.
3. The JSE processes the request and returns the result to the JAX-RPC servlet.
4. The JAX-RPC servlet converts the return value (or exception) into a SOAP message and sends it back to the client in the HTTP reply.

Vendors may generate special JAX-RPC servlets for each JSE, or multiplex all requests over a few general-purpose JAX-RPC servlets. The exact mechanics of the JAX-RPC servlet are not specified; vendors provide their own proprietary JAX-RPC servlets. That's OK, because you'll never deal directly with the JAX-RPC servlet anyway.

Because the JSE is embedded in a servlet, it can access the same resources the servlet can, via the JNDI Environment Naming Context (ENC). JSEs can access JDBC drivers, JMS providers, EJBs, J2EE connectors, other Web services, environment variables, the `ServletContext`, the `HttpSession`, and anything else a

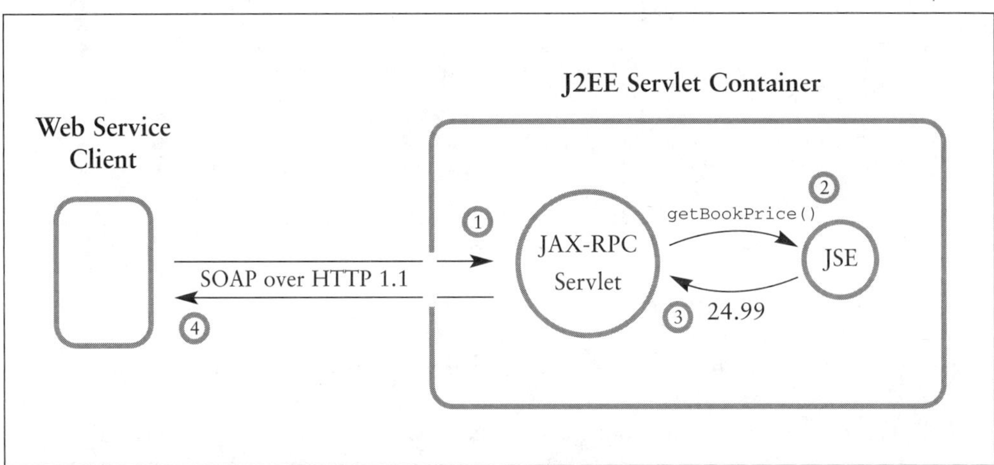

Figure 10–1 A JAX-RPC Servlet Delegates to a JSE

servlet can access. In addition, the JSE is allowed access to the actual SOAP message to which it's responding—which can be useful for examining header blocks and other information that is not explicitly passed as method parameters.

10.2.1 Servlets: The Foundation of JSE

The JAX-RPC service endpoint is built on the servlet programming model. Servlets have been evolving and improving since 1997. They have proven to be robust and efficient server-side components for processing HTTP requests for Web pages and, more recently, for Web service endpoints. One of the reasons servlets have been so successful is that, on the surface, they are extremely simple. When a Web browser makes a request for a Web page, it sends an HTTP GET (in most cases) to the servlet container system. The servlet container system picks an instance of the appropriate servlet to handle the HTTP request. The servlet instance is given an input stream representing the request and an output stream to send back a response to the browser. For example, the `HelloWorldServlet` (Listing 10–3) is designed to return a Web page that says, "Hello World!" At deployment time, it's assigned to handle all requests to the Web page address http://www.monson-haefel.com/jwsbook/helloworld.html.

Listing 10–3

A Simple Servlet

```
package com.jwsbook.jaxrpc;

import javax.servlet.http.*;
import javax.servlet.*;

public class HelloWorldServlet extends javax.servlet.http.HttpServlet {
  protected void doGet(HttpServletRequest req,
                       HttpServletResponse resp)
  throws ServletException,java.io.IOException {

    java.io.Writer outStream = resp.getWriter();
    outStream.write("<html><body>Hello World!</body></html>");
  }
}
```

This is a really basic servlet that illustrates the simplicity and elegance of the servlet programming model. It's possible to create far more complex servlets that can obtain more information from the calling browser and send far more sophisticated content back, but even those advanced capabilities build on the simple programming model illustrated in Listing 10–3. In a nutshell, servlets focus on processing HTTP requests as input and output streams.

When servlets were first introduced back in 1997, it was a fairly radical approach to a problem that had traditionally been solved using CGI (Common Gateway Interface). As servlets increased in popularity and attracted a broader audience, Sun decided to make things a little easier for less sophisticated developers by introducing JavaServer Pages (JSPs), which combine HTML with specialized tags and Java code. While JSPs today are perhaps more popular than servlets, it's important to understand that JSPs are in fact servlets. The only difference is the source code. To develop servlets, you create Java source files. To develop JSPs, you write everything in HTML and JSP tags—which is then compiled into a servlet. When you're talking about servlets and JSP, you are really talking about the same thing.

This is also true of JAX-RPC service endpoints. On the surface they look like a whole new type of component, and officially they are—but under the covers, JSEs are built on the servlet programming model.

10.2.2 JNDI Environment Naming Context

All J2EE components, including servlets, and therefore JSEs, have access to a private set of environment variables and resources using **JNDI** (Java Naming and Directory Interface). JNDI is usually used for access to a naming or directory service. A naming service binds objects or resources to names. A typical example of a naming service is DNS (Domain Name System), which maintains a distributed database that maps Internet domain names to IP addresses—you use DNS every time you look up a Web page with your browser. A directory service also binds names to objects or resources and can organize bindings into a directory structure analogous to the directory structure used by your file system. Examples of directory systems include LDAP (Lightweight Directory Access Protocol) and its more complex ancestor X.500.

J2EE defines a very simple directory service, called the **JNDI Environment Naming Context (JNDI ENC)**, which allows developers to bind resources (JDBC and JMS connection factories, for example), enterprise beans, Web service endpoints, and environment variables into a directory structure. The JNDI ENC is frequently used to gain access to a JDBC connection, so data can be read from and and written to a relational database. For example, in Listing 10–4 we beef up the `BookQuote` JSE implementation class by adding code that uses the JNDI ENC to obtain a JDBC connection, then using that connection to fetch the wholesale price of a book from a database.

Listing 10–4

A JSE Using the JNDI ENC to Get a JDBC Connection

```
package com.jwsbook.jaxrpc;

public class BookQuote_Impl_2 implements BookQuote {
  public float getBookPrice(String isbn){
    java.sql.Connection jdbcConnection = null;
```

```
    java.sql.Statement sqlStatement = null;
    java.sql.ResultSet resultSet;
    try {
      javax.naming.InitialContext jndiEnc =
                                 new javax.naming.InitialContext();
      javax.sql.DataSource dataSource = (javax.sql.DataSource)
                  jndiEnc.lookup("java:comp/env/jdbc/DataSource");
      jdbcConnection = dataSource.getConnection();
      sqlStatement = jdbcConnection.createStatement();
      resultSet = sqlStatement.executeQuery(
        "SELECT wholesale FROM CATALOG WHERE isbn = \'"+isbn+"\'");

      if(resultSet.next()){
        float price = resultSet.getFloat("wholesale");
        return price;
      }
      return 0;// zero means it's not stocked.
    }catch (java.sql.SQLException se) {
      throw new RuntimeException("JDBC access failed");
    }catch (javax.naming.NamingException ne){
      throw new RuntimeException("JNDI ENC access failed");
    }
  }
}
```

The JNDI ENC is a standard service available to all J2EE components, but each component has a unique view of the service. A component may access its own view of the JNDI ENC, but not the view of any other component. Every component's view of the JNDI ENC is fixed at deployment time and is immutable, which means that it's read-only. You cannot insert, remove, or modifiy values in the JNDI ENC at runtime.

The `InitialContext` object represents the root of the JNDI ENC hierarchy. When a JSE creates a new `InitialContext`, the servlet container automatically intervenes—under the covers—to return the root of the JNDI ENC for that JSE component. Every JSE, just like every servlet, has its own view of the JNDI ENC, which you configure before deploying the JSE. The following snippet from Listing 10–4 shows how the JNDI `InitialContext` object is created.

```
javax.naming.InitialContext jndiEnc =
                           new javax.naming.InitialContext();
```

The `InitialContext` defines an abundance of methods for perusing subcontexts (subdirectories), binding objects to subcontexts, and creating and removing subcontexts. Most of these methods will not work on the JNDI ENC itself, however, because the JSE's view of the JNDI ENC is immutable. The JSE cannot modify it in any way. In most cases the only method of `InitialContext` you are likely to use is the `lookup()` method, which takes a directory path as its only argument and returns whatever object is bound to that path. The following snippet from Listing 10–4 shows how the JSE invokes `lookup()` to obtain a reference to a JDBC `DataSource`.

```
javax.sql.DataSource ds = (javax.sql.DataSource)
                    jndiEnc.lookup("java:comp/env/jdbc/DataSource");
```

Resources like the JDBC `DataSource` in the previous example are bound to names that you declare in the deployment descriptor of the JSE. The root context of the JNDI ENC is always `"java:comp/env"`, but you can define any path relative to the root context you want. For example, you could have bound the JDBC `DataSource` to `"java:comp/env/mydirectory/database/BookDatabase"`. There are, however, naming conventions that most J2EE projects follow: JDBC `DataSource` objects are placed under the `"/jdbc"` subcontext; references to EJB objects are placed under the `"/ejb"` subcontext; JavaMail uses the `"/mail"` subcontext; JMS uses the `"/jms"` subcontext; and Web services use the `"/services"` subcontext. At the end of a directory path is the name that you assign to the object being referred to. There are no conventions for that name, except that it should be descriptive. This book tends to use names that describe the type of object being returned or the identity of the resource—for example, `DataSource` for a JDBC `DataSource`.

In the preceding example, the JSE uses the JNDI ENC to gain access to a JDBC `DataSource` object, which is a factory for creating JDBC connections, as shown in this snippet from Listing 10–4:

```
javax.sql.DataSource dataSource = (javax.sql.DataSource)
                    jndiEnc.lookup("java:comp/env/jdbc/DataSource");
jdbcConnection = dataSource.getConnection();
```

Looking up a resource factory and then using it to obtain resource connections is the normal pattern when using the JNDI ENC. For example, you can use the JNDI ENC to obtain a JMS `ConnectionFactory`, a JavaMail `Session`, or a J2EE `ConnectionFactory`. See Listings 10–5 through 10–7.

Listing 10–5

Using the JNDI ENC to Access a JMS `ConnectionFactory`

```
javax.naming.InitialContext jndiEnc = new javax.naming.InitialContext();
javax.jms.ConnectionFactory conFactory =(javax.jms.ConnectionFactory)
  jndiEnc.lookup("java:comp/env/jms/ConnectionFactory");
javax.jms.Connection connection =
  conFactory.createConnection(username,password);
```

Listing 10–6

Using the JNDI ENC for Access to a JavaMail `Session` *Object*

```
javax.naming.InitialContext jndiEnc = new javax.naming.InitialContext();
javax.mail.Session session = (javax.mail.Session)
  jndiEnc.lookup("java:comp/env/mail/Session");
javax.mail.internet.MimeMessage email = new
  javax.mail.internet.MimeMessage(session);
```

Listing 10–7

Using the JNDI ENC for Access to an Arbitrary J2EE Connector

```
javax.naming.InitialContext jndiEnc = new javax.naming.InitialContext();
javax.resource.cci.ConnectionFactory factory =
 (javax.resource.cci.ConnectionFactory)
   jndiEnc.lookup("java:comp/env/connector/VendorX");
javax.resource.cci.Connection con = factory.getConnection();
```

You can also use the JNDI ENC to access EJBs. For example, instead of using JDBC to access the database directly, you might use a Book EJB, an entity bean that represents an individual book in the database. Listing 10–8 shows how the BookQuote JSE would access the Book EJB to get the wholesale price and return it to the requester.

Listing 10–8

A JSE Implementation Object Using EJB

```
package com.jwsbook.jaxrpc;
import  jwsed1.support.BookLocal;
import  jwsed1.support.BookHomeLocal;

public class BookQuote_Impl_3 implements BookQuote {
  public float getBookPrice(String isbn){
    try {
      javax.naming.InitialContext jndiEnc =
                     new javax.naming.InitialContext();
      BookHomeLocal bookHome =(BookHomeLocal)
                     jndiEnc.lookup("java:comp/env/ejb/BookHomeLocal");
      BookLocal book = bookHome.findByPrimaryKey(isbn);
      return book.getWholesalePrice();
    }catch(javax.naming.NamingException ne){
      throw new RuntimeException("JNDI ENC access failed");
    }catch(java.rmi.RemoteException re){
```

```
            throw new RuntimeException("Problem invoking operation on Book EJB");
        }catch(javax.ejb.FinderException fe){
            throw new RuntimeException("Cannot find Book EJB");
        }
    }
}
```

You can also use the JNDI ENC to access other Web services via the JAX-RPC programming model. For example, the `BookQuote` JSE might obtain the pricing information from a legacy system such as CICS or IMS by way of some other Web service written in some other programming language. Listing 10–9 illustrates.

Listing 10–9

A JSE Implementation Object Using JAX-RPC Generated Stubs

```
package com.jwsbook.jaxrpc;
import jwsed1.support.CatalogPort;
import jwsed1.support.ImsCatalogService;

public class BookQuote_Impl_4 implements BookQuote {
  public float getBookPrice(String isbn){
    try {
      javax.naming.InitialContext jndiEnc = new javax.naming.InitialContext();
      ImsCatalogService webService =(ImsCatalogService)
              jndiEnc.lookup("java:comp/env/service/ImsCatalogService");
      CatalogPort catalog = webService.getCatalogPort();
      return catalog.getWholesalePrice(isbn);
    }catch (javax.xml.rpc.ServiceException se) {
            throw new RuntimeException("JAX-RPC ServiceException thrown");
    }catch (javax.xml.rpc.JAXRPCException je) {
            throw new RuntimeException("JAXRPCException thrown");
    }catch (java.rmi.RemoteException re){
            throw new RuntimeException("RemoteException thrown");
    }catch (javax.naming.NamingException ne){
            throw new RuntimeException("NamingException thrown");
    }
  }
}
```

The `ImsCatalogService` and `CatalogPort` interfaces and the code that implements them are generated at deployment time by the J2EE vendor's JAX-RPC toolkit. This is a hypothetical example that I won't elaborate on. The steps for creating JAX-

RPC generated stubs like this one are discussed in detail in Section 12.1: Generated Stubs.

A JSE can also access environment variables from the JNDI ENC. Environment variables are static; they cannot be changed. They can be of any Java primitive wrapper type (`Byte`, `Character`, `Short`, `Integer`, `Long`, `Float`, or `Double`) or a `String` value. Environment variables are often used for configuring variables used by a JSE. Listing 10–10 illustrates how the JNDI ENC can be used to obtain both numerical and `String` values.

Listing 10–10

Accessing Environment Variables from a JSE

```
javax.naming.InitialContext jndiEnc = new javax.naming.InitialContext();
Double maxValue = (Double)jndiEnc.lookup("java:comp/env/max_value");
Boolean flag = (Boolean)jndiEnc.lookup("java:comp/env/the_flag");
String name = (String)jndiEnc.lookup("java:comp/env/some_name");
```

You configure the JNDI ENC at deployment time, coding XML elements of the deployment descriptor to identify the resources, EJBs, Web services, and environment variables, and bind them to specific path names for a specific JSE. Part VII: Deployment describes in detail the deployment descriptors and the JNDI ENC, but Listing 10–11 illustrates how the declarations are defined in the deployment descriptor for a JSE.

Listing 10–11

A Deployment Descriptor for a JSE (Abbreviated)

```
<web-app>
  <display-name>BookQuoteJSE</display-name>
  ...
  <resource-ref>
    <res-ref-name>jdbc/BookDatabase</res-ref-name>
    <res-type>javax.sql.DataSource</res-type>
    <res-auth>Container</res-auth>
  </resource-ref>
  <env-entry>
    <env-entry-name>max_value</env-entry-name>
    <env-entry-type>java.lang.Double</env-entry-type>
    <env-entry-value>3929.22</env-entry-value>
  </env-entry>
  <ejb-local-ref>
    <ejb-ref-name>/ejb/BookHomeLocal</ejb-ref-name>
    <ejb-ref-type>Entity</ejb-ref-type>
```

```
        <local-home>jwsed1.support.BookHomeLocal</local-home>
        <local>jwsed1.support.BookLocal</local>
        <ejb-link>BookEJB</ejb-link>
    </ejb-local-ref>
    ...
</web-app>
```

When the JSE is deployed, the container will ensure that the resources, EJBs, and Web services declared in the deployment descriptor are live, working references. When you look up a JDBC `DataSource`, you will receive a live connection to a database. Similarly, when you look up an EJB or Web service, you will receive a working reference to an EJB or a Web service endpoint. The person who deploys the JSE into the J2EE application server is responsible for mapping the resource, EJB, and Web service references to actual resources, using tools provided by the J2EE vendor. In the case of a JDBC `DataSource`, for example, the deployer must map the `DataSource` object to an actual database using a specific JDBC driver.

Every J2EE vendor differs in the exact mechanics of how these mappings are achieved. In most cases, however, the vendor will provide ancillary configuration files (as BEA WebLogic does) or a graphical user interface (GUI) tool (as IBM WebSphere does).

10.2.3 The `ServletEndpointContext` and `ServiceLifecycle` Interfaces

In addition to the JNDI ENC there is another API that a JSE can use to interact with its environment, the `ServletEndpointContext`. This is an interface to the servlet container system itself. It provides the JSE with access to the underlying `ServletContext`, SOAP messages, and other information.

10.2.3.1 Using the Life-Cycle Methods `init()` *and* `destroy()`

To take advantage of the `ServletEndpointContext`, the JSE must implement the optional `javax.xml.rpc.server.ServiceLifecyle` interface, which defines two methods, as shown in Listing 10–12.

Listing 10–12

The `javax.xml.rpc.server.ServiceLifecycle` *Interface*

```
package javax.xml.rpc.server;
import javax.xml.rpc.ServiceException;

public interface ServiceLifecycle {
    public void init(Object context) throws ServiceException;
    public void destroy();
}
```

The init() method is called at the beginning of a JSE's life, just after it's instantiated by the container system, before it begins handling incoming SOAP requests. When the servlet container calls the init() method, the JSE is given a reference to its ServletEndpointContext. The servlet container calls the destroy() method at the end of the JSE's life, just before it is removed from service.

Depending on the J2EE vendor and the threading model used, a servlet container may use a single JSE instance to handle all incoming requests, or multiple instances—this subject is discussed in more detail in Section 10.3. When a new instance of a JSE is needed, one is instantiated and its init() method is called. The init() method is called only once in the life of a JSE instance. If the servlet container has more JSE instances than it needs for a particular Web service endpoint, it may choose to evict some of the instances from memory to conserve resources. Each JSE instance's destroy() method is called when the servlet container evicts it, when the JSE is removed from service, or when the J2EE server is shut down.

Because init() is called at the beginning of the JSE instance's life, and destroy() is called at the end, it makes sense to use these methods to obtain and release resources that will be used for the entire life of the instance. For example, instead of the JSE creating a new InitialContext and looking up the JDBC DataSource every time getBookPrice() is called, as in Listing 10–4, its init() method can create the InitialContext just once, and use it immediately to obtain a reference to the JDBC DataSource. The DataSource reference can then be held in an instance variable for the life of the JSE and reused as needed. Later, when the JSE instance is about to be removed from service, its destroy() method can release the DataSource by setting the reference to it to null. Listing 10–13 shows the BookQuote JSE implementing the ServiceLifecycle interface. It obtains its JDBC DataSource in init() and releases it in destroy(). In init() it also obtains a reference to its ServletEndpointContext.

Listing 10–13

A JSE Implementing the ServiceLifecycle *Interface*

```
package com.jwsbook.jaxrpc;
import javax.naming.InitialContext;
import javax.naming.NamingException;
import javax.xml.rpc.server.ServletEndpointContext;
import javax.xml.rpc.server.ServiceLifecycle;
import javax.xml.rpc.ServiceException;

public class BookQuote_Impl_5 implements BookQuote, ServiceLifecycle {
  javax.sql.DataSource dataSource;
  ServletEndpointContext endPtCntxt;

  public void init(Object context) throws ServiceException{
```

```java
    try{
      endPtCntxt = (ServletEndpointContext)context;
      InitialContext jndiEnc = new InitialContext();
      javax.sql.DataSource dataSource = (javax.sql.DataSource)
                          jndiEnc.lookup("java:comp/env/jdbc/BookDatabase");
    }catch(NamingException ne){
      throw new ServiceException("Cannot initialize JNDI ENC", ne);
    }
  }
  public float getBookPrice(String isbn){
    java.sql.Connection jdbcConnection = null;
    java.sql.Statement sqlStatement = null;
    java.sql.ResultSet resultSet;
    try {
      jdbcConnection = dataSource.getConnection();
      sqlStatement = jdbcConnection.createStatement();
      resultSet = sqlStatement.executeQuery(
        "SELECT wholesale FROM CATALOG WHERE isbn = \'"+isbn+"\'");

      if(resultSet.next()){
        float price = resultSet.getFloat("wholesale");
        return price;
      }
      return 0;// zero means it's not stocked.
    }catch (java.sql.SQLException se) {
      throw new RuntimeException("JDBC access failed");
    }
  }
  public void destroy( ){
    dataSource = null;
  }
}
```

In actual practice, you probably don't need to set the `DataSource` reference to `null` when you are done using it. The container should clean it up for you automatically. Setting the `DataSource` reference to `null` in this example demonstrates the basic purpose of the `destroy()` method: to release resources before the JSE instance is destroyed.

You may be asking yourself, "Why does the `init()` method declare the context parameter as an `Object` type and not a `ServletEndpointContext`?" Good question! The `ServiceLifecycle` interface is intended to be a general-purpose interface that can be used outside of J2EE and a servlet container system—it might be running in some other type of container. JAX-RPC defines the context parameter as an `Object` type, so the interface is compatible with other, unanticipated or proprietary, container systems. In J2EE Web services, however, the JAX-RPC service endpoint is the only kind of component that implements the `ServiceLifecycle` interface, and because it runs in a servlet container, it naturally makes use of the `ServletEndpointContext`.

10.2.3.2 *Using the* `ServletEndpointContext` *Interface*

A JSE instance obtains a reference to its `ServletEndpointContext` when its `init()` method is invoked—assuming it implements the `ServiceLifecyle` interface. The servlet container calls `init()` only once on each instance, so the JSE instance must preserve the reference in an instance variable if it wants to have access to it later.

The `ServletEndpointContext` is the JSE's interface to its servlet container. It provides access to the identity of the client making a request, session data, the servlet context, and the message context used by JAX-RPC handlers. To make these services available, the servlet container must provide an implementation of the `ServletEndpointContext` interface at runtime. The interface is shown in Listing 10–14.

Listing 10–14

The `javax.xml.rpc.server.ServletEndpointContext` *Interface*

```
package javax.xml.rpc.server;
public interface ServletEndpointContext {
    public java.security.Principal getUserPrincipal();
    public boolean isUserInRole(String role);
    public javax.xml.rpc.handler.MessageContext getMessageContext();
    public javax.Servlet.http.HttpSession getHttpSession()
      throws javax.xml.rpc.JAXRPCException;
    public javax.Servlet.ServletContext getServletContext();
}
```

Although a JSE instance maintains a reference to the same `ServletEndpointContext` object throughout its life, the values returned by its methods will change with every new SOAP request. The information obtained by the `ServletEndpointContext` is actually obtained via the JAX-RPC servlet that wraps the JSE instance. The `Principal` and `HttpSession` objects, returned by the `getUserPrincipal()` and `getHttpSession()` methods, are obtained from the servlet's `doPost()` method's `HttpServletRequest` parameter. Similarly, the `ServletContext`, returned by the `getServletContext()` method, is a reference to the JAX-RPC servlet's `ServletContext`. The JAX-RPC servlet also instantiates and manages the `MessageContext`, returned by `getMessageContext()`, which is used by the JAX-RPC handler chain.

10.2.3.2.1 The `getUserPrincipal()` and `isUserInRole()` Methods

The `ServiceEndpointContext.getUserPrincipal()` method returns the identity of the sender, the SOAP client that is making the request. The `java.security.Principal` object represents the identity of the application that is sending the SOAP message and is available only if the JSE was configured to use either HTTP Basic Authentication (BASIC-AUTH) or Symmetric HTTP. If no authentication is used, the `getUserPrincipal()` method returns `null`.

BASIC-AUTH requires that the SOAP sender provide a user-id and password, which are passed to the servlet container in a special HTTP request message. The servlet container will use the user-id and password to authenticate the SOAP sender against some kind of user database. The `Principal` object is derived from the identity obtained from the database. BASIC-AUTH can be set up during deployment and is usually used in combination with SSL (using the HTTPS protocol) for confidentiality (so the password is concealed when it's passed to the server). BASIC-AUTH is the most commonly used type of authentication.

Symmetric HTTP is a more sophisticated authentication mechanism, and more reliable because it's more difficult for hackers to fake. Symmetric HTTP requires both the servlet container and the SOAP sender to authenticate each other using X.509 digital certificates.[1] While Symmetric HTTP is stronger than BASIC-AUTH, it also requires more sophisticated SOAP clients, that can maintain and utilize X.509 digital certificates—a feature that most SOAP toolkits today do not support. This type of authentication is not very common.

Once a SOAP sender has been authenticated, using BASIC-AUTH or Symmetric HTTP, the same `Principal` object can be associated with the SOAP sender's subsequent messages by using session tracking, via SSL, cookies, or some other session-tracking method. Maintaining this association precludes having to reauthenticate every time the SOAP sender makes a request.

Regardless of the authentication mechanism used, the `Principal` represents the identity of the SOAP sender and the JSE can use it for logging. The `Principal` object may be propagated (for authorization) to any resources or EJBs accessible by the JSE, depending on the `run-as` and `res-auth` deployment settings in the deployment descriptor. See Part VII: Deployment for details.

A `Principal` may represent a specific person or system that assumes a variety of roles. For example, a bank employee might assume roles such as Teller, Bank Manager, and Employee. Roles are assigned to `Principals` using vendor-specific security tools. You can test callers to see if they belong to a specific role—assuming they have been authenticated—by calling the `isUserInRole()` method.

[1] Internet Engineering Task Force, *RFC 2459: Internet X.509 Public Key Infrastructure Certificate and CRL Profile* (1999). Available at http://www.ietf.org/rfc/rfc2459.txt.

10.2.3.2.2 The `getHttpSession()` Method

The `ServletEndpointSession.getHttpSession()` method returns a `javax.Servlet.http.HttpSession` object, which represents an **HTTP session** that is associated with the SOAP sender. An HTTP session is a continuing conversation between the SOAP sender and the servlet container. It's an identifier that allows the servlet container to associate multiple HTTP requests with a specific SOAP sender. Session tracking is not used with Web services very much today, but customary practice will probably change as implementations become more complex and the technology matures. When HTTP session tracking is used, it's usually done with either cookies or SSL.[2]

Cookies are identifiers that are sent from the servlet container to the SOAP sender and are associated with a specific host, such as monson-haefel.com. Every time the SOAP sender makes an HTTP request, it includes the cookie, which allows the servlet container to match the request to a specific session. If HTTP Basic Authentication is used, the cookie will be established at that time. Cookies do not require authentication, however. Anonymous SOAP senders can also be assigned cookies so that the servlet container can track requests within a single session. The servlet container doesn't know who all the SOAP clients are, but does know which requests come from which client.

SSL (Secure Sockets Layer) uses encryption keys to establish a secure communication channel between an HTTP client and an HTTP server. Basically, the client and server agree to use a private encryption key for the duration of the session, so that all messages are encrypted and decrypted using that key. All this is done behind the scenes and is fairly quick. You have probably used SSL while sending credit card or other personal information to a Web site like Amazon.com. When your Web browser shows a closed lock in a corner of the frame, it's telling you that you have a secure SSL connection with the Web site. As long as the lock symbol is closed, all the HTTP traffic between your browser and the HTTP Web server is encrypted and cannot be read by other parties.[3] A SOAP application can use the same mechanism for confidential communications with a JSE. SSL has session tracking built right into the protocol, so when SSL is used, you get session tracking as a bonus.

Regardless of the mechanism used to track a session, the `HttpSession` object is used to represent the session itself. The `HttpSession` object allows the JSE to view and change information about the session, such as the session identifier, creation time, last access time, and when the session will time out. In addition, the JSE can associate custom **attributes** with a session, so that it can maintain state across invocations by the same client. An attribute is a name-value pair, where the value is any

[2] URL rewriting and session tracking based on hidden forms are not used in SOAP-based Web services because they require the exchange of HTML, which isn't used in SOAP communications.

[3] When SSL is used with HTTP, it's called HTTPS.

serializable object. If HTTP session tracking is not used, `ServletEndpointContext.getHttpSession()` will return `null`.

In theory, Web services are supposed to be completely stateless, so the use of sessions and the storage of data associated with sessions are somewhat controversial. That said, there are circumstances in which session tracking and session data are necessary to improve the usability or performance of a Web service. For example, a Web service might use session tracking to ensure that clients receive information in their native language or currency. Most clients in the United States use English and the dollar, while those in France use French and the euro. Initially, the Web service might fetch language and currency preferences from the database, but once these are obtained they can be cached in the `HttpSession` to avoid repeated access to the database for the same information. In Listing 10–15, the `InternationalJSE_Impl` type uses the `HttpSession` object to track language and currency preferences of a specific client session.

Listing 10–15

Using an `HttpSession` *to Cache Session-Specific Data*

```
package com.jwsbook.jaxrpc;
...
public class InternationalJSE_Impl implements InternationalJSE,
javax.xml.rpc.server.ServiceLifecycle {
  javax.sql.DataSource dataSource;
  ServletEndpointContext servletEndpointContext;

  public void init(Object context) throws ServiceException{
    ...
  }
  public void destroy(){
    ...
  }
  public void someMethod( ) {
    HttpSession httpSession = servletEndpointContext.getHttpSession();
    Principal principal = servletEndpointContext.getUserPrincipal();
    if( httpSession != null){
      // Get preferences from HttpSession object
      String language_preference = (String)
                                 httpSession.getAttribute("language");
      String currency_preference = (String)
                                 httpSession.getAttribute("currency");
      if( language_preference == null || currency_preference == null) {
        // Get preferences from database and initialize session data
        java.sql.Connection jdbcConnection = null;
```

```
            java.sql.Statement sqlStatement = null;
            java.sql.ResultSet resultSet;
            try {
              jdbcConnection = dataSource.getConnection();
              sqlStatement = jdbcConnection.createStatement();
              resultSet = sqlStatement.executeQuery(
                         "SELECT language, currancy FROM PREFERENCES "+
                         "WHERE Principal = "+principal.getName());
              if(resultSet.next()){
                language_preference = resultSet.getString("language");
                currency_preference = resultSet.getString("currency");
                // set attributes on HttpSession to avoid DB access.
                httpSession.setAttribute("language", language_preference);
                httpSession.setAttribute("language", currency_preference);
              }
            }catch (java.sql.SQLException se) {
                // handle SQLException
            }
          }
        }
        // Use the language and currency preferences in further processing
    }
}
```

The session logic in Listing 10–15 could be used in any Web service to obtain and cache the language and currency preferences of each SOAP sender. If the HTTP session is being tracked, the JSE can obtain the preferences from the database on the first access, then store them in the `HttpSession` object, where it can get them for any subsequent requests by the same SOAP sender.

10.2.3.2.3 The `getServletContext()` Method

The `ServletEndpointContext.getServletContext()` method returns the `ServletContext` object owned by the JAX-RPC servlet that wraps the JSE instance. The `ServletContext` acts as an interface to the servlet container system and provides access to name-value attributes, initialization parameters, files, files' MIME types, path-URL conversions, container version and brand information, logging, and a `RequestDispatcher` (which allows one servlet to call another servlet, JSP, or HTML page). The usefulness of the `ServletContext` to a JSE depends in large part on the specific needs of your Web service. Most JSEs will not need to use the `ServletContext` except for accessing initialization parameters and perhaps logging. If you need the other methods, they're available to you.

Table 10–1 lists and describes some of the methods defined by the `ServletContext` interface.

Table 10–1 `ServletContext` Methods

`javax.Servlet.ServletContext`	**Description**
`getInitParameter(String)`	Returns the `String` value of an initialization parameter set in the deployment descriptor. Returns `null` if there is no matching value.
`getInitParameterNames()`	Returns an `Enumeration` of all the named initialization parameters set in the deployment descriptor.
`getAttribute(String)`	Returns the `Object` value of a name-value pair. The servlet container or an individual servlet may set attributes, which are available to any servlet, JSP, or JSE in the same context.
`setAttribute(String, Object)`	Sets an attribute for this context. The attribute value can be any type of `Object` and will be accessible to any servlet, JSP, or JSE in the same context.
`removeAttribute(String)`	Removes an attribute from this context.
`log(String)`	Writes a text message to the servlet log file.
`log(String, Throwable)`	Writes a text message and stack trace for the `Throwable` (`Exception` or `Error`) to the servlet log file.
`getResource(String)`	Returns a `java.net.URL` object for a specific resource located in the servlet's file system or a WAR file. The path must begin with a forward slash (`'/'`).
`getResourcePaths(String)`	Returns a `java.util.Set` of the paths of all the resources available, relative to the path passed to the method. The path must begin with a forward slash (`'/'`).
`getResourceAsStream(String)`	Returns the resource (GIF, JPEG, HTML, or XML file, for instance) located at the path passed into the method as a `java.io.InputStream`.
`getMimeType(String)`	Returns the MIME type of the specified file at a given path.
`getNamedDispatcher(String)`	Returns a `javax.Servlet.RequestDispatcher`, which can be used to forward requests to other servlets, JSPs, HTML files, or JSEs.
`getContext(String)`	Returns a `javax.Servlet.ServletContext` object for a Web application located at a specified URL.
`getRealPath(String)`	Returns the absolute path, as a `String`, for a given relative path.
`getServletContextName()`	Returns the display name, as specified in the `web.xml` deployment descriptor of the Web application to which this servlet belongs.
`getServletInfo()`	Returns the name and version number of the servlet container.
`getMajorVersion()`	Returns the major version of the Java Servlets API this container supports.
`getMinorVersion()`	Returns the minor version of the Java Servlets API this container supports.

10.2.3.2.4 The `getMessageContext()` Method

The `ServletEndpointContext.getMessageContext()` method returns a `javax.xml.rpc.handler.MessageContext` object that is used to share information among handler objects and the JSE implementation object. Message handlers are designed to pre- and post-process the SOAP messages exchanged between J2EE port components (JSEs and EJB endpoints) and SOAP clients. A port component can be configured to use a chain of handler objects, each of which does some pre- and/or post-processing on the SOAP message. Handler objects in a chain share information during the processing of a message using the `MessageContext`, which defines methods for setting and accessing properties in the form of name-value pairs. The `MessageContext` is covered in detail in Chapter 14.

10.3 Multi-threading and JSEs

Servlets, and therefore JSEs, support two basic threading models: multi-threaded and single-threaded. To understand these two programming models you have to understand Java threading—if you don't, I recommend you read up on the subject before tackling this section. A good book on threading is the second edition of *Concurrent Programming in Java: Design Principles and Patterns,* by Doug Lea.

When a JSE is multi-threaded, all client requests access exactly the same JAX-RPC servlet and JSE instance. Each client request is associated with its own thread of execution, and many threads will access the same JSE instance simultaneously. This model allows a single instance to support hundreds of clients, but it also requires care when accessing instance or class-level variables. Because all threads see the same instance and class variables, access to these variables should be avoided or synchronized using synchronized methods or blocks.

When a JSE is single-threaded, the servlet container normally maintains a pool of JAX-RPC servlets, and therefore JSE instances, then plucks them from the pool to handle client requests. Each simultaneous client request accesses a different JSE instance, so you never have multiple threads accessing the same JSE instance at the same time. Once a client request ends, the JSE instance is returned to the pool so that it can be used to handle another request. You don't have to worry about instance variables; they can be accessed freely without using synchronization. You should avoid creating static variables, on the other hand, or synchronize access to them, just as in the multi-threaded model. The single-threaded programming model has turned out to work poorly in practice because it degrades performance and introduces resource-management problems the multi-threaded model doesn't suffer from. For the most part, servlet experts recommend that you do not use the single-threaded programming model.

The single-threaded model was deprecated as of Java Servlets 2.4, which is the specification supported by J2EE 1.4. In the future the single-threaded model will be phased out of the specification, and only the multi-threaded model will be supported. You can still use the single-threaded model—that's why it's covered in this book—but it's discouraged by the specification.

Which threading model a JAX-RPC servlet and its JSE use depends on whether the JAX-RPC servlet implements the `javax.Servlet.SingleThreadModel` interface. A JSE that implements the `SingleThreadModel` interface can be accessed by only one thread at a time—the assumption being that a pool of instances will be used to service requests.

Currently there is no vendor-agnostic way to specify whether a JSE should use a single- or multi-threaded programming model. Your vendor may provide some method for specifying the threading model, or it may support only one threading model for JSEs. Consult your vendor's documentation for details.

10.4 Wrapping Up

JSEs are fairly simple to implement. You only need to define a Java implementation class and an endpoint interface. This simplicity masks a fairly complex and powerful runtime environment available to JSEs, however. Because a JSE is actually embedded in a JAX-RPC servlet, it can exploit the powerful servlet container system that has proven so useful in Web application development since 1997. The JSE effectively has access to most, if not all, of the same resources and APIs a servlet has at runtime.

As you learned in this chapter, a JSE can use the JNDI ENC to access JDBC drivers, JMS, J2EE connectors, EJBs, environment entries, and other Web services. If the JSE implements the `ServiceLifecycle` interface, it will be given a reference to the `ServletEndpointContext`, which provides the JSE with an API for accessing the `Principal`, the `HttpSession`, and the `ServletContext` of the JAX-RPC servlet, as well as the `MessageContext` used by the JSE's handlers.

The JSE is one of two types of Web service that can be deployed in J2EE. The other is the EJB endpoint, which is a stateless session bean that can process SOAP messages just as the JSE can. The main difference is that the EJB endpoint provides more robust transaction-processing capabilities, which tend to be useful when accessing resources that require distributed transactions, or when managing the interaction of several resources and enterprise beans. EJB endpoints are discussed in more detail in Chapter 11. In most cases, though, you will not need the robust transaction-processing capabilities of an EJB endpoint. Because the EJB endpoint programming model is more complex than the JSE programming model, and because EJBs tend to introduce more overhead and less throughput, it's best to avoid them unless you really need them.

If you have read this entire chapter, then you know enough about JSEs to be truly dangerous, which means you have enough knowledge to implement a Web service but you should learn more before implementing a production system. You don't have to read every chapter in this part of the book now, but you should study the other chapters when you have time. As always, read what you need, and use the rest as reference during development.

Chapter 11

JAX-RPC EJB Endpoints

Enterprise JavaBeans provides a richer, but more complex, programming model for developing J2EE Web services than the JAX-RPC service endpoint (JSE) programming model discussed in Chapter 10. The complexity of Enterprise JavaBeans (EJB) comes from its additional responsibilities for automatically managing the scope of transactions.

You should consider this chapter on EJB endpoints (EJBs that act as Web services) to be an advanced chapter. The bulk of it assumes you already have a good understanding of the EJB programming model. If you don't, you should read Section 11.1 to get a better understanding of transactions and EJB. The end of the primer provides some guidance on what else to do if you don't have prior experience with EJB. If you are already somewhat familiar with EJB and have used it in some capacity, you can skip the primer or treat it as a refresher. You'll find the section following the primer helpful when developing EJB endpoints. If you don't think you'll ever need to use EJBs, feel free to skip this chapter completely.

11.1 An Enterprise JavaBeans Primer

To understand and appreciate why EJB is important, you have to understand some basic concepts about transactions. The first part of this section describes transactions, while the second part provides an overview of EJB as a transactional system.

11.1.1 Transactions in a Nutshell

In a nutshell, a **transaction** represents a series of operations on a database (or on another resource) that are grouped together and treated as a single unit. Consider a scenario in which you have a JDBC database connection and want to perform three SQL operations, an INSERT, an UPDATE, and a DELETE. Without grouping the operations together in a transaction, each operation would be distinct and independent of the others. The INSERT and DELETE operations might execute without a problem, but the UPDATE operation might fail because of some integrity constraint. If the three operations are not grouped together in a transaction, the failure of the UPDATE will have no effect on the INSERT or DELETE operations. If you group the operations into a single transaction, however, then all three will either succeed or fail together. For example, if the UPDATE fails for any reason, then the INSERT and DELETE will also fail.

Let's consider a more concrete example. If a banking system transfers $100.00 from Account A to Account B, there are three database operations: two UPDATEs and one INSERT. The first UPDATE decreases the balance of Account A by $100.00. The second UPDATE increases the balance of Account B by $100.00. The INSERT creates an audit record that preserves the details of the transaction. If you don't group these operations into a single transaction, and any of them fails, serious side effects can occur. For example, if the first UPDATE decreases the balance of Account A by $100.00, but the second UPDATE fails to increase the balance of Account B, you effectively lose $100.00 of a customer's money. If one operation fails, you want all three to fail, so that your database is consistent with reality.

It's better to abandon all three operations than to allow some operations to succeed while others fail. A transaction groups the database operations together so you can be sure that they will all succeed or fail together. The terminology is very suggestive: An abandoned transaction is **rolled back,** meaning that any partial changes are undone. A successful transaction is **committed,** meaning that the changes made by all operations are permanent.

To group several database operations into a transaction, you need a mechanism to demarcate the beginning and end of a transaction explicitly, so that all operations performed between the beginning and end are parts of the same transaction. **Transactional resource APIs** such as JDBC and JMS usually offer some mechanism for starting and ending transactions. For example, in JDBC you can use a Transactional Connection object that groups all operations on the same database into a single transaction demarcated by a call to `Connection.commit()`, as shown in Listing 11–1—all operations between a call to `Connection.commit()` are grouped into a single transaction.

Listing 11–1

Using the JDBC Transactional Facilities

```
java.sql.Connection jdbcConnection = DriverManager.getConnection("");


Statement op_1 = jdbcConnection.createStatement( );
op_1.executeUpdate("UPDATE account SET balance = balance-"
```

```
                                 +transfer_amount+" WHERE   account_number = "
                                 +accountA);
Statement op_2 = jdbcConnection.createStatement( );
op_2.executeUpdate("UPDATE account SET balance = balance+"
                                 +transfer_amount+" WHERE   account_number = "
                                 +accountB);
Statement op_3 = jdbcConnection.createStatement( );
op_3.executeUpdate("INSERT INTO transfer_audit ("
                                 +accountA+","+accountB+","+transfer_amount+","
                                 +new java.sql.Date()+")");

jdbcConnection.commit();
```

Using an API's transaction methods works well if you are accessing only a single resource because the resource itself (usually a database) will take care of managing the transaction. If, however, you are accessing two different databases, or two different resources—JDBC and JMS, for example—and you want the operations performed by both resources to be part of the same transaction, then you have to use the **Java Transaction API (JTA)** to group all the operations into a single transaction. Listing 11–2 uses JTA with JDBC and JMS.

Listing 11–2

Using JTA with JDBC and JMS

```
javax.transaction.UserTransaction userTransaction =
              (javax.transaction.UserTransaction)
               jndiEnc.lookup("java:comp/UserTransaction");
userTransaction.begin();
try{

  Statement op_1 = jdbcConnection.createStatement( );
  op_1.executeUpdate("UPDATE account SET balance = balance-"
                        +transfer_amount+" WHERE   account_number = "
                        +accountA);
  Statement op_2 = jdbcConnection.createStatement( );
  op_2.executeUpdate("UPDATE account SET balance = balance+"
                        +transfer_amount+" WHERE   account_number = "
                        +accountB);
  Statement op_3 = jdbcConnection.createStatement( );
  op_3.executeUpdate("INSERT INTO transfer_audit ("
                        +accountA+","+accountB+","+transfer_amount+","
                        +new java.sql.Date(System.currentTimeMillis())+")");
```

```
    MessageProducer producer = jmsSession.createProducer(destinationA);
    TextMessage message =
    jmsSession.createTextMessage("$"+transfer_amount+" transferred from "
                            +accountA+" to "
                            +accountB);
    producer.send(message);

    userTransaction.commit();
}catch(SQLException sqle){
      userTransaction.rollback();
      // other error-handling code follows
}
```

The `UserTransaction.begin()` method marks the beginning of the transaction, and `UserTransaction.commit()` marks the end. Any JDBC and JMS operations performed between the `begin()` and `commit()` method calls are included in the same transaction. The `UserTransaction.commit()` method commits the changes made with the JDBC connection to the database and completes the delivery of the JMS message. If any of the operations throws a `SQLException`, the `UserTransaction.rollback()` method rolls the transaction back—that is, abandons all the operations.

The use of JTA appears fairly simple, but it can be difficult to use correctly. It requires a good understanding of both transactions and the resources used by the application developer. To make life easier, Enterprise JavaBeans handles transaction demarcation implicitly. When using EJB, you don't need to use JTA or call the `begin()`, `commit()`, or `rollback()` methods—the EJB container system will take care of all these chores for you automatically. In addition, a transaction that is started by one EJB can be propagated to other EJBs automatically—a very powerful feature.

11.1.2 Understanding EJB

Initially, EJB was introduced by Sun Microsystems in 1998 to compete with two leading RPC (Remote Procedure Call) technologies: MTS (Microsoft Transaction Server) and CORBA (Common Object Request Broker Architecture). Both of these distributed-object systems allow objects on one machine to invoke the methods of other objects on another machine, across a network. EJB borrowed from both MTS and CORBA, but is conceptually closer to MTS's model of a component transaction manager than to CORBA's. Since its debut, EJB has continued to grow and improve, while MTS has been rebranded and CORBA has diminished in popularity. Although EJB currently has a lead over its rivals, they are forever nipping at its heels. CORBA has actually evolved a very similar but somewhat broader component technology called the CCM (Common Component Model), while Microsoft has recently incorporated the MTS functionality into its .NET platform.

11.1.2.1 *What Is EJB?*

Enterprise JavaBeans is a server-side component model for transactional systems. It provides an API for developing business components whose transactions, resources, and security are managed automatically at runtime by a J2EE application server. As an EJB developer you can model your business in Java objects, with methods and fields representing the business logic and data. Meanwhile, the J2EE application server takes care of all the hard stuff, like transaction management, persistence, security, resources, and threading, for you automatically—which makes your job a lot easier: Freed of these concerns, you can focus on modeling the business logic and data.

11.1.2.2 *Why Use EJB?*

To start with, EJB makes the most sense if your system is highly transactional. If it does a lot of updates and deletes to a database, EJB may be a good idea because EJB is designed to address transactions from the ground up. It is, fundamentally, a transaction component model. Solid support for transaction processing is not the only criterion, however. Even if the system you are building does not make many changes to the database, EJB may still be a good choice. The powerful new **container-managed persistence** (**CMP**) of EJB 2.0 and 2.1 helps you model fairly complex business domains and allows you to combine business logic with implicit management of data persistence.

Although the business modeling capabilities of CMP entity beans are attractive reasons for using EJB in the first place, they don't provide any direct motivation for using EJBs as Web service endpoints because only stateless session beans can be used as Web services, not CMP entity beans. That said, stateless session beans still offer the benefits of automatic transaction management, and they work well with CMP entity beans. In other words, stateless session beans make for a fine interface into an EJB-based business application. If your Web service needs to interact with CMP entity components, then using an EJB endpoint (a stateless session bean that acts as a Web service) can be beneficial.

11.1.2.3 *RPC Components: Stateless, Stateful, and Entity Beans*

EJB provides four component models on which you can build your business system: stateless and stateful session beans, entity beans, and message-driven beans. The first three are **RPC** (Remote Procedure Call) components. An RPC component defines a set of methods applications can call across a network. RPC technology has been around for over 20 years and is the basis of DCE RPC, CORBA, DCOM, and most recently SOAP.

A **stateless session bean** is used to model service-oriented components that have no persistent state and are more procedural in nature than object-oriented. This component model is the basis of the EJB endpoint, which allows a bean to act as a Web service. You'll learn a lot more about stateless session beans and EJB endpoints later in this chapter. A stateless session bean will frequently access entity beans, which model the persistent state of the business application. They can coordinate the interaction of entity beans to accomplish some task, like processing a purchase order or accessing the wholesale price of a book.

A **stateful session bean** is a business object that represents a session with a client. When a client accesses a stateful bean it gets exclusive access to its own instance, which it can reuse over and over for the life of the session. A stateful bean can store data in memory from one invocation to the next, which allows it to maintain session state relative to the client using it. A stateful bean, like a stateless session bean, will often make use of entity beans—and stateless session beans as well—to accomplish its tasks. It's considered a bad design practice, however, for any other type of bean (stateless, stateful, entity, or message-driven) to make calls on a stateful session bean, because it represents a client's session.

An **entity bean** models a persistent business object, which is any business object whose data is stored in a database, such as Customer, Invoice, or Book. Entity beans come in two flavors, container-managed persistence (CMP) and bean-managed persistence (BMP). Since EJB 2.0 was released, CMP has become a very popular way of developing persistent business objects. The process of reading and writing a CMP entity's state to the database is managed automatically by the J2EE application server, according to mappings defined by the EJB developer at design time. BMP entity beans are used less often because they require the developer to write the logic for preserving the state of the entity. BMP is useful in situations where CMP won't work; for example, when an entity's state is derived from two or more resources. Entity beans will sometimes access stateless session beans, but most of the time they operate on their own state, or that of related entity beans.

For the past couple of years the standard way to access the RPC components (stateless, stateful, and entity beans) from remote clients has been to use CORBA IIOP (Internet Inter-ORB Protocol). The EJB specification authors chose IIOP as the standard protocol for accessing RPC components because it was mature, functional, and platform-neutral. It was also a good marketing decision because it gives the impression of better interoperability between brands of J2EE application servers. Listing 11–3 shows a J2EE client application accessing an EJB remotely using IIOP.

Listing 11–3

Using Java RMI-IIOP to Access an EJB

```
javax.naming.InitialContext jndiEnc = new javax.naming.InitialContext();
Object remoteRef =  jndiEnc.lookup("java:comp/env/ejb/BookQuoteHome");
BookQuoteHomeRemote ejbHome = (BookQuoteHomeRemote)
 javax.rmi.PortableRemoteObject.narrow( remoteRef, BookQuoteHomeRemote.class);

BookQuoteRemote bookQuote = ejbHome.create( );
float price = bookQuote.getBookPrice( isbn );
```

The use of CORBA IIOP to access EJBs is not the focus of this book, but the example illustrates how the BookQuote service can be manifested as an EJB and accessed via CORBA IIOP by remote clients. Later you'll see how to develop the BookQuote service as an EJB endpoint, so that it can be accessed using SOAP rather than IIOP.

11.1.2.4 *Asynchronous Components: The Message-Driven Bean*

Message-driven beans (**MDBs**) are used for processing asynchronous messages from some type of messaging system, usually a Java Message Service (JMS) provider. JMS is used for **enterprise messaging systems,** which use proprietary protocols to deliver messages between applications. This "message-oriented middleware" is kind of like e-mail for applications, but message delivery and consumption are more robust.

All J2EE 1.4 application servers are required to support JMS-based message-driven beans, but they may also support other, unspecified, messaging systems. Support for non-JMS messaging systems is made possible by the new asynchronous capabilities of the J2EE Connector Architecture 1.5, which allows asynchronous messaging systems to be plugged into any J2EE 1.4 platform.

It's possible, even likely, that J2EE vendors will begin to introduce message-driven bean types that can process SOAP messages. At this time, however, no standard J2EE MDB component for processing SOAP messages has been specified.

Although the Java API for XML Messaging (JAXM) is a JSR-approved API for asynchronus SOAP messaging, it is not an official part of J2EE. What's more, it's not supported by major J2EE vendors, who see it as unnecessary because it overlaps with JMS and JAX-RPC. It's unlikely that JAXM will be very successful in its current incarnation.

11.1.2.5 *The EJB Container System*

EJBs are managed and run in an EJB container system inside a J2EE application server. The EJB container system is responsible for managing concurrency, transactions, resources, remote access—basically the entire environment of EJBs at runtime. When a client makes a remote call on an EJB, the EJB container intercepts the call and delegates it to the proper EJB instance. The process of intercepting and delegating remote calls to EJBs is complex.

When the EJB container intercepts a remote call to an EJB, it will pick an EJB instance from an instance pool to handle the call. Except for stateful session beans, the EJB instances are pooled so that a few instances can serve many clients. Once an instance is selected from the pool, the EJB container will examine the transaction and security policies for the method invoked. There are several transaction policies that the EJB developer can specify for each of an EJB's methods, but at runtime there are only three possible outcomes with regard to transactions: a new transaction is started just before the call is delegated to the EJB, an existing transaction is propagated to the EJB, or there is no transaction.

If a new transaction is started, the EJB container begins the transaction just before it calls the method, and then attempts to commit the transaction immediately after the method returns. Within the method itself the EJB can access JDBC drivers, JMS providers, or any other type of transactional resource, and be assured that all the operations performed will be parts of the same transaction, and will either succeed or fail together.

Another possibility is that the client that made the call has already started a transaction, and the EJB receiving the call is set up to join the transaction, so that all the operations performed by the EJB instance become a part of the client's transaction. This process is called **transaction propagation** because the transaction spreads from the client to the EJB instance. Transaction propagation most often occurs when one EJB calls another to do some work. Propagating the transaction ensures that all the tasks performed by both EJBs are parts of the same transaction.

Transaction propagation is a powerful concept and is one of the most important reasons for using EJB in the first place. Because transactions can propagate between EJBs automatically, you can have multiple EJBs collaborate to achieve a task, without having to worry about system failures creating inconsistent results. If any of the operations performed by any of the EJBs fails, all the operations performed by all the EJBs fail. As an example, let's reconstruct the banking example used in Section 11.1.1. Imagine that a bank deploys three different EJBs: a stateless session EJB called MoneyTransfer EJB; an entity EJB called Account EJB; and another entity EJB called TransferAudit EJB. A remote client obtains a reference to the MoneyTransfer EJB and requests that $100.00 be transferred from Account A to Account B, as shown Listing 11–4.

Listing 11–4

The Remote Client View of a MoneyTransfer EJB

```
javax.naming.InitialContext jndiEnc = new javax.naming.InitialContext();
Object remoteRef =  jndiEnc.lookup("java:comp/env/ejb/MoneyTransferHome");
MoneyTransferHome ejbHome = (MoneyTransferHome)
 javax.rmi.PortableRemoteObject.narrow( remoteRef, MoneyTransferHome.class);

MoneyTransfer moneyTransfer = ejbHome.create( );

moneyTransfer.transfer(accountA,accountB,100.00d);
```

When the EJB container system intercepts this request from the remote client, it will pick an instance of the MoneyTransfer EJB from the instance pool to service the call. Just before calling the `transfer()` method on the instance, the EJB container will start a new transaction. The instance itself uses two Account EJBs and one TransferAudit EJB to do the actual transfer of funds, as in Listing 11–5.

Listing 11–5

The MoneyTransferEJB *class*

```
package jwsed1.support;
import javax.ejb.SessionContext;
import javax.naming.InitialContext;
import java.util.Date;
import java.security.Principal;

public class MoneyTransferEJB implements javax.ejb.SessionBean {
  SessionContext ejbContext;
  public void create( ){}

  public void transfer(int acctA, int acctB, double amount){
    try{
      if(amount > 100000.0d && !ejbContext.isCallerInRole("BankManager")){
       Principal principal = ejbContext.getCallerPrincipal();
       throw new AuthorizationException(principal.getName()+
               " is not authorized to transfer over $100,000.00");
      }

      InitialContext jndiEnc = new InitialContext( );
      AccountHomeLocal acctHome = (AccountHomeLocal)
                 jndiEnc.lookup("java:comp/env/ejb/AccountHome");
      AccountLocal accountA = acctHome.findByPrimarykey( acctA );
      AccountLocal accountB = acctHome.findByPrimarykey( acctB );

      accountA.withdraw( amount );
      accountB.deposit( amount );

      TransferAuditHomeLocal taHome = (TransferAuditHomeLocal)
                 jndiEnc.lookup("java:comp/env/ejb/TransferAuditHome");

      TransferAuditLocal audit =
        taHome.createAudit( accountA, accountB, amount, new Date());
    }catch(Exception e){
      throw new javax.ejb.EJBException(e);
    }
  }
  ...
}
```

The MoneyTransfer EJB finds the entity beans that represent Accounts A and B, and then proceeds to withdraw $100.00 from A and deposit $100.00 in B. After transferring the funds, the MoneyTransfer EJB creates a new TransferAudit EJB to represent the transfer. Each of the entity beans used in this example represents a row in a relational database table, which is how entities usually map to databases. Withdrawing or depositing money in an account effectively performs a database UPDATE, subtracting an amount from or adding it to the `balance` column of the `ACCOUNT` table. Creating a new TransferAudit EJB causes a database INSERT to add a new row in the `TRANSFER_AUDIT` table.

The transaction that was started just before the EJB container invoked the `transfer()` method of the TransferMoney EJB instance is propagated to all the operations performed on the Account EJBs, and to the creation of the TransferAudit EJB. If any one of these operations fails for any reason, or if the `transfer()` method throws an exception, the entire transaction is rolled back (aborted). We avoid a situation in which, for example, the withdrawal from Account A is made but the deposit to Account B is not. Either all the operations succeed, or they all fail together. As you can see, using EJB to transfer money from one account to another is a bit more object-oriented than using raw SQL and JDBC, as illustrated earlier in this section. In addition, you don't have to worry about explicitly starting a new transaction and managing transaction commits and rollbacks—the EJB container handles these chores for you.

The EJB container also automatically takes care of security authentication and authorization. For example, the EJB container can authenticate callers to make sure they are who they say they are. Once a caller is authenticated, the EJB container can apply authorization security policies to make sure that the client is authorized to make a transfer. For example, you would want only a bank teller to be authorized to transfer money from one account to another.

11.1.3 Where to Go from Here

It's not the purpose of this book to teach you Enterprise JavaBeans. The topic is simply too large and complex to do it justice in a book on J2EE Web Services. I hope the preceding sections have given you some insight into how EJB is used, why it's important, and some of the automatic transaction capabilities you get with EJB.

To really understand EJB you'll have to read a book dedicated to the subject; otherwise you are likely to do more damage than good when using it. The learning curve for EJB is fairly steep; you'll need to invest some time learning about it. If you think that EJB is the way to go, consider reading my book *Enterprise JavaBeans*, Fourth Edition (O'Reilly 2004). It will provide you with a gentle but comprehensive tutorial on the subject, and help you understand the underlying technology and programming model.

11.2 Enterprise JavaBeans Web Services

In J2EE 1.4 you can deploy a stateless session bean as a Web service endpoint that can process SOAP messages as RPC calls. Making a stateless session bean accessible as a Web service involves basically the same process used to deploy a stateless bean with a remote or local interface. The only big difference is that you define an **endpoint interface** that extends `javax.rmi.Remote`, instead of a **remote interface** that extends `javax.ejb.EJBObject`, or a **local interface** that extends `javax.ejb.EJBLocalObject`. In addition, you do not define a home interface, because an EJB endpoint does not have one.

An EJB endpoint can be a brand-new stateless session bean developed specifically to serve as a Web service endpoint, or you can re-deploy an existing stateless session bean so that it doubles as an endpoint. As long as you observe the restrictions on endpoint interfaces imposed by the JAX-RPC specification, you can turn a stateless session bean into a Web service endpoint with very little effort. In fact, a single stateless session bean can conceivably service remote, local, and endpoint clients simultaneously.

11.2.1 A Simple Example

The easiest way to show you how to deploy a stateless session bean as a Web service endpoint is to use an example. In this case we'll deploy the BookQuote Web service as an EJB endpoint. In reality, BookQuote is so simple it's best deployed as a JSE; it does not need the complex transaction management capabilities provided by Enterprise JavaBeans. It's an example that should be familiar to you by now, though, so using it at this point will allow you to focus on the mechanics of defining an EJB endpoint.

11.2.1.1 The Endpoint Interface

EJB developers usually start by developing a component's interface, which defines the business methods that clients can invoke on the EJB at runtime. If we wanted the EJB to be accessible via Java RMI-IIOP, we would create a remote interface that extends `javax.ejb.EJBObject`. If we wanted the EJB to be accessible to co-located beans (other components deployed in the same J2EE application), we would use a local interface that extends `javax.ejb.EJBLocalObject`. In this case, however, we want the EJB to be accessible to SOAP clients, so we'll define an endpoint interface that extends the `java.rmi.Remote` interface. The endpoint interface defines the Web service operations that SOAP clients can call on the EJB. As shown in Listing 11–6, the BookQuote Web service declares a single operation, defined by the `getBookPrice()` method.

Listing 11–6

An Endpoint Interface

```
package com.jwsbook.jaxrpc;

public interface BookQuote extends java.rmi.Remote {
  public float getBookPrice(String isbn) throws java.rmi.RemoteException;
}
```

The endpoint interface defined here is identical to the one defined for the JSE in Chapter 10. That they're exactly the same is telling: It illustrates that from the SOAP client's perspective there is no difference between a JSE and an EJB endpoint Web service.

The endpoint interface must comply with the rules for WSDL-to-Java mapping defined by the JAX-RPC specification. These rules are not all that complicated as long as you stick with primitive types. Classes and arrays are also supported, but they require a little more work. Complete coverage of WSDL-to-Java mapping is given in Chapter 15.

Every business method defined in the endpoint interface must declare the `java.rmi.RemoteException` in its `throws` clause. `RemoteException` is used to report any networking problems associated with processing a client's SOAP request. SOAP clients will not use the EJB endpoint interface directly. Instead SOAP clients will use the WSDL document associated with the EJB endpoint to generate their own service interface. If the client is a Java client, then you will probably use the JAX-RPC compiler to generate the client's own endpoint interface and stubs as I explained in Section 12.1: Generated Stubs. If the client is a .NET application or a Perl program or some other kind of client, you'll use some other SOAP toolkit to generate appropriate service interfaces to the Web service. The real purpose of the endpoint interface is to declare the Web service operations supported by the EJB endpoint, and any faults those operations may generate.

At deployment time the J2EE application server's deployment tools can examine the endpoint interface, along with other information provided by deployment descriptors, and use it to generate the `portType` and `message` definitions of the WSDL document. For example, the `BookQuote` endpoint interface maps to the definitions in Listing 11–7.

Listing 11–7

The WSDL Generated from the `BookQuote` *Interface*

```
<?xml version="1.0" encoding="utf-8"?>
<definitions xmlns="http://schemas.xmlsoap.org/wsdl/"
  xmlns:xsd="http://www.w3.org/2001/XMLSchema"
  xmlns:tns="http://www.Monson-Haefel.com/ed1/BookQuote"
```

```
  targetNamespace="http://www.Monson-Haefel.com/ed1/BookQuote" ...>
  <message name="getBookPriceRequest">
    <part name="isbn" type="xsd:string"/>
  </message>
  <message name="getBookPriceResponse">
    <part name="result" type="xsd:float"/>
  </message>
  <portType name="BookQuote">
    <operation name="getBookPrice">
      <input message="tns:getBookPriceRequest"/>
      <output message="tns:getBookPriceResponse"/>
    </operation>
  </portType>
  ...
</definitions>
```

11.2.1.2 The Bean Class

Once you've defined the endpoint interface, you can define the bean class, which will do the actual work of processing BookQuote Web service requests. Listing 11–8 defines the `BookQuoteBean` class.

Listing 11–8

The EJB Endpoint Bean Class

```
package com.jwsbook.jaxrpc;
import javax.ejb.SessionContext;

public class BookQuoteBean_1 implements javax.ejb.SessionBean {
  public void ejbCreate( ){}

  public float getBookPrice(String isbn) {
    return 24.99f;
  }

  public void setSessionContext(SessionContext cntxt){}
  public void ejbActivate() {}
  public void ejbPassivate() {}
  public void ejbRemove(){}
}
```

Although the bean class must implement all methods defined in the endpoint interface, it's not required to implement the interface itself. This is in keeping with the EJB platform convention of not implementing remote or local interfaces. It doesn't hurt anything to make the bean class implement the endpoint interface, though, because unlike the remote and local interfaces, the endpoint interface defines only business methods—it doesn't inherit EJB object methods. In any case, whether you choose to extend the endpoint interface explicitly or not, the bean class must implement methods that match the endpoint interface methods exactly. The only exception to this rule is the `Exception` types thrown by the bean class's methods. Each method in the implementation class must throw the same exceptions that the corresponding methods in the interface throw—except one: `java.rmi.RemoteException`. The endpoint bean's methods must never declare `RemoteException`.

A SOAP client will use the WSDL document associated with the EJB endpoint to send an appropriate SOAP message to the J2EE application server that hosts the EJB endpoint. Figure 11–1 shows how an EJB endpoint processes a SOAP message sent from a Web service client.

Invoking an EJB Web service as illustrated in Figure 11–1 proceeds as follows:

1. The Web service client sends a SOAP message to the EJB container hosting the EJB endpoint.
2. When the EJB container receives the SOAP message, it extracts the parameters from the message, then invokes the corresponding method of an EJB instance.
3. The EJB endpoint processes the request. If there is a return value, the EJB container constructs a SOAP reply message. If the endpoint method throws an exception, the EJB container generates an appropriate SOAP fault message.
4. The EJB container sends the SOAP reply or fault message back to the Web service client.

Every stateless session bean, whether it's used as a Web service endpoint or not, must define a bean class that implements the `javax.ejb.SessionBean` interface. The `SessionBean` interface defines a number of callback methods the container uses to interact with the bean. The purpose of these callback methods is discussed in detail later, in Section 11.2.2.2.

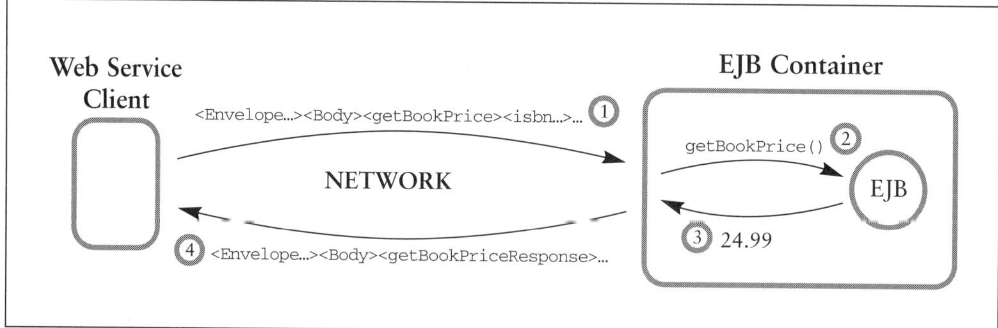

Figure 11–1 An EJB Endpoint Handling a SOAP Call

In addition to the callback methods, an EJB endpoint's bean class must declare an `ejbCreate()` method. This may perform initialization work that cannot be done in the `setSessionContext()` method. Specifically, it can access the EJB object, EJB home, and `TimerService` objects that are not available in the `setSessionContext()` method.

The `ejbCreate()` method must not declare any parameters because it's called by the container rather than a client, so there are no arguments to pass to it. If you find the purpose of the `ejbCreate()` method in stateless session beans a bit ambiguous, be content—you are not alone. The reason it's there has to do with providing a programming model that is consistent with other bean types, especially the stateful session bean, whose `ejbCreate()` method is actually directly linked to calls made on its EJB home. Because EJB endpoints do not have a home interface, the role of the `ejbCreate()` method is further marginalized. You must define it, however, if you want your EJB to deploy, so simply accept it as "one of those things" and implement it with an empty method body.

11.2.1.3 Deployment Descriptors and Packaging

In addition to the endpoint interface and the bean class, the EJB developer must provide a **deployment descriptor,** and will usually need to **package** the EJB endpoint in a JAR file. In many cases a J2EE deployment tool will do this automatically. All you'll need to do is fill in fields related to security and transactions and then choose some deployment option from the GUI. It's always helpful, however, to have some idea of what is in the deployment descriptor because it helps you understand the information used by the container—and you may have to write the deployment descriptor by hand if your J2EE deployment tool doesn't do it for you.

The deployment descriptors and packaging are discussed in more detail in Part VII. The whole deployment process is a bit complicated. Fundamentally, there are at least two basic deployment descriptors you must create for an EJB endpoint:

The `ejb-jar.xml` deployment descriptor declares the bean class, the local and remote interfaces, and the endpoint interface. In addition, it declares the JNDI ENC references to other beans, resources, Web services, and environment variables. Finally, it declares the security and transaction attributes of the EJB.

The `webservices.xml` deployment descriptor describes each Web service endpoint and links these descriptions to an endpoint, either JSE or EJB. In either case `webservices.xml` declares the location of the WSDL document, the `port` definition associated with the endpoint, the JAX-RPC mapping file, the endpoint interface, and a link to the actual component.

In addition to `ejb-jar.xml` and `webservices.xml`, the deployment tool will generate a JAX-RPC mapping file, which defines more complex mappings, between Java objects used as parameters and return values on one hand, and the XML types used in SOAP and WSDL on the other.

The deployment descriptors, endpoint interface, user-defined types, and bean class are all packaged together in a JAR file according to the packaging conventions described in the EJB and Web Services for J2EE 1.1 specification. Again, all this is covered in more detail in Part VII.

11.2.2 The EJB Runtime Environment

At runtime an EJB can access resources, other EJBs, and Web services using its JNDI ENC. (If you're not familiar with the JNDI Environment Naming Context, you should read Section 10.2.2 before proceeding into this section.) In addition, an EJB can interact with its container via callback methods and the `SessionContext` interface. Transactions and security are managed automatically by the EJB container system, which is responsible for starting and ending new transactions, propagating client transactions, authenticating and authorizing clients, and propagating both transactions and security identities from one EJB to the next. The following sections provide a detailed explanation of the EJB's interface to the container, as well as a detailed discussion of transaction and security attributes.

11.2.2.1 The JNDI Environment Naming Context

We can beef up the `BookQuote` bean class by using the JNDI ENC to obtain a JDBC connection, which can then be used to fetch the wholesale price of a book from a database. Listing 11–9 illustrates.

Listing 11–9

An EJB Endpoint That Uses JDBC

```
package com.jwsbook.jaxrpc;
import javax.ejb.SessionContext;

public class BookQuoteBean_2 implements javax.ejb.SessionBean {
  SessionContext ejbContext;
  public void ejbCreate( ){}

  public float getBookPrice(String isbn){
    java.sql.Connection jdbcConnection = null;
    java.sql.Statement sqlStatement = null;
    java.sql.ResultSet resultSet;
    try {
      javax.naming.InitialContext jndiEnc =
                                  new javax.naming.InitialContext();
      javax.sql.DataSource dataSource = (javax.sql.DataSource)
                  jndiEnc.lookup("java:comp/env/jdbc/DataSource");
      jdbcConnection = dataSource.getConnection();
      sqlStatement = jdbcConnection.createStatement();
      resultSet = sqlStatement.executeQuery(
        "SELECT wholesale FROM CATALOG WHERE isbn = \'"+isbn+"\'");
```

```
            if(resultSet.next()){
              float price = resultSet.getFloat("wholesale");
              return price;
            }
            return 0;// zero means its not stocked.
        }catch (java.sql.SQLException se) {
            throw new RuntimeException("JDBC access failed");
        }catch (javax.naming.NamingException ne){
            throw new RuntimeException("JNDI ENC access failed");
        }
    }
    ...
}
```

Obviously, this implementation is far more useful than simply returning a literal value. Wholesale prices are actually obtained from a relational database, which can provide up-to-date wholesale pricing on any book in Monson-Haefel Books' catalog. The JNDI ENC used by EJB endpoints is pretty much the same as the JNDI ENC used by the JSE. For a more detailed explanation of the JNDI ENC, see Section 10.2.2.

11.2.2.2 The `SessionBean` *Interface*

A stateless session bean class must implement the `javax.ejb.SessionBean` interface. The container uses this interface to alert the bean to events in its life cycle. Its definition is shown in Listing 11–10.

Listing 11–10

The `javax.ejb.SessionBean` *Interface*

```
package javax.ejb;
public interface SessionBean extends javax.ejb.EnterpriseBean {
    public void setSessionContext(SessionContext cntxt);
    public void ejbActivate();
    public void ejbPassivate();
    public void ejbRemove();
}
```

A stateless session bean's life cycle is really very simple. Initially the EJB container system might create a few stateless session beans for each deployment, and keep them in an instance pool, ready to handle requests. A specified procedure is followed while creating new instances and preparing them to service requests as illustrated in Figure 11–2.

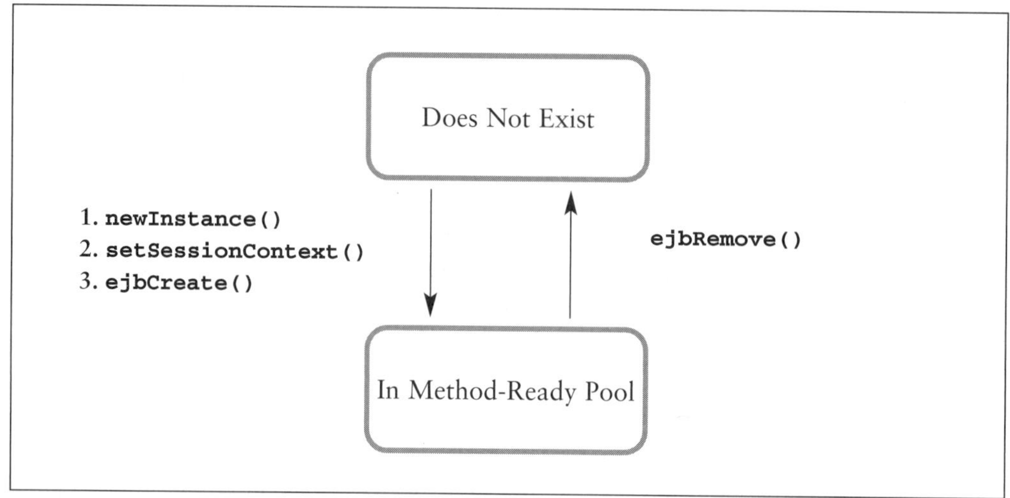

Figure 11–2 Stateless Session Bean Life Cycle

Creation of each bean instance entails three method calls, in this order:

1. The EJB container instantiates the bean class by calling its `newInstance()` method (this is equivalent to using a no-arg constructor).
2. The container then calls the bean's `setSessionContext()` method—just this once in the life of the bean instance.
3. At some point before the bean instance handles its first client request, the container calls its `ejbCreate()` method—again, only this one time.

After these three methods have been called, the bean instance enters the **method-ready pool,** at which point it is all set to process client requests. As the EJB container receives SOAP messages, it matches them up with the appropriate EJB, then selects an instance of that EJB from the method-ready pool. The SOAP call is delegated to the corresponding method of the instance. After the method returns, the bean instance is returned to the instance pool, ready for another request.

A stateless instance must not maintain client-specific state information between method invocations because, with every request, it may be serving a completely different client. It's for this reason that a stateless session bean is stateless.

Eventually the instance life cycle will come to an end, typically for one of three reasons: The J2EE application server is shut down, the EJB container reduces the number of instances in the pool to conserve resources, or an unexpected failure causes the J2EE application server to go down. In the first two cases, where the instance life cycle ends naturally, the EJB container will call the bean's `ejbRemove()` method to notify the instance that it's about to be dereferenced and made eligible for garbage collection. At that point, the bean instance should close any resources it has opened. In the event of an unanticipated shutdown, the bean instance is simply lost when the process that is running the EJB container's VM ends.

Although the `ejbActivate()` and `ejbPassivate()` callback methods are useful to stateful session beans (which also implement the `SessionBean` interface), they are not used with stateless session beans. Because they are part of the `SessionBean` interface, the stateless bean class must implement them, so just provide an empty implementation for each.

11.2.2.3 The `SessionContext`

The `SessionContext` provides the EJB endpoint instance with some information and access to functionality that may be useful while serving SOAP clients. The EJB instance receives the `SessionContext` when its `setSessionContext()` method is called. Because this method is called only once in the life of an instance, it must store the reference to the `SessionContext` in an instance variable if it wants to use it later, as in this snippet from Listing 11–9:

```
package com.jwsbook.jaxrpc;
import javax.ejb.SessionContext;

public class BookQuoteBean_2 implements javax.ejb.SessionBean {
  SessionContext ejbContext;
  ...
  public void setSessionContext(SessionContext cntxt){
    ejbContext = cntxt;
  }
  ...
}
```

The `SessionContext` is an interface implemented by the container. The information and functionality provided by `SessionContext` changes depending on the how the EJB is deployed, what SOAP client is being served, and from which method it's accessed. The `SessionContext` interface extends the `javax.ejb.EJBContext` interface. The methods provided by both interfaces are shown in Listing 11–11. The methods that `SessionContext` itself declares are in boldface; the rest are inherited from `EJBContext`. Several methods in the `EJBContext` interface have been deprecated and are no longer used; these methods are not shown.

Listing 11–11

The `javax.ejb.SessionContext` *Interface (with Inherited Methods)*

```
package javax.ejb;
import java.security.Principal;
```

```
public interface SessionContext extends EJBContext {

    public EJBLocalObject getEJBLocalObject();
    public EJBObject getEJBObject();

    public EJBLocalHome getEJBLocalHome();
    public EJBHome getEJBHome();

    public Principal getCallerPrincipal();
    public boolean isCallerInRole(String roleName);

    public UserTransaction getUserTransaction();
    public boolean getRollbackOnly();
    public void setRollbackOnly();

    public MessageContext getMessageContext();
    public TimerService getTimerService();

}
```

The EJB object methods, `getEJBObject()` and `getEJBLocalObject()`, and the EJB home methods, `getEJBHome()` and `getEJBLocalHome()`, return references to the EJB's remote and local interfaces. If you deploy the EJB as a Web services endpoint and do not define a remote or local interface, these methods will throw a `java.lang.IllegalStateException` when called.

The `SessionContext.getCallerPrincipal()` method returns a `javax.security.Principal` object, which represents the SOAP client's security identity. This method will return a `Principal` only if the SOAP client was authenticated before the call was dispatched to the bean instance. The `Principal` may be used for logging and other activities. The J2EE application server may use HTTP Basic Authentication or Symmetric HTTP to authenticate a SOAP client. These authentication mechanisms were discussed in detail in Section 10.2.3.2.1.

A caller's `Principal` may be associated with one or more **roles.** A role is a logical grouping of security identities, and a single `Principal` can be associated with many different roles. For example, a bank employee identified by `Principal` X might be associated with the three security roles of Teller, Bank Manager, and Human Resources Manager. Roles can be used to determine whether a `Principal` is authorized to perform a specific action. You can determine whether a `Principal` is associated with a specific role by invoking the `isCallerInRole()` method. The following snippet from Listing 11–5 shows how to ensure that only a `Principal` associated with the `BankManager` role may transfer more than $100,000.00 from one account to another.

```
package jwsed1.support;
import javax.ejb.SessionContext;
import javax.naming.InitialContext;
import java.util.Date;
import java.security.Principal;

public class MoneyTransferEJB implements javax.ejb.SessionBean {
  SessionContext ejbContext;
  public void create( ){}

  public void transfer(int acctA, int acctB, double amount){
    try{
      if(amount > 100000.0d && !ejbContext.isCallerInRole("BankManager")){
       Principal principal = ejbContext.getCallerPrincipal();
       throw new AuthorizationException(principal.getName()+
              " is not authorized to transfer over $100,000.00");
      }
      ...
  }
  ...
}
```

The `SessionContext.getUserTransaction()` method returns a `javax.transaction.UserTransaction` that can be used to begin, commit, and roll back transactions. This object is necessary if you want your EJB to manage its own transactions rather than using method-level declarative transactions. In practice, **bean-managed transactions** are rarely used, and the `UserTransaction` object is generally not needed. The EJB container provides a much simpler declarative transaction-management system tied to the methods themselves. **Container-managed transactions** allow you to declare, at development time, the transactional characteristics of methods.

The `SessionContext.getRollbackOnly()` method allows you to check the status of a container-managed transaction. This method will return `true` if the transaction has been marked for rollback. As you learned in Section 11.1, transactions can be propagated from one EJB to the next. Along the way, any one of them may invoke the `setRollbackOnly()` method, to mark the transaction for rollback and thus ensure that the transaction cannot commit. Another way to roll back a transaction is to throw a `javax.ejb.EJBException` or some other `java.lang.RuntimeException`. `RuntimeExceptions` always force a transaction to roll back and will also evict the offending instance from memory, ensuring that unstable bean instances are not used to handle subsequent client requests.

The `SessionContext.getMessageContext()` method allows an EJB endpoint to access a SAAJ representation of the SOAP message it's processing. In addition, it provides access to any properties set by its handler chain. This method is available only on the J2EE 1.4 platform. `getMessageContext()` returns a `MessageContext` object, which is discussed in detail in Section 14.3.4.

The `SessionContext.getTimerService()` method returns an interface to the EJB Timer Service in the form of a `TimerService` object. This method is available only on the J2EE 1.4 platform. The EJB Timer Service allows you to schedule an EJB to receive a callback method at a specific time, or at repeating intervals. These features are convenient for scheduling-type operations.

11.3 Wrapping Up

Using an EJB as a Web service endpoint can be a bit like using a sledgehammer to pound in a nail; it can be overkill if your Web service doesn't require automatic transaction management. In many cases, a Web service just performs simple reads or updates to a single database. In these cases, you want as light an implementation as possible, and the far simpler JSE may be preferable to an EJB endpoint—especially if the operations are read-only. For simple Web services like BookQuote, a JSE will achieve higher throughput than an EJB endpoint, because EJB containers tend to introduce a certain amount of overhead while managing transactions and security.

That said, there is nothing better than EJB when it comes to highly transactional services. If your Web service will be modifying data via resources like JDBC and JMS, or coordinating the activities of other EJBs that modify data, then it's a good idea to use an EJB endpoint. Only EJB endpoints are designed to handle the heavy transactional loads associated with this kind of work.

Enterprise JavaBeans is a very complex technology. Although it tends to make transaction management safer and, in the case of CMP entity beans, persistence easier, it requires significant investment of time to understand and master. If you think you will need to use EJB endpoints but you have no experience with EJB, then you should pick up a good book on the subject and study it carefully first.

Chapter 12
JAX-RPC Client APIs

JAX-RPC defines three programming models that Java applications can use to access Web services: **generated stubs, dynamic proxies,** and **DII.** Of these, the one you're most likely to use is generated stubs. Dynamic proxies and DII are interesting but less practical for most development efforts. That said, this chapter pays a great deal of attention to all three programming models so you can become familiar with each, and apply them as you see fit.

12.1 Generated Stubs

The purpose of the **generated stub** programming model is to provide object façades for accessing Web service endpoints. In other words, generated stubs make Web service endpoints look like local Java objects. A generated stub is created by a utility called a **JAX-RPC compiler.** J2EE vendors provide their own JAX-RPC compilers, some as command-line utilities, some built into GUI deployment tools. Regardless of the interface they use, all JAX-RPC compilers do essentially the same thing: They read a WSDL document and generate from it at least two Java class files, an **endpoint interface** and a **generated stub class.** The endpoint interface extends `java.rmi.Remote` and defines the methods that can be invoked on the Web service endpoint. The generated stub class implements the endpoint interface. At runtime an instance of the generated stub class converts each method invocation made on the remote interface into a SOAP 1.1 message, and sends it to the Web service endpoint. The generated stub also converts each SOAP reply message into a method return value, or throws an exception if the reply message is a SOAP fault.

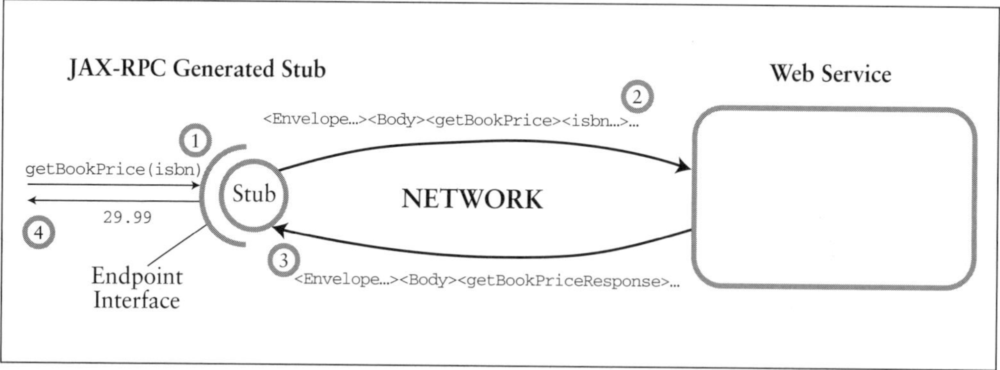

Figure 12–1 A Generated Stub Communicates with a Web Service

For example, you could use a generated stub to invoke operations on either of the BookQuote endpoints that you developed in Chapters 10 and 11. The endpoint interface would model the BookQuote endpoint by defining a single method, `getBookPrice()`, which accepts a `String` parameter containing a book's ISBN, and returns the wholesale price as a `float` type. The generated stub is responsible for sending SOAP messages to the BookQuote endpoint and processing SOAP reply messages sent back from the endpoint. Figure 12–1 illustrates.

The endpoint interface and stub class are generated from the WSDL document that describes the Web service endpoint. A JAX-RPC compiler will read the WSDL document and generate an endpoint interface that represents the abstract `portType`, and a generated stub class that implements the network protocol and SOAP messaging style described by the `binding` and `port` definitions.[1]

The JAX-RPC specification defines a detailed mapping between WSDL and generated stubs. It includes rules for mapping the abstract `message`, `operation`, and `portType` definitions, as well as XML schema types (simple and complex), to JAX-RPC endpoint interfaces. The full complement of rules for these mappings is quite complex. Chapter 15 provides detailed coverage, but in this section I'll keep it simple by using the most basic WSDL definitions and XML schema types.

12.1.1 The Endpoint Interface

The endpoint interface is derived from the WSDL `portType` definition, and each of the interface's methods represents a WSDL `operation` definition. To illustrate I'll use the WSDL document defined for the BookQuote Web service, shown in Listing 12–1.

[1] In some cases the binding may also influence the definition of the endpoint interface.

Listing 12–1

The WSDL Document for the BookQuote Web Service

```
<?xml version="1.0" encoding="UTF-8"?>
<definitions name="BookQuoteWS"
 targetNamespace="http://www.Monson-Haefel.com/jwsbook/BookQuote"
 xmlns:mh="http://www.Monson-Haefel.com/jwsbook/BookQuote"
 xmlns:soapbind="http://schemas.xmlsoap.org/wsdl/soap/"
 xmlns:xsd="http://www.w3.org/2001/XMLSchema"
 xmlns="http://schemas.xmlsoap.org/wsdl/">

  <!-- message elements describe the input and output parameters -->
  <message name="GetBookPriceRequest">
    <part name="isbn" type="xsd:string" />
  </message>
  <message name="GetBookPriceResponse">
    <part name="price" type="xsd:float" />
  </message>

  <!-- portType element describes the abstract interface of a Web service -->
  <portType name="BookQuote">
    <operation name="getBookPrice">
      <input name="isbn" message="mh:GetBookPriceRequest"/>
      <output name="price" message="mh:GetBookPriceResponse"/>
    </operation>
  </portType>

  <!-- binding tells us which protocols and encoding styles are used  -->
  <binding name="BookQuote_Binding" type="mh:BookQuote">
    <soapbind:binding style="rpc"
     transport="http://schemas.xmlsoap.org/soap/http"/>
    <operation name="getBookPrice">
      <soapbind:operation style="rpc"
       soapAction="http://www.Monson-Haefel.com/jwsbook/BookQuote"/>
        <input>
          <soapbind:body use="literal"
           namespace="http://www.Monson-Haefel.com/jwsbook/BookQuote" />
        </input>
        <output>
          <soapbind:body use="literal"
           namespace="http://www.Monson-Haefel.com/jwsbook/BookQuote" />
        </output>
    </operation>
```

```
  </binding>

  <!-- service tells us the Internet address of a Web service -->
  <service name="BookQuoteService">
    <port name="BookQuotePort" binding="mh:BookPrice_Binding">
      <soapbind:address
       location="http://www.Monson-Haefel.com/jwsbook/BookQuote" />
    </port>
  </service>

</definitions>
```

A JAX-RPC compiler will take the portType and operation definitions in this WSDL document and generate the endpoint interface shown in Listing 12–2.

Listing 12–2

The Endpoint Interface Generated from the WSDL Document in Listing 12–1

```
package com.jwsbook.jaxrpc;

public interface BookQuote extends java.rmi.Remote {
  public float getBookPrice(String isbn) throws java.rmi.RemoteException;
}
```

The name of the endpoint interface comes from the portType name. Similarly, there is a one-to-one mapping between methods defined in the endpoint interface and operation definitions declared by the portType. The parameters and return value of each endpoint method are derived from message definitions that the portType refers to in the input and output elements of an operation element. Each parameter name and type derives from a part of the input message, and the return type derives from the part of the output message. It's important to stress that this is a very simple mapping. More complex mappings may involve complex types, arrays, and multiple OUT and INOUT parameter types, all of which are covered in Chapter 15.

12.1.2 The Generated Stub

The JAX-RPC compiler will also generate the stub class that implements the endpoint interface. An instance of the generated stub class (routinely shortened to "the stub") is responsible for translating method calls into SOAP communications with the Web service endpoint. It will perform this translation according to the WSDL binding associated with the portType, which describes the style of messaging (rpc or document) and the type of encoding (always Literal in BP-conformant Web services). The stub will use the soap:address element specified by the WSDL port definition as the URL of the Web service.

In addition to implementing the endpoint interface, the stub class will also implement the javax.xml.rpc.Stub interface, which defines methods for reading and setting properties relating to network communication and authentication. Using these, an application can set the endpoint address, user name, password, and so on at runtime. The Stub interface appears in Listing 12–3.

Listing 12–3

The javax.xml.rpc.Stub *Interface*

```
package javax.xml.rpc;
import java.util.Iterator;

public interface Stub {

    // Standard property: The Web service's Internet address.
    public static String ENDPOINT_ADDRESS_PROPERTY;
    // Standard property: Password for authentication.
    public static String PASSWORD_PROPERTY;
    // Standard property: User name for authentication.
    public static String USERNAME_PROPERTY;
    // Standard property: Boolean flag for maintaining an HTTP session.
    public static String SESSION_MAINTAIN_PROPERTY;

    // Given a property name, get its value.
    public Object _getProperty(java.lang.String name);
    // Get the names of all the properties the stub supports.
    public Iterator _getPropertyNames();
    // Configure a property on the stub.
    public void _setProperty(java.lang.String name, java.lang.Object value);

}
```

For the most part, you won't use the property methods of the Stub interface. A few of the properties are standard (including all the ones that appear in Listing 12–3), while others are vendor-specific and will be defined in your vendor's documentation.

12.1.3 Service Interfaces

The JAX-RPC compiler can, as an option, generate a **service interface** representing the service definition from a WSDL document, and a class that implements this interface. A J2EE component can use an instance of the service interface, called a

service, to obtain a reference to a specific generated stub. The service interface defines an accessor for every `port` declared by the `service` definition. For example, the service interface generated from the BookQuote WSDL document would look like Listing 12–4.

Listing 12–4

The Service Interface Generated from the WSDL Document in Listing 12–1

```
package com.jwsbook.jaxrpc;

public interface BookQuoteService extends javax.xml.rpc.Service{
    public BookQuote getBookQuotePort()
    throws javax.xml.rpc.ServiceException;
}
```

The name of the service interface, in this case `BookQuoteService`, comes from the `name` attribute of the WSDL `service` definition. The accessor method, `getBookQuotePort()`, gets its method name from the `name` attribute of the WSDL `port` element. The return type is the endpoint interface type that the JAX-RPC compiler generated for the corresponding `portType`, in this case the `BookQuote` endpoint interface.

The service interface is implemented by a class generated by the JAX-RPC compiler. An instance of this class instantiates and preconfigures generated stubs requested by the client. In J2EE, the service is bound to the JNDI ENC (Environment Naming Context), and is used to obtain a reference to the generated stub. Think of the service as a factory for generated stubs.

The service interface extends the `javax.xml.rpc.Service` interface, which defines methods normally used with the dynamic proxy and DII programming models covered later in this chapter. We'll examine `javax.xml.rpc.Service` in detail at that time.

12.1.4 Using a Generated Stub in J2EE

Once you've generated the endpoint interfaces, the stubs, and the service, a J2EE component can use them to access the Web service endpoint described by the original WSDL document. The generated stub is "hard-wired" to use the protocol and network address described by the WSDL document, so all a client needs to do is obtain a reference to the stub from the service.

A standard J2EE component (J2EE client application, EJB, servlet, JSP, or JSE) can obtain a reference to any service from its JNDI ENC, so from a developer perspective it's easy to access the service and obtain a generated stub. For example, Listing 12–5 is a J2EE servlet that is deployed with a reference to the `BookQuote Service` registered in its JNDI ENC.

Listing 12–5

Using a Generated Stub from a Servlet

```
package com.jwsbook.jaxrpc;
import javax.servlet.http.*;
import javax.servlet.*;
import javax.naming.InitialContext;

public class BookQuoteServlet_1 extends javax.servlet.http.HttpServlet {
  protected void doGet(HttpServletRequest req, HttpServletResponse resp)
  throws ServletException,java.io.IOException {
    try{
      String isbn = req.getParameter("isbn");

      InitialContext jndiContext = new InitialContext();

      BookQuoteService service = (BookQuoteService)
      jndiContext.lookup("java:comp/env/service/BookQuoteService");

      BookQuote bookQuote = service.getBookQuotePort();

      float price = bookQuote.getBookPrice( isbn );

      java.io.Writer outStream = resp.getWriter();
      outStream.write("<html><body>The wholesale price for ISBN:"+isbn+
                      " = "+price+"</body></html>");
    }catch(javax.naming.NamingException ne){
      throw new ServletException(ne);
    }catch(javax.xml.rpc.ServiceException se){
      throw new ServletException(se);
    }
  }
}
```

This servlet first obtains a reference to the default JNDI ENC by instantiating a new `javax.naming.InitialContext` object. As you recall from Section 10.2.2, when a J2EE component creates a new instance of the `InitialContext`, the J2EE container intervenes and returns the root context of the JNDI ENC for that component.

At deployment time the implementation class of the `BookQuoteService` interface is assigned to the JNDI namespace `"java:comp/env/service/BookQuote Service"` by a **service reference element.** The service reference element is covered in detail in Section 22.5, but a quick peek now won't hurt. A JAX-RPC Web service is declared in a service-ref element of the deployment descriptor of a J2EE component. Listing 12–6 shows an example of a service-ref element.

Listing 12–6

A service-ref *Element*

```
<service-ref xmlns:mh="http://www.Monson-Haefel.com/jwsbook/BookQuote" >
    <service-ref-name>service/BookQuoteService</service-ref-name>
    <service-interface>com.jwsbook.jaxrpc.BookQuoteService</service-interface>
    <wsdl-file>BookQuote.wsdl</wsdl-file>
    <service-qname>mh:BookQuoteService</service-qname>
</service-ref>
```

At this point, don't worry about how the service-ref element is declared. The important thing to understand is that the service-ref element declares the JAX-RPC service as a resource available to the J2EE component. At deployment time the deployer will take care of actually binding the service to the JNDI ENC so it can be accessed at runtime.

The service interface will include a method that returns the generated stub. In this case, the BookQuoteService.getBookQuotePort() method returns the BookQuote stub. The stub methods can be invoked as many times as needed. The J2EE component can hold the service reference in an instance variable, so it doesn't need to use the JNDI ENC to get it again. The generated stub reference can also be kept in an instance variable and reused as needed. The BookQuoteServlet_2 shown in Listing 12–7 improves on BookQuoteServlet_1 (Listing 12–5) by caching and reusing the BookQuote generated stub.

Listing 12–7

Caching the JAX-RPC Generated Stub

```
package com.jwsbook.jaxrpc;
import javax.servlet.http.*;
import javax.servlet.*;
import javax.naming.InitialContext;

public class BookQuoteServlet_2 extends javax.servlet.http.HttpServlet {
  // A generated stub reference maintained for the life of the servlet
  BookQuote bookQuote;

  private BookQuote getStub() throws javax.naming.NamingException,
  javax.xml.rpc.ServiceException{
    if(bookQuote == null){
      InitialContext jndiEnc = new InitialContext();
```

```
        BookQuoteService service = (BookQuoteService)
            jndiEnc.lookup("java:comp/env/service/BookQuoteService");
        bookQuote = service.getBookQuotePort();
      }
      return bookQuote;
    }
  protected void doGet(HttpServletRequest req, HttpServletResponse resp)
  throws ServletException,java.io.IOException {
    try{
      String isbn = req.getParameter("isbn");

      float price = getStub().getBookPrice( isbn );

      java.io.Writer outStream = resp.getWriter();
      outStream.write("<html><body>The wholesale price for ISBN:"+isbn+
                      " = "+price+"</body></html>");
    }catch(javax.naming.NamingException ne){
      throw new ServletException(ne);
    }catch(javax.xml.rpc.ServiceException se){
      throw new ServletException(se);
    }
  }
}
```

While `BookQuoteServlet_2` isn't going to win any visual design contests, it does illustrate good program design when using generated stubs from J2EE components: The servlet's private helper method, `getStub()`, obtains the generated stub only once in the life of the component, and stores it in an instance variable to be reused as needed. The stub reference is lightweight and does not maintain a connection to a Web service—it reconnects briefly every time it's used[2]—so it doesn't consume extra resources while it's inactive. In fact, you should get better performance out of your J2EE component by maintaining a reference to a stub rather than fetching a new one with every request. This approach can be used with any of the J2EE components (J2EE application components, servlets, JSPs, EJBs, and JSEs).

When any of the stub's methods is invoked it will convert the method call into a SOAP message and send that message to the Web service endpoint. The WS-I Basic Profile 1.0 requires the use of an HTTP 1.1 POST to send a SOAP 1.1 message to the Web service.[BP] When the `BookQuote` stub's `getBookPrice()` method is invoked, the SOAP message sent to the Web service will look something like the one in Listing 12–8.

[2] This statement is true of JAX-RPC stubs that use HTTP 1.1, which is a connectionless protocol. All JAX-RPC providers must support HTTP 1.1 with SOAP, but may also support other protocols.

Listing 12–8

The SOAP Message Produced by the `BookQuote` *Generated Stub*

```
<?xml version="1.0" encoding="UTF-8"?>
<soap:Envelope
 xmlns:soap="http://schemas.xmlsoap.org/soap/envelope/"
 xmlns:mh="http://www.Monson-Haefel.com/jwsbook/BookQuote">
   <soap:Body>
      <mh:getBookPrice>
          <isbn>0321146182</isbn>
      </mh:getBookPrice>
   </soap:Body>
</soap:Envelope>
```

When the Web service replies, it sends a SOAP message back to the stub using an HTTP reply message. A normal reply from the BookQuote Web service would look like Listing 12–9.

Listing 12–9

The SOAP Reply Message from the BookQuote Web Service

```
<?xml version="1.0" encoding="UTF-8"?>
<soap:Envelope
 xmlns:soap="http://schemas.xmlsoap.org/soap/envelope/"
 xmlns:mh="http://www.Monson-Haefel.com/jwsbook/BookQuote">
   <soap:Body>
      <mh:getBookPriceResponse>
          <price>29.99</price>
      </mh:getBookPriceResponse>
   </soap:Body>
</soap:Envelope>
```

When the stub receives the SOAP reply message, it will extract its return value from the message or, if the message contains a fault, it will throw the appropriate Java exception.

The servlet examples in Listings 12–5 and 12–7 demonstrate how a J2EE servlet accesses a generated stub. The code used to access generated stubs from other J2EE components is exactly the same. They all use the JNDI ENC to get a reference to a service, from which they get a reference to the generated stub.

You can also use JAX-RPC from non-J2EE clients. This flexibility makes learning about JAX-RPC much easier because you don't have to deploy a servlet or EJB to try out some client code. Listing 12–10 shows you how to use JAX-RPC from a plain old J2SE application.

Listing 12–10

Accessing a Generated Stub from a Non-J2EE Client

```
package com.jwsbook.jaxrpc;
import javax.naming.InitialContext;

public class JaxRpcExample_1 {
  public static void main(String [] args) throws Exception{
    String isbn = args[0];

    BookQuoteService service = (BookQuoteService)
    ServiceFactory.loadService(com.jwsbook.jaxrpc.BookQuoteService.class);

    BookQuote bookQuote = service.getBookQuotePort();

    float price = bookQuote.getBookPrice( isbn );

    System.out.println("The price is = "+price);
  }
}
```

`JaxRpcExample_1` uses the static method `ServiceFactory.loadService()` to obtain a reference to the service object. This method can be used in non-J2EE clients only; J2EE components must use the JNDI ENC instead. Two overloaded versions of the `loadService()` method provide more specific information, including properties. Properties are vendor-specific, so use this method with care to avoid portability problems.

BookQuote is a Request/Response Web service, but generated stubs can also use One-Way messaging. If they do, their methods all return `void`. In Listing 12–11, the `foo` operation is defined with only an input message part, but its binding indicates that it uses RPC/Literal messaging.

Listing 12–11

A WSDL Document for a One-Way Web Service

```
<?xml version="1.0" encoding="utf-8"?>
<definitions xmlns="http://schemas.xmlsoap.org/wsdl/"
 xmlns:soap="http://schemas.xmlsoap.org/wsdl/soap/"
 xmlns:xsd="http://www.w3.org/2001/XMLSchema"
 xmlns:tns="http://www.Monson-Haefel.com/jwsbook/Foo"
 targetNamespace="http://www.Monson-Haefel.com/jwsbook/Foo">
  <message name="bar">
    <part name="value" type="xsd:string"/>
```

```
  </message>
  <portType name="Foo">
    <operation name="setBar">
      <input message="tns:bar"/>
    </operation>
  </portType>
  <binding name="FooBinding" type="tns:Foo">
    <soap:binding style="rpc"
        transport="http://schemas.xmlsoap.org/soap/http"/>
    <operation name="setBar">
      <soap:operation soapAction="" style="rpc"/>
      <input>
        <soap:body use="literal"
            namespace="http://www.Monson-Haefel.com/jwsbook/Foo"/>
      </input>
    </operation>
  </binding>
  ...
</definitions>
```

After compilation, the method in the endpoint interface has a return type of `void`, as shown in Listing 12–12.

Listing 12–12

The Endpoint Interface Generated from the WSDL Document in Listing 12–11

```
package com.jwsbook.jaxrpc;

public interface Foo extends java.rmi.Remote {
    public void setBar(String value) throws java.rmi.RemoteException;
}
```

Although the endpoint interface is semantically a one-way operation style, the underlying stub may in fact be using HTTP 1.1, which is a Request/Response protocol. In this case, the method returns after the stub receives the HTTP reply code (for example, `200` for OK) but it doesn't return any application data to the client. We don't have to handle a return value if there isn't a need for one, but we have some assurance that the SOAP message was received.

12.2 Dynamic Proxies

A **dynamic proxy,** as the name suggests, is created dynamically at runtime rather than generated statically at deployment time. Other than the method of accessing them, you use dynamic proxies to invoke Web service operations the same way you use generated stubs. The benefits of using dynamic proxies instead of generated stubs are not clear—it's probably best to stick with generated stubs. That said, it's important to know what your options are when using JAX-RPC.

12.2.1 Using a Dynamic Proxy

`JaxRpcExample_2`, in Listing 12–13, is a J2EE client application that shows how you can use a dynamic proxy to invoke the BookQuote Web service.

Listing 12–13

Using a Dynamic Proxy

```
package com.jwsbook.jaxrpc;
import javax.naming.InitialContext;

public class JaxRpcExample_2 {
  public static void main(String [] args) throws Exception{
    String isbn = args[0];

    InitialContext jndiContext = new InitialContext();

    javax.xml.rpc.Service service = (javax.xml.rpc.Service)
    jndiContext.lookup("java:comp/env/service/Service");

    BookQuote BookQuote_proxy = (BookQuote)
                              service.getPort(BookQuote.class);

    float price = BookQuote_proxy.getBookPrice( isbn );

    System.out.println("The price is = "+price);
  }
}
```

There is at least one significant difference between using a dynamic proxy and using a generated stub: You don't need a generated service interface. With dynamic proxies you can use the generic service interface `javax.xml.rpc.Service`. This interface defines two methods that can be used with dynamic proxies, shown in Listing 12–14.

Listing 12–14

The `javax.xml.rpc.Service` *Type's Dynamic Proxy Methods*

```
package javax.xml.rpc;

public interface Service {
```

```
    public java.rmi.Remote getPort(java.lang.Class endpointInterface)
    throws javax.xml.rpc.ServiceException;

    public java.rmi.Remote getPort(javax.xml.namespace.QName portName,
                                   java.lang.Class endpointInterface)
    throws javax.xml.rpc.ServiceException;

    ...
}
```

The whole point of dynamic proxies is that they are generated dynamically the first time you use them. At runtime the JAX-RPC provider (the vendor implementation) will read the WSDL document and generate a proxy to implement the endpoint interface at the moment the `getPort()` method is invoked. It may do so every time `getPort()` is invoked, but it will probably cache proxies for subsequent requests. The J2EE container generates the proxy by matching the endpoint interface passed into the `getPort()` method with a matching `portType` definition in the WSDL document, or by examining the JAX-RPC mapping file (covered in Chapter 24). If it finds a matching `portType`, it uses the `binding` and `port` definitions associated with that `portType` to create a class that implements the endpoint interface.

Of course this isn't a guessing game. When you deploy a J2EE component that uses a JAX-RPC dynamic proxy, you include a `service-ref` element in the deployment descriptor that tells the J2EE container which WSDL document you're using. Listing 12–15 shows a snippet of such a `service-ref` element.

Listing 12–15

A `service-ref` Element for a Dynamic Proxy

```
<service-ref xmlns:mh="http://www.Monson-Haefel.com/jwsbook/BookQuote" >
    <service-ref-name>service/Service</service-ref-name>
    <service-interface>javax.xml.rpc.Service</service-interface>
    <wsdl-file>BookQuote.wsdl</wsdl-file>
    <service-qname>mh:BookQuoteService</service-qname>
</service-ref>
```

You probably noticed that the `service-interface` is the generic `javax.xml.rpc.Service` interface customarily used with dynamic proxies. The `Service` interface is associated with a specific `service` definition in the WSDL document via the `service-qname` element in the `service-ref`. That way if the WSDL document defines more than one `service`, the J2EE container system can tell which `service` definition this `service-ref` is referring to. The `service-ref` element is declared in the deployment descriptor of the J2EE component. All this is covered in more detail in Chapter 23: Web Service Descriptors.

If there is only one `port` defined for the matching `portType`, the `getPort(Class)` method will create a dynamic proxy for that `port` definition. As you learned in Chapter 5, though, a single `portType` definition in a WSDL document may be the basis of more than one `port` definition. One WSDL `port` may use an RPC/Encoded binding, while another uses RPC/Literal. For example, review Listing 12–16 and assume the `BookQuote_EncodedBinding` uses RPC/Encoded SOAP 1.1 over HTTP, while the `BookQuote_LiteralBinding` uses RPC/Literal SOAP 1.1 over HTTP.

The use of RPC/Encoded messaging mode is prohibited by the Basic Profile, so this example should be considered as illustrative only.

Listing 12–16

A WSDL `service` *Element That Declares Two* `port` *Elements*

```
<?xml version="1.0" encoding="utf-8"?>
<definitions xmlns="http://schemas.xmlsoap.org/wsdl/"
 xmlns:soap="http://schemas.xmlsoap.org/wsdl/soap/"
 xmlns:xsd="http://www.w3.org/2001/XMLSchema"
 xmlns:mh="http://www.Monson-Haefel.com/jwsbook/BookQuote"
 targetNamespace="http://www.Monson-Haefel.com/jwsbook/BookQuote">
 ...
 <service name="BookQuote">
   <port name="BookQuoteEncodedPort" binding="mh:BookQuote_EncodedBinding">
     <soap:address location="http://www.Monson-Haefel/jwsbook/BookQuote/Encoded"/>
   </port>
   <port name="BookQuoteLiteralPort" binding="mh:BookQuote_LiteralBinding">
     <soap:address location="http://www.Monson-Haefel/jwsbook/BookQuote/Literal"/>
   </port>
 </service>
</definitions>
```

In this case the `binding` definition used to create the proxy depends on the JAX-RPC mapping file, which pinpoints the exact WSDL `binding` definition to use in cases where a WSDL `service` defines multiple ports. Listing 12–17 shows a snippet from a JAX-RPC mapping file that determines which WSDL `binding` should be used for the `service` element in Listing 12–16. The JAX-RPC mapping file is covered in detail in Chapter 24: JAX-RPC Mapping Files.

Listing 12–17

A Portion of a JAX-RPC Mapping File

```
<?xml version='1.0' encoding='UTF-8' ?>
<java-wsdl-mapping
  xmlns="http://java.sun.com/xml/ns/j2ee"
```

```
  xmlns:mh="http://www.Monson-Haefel.com/jwsbook/BookQuote"...>
  ...
  <service-endpoint-interface-mapping>
    <service-endpoint-interface>com.jwsbook.jaxrpc.BookQuote
    </service-endpoint-interface>
    <wsdl-port-type>mh:BookQuote</wsdl-port-type>
    <wsdl-binding>mh:BookQuote_LiteralBinding</wsdl-binding>
    ...
  </service-endpoint-interface-mapping>
</java-wsdl-mapping>
```

As an alternative, you can use the `Service.getPort(QName, Class)` method to create a dynamic proxy for the correct WSDL `port` and `binding`. In Listing 12–18 `JaxRpcExample_3` uses this method to request a dynamic proxy for the `BookQuoteLiteralPort` WSDL `port` definition.

Listing 12–18

Another Way of Using a Dynamic Proxy

```
package com.jwsbook.jaxrpc;
import javax.naming.InitialContext;
import javax.xml.namespace.QName;

public class JaxRpcExample_3 {
  public static void main(String [] args) throws Exception{
    String isbn = args[0];

    InitialContext jndiContext = new InitialContext();

    javax.xml.rpc.Service service = (javax.xml.rpc.Service)
    jndiContext.lookup("java:comp/env/service/Service");

    QName portName =
          new QName("http://www.Monson-Haefel/jwsbook/BookQuote",
          "BookQuoteLiteralPort");

    BookQuote BookQuote_proxy = (BookQuote)
                              service.getPort(portName, BookQuote.class);

    float price = BookQuote_proxy.getBookPrice( isbn );

    System.out.println("The price is = "+price);
  }
}
```

The QName class is defined in the javax.xml.namespace package (it's currently the only class in that package). An instance of this class represents an XML name. QName declares two constructors and a few accessor methods, as shown in Listing 12–19.

Listing 12–19

The javax.xml.namespace.QName *Class (Abbreviated)*

```
package javax.xml.namespace;

public class QName implements java.io.Serializable {
    public QName(String localPart) {…}
    public QName(String namespaceURI, String localPart){…}
    public String getNamespaceURI(){…}
    public String getLocalPart(){…}
    public static QName valueOf(String qualfiedName){…}
}
```

The constructors and accessors are pretty self-explanatory. The localPart is equal to the name assigned to the port, and namespaceURI is the XML namespace of the port. The static QName.valueOf() method allows you to create an instance of the port's QName from a single String value formatted as "{namespaceURI}local Part". The XML namespace of the port is nested in braces to separate it from the local name. The following code snippet creates two identical QNames in different ways, using a constructor, and using the static valueOf() method.

```
// Use constructor
QName qname1 = new QName("http://www.Monson-Haefel/jwsbook/BookQuote",
                         "BookQuoteLiteralPort");

// Use static valueOf() method
String s = "{http://www.Monson-Haefel/jwsbook/BookQuote}BookQuoteLiteralPort";
QName qname2 = QName.valueOf(s);
```

Dynamic proxies are usually used with the generic Service interface. You can also obtain them from generated service implementations, because generated service interfaces, like BookQuoteService in Listing 12–4, must extend the javax .xml.rpc.Service interface, and so support all the Service interface methods, including the getPort() methods for obtaining dynamic proxies.

The Service.getPort() methods may return a generated stub instead of a dynamic proxy. If you deploy a J2EE component that uses generated stubs and then make a call to the Service.getPort() method, you'll probably get back a stub rather than a dynamic proxy—it's difficult to tell the difference, because both dynamic proxies and generated stubs implement the javax.xml.rpc.Stub interface.

The endpoint interface used to create a dynamic proxy can be generated (using a JAX-RPC compiler), or it can be hand-coded by the developer. Either way it must conform to the JAX-RPC specification for mappings between WSDL and Java, and between XML and Java. These are covered in more detail in Chapter 15.

12.2.2 Under the Covers

Beneath the surface, the J2EE container system uses the J2SE Reflection API defined by the `java.lang.reflect` package to generate dynamic proxies. Specifically, it uses the `java.lang.reflect.Proxy` class, and implementations of the `java.lang.reflect.InvocationHandler` interface to create JAX-RPC dynamic proxies.

The dynamic proxy class extends the `java.lang.reflect.Proxy` class, so you have access to the methods defined by `Proxy`. As an application developer you won't need to use these methods, but knowing that dynamic proxies are a type of `java.lang.relect.Proxy` can be useful in rare situations.

12.3 DII

The **Dynamic Invocation Interface** (**DII**) defines an API for invoking operations on Web service endpoints. Unlike generated stubs and dynamic proxies, DII doesn't use an endpoint interface that is different for every `portType`. Instead, DII uses a fixed API that can be used to invoke operations on just about any endpoint. This makes the DII **toolable,** meaning it can be used by applications that automatically discover and invoke Web service operations.

12.3.1 Using DII with a WSDL Document

DII can be used with or without a WSDL document. If a WSDL document is available, it's much simpler to use because the details about the Web service operation being invoked can be derived from the WSDL document. To illustrate I'll use the `BookQuote.wsdl` document in Listing 12–20 as a guide.

Listing 12–20

The BookQuote WSDL Document

```
<?xml version="1.0" encoding="UTF-8"?>
<definitions name="BookQuoteWS"
 targetNamespace="http://www.Monson-Haefel.com/jwsbook/BookQuote"
 xmlns:mh="http://www.Monson-Haefel.com/jwsbook/BookQuote"
 xmlns:soapbind="http://schemas.xmlsoap.org/wsdl/soap/"
 xmlns:xsd="http://www.w3.org/2001/XMLSchema"
 xmlns="http://schemas.xmlsoap.org/wsdl/">
```

```
  <!-- message elements describe the input and output parameters -->
  <message name="GetBookPriceRequest">
    <part name="isbn" type="xsd:string" />
  </message>
  <message name="GetBookPriceResponse">
    <part name="price" type="xsd:float" />
  </message>

  <!-- portType element describes the abstract interface of a Web service -->
  <portType name="BookQuote">
    <operation name="getBookPrice">
      <input name="isbn" message="mh:GetBookPriceRequest"/>
      <output name="price" message="mh:GetBookPriceResponse"/>
    </operation>
  </portType>

  <!-- binding tells us which protocols and encoding styles are used  -->
  <binding name="BookQuote_Binding" type="mh:BookQuote">
    <soapbind:binding style="rpc"
     transport="http://schemas.xmlsoap.org/soap/http"/>
    <operation name="getBookPrice">
      <soapbind:operation style="rpc"
       soapAction="http://www.Monson-Haefel.com/jwsbook/BookQuote"/>
        <input>
          <soapbind:body use="literal"
           namespace="http://www.Monson-Haefel.com/jwsbook/BookQuote" />
        </input>
        <output>
          <soapbind:body use="literal"
           namespace="http://www.Monson-Haefel.com/jwsbook/BookQuote" />
        </output>
    </operation>
  </binding>

  <!-- service tells us the Internet address of a Web service -->
  <service name="BookQuoteService">
    <port name="BookQuotePort" binding="mh:BookQuote_Binding">
      <soapbind:address
       location="http://www.Monson-Haefel.com/jwsbook/BookQuote" />
    </port>
  </service>

</definitions>
```

Using the WSDL document in Listing 12–20 as a guide, we can access the BookQuote Web service using DII. In Listing 12–21 `JaxRpcExample_4` illustrates how to use DII to call the `getBookPrice` operation of the BookQuote Web service.

Listing 12–21

Using the DII with a WSDL Document

```
package com.jwsbook.jaxrpc;
import javax.naming.InitialContext;
import javax.xml.rpc.Service;
import javax.xml.rpc.Call;
import javax.xml.namespace.QName;

public class JaxRpcExample_4 {
  public static void main(String [] args) throws Exception{
    String isbn = args[0];

    InitialContext jndiContext = new InitialContext();

    javax.xml.rpc.Service service = (javax.xml.rpc.Service)
    jndiContext.lookup("java:comp/env/service/Service");

    QName portName =
     new QName("http://www.Monson-Haefel.com/jwsbook/BookQuote",
               "BookQuotePort");
    QName operationName =
     new QName("http://www.Monson-Haefel.com/jwsbook/BookQuote",
               "getBookPrice");

    Call call = service.createCall(portName,operationName);

    Object [] inputParams = new Object[]{isbn};

    Float price = (Float)call.invoke(inputParams);

    System.out.println("The price is = "+price.floatValue());
  }
}
```

The `javax.xml.rpc.Call` interface represents a Web service operation that can be invoked or called using the `Call.invoke()` method. `JaxRpcEample_4` first obtains a `javax.xml.rpc.Service` object from the JNDI ENC. As with generated stubs and dynamic proxies, the `Service` type is bound to the JNDI ENC using a service-ref element in a deployment descriptor. The service-ref element associates the Service type with a specific WSDL service element for a specific WSDL document, in this case BookQuote.wsdl. The WSDL document must be stored in the J2EE component's JAR file. wsdl-file specifies a path to the WSDL document, relative to the root of that JAR file.

```
<service-ref xmlns:mh="http://www.Monson-Haefel.com/jwsbook/BookQuote" >
    <service-ref-name>service/Service</service-ref-name>
    <service-interface>javax.xml.rpc.Service</service-interface>
    <wsdl-file>META-INF/BookQuote.wsdl</wsdl-file>
    <service-qname>mh:BookQuoteService</service-qname>
</service-ref>
```

Using the Service object, you can create a Call object for a specific WSDL port and operation. You use javax.xml.namespace.QName objects to identify the WSDL port and operation (go back to Section 12.2.1 if you need to review what you learned about the QName type). The following snippet from Listing 12–21 illustrates how the QName objects are used to identify the proper WSDL port and operation.

```
QName portName =
  new QName("http://www.Monson-Haefel.com/jwsbook/BookQuote",
            "BookQuotePort");
QName operationName =
  new QName("http://www.Monson-Haefel.com/jwsbook/BookQuote",
            "getBookPrice");

Call call = service.createCall(portName,operationName);
```

The Call object is associated with a specific WSDL operation of a specific port, from which it derives the proper operation style (RPC or Document) and encoding (for example, Literal). The Call object uses this information to construct the SOAP message it sends to the Web service. DII, like all JAX-RPC APIs, is required to support RPC/Literal, Document/Literal, and RPC/Encoded SOAP 1.1 messaging over HTTP 1.1. Although JAX-RPC requires vendors to support RPC/Encoded, it is prohibited by the WS-I Basic Profile.

Once the Call object is created, its invoke() method can be executed using the proper arguments as shown in the following snippet from Listing 12–21. In this case the Call object is associated with the getBookPrice operation of the BookQuote Web service, which defines only a single String type input parameter, an ISBN.

```
Object [] inputParams = new Object[]{isbn};

Float price = (Float)call.invoke(inputParams);
```

If the input message of the portType defines several part elements (parameters), then a value for each of those parameters is passed into the invoke() method using the Object array. The order that parameters are placed in the Object array depends on the parameterOrder attribute of the WSDL operation element in the portType. For example, in Section 5.2.3.1 the getBulkBookPrice operation was used as an example of an operation that defined a parameterOrder. A fragment of the WSDL document for that operation is shown in Listing 12–22.

Listing 12–22

The WSDL Document Definition for the getBulkBookQuote *Operation*

```
<message name="GetBulkBookPriceRequest">
  <part name="isbn" type="xsd:string"/>
  <part name="quantity" type="xsd:int"/>
</message>
<message name="GetBulkBookPriceResponse">
  <part name="prices" type="titan:prices" />
</message>
<portType name="GetBulkBookPrice" >
  <operation name="getBulkBookPrice" parameterOrder="isbn quantity">
     <input name="request" message="titan:GetBulkBookPriceRequest"/>
     <output name="prices" message="titan:GetBulkBookPriceResponse"/>
  </operation>
</portType>
```

In this case the parameters passed into the Call.invoke() method must be in the order defined by the parameterOrder attribute. In addition, the quantity must be a java.lang.Integer value instead of a primitive int—you can't put a primitive into an Object array. The following code snippet illustrates.

```
public static void main(String [] args) throws Exception{

   String isbn = args[0];
   Integer quantity = new Integer(args[1]);
   ...

   Object [] inputParams = new Object[]{isbn, quantity};

   Float price = (Float) call.invoke(inputParams);
}
```

The operation return value is always returned by the invoke() method. To retrieve the values of OUT and INOUT parameters, after the invoke() method is called you have to invoke the Call.getOutputValues() method, as here:

```
java.util.List outputParams = call.getOutputValues();
```

The returned `List` object contains all the OUT and INOUT arguments returned in the SOAP reply message. The OUT and INOUT parameters are used by Web service endpoints written in other programming languages—the Java programming language natively supports IN parameters and return values, but requires special facilities for handling OUT and INOUT parameters. The OUT and INOUT parameters are discussed in more detail in Section 15.3: Holders.

12.3.2 Using DII without a WSDL Document

The Basic Profile requires that Web service endpoints provide a WSDL document that describes the Web service. You may need to interact with a non-conformant Web service, however, in which case you can use the DII's facilities for messaging without a WSDL document. This topic is covered in more detail in Appendix H: Using JAX-RPC DII without a WSDL Document.

12.3.3 Using One-Way Messaging with DII

DII can be used to send One-Way messages as well as Request/Response messages. If you are sending an RPC/Literal message that does not require a reply message, you can simply use the `invokeOneWay()` method instead of `invoke()`. The only difference is that `invokeOneWay()` has no return value (or output values) and does not block, waiting for a reply (other than the HTTP reply with code `200`). This snippet shows how `invokeOneWay()` is called—it's very similar to a call to `invoke()`:

```
Object [] inputParams = new Object[]{value1, value2,…};
call.invokeOneWay(inputParams);
```

12.3.4 JAX-RPC Standard Properties and Constants

The JAX-RPC API defines a number of properties and constants that are used frequently with DII. You can see examples of these constants in use in Appendix H. This section simply provides a reference for you when using DII.

The `javax.xml.rpc.Call` class defines seven constants corresponding to standard properties, most of which are optional. Table 12–1lists each constant, its value, whether it's required to be supported by JAX-RPC vendors, and the meaning of the property.

Many of the standard properties need not be supported by JAX-RPC implementations, but most are. If a property is not supported, the `Call.setProperty()` method will throw a `javax.xml.rpc.JAXRPCException`. Just because a property must be supported doesn't mean it has to be declared. In fact, the Web Services for J2EE 1.1 specification discourages the use of the `USERNAME_PROPERTY` and `PASSWORD_PROPERTY` in J2EE, because the J2EE container usually handles authentication automatically.

Table 12–1 Constants Representing Standard Properties

`javax.xml.rpc.Call` **Constant = Property Value**	**Support Required**	**Definition**
`ENCODINGSTYLE_URI_PROPERTY = javax.xml.rpc.encodingstyle.namespace.uri`	No	Declares the encoding style used. The default value is SOAP 1.1 Encoding: http://schemas.xmlsoap.org/soap/encoding/.
`OPERATION_STYLE_PROPERTY = javax.xml.rpc.soap.operation.style`	No	Declares the operation style. The only values accepted are `"rpc"` and `"document"`.
`SOAPACTION_USE_PROPERTY = javax.xml.rpc.soap.http.soapaction.use`	No	Declares whether or not the `SOAPAction` header is used in the HTTP request. The value can be `true` or `false`. The default is `false`.
`SOAPACTION_URI_PROPERTY = javax.xml.rpc.soap.http.soapaction.uri`	No	If `SOAPAction` is used, declares the value of the `SOAPAction`.
`SESSION_MAINTAIN_PROPERTY = javax.xml.rpc.j session.maintain`	Yes	Declares whether the `Call` object must support session tracking (for example, cookies). The value can be `true` or `false`. The default is `false`.
`USERNAME_PROPERTY = javax.xml.rpc.security.auth.username`	Yes	Declares the user name for authentication.
`PASSWORD_PROPERTY = javax.xml.rpc.security.auth.password`	Yes	Declares the password for authentication.

JAX-RPC also defines the `javax.xml.rpc.NamespaceConstants` type, which contains a bunch of other SOAP 1.1 XML namespace URIs and prefix constants that are commonly used (see Table 12–2).

While the URI constants defined by the `NamespaceConstants` class are very useful, the prefix constants are less important. In XML, and therefore SOAP, you can pretty much use any prefixes you want. The industry tends to use a common set, however, such as those prefixes used in `NamespaceConstants`. The exception is the prefix used for the `Envelope` namespace, which varies from one vendor to the next, and includes prefixes like `SOAP-ENV`, `env`, `soapenv`, and others. Again, it's not that important. You can use any prefix you want.

Constructing `QName` objects is kind of a pain, so JAX-RPC provides the `javax.xml.rpc.encoding.XMLType` class that defines a couple of dozen final static `QName` constant values for the most common XML schema and SOAP 1.1 types. Table 12–3 lists them.

Table 12–2 Namespace Constants

javax.xml.rpc.NamespaceConstants	String **Value**
NSPREFIX_SOAP_ENVELOPE	soapenv
NSURI_SOAP_ENVELOPE	http://schemas.xmlsoap.org/soap/envelope/
NSPREFIX_SOAP_ENCODING	soapenc
NSURI_SOAP_ENCODING	http://schemas.xmlsoap.org/soap/encoding/
NSPREFIX_SCHEMA_XSD	xsd
NSURI_SCHEMA_XSD	http://www.w3.org/2001/XMLSchema
NSPREFIX_SCHEMA_XSI	xsi
NSURI_SCHEMA_XSI	http://www.w3.org/2001/XMLSchema-instance
NSURI_SOAP_NEXT_ACTOR	http://schemas.xmlsoap.org/soap/actor/next

Table 12–3 QName Constants Available in javax.xml.rpc.encoding.XMLType

Constant Field	Value
XSD_STRING	xsd:string
XSD_FLOAT	xsd:float
XSD_BOOLEAN	xsd:boolean
XSD_DOUBLE	xsd:double
XSD_INTEGER	xsd:integer
XSD_INT	xsd:int
XSD_LONG	xsd:long
XSD_SHORT	xsd:short
XSD_DECIMAL	xsd:decimal
XSD_BASE64	xsd:base64Binary
XSD_HEXBINARY	xsd:hexBinary
XSD_BYTE	xsd:byte
XSD_DATETIME	xsd:dateTime
XSD_QNAME	xsd:Qname
SOAP_STRING	soapenc:string
SOAP_FLOAT	soapenc:float
SOAP_BOOLEAN	soapenc:boolean
SOAP_DOUBLE	soapenc:double
SOAP_INT	soapenc:int
SOAP_LONG	soapenc:long
SOAP_SHORT	soapenc:short
SOAP_BASE64	soapenc:base64
SOAP_BYTE	soapenc:byte
SOAP_ARRAY	soapenc:Array

The constants that have an `xsd` prefix belong to the XML schema namespace (`xmlns:xsd="http://www.w3.org/2001/XMLSchema"`), while the constants prefixed with `soapenc` belong to the SOAP 1.1 Encoding namespace (`xmlns:soapenc="http://schemas.xmlsoap.org/soap/encoding"`).

Other than the `soapenc:Array` type, the only difference between a SOAP Encoding type and an XML schema document type is that the SOAP Encoding types are *nillable;* that is, they can take on null values. Because they are nillable, they are mapped to Java's primitive wrapper types, which can be null, rather than to the underlying primitive types, which can't. Using JAX-RPC with SOAP encoding is covered in Appendix G.

12.4 Wrapping Up

The first section of this chapter explained the basics of using generated stubs to access SOAP-based Web services. I say "the basics" because it didn't touch on several other topics you'll probably need to know over the course of your development work. For example, how are complex types, arrays, faults, and OUT and INOUT parameters handled? These types of questions are addressed in Chapter 15. Other topics are also important for you to know, like message handlers used to process header blocks, covered in Chapter 14.

Generated stubs are going to be the mainstay of your J2EE Web service client development. As you use generated stubs (or any other JAX-RPC API) you may occasionally encounter problems making them work with other Web service platforms. Web services interoperability is a moving target that has not been fully addressed by Web service technologies. SOAP and WSDL certainly go a long way toward interoperability, but there are enough "corner cases" to cause at least a few interoperability headaches. The WS-I Basic Profile 1.0 has done much to smooth out the interoperability wrinkles that tend to pop up.

DII is an interesting API that can be useful for tool vendors, but is generally not very useful to the average application developer. You are much better off using generated stubs, as they provide a simpler and more productive programming model and you can optimize them to be much faster than DII. It should be noted, however, that some JAX-RPC implementations actually use the DII libraries inside generated stubs and dynamic proxies to marshal method calls into SOAP messages. This approach allows the vendor to reuse DII, but it can decrease performance compared to optimized static code in generated stubs.

Chapter 13

SAAJ

To read and manipulate SOAP header blocks in JAX-RPC you have to use **message handlers,** which are covered in Chapter 14. Message handlers, however, use **SOAP with Attachments API for Java (SAAJ)**, version 1.2, to represent an XML SOAP message. Therefore, you need to understand how to use SAAJ before you can learn how to use message handlers. It's the purpose of this chapter to teach you how to create, read, and manipulate SOAP messages using SAAJ. While SAAJ is central to the JAX-RPC Message Handler API, it's also useful by itself. In fact, it's easier to understand SAAJ by discussing it outside the context of JAX-RPC. This chapter explains the SAAJ programming model and explains how to use it as a standalone API. Chapter 14: Message Handlers explains how to use SAAJ with JAX-RPC.

SAAJ is an API-based SOAP toolkit, which means that it models the structure of SOAP messages. SAAJ models **SOAP Messages with Attachments** (**SwA**) in Java. SwA is the MIME message format for SOAP.[1] For all practical purposes SwA is a standard and is used throughout the Web services industry. While SAAJ models plain SOAP messages as well as SwA, the WS-I Basic Profile does not endorse SwA, so it's not covered in this part of the book. You're very likely to encounter SwA messaging at some time, though, so this book provides detailed coverage of SAAJ's support for SwA in Appendix F.

SAAJ (rhymes with "page") is an API you can use to create, read, or modify SOAP messages using Java. It includes classes and interfaces that model the SOAP `Envelope`,

[1] The SwA specification is actually a Note maintained by the World Wide Web Consortium (W3C). A W3C "Note" is not a finished specification (which W3C calls a "Recommendation"), but simply a suggestion or a work in progress.

`Body`, `Header`, and `Fault` elements, along with XML namespaces, elements, and attributes, and text nodes and MIME attachments. SAAJ is similar to JDBC, in that it's a hollow API. You can't use it by itself; you need a vendor implementation. Each J2EE vendor will provide its own SAAJ implementation. They should all function the same way, although some may be more efficient than others.

You can use SAAJ to manipulate simple SOAP messages (just the XML without any attachments) or more complex SOAP messages with MIME attachments. SAAJ is used in combination with JAX-RPC (Java API for XML-based RPC), which is the J2EE standard API for sending and receiving SOAP messages. SAAJ can also be used independently of JAX-RPC and has its own, optional facilities for basic Request/Response-style messaging over HTTP or other protocols.

> ***SAAJ's network communication is based on the*** `java.net.URL` ***class, which can be extended to support any network protocol, not just HTTP. HTTP is the only protocol actually sanctioned by the Basic Profile, however.***

Java developers can use SAAJ to work with SOAP messages within any SOAP application, including initial senders, intermediaries, and ultimate receivers. For example, you might develop a SOAP intermediary that processes a specific header block before sending the message on to the next receiver. Using SAAJ you can easily examine a SOAP message, extract the appropriate header block, then send the message along to the next node in the message path. Similarly, an ultimate receiver can use SAAJ to process the application-specific content of the SOAP body.

SAAJ is based on the Abstract Factory Pattern,[2] which means SAAJ is a family of types in which each type of object is manufactured by another type in the SAAJ family. The root of the Abstract Factory Pattern in SAAJ is the `MessageFactory` class. It's responsible for manufacturing an instance of itself, which can in turn be used to manufacture a `SOAPMessage`. A `SOAPMessage` contains a `SOAPPart`, which represents the SOAP document, and zero or more `AttachmentPart` objects, which represent MIME attachments (such as GIFs and PDFs).

The `SOAPPart` contains a family of objects that model the SOAP document, including the `Envelope`, `Header`, and `Body` elements. You can obtain a clearer understanding of SAAJ by examining the basic structure of the SAAJ API alongside a diagram of an SwA message. As you can see from Figure 13–1, the SAAJ API models the exact structure of an SwA message.

SAAJ 1.2 is also based, in part, on the W3C Document Object Model (DOM), version 2. This relationship is explained in more detail in Section 13.6: SAAJ 1.2 and DOM 2.

[2] Erich Gamma, et al. *Design Patterns: Elements of Reusable Object-Oriented Software.* Reading, MA: Addison-Wesley, 1995, p. 87.

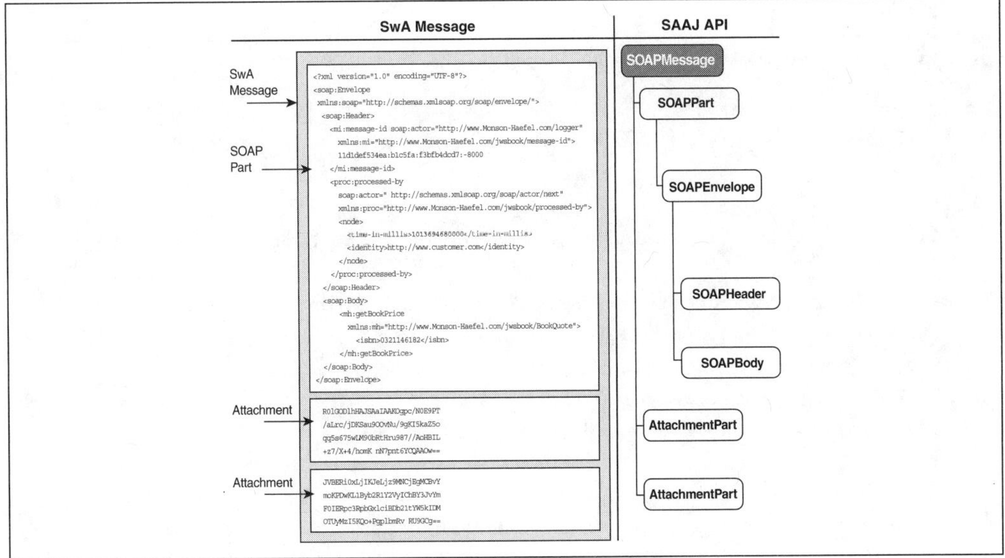
SwA Message
SAAJ API
SwA Message
SOAP Part
Attachment
Attachment
<?xml version="1.0" encoding="UTF-8"?>
<soap:Envelope
xmlns:soap="http://schemas.xmlsoap.org/soap/envelope/">
<soap:Header>
<mi:message-id soap:actor="http://www.Monson-Haefel.com/logger"
xmlns:mi="http://www.Monson-Haefel.com/jwsbook/message-id">
11d1def534ea:b1c5fa:f3bfb4dcd7:-8000
</mi:message-id>
<proc:processed-by
soap:actor=" http://schemas.xmlsoap.org/soap/actor/next"
xmlns:proc="http://www.Monson-Haefel.com/jwsbook/processed-by">
<node>
<time-in-millis>1013694680000</time-in-millis>
<identity>http://www.customer.com</identity>
</node>
</proc:processed-by>
</soap:Header>
<soap:Body>
<mh:getBookPrice
xmlns:mh="http://www.Monson-Haefel.com/jwsbook/BookQuote">
<isbn>0321146182</isbn>
</mh:getBookPrice>
</soap:Body>
</soap:Envelope>
R0lGODlhHAJSAaIAAKOgpc/N0E9PT
/aLrc/jDKSau9OOvNu/9gKI5kaZ5o
qq5s675wLM90bRtHru987//AoHBIL
+z7/X+4/homK nN7pnt6YCQAAOw==
JVBERi0xLjIKJeLjz9MNCjEgMCBvY
moKPDwKL1Byb2R1Y2VyIChBY3JvYm
F0IERpc3RpbGxlciBDb21tYW5kIDM
OTUyMzI5KQo+PgplbmRv RU9GCg==
SOAPMessage
SOAPPart
SOAPEnvelope
SOAPHeader
SOAPBody
AttachmentPart
AttachmentPart

Figure 13–1 Comparing the SAAJ Types to an SwA Message

13.1 A Simple SAAJ Example

The best way to learn SAAJ is to jump right in and build a simple SOAP message using the API. Listing 13–1 shows the BookQuote request message you've seen before.

Listing 13–1

A Simple SOAP Message

```
<?xml version="1.0" encoding="UTF-8"?>
<soap:Envelope
 xmlns:soap="http://schemas.xmlsoap.org/soap/envelope/"
 xmlns:mh="http://www.Monson-Haefel.com/jwsbook/BookQuote">
   <soap:Body>
      <mh:getBookPrice>
          <isbn>0321146182</isbn>
      </mh:getBookPrice>
   </soap:Body>
</soap:Envelope>
```

`SaajExample_1` in Listing 13–2 uses the SAAJ API to create the SOAP message, which is semantically equivalent to the SOAP message shown in Listing 13–1.

Listing 13–2

Using SAAJ to Create a Simple SOAP Message

```
package com.jwsbook.saaj;
import javax.xml.soap.*;

public class SaajExample_1 {
  public static void main(String [] args) throws SOAPException{

    MessageFactory msgFactory = MessageFactory.newInstance();
    SOAPMessage message = msgFactory.createMessage();
    message.getSOAPHeader().detachNode();
    SOAPBody body = message.getSOAPBody();
    SOAPElement getBookPrice = body.addChildElement(
                        "getBookPrice",
                        "mh",
                        "http://www.Monson-Haefel.com/jwsbook/BookQuote");
    getBookPrice.setEncodingStyle(SOAPConstants.URI_NS_SOAP_ENCODING);
    SOAPElement isbn = getBookPrice.addChildElement("isbn");
    isbn.addTextNode("0321146182");

    SaajOutputter.writeToScreen(message);
  }
}
```

To run `SaajExample_1` and the rest of the examples in this book, you'll need to have a J2EE platform installed, the proper classpaths set up, and supporting Web services deployed. You'll know if `SaajExample_1` is working properly by the lack of error messages—if there is a problem a `SOAPException` will be thrown and displayed on the output screen.

The rest of this chapter will use `SaajExample_1` and similar examples to discuss the SAAJ API and how to use its various classes and interfaces. Although you will frequently use the SAAJ API inside J2EE message handlers for JAX-RPC service endpoints and EJB endpoints, the examples in this chapter are standalone applications. This approach spares you the arduous process of deploying a J2EE component every time you want to test an example.

13.2 Creating a SOAP Message

To create a simple SOAP document, you obtain a new `SOAPMessage` object from a `MessageFactory` object, as shown in this snippet from `SaajExample_1` (Listing 13–2):

```
MessageFactory msgFactory = MessageFactory.newInstance();
SOAPMessage message = msgFactory.createMessage();
```

Although you will usually work with basic SOAP messages, without attachments, the SAAJ API models SwA, not just SOAP. Appendix F: SAAJ Attachments shows how to create an SwA message in which the SOAP document is treated as a MIME part, and accessed via the `SOAPMessage.getSOAPPart()` method.

13.2.1 The `MessageFactory` Class

The `MessageFactory` is the root factory of SAAJ. It's the class you will start with each time you create a SOAP message. `MessageFactory` is an abstract class that contains three methods, as shown in Listing 13–3 (the implementations are omitted).

Listing 13–3

The `javax.xml.soap.MessageFactory` *Class*

```
package javax.xml.soap;

public abstract class MessageFactory {

  private static final String DEFAULT_MESSAGE_FACTORY =
          "com.sun.xml.messaging.saaj.soap.MessageFactoryImpl";

  private static final String MESSAGE_FACTORY_PROPERTY =
          "javax.xml.soap.MessageFactory";

  public static MessageFactory newInstance() throws SOAPException;

  public SOAPMessage createMessage() throws SOAPException;

  public SOAPMessage createMessage(MimeHeaders headers,java.io.InputStream in)
  throws SOAPException;
}
```

13.2.1.1 The `newInstance()` *Method*

The `MessageFactory` class itself is abstract and cannot be instantiated. Its `newInstance()` method creates an object that is actually a subtype of `MessageFactory`. By default, the instance is of a proprietary type provided by Sun Microsystems, when SAAJ is employed as a standalone API.

13.2.1.2 The `createMessage()` *Method*

In addition to the `newInstance()` method, the `MessageFactory` has two `createMessage()` methods. The first takes no arguments, and is the one used in

SaajExample_1. It simply creates a new SOAPMessage. The following code line from Listing 13–2 shows how the createMessage() method is used in an application.

```
SOAPMessage message = msgFactory.createMessage();
```

In this case the SOAPMessage object is generated from scratch, and contains only the framework of a SOAP message. If you were to dump the contents of the SOAPMessage instance to the screen, it would look something like the following.

```
<?xml version="1.0" encoding="UTF-8"?>
<soap:Envelope xmlns:soap="http://schemas.xmlsoap.org/soap/envelope/">
  <soap:Header/>
  <soap:Body/>
</soap:Envelope>
```

Notice that the main message elements, Envelope, Header, and Body, are present, the last two empty. These are supplied as a convenience for the developer. Once the SOAPMessage is created, all you need to do is fill in the blanks using the SAAJ API.

13.2.1.3 The createMessage *Method with Parameters*

The MessageFactory's second create method can construct a SAAJ representation of an existing SOAP message, instead of building a new one from scratch. The following snippet from Listing 13–3 shows the createMessage() method declaration.

```
public abstract class MessageFactory {
  ...
  public SOAPMessage createMessage(MimeHeaders headers,java.io.InputStream in)
  throws SOAPException;
}
```

The MimeHeaders parameter holds one or more MIME headers. A MIME header is a name-value pair that describes the contents of a MIME block. For example, a SOAP document might have a MIME header with a name-value pair of "Content -Type = text/xml".

The InputStream parameter can be any kind of stream. For example it could be a network stream from a socket connection, an IO stream from a JDBC connection, or a simple file stream. The data obtained from the InputStream parameter must be a valid SOAP or SwA message. For example, suppose a file called soap.xml contains a SOAP document like the one shown in Listing 13–4.

Listing 13–4

The soap.xml *File*

```
<?xml version="1.0" encoding="UTF-8"?>
<soap:Envelope
```

```
 xmlns:soap="http://schemas.xmlsoap.org/soap/envelope/"
 xmlns:mh="http://www.Monson-Haefel.com/jwsbook/BookQuote">
   <soap:Body>
      <mh:getBookPrice>
          <isbn>0321146182</isbn>
      </mh:getBookPrice>
   </soap:Body>
</soap:Envelope>
```

Using a `FileInputStream`, the `MessageFactory` class can read the `soap.xml` file and generate a SAAJ object graph of the SOAP message it contains. In Listing 13–5 `SaajExample_2` uses the `MessageFactory` class to read the file and generate a `SOAPMessage`.

Listing 13–5

Building a SAAJ Object Graph from a File

```
package com.jwsbook.saaj;
import java.io.FileInputStream;
import javax.xml.soap.*;

public class SaajExample_2 {
   public static void main(String [] args)
   throws SOAPException, java.io.IOException{

        MessageFactory msgFactory = MessageFactory.newInstance();

        MimeHeaders mimeHeaders = new MimeHeaders();
        mimeHeaders.addHeader("Content-Type","text/xml; charset=UTF-8");

        FileInputStream file = new FileInputStream("soap.xml");

        SOAPMessage message = msgFactory.createMessage(mimeHeaders, file);

        file.close();
        SaajOutputter.writeToScreen(message);
    }
}
```

In `SaajExample_2` the MIME header `"Content-Type=text/xml;charset =UTF-8"` is added to an instance of `MimeHeaders`, which is the first parameter of the `createMessage()` method. The second parameter is an instance of `FileInput Stream` that points to the `soap.xml` file.

To summarize: You can use `MessageFactory` to create new SOAP messages from scratch or from an existing SOAP message obtained from some type of input stream. In many cases, however, you will use SAAJ in combination with JAX-RPC, as explained in Chapter 14, and receive a complete SAAJ message automatically. In such cases you will not need to use either of the `createMessage()` methods.

13.2.2 `SaajOutputter` Classes

To become skilled with SOAP, you must be able to read the SOAP messages generated by SAAJ, so this book uses a custom-built class called `SaajOutputter` to write `SOAPMessage` objects out in a nice, readable format. The following snippet shows how `SaajOutputter` is used.

```
MessageFactory msgFactory = MessageFactory.newInstance();
SOAPMessage message = msgFactory.createMessage();
SaajOutputter.writeToScreen(message);
```

`SaajOutputter` is not a part of the SAAJ API. It was developed specifically for this book and belongs to the `com.jwsbook.saaj` package, the example code for this chapter. As an alternative you can simply use the `SOAPMessage.writeTo()` method (using `System.out` as the parameter), but the output will have no line breaks and won't be as easy to read.

> `SaajOutputter` ***is a simple hack that works only when the*** `SOAPMessage` ***does not contain attachments. If the*** `SOAPMessage` ***contains attachments, use*** `SOAPMessage.writeTo()` ***instead of*** `SaajOutputter`.

13.2.3 The `SOAPMessage` Class

In many cases, the SOAP message you're working with will not have attachments and will not need the MIME message format. The SAAJ implementations are smart enough to recognize when no attachments are added, and omit the MIME packaging when writing the message. If you look closely at `SaajExample_1` (Listing 13–2), you'll notice that no MIME attachments are added, and that the output of the program is strictly XML and doesn't include any MIME headers or boundaries. When `SaajExample_1` executed, the SAAJ toolkit realized that no attachments had been added, so it didn't enforce the use of the MIME message format.

Most of the methods defined by the `SOAPMessage` class are related to SwA MIME parts; these are covered in Appendix F: SAAJ Attachments. The only methods that are relevant to this chapter are `writeTo()`, `getSOAPBody()`, `getSOAPHeader()`, `getProperty()`, and `setProperty()`.

13.2.3.1 *The* `writeTo()` *Method*

The `SOAPMessage.writeTo()` method simply writes the message represented by the `SOAPMessage` object to an output stream. If the `SOAPMessage` has no attachments, `writeTo()` will write only the XML SOAP part of the message to the stream. For example, in the following code snippet a `SOAPMessage` writes its contents to `System.out` (the screen) using `writeTo()`.

```
MessageFactory msgFactory = MessageFactory.newInstance();
SOAPMessage soapMessage = msgFactory.createMessage();
soapMessage.writeTo(System.out);
```

The output from the `SOAPMessage.writeTo()` method is the default content of the SOAP message without line breaks. The lack of line breaks and white space (except between the XML declaration and the SOAP message) creates a tight stream of text. Because SOAP message are, in practice, processed by software and not read by people, readability is not important; eliminating line breaks and unnecessary white space is considered more efficient.

13.2.3.2 *The* `getSOAPBody()` *and* `getSOAPHeader()` *Methods*

The root MIME part of any SwA message is always the XML SOAP document; this is covered in more detail in Appendix F. The `getSOAPPart()` method allows you to access the SOAP MIME part directly, as shown in this snippet.

```
MessageFactory msgFactory = MessageFactory.newInstance();
SOAPMessage message = msgFactory.createMessage();
SOAPPart soap = message.getSOAPPart();
```

Accessing the `SOAPBody` and `SOAPHeader` via the `SOAPPart` is not necessary, however, if the SOAP message does not use attachments, as will be the case with BP-conformant Web services. When there are no attachments, you can simply use the `getSOAPBody()` and `getSOAPHeader()` methods to access those elements in the SOAP message directly. The following snippet from `SaajExample_1` shows how these methods are used.

```
MessageFactory msgFactory = MessageFactory.newInstance();
SOAPMessage message = msgFactory.createMessage();
message.getSOAPHeader().detachNode();
SOAPBody body = message.getSOAPBody();
```

The examples in this chapter use the `getSOAPBody()` and `getSOAPHeader()` methods. In Appendix F: SAAJ Attachments, the `getSOAPPart()` and getSOAPEnvelope() methods are used. The detachNode() method simply removes the Header element from the SOAP message—SAAJ always includes the Header by default. Header blocks are not used in this example, so the Header element is not needed.

13.2.3.3 The getProperty() *and* setProperty() *Methods*

The SOAPMessage type also defines the setProperty() and getProperty() methods, which are used to set and obtain standard and vendor-specific properties of a SOAPMessage object. There are two standard properties:

- javax.xml.soap.CHARACTER_SET_ENCODING can be either "UTF-8" or "UTF-16" in applications that conform with the BP. The default is "UTF-8".[BP]
- javax.xml.soap.WRITE_XML_DECLARATION can have a value of "true" or "false". If it's "true", then the XML declaration is included in the SOAP message; if "false", it is not. The default is "false". Web service endpoints must accept SOAP 1.1 messages with or without an XML declaration.[BP]

As an example, the following snippet modifies SaajExample_2 (Listing 13–5) so that it sets the values of CHARACTER_SET_ENCODING and WRITE_XML_DECLARATION to "UTF-16" and "true" respectively.

```
FileInputStream file = new FileInputStream("soap.xml");
SOAPMessage message = msgFactory.createMessage(mimeHeaders, file);

message.setProperty("javax.xml.soap.CHARACTER_SET_ENCODING", "UTF-16");
message.setProperty("javax.xml.soap.WRITE_XML_DECLARATION", "true");
```

With these properties set, the output for SaajExample_2 would be an XML document in UTF-16 with an XML document declaration, as follows:

```
<?xml version="1.0" encoding="UTF-16"?>
<soap:Envelope
 xmlns:soap="http://schemas.xmlsoap.org/soap/envelope/"
 xmlns:mh="http://www.Monson-Haefel.com/jwsbook/BookQuote">
   <soap:Body>
      <mh:getBookPrice>
          <isbn>0321146182</isbn>
      </mh:getBookPrice>
   </soap:Body>
</soap:Envelope>
```

This SOAP message is exactly the same as the one in Listing 13–4, except that it includes the XML declaration shown in bold. XML declarations are explained in more detail in Section 2.1.2.1 and Section 4.1. The fact that the SOAP message is encoded using UTF-16 rather than UTF-8 is not visible to the eye.

13.3 Working with SOAP Documents

SAAJ provides a number of interfaces you can use to construct a simple SOAP document. This section covers most of these types; the SOAP fault types are covered in Section 13.4. Figure 13–2 is an inheritance class diagram that shows all the SOAP document elements. The gray types are fault types, which are covered later.

A SOAP message or document is an XML instance composed of elements and attributes. As a convenience each of the major parts of a SOAP document has a corresponding type in SAAJ. The `Envelope` is represented by `SOAPEnvelope`, the `Header` is represented by `SOAPHeader`, the `Body` by `SOAPBody`, and so on. The `SOAPElement` type is used for application-specific elements that don't belong to the SOAP 1.1 namespace. Figure 13–3 shows the correlation between SOAP elements and SAAJ types.

13.3.1 The `SOAPPart` and `SOAPEnvelope` Types

When working with SwA messages you will frequently make use of the `SOAPPart` and `SOAPEnvelope` types. The `SOAPPart` represents the root MIME part of an SwA message, which is always the SOAP XML document. You access the `SOAPPart` of an SwA message by invoking the `SOAPMessage.getSOAPPart()` method.

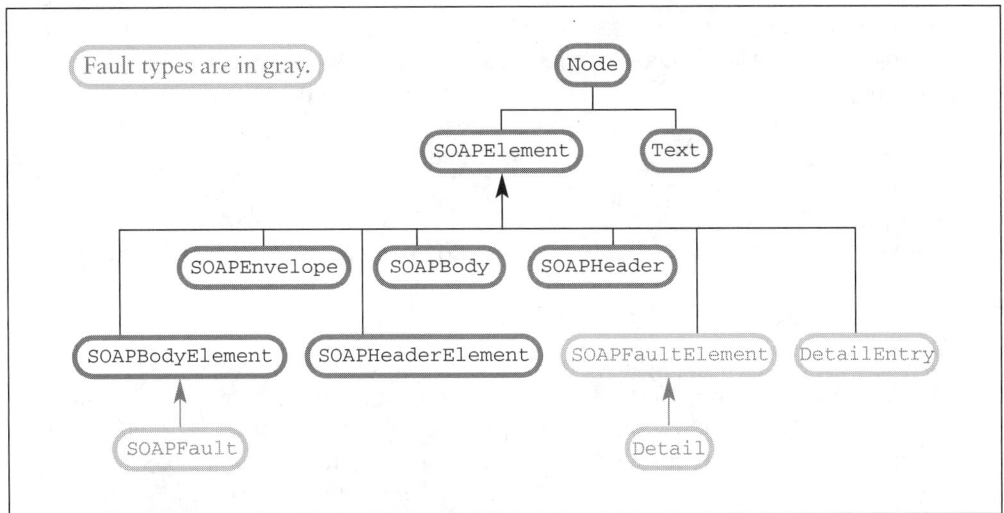

Figure 13–2 Inheritance Diagram of SAAJ SOAP Types

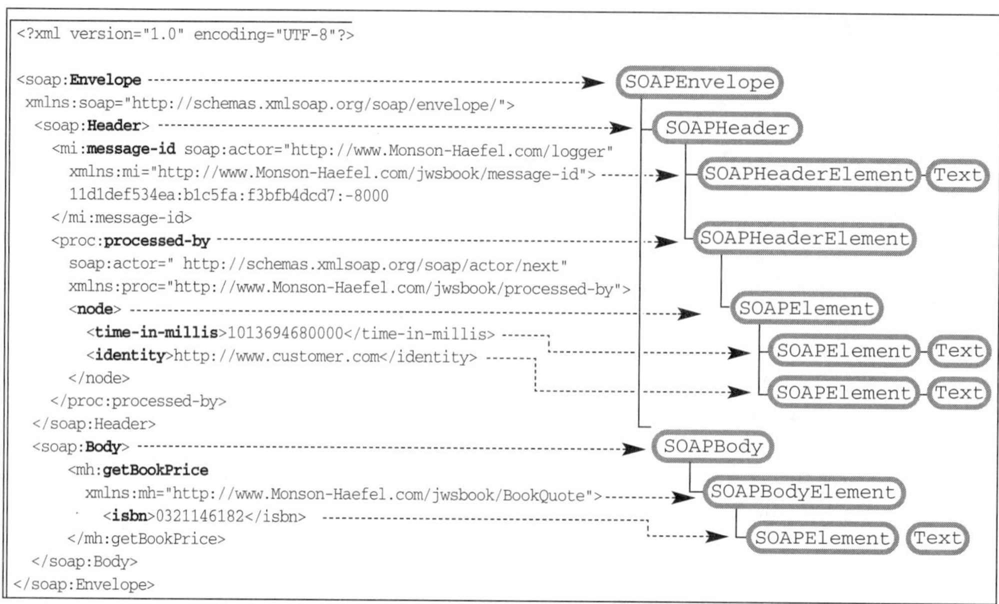
<?xml version="1.0" encoding="UTF-8"?>
<soap:Envelope
xmlns:soap="http://schemas.xmlsoap.org/soap/envelope/">
<soap:Header>
<mi:message-id soap:actor="http://www.Monson-Haefel.com/logger"
xmlns:mi="http://www.Monson-Haefel.com/jwsbook/message-id">
11d1def534ea:b1c5fa:f3bfb4dcd7:-8000
</mi:message-id>
<proc:processed-by
soap:actor=" http://schemas.xmlsoap.org/soap/actor/next"
xmlns:proc="http://www.Monson-Haefel.com/jwsbook/processed-by">
<node>
<time-in-millis>1013694680000</time-in-millis>
<identity>http://www.customer.com</identity>
</node>
</proc:processed-by>
</soap:Header>
<soap:Body>
<mh:getBookPrice
xmlns:mh="http://www.Monson-Haefel.com/jwsbook/BookQuote">
<isbn>0321146182</isbn>
</mh:getBookPrice>
</soap:Body>
</soap:Envelope>
SOAPEnvelope
SOAPHeader
SOAPHeaderElement
Text
SOAPHeaderElement
SOAPElement
SOAPElement
Text
SOAPElement
Text
SOAPBody
SOAPBodyElement
SOAPElement
Text

Figure 13–3 Comparing the SAAJ Type System to a SOAP Document

Because the BP doesn't support SwA, you may never need to access the `SOAPPart`, because you may never use SwA. That said, Appendix F: SAAJ Attachments provides a detailed discussion of the `SOAPPart`, in case you ever need to transmit or process SwA messages.

You can obtain a reference to the `SOAPEnvelope` by invoking the `getEnvelope()` method of a `SOAPPart`. The `SOAPEnvelope` represents the root of the XML SOAP document. It includes methods for accessing or creating the `SOAPHeader` and `SOAPBody`. Unless you're working with attachments, you won't usually need to deal with the `SOAPEnvelope` type, because SAAJ constructs the `SOAPEnvelope` automatically when you create a new `SOAPMessage` object. In addition, you can access the `SOAPBody` and `SOAPHeader` types directly from the `SOAPMessage` object.

13.3.2 The `SOAPFactory` Class and `Name` Types

The `SOAPFactory` provides two factory methods for creating `Name` type objects. As you already know from Section 2.2: XML Namespaces, the name of an element or attribute dictates which XML namespace it belongs to. The `Name` type is simply an abstraction of an XML qualified name. For example, in Listing 13–6 `SaajExample_3` shows how the `SOAPFactory` is used to create the `getBookPrice` and `isbn` elements in the `BookPrice` SOAP message.

Listing 13–6

Creating and Using Name *Objects*

```
package com.jwsbook.saaj;
import javax.xml.soap.*;

public class SaajExample_3 {
  public static void main(String [] args)
  throws SOAPException, java.io.IOException{

    MessageFactory msgFactory = MessageFactory.newInstance();
    SOAPMessage message = msgFactory.createMessage();
    SOAPFactory soapFactory = SOAPFactory.newInstance();

    Name getBookPrice_Name = soapFactory.createName("getBookPrice","mh",
                     "http://www.Monson-Haefel.com/jwsbook/BookQuote");
    Name isbnName = soapFactory.createName("isbn");

    SOAPBody body = message.getSOAPBody();
    SOAPBodyElement getBookPrice_Element =
                    body.addBodyElement(getBookPrice_Name);
    getBookPrice_Element.addChildElement( isbnName );

    SaajOutputter.writeToScreen(message);
  }
}
```

The following code shows the output from `SaajExample_3`: a SOAP document that contains the XML names corresponding to ones created using the `SOAPFactory` object.

```
<?xml version="1.0" encoding="UTF-8"?>
<soap:Envelope
 xmlns:soap="http://schemas.xmlsoap.org/soap/envelope/"
 xmlns:mh="http://www.Monson-Haefel.com/jwsbook/BookQuote">
   <soap:Body>
      <mh:getBookPrice>
          <isbn/>
      </mh:getBookPrice>
   </soap:Body>
</soap:Envelope>
```

The preceding SOAP message is not complete (it's missing a value for the isbn element), but it does demonstrate how you can add new elements via Name objects created by the SOAPFactory. There is another way to add new elements without having to create Name objects first. This technique was demonstrated in Saaj Example_1, and I'll expand on it when we talk about the SOAPElement methods.

Remember that a Name type represents an XML qualified name. The SOAP Envelope or the SOAPFactory can create Name objects—the SOAPFactory is a general-purpose factory class. When a Name object is created, it's assigned either a local name or a fully qualified name that includes the local name, a prefix, and a URI identifying the XML namespace. Listing 13–7 shows the definition of the Name interface, which declares four methods for obtaining various parts of the XML name as String values.

Listing 13–7

The javax.xml.soap.Name *Interface*

```
package javax.xml.soap;

public interface Name {

   public String getLocalName();
   public String getPrefix();
   public String getQualifedName();
   public String getURI();

}
```

Each Name object is associated with an element or attribute. For example, in Listing 13–8 the getBookPrice element declares a local name, prefix, for an XML namespace.

Listing 13–8

XML Namespaces in a SOAP Document

```
<?xml version="1.0" encoding="UTF-8"?>
<soap:Envelope
 xmlns:soap="http://schemas.xmlsoap.org/soap/envelope/"
 xmlns:mh="http://www.Monson-Haefel.com/jwsbook/BookQuote">
   <soap:Body>
      <mh:getBookPrice>
          <isbn/>
      </mh:getBookPrice>
   </soap:Body>
</soap:Envelope>
```

Table 13–1 `Name` Properties for the `getBookPrice` Element in Listing 13–8

Method	Return Value
`getLocalName()`	`"getBookPrice"`
`getPrefix()`	`"mh"`
`getQualifiedName()`	`"mh:getBookPrice"`
`getURI()`	`"http://www.Monson-Haefel.com/jwsbook/BookQuote"`

The `String` values returned by the `Name` object associated with the `getBookPrice` element in Listing 13–8 are shown in Table 13–1.

While the `Name` object obtained from the `getBookPrice` element has values for each accessor, the `Name` object for the `isbn` element would contain only a local name and qualified name of `"isbn"`—it would not contain a prefix or a URI. In other words, the `Name` object is a very literal representation of the XML name used in the corresponding SOAP document; it is not derived and will not contain inherited namespaces or prefixes. In the absence of a prefix, the qualified name is equal to the local name. Table 13–2 shows the `String` values that will be returned when invoking the methods of the `Name` object that represents the `isbn` element.

Table 13–2 `Name` Properties for the `isbn` Element in Listing 13–8

Method	Return Value
`getLocalName()`	`"isbn"`
`getPrefix()`	`null`
`getQualifiedName()`	`"isbn"`
`getURI()`	`null`

13.3.3 The `SOAPElement` Type

The application-specific elements, those that are not part of the SOAP 1.1 XML namespace, are represented directly by objects of the `SOAPElement` type. This type can represent any XML element. It contains methods for accessing the child elements, attributes, namespace information, and so on. Just as an XML element may contain other XML elements, a `SOAPElement` may contain other `SOAPElement` objects. The `SOAPElement` type models a hierarchical structure that corresponds to the hierarchical structure of XML. As you saw in Figure 13–2, the `SOAPElement` type is the supertype of the other SOAP types, including `SOAPEnvelope`, `SOAPBody`, `SOAPBodyElement`, `SOAPHeader`, `SOAPHeaderElement`, and the fault elements, which are covered later. The `Node` type is the supertype of `SOAPElement`.

As the supertype of all other SOAP element types, `SOAPElement` contains a number of useful methods you can use to create and access child elements, attributes, namespace declarations, the element name, and the encoding style. Listing 13–9 shows the definition of the `SOAPElement` type.

Listing 13–9

The `javax.xml.soap.SOAPElement` *Interface*

```
package javax.xml.soap;
import java.util.Iterator;

public interface SOAPElement extends Node, org.w3c.dom.Element {
    public SOAPElement addAttribute(Name name, String value)
      throws SOAPException;
    public SOAPElement addChildElement(Name name) throws SOAPException;
    public SOAPElement addChildElement(SOAPElement element)
      throws SOAPException;
    public SOAPElement addChildElement(String localName) throws SOAPException;
    public SOAPElement addChildElement(String localName, String prefix)
      throws SOAPException;
    public SOAPElement addChildElement(String localName, String prefix,
                                       String uri) throws SOAPException;
    public SOAPElement addNamespaceDeclaration(String prefix, String uri)
      throws SOAPException;
    public SOAPElement addTextNode(String text);
    public Iterator getAllAttributes();
    public String getAttributeValue(Name name);
    public Iterator getChildElements();
    public Iterator getChildElements(Name name);
    public Name getElementName();
    public String getEncodingStyle();
    public Iterator getNamespacePrefixes();
    public String getNamespaceURI(String prefix);
    public Iterator getVisableNamespacePrefixes();
    public boolean removeAttribute(Name name);
    public boolean removeNamespaceDeclaration(String prefix);
    public boolean removeContents();
    public void setEncodingStyle(String encodingStyle);
}
```

Most of the methods defined in `SOAPElement` are self-explanatory and won't be covered in any detail here. The SAAJ API provides concise definitions of each method, in case the behavior is not obvious to you. In Listing 13–10, `SaajExample_4` shows a SOAP message being created by an initial sender. `SaajExample_4` makes extensive use of the `SOAPElement` interface and methods.

Listing 13–10

Using the `SOAPElement` *Type*

```
package com.jwsbook.saaj;
import javax.xml.soap.*;

public class SaajExample_4 {
  public static void main(String [] args) throws SOAPException {

    // Create SOAPMessage
    MessageFactory msgFactory = MessageFactory.newInstance();
    SOAPMessage message = msgFactory.createMessage();
    SOAPElement header = message.getSOAPHeader();

    // Create message-id header block
    SOAPElement msgIdHeader = (SOAPElement)
      header.addChildElement("message-id","mi",
                         "http://www.Monson-Haefel.com/jwsbook/message-id");
    String uuid = new java.rmi.dgc.VMID().toString();
    msgIdHeader.addTextNode(uuid);


    // Create processed-by header block
    SOAPElement prcssdByHeader = (SOAPElement)
      header.addChildElement("processed-by","proc",
                       "http://www.Monson-Haefel.com/jwsbook/processed-by");
    SOAPElement node = prcssdByHeader.addChildElement("node");
    SOAPElement time = node.addChildElement("time-in-millis");
    long millis = System.currentTimeMillis();
    time.addTextNode(String.valueOf(millis));
    SOAPElement identity = node.addChildElement("identity");
    identity.addTextNode("SaajExample_4");

    // Create getBookPrice RPC call
    SOAPElement body = message.getSOAPBody();
    SOAPElement getBookPrice = body.addChildElement("getBookPrice","mh",
                            "http://www.Monson-Haefel.com/jwsbook/BookQuote");
    SOAPElement isbn = getBookPrice.addChildElement("isbn");
    isbn.addTextNode("0321146182");
```

```
        SaajOutputter.writeToScreen(message);
    }
}
```

Although SAAJ provides special types for SOAP `Header`, `Body`, and header-block elements, it's frequently more convenient to use the `SOAPElement` supertype. `SaajExample_4` provides an example: It creates the header blocks using `SOAPElement.addChildElement()` instead of `SOAPHeader.addHeaderElement()` because it's easier (you don't have to create a `Name` object).

```
// Create message-id header block
SOAPElement msgIdHeader = (SOAPElement)
  header.addChildElement("message-id","mi",
                        "http://www.Monson-Haefel.com/jwsbook/message-id");
...

// Create processed-by header block
SOAPElement prcssdByHeader = (SOAPElement)
  header.addChildElement("processed-by","proc",
                        "http://www.Monson-Haefel.com/jwsbook/processed-by");
```

Naturally, the more familiar you are with the methods of `SOAPElement` and its derived types, the easier and more efficient your code becomes.

It's important to note that each of the `addChildElement()` methods returns a `SOAPElement`. If you use the overloading of `addChildElement()` that expects another `SOAPElement`, the instance returned may not be the same one you passed into the method. Be careful not to use the original reference after you pass it to `addChildElement()`; modifying it may not have the desired effect. For example:

```
SOAPElement child = … // get SOAPElement from somewhere
element.addChildElement( child );
child.addAttribute( attribName, attribValue );
```

This code may not actually add the attribute to the child as you might expect, because `addChildElement()` may have copied the child when adding it to the parent element, and returned the copy rather than the original. You should always use the `SOAPElement` returned by the `addChildElement()` method if you need to modify a `SOAPElement` object after you add it, thus:

```
SOAPElement child = // get SOAPElement from somewhere
child = element.addChildElement( child );
child.addAttribute( attribName, attribValue );
```

13.3.4 The `Node` Type

The supertype of the `SOAPElement` type, and therefore all of its subtypes, is `Node` (see Figure 13–2). The `Node` interface provides a few useful methods for navigating through a hierarchical tree of elements, removing nodes from the tree, and marking nodes for "recycling." Listing 13–11 shows the interface definition for the Node type.

Listing 13–11

The javax.xml.soap.Node *Interface*

```
package javax.xml.soap;

public interface Node extends org.w3c.dom.Node {
    public void detachNode();
    public SOAPElement getParentElement()
      throws java.lang.UnsupportedOperationException;
    public String getValue();
    public void setValue(String value)
      throws java.lang.IllegalStateException;
    public void recycleNode();
    public void setParentElement(SOAPElement parent)
      throws SOAPException;
}
```

The detachNode() method is frequently used to remove the SOAPHeader object from a newly created SOAP message. When a SOAPMessage is first created, it automatically contains Envelope, Header, and Body elements. If the SOAP message you are constructing will not be using any header blocks, then removing the Header element is a good idea. You may have noticed that SaajExample_1 (Listing 13–2) used detachNode() for this purpose:

```
message.getSOAPHeader().detachNode();
```

The recycleNode() method is a bit odd. It's supposed to help the underlying SAAJ implementation conserve resources—no harm in that, but with recent improvements in JVM garbage collection it hardly seems necessary. It's difficult to determine the overhead of using this method compared to simply dereferencing a node to release it for garage collection, but you may want to err on the side of resource conservation, and call recycleNode() if you detach a node you won't be using further. The following snippet illustrates.

```
SOAPHeader header = message.getSOAPHeader();
header.detachNode();
header.recycleNode();
```

The behavior of the setValue() method depends on the type of Node. If it's a Text type, setValue() assigns the String argument to be the value of the text. If setValue() is invoked on an Element, then it will assign the String argment to the `Text` node contained by the `Element`. If the `Element` object has no children, the `setValue()` method will create a child `Text` node. If, however, the `Element` object has another `Element` object as its child, or multiple children of any type, then `setValue()` will throw a `java.lang.IllegalStateException`.

13.3.5 The `SOAPHeader` Type

In Chapter 4 you learned that the SOAP `Header` element may have zero or more header blocks. In SAAJ, the `SOAPHeader` type represents the `Header` element, and the `SOAPHeaderElement` type represents an individual header block. `SOAPHeader` provides methods for adding, examining, and removing `SOAPHeaderElement` objects—effectively adding, examining, or removing header blocks from the SOAP document. For example, we can insert the `message-id` header block into a SOAP message as shown in bold in Listing 13–12.

Listing 13–12

Adding a Header Block to a SOAP Message

```
package com.jwsbook.saaj;
import javax.xml.soap.*;

public class SaajExample_5 {
  public static void main(String [] args) throws SOAPException {
    // Create SOAPMessage
    MessageFactory msgFactory = MessageFactory.newInstance();
    SOAPMessage message = msgFactory.createMessage();
    SOAPHeader header = message.getSOAPHeader();

    // Create message-id header block
    SOAPHeaderElement msgId = (SOAPHeaderElement)
      header.addChildElement("message-id","mi",
                          "http://www.Monson-Haefel.com/jwsbook/message-id");
    String uuid = new java.rmi.dgc.VMID().toString();
    msgId.addTextNode(uuid);
    msgId.setActor("http://www.Monson-Haefel.com/logger");
    msgId.setMustUnderstand(false);


    // Create getBookPrice RPC call
    SOAPBody body = message.getSOAPBody();
    SOAPElement getBookPrice = body.addChildElement(
                          "getBookPrice",
                          "mh",
                          "http://www.Monson-Haefel.com/jwsbook/BookQuote");
```

```
        SOAPElement isbn = getBookPrice.addChildElement("isbn");
        isbn.addTextNode("0321146182");
        SaajOutputter.writeToScreen(message);
    }
}
```

SOAPHeader.addChildElement() adds the root element of the header block, in this case the message-id element. The header block should be assigned a namespace and possibly an actor. Here we have assigned it both a namespace, "http://www.Monson-Haefel.com/jwsbook/message-id", and an actor, "http://www.Monson-Haefel.com/logger". As you learned in Chapter 4, the actor attribute specifies a role that should process the header block. The call to java.rmi.dgc.VMID() is a simple hack to obtain a unique ID.

> ***There are multiple*** addChildElement() ***methods. If you pass a*** SOAPHeaderElement ***parameter, you can add the whole header block, not just its root. The*** addChildElement() ***method is defined by the*** SOAPElement ***class, which is the supertype of*** SOAPHeader. ***The*** SOAPElement ***is discussed in more detail in Section 13.3.3.***

The output of SaajExample_5 would look something like this:

```
<?xml version="1.0" encoding="UTF-8"?>
<soap:Envelope xmlns:soap="http://schemas.xmlsoap.org/soap/envelope/"
 xmlns:mh="http://www.Monson-Haefel.com/jwsbook/BookQuote">
  <soap:Header>
    <mi:message-id xmlns:mi="http://www.Monson-Haefel.com/jwsbook/message-id"
     soap:actor="http://www.Monson-Haefel.com/logger"
     soap:mustUnderstand="0">
       11d1def534ea1be0:b1c5fa:f3bfb4dcd7:-8000
    </mi:message-id>
  </soap:Header>
  <soap:Body>
    <mh:getBookPrice>
      <isbn>0321146182</isbn>
    </mh:getBookPrice>
  </soap:Body>
</soap:Envelope>
```

In addition to adding header blocks, the SOAPHeader type allows us to examine and remove specific header blocks. SOAP receivers use this functionality to access all header blocks, header blocks associated with a particular actor, or only those header blocks with mustUnderstand equal to true for a particular actor. The SOAPHeader class provides five methods for examining or extracting (accessing or removing) header blocks. These methods are shown in bold in the Listing 13–13, which is the definition of the `SOAPHeader` class.

Listing 13–13

The `javax.xml.SOAPHeader` *Interface*

```
package javax.xml.soap;
import java.util.Iterator;

public interface SOAPHeader extends SOAPElement {
    public SOAPHeaderElement addHeaderElement( Name name )
    throws SOAPException;
    public Iterator extractHeaderElements(String actor);
    public Iterator examineHeaderElements(String actor);
    public Iterator examineMustUnderstandHeaderElements(String actor);
    public Iterator examinAllHeaderElements();
    public Iterator extractAllHeaderElements();
}
```

All of these methods return a `java.util.Iterator` whose elements are `SOAPHeaderElement` objects. For example, the following SOAP message contains two header blocks (`message-id` and `processed-by`), each with a different `actor` attribute.

```
<?xml version="1.0" encoding="UTF-8"?>
<soap:Envelope xmlns:soap="http://schemas.xmlsoap.org/soap/envelope/">
   <soap:Header>
      <mi:message-id soap:actor="http://www.Monson-Haefel.com/logger"
         xmlns:mi="http://www.Monson-Haefel.com/jwsbook/message-id">
          11d1def534ea1be0:b1c5fa:f3bfb4dcd7:-8000
      </mi:message-id>
      <proc:processed-by
         soap:actor="http://schemas.xmlsoap.org/soap/actor/next"
         xmlns:proc="http://www.Monson-Haefel.com/jwsbook/processed-by">
         <node>
            <time-in-millis>1013694684723</time-in-millis>
            <identity>http://local/SOAPClient2</identity>
         </node>
      </proc:processed-by>
   </soap:Header>
   <soap:Body>
       <!-- application-specific data goes here -->
  </soap:Body>
</soap:Envelope>
```

Upon receiving this SOAP message, a SOAP node will request all header blocks that are associated with the standard next actor so that those headers can be processed. The following snippet shows code for extracting and processing SOAPHeaderElement objects associated with the next actor role.

```
SOAPHeader header = message.getSOAPHeader();
String actor = "http://schemas.xmlsoap.org/soap/actor/next";
Iterator headerBlocks = header.extractHeaderElements( actor );
while(headerBlocks.hasNext()){
    SOAPHeaderElement block = (SOAPHeaderElement)headerBlocks.next();
    if(block.getElementName().getLocalName().equals("processed-by")){
            SOAPElement node = block.addChildElement("node");

            // do something useful with header blocks and then discard them
    }
}
```

Obviously, the ability to examine, modify, and remove header blocks is a very important feature of SAAJ, one receivers (such as JAX-RPC handlers) will use extensively as they process incoming messages. As you learned in Chapter 4, intermediaries are required to remove any header block targeted to a role they play. The extractHeaderElements() method enables a receiver to fulfill that obligation in one operation. Chapter 4 also mentioned, though, that some receivers will feign removal and insertion of the same header block, by simply modifying it. In such cases the receiver invokes examineHeaderElements() instead of extractHeaderElements(). This method allows the node to search for and access header blocks easily, without removing them.

13.3.6 The SOAPHeaderElement Type

SOAPHeaderElement is an abstraction of a header block that lets us create and examine the attributes and child elements of a particular header block. Each header block may have an actor attribute, a mustUnderstand attribute, or both, in addition to child elements and other attributes. The definition of the SOAPHeaderElement is shown in Listing 13–14 (its methods for accessing child elements and other attributes are defined in its supertype, SOAPElement).

Listing 13–14

The javax.xml.soap.SOAPHeaderElement *Interface*

```
package javax.xml.soap;

public interface SOAPHeaderElement extends SOAPElement {
    public String getActor();
```

```
    public boolean getMustUnderstand();
    public void setActor(String actorURI);
    public void setMustUnderstand(boolean flag);
}
```

The SOAPHeaderElement methods are employed when modifying and examining header blocks. For example, when creating the message-id header block, we use these methods to set the value of the actor and mustUnderstand attributes, as shown in the following snippet from SaajExample_5 (Listing 13–12).

```
// Create message-id header block
SOAPHeaderElement msgId = (SOAPHeaderElement)
  header.addChildElement("message-id","mi",
                        "http://www.Monson-Haefel.com/jwsbook/message-id");
String uuid = new java.rmi.dgc.VMID().toString();
msgId.addTextNode(uuid);
msgId.setActor("http://www.Monson-Haefel.com/logger");
msgId.setMustUnderstand(false);
```

In addition to the actor and mustUnderstand attributes, a SOAPHeaderElement may also contain one or more SOAPElement objects, which represent the child elements of the header block.

13.3.7 The SOAPBody Type

As its names suggests, the SOAPBody type represents the SOAP Body element. Of its four methods, three deal with SOAP faults and one with the Body of a non-fault SOAP message. Listing 13–15 shows the definition of the SOAPBody interface.

Listing 13–15

The javax.xml.soap.SOAPBody *Interface*

```
package javax.xml.soap;

public interface SOAPBody extends SOAPElement {
  public SOAPBodyElement addBodyElement(Name name) throws SOAPException;
  public SOAPBodyElement addDocument(org.w3c.dom.Document doc)
    throws SOAPException;
  public SOAPFault addFault() throws SOAPException;
  public SOAPFault addFault(Name faultcode, String faultString,
                            java.util.Locale local) throws SOAPException;
  public SOAPFault addFault(Name faultcode, String faultString)
    throws SOAPException;
  public SOAPFault getFault();
```

```
  public boolean hasFault();
}
```

The SOAPBody type is used in several of the earlier examples. The following snippet from SaajExample_3 (Listing 13–6) shows how SAAJ can be used to create a SOAP body with contents.

```
Name getBookPrice_Name = soapFactory.createName("getBookPrice","mh",
                          "http://www.Monson-Haefel.com/jwsbook/BookQuote");
Name isbnName = soapFactory.createName("isbn");

SOAPBody body = message.getSOAPBody();
SOAPBodyElement getBookPrice_Element =
                body.addBodyElement(getBookPrice_Name);
getBookPrice_Element.addChildElement( isbnName );
```

The addFault(), getFault(), and hasFault() methods are discussed in Section 13.4: Working with SOAP Faults. The addDocument() method is discussed in Section 13.6: SAAJ 1.2 and DOM 2.

13.3.8 The SOAPBodyElement Type

SOAPBodyElement extends SOAPElement and doesn't add any methods of its own, as you see in Listing 13–16.

Listing 13–16

The javax.xml.soap.SOAPBodyElement *Interface*

```
package javax.xml.soap;
public interface SOAPBodyElement extends SOAPElement {}
```

Although it may seem a bit silly to define a SOAPBodyElement type that adds no methods—SOAPElement would seem to suffice—this empty type may be beneficial in the future. As the SOAP protocol evolves, the SOAPBodyElement will already be present as a construct for adding new functionality (methods), without breaking backward-compatibility of existing code. In addition, the SOAPBodyElement type, which is also the base type of the SOAPFault, suggests type safety by restricting the type of SOAPElement object a SOAPBody can contain.

A SOAPBodyElement can be added to a SOAPBody object using a Name object, as shown in the following snippet from SaajExample_3.

```
Name getBookPrice_Name = soapFactory.createName("getBookPrice","mh",
                          "http://www.Monson-Haefel.com/jwsbook/BookQuote");
...
```

```
SOAPBodyElement getBookPrice_Element =
                body.addBodyElement(getBookPrice_Name);
```

13.3.9 The `Text` Type

The `Text` type is an extension of `Node` that represents literal text contained by an element or a comment. The interface definition of `Text` requires familiarity with `Node` to be useful, because the subtype adds only a single method, `isComment()`, as shown in Listing 13–17.

Listing 13–17

The `javax.xml.soap.Text` *Interface*

```
package javax.xml.soap;

public interface Text extends Node, org.w3c.dom.Text {
    public boolean isComment();
}
```

You have to use the methods `getValue()` and `setValue()` defined by the `Node` supertype to retrieve and set the contents of a `Text` object. To access a `Text` object from an element use `Node.getValue()`, which will return a `String` value if the element contains a `Text` node, or `null` if it doesn't. For example, we could retrieve the ISBN number from the `isbn` element as follows:

```
SOAPElement isbn = getBookPrice.addChildElement("isbn");
...
isbn.addTextNode("0321146182");
...
Text textValue = isbn.getValue();
```

For some reason the `addTextNode()` method returns a `SOAPElement` rather than the `Text` node itself. I suspect this was done to aid in changing calls, but its effectiveness is debatable.

There is no obvious way to add a comment to a SOAP message without reverting to the DOM object model. Of course, SOAP messages are not meant for human consumption, so this lack is not a big problem.

13.3.10 The `SOAPConstants` Class

Certain XML namespaces will not change and will be used over and over again. The values of these namespaces are assigned to constants as a convenience for the developer. Specifically, the `SOAPConstants` class defines constants for the SOAP 1.1 namespace, the namespace of the standard `next` actor attribute value, and the namespace of standard SOAP encoding. Table 13–3 shows the `SOAPConstants` fields and their values.

Table 13–3 Namespace Constants

SOAPConstants **Field Name**	**XML Namespace** **String Value**
SOAPConstants.URI_NS_SOAP_ENCODING	"http://schemas.xmlsoap.org/soap/encoding/"
SOAPConstants.URI_NS_SOAP_ENVELOPE	"http://schemas.xmlsoap.org/soap/envelope/"
SOAPConstants.URI_SOAP_ACTOR_NEXT	"http://schemas.xmlsoap.org/soap/actor/next"

You can see how `SOAPConstants` is used in some of the examples in this chapter; for example, `SaajExample_4` uses the constant for the `next` SOAP actor, as shown in this code snippet:

```
prcssdBy.setActor(SOAPConstants.URI_SOAP_ACTOR_NEXT);
prcssdBy.setMustUnderstand(true);
```

The `URI_NS_SOAP_ENCODING` constant is used to set the encoding style to RPC/Encoding. As I noted in Part II, the BP doesn't support this messaging mode, so you should avoid it.

13.3.11 The `SOAPException` Class

`SOAPException` is used to report errors encountered by the SOAP toolkit while attempting to perform some operation. Many of the methods that manufacture objects throw this exception because they affect the structure of the SOAP message. *Remember: A* `SOAPException` *does not represent a SOAP fault generated by the receiver.* A SOAP fault will always be received as a `SOAPMessage` (see Section 13.4).

A `SOAPException` may contain an embedded exception if the error was caused by a subsystem like I/O or an XML parser. It may also contain a reason message. A skeletal definition of `SOAPException` is shown in Listing 13–18 (the method bodies have been omitted for brevity).

Listing 13–18

The `javax.xml.soap.SOAPException` *Class*

```
package javax.xml.soap;

public class SOAPException extends Exception {

    public SOAPException(){…}
    public SOAPException(String reason){…}
    public SOAPException(String reason, Throwable cause){…}
    public SOAPException(Throwable cause){…}

    public Throwable getCause(){…}
```

```
    public getMessage(){…}
    public Throwable initCause(Throwable cause){…}
}
```

13.3.12 The `SOAPFactory` and `SOAPElement` Types

The `SOAPFactory` class is provided for the developer's convenience. It's a nice thing to have around because it allows you to create a `SOAPElement` independent of context. In other words, you can use it to create detached instances of the `SOAPElement` type. Listing 13–19 shows the definition of `SOAPFactory` (the method bodies have been omitted for brevity).

Listing 13–19

The `javax.xml.soap.SOAPFactory` *Class*

```
package javax.xml.soap;

public abstract class SOAPFactory {

    ...
    public abstract  SOAPElement createElement(Name name)
      throws SOAPException{…}
    public abstract  SOAPElement createElement(String localName)
      throws SOAPException{…}
    public abstract  SOAPElement createElement(String localName,
                                              String prefix, String uri)
       throws SOAPException{…}
    ...
}
```

`SOAPFactory` can be used to construct portions of a SOAP message independent of a `SOAPMessage` object. For example, you might use it to construct a specialized header block in one module, which can be added to a SOAP document in some other module. As a demonstration, in Listing 13–20 `SaajExample_6` creates a SOAP message but uses a separate class, the `MessageIDHeader` class, to construct the `message-id` header block.

Listing 13–20

Delegating Header-Block Creation to a `MessageIDHeader`

```
package com.jwsbook.saaj;
import javax.xml.soap.*;

public class SaajExample_6 {
```

```
  public static void main(String [] args) throws SOAPException {

    // Create SOAPMessage
    MessageFactory msgFactory = MessageFactory.newInstance();
    SOAPMessage message = msgFactory.createMessage();
    SOAPHeader header = message.getSOAPHeader();

    // Create message-id header block
    SOAPElement msgId =  MessageIDHeader.createHeaderBlock();
    SOAPHeaderElement msgId_header =
            (SOAPHeaderElement)header.addChildElement(msgId);
    msgId_header.setActor("http://www.Monson-Haefel.com/logger");

    SaajOutputter.writeToScreen(message);
  }
}
```

The `MessageIDHeader` class in Listing 13–21 uses the `SOAPFactory` to create an isolated header block that can be generated for any SOAP application that needs it.

Listing 13–21

Using `SOAPFactory` *to Create a Header Block*

```
package com.jwsbook.saaj;
import javax.xml.soap.*;

public class MessageIDHeader {
  public static SOAPElement createHeaderBlock() throws SOAPException{

    SOAPFactory factory = SOAPFactory.newInstance();
    SOAPElement msgId = factory.createElement("message-id","mi",
                     "http://www.Monson-Haefel.com/jwsbook/message-id");

    String messageid = new java.rmi.dgc.VMID().toString();

    msgId.addTextNode( messageid );
    return msgId;
  }

}
```

The `java.rmi.dgc.VMID` ***does a fairly good job of generating unique identifiers. It's convenient because it's found in the core libraries, but it's not perfect and is not recommended for use in production systems.***

The output from `SaajExample_6` would look something like the following (the text value of `message-id` would differ):

```
<?xml version="1.0" encoding="UTF-8"?>
<soap:Envelope xmlns:soap="http://schemas.xmlsoap.org/soap/envelope/">
  <soap:Header>
    <mi:message-id xmlns:mi="http://www.Monson-Haefel.com/jwsbook/message-id"
                   soap:actor="http://www.Monson-Haefel.com/logger">
       11d1def534ea1be0:194a4e:f3c05ce67a:-8000
    </mi:message-id>
  </soap:Header>
  <soap:Body/>
</soap:Envelope>
```

`SOAPFactory` makes it fairly easy to modularize the construction of SOAP messages, especially SOAP headers, which are specialized and often used across a variety of SOAP applications. For example, at Monson-Haefel Books almost every Web service requires that a `message-id` header block be included for logging purposes. A class like `MessageIDHeader` can be reused throughout the system to generate the `message-id` header block.

13.4 Working with SOAP Faults

As you know from Chapter 4, faults are a special kind of SOAP message that contains error information. SOAP faults are always delivered from the receiver back to the sender. In SAAJ, SOAP fault messages are constructed in basically the same way as a plain SOAP message, except the `SOAPBody` object contains a `SOAPFault` instead of a `SOAPBodyElement`. `SOAPFault` is actually a subtype of `SOAPBodyElement` that specializes the behavior to support the structure of a SOAP `Fault` element. Several interfaces play a role in creating SOAP fault messages with SAAJ. Figure 13–4 shows these interfaces in the context of all the other SAAJ types.

13.4.1 The `SOAPFault` Type

Every instance of the `SOAPFault` type is contained by a `SOAPBody` element. It describes an error generated by the receiver while processing a SOAP message.

The `SOAPFault` interface (Listing 13–22) defines several methods for setting and getting the `faultactor`, `faultcode`, and `faultstring` (description) elements of the `Fault` element, as well as creating and accessing `detail` elements.

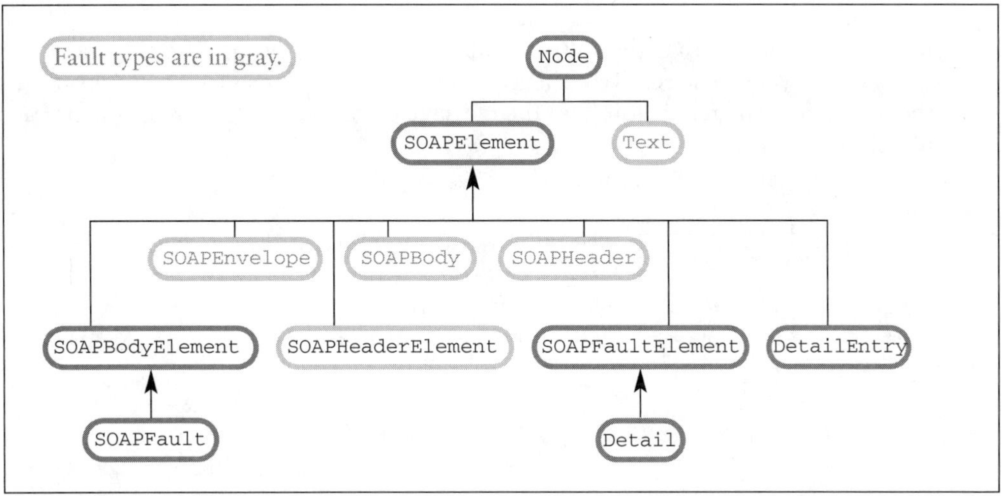

Figure 13–4 Inheritance Diagram of SAAJ SOAP Fault Types (Fault types are in gray.)

Listing 13–22

The `javax.xml.soap.SOAPFault` *Interface*

```
package javax.xml.soap;
import java.util.Locale;

public interface SOAPFault extends SOAPBodyElement {

    public Detail addDetail() throws SOAPException;
    public Detail getDetail();
    public String getFaultActor();
    public String getFaultCode();
    public Name getFaultCodeAsName();
    public String getFaultString();
    public Locale getFaultStringLocale();
    public void setFaultActor(String faultActor) throws SOAPException;
    public void setFaultCode(String faultCode) throws SOAPException;
    public void setFaultCode(Name faultCode) throws SOAPException;
    public void setFaultString(String faultString) throws SOAPException;
    public void setFaultString(String faultString, Locale local)
     throws SOAPException;

}
```

As an example, imagine that the ultimate receiver of the BookQuote SOAP message determines that the ISBN number declared in the `Body` of an incoming message is invalid. The receiver will generate a SOAP Fault message and deliver it to the sender immediately before it in the message path. The Fault message might look like the one in Listing 13–23.

Listing 13–23

A SOAP Fault Message

```
<?xml version="1.0" encoding="UTF-8"?>
<soap:Envelope xmlns:soap="http://schemas.xmlsoap.org/soap/envelope/">
  <soap:Body>
    <soap:Fault>
      <faultcode>soap:Client</faultcode>
      <faultstring>The ISBN contains an invalid character(s)</faultstring>
      <faultactor>
        http://www.Monson-Haefel.omc/BookQuote_WebService
      </faultactor>
      <detail>
        <mh:InvalidIsbnFaultDetail
                xmlns:mh="http://www.Monson-Haefel.com/jwsbook/BookQuote">
          <offending-value>19318224-D</offending-value>
          <conformance-rules>
                The first nine characters must be digits. The last
                character may be a digit or the letter 'X'. Case is not
                important.
          </conformance-rules>
        </mh:InvalidIsbnFaultDetail>
      </detail>
    </soap:Fault>
  </soap:Body>
</soap:Envelope>
```

This fault message can be constructed fairly easily using SAAJ, as shown in Listing 13–24, `SaajExample_7`.

Listing 13–24

Building a Fault Message with SAAJ

```
package com.jwsbook.saaj;
import javax.xml.soap.*;

public class SaajExample_7 {
```

```
public static void main(String [] args) throws SOAPException {
    // Create SOAPMessage
    MessageFactory msgFactory = MessageFactory.newInstance();
    SOAPMessage message = msgFactory.createMessage();
    message.getSOAPHeader().detachNode();

    // Create Fault message
    SOAPBody body = message.getSOAPBody();

    SOAPFault fault = body.addFault();
    fault.setFaultCode("soap:Client");
    fault.setFaultString("The ISBN contains an invalid character(s)");
    fault.setFaultActor("http://www.Monson-Haefel.org/BookQuote_WebService");

    Detail detail = fault.addDetail();
    SOAPFactory soapFactory = SOAPFactory.newInstance();
    Name errorName = soapFactory.createName(
                     "InvalidIsbnFaultDetail","mh",
                     "http://www.Monson-Haefel.com/jwsbook/BookQuote");

    DetailEntry detailEntry = detail.addDetailEntry(errorName);
    SOAPElement offendingValue =
      detailEntry.addChildElement("offending-value");
    offendingValue.addTextNode("19318224-D");
    SOAPElement conformanceRules =
      detailEntry.addChildElement("conformance-rules");
    conformanceRules.addTextNode(
       "The first nine characters must be digits.  The last character "+
       "may be a digit or the letter 'X'. Case is not important.");

    SaajOutputter.writeToScreen(message);
  }
}
```

Version 1.2 of SAAJ modified the `SOAPFault` interface and added a couple of methods that are QName-oriented. For example, when you call the `setFaultCode()` method, you can pass it a `Name` parameter that represents a proper QName, instead of a `String`. The following snippet illustrates.

```
SOAPFault fault = body.addFault();
SOAPFactory soapFactory = SOAPFactory.newInstance();

Name faultCode = soapFactory.createName("Client","soap",
```

```
                                SOAPConstants.URI_NS_SOAP_ENVELOPE);
fault.setFaultCode(faultCode);
fault.setFaultString("The ISBN contains an invalid character(s)");
```

You can also access fault codes as either `String` values or `Name` objects. The `getFaultCodeAsName()` method returns the fault code as a SAAJ `Name` object, rather than a `String` value. This book tends to use the `String` methods because they are easier to read in example code, but use the `Name` object methods if you wish.

To support international applications, the `getFaultString()` and `setFaultString()` methods are complemented by `java.util.Locale` style methods, namely `getFaultStringLocale()` and an overloading of `setFaultString()` that expects both a `String` and a `Locale`. These methods access or assign an `xml:lang` attribute to the `faultstring` value. If you do not use a `Locale` method, the default locale is used. A `java.util.Locale` represents a geographic, cultural, or political region (for example, the French-speaking area of Canada, or Simplified Chinese).

> ***The legal values for the `xml:lang` attribute are specified in the IETF standard RFC 1766 and its successors (currently RFC 3066), which are based in part on ISO 639:1988. Language values begin with a primary two-character language identifier, optionally followed by a series of hyphen-delimited sub-ids for country or dialect identification; the ids are not case-sensitive. Examples include `"en-us"` for United States English and `"fr-ca"` for Canadian French. You don't have to use the sub-ids if the nature of the application doesn't require you to; `"en"` or `"fr"` by itself is fine.***

The simplest way to add a `SOAPFault` to a message is to use the overloaded `addFault()` methods, which allow you to initialize the fault code, fault string, and language (`Locale`) of the fault string when it's created. For example, the following snippet shows how to create a complete `SOAPFault` object in one operation.

```
SOAPFactory soapFactory = SOAPFactory.newInstance();

Name faultCode = soapFactory.createName("Client","soap",
                            SOAPConstants.URI_NS_SOAP_ENVELOPE);
SOAPFault fault = body.addFault(faultCode,
                               "The ISBN contains an invalid character(s)",
                               Locale.US);
```

If you're using the default `Locale`, you can just invoke the `addFault(Name,String)` overloading of the method instead of passing the default `Locale` object explicitly.

13.4.2 The Detail Type

A SOAPFault object contains an object of type Detail, which in turn contains one or more DetailEntry objects. As shown in Listing 13–25, the Detail type defines two methods: one for adding new DetailEntry objects and one for accessing existing ones.

Listing 13–25

The javax.xml.soap.Detail *Interface*

```
package javax.xml.soap;
import java.util.Iterator;

public interface Detail extends SOAPFaultElement {
    public DetailEntry addDetailEntry(Name name) throws SOAPException;
    public Iterator getDetailEntries()
}
```

The Detail object was used in SaajExample_7, as shown in the following snippet from Listing 13–24.

```
Detail detail = fault.addDetail();
Name errorName = envelope.createName("InvalidIsbnFaultDetail","mh",
                         "http://www.Monson-Haefel.com/jwsbook/BookQuote");

DetailEntry detailEntry = detail.addDetailEntry(errorName);
```

13.4.3 The SOAPFaultElement Type

SOAPFaultElement is the supertype of SOAPDetail type (see Figure 13–4). It defines no methods or fields; it's an empty interface. It provides the same kind of typing benefit that SOAPBodyElement does: some assurance of backward-compatibility if the SOAP protocol changes, and some type safety. Its definition appears in Listing 13–26.

Listing 13–26

The javax.xml.soap.SOAPFaultElement *Interface*

```
package javax.xml.soap;
public interface SOAPFaultElement extends SOAPElement {}
```

SOAPFaultElement is not usually used directly in your code, but it has utility because it extends SOAPElement, and thus inherits all the methods of that interface.

13.4.4 The `DetailEntry` Type

`DetailEntry`, defined in Listing 13–27, is another empty interface. It has no methods or fields, and is useful only for type safety (the `Detail` object may contain `DetailEntry` objects only). Its supertype, `SOAPElement`, defines all the methods you need to work with detail entries. It also offers some flexibility for the future, if new versions of SOAP add new restrictions on detail elements.

Listing 13–27

The `javax.xml.soap.DetailEntry` *Interface*

```
package javax.xml.soap;
public interface DetailEntry extends SOAPElement {}
```

13.5 Sending SOAP Messages with SAAJ

Building SOAP messages with SAAJ wouldn't be very useful if you didn't send them anywhere. Usually SAAJ is used in combination with JAX-RPC, but it's not dependent on JAX-RPC.

SAAJ comes with its own, fairly simple and limited, message-delivery system, which is a part of the basic API. Using SAAJ you can exchange Request/Response-style SOAP messages with a Web service over HTTP. You can also use SAAJ's native message delivery system with any other kind of URL-based protocol, depending on what your vendor supports—but remember that HTTP is the only protocol sanctioned by the Basic Profile.

SAAJ's native message-delivery system is so simple that it takes only a few lines of code to send and receive SOAP messages. In fact it's so simple that there is not much to explain. You simply create a `SOAPConnection` and send the message. `SaajExample_8` in Listing 13–28 demonstrates this procedure.

Listing 13–28

Using SAAJ to Send and Receive SOAP Messages

```
package com.jwsbook.saaj;
import javax.xml.soap.*;
import java.net.URL;
import java.io.FileInputStream;

public class SaajExample_8 {
  public static void main(String [] args) throws SOAPException,
    java.io.IOException{
```

```
    // Build a SOAPMessage from a file
    MessageFactory msgFactory = MessageFactory.newInstance();
    MimeHeaders mimeHeaders = new MimeHeaders();
    mimeHeaders.addHeader("Content-Type","text/xml; charset=UTF-8");
    FileInputStream file = new FileInputStream("soap.xml");
    SOAPMessage requestMsg = msgFactory.createMessage(mimeHeaders, file);
    file.close();

    // Send the SOAP message to the BookQuote Web service
    SOAPConnectionFactory conFactry = SOAPConnectionFactory.newInstance();
    SOAPConnection connection = conFactry.createConnection();
    URL url = new URL(args[0]);
    SOAPMessage replyMsg =connection.call(requestMsg, url);

    // Print out the reply message
    SaajOutputter.writeToScreen(replyMsg);
  }
}
```

SaajExample_8 builds a SOAP message from a file (soap.xml), then sends the message to the URL you provide as an argument. The SOAPConnection object creates an HTTP connection to the specified URL and sends the SOAP message to the Web service as an HTTP POST message. The HTTP reply that's sent from the Web service back to the SOAPConnection object will contain a SOAP message, a SOAP fault, or an HTTP error code; in the last case a SOAPException is thrown.

The SOAP reply message is returned by the SOAPConnection.call() method as a SOAPMessage object, which can be accessed using the SAAJ API. SaajExample_8 writes the reply SOAP message to the screen. It will look something like this:

```
<?xml version="1.0" encoding="UTF-8"?>
<soap:Envelope xmlns:soap="http://schemas.xmlsoap.org/soap/envelope/"
xmlns:ns0="http://www.Monson-Haefel.com/jwsbook/BookQuote" >
  <soap:Body>
    <ns0:getBookPriceResponse>
      <result>24.99</result>
    </ns0:getBookPriceResponse>
  </soap:Body>
</soap:Envelope>
```

SAAJ's native messaging service is optional, so your vendor may not support it; if so, the SOAPConnection.call() method may not work. Check your vendor's documentation to determine whether it's supported.

13.6 SAAJ 1.2 and DOM 2

SAAJ 1.1, the first official version of SAAJ, was not as flexible as it could have been. Vendors and developers complained that it should have been based on DOM 2. They claimed—rightly—that a DOM-based SAAJ would be a more flexible API, would make it easier to work with arbitrary XML document fragments, and would allow SAAJ to work well with DOM. In recognition of version 1.1's shortcomings, SAAJ 1.2 redefines the API so that it's an extension of the DOM 2 Java object model. SAAJ is now a lot more powerful, because you can use it to create and manipulate SOAP messages, but you can also take advantage of low-level DOM 2 functionality as the need arises. In addition, you can import `Nodes` from a DOM 2 document into a SOAP message, which is useful when working with JAX-RPC message handlers and Document/Literal payloads.

This section assumes you are already familiar with DOM 2. If you're not, then you should take time out to read Chapter 21: DOM 2 now, or this section is not going to make much sense to you. Chapter 21 will teach some of the basics about the DOM 2 programming API and how it's used. To find out where you can learn still more about DOM, see the introduction to Part VI: JAXP.

Aligning SAAJ 1.2 with DOM 2 didn't really complicate the SAAJ API too much. In most cases interfaces were simply redefined to extend DOM 2 interface types like `Document`, `Element`, and `Text`. Figure 13–5 shows how SAAJ 1.2 types inherit from DOM 2 types.

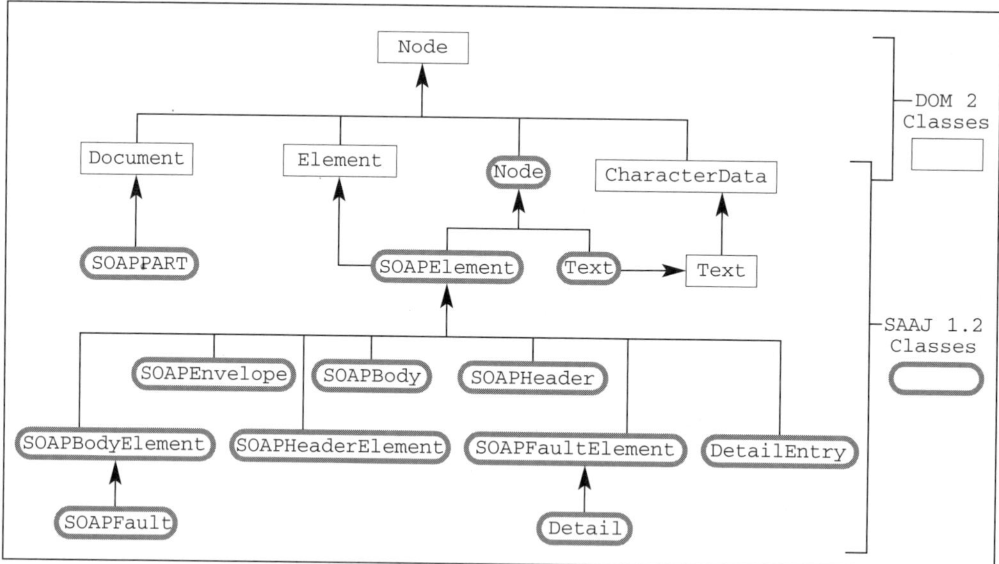

Figure 13–5 SAAJ 1.2 and DOM 2 Inheritance Diagram (DOM types are in gray, SAAJ types in black.)

SaajExample_9 in Listing 13–29 is a simple example of how you can use SAAJ 1.2 and DOM 2 in concert to construct a Document/Literal SOAP message.

Listing 13–29

Importing a DOM Element into a SAAJ 1.2 SOAPMessage

```
package com.jwsbook.saaj;
import javax.xml.parsers.DocumentBuilderFactory;
import javax.xml.parsers.DocumentBuilder;
import org.w3c.dom.Document;
import org.w3c.dom.Element;
import org.w3c.dom.Node;
import javax.xml.soap.*;

public class SaajExample_9 {
  public static void main(String [] args) throws Exception{

    // Read an XML document from a file into a DOM tree using JAXP.
    String filePath = args[0];
    DocumentBuilderFactory factory = DocumentBuilderFactory.newInstance();
    DocumentBuilder parser = factory.newDocumentBuilder();
    Document xmlDoc = parser.parse(filePath);

    // Create a SAAJ SOAPMessage object. Get the SOAPBody and SOAPPart.
    MessageFactory msgFactory = MessageFactory.newInstance();
    SOAPMessage message = msgFactory.createMessage();
    SOAPPart soapPart = message.getSOAPPart();
    SOAPBody soapBody = soapPart.getEnvelope().getBody();

    // Import the root element and append it to the body of the SOAP message.
    Node elementCopy =
      soapPart.importNode(xmlDoc.getDocumentElement(), true);
    soapBody.appendChild(elementCopy);

    // Output SOAP message.
    SaajOutputter.writeToScreen(message);
  }
}
```

SaajExample_9 reads an XML document from a file and has a DOM provider parse it into a Document object. It also creates a new SOAPMessage object. The application imports the root of the XML document into the SOAPPart (using the Document.importNode() method) and subsequently appends the imported copy to the SOAPBody (using the Node.appendNode() method).

As an alternative to using the `importNode()` method, you can use the `SOAPBody.addDocument()` method, which requires a lot less code, but has a significant side effect. When you call `SOAPBody.addDocument()`, the root element of the `Document` is actually moved (not copied) to become a child of the `SOAPBody`. In other words, the root element is physically reassigned to the `SOAPMessage` object. As you learned earlier in chapter 21, a `Node` cannot refer to more than one `Document` object, so moving the root element to the `SOAPMessage` (specifically to the `SOAPPart`) invalidates the source `Document`—there is no longer a root element that refers to it. In Listing 13–30, `SaajExample_10` shows how you can use `SOAPBody.addDocument()`.

Listing 13–30

Moving a DOM Root Element to a SAAJ 1.2 `SOAPMessage`

```
package com.jwsbook.saaj;
import javax.xml.parsers.DocumentBuilderFactory;
import javax.xml.parsers.DocumentBuilder;
import org.w3c.dom.Document;
import org.w3c.dom.Element;
import javax.xml.soap.*;

public class SaajExample_10 {
  public static void main(String [] args) throws Exception{

    // Read an XML document from a file into a DOM tree using JAXP.
    String filePath = args[0];
    DocumentBuilderFactory factory = DocumentBuilderFactory.newInstance();
    DocumentBuilder parser = factory.newDocumentBuilder();
    Document xmlDoc = parser.parse(filePath);

    // Create a SAAJ SOAPMessage object. Get the SOAPBody.
    MessageFactory msgFactory = MessageFactory.newInstance();
    SOAPMessage message = msgFactory.createMessage();
    SOAPBody soapBody = message.getSOAPPart().getEnvelope().getBody();

    // Append the root element of the XML doc to the body of the SOAP message.
    soapBody.addDocument(xmlDoc);

    // Output SOAP message.
    jwsed1.SaajOutputter.writeToScreen(message);
  }
}
```

13.7 Wrapping Up

Using SAAJ makes it fairly easy to construct SOAP messages from scratch, and to peruse SOAP messages received from other nodes. While SAAJ is normally used in combination with JAX-RPC or some other API, it can also be used independently, which is why it's a separate API from JAX-RPC.

JAX-RPC's Message Handler API depends heavily on SAAJ to represent incoming and outgoing SOAP messages so that you can manipulate SOAP header blocks. The next chapter explains in detail how to use SAAJ with JAX-RPC message handlers.

This chapter covered the construction of simple SOAP documents using SAAJ, but SAAJ is also designed to model SOAP Messages with Attachments (SwA), the MIME format used to deliver SOAP messages that refer to XML and non-XML data. Because the Basic Profile doesn't support SwA, this subject is addressed in Appendix F: SAAJ Attachments.

Chapter 14
Message Handlers

Message handlers allow you to manipulate SOAP messages that are sent and received by JAX-RPC clients and Web service endpoints. They can be used with generated stubs, dynamic proxies, the DII, JAX-RPC service endpoints (JSEs), and EJB endpoints. If you've worked with servlet filters, message handlers will be familiar to you.

You may have noticed that none of the JAX-RPC client APIs (generated stubs, dynamic proxies, or DII) provide support for SOAP header blocks. In other words, if you use a generated stub or any other JAX-RPC client API to send a SOAP message, there's no obvious mechanism for adding header-block information. The same is also true of JAX-RPC Web service endpoints (JSEs and EJB endpoints). The primary purpose of message handlers is to provide a mechanism for adding, reading, and manipulating header blocks in SOAP messages that JAX-RPC clients and Web service endpoints send and receive.

Message handlers operate behind the scenes, and are managed by the J2EE container system. At runtime the message handlers are not visible to your application code—they are applied automatically by the JAX-RPC runtime system. When you send a SOAP message using a JAX-RPC client API, the JAX-RPC runtime will filter the outgoing SOAP message through a chain of message handlers before sending it across the network to the Web services. Similarly, any SOAP reply messages received by a JAX-RPC client will be filtered through the same chain of message handlers before the result is returned to your application code. Figure 14–1 shows where the handler chain fits into the JAX-RPC runtime for a generated stub and a J2EE Web service endpoint.

14.1 A Simple Example

To illustrate how message handlers work, we'll develop a very simple message handler that adds a `message-id` header block to a SOAP message that is produced by a generated stub. The `message-id` header block adds a unique identifier to a message sent by the JAX-RPC client so that it can be logged by SOAP nodes that process it—`message-ids` help with debugging and provide audit trails. We're talking about the same `message-id` header block introduced in Chapter 4: SOAP.

14.1.1 Defining a Message-Handler Class

All message handlers must implement the `javax.xml.rpc.handler.Handler` interface, which provides methods for processing SOAP requests, replies, and fault messages. Listing 14–1 shows the interface definition for the `Handler` type.

Listing 14–1

The `javax.xml.rpc.handler.Handler` *Interface*

```
package javax.xml.rpc.handler;

public interface Handler {
    public boolean handleRequest(MessageContext context);
    public boolean handleResponse(MessageContext context);
```

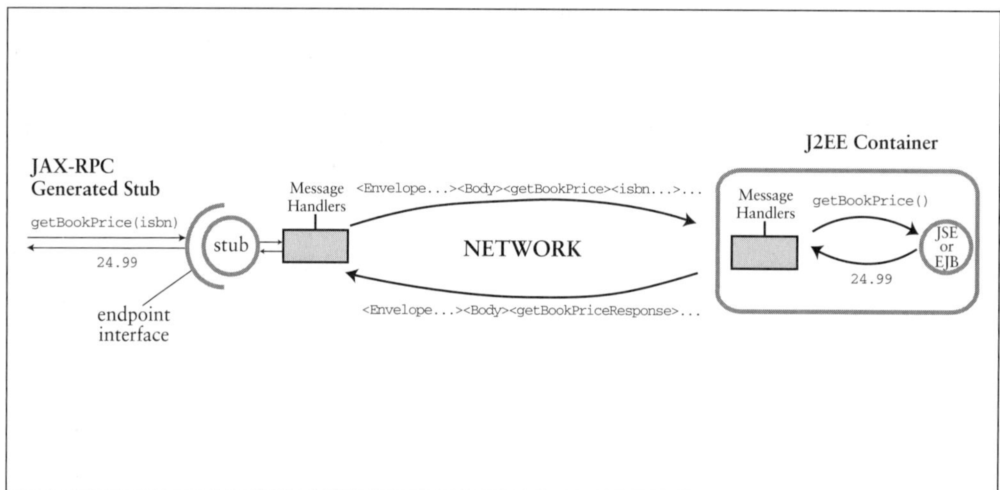

Figure 14–1 Message Handlers in the Invocation Loop

```
    public boolean handleFault(MessageContext context);
    public void init(HandlerInfo config) ;
    public void destroy();
    public QName[] getHeaders();
}
```

We'll examine all of these methods in detail later, but for now all we're concerned with is the `handleRequest()` method, which allows us to add the `message-id` header block to the SOAP message before it's sent across the network. In many cases, you won't need to implement all the methods defined by the `Handler` interface, so the JAX-RPC API provides an abstract class, `javax.xml.rpc.handler.GenericHandler`, that "stubs out" all the methods of the `Handler` interface. Extending the `GenericHandler` class allows you to implement the methods you're interested in and ignore the rest. The `message-id` handler developed in this example will extend the `GenericHandler` class, so we need to implement only the `handleRequest()` and `getHeaders()` methods. Listing 14–2 shows the `MessageIDHandler` class, our implementation of the `message-id` handler.

Listing 14–2

A Simple Message Handler

```
package com.jwsbook.jaxrpc;
import javax.xml.rpc.handler.MessageContext;
import javax.xml.rpc.handler.soap.SOAPMessageContext;
import javax.xml.namespace.QName;
import javax.xml.soap.SOAPFactory;
import javax.xml.soap.SOAPMessage;
import javax.xml.soap.SOAPHeader;
import javax.xml.soap.SOAPHeaderElement;
import javax.xml.soap.Name;

public class MessageIDHandler extends javax.xml.rpc.handler.GenericHandler{

  QName [] headerNames = null;

  public QName [] getHeaders(){
    if(headerNames == null){
      QName myHeader =
        new QName("http://www.Monson-Haefel.com/jwsbook/message-id",
                  "message-id");
      headerNames = new QName[]{ myHeader };
    }
    return headerNames;
```

```
  }
  public boolean handleRequest(MessageContext context){
    String messageID = new java.rmi.dgc.VMID().toString();

    try{

      SOAPMessageContext soapCntxt = (SOAPMessageContext)context;
      SOAPMessage message = soapCntxt.getMessage();
      SOAPHeader header = message.getSOAPPart().getEnvelope().getHeader();

      Name blockName = SOAPFactory.newInstance().createName(
                     "message-id","mi",
                     "http://www.Monson-Haefel.com/jwsbook/message-id");
      SOAPHeaderElement headerBlock = header.addHeaderElement(blockName);
      headerBlock.setActor("http://www.Monson-Haefel.com/logger");
      headerBlock.addTextNode( messageID );
      return true;

    }catch(javax.xml.soap.SOAPException se){
         throw new javax.xml.rpc.JAXRPCException(se);
    }
  }
}
```

While the `MessageIDHandler` isn't as simple as a "Hello World!" type example, it's about a simple as you can get when writing a `Handler` class. I'll examine the `MessageIDHandler` in pieces so that it's easier to understand.

The first thing we need to do is to identify the header blocks that the `MessageIDHandler` will process. Every `Handler` class must implement the `getHeaders()` method, which returns an array of header-block element names that the `Handler` should process. The JAX-RPC runtime will use this list of names to determine whether it has a message handler that matches a header block of an incoming message. The following snippet from Listing 14–2 shows the implementation of the `getHeaders()` method defined by the `MessageIDHandler` class.

```
QName [] headerNames = null;

public QName [] getHeaders(){
  if(headerNames == null){
    QName myHeader =
      new QName("http://www.Monson-Haefel.com/jwsbook/message-id",
               "message-id");
    headerNames = new QName[]{ myHeader };
```

```
    }
    return headerNames;
  }
```

The `getHeaders()` method always returns an array of `QName` objects, each of which represents a header block that the message handler is designed to process. Usually a message handler will process only one type of header block, but it's possible for a single message handler to process several different types (perhaps different versions of the same header block), which is why `getHeaders()` returns an array of `QName` objects. In this example, we are processing only the `message-id` header block, so our `QName` array contains a single entry. This class implements `getHeaders()` in a way that ensures it will create the `QName` array only once; subsequent calls return the array that was created the first time through.

The real meat of `MessageIDHeader` is in its `handleRequest()` method, which adds a `message-id` header block to an outgoing SOAP message. The method begins by creating a `java.rmi.dgc.VMID` instance, which represents a unique id based on the Internet address of the caller, an object id, a count, and a millisecond time stamp. The details of the `VMID` class are not important. It's used here because it's the simplest way to create a unique id for this example. The following snippet from Listing 14–2 shows the line that creates the unique id.

```
public boolean handleRequest(MessageContext context){
  String messageID = new java.rmi.dgc.VMID().toString();
  ...
}
```

Now armed with a unique id, all we need to do is insert a `message-id` header block into the outgoing SOAP message. Using SAAJ, `handleRequest()` adds a new `message-id` header block to the outgoing SOAP message and sets the element's value equal to the unique id generated by the `VMID` object (see the next snippet). When `handleRequest()` is done, it returns `true`, to indicate that it processed the message successfully. If the SAAJ API throws a `SOAPException`, the method catches it and throws a `javax.xml.rpc.JAXRPCException`, a kind of `java.lang.RuntimeException`, which causes the message delivery to fail. The following shows the complete definition of the `handleRequest()` method from Listing 14–2.

```
public boolean handleRequest(MessageContext context){
  String messageID = new java.rmi.dgc.VMID().toString();

  try{

    SOAPMessageContext soapCntxt = (SOAPMessageContext)context;
    SOAPMessage message = soapCntxt.getMessage();
```

```
        SOAPHeader header = message.getSOAPPart().getEnvelope().getHeader();

        Name blockName = SOAPFactory.newInstance().createName(
                             "message-id","mi",
                             "http://www.Monson-Haefel.com/jwsbook/message-id");
        SOAPHeaderElement headerBlock = header.addHeaderElement(blockName);
        headerBlock.setActor("http://www.Monson-Haefel.com/logger");
        headerBlock.addTextNode( messageID );
        return true;

      }catch(javax.xml.soap.SOAPException se){
        throw new javax.xml.rpc.JAXRPCException(se);
      }
    }
```

The `handleRequest()` method, like the other `handleXXX()` methods of the `Handler` interface, declares its parameter to be a `javax.xml.rpc.handler.MessageContext`. This is a protocol-agnostic interface that describes a message. Because JAX-RPC is almost always used for SOAP messaging, however, the actual object implementing this interface will usually be an instance of the `javax.xml.rpc.handler.soap.SOAPMessageContext` interface, which extends `MessageContext`, adding support for accessing `actor` roles and `javax.xml.soap.SOAPMessage` objects.

In Chapter 13: SAAJ you learned that `SOAPMessage` objects represent SOAP messages, which may include attachments. Using the SAAJ API you can access and modify any part of the SOAP message before it's sent over the network, or after it's received from the network. When a JAX-RPC client invokes a method (for example, an endpoint method on a generated stub) to send a SOAP message, the JAX-RPC runtime will first marshal the arguments of the call into an XML SOAP message, then place that SOAP message in a SAAJ `SOAPMessage` object. Once the `SOAPMessage` object is constructed, it's passed into the chain of message handlers.

14.1.2 Defining a WSDL Document

In this example we are going to use the `MessageIDHandler` with a generated stub for the BookQuote Web service, like the one created in Section 12.1: Generated Stubs. The first thing we will do is define a WSDL document and use it to generate the stub and the endpoint interface. We will modify the BookQuote WSDL document defined in Chapter 12, so that it includes the definition of the `message-id` header block as shown in Listing 14–3 (changes are in bold).

Listing 14–3

A WSDL Document That Defines a Header Block

```
<?xml version="1.0" encoding="utf-8"?>
<definitions xmlns="http://schemas.xmlsoap.org/wsdl/"
 xmlns:xsd="http://www.w3.org/2001/XMLSchema"
 xmlns:soapbind="http://schemas.xmlsoap.org/wsdl/soap/"
 xmlns:mh="http://www.Monson-Haefel.com/jwsbook/BookQuote"
 xmlns:mi="http://www.Monson-Haefel.com/jwsbook/message-id"
 targetNamespace="http://www.Monson-Haefel.com/jwsbook/BookQuote">
  <types>
    <schema targetNamespace="http://www.Monson-Haefel.com/jwsbook/message-id"
     xmlns="http://www.w3.org/2001/XMLSchema">
      <element name="message-id" type="string"/>
    </schema>
  </types>

  <message name="Headers">
    <part name="message-id" element="mi:message-id"/>
  </message>
  <message name="getBookPrice">
    <part name="isbn" type="xsd:string"/>
  </message>
  <message name="getBookPriceResponse">
    <part name="result" type="xsd:float"/>
  </message>
  <portType name="BookQuote">
    <operation name="getBookPrice">
      <input message="mh:getBookPrice"/>
      <output message="mh:getBookPriceResponse"/>
    </operation>
  </portType>
  <binding name="BookQuoteSoapBinding" type="mh:BookQuote">
    <soapbind:binding style="rpc"
        transport="http://schemas.xmlsoap.org/soap/http"/>
    <operation name="getBookPrice">
      <soapbind:operation soapAction="" style="rpc"/>
      <input>
        <soapbind:header message="mh:Headers" part="message-id"
                         use="literal"/>
        <soapbind:body use="literal"
          namespace="http://www.Monson-Haefel.com/jwsbook/BookQuote" />
      </input>
```

```
      <output>
        <soapbind:body use="literal"
          namespace="http://www.Monson-Haefel.com/jwsbook/BookQuote" />
      </output>
    </operation>
  </binding>

  <!-- service tells us the Internet address of a Web service -->
  <service name="BookPriceService">
    <port name="BookPrice_Port" binding="mh:BookQuoteSoapBinding">
      <soapbind:address
       location="http://www.Monson-Haefel.com/jwsbook/BookQuote" />
    </port>
  </service>
</definitions>
```

Notice that the WSDL `message` definition labeled `Headers` is not included in the `portType` definition, but it is included in the `binding` definition—the typical pattern for defining headers in WSDL. As a result, the `Headers` message is included in the SOAP message, but it's not part of the abstract interface from which JAX-RPC endpoints are generated.

14.1.3 Generating the Service and Endpoint Interfaces

Using the WSDL document defined in Listing 14–3, we can generate the service and endpoint interfaces and their implementations. The endpoint interface is defined as in Listing 14–4.

Listing 14–4

The Endpoint Interface

```
package com.jwsbook.jaxrpc;

public interface BookQuote extends java.rmi.Remote {
  public float getBookPrice(String isbn) throws java.rmi.RemoteException;
}
```

Notice that the endpoint interface in Listing 14–4 is identical to the endpoint interfaces in previous chapters—it doesn't define any `message-id` header block parameter.

The generated service interface is also the same as you've seen in previous chapters. Listing 14–5 shows the `BookQuoteService` definition.

Listing 14–5

The Service Interface

```
package com.jwsbook.jaxrpc;

public interface BookQuoteService extends javax.xml.rpc.Service{
    public BookQuote getBookQuotePort()
    throws javax.xml.rpc.ServiceException;
}
```

As you can see from these two listings, there are no methods for accessing message handlers, nor is there a `message-id` parameter in the `getBookPrice()` method. The application of the `MessageIDHandler` by the JAX-RPC runtime is automatic and hidden. The `MessageIDHandler`'s `handleRequest()` method is invoked after `getBookPrice()` is called, but before the SOAP message is sent across the network.

14.1.4 Configuring Message Handlers

There are basically two ways that you can configure the JAX-RPC runtime to use message handlers: In a J2EE environment you must configure them using Web services deployment descriptors. In standalone applications you can add them programmatically at runtime, using the JAX-RPC API. Because this book is about J2EE Web Services, we'll focus on the path J2EE requires you to follow.

Web services deployment descriptors are covered in detail in Part VII: Deployment, but it's worth introducing the configuration of message handlers here because you'll need it to understand how message handlers are processed at runtime. In particular we'll be looking at the order in which handlers are processed, in Section 14.2. In this section we want to focus on the declaration of the `handler` element, which describes a JAX-RPC handler.

Message handlers are configured in different locations, depending on which type of component you use. In this case we are interested in configuring message handlers using the `service-ref` descriptor element, which is used by J2EE components (servlets, EJBs, JSEs, and the like).

In J2EE 1.4 the `service-ref` element is nested in the J2EE component's deployment descriptor, along with other JNDI ENC elements, like `env-entry` and `resource-ref`. Listing 14–6 shows an example of a `service-ref` element used in J2EE 1.4.

Listing 14–6

Declaring Message Handlers in the `service-ref` *Element*

```
<service-ref xmlns:mh="http://www.Monson-Haefel.com/jwsbook/BookQuote"
             xmlns:mi="http://www.Monson-Haefel.com/jwsbook/messsage-id" >
  <service-ref-name>service/BookQuoteService</service-ref-name>
```

```
  <service-interface>com.jwsbook.jaxrpc.BookQuoteService
  </service-interface>
  <wsdl-file>META-INF/BookQuote.wsdl</wsdl-file>
  <jaxrpc-mapping-file>META-INF/mapping.xml</jaxrpc-mapping-file>
  <service-qname>mh:BookQuoteService</service-qname>
  <handler>
    <handler-name>MessageID</handler-name>
    <handler-class>com.jwsbook.jaxrpc.MessageIDHandler</handler-class>
    <soap-header>mi:message-id</soap-header>
    <soap-role>http://www.Monson-Haefel.com/logger</soap-role>
    <port-name>BookQuotePort</port-name>
  </handler>
</service-ref>
```

The `service-ref` element describes a reference to a JAX-RPC Web service endpoint. Basically, the `service-ref` element identifies the directory name of the service in the JNDI ENC, the endpoint and service interfaces, and the location of the WSDL document that describes the Web service. In addition, you can configure message handlers that are to be used in conjunction with the service reference. In Listing 4–6, the highlighted code configures the `MessageIDHandler` that is used to preprocess SOAP messages before sending them across the wire.

14.1.5 Using Message Handlers in a J2EE Component

Once you have developed one or more message handlers, defined the `service-ref` element, and generated the service implementation and endpoint stub, you are ready to deploy your J2EE component. `JaxRpcExample_6` (Listing 14–7) is a J2EE Application Client that uses a generated stub and the `MessageIDHandler` to call the BookQuote Web service.

Listing 14–7

Using a Generated Stub Configured to Use a Message Handler

```
package com.jwsbook.jaxrpc;
import javax.naming.InitialContext;

public class JaxRpcExample_6 {

  public static void main(String [] args) throws Exception{
      String isbn = args[0];

      InitialContext jndiContext = new InitialContext();

      BookQuoteService service = (BookQuoteService)
```

```
        jndiContext.lookup("java:comp/env/service/BookQuoteService");

        BookQuote BookQuote_stub = service.getBookQuotePort();

        float price = BookQuote_stub.getBookPrice( isbn );

        System.out.println("The price is = "+price);

    }
}
```

If `JaxRpcExample_6` looks familiar, it's because the code appears to be exactly the same as in `JaxRpcExample_1`, which was defined in Listing 12–10. There's a significant difference, however: The `JaxRpcExample_6` application is deployed with a message handler configured, so the SOAP messages it sends will include the `message-id` header block, as shown in Listing 14–8.

Listing 14–8

A SOAP Message with the `message-id` *Header Block*

```
<?xml version="1.0" encoding="UTF-8"?>
<soap:Envelope
 xmlns:soap="http://schemas.xmlsoap.org/soap/envelope/"
 xmlns:mi="http://www.Monson-Haefel.com/jwsbook/message-id"
 xmlns:mh="http://www.Monson-Haefel.com/jwsbook/BookQuote">
   <soap:Header>
      <mi:message-id soap:actor="http://www.Monson-Haefel.com/logger">
           deabc782dbbd11bf:29e357:f1ad93fdbf:-8000
      </mi:message-id>
   </soap:Header>
   <soap:Body>
      <mh:getBookPrice>
          <isbn>0321146182</isbn>
      </mh:getBookPrice>
   </soap:Body>
</soap:Envelope>
```

Remember: The JAX-RPC runtime adds the `message-id` header block after the `getBookPrice()` method is invoked, but before the SOAP message is sent across the network to the BookQuote Web service.

14.2 Handler Chains and Order of Processing

In some cases you will need to use several message handlers, each assigned to process a different header block. In these cases, the message handlers are **chained:** They process the SOAP message serially, one after another, in the order in which you declare them in the deployment descriptor.

For example, imagine that you use three message handlers: `MessageIDHandler`, `ProcessedByHandler`, and `ClientSecurityHandler`. The `MessageIDHandler` we've already discussed. The `ProcessedByHandler` is responsible for adding to the message the `processed-by` header block, which logs information about the nodes along the message path that process the message. This information is useful for debugging. The `ClientSecurityHandler` is responsible for adding an **XML digital signature** to the message. The digital signature reveals whether the `Body` of the message was tampered with en route.

> ***You can use an XML digital-signature[1] header block to verify the integrity of some portion of an XML document—for example, the contents of the*** `Body` ***element in a SOAP message. Basically, a digital signature performs a standard hash algorithm on the contents of the*** `Body` ***element, using a public key. If the contents of the*** `Body` ***element are tampered with on their way to the ultimate receiver, the change will be detected and the message can be rejected. An XML digital signature doesn't actually encrypt the message; it simply generates a unique sequence of bytes from the data that can be reproduced only if the data has not changed.***

The SOAP message that is processed by these three message handlers would look something like Listing 14–9 (elements of the digital-signature block are omitted for brevity).

Listing 14–9

A SOAP Message with Multiple Header Blocks

```
<?xml version="1.0" encoding="UTF-8"?>
<soap:Envelope
 xmlns:soap="http://schemas.xmlsoap.org/soap/envelope/"
 xmlns:mi="http://www.Monson-Haefel.com/jwsbook/message-id"
 xmlns:proc="http://www.Monson-Haefel.com/jwsbook/processed-by"
 xmlns:sec="http://schemas.xmlsoap.org/soap/security/2000-12"
 xmlns:mh="http://www.Monson-Haefel.com/jwsbook/BookQuote">
   <soap:Header>
```

[1] World Wide Web Consortium, "SOAP Security Extensions: Digital Signature," W3C Note, February 2001. Available at http://www.w3.org/TR/SOAP-dsig/.

```
      <mi:message-id soap:actor="http://www.Monson-Haefel.com/logger">
           deabc782dbbd11bf:29e357:f1ad93fdbf:-8000
      </mi:message-id>
      <proc:processed-by
        soap:actor="http://schemas.xmlsoap.org/soap/actor/next">
        <node>
          <time-in-millis>1013694684723</time-in-millis>
          <identity>http://www.client.com/JaxRpcExample_6</identity>
        </node>
      </proc:processed-by>
      <sec:Signature>
        <ds:Signature xmlns:ds="http://www.w3.org/2000/09/xmldsig#">
          <ds:SignedInfo>
            ...
          </ds:SignedInfo>
          <ds:SignatureValue>CFFOMFCtVLrklR...</ds:SignatureValue>
        </ds:Signature>
      </sec:Signature>
   </soap:Header>
   <soap:Body>
      <mh:getBookPrice>
          <isbn>0321146182</isbn>
      </mh:getBookPrice>
   </soap:Body>
</soap:Envelope>
```

For a J2EE client to use all three of the message handlers, they all must be declared in the `service-ref` element, as in Listing 14–10.

Listing 14–10

A `service-ref` *Element Declaring Multiple Message Handlers*

```
<service-ref>
  <service-ref-name>service/BookQuoteService</service-ref-name>
  ...
  <handler>
    <handler-name>MessageID</handler-name>
    <handler-class>com.jwsbook.jaxrpc.MessageIDHandler</handler-class>
    <soap-header>mi:message-id</soap-header>
    <soap-role>http://www.Monson-Haefel.com/logger</soap-role>
    <port-name>BookQuotePort</port-name>
  </handler>
  <handler>
```

```
    <handler-name>ProcessedBy</handler-name>
    <handler-class>com.jwsbook.jaxrpc.ProcessedByHandler</handler-class>
    <soap-header>proc:processed-by</soap-header>
    <soap-role>http://schemas.xmlsoap.org/soap/actor/next</soap-role>
    <port-name>BookQuotePort</port-name>
  </handler>
  <handler>
    <handler-name>ClientSecurityHandler</handler-name>
    <handler-class>com.jwsbook.jaxrpc.ClientSecurityHandler
    </handler-class>
    <soap-header>sec:Signature</soap-header>
    <port-name>BookQuotePort</port-name>
  </handler>
</service-ref>
```

When the J2EE client sends a SOAP message, the message handlers will process the outgoing message in the order specified in the `service-ref` element. Figure 14–2 illustrates.

Message handlers can process both outgoing and incoming messages. When a client application sends SOAP messages, the `handleRequest()` method of each message handler processes the outgoing messages, while the `handleResponse()` method processes incoming messages (the replies from the Web service). All the message handlers have an opportunity to process both outgoing and incoming messages, in the order in which they are configured. When the Web service endpoint sends a reply back to the client, the message handlers process it in the reverse order that they processed the corresponding request. For example, if you configure message handlers A, B, and C, in that order, to implement both the `handleRequest()` and `handleResponse()` methods, they will process requests and reply messages as shown in Figure 14–3.

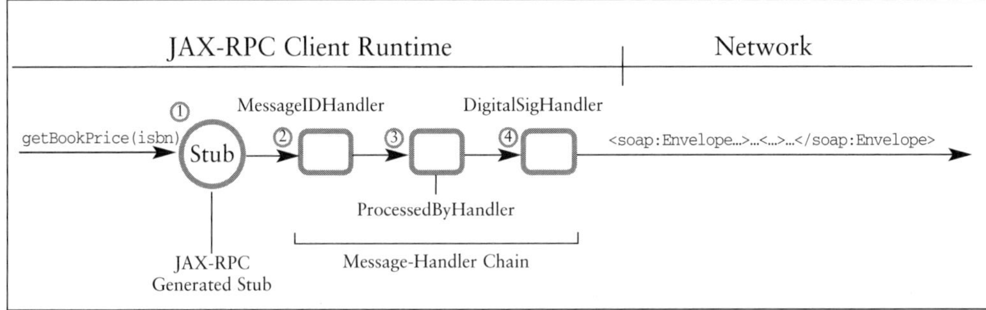

Figure 14–2 Message-Handler Chain: Sender Processing Outgoing Messages

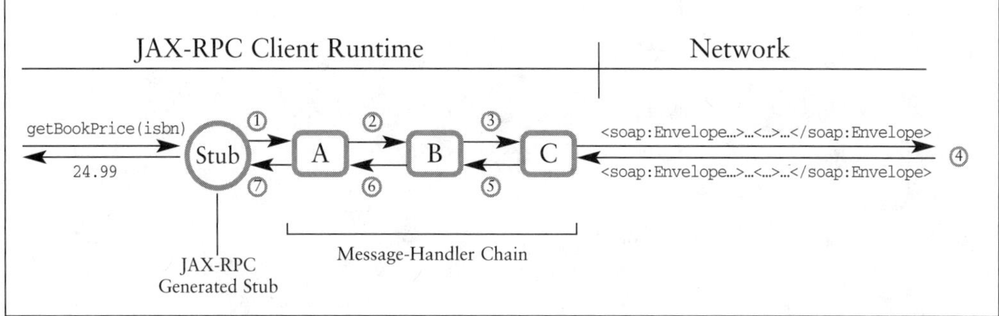

Figure 14–3 Message-Handler Chain: Processing Order for Sender's Outgoing and Incoming Messages

JSEs and EJB endpoints also use message handlers. You could, for example, configure the BookQuote JSE developed in Chapter 10: JAX-RPC Service Endpoints to use message handlers in the same way a J2EE client does, with one significant difference: The `handleRequest()` method of each message handler will process the incoming messages—those sent by the client—while the `handleResponse()` method will process the outgoing messages—the replies sent back to the client. In other words, SOAP requests are outgoing messages for clients but incoming messages for endpoints, and SOAP replies are outgoing messages for endpoints but incoming messages for clients. This all makes sense, because a SOAP request goes to a Web service, while the SOAP reply goes back to a client.

Message handlers for Web service endpoints process messages in the order they are declared in the J2EE component's `webservice.xml` deployment descriptor. This file is a separate document that describes the Web service aspects of a J2EE component. When you develop a JSE or an EJB endpoint, you must define a `webservice.xml` deployment descriptor. Web services deployment descriptors are covered in detail in Chapter 23.

For example, imagine that the BookQuote JSE discussed in Chapter 10 uses two message handlers to process header blocks, the `LoggerHandler` and the `Server SecurityHandler`. The `LoggerHandler` is designed to record SOAP request messages to a database for audit or debugging purposes. It's associated with both the `next` actor role and the `http://www.Monson-Haefel.com/logger` role, so it processes both the `message-id` and `processed-by` header blocks. The `Server SecurityHandler` is designed to examine and confirm digital signatures of incoming request messages and generate XML digital signatures for outgoing reply messages.

The message handlers for JSEs and EJB endpoints are configured in the `webservices.xml` deployment descriptor in the same way that JAX-RPC clients' message handlers are configured in the `service-ref` element. Listing 14–11, excerpted from the BookQuote JSE's deployment descriptor, shows how `LoggerHandler` and `ServerSecurityHandler` are configured.

Listing 14–11

Declaring Message Handlers in a `webservices.xml` *File*

```
<webservices ...
  xmlns:ds="http://schemas.xmlsoap.org/soap/security/2000-12"
  xmlns:proc="http://www.Monson-Haefel.com/jwsbook/processed-by"
  xmlns:mi="http://www.Monson-Haefel.com/jwsbook/message-id" ...>
  <webservice-description>
    <webservice-description-name>BookQuote</webservice-description-name>
    ...
    <port-component>
      <port-component-name>BookQuoteJSE</port-component-name>
      ...
      <handler>
        <handler-name>Logger</handler-name>
        <handler-class>com.jwsbook.jaxrpc.LoggerHandler</handler-class>
        <soap-header>mi:message-id</soap-header>
        <soap-header>proc:processed-by</soap-header>
        <soap-role>http://www.Monson-Haefel.com/logger</soap-role>
      </handler>
      <handler>
        <handler-name>ServerSecurityHandler</handler-name>
        <handler-class>com.jwsbook.jaxrpc.ServerSecurityHandler
        </handler-class>
        <soap-header>ds:Signature</soap-header>
      </handler>
    </port-component>
  </webservice-description>
</webservices>
```

`LoggerHandler` is designed to process both the `message-id` and the `processed-by` header blocks of incoming (request) messages. The implementation of this handler is shown later in this section. The `LoggerHandler` will process only incoming request messages, not outgoing replies. The `ServerSecurityHandler` is designed to process both request and reply messages. Its `handleRequest()` method will examine and confirm XML digital signatures on incoming messages, while its `handleResponse()` method will generate XML digital signatures for outgoing messages. Figure 14–4 shows the order in which the JSE's message handlers process header blocks.

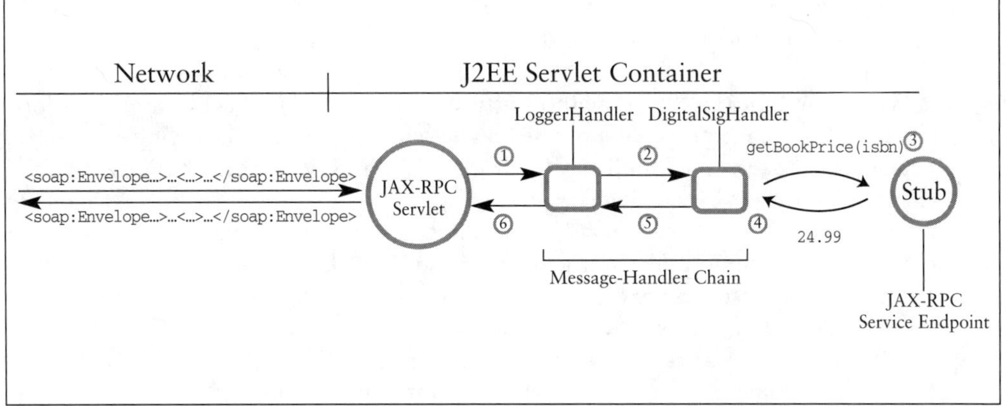

Figure 14–4 Message-Handler Chain: Processing Order for Receiver's Incoming and Outgoing Messages

A detailed discussion of the handler configuration for the `webservices.xml` deployment descriptor is covered in Chapter 23.

14.2.1 Return Values and Order of Processing

The return value of each of the `handleXXX()` methods defined by the `Handler` interface (`handleRequest()`, `handleResponse()`, and `handleFault()`) is a primitive `boolean` value. Listing 14–12 illustrates (return types shown in bold).

Listing 14–12

The `javax.xml.rpc.handler.Handler` *Return Types*

```
package javax.xml.rpc.handler;

public interface Handler {
    public boolean handleRequest(MessageContext context);
    public boolean handleResponse(MessageContext context);
    public boolean handleFault(MessageContext context);
    public void init(HandlerInfo config) ;
    public void destroy();
    public QName[] getHeaders();
}
```

When a `handleXXX()` method returns `true`, it indicates that processing proceeded without a problem and that normal processing of the SOAP message should continue.

When any `handleXXX()` method returns `false`, the JAX-RPC runtime short-circuits the message processing by the handler chain. The exact behavior depends on which `handleXXX()` method returned `false`, and on whether it happened on the client side or the server side. The various scenarios are described in the following paragraphs. One thing to keep in mind is that returning `false` from a `handleXXX()` method does not generate a SOAP fault message. A fault message is generated when a `handleXXX()` method throws an exception—such cases will be covered shortly, in Section 14.2.2.

When a `handleRequest()` method on a JSE or EJB endpoint returns `false`, the JAX-RPC runtime immediately aborts the normal processing of the SOAP message and sends it back through the handler chain in the direction it came from, starting from the current message handler. For example, imagine that message handlers A, B, and C are processing messages for a J2EE Web service endpoint (JSE or EJB endpoint), and that, while processing a SOAP message, B's `handleRequest()` method returns `false`. In this case, the SOAP message does not reach handler C or the service endpoint. Instead, it is immediately processed by handler B's `handleResponse()` method, and then by handler A's `handleResponse()` method, whereupon it's sent back across the network to the client-side handler chain (see Figure 14–5).

Before a server-side handler's `handleRequest()` method returns `false`, it must change the SOAP request message into a SOAP reply message. That way, when the message goes back up the handler chain, it's in the form of a SOAP reply message, as the handlers who receive it expect.

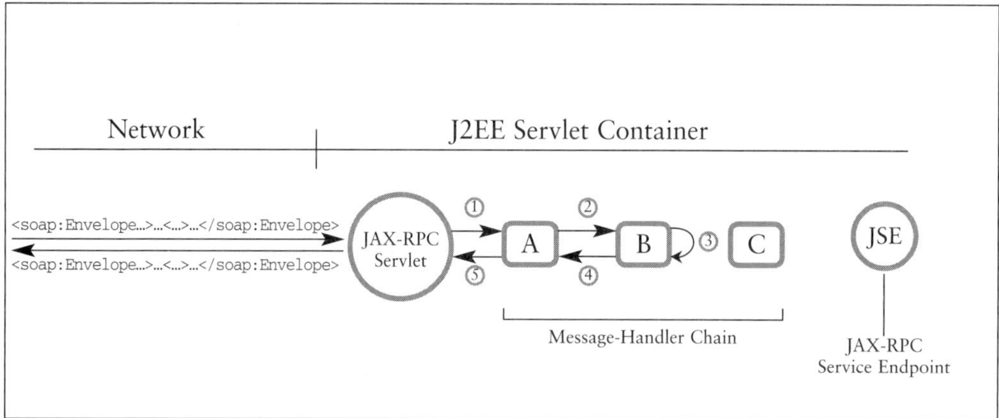

Figure 14–5 Order of Processing When a Server-Side `handleRequest()` Method Returns `false`

Using a `false` ***return value to cut the message path short might be useful when a handler caches reply information. You can design a handler to cache frequently requested data—and update it periodically—to reduce the number of database accesses.***

A `false` return from a message-handler method on the client side has pretty much the same effect it has on the server side. If a client-side `handleRequest()` method returns `false`, the SOAP message is never sent over the network; it just reverses direction and is changed into a reply message.

The behavior is quite different when the `false` return is from a response-handling method. When a server-side `handleResponse()` method returns `false`, the SOAP message does not reverse direction. Instead, the message skips the rest of the message handlers in the chain and the JAX-RPC servlet sends it straight back to the client. Figure 14–6 illustrates. In this case, handler B returns `false`, which causes the SOAP message to bypass handler A and go directly to the SOAP client.

As on the server side, returning `false` from a client-side `handleResponse()` message causes the SOAP response to skip over the remaining message handlers in the chain and go straight to the client. A handler would do this if it determined that a SOAP reply message needed no further processing.

Returning `false` from a `handleFault()` method on the server side has the same effect as returning `false` from a server-side `handleResponse()` method; the fault message just skips the rest of the handlers and is sent across the network to the client. On the client side, returning `false` from a `handleFault()` method has the same effect as returning `false` from a `handleResponse()` method: The fault message skips the rest of the handlers, and returns directly to the client as a `Remote`

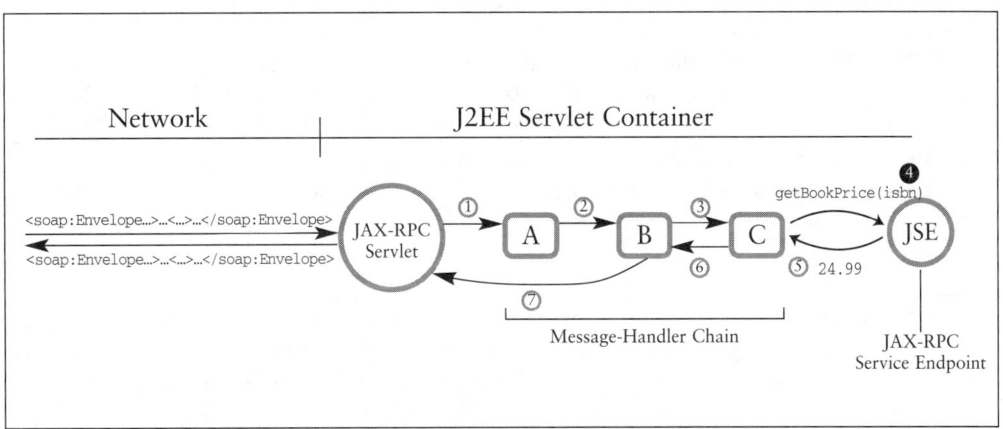

Figure 14–6 Order of Processing When a Server-Side `handleResponse()` Method Returns `false`

Exception or some type of application exception (a SOAP fault exception defined by the developer).

Short-circuiting (also called "blocking") a handler chain by returning false is tricky business. You should use this technique only if you are certain of what you're doing, because if you do it incorrectly it can introduce bugs into your application code that are difficult to track down.

While short-circuiting message-handler chains is discouraged for normal processing, it's a good approach to fault handling—if you do it the right way. In the event of a fault (for example, an erroneous header block), don't return false from the handler that detected the error, throw an exception. Only return false to avoid processing by subsequent headers.

14.2.2 Exceptions and Order of Processing

There are basically two kinds of exceptions that a handleXXX() method can throw: javax.xml.rpc.soap.SOAPFaultException and javax.xml.rpc.JAXRPCException. A SOAPFaultException is used to indicate that a SOAP fault has occurred—that the SOAP message is incorrect or could not be processed. A JAXRPCException is used when some type of runtime error occurs that prevents the message handler from functioning properly.

14.2.2.1 The SOAPFaultException *Type*

A SOAPFaultException can be thrown only by the handleRequest() methods of a handler chain on the server side, when a message handler encounters a problem with the SOAP message itself. Perhaps the header block is structured improperly or the message contains invalid values. For example, if the ServerSecurityHandler discovers that the XML digital signature is invalid (indicating that the message has been tampered with), it throws a SOAPFaultException.

When a server-side handler throws a SOAPFaultException from its handleRequest() method, the JAX-RPC runtime will short-circuit the handler chain and reverse the direction of message flow back up the message chain, just as it does when the handleRequest() method returns false (see Figure 14–5). As the message flows back up the handler chain, it's processed by the handleFault() methods of each handler in the chain, however, rather than by the handleResponse() methods.

SOAPFaultExceptions are never thrown from the handleResponse() method of a server-side handler chain, or from any method of the client-side handler chain. In other words, SOAPFaultExceptions are thrown only from the handleRequest() methods of server-side message handlers. This restriction makes sense if you think about it.

On the client side, handleResponse() is processing a SOAP reply message from a Web service endpoint—you never generate a fault message on a SOAP reply. On the server side, the handleResponse() method is processing a reply the server is sending to the client—the presumption is that the server will not find fault with its own outgoing messages.

On the client the handleRequest() method never throws a SOAPFaultException because the client just generated the request—the client wouldn't find fault in its own request.

Again, the only method that throws a SOAPFaultException is the server-side handleRequest(). That's because the server-side handleRequest() method is processing a message coming from the client, which may contain an error.

If I lost you here, I suggest you read these paragraphs a couple more times and think about the logic for a while. It seems a little convoluted, but it begins to make sense after you've had time to process it.

14.2.2.2 The JAXRPCException *Type*

A message handler should throw a JAXRPCException whenever it encounters a problem processing a SOAP message that is not related to the message's contents—for example, when it cannot do its own processing because a JDBC method throws a SQLException.

The impact of a JAXRPCException depends, in part, on whether it's thrown from a handler on the client side or on the server side. On the server side a JAXRPCException always results in a SOAP fault being generated and sent back to the client (assuming Request/Response messaging). The SOAP fault message has a fault code of "soap:Server" to indicate that the problem is not related to the SOAP message itself, that it results from some server-side error. All handler methods on the server side (handleRequest(), handleResponse(), and handleFault()) behave the same way.

As on the server side, on the client side a JAXRPCException indicates that the client-side JAX-RPC runtime encountered some error sending or receiving the SOAP message that's unrelated to the message contents. Perhaps there was a class loader problem or an array overflow. When a JAXRPCException is thrown, the JAX-RPC runtime simply returns a java.rmi.RemoteException, or one of its subtypes, to the client. All client-side handler methods (handleRequest(), handleResponse(), and handleFault()) behave the same way.

Regardless of whether a JAXRPCException is thrown on the client side or on the server side, it always stops the processing by message handlers in the chain. Once a message handler throws a JAXRPCException, no other handlers will get to process that SOAP message. On the client side a RemoteException type is immediately thrown to the client application. On the server side a SOAP fault is immediately sent to the client.

The JAXRPCException is a subtype of java.lang.RuntimeException. If your message handler throws any type of RuntimeException, it will be handled by the JAX-RPC runtime system the same way a JAXRPCException would.

14.3 The Handler Runtime Environment

Handlers operate in the same context as the J2EE component they are serving, which means they execute in the same transaction and security scope, as well as threading policy of the J2EE component. In addition, by way of the JNDI ENC, a handler enjoys access to the same resources as the J2EE component it serves. Technically, a message handler is an extension of the component it serves, but from a developer perspective a message handler is itself a component, with its own behavior and life cycle.

14.3.1 Statelessness and Multi-threading

Message handlers are stateless objects, which means that they do not maintain session state between invocations. This statelessness allows the JAX-RPC runtime more freedom in how it manages message-handler instances. It might pool them, for example, or allow multiple threads to access the same handlers at the same time. A lot of this depends on the runtime environment of the J2EE Web service component that the handler is serving. For example, a JSE runs in a servlet container and can be either single-threaded or multi-threaded. In a single-threaded model, a JSE will process only one request at a time. A pool of JSEs can process multiple client requests. In a multi-threaded model, a single JSE can process many requests simultaneously, with each thread executing in its own context. By contrast, in EJB endpoints requests are always single-threaded, so a single EJB endpoint instance processes only one request at a time—the EJB container uses a pool of instances to process many simultaneous requests. Message handlers that serve JSEs and J2EE application clients may be single- or multi-threaded, but message handlers that serve EJB endpoints are always single-threaded.

Because the threading model of a message handler varies, and because Web services are inherently stateless services, message handlers are stateless. This doesn't mean that message handlers can't have instance variables. They can. It just means that they cannot maintain state between method invocations. For example, it would be a mistake to assume that the message-handler instance that processed a SOAP request message will also process the reply to it. One instance may process the request, while another processes the reply.

Although message handlers are stateless, it is possible to exchange information, or state, between message handlers, using the `MessageContext` ***object, which is discussed in Section 14.3.4.***

In most cases, instance variables in message handlers maintain references to resources that are not associated with specific SOAP messages. A reference to a JDBC `DataSource` object is a good example. A `DataSource` is used to obtain a pooled connection to a relational database, and is useful if a handler needs to access or write information to a database in order to process the headers of a message. The `LoggerHandler`, for example, might use JDBC to log SOAP messages. Another example is a `ClientSecurityHandler`, which might maintain a reference to the client's `java.security.KeyPair`, to use it for generating XML digital signatures.

While maintaining resources in instance variables is convenient, it poses risks. You should ensure that any object an instance variable refers to can tolerate access from multiple threads, because it's possible that the message handler will be used in a multi-threaded environment. For example, maintaining a reference to a JDBC `DataSource` is fine, because the `javax.sql.DataSource` object can handle multiple threads—each thread receives its own JDBC `Connection` object. Similarly, the `java.security.KeyPair` is not a problem. It's not a good idea, however, to maintain a JDBC `Connection` reference. Although some JDBC vendors support concurrent use of a `Connection` object by multiple threads, others employ synchronization to serialize access to it. If many threads attempt to use the same `Connection` object, the JDBC driver that serializes access will become a major bottleneck.

14.3.2 JNDI Environment Naming Context

Message handlers always execute in the context of the component they are serving, which means that they have access to the JNDI ENC of the component. A message handler has access to any resources, EJB references, Web service references, or environment variables that are configured for the J2EE component it's serving. Listing 14–13 shows how a message handler might use the JNDI ENC to access a database.

Listing 14–13

Using JNDI ENC and JDBC from a Message Handler

```
package com.jwsbook.jaxrpc;
import javax.xml.namespace.QName;
import javax.xml.rpc.handler.*;
import javax.xml.rpc.handler.soap.*;
import javax.xml.soap.*;
import java.util.*;
import javax.sql.DataSource;
import java.sql.Connection;
import java.sql.Statement;
import javax.naming.InitialContext;
import com.jwsbook.saaj.SaajOutputter;

public class LoggerHandler extends javax.xml.rpc.handler.GenericHandler{
  QName [] headerNames = null;
  javax.sql.DataSource dataSource;
```

```
    public QName [] getHeaders(){...}

    public boolean handleRequest(MessageContext context){
      String messageID = null;

      try{
        SOAPMessageContext soapCntxt = (SOAPMessageContext)context;
        SOAPMessage message = soapCntxt.getMessage();
        SOAPHeader header = message.getSOAPPart().getEnvelope().getHeader();

        Iterator allHeaders = header.getChildElements();
        while(allHeaders.hasNext()){
          SOAPElement headerBlock = (SOAPElement)allHeaders.next();
          Name headerName = headerBlock.getElementName();
          if(headerName.getLocalName().equals("message_id")){
            messageID = header.getValue();
          }
        }
        if(dataSource == null){
          InitialContext jndiEnc = new InitialContext();
          dataSource = (DataSource)
                       jndiEnc.lookup("java:comp/env/jdbc/MyDatabase");
        }

        String soapMessage = SaajOutputter.writeToString(message);
        try{
          Connection conn = dataSource.getConnection();
          Statement stmt = conn.createStatement();
          stmt.executeUpdate("INSERT INTO soap_log ("
                             +messageID+","
                             +System.currentTimeMillis()+","
                             +soapMessage+")");
          conn.close();
          return true;
        }catch(java.sql.SQLException sqe){
           throw new javax.xml.rpc.JAXRPCException(sqe);
        }
      }catch(javax.xml.soap.SOAPException se){
        throw new javax.xml.rpc.JAXRPCException(se);
      }catch(javax.naming.NamingException ne){
        throw new javax.xml.rpc.JAXRPCException(ne);
      }
    }
  }
```

Some of the superfluous detail was removed from this listing, but the most important part of this example is shown in bold. The `handleRequest()` method of the `LoggerHandler` class uses the `javax.naming.InitialContext` object to access the JNDI ENC of the J2EE component. The JNDI ENC provides the message handler with access to a `javax.sql.DataSource` object, which it keeps in an instance variable so that it needs to fetch the object only once in its life. The `DataSource` object is used to create a `java.sql.Connection`, which in turn is used to log the incoming SOAP message to the database.

You may have noticed that subsystem (JDBC, JNDI, or SAAJ) exceptions are caught and rethrown as `javax.xml.rpc.JAXRPCException` ***types. This behavior is in keeping with the rules for handling server-side errors outlined earlier, in Section 14.2.2.2.***

The functionality of the JNDI ENC is the same across J2EE components (EJBs, servlets, JSPs, and JSEs) and is addressed in detail in Section 10.2.2: JNDI Environment Naming Context.

14.3.3 A Message Handler's Life Cycle

A message handler's life cycle is delimited by its `init()` and `destroy()` methods, which appear in bold in the `Handler` interface definition in Listing 14–14.

Listing 14–14

The `javax.xml.rpc.handler.Handler` *Life-Cycle Methods*

```
package javax.xml.rpc.handler;

public interface Handler {
   public void init(HandlerInfo config) ;
   public QName[] getHeaders();
   public boolean handleRequest(MessageContext context);
   public boolean handleResponse(MessageContext context);
   public boolean handleFault(MessageContext context);
   public void destroy();
}
```

Before a message-handler instance is allowed to process SOAP messages, the JAX-RPC runtime invokes its `init()` method. The message handler must include a no-argument constructor so that the J2EE container can instantiate it using the `Class.newInstance()` method—if no constructors are defined, the default constructor of a class is a no-arg constructor. The `init()` method takes a single parameter, `HandlerInfo`, which provides the handler with configuration information that it may need to process messages. The `init()` method is invoked only once in the life of an instance.

The `javax.xml.rpc.handler.HandlerInfo` class provides a message handler with configuration information, in the form of a `java.util.Map` object, when it's initialized. The configuration `Map` is accessed via the `HandlerInfo` object's `getHandlerConfig()` method, which appears in bold in Listing 14–15.

Listing 14–15

The `javax.xml.rpc.handler.HandlerInfo` *Class (Abbreviated)*

```
package javax.xml.rpc.handler;

public class HandlerInfo implements java.io.Serializable {
    public HandlerInfo() {...}
    public HandlerInfo(Class handlerClass, java.util.Map config,
                       QName[] headers) {...}

    public java.util.Map getHandlerConfig(){...}

    public Class getHandlerClass() {...}
    public QName[] getHeaders(){...}

    public void setHandlerClass(java.lang.Class handlerClass){...}
    public void setHandlerConfig(java.util.Map config){...}
    public void setHeaders(QName[] headers){...}
}
```

The `HandlerInfo` class defines a couple of constructors, and several other methods for accessing and changing the message handler's `Class` type, its configuration, and names of header blocks, but as a J2EE developer the only methods you are likely to use are the `getHandlerConfig()` and `getHeaders()` methods. Your code won't call the others, because in J2EE the message handlers and their `HandlerInfo` objects are constructed automatically by the JAX-RPC runtime, based on the configuration you define in the deployment descriptors. Because J2EE takes care of constructing the handler chain and the `HandlerInfo` objects automatically, the `HandlerInfo` class's `setHandlerClass()`, `setHandlerConfig()`, and `setHeaders()` methods simply don't work in J2EE; they are ignored. (These methods are useful in standalone applications where deployment descriptors are not used.) In J2EE, the `Class` and configuration `Map` are defined in the deployment descriptor, and the header-block `QName` objects are defined by the message handler's implementation of the `getHeaders()` method.

Listing 14–16 shows possible configuration information for `ClientSecurityHandler`, which uses the Java Security Architecture to generate XML digital-signature header blocks.

Listing 14–16

Configuring the Initialization Parameters of a Message Handler

```
<handler xmlns:ds="http://schemas.xmlsoap.org/soap/security/2000-12">
   <handler-name>ClientSecurityHandler</handler-name>
   <handler-class>com.jwsbook.jaxrpc.ServerSecurityHandler</handler-class>
   <init-param>
       <param-name>KeyAlgorithm</param-name>
       <param-value>DSA</param-value>
   </init-param>
   <init-param>
       <param-name>KeySize</param-name>
       <param-value>512</param-value>
   </init-param>
   <init-param>
       <param-name>SignatureAlgorithm</param-name>
       <param-value>SHA1</param-value>
   </init-param>
   <soap-header>ds:Signature</soap-header>
 </handler>
```

The `ClientSecurityHandler` creates a `KeyPair` object and a `Signature` object based on the initialization parameters. The `KeyPair` and `Signature` are used to sign SOAP messages and construct XML digital-signature header blocks. A snippet of the `ClientSecurityHandler` is shown in Listing 14–17.

Listing 14–17

A Message Handler Uses Its Initialization Parameters

```
package jwsed1.part5_jaxprc;
import java.security.*;
import javax.xml.namespace.QName;

public class ClientSecurityHandler extends javax.xml.rpc.handler.GenericHandler {
  java.security.KeyPair keyPair;
  java.security.Signature signature;
  QName [] headerNames = null;

  public QName [] getHeaders(){...}

  public void init(javax.xml.rpc.handler.HandlerInfo info ){
    try{
        java.util.Map map = info.getHandlerConfig();
```

```
      String keyAlgorithm = (String)map.get("KeyAlgorithm");
      String sigAlgorithm = (String)map.get("SignatureAlgorithm");
      int keySize = Integer.parseInt((String)map.get("KeySize"));

      KeyPairGenerator generator = KeyPairGenerator.getInstance(keyAlgorithm);
      generator.initialize(keySize);
      keyPair = generator.generateKeyPair();

      signature = Signature.getInstance(sigAlgorithm);
      signature.initSign(keyPair.getPrivate());
    }catch(java.security.GeneralSecurityException se){
      throw new javax.xml.rpc.JAXRPCException(se);
    }
  }
  ...
}
```

When a handler instance is no longer needed by the JAX-RPC runtime, its `Handler.destroy()` method is called just before it is discarded. This method gives the handler an opportunity to free up any resources it was using during its life (JDBC connections, JMS connections, and so forth). In the `ClientSecurityHandler` class, the `destroy()` method is unimplemented because there are no live resources. If a handler maintains a reference to JDBC `DataSource` or some other resource, however, it might be prudent to close it or set the reference to `null` in the `destroy()` method.

14.3.4 The `MessageContext` Type

In Section 14.1.1 you learned that a `SOAPMessageContext` object is passed to each of the `handleXXX()` methods of the `Handler` interface. You also learned that `SOAPMessageContext` defines a method for accessing the `SOAPMessage` object. In addition, the `SOAPMessageContext` defines a method named `getRoles()`. This method tells you which roles the entire message-handler chain is able to process on the SOAP message. It's not likely you'll use this method much, but it's there if you need it.

You can also take advantage of the property methods defined by the `SOAPMessageContext` type's supertype, `MessageContext`. During the course of a message handler's life it will be used to process many different SOAP requests, replies, and sometimes fault messages. As you've learned, message handlers are stateless, but in some cases you will want to pass information specific to a SOAP message from one message handler to the next in a handler chain. This is where the property methods of `javax.xml.rpc.handler.MessageContext` come in handy.

First take a look at Listing 14–18, which shows the definition of the `SOAPMessageContext` class with its inherited `MessageContext` property methods in bold.

Listing 14–18

The `javax.xml.rpc.handler.soap.SOAPMessageContext` *Property Methods*

```
package javax.xml.rpc.handler.soap;
import javax.xml.soap.SOAPMessage;
import java.util.Iterator;

public interface SOAPMessageContext extends javax.xml.rpc.handler.MessageContext {
   public SOAPMessage getMessage();
   public void setMessage(SOAPMessage message);
   public String[] getRoles();

   public boolean containsProperty(String name);
   public Object getProperty(String name);
   public Iterator getPropertyNames();
   public void removeProperty(String name);
   public void setProperty(String name, Object value);
}
```

As a SOAP message passes from one message handler to the next in a handler chain, the `SOAPMessageContext` object that carries it can also carry properties. Any message handler in the chain can read, add, update, or remove these properties—and use them to pass information about the message to the next handler in the chain. Once the Web service consumes a SOAP message, the `SOAPMessageContext` object and its properties are discarded. If you need to pass information between message handlers while processing a SOAP message, use the property methods defined in the `MessageContext` interface and inherited by the `SOAPMessageContext`.

In most cases the only objects that need access to the `SOAPMessageContext` are the message-handler objects, but a JSE can also access the `SOAPMessageContext` via its `ServiceEndpointContext`, as shown in the following code snippet.

```
public class BookQuoteImpl implements BookQuote {
    ...
    ServletEndpointContext endPtCntxt;

    public void init(Object context) throws ServiceException{
       try{
         endPtCntxt = (ServiceEndpointContext)context;
         ...
    }
    public float getBookPrice(String isbn) {

         SOAPMessageContext msgCntxt = endPtCntxt.getMessageContext();
```

```
        ...
    }
...
}
```

The JSE can use the `SOAPMessageContext` and its property methods to obtain information from its message handlers that may not be communicated in headers themselves. The JSE can also access the `SOAPMessage` object via the `SOAPMessageContext`. See Section 10.2.3.2 for more details about the `ServletEndpointContext` type.

In J2EE 1.4 an EJB endpoint can access the `SOAPMessageContext` object via the `SessionContext` reference, which is handed to the EJB endpoint at the beginning of its life cycle. The following snippet shows an EJB endpoint accessing the `SOAPMessageContext` from the `SessionContext` object.

```
package com.jwsbook.jaxrpc;
import javax.ejb.SessionContext;
import javax.xml.rpc.handler.soap.SOAPMessageContext;

public class BookQuoteBean implements javax.ejb.SessionBean {
    SessionContext sessionContext;

    public void setSessionContext(SessionContext cntxt){
        sessionContext = cntxt;
    }

    public void ejbCreate(){}

    public float getBookQuote(String isbn) {
        SOAPMessageContext msgCntxt = (SOAPMessageContext)
          sessionContext.getMessageContext();
        ...

    }

    public void ejbActivate() {}
    public void ejbPassivate() {}
    public void ejbRemove(){}
}
```

See Section 11.2.2.3 for more details about the `SessionContext`.

14.4 Wrapping Up

Message handlers offer an interesting, if somewhat complicated, solution to the problem of handling header blocks in SOAP messaging. The design allows you to plug in message handlers for different header blocks easily. Message handlers benefit from the same robust operation environment enjoyed by the J2EE components they serve, because they are extensions of the J2EE components. Alas, message handlers are kind of easy to mess up. You have to remember that they cannot maintain state from one invocation to the next. In addition, message handlers may be used by multi-threaded J2EE clients or JSEs, in which case you must consider thread synchronization and contention. If you keep those concerns in mind, though, you should be able to develop very robust and powerful messaging handlers for processing just about any type of header block, industry-standard or proprietary.

Chapter 15

Mapping Java to WSDL and XML

As you learned in Chapter 5, WSDL documents describe a Web service so that, using SOAP, applications can access it from different operating systems and programming languages. WSDL names the operations that can be invoked and describes the exact format of SOAP messages, the Internet protocol used (for example, HTTP) and the Internet addresses of Web service endpoints.

JAX-RPC defines a J2EE standard programming model developers use to exchange SOAP messages based on WSDL document definitions. Specifically, JAX-RPC defines how developers can use WSDL documents to generate endpoint and service interfaces, and the classes that implement them. JAX-RPC can also be used to generate WSDL documents from endpoint interface definitions and configuration files. It's the purpose of this section to delve into the details of the JAX-RPC mapping of Java code to WSDL and XML documents.

The mapping between WSDL and Java was covered to some extent in Section 12–1: Generated Stubs, but this chapter will go into more depth—after covering the basics—including detailed coverage of the mapping between XML types declared by `message` definitions and the parameters of endpoint methods that employ the RPC/Literal and Document/Literal messaging modes.

This chapter will not attempt to teach you about WSDL or XML; it's assumed that you understand these technologies already. If any XML or WSDL features are unfamiliar, you can review the coverage of them in Chapter 3: The W3C XML Schema Language and Chapter 5: WSDL.

15.1 Mapping WSDL to Java

A WSDL document has both **abstract definitions** and **implementation definitions.** The abstract definitions are declared in the `types`, `message`, and `portType` elements. They're considered abstract because they define what the Web service looks like (operation names, data types, and the like) but not the message formats and protocols used to access an endpoint. The `binding` and `service` are considered implementation definitions because they tell us how the abstract definitions are bound to a specific SOAP messaging mode, Internet protocol, and Internet address.

There is a one-to-one mapping between a `portType` and a JAX-RPC endpoint interface. The mapping is not complex, and it applies only to One-Way and Request/Response operation styles; JAX-RPC doesn't provide a mapping for the Solicit/Response or Notification operation styles.

A lot of this chapter uses the traditional "Foo" and "Bar" example names, which are convenient because they allow you to focus your attention on the mapping rather than the business case. Package names are omitted from some of the Java definitions, because mapping a Java package to an XML namespace requires a special configuration file called a **JAX-RPC mapping file.** Mapping files are introduced briefly in this chapter, but covered fully only in Chapter 24. In addition, many of the listings show fragments of WSDL documents instead of complete documents, to make the chapter easier to read. You should be able to recognize the relevant elements and their meanings, without a complete WSDL document to look at.

Listing 15–1 shows a simple WSDL `portType` definition, which we can use to demonstrate the mapping between a WSDL document and an endpoint interface.

Listing 15–1

A Simple `portType` *Definition*

```
<?xml version="1.0" encoding="UTF-8"?>
<definitions name="FooWS"
 targetNamespace="http://www.Monson-Haefel.com/jwsbook/Foo"
 xmlns:mh="http://www.Monson-Haefel.com/jwsbook/Foo"
 xmlns:xsd="http://www.w3.org/2001/XMLSchema"
 xmlns="http://schemas.xmlsoap.org/wsdl/">

  <message name="fooRequest">
    <part name="param1" type="xsd:string"/>
  </message>
  <message name="fooResponse">
    <part name="param2" type="xsd:float"/>
  </message>
  <portType name="FooBar">
    <operation name="foo" >
```

```
    <input message="mh:fooRequest"/>
    <output message="mh:fooResponse"/>
  </operation>
</portType>
```

This portType definition describes a Web service operation that takes a single xsd:string type as input and returns an xsd:float type value as output. When a JAX-RPC compiler reads this portType definition, it will generate the endpoint interface in Listing 15–2.

Listing 15–2

The Endpoint Interface Generated from the portType *Defined in Listing 15–1*

```
public interface FooBar extends java.rmi.Remote {
    public float foo(java.lang.String param1)
    throws java.rmi.RemoteException;
}
```

As you learned in Section 12.1: Generated Stubs, the endpoint interface always extends the java.rmi.Remote interface, and each method defined by the endpoint interface declares the java.rmi.RemoteException in its throws clause.

The portType name is mapped directly to the endpoint interface name. Similarly, the operation names and the part names are mapped to method and parameter names of the endpoint interface. The mapping is always one-to-one, character-for-character, unless the name is illegal in Java, in which case the mapping is subject to certain name-collision rules.[1] It's also possible to deviate from this strict one-to-one mapping of names by specifying different names for methods in a JAX-RPC mapping file. This variation is explained in detail in Chapter 24.

15.1.1 WSDL-to-Endpoint Interfaces

Although the SOAP messages used for RPC/Literal and Document/Literal differ, the JAX-RPC endpoint interface generated for these two messaging modes are almost always identical, especially when you base the part elements of your message definitions on simple XML schema built-in types. The inputs and outputs are the same, it's simply the method of serialization that is different. Because the endpoint interface is concerned only with inputs and outputs, and not with the SOAP message format, the endpoint interface tends to be the same no matter which message mode you are using. The following sections describe the mapping between portType definitions and endpoint interfaces for RPC/Literal and Document/Literal WSDL bindings.

[1] For details see the JAX-RPC (Java API for XML-based RPC) Specification, version 1.1, section 4.3.12: Name Collisions.

15.1.2 Declaring Multiple Parts

The input message declared by the WSDL `portType` describes the parameters of an endpoint method, while the output message describes the return value, as well as INOUT and OUT parameters, if any. When the input message declares multiple `part` elements, the corresponding endpoint method will have multiple parameters. Listing 15–3 shows a `portType` whose input message has three `part` elements.

Listing 15–3

A WSDL `portType` *with Multiple Input Parameters*

```
<?xml version="1.0" encoding="UTF-8"?>
<definitions name="FooWS"
 targetNamespace="http://www.Monson-Haefel.com/jwsbook/Foo"
 xmlns:mh="http://www.Monson-Haefel.com/jwsbook/Foo"
 xmlns:xsd="http://www.w3.org/2001/XMLSchema"
 xmlns="http://schemas.xmlsoap.org/wsdl/">

<message name="fooRequest">
  <part name="param1" type="xsd:string"/>
  <part name="param2" type="xsd:int" />
  <part name="param3" type="xsd:boolean" />
</message>
<message name="fooResponse">
  <part name="param4" type="xsd:float"/>
</message>
<portType name="FooBar">
  <operation name="foo" >
    <input message="mh:fooRequest"/>
    <output message="mh:fooResponse"/>
  </operation>
</portType>
```

The endpoint generated form this `portType` definition is shown in Listing 15–4.

Listing 15–4

The Endpoint Interface Generated from the `portType` *Defined in Listing 15–3*

```
public interface FooBar extends java.rmi.Remote {
    public float foo(String param1, int param2, boolean param3)
    throws java.rmi.RemoteException;
}
```

It's also possible to define a `portType` whose output message has multiple parts, as shown in Listing 15–5.

Listing 15–5

A WSDL `portType` *with Multiple Output Parameters*

```
<?xml version="1.0" encoding="UTF-8"?>
<definitions name="FooWS"
 targetNamespace="http://www.Monson-Haefel.com/jwsbook/Foo"
 xmlns:mh="http://www.Monson-Haefel.com/jwsbook/Foo"
 xmlns:xsd="http://www.w3.org/2001/XMLSchema"
 xmlns="http://schemas.xmlsoap.org/wsdl/">

<message name="fooRequest">
  <part name="param1" type="xsd:string"/>
</message>
<message name="fooResponse">
  <part name="param2" type="xsd:int" />
  <part name="param3" type="xsd:boolean" />
  <part name="param4" type="xsd:float"/>
</message>
<portType name="FooBar">
  <operation name="foo" >
    <input message="mh:fooRequest"/>
    <output message="mh:fooResponse"/>
  </operation>
</portType>
```

You'll see a big change in the resulting endpoint interface when the output message declares multiple parts, as it does here. Normally, a Java method may declare multiple input parameters but only a single return type. By contrast, other programming languages, including C++ and C#, can declare multiple return types in the form of INOUT and OUT parameters. Because WSDL is language-agnostic, it allows Web services to define INOUT and OUT parameters in addition to the IN parameters typically used in Java. JAX-RPC overcomes Java's limitations, and accommodates INOUT and OUT parameters through the use of special wrapper classes, called **holders.** The `portType` definition in Listing 15–5 would result in the endpoint definition shown in Listing 15–6.

Listing 15–6

The Endpoint Interface Generated from the `portType` *Defined in Listing 15–5*

```
public interface FooBar extends java.rmi.Remote {
    public void foo(java.lang.String param1,
                    javax.xml.rpc.holders.IntHolder param2,
                    javax.xml.rpc.holders.BooleanHolder param3,
```

```
                    javax.xml.rpc.holders.FloatHolder param4)
    throws java.rmi.RemoteException;
}
```

Here, `param1` is a normal IN parameter, declared as a `part` of the input message. Because it's an IN parameter, the generated interface can use a conventional core-Java type to declare it: `String`. The other parameters, however, are declared as `parts` of the output message, and must enable the Web service to pass information back to the client. Core-Java types won't do, so the interface declares these parameters using `javax.xml.rpc.holders.Holder` types. Section 15.3 discusses holder types and IN, INOUT, and OUT parameters in detail.

15.1.3 Defining Multiple Operations

A WSDL `portType` may define multiple operations, each of which maps to a different method in an endpoint interface. The `portType` in Listing 15–7 defines two methods.

Listing 15–7

A WSDL `portType` *with Multiple Operations*

```
<?xml version="1.0" encoding="UTF-8"?>
<definitions name="FooWS"
 targetNamespace="http://www.Monson-Haefel.com/jwsbook/Foo"
 xmlns:mh="http://www.Monson-Haefel.com/jwsbook/Foo"
 xmlns:xsd="http://www.w3.org/2001/XMLSchema"
 xmlns="http://schemas.xmlsoap.org/wsdl/">

<message name="fooRequest">
  <part name="param1" type="xsd:string"/>
</message>
<message name="barRequest">
  <part name="param2" type="xsd:float"/>
</message>
<message name="fooBarResponse">
  <part name="param3" type="xsd:int" />
</message>
<portType name="FooBar">
  <operation name="foo" >
    <input message="mh:fooRequest"/>
    <output message="mh:fooBarResponse"/>
  </operation>
  <operation name="bar" >
    <input message="mh:barRequest"/>
```

```
    <output message="mh:fooBarResponse"/>
  </operation>
</portType>
```

In this case the two operations, `foo` and `bar`, use different input messages but the same output message. The result is an endpoint interface with two methods, `foo()` and `bar()`, as shown in Listing 15–8.

Listing 15–8

The Endpoint Interface Generated from the `portType` *Defined in Listing 15–7*

```
public interface FooBar extends java.rmi.Remote {
    public int foo(String param1) throws java.rmi.RemoteException;
    public int bar(float param2) throws java.rmi.RemoteException;
}
```

This listing demonstrates that endpoint interfaces can support multiple `operation` elements—and that `message` definitions can be reused.

JAX-RPC compilers also support operation overloading in WSDL as long as the operations define different input messages, output messages, or both. Basically, JAX-RPC follows the standard Java rules for operation overloading. Operation overloading is not allowed by the WS-I Basic Profile 1.0,[BP] however, so we won't bother discussing it in this book.

15.1.4 One-Way Messaging

JAX-RPC explicitly supports both Request/Response and One-Way messaging. A `portType` indicates that it uses Request/Response messaging by listing an `input` message followed by an `output` message, and that it uses One-Way messaging by listing only an `input` message. Most of the examples throughout this section use Request/Response messaging, but you will also use One-Way messaging. To do so, simply omit the output message from the `portType` definition, as in Listing 15–9.

Listing 15–9

A WSDL `portType` *That Uses One-Way Messaging*

```
<?xml version="1.0" encoding="UTF-8"?>
<definitions name="FooWS"
 targetNamespace="http://www.Monson-Haefel.com/jwsbook/Foo"
 xmlns:mh="http://www.Monson-Haefel.com/jwsbook/Foo"
 xmlns:xsd="http://www.w3.org/2001/XMLSchema"
 xmlns="http://schemas.xmlsoap.org/wsdl/">

<message name="fooRequest">
```

```
  <part name="param1" type="xsd:string"/>
</message>
<portType name="FooBar">
  <operation name="foo" >
    <input message="mh:fooRequest"/>
  </operation>
</portType>
```

Regardless of the binding you use, RPC/Literal or Document/Literal, this `portType` will result in an endpoint interface that looks like the one in Listing 15–10. Notice `foo()`'s return type. One-Way endpoint interface methods always return `void`.

Listing 15–10

The Endpoint Interface Generated from the `portType` *Defined in Listing 15–9*

```
public interface FooBar extends java.rmi.Remote {
    public void foo(String param1) throws java.rmi.RemoteException;
}
```

It's important to understand two things about One-Way messaging in JAX-RPC. First, you cannot define faults. Conceptually, the Web service (receiver) is not supposed to respond to the client (sender). Second, when using an HTTP SOAP binding, the underlying protocol is still Request/Response HTTP, but the reply is limited to HTTP success or failure codes. An HTTP success code (for example, `200 OK`) will result in a successful return of the method, while a failure code such as `500` will generally cause a `java.rmi.RemoteException` to be thrown. HTTP success and failure codes are discussed in detail in Section 4.7.2.

15.2 Mapping XML Schema to Java

J2EE vendors that implement Web services must follow the conventions for mapping between XML and Java mandated by the JAX-RPC specification. This section covers these rules in detail. In addition to the JAX-RPC XML-to-Java mapping, vendors are free to offer alternatives such as conformance with JAXB (Java Architecture for XML Binding) or a proprietary framework. Such alternatives are not standard, however, and are not discussed in this book.

When a JAX-RPC compiler is given a WSDL document, it automatically generates an endpoint interface that matches the `portType` of the WSDL document. It may also generate custom JavaBeans components and special `javax.xml.rpc.holders.Holder` types for parameters and return values, depending on the complexity of the `message` definitions used by the `portType`. This section covers the mapping between WSDL `message` and `types` definitions, and the parameters of endpoint interfaces generated by the JAX-RPC compiler.

In this section we mix "FooBar" examples with examples related to Web services offered by the fictitious company Monson-Haefel Books.

15.2.1 XML Schema Built-in Simple Types

The easiest WSDL documents to model in Java are those that use simple XML schema built-in types as parameters, and that define only one `part` for outgoing `message` definitions. The BookQuote `portType` example used throughout this chapter is very simple, as Listing 15–11 shows.

Listing 15–11

A Simple WSDL `portType` *Definition*

```
<?xml version="1.0" encoding="UTF-8"?>
<definitions name="BookQuoteWS"
 targetNamespace="http://www.Monson-Haefel.com/jwsbook/BookQuote"
 xmlns:mh="http://www.Monson-Haefel.com/jwsbook/BookQuote"
 xmlns:xsd="http://www.w3.org/2001/XMLSchema"
 xmlns="http://schemas.xmlsoap.org/wsdl/">

<message name="getBookPriceRequest">
  <part name="isbn" type="xsd:string"/>
</message>
<message name="getBookPriceResponse">
  <part name="result" type="xsd:float"/>
</message>
<portType name="BookQuote">
  <operation name="getBookPrice">
    <input message="mh:getBookPriceRequest"/>
    <output message="mh:getBookPriceResponse"/>
  </operation>
</portType>
```

The `operation` element defines `input` and `output` messages, each of which has only one `part`. The `part` elements in both messages declare simple XML schema built-in types. This WSDL `portType` is easily mapped to a Web services endpoint interface as in Listing 15–12.

Listing 15–12

The Endpoint Interface Generated from the `portType` *Defined in Listing 15–11*

```
public interface BookQuote extends java.rmi.Remote {
    public float getBookQuote(String isbn) throws java.rmi.RemoteException;
}
```

As you can see, the JAX-RPC compiler mapped the `xsd:string` to a Java `java.lang.String` type, and the `xsd:float` to a Java primitive `float` type. Simple, no? Many of the XML schema built-in types map cleanly to Java primitive types. Table 15–1 shows how some of the XML schema built-in simple types map to common Java primitive types.

Table 15–1 Mapping: XML Schema Built-in Types to Java Primitive Types

XML Schema Built-in Type	Java Primitive Type
`xsd:byte`	`byte`
`xsd:boolean`	`boolean`
`xsd:short`	`short`
`xsd:int`	`int`
`xsd:long`	`long`
`xsd:float`	`float`
`xsd:double`	`double`

Other XML schema built-in types map to standard Java classes like `String`, `Calendar`, and `BigDecimal`, or to primitive byte arrays. Table 15–2 shows these additional mappings.

Table 15–2 Mapping: XML Schema Built-in Types to Non-primitive Java Types

XML Schema Built-in Type	Java Class Type
`xsd:string`	`java.lang.String`
`xsd:dateTime`	`java.util.Calendar`
`xsd:integer`	`java.math.BigInteger`
`xsd:decimal`	`java.math.BigDecimal`
`xsd:QName`	`java.xml.namespace.QName`
`xsd:base64Binary`	`byte[]`
`xsd:hexBinary`	`byte[]`

15.2.2 XML Schema Complex Types

In some cases, a message `part` definition is based on an XML schema complex type. For example, a `part` might use a complex type that provides a more comprehensive representation of a book, including author, title, and ISBN. Listing 15–13 illustrates.

Listing 15–13

A WSDL `portType` *That Refers to an XML Complex Type*

```
<?xml version="1.0" encoding="UTF-8"?>
<definitions name="BookQuoteWS"
 targetNamespace="http://www.Monson-Haefel.com/jwsbook/BookQuote"
 xmlns:mh="http://www.Monson-Haefel.com/jwsbook/BookQuote"
 xmlns:xsd="http://www.w3.org/2001/XMLSchema"
 xmlns="http://schemas.xmlsoap.org/wsdl/">

<types>
   <xsd:schema
    targetNamespace="http://www.Monson-Haefel.com/jwsbook/BookQuote">
     <xsd:complexType name="Book">
       <xsd:sequence>
         <xsd:element name="title"          type="xsd:string"/>
         <xsd:element name="isbn"           type="xsd:string"/>
         <xsd:element name="authors"        type="xsd:string"
                                            maxOccurs="unbounded"/>
       </xsd:sequence>
     </xsd:complexType>
  </xsd:schema>
</types>
<message name="getBookPriceRequest">
  <part name="book" type="mh:Book"/>
</message>
<message name="getBookPriceResponse">
  <part name="result" type="xsd:float"/>
</message>
<portType name="BookQuote">
  <operation name="getBookPrice">
    <input message="mh:getBookPriceRequest"/>
    <output message="mh:getBookPriceResponse"/>
  </operation>
</portType>
```

The endpoint interface that would be generated from this WSDL definition is shown in Listing 15–14.

Listing 15–14

The Endpoint Interface Generated from the `portType` *Defined in Listing 15–13*

```
public interface BookQuote extends java.rmi.Remote {
    public float getBookQuote(Book book) throws java.rmi.RemoteException;
}
```

The JAX-RPC compiler generates the Book-type parameter to model the Book complex type defined in the WSDL document (Listing 15–13). Complex types are mapped to JavaBeans class definitions, where the name of the bean class is the name of the XML schema complex type. Bean properties map to the elements of the complex type. For example, the Book XML schema complex type would map to the Java bean class in Listing 15–15.

Listing 15–15

The Java Bean Class Generated from the XML Schema Book *Type Defined in Listing 15–13*

```
public class Book {
    private String title;
    private String isbn;
    private String [] authors;

    public void Book(){}

    public String getTitle() { return title;}
    public void setTitle(String title){ this.title = title;}

    public String getIsbn() {return isbn;}
    public void setIsbn(String isbn){this.isbn = isbn;}

    public String [] getAuthors(){ return authors;}
    public void setAuthors(String [] authors){this.authors = authors;}
}
```

As you can see, the mapping is not rocket science. Built-in XML schema types are translated into Java primitive and class types as indicated in Tables 15–1 and 15–2 (and Table 15–3, which appears later). Anytime the type's maxOccurs attribute is greater than one, the JAX-RPC will map to an array type.[2] For example, the authors element (Listing 15–13), which declares maxOccurs as unbounded, is manifested as a String array in the Book class. In general, minOccurs attribute values other than "0" are ignored—there is no standard way to support minOccurs in Java.

You can even map complex types that include elements of other complex types into Java beans. For example, we can make the authors element use a complex type, Author, as shown in Listing 15–16.

[2] JavaBeans aficionados: You'll notice that JAX-RPC doesn't use indexed properties.

Listing 15–16

A WSDL types *Element That Declares an Array of Complex Types*

```
<?xml version="1.0" encoding="UTF-8"?>
<definitions name="BookQuoteWS"
 targetNamespace="http://www.Monson-Haefel.com/jwsbook/BookQuote"
 xmlns:mh="http://www.Monson-Haefel.com/jwsbook/BookQuote"
 xmlns:xsd="http://www.w3.org/2001/XMLSchema"
 xmlns="http://schemas.xmlsoap.org/wsdl/">

<types>
   <xsd:schema
    targetNamespace="http://www.Monson-Haefel.com/jwsbook/BookQuote">
     <xsd:complexType name="Book">
       <xsd:sequence>
         <xsd:element name="title"          type="xsd:string"/>
         <xsd:element name="isbn"           type="xsd:string"/>
         <xsd:element name="authors"        type="mh:Author"
                                            maxOccurs="unbounded"/>
       </xsd:sequence>
     </xsd:complexType>
     <xsd:complexType name="Author">
       <xsd:sequence>
         <xsd:element name="firstName"          type="xsd:string"/>
         <xsd:element name="lastName"            type="xsd:string"/>
         <xsd:element name="middleInitial"       type="xsd:string"/>
       </xsd:sequence>
     </xsd:complexType>
  </xsd:schema>
</types>
```

In this case the Author complex type would have its own corresponding Java bean class, as shown in Listing 15–17.

Listing 15–17

The Java Bean Class Generated from the XML Schema Author *Type Defined in Listing 15–16*

```
public class Author {
    private String firstName;
    private String lastName;
    private String middleInitial;
```

```
    public String getFirstName() { return firstName;}
    public void setFirstName(String firstName){this.firstName = firstName;}

    public String getLastName() { return lastName;}
    public void setLastName(String lastName){this.lastName = lastName;}

    public String getMiddleInitial() { return middleInitial;}
    public void setMiddleInitial(String middleInitial){
           this.middleInitial = middleInitial;
    }
}
```

The `Book` Java bean class would refer to an array of `Author` Java beans, as in Listing 15–18.

Listing 15–18

The Java Bean Class Generated from the XML Schema `Book` *type Defined in Listing 15–16*

```
public class Book {
    private String title;
    private String isbn;
    private Author [] authors;

    public String getTitle() { return title;}
    public void setTitle(String title){ this.title = title;}

    public String getIsbn() {return isbn;}
    public void setIsbn(String isbn){this.isbn = isbn;}

    public Author [] getAuthors(){ return authors;}
    public void setAuthors(Author [] authors){this.authors = authors;}
}
```

15.2.3 Arrays

There are several ways to declare arrays in a WSDL document, including the use of `maxOccurs` greater than one for elements in a structure, as just illustrated, SOAP RPC/Encoding arrays, and WSDL modifiers for RPC/Encoded arrays. JAX-RPC supports all of these, but the Basic Profile supports `maxOccurs` values greater than one only for elements in a structure. The other types of arrays are explicitly forbidden.[BP]

15.2.4 Enumerations

An enumeration is a custom type that can represent a fixed set of values. Enumerations are supported by many programming languages (among them C, C++, and C#) but are not a native feature of Java.[3] Still, some WSDL documents may declare XML schema enumerations, so it's important that JAX-RPC support them. When a JAX-RPC compiler encounters an XML schema enumeration, it generates a Java class that models the enumeration appropriately.

In Section 3.2: Advanced XML Schema, we defined a state code enumeration. That example is used in the WSDL document shown in Listing 15–19.

Listing 15–19

A WSDL `portType` *That Refers to an Enumeration Type*

```
<?xml version="1.0" encoding="UTF-8"?>
<definitions name="FooWS"
 targetNamespace="http://www.Monson-Haefel.com/jwsbook/Foo"
 xmlns:mh="http://www.Monson-Haefel.com/jwsbook/Foo"
 xmlns:xsd="http://www.w3.org/2001/XMLSchema"
 xmlns="http://schemas.xmlsoap.org/wsdl/">


<types>
  <xsd:schema targetNamespace="http://www.Monson-Haefel.com/jwsbook/Foo">
    <xsd:simpleType name="USState">
      <xsd:restriction base="xsd:string">
        <xsd:enumeration value="AK"/> <!-- Alaska   -->
        <xsd:enumeration value="AL"/> <!-- Alabama  -->
        <xsd:enumeration value="AR"/> <!-- Arkansas -->
        <!-- and so on ... -->
      </xsd:restriction>
    </xsd:simpleType>
  </xsd:schema>
</types>
<message name="fooRequest">
  <part name="state" type="mh:USState"/>
</message>
<message name="fooResponse">
  <part name="param2" type="xsd:float"/>
</message>
```

[3] Enumerations may be added to J2SE 1.5.

```
<portType name="FooEnum">
  <operation name="foo">
    <input message="mh:fooRequest"/>
    <output message="mh:fooResponse"/>
  </operation>
</portType>
```

When the JAX-RPC compiler finds the definition of an XML schema enumeration type, it automatically generates a Java class with a standard set of methods and fields. Listing 15–20 shows the class it would generate for the `USState` enumeration type.

Listing 15–20

The Java Class Generated for the `USState` *Enumeration Type Defined in Listing 15–19*

```
public class USState {
    private String value;

    protected USState(String state) {
        value = state;
    }
    public static final String _AK = "AK";
    public static final String _AL = "AL";
    public static final String _AR = "AR";
    ...
    public static final USState AK = new USState(_AK);
    public static final USState AL = new USState(_AL);
    public static final USState AR = new USState(_AR);
    ...
    public String getValue() { return value;}

    public static USState fromValue(String other){
      if(other.equals(_AK)) return AK;
      else if(other.equals(_AL)) return AL;
      else if(other.equals(_AR)) return AR;
      ...
    }
    public boolean equals(Object obj) { ... }
    public int hashCode() { ... }
}
```

In the JAX-RPC endpoint interface the `foo()` method would take the `USState` class as its only parameter, as shown in Listing 15–21.

Listing 15–21

The Endpoint Interface Generated from the `portType` *Defined in Listing 15–19*

```
public interface FooEnum extends java.rmi.Remote {
    public float foo(USState state)
    throws java.rmi.RemoteException;
}
```

15.2.5 `SOAPElement`: Supporting Non-standard Types in Document/Literal Encoding

All the examples up to this point work the same way with either RPC/Literal or Document/Literal messaging mode. The only difference will be in the implementation of the stubs, which require different logic to marshal messages to and from SOAP. Fortunately, these differences are completely hidden from the developer. This section explains how endpoint interfaces are generated for Document/Literal messaging when unsupported XML schema types are used.

When the Document/Literal messaging mode is used, nodes exchange document fragments, rather than SOAP representations of RPC calls. An example is the PurchaseOrder Web service used by retailers to send purchase orders to Monson-Haefel Books. The PurchaseOrder Web service consumes SOAP messages that carry a `purchaseOrder` document fragment, based on the Purchase Order Markup Language discussed in Chapter 2: XML Basics. The PurchaseOrder Web service uses a One-Way operation style, where SOAP messages are sent without any expectation of a reply. The PurchaseOrder Web service is described by its own WSDL document, shown in Listing 15–22.

Listing 15–22

The WSDL Document for the PurchaseOrder Web Service

```
<?xml version="1.0" encoding="UTF-8"?>
<definitions xmlns="http://schemas.xmlsoap.org/wsdl/"
    xmlns:po="http://www.Monson-Haefel.com/jwsbook/PO"
    xmlns:soap="http://schemas.xmlsoap.org/wsdl/soap/"
    xmlns:xsd="http://www.w3.org/2000/10/XMLSchema"
    xmlns:mh="http://www.Monson-Haefel.com/jwsbook/PurchaseOrder"
    targetNamespace="http://www.Monson-Haefel.com/jwsbook/PurchaseOrder">

  <types>
    <xsd:schema targetNamespace="http://www.Monson-Haefel.com/jwsbook/PO">
    <xsd:import namespace="http://www.Monson-Haefel.com/jwsbook/PO"
      schemaLocation="http://www.Monson-Haefel.com/jwsbook/po.xsd"/>
    </xsd:schema>
  </types>
```

```
  <message name="PurchaseOrderMessage">
    <part name="body" element="po:purchaseOrder"/>
  </message>
  <portType name="PurchaseOrder">
    <operation name="submitPurchaseOrder">
      <input message="mh:PurchaseOrderMessage"/>
    </operation>
  </portType>
  <binding name="PurchaseOrderBinding" type="mh:PurchaseOrder">
    <soap:binding style="document"
        transport="http://schemas.xmlsoap.org/soap/http"/>
    <operation name="submitPurchaseOrder">
      <input>
        <soap:body use="literal"/>
      </input>
    </operation>
  </binding>
  <service name="PuchaseOrderService">
    <port name="PurchaseOrderPort" binding="mh:PurchaseOrderBinding">
      <soap:address
          location="http://www.Monson-Haefel.com/jwsbook/PurchaseOrder"/>
    </port>
  </service>
</definitions>
```

When a JAX-RPC toolkit generates a stub and an endpoint interface from this WSDL definition, it will usually define a method with a single Java bean argument representing the document fragment and a `void` return type. The endpoint interface for the PurchaseOrder Web service would look like the one in Listing 15–23.

Listing 15–23

The Endpoint Interface Generated from the `portType` *Defined in Listing 15–22*

```
public interface PurchaseOrder extends java.rmi.Remote {
    public void submitPurchaseOrder(PurchaseOrder purchaseOrder)
    throws java.rmi.RemoteException;
}
```

The return type for the `submitPurchaseOrder()` method is `void` because the operation style is One-Way (specified by the absence of an `output` element in the `portType` definition). The `PurchaseOrder` parameter's type is a Java bean class, which represents the `purchaseOrder` document fragment.

Most JAX-RPC compilers will generate the endpoint interface in this way, provided that the XML schema of the `purchaseOrder` document uses only JAX-

RPC **standard** XML schema types. All JAX-RPC compilers must support the standard XML schema types; the JAX-RPC specification calls all other XML schema types **non-standard.** In most cases the XML schemas you create or encounter will use JAX-RPC standard types. Occasionally, however, you may bump into an XML schema type that is not supported by your JAX-RPC compiler, in which case the compiler should switch to using the SAAJ `SOAPElement` type as a parameter instead of a Java bean class. In such cases, the endpoint interface will look like the one in Listing 15–24.

Listing 15–24

The `SOAPElement` *Type Used for a JAX-RPC Non-standard XML Schema Type*

```
public interface PurchaseOrder extends java.rmi.Remote {
    public void submitPurchaseOrder(javax.xml.soap.SOAPElement element)
    throws java.rmi.RemoteException;
}
```

The `submitPurchaseOrder()` method in Listing 15–24 defines a single parameter of type `javax.xml.soap.SOAPElement`. This is the SAAJ generic type for an XML element—you learned about it in Chapter 13. The `SOAPElement` type represents the `purchaseOrder` document fragment that is sent to the PurchaseOrder Web service. To use this service, a client must construct a `SOAPElement` object and pass it to the endpoint stub when invoking the `submitPurchaseOrder()` endpoint method.

I'll give you a demonstration of how the `SOAPElement` is constructed and passed to `submitPurchaseOrder()` in a little bit, but first we'll take a moment to reexamine a version of the Purchase Order Markup Language that uses a non-standard XML schema type.

The WSDL document for the PurchaseOrder Web service imports the XML schema for Purchase Order Markup using the `types` element. Importing it rather than embedding it allows you to reuse the XML schema in other applications, and helps ensure that there is a single, uniform source for the `PurchaseOrder` type. The following snippet from the PurchaseOrder WSDL document (Listing 15–22) shows the `import` statement in bold.

```
<?xml version="1.0" encoding="UTF-8"?>
<definitions xmlns="http://schemas.xmlsoap.org/wsdl/"
    xmlns:po="http://www.Monson-Haefel.com/jwsbook/PO"
    xmlns:soap="http://schemas.xmlsoap.org/wsdl/soap/"
    xmlns:xsd="http://www.w3.org/2000/10/XMLSchema"
    xmlns:mh="http://www.Monson-Haefel.com/jwsbook/PurchaseOrder"
    targetNamespace="http://www.Monson-Haefel.com/jwsbook/PurchaseOrder">

  <types>
```

```
    <xsd:schema targetNamespace="http://www.Monson-Haefel.com/jwsbook/PO">
      <xsd:import namespace="http://www.Monson-Haefel.com/jwsbook/PO"
              schemaLocation="http://www.Monson-Haefel.com/jwsbook/po.xsd"/>
    </xsd:schema>
  </types>
  ...
</definitions>
```

In Listing 15–25, the XML schema for Purchase Order Markup uses non-standard complex types, which should force a JAX-RPC compiler to use the SAAJ `SOAPElement` type as the parameter for the document fragment.

Listing 15–25

The XML Schema for the Purchase Order Markup Language with Non-standard XML Schema Types

```
<?xml version="1.0" encoding="UTF-8"?>
<schema xmlns="http://www.w3.org/2001/XMLSchema"
    xmlns:po="http://www.Monson-Haefel.com/jwsbook/PO"
    targetNamespace="http://www.Monson-Haefel.com/jwsbook/PO">

  <element name="purchaseOrder" type="po:PurchaseOrder"/>

  <complexType name="PurchaseOrder">
    <sequence>
      <element name="accountName" type="string"/>
      <element name="accountNumber" type="short"/>
      <group ref="po:shipAndBill"/>
      <element name="book" type="po:Book"/>
      <element name="total" type="float"/>
    </sequence>
  </complexType>
  <group name="shipAndBill">
      <sequence>
          <element name="shipTo" type="po:USAddress" maxOccurs="0"/>
          <element name="billTo" type="po:USAddress"/>
      </sequence>
  </group>
  <complexType name="USAddress">
    <sequence>
      <element name="name" type="string"/>
      <element name="street" type="string"/>
      <element name="city" type="string"/>
```

```
      <element name="state" type="string"/>
      <element name="zip" type="string"/>
    </sequence>
  </complexType>
  <complexType name="Book">
    <sequence>
      <element name="title" type="string"/>
      <element name="quantity" type="short"/>
      <element name="wholesale-price" type="float"/>
    </sequence>
  </complexType>
</schema>
```

You should pay special attention to the use of the `group` type shown in bold, because it's a JAX-RPC non-standard type. Support for this type is optional. If your JAX-RPC compiler doesn't support the `group` type, then it should generate an endpoint that uses the `SOAPElement` as a parameter. The strategy of using the `SOAPElement` type allows you to exchange messages with Web services even when the JAX-RPC compiler doesn't recognize their XML schema types. The downside to this strategy is that you have to construct the XML document fragment by hand using SAAJ.

Suppose the JAX-RPC compiler used for the PurchaseOrder Web service doesn't support `group`. Our application client can use SAAJ to construct a valid document fragment and deliver it to the Web service using JAX-RPC, as shown in `JaxRpcExample_7`, Listing 15–26.

Listing 15–26

Using a `SOAPElement` *for a Non-standard Type in Document/Literal Messaging*

```
package com.jwsbook.jaxrpc;
import javax.naming.InitialContext;
import javax.xml.soap.SOAPFactory;
import javax.xml.soap.SOAPElement;

public class JaxRpcExample_7 {
  public static void main(String [] args) throws Exception{
    InitialContext jndiContext = new InitialContext();
    PurchaseOrderService service = (PurchaseOrderService)
      jndiContext.lookup("java:comp/env/service/PurchaseOrderService");
    PurchaseOrder po_stub = service.getPurchaseOrderPort();

    SOAPElement xml_fragment = getPurchaseOrderXML();

    po_stub.submitPurchaseOrder( xml_fragment);
```

```
    }
    public static SOAPElement getPurchaseOrderXML()
    throws javax.xml.soap.SOAPException{
      SOAPFactory factory = SOAPFactory.newInstance();
      SOAPElement purchaseOrder =
      factory.createElement("purchaseOrder","po",
                           "http://www.Monson-Haefel.com/jwsbook/PO");

      purchaseOrder.addChildElement("accountName").addTextNode("Amazon.com");
      purchaseOrder.addChildElement("accountNumber").addTextNode("923");

      SOAPElement billingAddress =
        purchaseOrder.addChildElement("billingAddress");
      billingAddress.addChildElement("name").addTextNode("Amazon.com");
      billingAddress.addChildElement("street").addTextNode("1516 2nd Ave");
      billingAddress.addChildElement("city").addTextNode("Seattle");
      billingAddress.addChildElement("state").addTextNode("WA");
      billingAddress.addChildElement("zip").addTextNode("90952");

      SOAPElement book = purchaseOrder.addChildElement("book");
      book.addChildElement("title").addTextNode("J2EE Web Services");
      book.addChildElement("quantity").addTextNode("3000");
      book.addChildElement("wholesale-price").addTextNode("24.99");

      return purchaseOrder;
    }
}
```

Obviously, in a real-world application you would obtain the address and other values from a database or some other source, but in `JaxRpcExample_7`, they are hard-coded to keep the example simple. The main idea is that you pass the endpoint stub method a `SOAPElement`.

When it sends a SOAP message to the PurchaseOrder Web service, the stub simply places the XML fragment in the body of the SOAP message as shown in Listing 15–27.

Listing 15–27

The SOAP Message Generated by the Client in Listing 15–26

```
<soap:Envelope xmlns:soap="http://schemas.xmlsoap.org/soap/envelope/">
  <soap:Body>
    <po:purchaseOrder xmlns:po="http://www.Monson-Haefel.com/jwsbook/PO">
      <accountName>Amazon.com</accountName>
      <accountNumber>923</accountNumber>
      <billingAddress>
```

```
        <name>Amazon.com</name>
        <street>1516 2nd Ave</street>
        <city>Seattle</city>
        <state>WA</state>
        <zip>90952</zip>
      </billingAddress>
      <book>
        <title>J2EE Web Services</title>
        <quantity>3000</quantity>
        <wholesale-price>24.99</wholesale-price>
      </book>
    </po:purchaseOrder>
  </soap:Body>
</soap:Envelope>
```

In the PurchaseOrder Web service example, the operation style is One-Way, as indicated by the `portType` element (it doesn't define an `output` element), but generated stubs can also support the Request/Response operation style with the Document/Literal messaging mode. For example, the PurchaseOrder Web service could be redefined to return an XML document fragment, perhaps confirmation that the order has been placed. In this case we'd redefine the `portType` in the WSDL document to have an output message like the one shown in this snippet:

```
<portType name="PurchaseOrder">
   <operation name="submitPurchaseOrder">
     <input message="mh:PurchaseOrderRequest"/>
     <output message="mh:PurhaseOrderResponse" />
   </operation>
</portType>
```

Assuming that, like `PurchaseOrderRequest`, the `PurchaseOrderResponse` type is an XML document fragment that uses non-standard XML schema types, the toolkit would generate a `PurchaseOrder` endpoint interface whose method returns a `SOAPElement` instead of a `void` type, thus:

```
import javax.xml.soap.SOAPElement;

public interface PurchaseOrder extends java.rmi.Remote {
    public SOAPElement submitPurchaseOrder( SOAPElement element)
    throws java.rmi.RemoteException;
}
```

If the `PurchaseOrderResponse` message refers to an element that uses supported XML schema types, then the return type would probably be a Java bean type representing the XML document fragment, rather than a `SOAPElement` type.

15.2.6 `SOAPElement`: The `xsd:any` Element

In the W3C XML Schema Language the `xsd:any` element represents an element of arbitrary type. In other words, any kind of element can be used in an instance document whose XML schema declares the `xsd:any` element. When a WSDL `part` declares that its type uses an `xsd:any` element, the JAX-RPC compiler will use a `SOAPElement` to represent the `xsd:any` parameter or bean field. See, for example, the WSDL document in Listing 15–28.

Listing 15–28

Mapping the `xsd:any` *Type to the* `SOAPElement` *Type*

```
<?xml version="1.0" encoding="UTF-8"?>
<definitions name="FooWS"
 targetNamespace="http://www.Monson-Haefel.com/jwsbook/Foo"
 xmlns:mh="http://www.Monson-Haefel.com/jwsbook/Foo"
 xmlns:xsd="http://www.w3.org/2001/XMLSchema"
 xmlns="http://schemas.xmlsoap.org/wsdl/">

<types>
  <xsd:schema targetNamespace="http://www.Monson-Haefel.com/jwsbook/Foo">
     <xsd:complexType name="xmlFragment">
      <xsd:sequence>
       <xsd:any namespace="##any"/>
      </xsd:sequence>
     </xsd:complexType>
     <xsd:complexType name="ArbitraryXML">
       <xsd:sequence>
         <xsd:element name="label"          type="xsd:string"/>
         <xsd:element name="xmlFragment"    type="mh:xmlFragment"/>
       </xsd:sequence>
     </xsd:complexType>
  </xsd:schema>
</types>
<message name="fooRequest">
  <part name="isbn" type="mh:ArbitraryXML"/>
</message>
<message name="fooResponse">
  <part name="result" type="mh:xmlFragment"/>
</message>
<portType name="foo">
  <operation name="bar">
    <input message="mh:fooRequest"/>
    <output message="mh:fooResponse"/>
```

```
  </operation>
</portType>
```

The endpoint interface for this WSDL definition would be as follows:

```
public interface FooBar extends java.rmi.Remote {
    public javax.xml.soap.SOAPElement foo(ArbitraryXML xmlDoc)
    throws java.rmi.RemoteException;
}
```

The return type, `mh:xmlFragment`, is mapped to the `SOAPElement` type, and the parameter is of the type `ArbitraryXML`, a bean class whose `xmlFragment` field is of type `SOAPElement`.

```
import javax.xml.soap.SOAPElement;

public class ArbitraryXML {
    private String label;
    private SOAPElement xmlFragment;

    public String getLabel() { return label;}
    public void setLabel(String label){ this.label = label;}

    public SOAPElement getXmlFragment() {return xmlFragment;}
    public void setXmlFragment(SOAPElement xmlFragment){
      this.xmlFragment = xmlFragment;
    }
}
```

15.2.7 Nillable Elements

A `part` can refer to an element that is **nillable**, meaning that the element can be empty without causing a validation error. For example, in Listing 15–29 a `message` definition defines the ISBN number as a nillable `xsd:int` element.

Listing 15–29

A WSDL `portType` *That Refers to a Nillable Type*

```
<?xml version="1.0" encoding="UTF-8"?>
<definitions name="FooWS"
 targetNamespace="http://www.Monson-Haefel.com/jwsbook/Foo"
 xmlns:mh="http://www.Monson-Haefel.com/jwsbook/Foo"
 xmlns:xsd="http://www.w3.org/2001/XMLSchema"
 xmlns="http://schemas.xmlsoap.org/wsdl/">

<types>
```

```
    <xsd:schema targetNamespace="http://www.Monson-Haefel.com/jwsbook/Foo">
         <xsd:element name="nillable_int" type="xsd:int" nillable="true" />
    </xsd:schema>
  </types>
  <message name="fooRequest">
    <part name="quantity" element="mh:nillable_int"/>
  </message>
  <portType name="Foo">
    <operation name="bar">
      <input message="mh:fooRequest"/>
    </operation>
  </portType>
```

The implication is that the element in the SOAP message can be valid even when it's empty. An empty XML element maps to a `null` value in Java. Because primitive types cannot be `null`, nillable elements are mapped to Java primitive wrapper classes instead of to Java primitive types. Listing 15–30 shows the endpoint definition for the Foo `portType`.

Listing 15–30

The Endpoint Interface Generated from the `portType` *Defined in Listing 15–29*

```
public interface Foo extends java.rmi.Remote {
    public void bar(java.lang.Integer quantity)
    throws java.rmi.RemoteException;
}
```

For each of the XML schema built-in types that map to a Java primitive, there is a corresponding Java primitive wrapper that can be used if a nillable element is specified. Table 15–3 lists the nillable XML schema built-in types and their corresponding Java primitive wrappers.

Table 15–3 Mapping: XML Schema Nillable Built-in Types to Java Primitive Wrapper Types

XML Schema Built-in Type	Java Primitive Wrapper Type
`xsd:byte`	`java.lang.Byte`
`xsd:boolean`	`java.lang.Boolean`
`xsd:short`	`java.lang.Short`
`xsd:int`	`java.lang.Integer`
`xsd:long`	`java.lang.Long`
`xsd:float`	`java.lang.Float`
`xsd:double`	`java.lang.Double`

15.3 Holders

WSDL allows a Web service to declare IN, OUT, and INOUT parameters. While IN parameters are native to Java, OUT and INOUT are not. To accommodate OUT and INOUT parameters JAX-RPC defines the `javax.xml.rpc.holders.Holder` interface, which is implemented by classes called **holders**, whose instances act as wrappers for OUT and INOUT parameters at runtime.

To understand how OUT and INOUT parameters work, you'll first need to understand the differences between pass-by-copy, which is used by Java, and pass-by-reference, employed by other programming languages, like C++ and C#.

15.3.1 Pass-by-Copy: IN Parameters

The Java programming language uses **pass-by-copy** for all primitive values—and even object references—passed as arguments to method calls. The value passed is a copy of the value held by the variable used in the method invocation, not the original variable itself. For example, when a Java program invokes the `foo()` method shown in Listing 15–31, the arguments passed into the method (a primitive `int` and a reference to `java.util.Date` object) are copies of the values held by the instance variables `myInt` and `myDate`.

Listing 15–31

Invoking `foo`*: Pass-by-Copy*

```
int myInt = 1;
Date myDate = new Date();

someObject.foo( myInt, myDate);
```

One advantage of pass-by-copy is that the value held by `myInt` and the object reference held by `myDate` will not change, no matter what the method `foo()` does to the two parameters passed in. This is not to say that the `Date` object that `myDate` refers to won't change. Its instance data may be modified by `foo()`, using the reference it received as a parameter—but `foo()` cannot change the object reference held by the variable `myDate`. For example, let's say that `foo()` assigns a new `int` value to the first parameter and a new `Date` to the second parameter as shown in Listing 15–32.

Listing 15–32

Assigning Values to the IN Parameters

```
public void foo(int param1, java.util.Date param2){
    param1 = 5;
    param2= new java.util.Date(0);
}
```

The Date object that was passed into foo() in Listing 15–31 represented today's date and time, but foo() replaces the Date reference passed in param2 with a reference to a new Date object, initialized to zero milliseconds from the "epoch date," so the new Date object represents January 1, 1970, 00:00:00 GMT.[4] Although param2 now holds a reference to the new Date object, which represents the epoch date, the calling method's variable, myDate, continues to refer to the Date object that represents today. In other words, any changes made to parameters are strictly local to the method and have no impact on the calling program. The same rule applies to the primitive value. Although param1 is assigned a new value (5), the myInt variable in Listing 15–31 still contains its original value (1). This may seem obvious to you if you've been programming in Java for a while, because this pass-by-copy behavior is how Java works. Java supports pass-by-copy exclusively.

In general OO programming parlance, pass-by-copy parameters are known as *IN* parameters. Most, if not all, modern programming languages support IN parameters. Some OO languages, like C# and C++, also support INOUT and OUT parameters, which are significantly different from the IN parameters supported by Java. INOUT and OUT parameters are covered in the next section.

15.3.2 Pass-by-Reference: INOUT and OUT Parameters

Some programming languages allow you to **pass by reference,** rather than by copy. When a variable is passed by reference, the parameter refers to the same variable, the same memory location, as the argument passed into the invocation. It is not just a copy, it's a pointer to exactly the same thing. Anything that's done to the parameter, including assigning it a new value, will be reflected in the variable it represents.

> ***To demonstrate pass-by-reference I've chosen to use C#, Microsoft's new OO programming language, because it provides native support for pass-by-reference, yet its syntax is very similar to Java's.***

For example, in C# you can declare that a parameter is pass-by-reference using the ref keyword as shown in Listing 15–33.

Listing 15–33

Declaring an INOUT Parameter in C#

```
// C# code
public void Foo(int param1, ref System.DateTime param2){
    param1 = 5;
```

[4] The time a Date object returns when its toString() method is invoked will be local to your time zone, so the "epoch" occurs at a different time relative to your time zone. In California, for example, setting the date to zero milliseconds will result in a time that is "December 31, 1969, 16:00:00 PST" because California time is eight hours behind GMT (Greenwich Mean Time).

```
    param2 = new Date(1970,1,1);
}
```

When this method is invoked, the variable in the calling method that refers to the `DateTime` object passed to `Foo()` will change when the new `DateTime` is assigned to `param2`. For example, in Listing 15–34 a fragment of a C# program calls the `Foo()` method defined in Listing 15–33.

Listing 15–34

Pass-by-Reference with an INOUT Parameter

```
// C# code
int myInt = 1;
System.DateTime myDate = System.DateTime.NOW;

someObject.Foo( myInt, myDate);
```

Although `myDate` starts out referring to a `DateTime` object that represents today's date (`NOW`), `Foo()` changes `myDate` to refer to a completely different `DateTime` object, one that represents January 1, 1970. This is an example of pass-by-reference, where any change made to the reference held by the parameter is reflected by the variable used as an argument to that parameter. This is an example of an INOUT parameter, a parameter that is passed by reference into the method and back out again.

In some programming languages, such as C#, it's also possible to specify an OUT parameter, which ignores the value passed in (the parameter is unassigned) but can assign a value to the parameter and pass it back out to the calling program. An OUT parameter is more like a return value than a parameter. Values pass out of a method, but not into it. For example, we can redefine `Foo()` to use an `out` parameter for the `DateTime` argument, as shown in Listing 15–35.

Listing 15–35

Declaring OUT Parameters in C#

```
// C# code
public void Foo(out int param1, out System.DateTime param2){
    param1 = 5;
    param2 = new System.DateTime(1970,1,1);
}
```

If you invoke this method as shown in Listing 15–36, then the `myInt` variable starts out as `1` before the method is invoked, but ends up as `5` after the method executes. Similarly, the `myDate` variable starts out pointing to one `DateTime` object and ends up pointing to a different object after the method completes.

Listing 15–36

Invoking `Foo`*: Pass-by-Reference with an OUT Parameter*

```
// C# code
int myInt = 1;
System.DateTime myDate = System.DateTime.NOW;

someObject.Foo( myInt, myDate);
```

The changes to the calling code's variables are the same as when the parameters were INOUT. The thing that makes an OUT parameter different is that the method has no access to the values the variables had before the method is invoked.

15.3.3 Holders: Supporting INOUT and OUT Parameters in JAX-RPC

The Java programming language doesn't use pass-by-reference, and supports only IN parameters. In some cases, though, you may need to use Java to communicate with Web services written in languages that support INOUT and OUT parameters. To make such communications possible, JAX-RPC provides **holders,** classes that implement the `javax.xml.rpc.holders.Holder` interface.

There is nothing elegant about the `Holder` interface and its subclasses. It simply provides a Band-Aid to support pass-by-reference in Java. Essentially, a `Holder` is an object that wraps around the argument you're passing. This mechanism allows the JAX-RPC runtime to change the value held by a `Holder` object before the method returns, so that you can extract the INOUT or OUT parameter value passed back from the Web service.

For example, let's suppose that a .NET Web service written in C# defines an RPC operation, `Foo()`, which declares an INOUT `int` parameter and an OUT `DateTime` parameter. In C# this method would look like Listing 15–37.

Listing 15–37

A C# Web Service Class That Uses OUT and INOUT Parameters

```
public class FooBar {
    public void Foo(ref int param1, out System.DateTime param2){
        param1 = param1 + 5;
        param2 = new System.DateTime(1970,1,1);
    }
}
```

The Web service would publish a WSDL document that represents the Web service endpoint in Listing 15–37. The JAX-RPC compiler would use this WSDL document to generate a JAX-RPC endpoint interface and stub for communicating with the .NET Web service. The endpoint interface is shown in Listing 15–38.

Listing 15–38

A JAX-RPC Endpoint Interface That Supports INOUT and OUT Parameters

```
import javax.xml.rpc.holders.IntHolder;
import javax.xml.rpc.holders.CalendarHolder;

public interface FooBar extends java.rmi.Remote {
    public void foo(IntHolder param1, CalendarHolder param2)
    throws java.rmi.RemoteException;
}
```

The `FooBar` endpoint interface in Listing 15–38 declares two arguments in its `foo()` method. The first is a `Holder` type for `xsd:int` values, while the second is a `Holder` type for `xsd:dateTime` types. To invoke the endpoint method you create two new `Holder` objects (an `IntHolder` and a `CalendarHolder`) and pass them into the `foo()` method of the JAX-RPC stub as illustrated in Listing 15–39.

Listing 15–39

Invoking the `foo()` *Method Defined by Listing 15–38*

```
IntHolder intHolder = new IntHolder( 10 );
CalendarHolder calendarHolder = new CalendarHolder();

FooBar fooBarStub = fooBarService.getFooBarPort();

fooBar.foo(intHolder, calendarHolder);

System.out.println("IntHolder = "+intHolder.value);
System.out.println("CalendarHolder = "+calendarHolder.value);
```

Before the method call, the value of `intHolder` is `10` and the value of `calendarHolder` is `null`. After `foo()` executes, however, `intHolder` contains the value `15` and `calendarHolder` contains a representation of the date January 1, 1970. The values are modified by the `foo()` method defined in Listing 15–37. Note that the value of a `Holder` type is always available via the public instance variable named `value`.

15.3.4 Mapping Holder Types from WSDL

The C# examples help explain why `Holder` types are needed, but JAX-RPC generates stubs from WSDL documents, not from C# code, so it's important to understand how INOUT and OUT parameters are defined in WSDL and mapped to JAX-RPC endpoints. It's fairly easy to tell whether a WSDL operation uses INOUT or OUT parameters by examining the `parameterOrder` attribute of the `operation` and comparing the `part` elements defined by the `input` and `output` messages.

15.3.4.1 Examples

The easiest way to learn how JAX-RPC maps IN, INOUT, and OUT parameter types to Java is to see a couple of simple examples. The `foo()` Web service method could be defined in a WSDL `portType` as shown in Listing 15–40.

Listing 15–40

A WSDL Document That Declares an INOUT Parameter

```
<?xml version="1.0" encoding="UTF-8"?>
<definitions name="FooWS"
 targetNamespace="http://www.Monson-Haefel.com/jwsbook/Foo"
 xmlns:mh="http://www.Monson-Haefel.com/jwsbook/Foo"
 xmlns:xsd="http://www.w3.org/2001/XMLSchema"
 xmlns="http://schemas.xmlsoap.org/wsdl/">

<message name="fooRequest">
  <part name="param1" type="xsd:int"/>
</message>
<message name="fooResponse">
  <part name="param1" type="xsd:int"/>
  <part name="param2" type="xsd:dateTime"/>
</message>
<portType name="FooBar">
  <operation name="foo" parameterOrder="param1 param2">
    <input message="mh:fooRequest"/>
    <output message="mh:fooResponse"/>
  </operation>
</portType>
```

When a JAX-RPC compiler reads the `portType` definition in Listing 15–40, it will notice that the `part` element labeled `param1` is declared in both the `input` and `output` messages, `fooRequest` and `fooResponse`. Any time a `part` is declared in both `input` and `output` the JAX-RPC compiler knows it is an INOUT parameter, and will require a `Holder` type. In this case, the `part` specifies that `param1` is an INOUT parameter of type `xsd:int`, which maps to the `javax.xml.rpc.holders.IntHolder` type.

The JAX-RPC compiler will also notice that one of the `part` elements is defined in the `output` message but not the `input` message, indicating that it is either a return value or an OUT parameter. If it should be an OUT parameter, then the `part` label will be listed in the `parameterOrder` attribute of the `operation` element. If the `part` should be a return value, it will not be listed in the `parameterOrder` attribute. In Listing 15–40 `param2` is an OUT parameter, because it's listed in `parameterOrder`.

Based on the WSDL definition in Listing 15–40, a JAX-RPC compiler will generate an endpoint as shown in Listing 15–41.

Listing 15–41

The Endpoint Interface Generated from the `portType` *Defined in Listing 15–40*

```
import javax.xml.rpc.holders.IntHolder;
import javax.xml.rpc.holders.CalendarHolder;

public interface FooBar extends java.rmi.Remote {
    public void foo(IntHolder param1, CalendarHolder param2)
    throws java.rmi.RemoteException;
}
```

Notice that `foo()`'s return type is `void`. When all the `part` elements are listed in the `parameterOrder` attribute, there is no return value. If the `parameterOrder` attribute is omitted, the JAX-RPC compiler will assume that the `param2 part` element is a return value and will generate an endpoint interface like the one in Listing 15–42.

Listing 15–42

The Endpoint Interface Generated from Listing 15–40 if the `parameterOrder` *Attribute Is Omitted*

```
import javax.xml.rpc.holders.IntHolder;

public interface FooBar extends java.rmi.Remote {
    public java.util.Calendar foo(IntHolder param1)
    throws java.rmi.RemoteException;
}
```

Although this endpoint interface looks different from the one before it, it's semantically equivalent because both interfaces have an INOUT parameter and an OUT parameter. A return value is simply an OUT parameter that does not require the use of a `Holder` class.

Any `part` that is declared in the input message but not the output message is an IN parameter, and doesn't require a `Holder` class because Java automatically supports IN parameters.

You can mix IN, INOUT, and OUT parameters as much as you want, as long as you describe them in WSDL properly. For example, the `portType` definition in Listing 15–43 describes a Web service that has all three kinds of parameters.

Listing 15–43

A WSDL `portType` *Definition That Declares IN, INOUT, and OUT Parameters*

```
<?xml version="1.0" encoding="UTF-8"?>
<definitions name="FooWS"
 targetNamespace="http://www.Monson-Haefel.com/jwsbook/Foo"
 xmlns:mh="http://www.Monson-Haefel.com/jwsbook/Foo"
 xmlns:xsd="http://www.w3.org/2001/XMLSchema"
 xmlns="http://schemas.xmlsoap.org/wsdl/">

<message name="fooRequest">
  <part name="param1" type="xsd:int"/>
  <part name="param2" type="xsd:double"/>
</message>
<message name="fooResponse">
  <part name="param2" type="xsd:double"/>
  <part name="param3" type="xsd:dateTime"/>
  <part name="param4" type="xsd:float" />
</message>
<portType name="FooBoo">
  <operation name="foo" parameterOrder="param1 param2 param3">
    <input message="mh:fooRequest"/>
    <output message="mh:fooResponse"/>
  </operation>
</portType>
```

From this `portType` definition a JAX-RPC compiler would generate the JAX-RPC endpoint interface shown in Listing 15–44.

Listing 15–44

The Endpoint Interface Generated from the `portType` *Defined in Listing 15–43*

```
import javax.xml.rpc.holders.DoubleHolder;
import javax.xml.rpc.holders.CalendarHolder;

public interface FooBoo extends java.rmi.Remote {
    public float foo(int param1, DoubleHolder param2, CalendarHolder param3)
    throws java.rmi.RemoteException;
}
```

The JAX-RPC compiler always lists the parameters in the order specified by the `parameterOrder` attribute. In this case the order is `param1`, `param2`, `param3`. The following list explains the kind of parameter that each WSDL `part` in Listing 15–43 represents.

* The param1 part is referred to only by the input message (fooRequest), so it's an IN parameter, which doesn't need a Holder type.
* The param2 part is listed by the parameterOrder attribute and referred to by both the input and output messages, so it's an INOUT parameter, which requires a Holder class (DoubleHolder).
* The param3 part is listed by the parameterOrder attribute and referred to only by the output message (fooResponse), and it's listed in the parameterOrder attribute, so it's an OUT parameter, which requires a Holder class (CalendarHolder).
* The param4 part is referred to only by the output message, so it's an OUT parameter too; but it's not listed by the parameterOrder attribute, so it's the return type of the method, which doesn't need a Holder type.

15.3.4.2 Rules for Mapping parts *to Method Parameters*

JAX-RPC compilers follow established rules when mapping a WSDL portType definition to parameters and return types of an endpoint interface. The rules depend, in part, on whether a part name is listed in the parameterOrder attribute. If it is, then it's considered **listed;** if not, then it's **unlisted.** These terms are used in the rules below. The term "parameter" is used to refer to both the part elements of input and output messages as well as the parameters of an endpoint method.

1. If a part is declared only by the input message, then it's an IN parameter, which doesn't require a holder.
2. If a parameter is declared by both the input and output messages, then it's an INOUT parameter, which requires a holder.
3. If a part is declared only by the output message, then it's an OUT parameter, which requires a holder (unless it's a return value; see rule #6).
4. The parameterOrder attribute dictates the order of parameters in the endpoint method.
5. If the parameterOrder attribute is declared, then all input message parameters must be listed. The output message parameters may or may not be listed.
6. If there is a single unlisted output parameter, then that parameter is the return type of the method. Otherwise the return type is void.
7. Parameters are declared in the endpoint method in the order they are listed, followed by unlisted parameters.
8. Unlisted parameters are ordered as follows: Parameters declared in the input message are listed first, followed by parameters declared by the output message. Unlisted INOUT parameters, those that are declared by both the input and output messages, are listed in the order they are declared in the input message.

The parameterOrder attribute is actually optional; if it's not declared, then all the parameters follow the rules for unlisted parameters (rule #8).

15.3.4.3 Standard Holder Types

JAX-RPC provides a dozen or so standard `Holder` classes in the `javax.xml.rpc.holders` package. These types must be used for INOUT and OUT parameters that map to Java primitive types. The `Holder` types are listed in Table 15–4, along with the corresponding non-holder Java types and XML schema types, the types declared in WSDL documents:

Table 15–4 Standard `Holder` Classes for XML Schema Built-in Types

XML Schema Built-in Type	IN Java Type	INOUT and OUT JAX-RPC Holder Type
`xsd:byte`	`byte`	`ByteHolder`
`xsd:boolean`	`boolean`	`BooleanHolder`
`xsd:short`	`short`	`ShortHolder`
`xsd:int`	`int`	`IntHolder`
`xsd:long`	`long`	`LongHolder`
`xsd:float`	`float`	`FloatHolder`
`xsd:double`	`double`	`DoubleHolder`
`xsd:string`	`java.lang.String`	`StringHolder`
`xsd:dateTime`	`java.util.Calendar`	`CalendarHolder`
`xsd:integer`	`java.math.BigInteger`	`BigIntegerHolder`
`xsd:decimal`	`java.math.BigDecimal`	`BigDecimalHolder`
`xsd:QName`	`java.xml.namespace.QName`	`QNameHolder`
`xsd:base64Binary`	`byte[]`	`ByteArrayHolder`
`xsd:hexBinary`	`byte[]`	`ByteArrayHolder`

In addition to the `Holder` classes listed in Table 15–4, there is also a set of `Holder` types defined for nillable built-in types; these are listed in Table 15–5.

Table 15–5 Standard `Holder` Classes for Nillable XML Schema Built-in Types

XML Schema Built-in Type	IN Java Type	INOUT and OUT JAX-RPC Holder Type
`xsd:byte` (nillable)	`java.lang.Byte`	`ByteWrapperHolder`
`xsd:boolean` (nillable)	`java.lang.Boolean`	`BooleanWrapperHolder`
`xsd:short` (nillable)	`java.lang.Short`	`ShortWrapperHolder`
`xsd:int` (nillable)	`java.lang.Integer`	`IntegerWrapperHolder`
`xsd:long` (nillable)	`java.lang.Long`	`LongWrapperHolder`
`xsd:float` (nillable)	`java.lang.Float`	`FloatWrapperHolder`
`xsd:double` (nillable)	`java.lang.Double`	`DoubleWrapperHolder`

The standard holder types all follow the same design, which includes the definition of a no-argument constructor, a single-argument constructor, and a public instance field named `value`. The type used for the `value` field and the parameter of the single-argument constructor is the type that's held by the wrapper. For example, Listing 15–45 shows the definition of `javax.xml.rpc.holders.IntHolder`.

Listing 15–45

The `javax.xml.rpc.holders.IntHolder` *Class*

```
package javax.xml.rpc.holders;

public class IntHolder extends javax.xml.rpc.holders.Holder {
    public int value;

    public IntHolder(){
    }
    public IntHolder(int myint){
        value = myint;
    }
}
```

The other standard holder classes follow exactly the same pattern. All holder classes must extend the `javax.xml.rpc.holders.Holder` interface, which is defined in Listing 15–46. As you can see, the `Holder` interface is purely a typing, or "marker," interface: It defines no methods.

Listing 15–46

The `javax.xml.rpc.holders.Holder` *Interface*

```
package javax.xml.rpc.holders;

public interface Holder {
}
```

15.3.4.4 Generated Holder Types

When the JAX-RPC compiler encounters an INOUT or OUT parameter of a type not already supported by the standard holder classes, it will generate a custom `Holder` type specifically for that parameter.

For example, earlier in this chapter, in Listing 15–13, the complex type `Book` was defined as a parameter in a WSDL document. As you saw in Listing 15–15, the JAX-RPC compiler will generate a Java bean for this complex type—and a custom `Holder` class for the bean as well, if it's an INOUT or OUT parameter. Listing 15–47 shows a WSDL document that declares the `Book` type as an INOUT parameter.

Listing 15–47

A WSDL Document That Declares a Complex Type as an INOUT Parameter

```
<?xml version="1.0" encoding="UTF-8"?>
<definitions name="FooWS"
 targetNamespace="http://www.Monson-Haefel.com/jwsbook/Foo"
 xmlns:mh="http://www.Monson-Haefel.com/jwsbook/Foo"
 xmlns:xsd="http://www.w3.org/2001/XMLSchema"
 xmlns="http://schemas.xmlsoap.org/wsdl/">

<types>
  <xsd:schema targetNamespace="http://www.Monson-Haefel.com/jwsbook/Foo">
    <xsd:complexType name="Book">
      <xsd:sequence>
        <xsd:element name="title" type="xsd:string"/>
        <xsd:element name="isbn" type="xsd:string"/>
        <xsd:element name="authors" type="mh:Author"
            maxOccurs="unbounded"/>
      </xsd:sequence>
    </xsd:complexType>
    <xsd:complexType name="Author">
      <xsd:sequence>
        <xsd:element name="firstName"          type="xsd:string"/>
        <xsd:element name="lastName"           type="xsd:string"/>
        <xsd:element name="middleInitial"      type="xsd:string"/>
      </xsd:sequence>
    </xsd:complexType>
  </xsd:schema>
</types>
<message name="fooRequest">
  <part name="book" type="mh:Book" />
</message>
<message name="fooResponse">
  <part name="book" type="mh:Book" />
</message>
<portType name="FooBar">
  <operation name="foo">
    <input message="mh:fooRequest"/>
    <output message="mh:fooResponse"/>
  </operation>
</portType>
```

Here the part labeled "book" is declared by both the input and output messages, so it's an INOUT parameter. When the JAX-RPC compiler generates an endpoint interface for the portType defined in Listing 15–47, it will automatically generate a Book Java bean that represents the Book XML schema type, as well as a specialized Holder class for the Java bean. As you can see in Listing 15–48, the foo endpoint method declares the BookHolder type to be its only parameter.

Listing 15–48

The Endpoint Interface Generated from the portType *Defined in Listing 15–47*

```
public interface FooBar extends java.rmi.Remote {
  public void foo(BookHolder book) throws java.rmi.RemoteException;
}
```

The BookHolder class is defined in Listing 15–49.

Listing 15–49

The Holder *Class Generated for the INOUT* Book *Parameter Defined in Listing 15–47*

```
public class BookHolder implements javax.xml.rpc.holders.Holder {
  public Book value;

  public BookHolder(){
    // no-arg contructor is required.
  }
  public BookHolder(Book myBook) {
    value = myBook;
  }
}
```

The class name of a generated holder will be the type of the generated bean followed by the word "Holder." Aggregated types do not need holders. The holder class is needed only for the containing type. For example, if the Book Java bean refers to another Java bean type, Author, the JAX-RPC compiler will not generate an AuthorHolder class, only a BookHolder class, because Book is the containing type.

In addition to generating holders for complex types, the JAX-RPC compiler will also generate holders for arrays that are used as INOUT or OUT parameters. For example, the WSDL document in Listing 15–50 uses a complex type array as an INOUT parameter.

Listing 15–50

A WSDL Document That Uses a WSDL Restricted Array as an INOUT Parameter

```
<?xml version="1.0" encoding="UTF-8"?>
<definitions name="FooWS"
 targetNamespace="http://www.Monson-Haefel.com/jwsbook/Foo"
 xmlns:mh="http://www.Monson-Haefel.com/jwsbook/Foo"
 xmlns:xsd="http://www.w3.org/2001/XMLSchema"
 xmlns="http://schemas.xmlsoap.org/wsdl/">

<types>
  <xsd:schema targetNamespace="http://www.Monson-Haefel.com/jwsbook/Foo">
    <xsd:complexType name="StringArray">
     <xsd:sequence>
       <xsd:element name="item" maxOccurs="unbounded"/>
     </xsd:sequence>
    </xsd:complexType>
  </xsd:schema>
</types>
<message name="fooRequest">
  <part name="strings" type="mh:StringArray" />
</message>
<message name="fooResponse">
  <part name="strings" type="mh:StringArray" />
</message>
<portType name="FooBar">
  <operation name="foo">
    <input message="mh:fooRequest"/>
    <output message="mh:fooResponse"/>
  </operation>
</portType>
```

In this case, the JAX-RPC compiler will generate an endpoint interface that declares a `StringArrayHolder` parameter, as shown in Listing 15–51.

Listing 15–51

The Endpoint Interface Generated from the `portType` *Defined in Listing 15–50*

```
public interface FooBar extends java.rmi.Remote {
    public void foo(StringArrayHolder strings)
    throws java.rmi.RemoteException;
}
```

The `StringArrayHolder` is defined in Listing 15–52.

Listing 15–52

The `Holder` *Class Generated for the INOUT Array Parameter Defined in Listing 15–50*

```
public final class StringArrayHolder implements javax.xml.rpc.holders.Holder
{
  public java.lang.String[] value;

  public StringArrayHolder(){
    // no-arg contructor is required.
  }
  public StringArrayHolder(java.lang.String[] myStrings) {
    this.value = value;
  }
}
```

15.4 Faults and Java Exceptions

All endpoint interface methods must declare the `java.rmi.RemoteException` type in their `throws` clause. The stub uses the `RemoteException` to report network communication errors, including TCP/IP communication problems, and problems with higher-level protocols like HTTP (for example, the familiar `404 Not Found` error). The `RemoteException` is also used for standard SOAP faults: `Server`, `Client`, and so on.

15.4.1 WSDL Faults and Application Exceptions

In addition to the mandatory `RemoteException` type, endpoint methods may declare application-specific exceptions that map to fault messages defined in the WSDL document. For example, the WSDL document for the BookQuote Web service could define a fault message for invalid ISBN numbers as shown in Listing 15–53.

Listing 15–53

A WSDL Document That Defines a Fault Message

```
<message name="InvalidIsbnFault">
  <part name="InvalidIsbn" type="xsd:string" />
</message>
```

```
<portType name="BookQuote">
  <operation name="getBookPrice">
    <input message="mh:getBookPriceRequest"/>
    <output message="mh:getBookPriceResponse"/>
    <fault name="InvalidIsbnFault" message="mh:InvalidIsbnFault"/>
  </operation>
</portType>
```

The mapping of faults to exceptions can get a little involved, but in this case it's fairly simple. The message name, `"InvalidIsbnFault"`, is mapped to an exception class of the same name, which extends `java.lang.Exception` as in Listing 15–54. A single accessor is defined for the `InvalidIsbnFault` exception class, `getInvalidIsbn()`—this method is based on the fault message's `part` definition.

Listing 15–54

The Exception Type Generated from the Fault Message Defined in Listing 15–53

```
public class InvalidIsbnFault extends java.lang.Exception {
  private String invalidIsbn;
  public InvalidIsbnFault(String invalidIsbn){
    super();
    this.invalidIsbn = invalidIsbn;
  }
  public String getInvalidIsbn(){
    return invalidIsbn;
  }
}
```

The `InvalidIsbnFault` type is a checked exception, so it must be declared in the `throws` clause of the endpoint method, as in Listing 15–55.

Listing 15–55

The Endpoint Interface Generated from the `portType` *Defined in Listing 15–53*

```
public interface BookQuote extends java.rmi.Remote {
  public float getBookPrice(String isbn)
   throws java.rmi.RemoteException, InvalidIsbnFault;
}
```

Although a fault message may have only a single `part`, that part may refer to an XML schema complex type, which allows for a richer set of data to be associated with the exception. The WSDL document in Listing 15–56 shows a complex type referred to by the fault message's `part` definition.

Listing 15–56

A WSDL Document That Defines a Fault Message with an XML Schema Complex Type

```
<?xml version="1.0" encoding="UTF-8"?>
<definitions name="BookQuoteWS"
 targetNamespace="http://www.Monson-Haefel.com/jwsbook/BookQuote"
 xmlns:mh="http://www.Monson-Haefel.com/jwsbook/BookQuote"
 xmlns:xsd="http://www.w3.org/2001/XMLSchema"
 xmlns="http://schemas.xmlsoap.org/wsdl/">

<types>
  <xsd:schema
    targetNamespace="http://www.Monson-Haefel.com/jwsbook/BookQuote">
    <xsd:complexType name="InvalidIsbnType">
       <xsd:sequence>
         <xsd:element name="offending-value" type="xsd:string"/>
         <xsd:element name="conformance-rules" type="xsd:string"/>
       </xsd:sequence>
    </xsd:complexType>
  </xsd:schema>
</types>
<message name="getBookPriceRequest">
  <part name="isbn" type="xsd:string"/>
</message>
<message name="getBookPriceResponse">
  <part name="result" type="xsd:float"/>
</message>
<message name="getBookPriceFault">
  <part name="fault" type="mh:InvalidIsbnType" />
</message>
<portType name="BookQuote">
  <operation name="getBookPrice">
    <input message="mh:getBookPriceRequest"/>
    <output message="mh:getBookPriceResponse"/>
    <fault name="fault" message="mh:getBookPriceFault"/>
  </operation>
</portType>
```

When a JAX-RPC compiler generates an application exception class from a fault message that's based on an XML schema complex type, it will derive the exception's name from the name of the complex type, rather than from the fault message name. For the WSDL document in Listing 15–56, the name of the fault will be

InvalidIsbnType, the same name as the complex type declared by the fault-message part. Listing 15–57 shows the application exception generated from the getBookQuoteFault message.

Listing 15–57

The Exception Type Generated from the Fault message *Defined in Listing 15–56*

```
public class InvalidIsbnType extends java.lang.Exception{
  private java.lang.String offendingValue;
  private java.lang.String conformanceRules;

  public InvalidIsbnType() {
    // no-arg constructor is required.
  }
  public InvalidIsbnType(String offendingValue,String conformanceRules){
    this.offendingValue = offendingValue;
    this.conformanceRules = conformanceRules;
  }
  public java.lang.String getOffendingValue() {
    return offendingValue;
  }
  public java.lang.String getConformanceRules() {
    return conformanceRules;
  }
}
```

The endpoint interface declares the InvalidIsbnType just as it does any other exception; see Listing 15–58.

Listing 15–58

The Endpoint Interface Generated from the portType *Defined in Listing 15–56*

```
public interface BookQuote extends java.rmi.Remote {
    public float getBookPrice(java.lang.String isbn)
    throws java.rmi.RemoteException, InvalidIsbnType;
}
```

If you use inheritance by extension, the JAX-RPC compiler will generate exception classes that represent both the base type and the extension type. For example, Listing 15–59 shows a types definition that defines the InvalidIsbnType type as extending the base type labeled FaultType.

Listing 15–59

A WSDL Document That Defines a Fault Complex Type and Its Base Type

```
<?xml version="1.0" encoding="UTF-8"?>
<definitions name="BookQuoteWS"
 targetNamespace="http://www.Monson-Haefel.com/jwsbook/BookQuote"
 xmlns:mh="http://www.Monson-Haefel.com/jwsbook/BookQuote"
 xmlns:xsd="http://www.w3.org/2001/XMLSchema"
 xmlns="http://schemas.xmlsoap.org/wsdl/">

<types>
  <xsd:schema
   targetNamespace="http://www.Monson-Haefel.com/jwsbook/BookQuote">
    <xsd:complexType name="FaultType">
       <xsd:sequence>
         <xsd:element name="error-code" type="xsd:int"/>
       </xsd:sequence>
    </xsd:complexType>
    <xsd:complexType name="InvalidIsbnType">
       <xsd:complexContent>
         <xsd:extension base="mh:FaultType" >
           <xsd:sequence>
             <xsd:element name="offending-value" type="xsd:string"/>
             <xsd:element name="conformance-rules" type="xsd:string"/>
           </xsd:sequence>
         </xsd:extension>
       </xsd:complexContent>
    </xsd:complexType>
  </xsd:schema>
</types>
```

From this `types` definition, the JAX-RPC compiler will generate the two exception types shown in Listings 15–60 and 15–61.

Listing 15–60

The Exception Type Based on the `FaultType` *Complex Base Type Defined in Listing 15–59*

```
public class FaultType extends Exception {
    private int errorCode;
```

```
    public FaultType(int errorCode) {
        this.errorCode = errorCode;
    }
    public int getErrorCode() {
        return errorCode;
    }
}
```

Listing 15–61

The Exception Type Based on the `InvalidIsbnType` *Complex Extended Type Defined in Listing 15–59*

```
public class InvalidIsbnType extends FaultType {
    private String offendingValue;
    private String conformanceRules;

    public InvalidIsbnType(int errorCode, String offendingValue,
                           String conformanceRules) {
        super(errorCode);
        this.offendingValue = offendingValue;
        this.conformanceRules = conformanceRules;
    }
    public java.lang.String getOffendingValue() {
        return offendingValue;
    }
    public java.lang.String getConformanceRules() {
        return conformanceRules;
    }
}
```

Although the JAX-RPC compiler generates both the base `FaultType` and its subtype, `InvalidIsbnType`, only the latter is declared in the endpoint interface, as shown in Listing 15–62.

Listing 15–62

The Endpoint Interface Generated from the `portType` *Defined in Listing 15–59*

```
public interface BookQuote extends java.rmi.Remote {
    public float getBookPrice(java.lang.String isbn)
    throws java.rmi.RemoteException, InvalidIsbnType;
}
```

Even though the base exception type is not used in this remote interface, it is generated anyway, to accommodate other operations that may explicitly throw the base type.

15.5 Wrapping Up

This chapter has explained in detail the default mappings between Java types and WSDL and XML types, but it doesn't tell the entire mapping story. In addition to the mappings described here, you will also need to use a JAX-RPC mapping file to help the JAX-RPC compiler and runtime understand the relationship between the Java interfaces and Java beans on one hand and the WSDL document and XML data types on the other. JAX-RPC mapping files are created as part of the deployment process, and are covered in Chapter 24. You are required to provide a JAX-RPC mapping file whenever you deploy a J2EE Web service client or service (JSE or EJB endpoint). It's possible that your J2EE application server will generate this mapping file automatically, in which case you are not required to understand its content.

Part V

JAXR

This part covers the use of **JAXR (Java API for XML Registries)** for access to UDDI registries. All of the examples in this part are executed against IBM's live UDDI test registry, so you can actually work with one of the four Universal Business Registry operator sites. You don't need to know UDDI to understand this part, but a solid background in UDDI makes you more fully aware of JAXR's benefits and limitations. If you want to learn more about UDDI, read Part III: UDDI.

Whether you'll need JAXR in your development efforts depends on the type of system you're writing. In many projects, you won't need JAXR because you won't need to access a UDDI registry, but there will certainly be plenty of developers that will work with a UDDI registry and need to create browsing tools, recovery code, or even dynamic access to a UDDI registry. For those folks (and other inquiring minds), the JAXR API provides a very convenient, object-oriented view of a UDDI registry.

In This Part

Chapter 16

Getting Started with JAXR

JAXR (**Java API for XML Registries**) is a client-side API for accessing different kinds of XML-based business registries, but is used predominantly for UDDI and ebXML registries. Actually, the data model of the API closely matches ebXML concepts and terminology, but it still works well for UDDI.

In some respects JAXR is analogous to JDBC. Where JDBC provides a vendor-neutral API for accessing any type of relational database, JAXR provides a vendor-neutral API for accessing any ebXML or UDDI registry. J2EE vendors will provide their own implementations of the JAXR API for accessing ebXML, UDDI, or other types of XML registry systems.

The JAXR API has two conformance levels: Level 0 and Level 1. Level 1 is a richer API that is designed for accessing ebXML registries. Level 0 provides fewer features and is intended for UDDI registries, which are less flexible than ebXML but more popular. The WS-I Basic Profile 1.0 sanctions the use of UDDI, but not ebXML. Because J2EE Web Services are aligned with the Basic Profile, this book covers only JAXR Level 0, the UDDI-compliant aspect of the API.

JAXR comes in two interdependent packages: The Query and Life Cycle API (`javax.xml.registry`) and the Information Model (`javax.xml.registry.infomodel`). The Query and Life Cycle API supports the UDDI Inquiry and Publishing APIs respectively. The Information Model (**infomodel** for short) provides business- and technical-object views that correspond to UDDI data structures (`businessEntity`, `bindingTemplate`, `tModel`, and so on). This part of the book covers both packages.

JAXR is very useful under certain circumstances. If you need to build a UDDI browsing tool, JAXR is a great choice for supporting the actual SOAP communications between the browser and the UDDI registry. JAXR is useful for implementing failover mechanisms, to handle gracefully the problem of a Web service endpoint becoming unavailable. The JAXR API can be used to look up the Web service in UDDI and determine whether an alternative access point is offered.

Some have proposed that UDDI provides a "self-organizing" system, where software automatically locates new business partners and interacts with those partners automatically. The concept of self-organizing systems is more fantasy than reality, however. In truth, there is not a lot of self-organizing going on in real-world implementations—most businesses don't trust software to create business relationships, which is the implication of a self-organizing system.

JAXR is a good API for developers to use for accessing a UDDI registry. A lot of the grunt work of communicating with a UDDI registry is hidden behind JAXR's APIs and infomodel. Essentially, you work with **business objects and technical objects,** which represent organizations, services, classification systems, and so on, without having to think in terms of SOAP messaging. This is a departure from other UDDI APIs like IBM's UDDI4J (UDDI for Java) open source project or Systinet's WASP UDDI API, both of which model the data structures and SOAP operations more closely.

16.1 Using a UDDI Test Registry

One nice thing about UDDI is that there is a public registry called the **UDDI Business Registry** (**UBR**) that you can use free of charge. The UBR can be accessed at four different **operator sites** hosted by Microsoft, IBM, SAP, and NTT. These organizations synchronize their UDDI registry entries so that an entry made on one system is replicated, after a period of time, on the other three. All the UBR operator sites except NTT's offer a test registry as well as a production registry. You will be using IBM's test registry for the examples in this chapter. The test registry is occasionally purged and is not replicated, but otherwise it behaves like a production UDDI registry, and is good for testing and learning.

The Web site for the IBM test registry is located at http://uddi.ibm.com/testregistry /registry.html. You will need to browse to that location and register before you can try out the examples in this chapter. When you register, you will choose a user-id and password. You'll need these to add, modify, and delete information about your organization in the test registry. Actually, the registration will give you rights to create business entries in the production registry as well, but don't do that until you're comfortable with JAXR and ready to create a real-world entry in the UBR.

To get started you'll need a **JAXR provider. A JAXR provider is a vendor's implementation of the JAXR API.** It's likely that your J2EE application server will include a JAXR provider, so all you'll need to do is locate it and include the provider JAR in your classpath.

16.2 Connecting to a UDDI Registry

Connecting to a UDDI registry with JAXR requires that you obtain a `ConnectionFactory`, configure its connection properties, and request a `Connection` object. J2EE application servers may take care of some of this work, such as configuration, automatically—depending on the vendor. The examples throughout this chapter use non-J2EE application clients, because it's easier for you to compile and execute the programs.

In a standalone application you have to configure the `ConnectionFactory` in your code. In Listing 16–1, `JaxrExample_1` shows how to connect to a UDDI registry—specifically the IBM Test Registry—from a non-J2EE application client. Subsequent sections will discuss these steps in more detail.

Listing 16–1

Connecting to a UDDI Registry

```
package com.jwsbook.jaxr;
import javax.xml.registry.ConnectionFactory;
import javax.xml.registry.Connection;
import javax.xml.registry.RegistryService;
import javax.xml.registry.BusinessLifeCycleManager;
import javax.xml.registry.infomodel.Organization;
import javax.xml.registry.infomodel.InternationalString;
import javax.xml.registry.JAXRException;
import java.net.PasswordAuthentication;
import java.util.Properties;
import java.util.Set;
import java.util.HashSet;

public class JaxrExample_1 {
  public static void main(String [] args) throws JAXRException {
    // Extract parameters.
    String userName = args[0];
    String password = args[1];

    // Connect to UDDI registry and authenticate.
    Connection connection = connectToRegistry(userName,password);

    // Close connection.
    connection.close();
  }
```

```
    public static Connection connectToRegistry(String userName,
                                               String password)
    throws JAXRException {
      // Create a ConnectionFactory.
      ConnectionFactory factory = ConnectionFactory.newInstance();

      // Configure the ConnectionFactory.
      Properties props = new Properties();
      props.setProperty("javax.xml.registry.lifeCycleManagerURL",
                        "https://uddi.ibm.com/testregistry/publishapi");
      props.setProperty("javax.xml.registry.queryManagerURL",
                        "http://uddi.ibm.com/testregistry/inquiryapi");
      props.setProperty("javax.xml.registry.security.authenticationMethod",
                      "UDDI_GET_AUTHTOKEN");
      factory.setProperties(props);

      // Connect to UDDI test registry.
      Connection connection = factory.createConnection();

      // Authenticate (log in) to the Publishing endpoint.
      PasswordAuthentication credential =
        new PasswordAuthentication(userName, password.toCharArray());
      Set credentials = new HashSet();
      credentials.add(credential);
      connection.setCredentials(credentials);

      return connection;
    }
}
```

JaxrExample_1 creates a ConnectionFactory, configures it, connects to a UDDI registry, and authenticates the user. The code for configuring and connecting to a UDDI registry is factored into the connectToRegistry() method, which is reused in the rest of the JAXR examples.

Once you have the JAXR provider installed and your classpath set up, you can run this program. You'll know it succeeded if you don't get any error messages—if there is a problem, a JAXRException will be thrown and displayed on the output screen. To run JaxrExample_1 from a command window, execute a command in the following format:

```
[prompt] java com.jwsbook.jaxr.JaxrExample_1 userName password
```

16.2.1 Obtaining a `ConnectionFactory`

Connecting to a UDDI registry is a simple matter for J2EE and non-J2EE applications alike. `JaxrExample_1` (Listing 16–1) is a standalone application client, and its first task is to use `ConnectionFactory.newInstance()` to create a `ConnectionFactory`:

```
// Create a ConnectionFactory.
ConnectionFactory factory = ConnectionFactory.newInstance();
```

This operation assumes either that you are using the JAXR reference implementation (packaged with the J2EE 1.4 SDK) or that you have specified a special JAXR system property that names the JAXR `ConnectionFactory` implementation class. Different vendors offer their own implementations of the `ConnectionFactory`, so if you're not using the JAXR RI, you'll need to specify the following system property, in any of several ways.

```
javax.xml.registry.ConnectionFactoryClass =vendors_connectionfactory_class
```

You can do it in your Java code by calling the `java.lang.System.setProperty()` method, or you can do it on the command line when you execute `JaxrExample_1`, as follows:

```
[prompt] java -Djavax.xml.registry.ConnectionFactoryClass=
some_class_name com.jwsbook.jaxr.JaxrExample_1  myUserID myPassword
```

You can also add the property to your operating system's registry—you must do so before opening a command window.

You don't need to set the `ConnectionFactoryClass` system property if you are using the reference implementation of JAXR.

16.2.2 Configuring the `ConnectionFactory`

Before you can use a `ConnectionFactory` to create a connection, you will need to configure the connection URLs. UDDI registries support two sets of Web service operations: Inquiry and Publishing. Inquiry is used to search and navigate the UDDI directory, while Publishing is used to add, modify, and delete information in the registry. All of the UBR operator sites have their own endpoints for Inquiry and Publishing—they are separate URLs—and three of them have different URLs for testing and production. The following outline shows the four UBR operator sites and their Inquiry and Publishing URLs, as listed at the UDDI.org Web site.

IBM

UBR Node

Home page = http://uddi.ibm.com/
Inquiry API = http://uddi.ibm.com/ubr/inquiryapi
Publishing API = https://uddi.ibm.com/ubr/publishapi

Test Node

Home page = http://uddi.ibm.com/testregistry/registry.html
Inquiry API = http://uddi.ibm.com/testregistry/inquiryapi
Publishing API = https://uddi.ibm.com/testregistry/publishapi

Microsoft

UBR Node

Home page = http://uddi.microsoft.com/
Inquiry API = http://uddi.microsoft.com/inquire
Publishing API = https://uddi.microsoft.com/publish

Test Node

Home page = http://test.uddi.microsoft.com/
Inquiry API = http://test.uddi.microsoft.com/inquire
Publishing API = https://test.uddi.microsoft.com/publish

SAP

UBR Node

Home page = http://uddi.sap.com/
Inquiry API = http://uddi.sap.com/uddi/api/inquiry
Publishing API = https://uddi.sap.com/uddi/api/publish

Test Node

Home page = http://udditest.sap.com/
Inquiry API = http://udditest.sap.com/UDDI/api/inquiry
Publishing API = https://udditest.sap.com/UDDI/api/publish

NTT

UBR Node

Home page = http://www.ntt.com/uddi/
Inquiry API = http://www.uddi.ne.jp/ubr/inquiryapi
Publishing API = https://www.uddi.ne.jp/ubr/publishapi

Except for NTT, all of the operator sites offer both a test node (UDDI registry) and access to a real-world UBR node. It's recommended that you do not do development work on a UBR node. Do all your development and testing on one of the test nodes. In the exercises in this book we're using IBM's test node.

To use the JAXR `ConnectionFactory` you have to configure its Inquiry and Publishing URLs so that the JAXR provider knows where to send Inquiry and Publishing SOAP messages. `JaxrExample_1` configures the Inquiry and Publishing URLs to connect to IBM's test node, as shown in the following snippet from Listing 16–1.

```
// Configure the ConnectionFactory.
Properties props = new Properties();
props.setProperty("javax.xml.registry.lifeCycleManagerURL",
                  "https://uddi.ibm.com/testregistry/publishapi");
props.setProperty("javax.xml.registry.queryManagerURL",
                  "http://uddi.ibm.com/testregistry/inquiryapi");
props.setProperty("javax.xml.registry.security.authenticationMethod",
                  "UDDI_GET_AUTHTOKEN");
factory.setProperties(props);
```

The property names used to configure the `ConnectionFactory` are standard properties that all JAXR vendors must support. There are actually several different standard properties you can use to configure the `ConnectionFactory`. These are listed in Table 16–1.

The `lifeCycleManagerURL` and `queryManagerURL` properties identify URLs of the Publishing and Inquiry Web services. The `authenticationMethod` can be one of a variety of values, but UBR registries use `UDDI_GET_AUTHTOKEN`, which indicates that an authorization token is to be passed with every Publishing operation (see Section 8.1.1: Authorization Operations for more details.) The `maxRows` property is pretty self-explanatory—you can limit the size of your result sets. The `postal AddressScheme` property is not covered in this book, but basically it sets the default structure of address values (U.S. address, Canadian address, and so on).[1]

Table 16–1 JAXR Standard Configuration Properties

JAXR Property Name	Description
`javax.xml.registry.lifeCycleManagerURL`	The URL of the UDDI's Publishing Web service.
`javax.xml.registry.queryManagerURL`	The URL of the UDDI's Inquiry Web service.
`javax.xml.registry.security.authenticationMethod`	The method of authentication used—the value allowed for UDDI is `UDDI_GET_AUTHTOKEN`.
`javax.xml.registry.uddi.maxRows`	The maximum number of rows to be returned by find operations.
`javax.xml.registry.postalAddressScheme`	The id of the `ClassificationScheme` (a `tModel`) that is used as the default address scheme for this connection.

[1] See the JAXR 1.0 specification for more details on the `postalAddressScheme` property; it's available at http://java.sun.com/xml/jaxr/index.html.

16.2.3 Connecting to the UDDI Registry

Once you've configured the `ConnectionFactory`, you can use it to create a `Connection` object, which represents a virtual connection to the UDDI directory.[2] UDDI SOAP messages use HTTP for inquiry and HTTPS for publishing—the inquiry SOAP messages are sent to the Inquiry URL while the publishing messages are sent to the Publishing URL. The following snippet from Listing 16–1 demonstrates how to create a Connection from a `ConnectionFactory`.

```
// Connect to UDDI test registry.
Connection connection = factory.createConnection();
```

That's pretty straightforward. You can also create a `FederatedConnection`, which can be used to query several different registries at the same time. To create a `FederatedConnection` you would first create two or more regular JAXR connections as above, then use those `Connection` objects to create a `Federated Connection` as shown in the following snippet.

```
Set connections = HashSet();
Connection con1 = factory1.createConnection();
connections.add(con1);
Connection con2 = factory2.createConnection();
connections.add(con2);
FederatedConnection federatedCon = factory3.createFederatedConnection( connections);
```

Once you have a `FederatedConnection`, search operations will be executed against all of the registries represented by the `FederatedConnection`—you'll be searching multiple registries at once. `FederatedConnection` objects are not covered further by this book for a couple of reasons: first, it's an optional feature that not all vendors will support; second, developers will rarely need to send the same query to multiple registries.

16.2.4 Authenticating to a UDDI Registry

Anyone can query the UBR at any operator site, but only registered users can publish data to the UBR. In order to register you have to browse the operator's UDDI Web site. Each operator site has different requirements for registering, but all basically request some information about you, including a user-id and password. The home pages of the operator sites where you can register were listed earlier in this chapter.

[2] UDDI uses HTTP, which is a "connectionless" protocol, meaning that TCP/IP connections are not actually maintained between requests. With every new request, a connection is formed temporarily, then dropped once the response is sent. That's why we say the JAXR `Connection` object represents a *virtual* connection.

Once you are registered with one of the UBR operators (IBM, Microsoft, SAP, or NTT) you can publish information to the UDDI registry. For this book I've used IBM's test registry—I suggest you do too, so that your practice sessions are consistent with mine. Once you are familiar with the JAXR, however, you can use any one of the operator sites, or a private UDDI registry.

If you're using JAXR from a J2EE component, then it's possible that your J2EE application server is configured to authenticate you automatically. This section assumes you have chosen to authenticate manually and will be passing the credentials for authentication explicitly in your code. You may not have to do it this way, provided your J2EE application server supports container-managed authentication with the JAXR provider. Consult your vendor's documentation to find out.

In order to execute publishing operations, which include adding, updating, and removing information in the UDDI directory, you'll need to authenticate (log in) to the registry. The following code from Listing 16–1 shows how to authenticate using a user name and password.

```
// Authenticate (log in) to the UDDI registry.
PasswordAuthentication credential =
        new PasswordAuthentication(userName, password.toCharArray());
Set credentials = new HashSet();
credentials.add(credential);
connection.setCredentials(credentials);
```

The `PasswordAuthentication` class is part of the Java Networking package (`java.net`). It provides a wrapper for a user name and password. Private UDDI registries may require a different kind of authentication. For example, if a registry mandates use of X.509 certificates, you must pass an instance of the `javax.security.auth.x500.X500PrivateCredential` class, which is part of the JAAS (Java Authentication and Authorization Service) API.

The use of Java security and JAAS to authenticate via X.509 credentials is too complex to cover here, but the following snippet of code gives you an idea of how it's done (the `KeyStore` represents a secure storage system for certificates and private keys).

```
// Authenticate using X.509 certificate
KeyStore ks = KeyStore.getInstance("JKS");
X509Certificate certificate = (X509Certificate)
                keyStore.getCertificate( userName );
PrivateKey privateKey = (PrivateKey)
                keyStore.getKey( userName, password.toCharArray());
X500PrivateCredential x500Credential =
                new X500PrivateCredential(certificate, privateKey);
Set credentials = new HashSet();
```

```
credentials.add(x500Credential);
connection.setCredentials(credentials);
```

16.2.5 Obtaining a JAXR Connection in J2EE

Up to this point we've focused mostly on non-J2EE JAXR clients. Standalone clients are the basis of all the examples in this part of the book because they are more focused and easier for you to work with. That said, this is a J2EE Web Services book, so some attention to the topic of accessing a JAXR `Connection` object from a J2EE component (such as an EJB, servlet, JSP, or JSE) is warranted.

For J2EE components you will access a JAXR `ConnectionFactory` from the component's JNDI Environment Naming Context (JNDI ENC), which is also used to access JAX-RPC endpoints, JDBC, JMS, J2EE Connectors, EJBs, and other resources. The following code snippet shows how a J2EE component would access a JAXR `ConnectionFactory` from the JNDI ENC.

```
InitialContext jndiEnc = new InitialContext();
ConnectionFactory factory = (ConnectionFactory)
   jndiEnc.lookup("java:comp/env/jaxr/UddiRegistry");
Connection connection = factory.createConnection();
...
```

From the component developer's perspective, accessing a UDDI connection may be easier in J2EE clients than in standalone applications, because you may not have to set the connection properties for Publishing and Inquiry APIs or authenticate explicitly. All that work is handled by the J2EE container system automatically. In addition, you won't need to close your connection explicitly, because the J2EE container manages the JAXR `Connection` objects automatically—but it's a good policy always to close your connections, even if you think the container will close them for you.

To use JAXR in J2EE you'll have to configure it as a resource in your component's deployment descriptor. The following snippet shows deployment descriptor elements used to configure JAXR for use in a JSE (JAX-RPC service endpoint).

```
<web-app>
    <display-name>SomeTypeOfJSE</display-name>
    ...
    <resource-ref>
         <res-ref-name>jaxr/UddiRegistry</res-ref-name>
         <res-type>javax.xml.registry.ConnectionFactory</res-type>
         <res-auth>Container</res-auth>
    </resource-ref>
  ...
```

The configuration of JAXR for other kinds of J2EE components looks the same as it does for this JSE. At deployment time the deployer will map the configuration properties for authentication and access to the Publishing and Inquiry APIs. The J2EE container will authenticate you automatically each time you use JAXR to access the Publishing API of a UDDI registry. How the deployer configures this information varies from one vendor to the next, as the interface for configuration of the properties in J2EE is not specified.

As you can see, there is not a whole lot to say about the J2EE support for JAXR other than that it may be easier from a developer's perspective. Remember that the examples in this chapter are for non-J2EE JAXR clients, so you need to configure and authenticate manually. The manner in which you create a `ConnectionFactory` and configure is the only difference between using JAXR from J2EE components and from non-J2EE components.

16.3 Using the `RegistryService` and `BusinessLifeCycleManager`

Once the connection is established and you are authenticated to the UDDI registry, you can obtain the `RegistryService` object, which represents the UDDI registry. You can then use the `RegistryService` object to get a reference to the `BusinessLifeCycleManager` object, which is used to add, modify, and delete information in the registry. In Listing 16–2, `JaxrExample_2` shows how to obtain the `RegistryService` and the `BusinessLifeCycleManager` objects, and create and save an `Organization` object in the UDDI registry.

Listing 16–2

Creating a new `Organization` *object*

```
package com.jwsbook.jaxr;
import javax.xml.registry.ConnectionFactory;
import javax.xml.registry.Connection;
import javax.xml.registry.RegistryService;
import javax.xml.registry.BusinessLifeCycleManager;
import javax.xml.registry.infomodel.Organization;
import javax.xml.registry.infomodel.InternationalString;
import javax.xml.registry.JAXRException;
import javax.xml.registry.JAXRResponse;
import javax.xml.registry.BulkResponse;
import java.net.PasswordAuthentication;
import java.util.Properties;
import java.util.Set;
import java.util.HashSet;
```

```
import java.util.Iterator;

public class JaxrExample_2 {
  public static void main(String [] args) throws JAXRException {
    // Extract parameters.
    String companyName = args[0];
    String userName = args[1];
    String password = args[2];
    // Connect to the UDDI registry and authenticate.
    Connection connection = connectToRegistry(userName,password);

    // Access the RegistryService and BusinessLifeCycle objects.
    RegistryService registry = connection.getRegistryService();
    BusinessLifeCycleManager lifeCycleMngr =
                            registry.getBusinessLifeCycleManager();

    // Create an Organization object and assign it a name.
    Organization myOrganization =
                lifeCycleMngr.createOrganization(companyName);

    // Save the Organization to the UDDI directory.
    Set organizationSet = new HashSet();
    organizationSet.add(myOrganization);
    BulkResponse response =
                lifeCycleMngr.saveOrganizations(organizationSet);

    // Check for registry exceptions.
    doExceptions(response);

    // Close connection.
    connection.close();
  }

  public static void doExceptions(BulkResponse rspns)
  throws JAXRException {
    if(rspns.getStatus()==JAXRResponse.STATUS_SUCCESS){
      System.out.println("\nProgram Complete: No problems reported!");
    }else {
      Iterator exceptions = rspns.getExceptions().iterator();
      while(exceptions.hasNext()){
        Exception je = (Exception)exceptions.next();
        System.out.println("\n***** BulkResponse Exceptions *****\n\n");
        je.printStackTrace();
```

```
            System.out.println("\n*********************************");
        }
      }
    }

    public static Connection connectToRegistry(String userName,
                                               String password)
    throws JAXRException {
        /* The code for this method is omitted for brevity. See
           Listing 16-1 for the implementation.*/
    }
}
```

From a command window, you can run `JaxrExample_2` as follows:

```
[prompt] java com.jwsbook.jaxr.JaxrExample_2 organizationName userName password
```

Make sure that the organization name doesn't include spaces, because in the command line a space is interpreted as a parameter separator. (Your command interpreter may let you use quotation marks to delimit a parameter that includes spaces.)

Don't concern yourself at the moment with the `BulkResponse` object or the `doExceptions()` method. I'll be covering use of `BulkResponse` in Section 16.4.

You can check to see whether your `Organization` was added to the UDDI registry by logging in to IBM's test registry and searching for the company you created. It's suggested that you keep track of the name you assigned your organization so that you can use it later—and when you are done with this part of the book you should delete your organization entry using the Web interface, to help keep the test registry as clean as possible.

If you are already logged in to the IBM test registry, the company may not show up on the default Publishing page until you log out and log back in.

16.3.1 The `RegistryService` Interface

The `RegistryService` is the principal interface in the JAXR API. The `RegistryService` represents the entire UDDI registry. You obtain it from the JAXR `Connection` object as in this snippet from `JaxrExample_2` (Listing 16–2).

```
// Access the RegistryService and BusinessLifeCycle objects.
RegistryService registry = connection.getRegistryService();
```

The `RegistryService` defines methods you can use to access different capabilities offered by a registry. Some of these methods can be used with UDDI and some cannot.

Listing 16–3 shows the RegistryService interface definition, which is followed by a short discussion of each method.

Listing 16–3

The javax.xml.registry.RegistryService *Interface*

```
package javax.xml.registry;
import java.util.*;
import javax.xml.registry.infomodel.*;

public interface RegistryService {
   // Returns the CapabilityProfile for the JAXR provider.
   CapabilityProfile getCapabilityProfile() throws JAXRException;

   // Returns the BusinessLifeCycleManager object.
   BusinessLifeCycleManager getBusinessLifeCycleManager()
     throws JAXRException;

   // Returns the BusinessQueryManager object.
   BusinessQueryManager getBusinessQueryManager() throws JAXRException;

   // This method is not applicable to UDDI.
   BulkResponse getBulkResponse(String requestId)
     throws InvalidRequestException, JAXRException;

   // Get the default postal scheme for PostalAddress.
   public ClassificationScheme getDefaultPostalScheme()  throws JAXRException;

   // This method sends an XML request in a registry-specific format.
   public String makeRegistrySpecificRequest(String request)
     throws JAXRException;
}
```

The getCapabilityProfile() method returns a CapabilityProfile object, which can tell you the JAXR specification version and the capability level (Level 0 or Level 1) of the JAXR provider.

The getBusinessLifeCycleManager() method returns a BusinessLifeCycleManager object, which you can use to add, modify, or delete information in the UDDI registry. Use of the BusinessLifeCycleManager is discussed in more detail shortly.

The getBusinessQueryManager() method returns a BusinessQueryManager object, which you can use to search for and retrieve information from the UDDI registry. The BusinessQueryManager is discussed in more detail in Chapter 19: The JAXR Inquiry and Publishing APIs.

The `getBulkResponse()` method is designed to access a response when asynchronous messaging is used. Because UDDI uses only Request/Response-style messaging, this method is not applicable to UDDI.

The `makeRegistrySpecificRequest()` method allows you to send an explicit XML document fragment in a SOAP message to the UDDI registry. This might be useful if the XML is already generated or if some facet of the request cannot be expressed using the JAXR API. The `Body` contents of the SOAP messages used in UDDI are detailed in Chapter 7: The UDDI Inquiry API.

The `RegistryService` also defines a method named `getDeclarativeQuery Manager()`, which facilitates sending dynamic queries to the registry in some type of declarative language (for example, SQL or OQL). This is a JAXR Level 1 method, however, that is not supported by UDDI because UDDI doesn't define a declarative query language.

16.3.2 Using the `BusinessLifeCycleManager`

When we discuss the functionality of the `BusinessLifeCycleManager`, we are, by extension, talking about the functionality of the `LifeCycleManager`, its superinterface. Many of the methods defined by `LifeCycleManager` are used to manufacture in-memory instances of JAXR information objects. The methods defined by the `BusinessLifeCycleManager` subtype are used to save, update, and delete information in the UDDI registry. A reference to the `BusinessLifeCycleManager` is obtained from the `RegistryService` object as shown in the following snippet from `JaxrExample_2` (Listing 16–2).

```
// Access the RegistryService and BusinessLifeCycle objects.
RegistryService registry = connection.getRegistryService();
BusinessLifeCycleManager lifeCycleMngr =
                              registry.getBusinessLifeCycleManager();
```

The next two sections examine the functionality defined by the `LifeCycle Manager` and the `BusinessLifeCycleManager`. Keep in mind that when you use a reference to a `BusinessLifeCycleManager`, you are also using a reference to a `LifeCycleManager`.

16.3.2.1 The `LifeCycleManager` *Interface*

The `LifeCycleManager` interface defines factory methods for creating instances of every type of information object, from `Organization` to `PersonName`. `Jaxr Example_2` (Listing 16–2) creates an `Organization` instance using one of the methods defined by the `LifeCycleManager` interface, as shown in the following snippet.

```
// Access the RegistryService and  BusinessLifeCycle objects.
RegistryService registry = connection.getRegistryService();
BusinessLifeCycleManager lifeCycleMngr =
```

```
                         registry.getBusinessLifeCycleManager();

// Create an Organization object and assign it a name.
Organization myOrganization =
            lifeCycleMngr.createOrganization(companyName);
```

When an information object (such as an `Organization`, `Service`, or `User`) is created by one of the `LifeCycleManager` factory methods, it is not automatically added to the UDDI registry; the factory methods simply instantiate the object type. An information object is not saved to the registry until you use the appropriate `saveXXX()` operation defined by the `BusinessLifeCycleManager` interface.

The ability to build an in-memory graph of JAXR objects and then save the entire graph to the registry with a single call is very convenient. It allows you to manipulate an entry without experiencing the latency of SOAP calls. Once the entry has been created or modified, you can save it to the UDDI registry. From the developer's perspective only one call to the registry is made, when the `saveXXX()` method is invoked. In reality, the JAXR provider may be using many different SOAP messages to update UDDI information, but all that work is done automatically when you call `saveXXX()`. Listing 16–4 shows the definition of the `LifeCycleManager` interface. All the methods defined by the `LifeCycleManager` are inherited by the `BusinessLifeCycleManager` interface. Some methods are overloaded, but for brevity I show only one signature for each method.

Listing 16–4

The `javax.xml.registry.LifeCycleManager` *Interface*

```
package javax.xml.registry;
import java.util.*;
import javax.xml.registry.infomodel.*;

public interface LifeCycleManager {

  // Create primary information objects.
  public Organization createOrganization(String name)
   throws JAXRException;
  public Service createService(String name) throws JAXRException;
  public ServiceBinding createServiceBinding() throws JAXRException;
  public Concept createConcept(RegistryObject parent,
                               InternationalString name,
                               String value) throws JAXRException;
  public Association createAssociation(RegistryObject targetObject,
                                       Concept associationType)
    throws JAXRException;
```

```
// Create demographic information objects.
public InternationalString createInternationalString(String s)
  throws JAXRException;
public LocalizedString createLocalizedString(Locale l,String s)
  throws JAXRException;
public User createUser() throws JAXRException;
public PersonName createPersonName(String fullName)
 throws JAXRException;
public EmailAddress createEmailAddress(String address)
 throws JAXRException;
public TelephoneNumber createTelephoneNumber() throws JAXRException;
public PostalAddress createPostalAddress(String streetNumber,
                                          String street,
                                          String city,
                                          String stateOrProvince,
                                          String country,
                                          String postalCode,
                                          String type)
 throws JAXRException;

// Creates taxonomy information objects.
public Classification createClassification(
                                        ClassificationScheme scheme,
                                         String name,String value)
 throws JAXRException;
public ClassificationScheme createClassificationScheme(
                                                     String name,
                                                     String description)
 throws JAXRException, InvalidRequestException;
public ExternalIdentifier createExternalIdentifier(
                        ClassificationScheme identificationScheme,
                        String name,String value)
 throws JAXRException;
public ExternalLink createExternalLink(String externalURI,
                                       String description)
 throws JAXRException;
public Slot createSlot(String name,String value,String slotType)
 throws JAXRException;
public SpecificationLink createSpecificationLink()
 throws JAXRException;

// General-purpose create, save, and delete methods.
public Object createObject(String interfaceName)
```

```
    throws JAXRException, InvalidRequestException,
          UnsupportedCapabilityException;
  BulkResponse saveObjects(Collection objects) throws JAXRException;
  BulkResponse deleteObjects(Collection keys) throws JAXRException;

  // Get a reference to the Registry Service.
  RegistryService getRegistryService() throws JAXRException;
}
```

You don't need to study these method definitions too closely; you'll be using most if not all of them in the following sections to create various JAXR information objects. As you can see, the methods have been divided up into general categories, including methods that create primary information objects, those that create taxonomy objects, and general-purpose save and delete operations. The `getRegistryService()` method provides access to the `RegistryService` that created the `LifeCycleManager`.

16.3.2.2 *The* `BusinessLifeCycleManager` *Interface*

You use the `BusinessLifeCycleManager` to add, update, and delete information in the UDDI registry. It represents the UDDI Publishing API discussed in detail in Chapter 8. It defines about a dozen methods, which can be used with a UDDI directory. These methods can be grouped into three general categories by their use: to add or update information objects; to delete information objects; to confirm and undo associations. Listing 16–5 shows the definition of the `BusinessLifeCycleManager` interface.

Listing 16–5

The `javax.xml.registry.BusinessLifeCycleManager` *Interface*

```
package javax.xml.registry;
import java.util.*;
import javax.xml.registry.infomodel.*;

public interface BusinessLifeCycleManager extends LifeCycleManager {

   // Add or update information objects in the UDDI registry.
   BulkResponse saveOrganizations(Collection organizations)
     throws JAXRException;
   BulkResponse saveServices(Collection services) throws JAXRException;
   BulkResponse saveServiceBindings(Collection bindings)
    throws JAXRException;
   BulkResponse saveConcepts(Collection concepts) throws JAXRException;
   BulkResponse saveClassificationSchemes(Collection schemes)
     throws JAXRException;
```

```
    BulkResponse saveAssociations(Collection associations,
                                  boolean replace)
      throws JAXRException;

    // Delete information objects from a UDDI registry.
    BulkResponse deleteOrganizations(Collection organizationKeys)
      throws JAXRException;
    BulkResponse deleteServices(Collection serviceKeys)
      throws JAXRException;
    BulkResponse deleteServiceBindings(Collection bindingKeys)
      throws JAXRException;
    BulkResponse deleteConcepts(Collection conceptKeys)
      throws JAXRException;
    BulkResponse deleteClassificationSchemes(Collection schemeKeys)
      throws JAXRException;
    BulkResponse deleteAssociations(Collection associationKeys)
      throws JAXRException;

    // Confirm/undo an association.
    public void confirmAssociation(Association assoc)
      throws JAXRException, InvalidRequestException;
    public void unConfirmAssociation(Association assoc)
      throws JAXRException, InvalidRequestException;
}
```

The saveXXX() methods defined in Listing 16–5 are used either to add a new information object to the UDDI registry, or to update an object already in the registry. In JaxrExample_2 (Listing 16–2) you used the saveOrganizations() method to add a new Organization to the UDDI registry. After you've added the Organization object to the registry, you must also save any subsequent changes to it, to keep the registry synchronized with the JAXR infomodel. For example, if you change the name of the Organization instance, you need to save that information for it to be updated in the UDDI registry. The following snippet illustrates how you might update and save an Organization object.

```
// Modify an Organization object.
InternationalString newName =
  lifeCycleMngr.createInternationalString("ACME Corperation");
organization.setName( newName );

// Update the UDDI registry.
Set organizationSet = new HashSet();
organizationSet.add(myOrganization);
BulkResponse response = lifeCycleMngr.saveOrganizations(organizationSet);
```

16.4 The `BulkResponse` Type

All of the `BusinessLifeCycleManager` save and delete methods (`saveOrganizations()`, `deleteOrganizations()`, and so on) return the `BulkResponse` type. So do most of the `BusinessQueryManager` type's `findXXX()` methods.

16.4.1 The `BulkResponse` Interface

The `BulkResponse` type is designed to carry a `Collection` of arbitrary values, the type of which depends on the method invoked. For example, the `BulkResponse` returned by the `BusinessQueryManager.findOrganizations()` method will contain a `Collection` of `Organization` objects. The `BulkResponse` returned by the `BusinessLifeCycleManager.saveOrganizations()` method, on the other hand, will contain a `Collection` of `Key` objects, one UUID key for each `Organization` that was saved. Listing 16–6 shows the definition of the `BulkResponse` type.

Listing 16–6

The `javax.xml.registry.BulkResponse` *Interface*

```
package javax.xml.registry;
import java.util.*;
import javax.xml.registry.infomodel.*;

public interface BulkResponse extends JAXRResponse {
   // Collection of objects returned as a response of a bulk operation.
   public Collection getCollection() throws JAXRException;

   // Collection of RegistryException instances for partial commit.
   public Collection getExceptions() throws JAXRException;

   // Determines this is a partial response due to large result set.
   public boolean isPartialResponse() throws JAXRException;
}
```

The `getExceptions()` method returns JAXR `RegistryException` types when the UDDI registry itself encounters an error. The `RegistryException` types contain codes that correspond to the UDDI SOAP fault message types, which are covered in Section 8.2: Fault Messages. There are three `RegistryException` subtypes: `SaveException`, `DeleteException`, and `FindException`. These correspond to the kind of method called. For example, `BusinessLifeCycle`

Manager.saveOrganizations() may return a BulkResponse containing one or more javax.xml.registry.SaveException types. Likewise, BusinessQueryManager.findOrganizations() might return a BulkResponse containing one or more javax.xml.registry.FindException types.

The isPartialResponse() method returns true when a BusinessQueryManager.findXXX() method produces a result set that is too large to return in full, and the BulkResponse contains only a portion of the results found by the query. The limit on results returned is determined by a policy set by the UDDI operator.

You can use the getStatus() method of the BulkResponse (declared by its supertype JAXRResponse) to determine whether the method performed successfully. The possible values for a UDDI registry are

- JAXRResponse.STATUS_SUCCESS
- JAXRResponse.STATUS_FAILURE

There are also JAXRResponse.STATUS_WARNING and JAXRResponse.STATUS_UNAVAILABLE values that don't apply to UDDI registries.

16.4.2 Handling the BulkResponse in Examples

Throughout this part of the book, all the example programs except JaxrExample_1 process the BulkResponse to determine whether the UDDI registry returned an exception. They do so by calling a doExceptions() method just before the connection is closed. The definition of this method is as follows:

```
public static void doExceptions(BulkResponse rspns) throws JAXRException {
  if(rspns.getStatus()==JAXRResponse.STATUS_SUCCESS){
     System.out.println("\nProgram Complete: No problems reported!");
  }else {
     Iterator exceptions = rspns.getExceptions().iterator();
     while(exceptions.hasNext()){
        Exception je = (Exception)exceptions.next();
        System.out.println("\n***** BulkResponse Exceptions *****\n\n");
        je.printStackTrace();
        System.out.println("\n**********************************");
     }
}
```

The purpose of this method is to display a stack trace for exceptions returned by the UDDI registry. If no exceptions are returned, the output is "Program Complete. No problems reported!" When you see this output, you know everything executed correctly.

16.5 Exceptions

The JAXR API has two mechanisms for returning exceptions. A method can throw them like any other exception, or return them in a `BulkResponse` object. Most of the JAXR `BusinessLifeCycleManager` and `BusinessQueryManager` return multiple results from a method. For example, `saveOrganizations()` returns a `Collection` of UUID `Key` objects, one for each `Organization` saved. When a JAXR Inquiry or Publishing method returns multiple results, it may return UDDI registry exceptions in a `Collection`, rather than just throw a single exception. These are accessed by calling `BulkResponse.getExceptions()`.

If, however, an abnormal condition is encountered by the client-side runtime of the JAXR implementation (for example, a `NullPointerException`), the method will throw a `JAXRException` instead of returning it in the `BulkResponse` object. In a nutshell, only SOAP faults generated by the UDDI registry are returned as exceptions in a `BulkResponse` object.

If the method returns only a single value (something other than `BulkResponse`), then all exceptions, even UDDI registry exceptions, are thrown directly from the method.

The UDDI registry exceptions are of type `javax.xml.registry.Registry Exception` or one of its subtypes: `SaveException`, `DeleteException`, and `FindException`. The messages returned with these exceptions provide fault codes and descriptions that correlate with the error codes shown in Table 8–3.

16.6 Wrapping Up

JAXR is not the only API for accessing a UDDI registry. IBM's open source UDDI4J (UDDI for Java) API and Systinet's WASP UDDI API are both examples of UDDI Java APIs. These alternatives offer a more UDDI-oriented interface, which can be advantageous if you are already familiar and comfortable with the UDDI data structures and programming APIs.

For developers not already steeped in UDDI, however, the JAXR API appears to be more intuitive and easier to use than other UDDI APIs. In addition, I believe that the JAXR API will be flexible enough to accommodate many of the changes UDDI is likely to undergo over the next couple of years—other APIs may be too brittle to accommodate changes easily because they are more tightly tied to the current UDDI programming model. Finally, JAXR is the only UDDI API that is actually a part of the J2EE platform, and for that reason alone it is likely to become the most popular Java UDDI API.

Chapter 17

The JAXR Business Objects

The purpose of JAXR is twofold: It models the data structures managed by ebXML and UDDI registries and it provides an API for searching registries and publishing data to registries. Because UDDI is the standard XML registry supported by the WS-I Basic Profile 1.0, and J2EE supports the BP, this chapter focuses on explaining the mapping between the JAXR information model and UDDI data structures (XML complex types).

> ***If you need JAXR to access an ebXML registry, you should consult the JAXR 1.0 specification available on Sun Microsystems' Web site.[1] You can also use the OASIS ebXML Registry Reference Implementation (ebxmlrr), an open source JAXR implementation for ebXML at SourceForge.[2]***

The JAXR information model was originally based on the ebXML data types and was later adapted to support UDDI. As a result you have to do some mental gymnastics to translate JAXR object types and fields into UDDI complex types and elements. This chapter and Chapter 18 will help you understand the mapping between the JAXR information model and the UDDI data structures. You don't need to study Chapter 6 in detail before reading this chapter, but occasionally you will need to refer to some of the material there to understand certain topics. I'll try to keep the shuffling between chapters to a minimum, but keep in mind that UDDI is a complex topic, which is why it required three chapters of its own.

[1] Java API for XML Registries, version 1.0, April 10, 2002, Appendix C: JAXR Mapping to ebXML Registry. Available at http://java.sun.com/xml/jaxr/index.html.

[2] See http://ebxmlrr.sourceforge.net/.

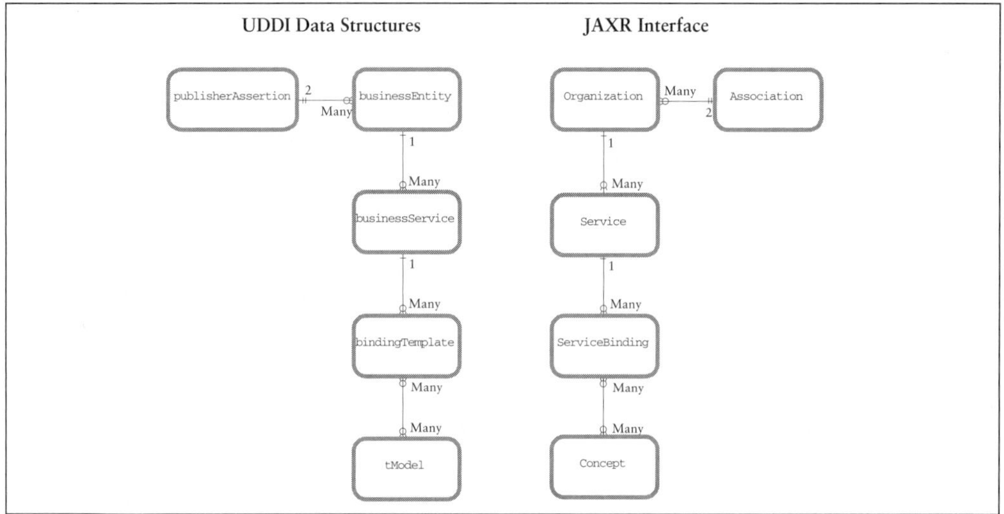

Figure 17–1 Mapping JAXR Object Types to UDDI Data Structures

Figure 17–1 is a visual representation of the mapping between the most significant UDDI data structures and JAXR object types. It's not a complete mapping, but it's a good start.

As you can see in the figure, the mapping between UDDI data structures and JAXR interface types is pretty easy to follow. The JAXR names are a little different (they're derived from ebXML), but the purposes of the types and their relationships are the same. As you get a little deeper into the fields of these types, you discover that JAXR has a richer, more object-oriented model than UDDI, because it must model both ebXML and UDDI.

I've broken this topic into two chapters according to the two types of data modeled by JAXR. This chapter covers those JAXR information objects that model business concepts: organization, contact, classification, and so on. Chapter 18 continues the discussion by covering those JAXR information objects that represent technical aspects of a Web service: protocol binding, specifications, and so on. The separation of topics is not perfect. For example, this chapter covers supertypes that are common to information objects discussed in both chapters. Similarly, Chapter 18 is primarily concerned with technical objects, but includes coverage of `Association`, which is a business type of object. It was more important to me to present the information model clearly than to be rigid about the categories.

The best way to understand the JAXR information model is to jump right in and examine the purposes and behavior of the different object types, starting with the ultimate base type, `RegistryObject`. This part of the book describes methods whose conformance is ranked Level 0 only, because these are the only methods applicable to UDDI. ebXML registries use both Level 0 and Level 1 methods.

17.1 The RegistryObject Interface

Most of the interfaces defined in the JAXR information model extend the javax.xml.registry.infomodel.RegistryObject interface. This interface defines about three dozen methods, only some of which are applicable to UDDI data types. Rather than waste your time talking about methods you may never use, I'll focus only on methods that apply to UDDI.

The RegistryObject methods that can be used with UDDI are typically get and set methods for accessing properties common to information objects, such as UUID, name, description, classification, external identifiers, and URLs. The usefulness and purpose of the various RegistryObject methods depends in large part on the type of information object on which they are invoked. Listing 17–1 is an abbreviated definition of the RegistryObject interface. It lists the basic properties that can be manipulated on a RegistryObject for a UDDI registry.

Listing 17–1

The javax.xml.registry.infomodel.RegistryObject *Interface*

```
package javax.xml.registry.infomodel;
import java.io.*;
import java.net.*;
import javax.xml.registry.*;
import java.util.*;

public interface RegistryObject extends ExtensibleObject  {

   //The universally unique ID (UUID) for this object.
   public Key getKey() throws JAXRException;
   public void setKey(Key key) throws JAXRException;

   //The name of this object.
   public InternationalString getName() throws JAXRException;
   public void setName(InternationalString name) throws JAXRException;

   //The text description for this object.
   public InternationalString getDescription() throws JAXRException;
   public void setDescription(InternationalString description)
    throws JAXRException;

   //The collection of Classifications for this object.
   public void setClassifications(Collection classifications)
    throws JAXRException;
```

```
    public Collection getClassifications() throws JAXRException;

    //The collection of ExternalIdentifiers for this object.
    public void setExternalIdentifiers(Collection externalIdentifiers)
     throws JAXRException;
    public Collection getExternalIdentifiers() throws JAXRException;

    //The collection of ExternalLinks for this object.
    public void setExternalLinks(Collection externalLinks)
     throws JAXRException;
    public Collection getExternalLinks() throws JAXRException;

    //The collection of Associations for this object.
    public void setAssociations(Collection associations)
     throws JAXRException;
    public Collection getAssociations() throws JAXRException;

    //The Organization that submitted this object.
    public Organization getSubmittingOrganization() throws JAXRException;

    //The LifeCycleManager that created this object.
    public LifeCycleManager getLifeCycleManager() throws JAXRException;
}
```

Rather than discuss each of these methods in the abstract, I'll introduce them in the context of the information objects in which they are used. The only methods discussed at this point are the `getKey()` and `setKey()` methods.

17.1.1 The UUID Key

The first time you save `RegistryObjects` of certain types (for example, `Organization` and `Concept`) to a UDDI registry, they will be assigned a **UUID** (Universally Unique Identifier) **key.** You can obtain the key the registry generated for an object by invoking `getKey()`. The circumstances under which you would use `setKey()` are pretty unusual; in most cases changing the key will cause an error, because the UUID must match an existing UUID of a UDDI data structure. The following snippet from Listing 17–1 shows the method signatures for the key property:

```
public interface RegistryObject extends ExtensibleObject  {

    //The universally unique ID (UUID) for this object.
    Key getKey() throws JAXRException;
    void setKey(Key key) throws JAXRException;
    ...
```

The JAXR object types that have a UUID key in UDDI are the following:

- `Organization`
- `Service`
- `ServiceBinding`
- `Concept`
- `ClassificationScheme`

Other `RegistryObject` types will also return a unique key, but those keys will be generated dynamically, and will represent a combination of other values relative to the object. These **faux keys** are considered "fake" because they have no real significance in the UDDI registry. They are generated to fill a gap between expected behavior of the JAXR API and the UDDI data model: JAXR requires every subtype of `RegistryObject` to return a key value when `getKey()` is invoked, but not all have genuine UUID keys they can return.[3] The following `RegistryObject` types return faux keys:

- `Association`
- `Classification`
- `ExternalIdentifier`
- `ExternalLink`
- `SpecificationLink`
- `User`

17.1.1.1 *Understanding UUIDs*

The primary data structures in UDDI all have UUID keys that are generated by the UDDI registry when an object is first added. The UUID is a hexadecimal-encoded number that is fairly long (about 30 characters), and is generated using a standard algorithm that will produce globally unique ids—there should not be duplicates even in other registries.[4] The following is an example of a UUID generated for an `Organization`—a subtype of the `RegistryObject`:

```
01B1FA80-2A15-11D7-9B59-000629DC0A53
```

The `Concept` and `ClassificationScheme` objects, which represent UDDI `tModels`, prefix their UUID values with the characters `uuid:`—the only infomodel types that do.

[3] The exact structure of faux keys is not specified, but the JAXR specification does suggest a convention that is detailed in Appendix D.11 of the specification, available at http://java.sun.com/xml/jaxr/index.html.

[4] The UUID algorithm is described in the ISO/IEC 11578:1996 standard, available at http://www.iso.ch.

17.1.1.2 *The* `Key` *Interface*

The UUID key property is based on the `javax.xml.registry.infomodel.Key` interface, which simply wraps around a `String` value. Listing 17–2 shows the definition of the `Key` type.

Listing 17–2

The `javax.xml.registry.infomodel.Key` *Interface*

```
package javax.xml.registry.infomodel;
import javax.xml.registry.*;

public interface Key {

  //Returns the UUID value of this key.
  public String getId() throws JAXRException;

  //Sets the UUID value associated with this key.
  public void setId(String id) throws JAXRException;
}
```

17.2 The `Organization` Information Object

The `Organization` object is the root of a UDDI business entry. It represents an instance of the UDDI `businessEntity` data structure discussed in Chapter 6: The UDDI Data Structures. In Chapter 16 the `JaxrExample_2` application created an `Organization`. This chapter too refers to `JaxrExample_2`, so its source code is reprinted in Listing 17–3 for your convenience.

Listing 17–3

Creating a new `Organization` *object*

```
package com.jwsbook.jaxr;
import javax.xml.registry.ConnectionFactory;
import javax.xml.registry.Connection;
import javax.xml.registry.RegistryService;
import javax.xml.registry.BusinessLifeCycleManager;
import javax.xml.registry.infomodel.Organization;
import javax.xml.registry.infomodel.InternationalString;
import javax.xml.registry.JAXRException;
import javax.xml.registry.JAXRResponse;
import javax.xml.registry.BulkResponse;
import java.net.PasswordAuthentication;
```

```
import java.util.Properties;
import java.util.Set;
import java.util.HashSet;
import java.util.Iterator;

public class JaxrExample_2 {
  public static void main(String [] args) throws JAXRException {
    // Extract parameters.
    String companyName = args[0];
    String userName = args[1];
    String password = args[2];

    // Connect to the UDDI registry and authenticate.
    Connection connection = connectToRegistry(userName,password);

    // Access the RegistryService and BusinessLifeCycle objects.
    RegistryService registry = connection.getRegistryService();
    BusinessLifeCycleManager lifeCycleMngr =
                              registry.getBusinessLifeCycleManager();

    // Create an Organization object and assign it a name.
    Organization myOrganization =
                 lifeCycleMngr.createOrganization(companyName);

    // Save the Organization to the UDDI directory.
    Set organizationSet = new HashSet();
    organizationSet.add(myOrganization);
    BulkResponse response =
                 lifeCycleMngr.saveOrganizations(organizationSet);

    // Check for registry exceptions.
    doExceptions(response);

    // Close the connection
    connection.close();
  }

  public static void doExceptions(BulkResponse rspns)
  throws JAXRException {
    if(rspns.getStatus()==JAXRResponse.STATUS_SUCCESS){
      System.out.println("\nProgram Complete: No problems reported!");
    }else {
      Iterator exceptions = rspns.getExceptions().iterator();
```

```
      while(exceptions.hasNext()){
        Exception je = (Exception)exceptions.next();
        System.out.println("\n***** BulkResponse Exceptions *****\n\n");
        je.printStackTrace();
        System.out.println("\n**********************************");
      }
    }
  }

  public static Connection connectToRegistry(String userName,
                                             String password)
  throws JAXRException {
    // Create a ConnectionFactory.
    ConnectionFactory factory = ConnectionFactory.newInstance();

    // Configure the ConnectionFactory.
    Properties props = new Properties();
    props.setProperty(
               "javax.xml.registry.lifeCycleManagerURL",
               "https://uddi.ibm.com/testregistry/publishapi");
    props.setProperty(
               "javax.xml.registry.queryManagerURL",
               "http://uddi.ibm.com/testregistry/inquiryapi");
    props.setProperty(
               "javax.xml.registry.security.authenticationMethod",
               "UDDI_GET_AUTHTOKEN");
    factory.setProperties(props);

    // Connect to UDDI test registry.
    Connection connection = factory.createConnection();

    // Authenticate (log in) to the Publishing endpoint.
    PasswordAuthentication credential =
      new PasswordAuthentication(userName, password.toCharArray());
    Set credentials = new HashSet();
    credentials.add(credential);
    connection.setCredentials(credentials);
    return connection;
  }
}
```

An `Organization` object contains a business name and description, contact information, industry categorizations and identification values, and a collection of zero or more BusinessService objects, each of which represents some type of electronic service—usually a Web service or Web site. JaxrExample_2 instantiates an instance of the Organization object with a specific company name and saves it to the UDDI registry:

```
// Create an Organization object and assign it a name.
Organization myOrganization =
            lifeCycleMngr.createOrganization(companyName);

// Save the Organization to the UDDI directory.
Set organizationSet = new HashSet();
organizationSet.add(myOrganization);
lifeCycleMngr.saveOrganizations(organizationSet);
```

The Organization interface defines about two dozen methods for adding information to and removing information from an Organization object. Not all of those methods are useful when working with a UDDI registry, however. Listing 17–4 shows the definition of the Organization interface, including only the methods that can be used with UDDI—ebXML-specific methods (Level 1) are omitted.

Listing 17–4

The javax.xml.registry.infomodel.Organization *Interface*

```
package javax.xml.registry.infomodel;
import javax.xml.registry.*;
import java.util.*;

public interface Organization extends RegistryObject {

    // User methods.
    public void addUser(User user) throws JAXRException;
    public void addUsers(Collection users) throws JAXRException;
    public void removeUser(User user) throws JAXRException;
    public void removeUsers(Collection users) throws JAXRException;
    public Collection getUsers() throws JAXRException;
    public User getPrimaryContact() throws JAXRException;
    public void setPrimaryContact(User primaryContact)
     throws JAXRException;

    // Service methods.
    public void addService(Service service) throws JAXRException;
    public void addServices(Collection services) throws JAXRException;
    public void removeService(Service service) throws JAXRException;
```

```
    public void removeServices(Collection services)
     throws JAXRException;
    public Collection getServices() throws JAXRException;
}
```

The `Organization` interface inherits the methods defined in its supertype, the `RegistryObject` interface, and makes use of some of them. These include accessor methods for name, description, external links, classifications, and external identifiers. These methods will be examined in detail in the sections to come. In addition, the `Organization` interface defines methods that fall into two categories: **user methods** and **service methods.**

User methods allow you to add, access, and remove `javax.xml.registry.infomodel.User` information objects to an `Organization` object. A `User` object represents a UDDI `contacts` element contained by a UDDI `businessEntity` data structure (see Section 6.1.5). Basically, the `User` object represents a contact person. An `Organization` may have one or more `User` objects, each of which represents a different kind of contact (technical support, sales, administration, and so on.) The `Organization` type also defines `setPrimaryContact()` and `getPrimaryContact()` methods, which have little meaning in UDDI. In ebXML there is the concept of a primary contact, but UDDI doesn't make such distinctions; when invoked, these methods simply operate on the first `User` in the collection of `User` objects in the `Organization`.

The service methods enable you to add, access, and remove `javax.xml.registry.infomodel.Service` objects. A `Service` object represents a UDDI `businessService` data structure (see Section 6.2). Each `Service` object represents some type of electronic service provided by the `Organization`, usually a Web page or a Web service.

17.2.1 `businessEntity`

It's important to remember that an `Organization` is simply an object representation of some type of data in a registry. In the case of UDDI, the `Organization` type corresponds to a data structure called `businessEntity`, which is defined by an XML schema as in Listing 17–5.

Listing 17–5

The XML Schema Type Definition for the UDDI `businessEntity` *Data Structure*

```
<schema targetNamespace="urn:uddi-org:api_v2"
            xmlns="http://www.w3.org/2001/XMLSchema"
            xmlns:uddi="urn:uddi-org:api_v2"
            version="2.03" id="uddi">
...
<element name="businessEntity" type="uddi:businessEntity"/>
```

```
<complexType name="businessEntity">
   <sequence>
      <element ref="uddi:discoveryURLs" minOccurs="0"/>
      <element ref="uddi:name" maxOccurs="unbounded"/>
      <element ref="uddi:description" minOccurs="0"
                                      maxOccurs="unbounded"/>
      <element ref="uddi:contacts" minOccurs="0"/>
      <element ref="uddi:businessServices" minOccurs="0"/>
      <element ref="uddi:identifierBag" minOccurs="0"/>
      <element ref="uddi:categoryBag" minOccurs="0"/>
   </sequence>
   <attribute name="businessKey" type="uddi:businessKey"
                  use="required"/>
   <attribute name="operator" type="string" use="optional"/>
   <attribute name="authorizedName" type="string" use="optional"/>
</complexType>
```

The `businessEntity` data structure is discussed in detail in Section 6.1. The data in the registry must adhere to this schema, but it may be stored in any format. Most UDDI registries use a relational database, but it's also possible to store the information in an object database or an XML database, among others. The rest of this section will address each of these elements (or fields), describing the methods used to access and modify them. Some of these methods are defined by the `Organization` interface, while others are inherited from the `Organization` interface's supertype, the `RegistryObject` interface.

17.2.2 `ExternalLinks`

The `externalLinks` property is a collection of `ExternalLink` objects, which wrap around URLs that point to information (resources) that is associated with the `Organization`, but outside the registry. UDDI operators are required to provide at least one `ExternalLink`, which points to the raw XML data that describes the underlying `businessEntity`.

Methods for adding, modifying, removing, and accessing `ExternalLink` objects are defined by `Organization`'s supertype, the `RegistryObject` interface, as shown in the expanded snippet from Listing 17–1.

```
public interface RegistryObject extends ExtensibleObject  {
   ...
   //The collection of ExternalLinks for this object.
   public void addExternalLink(ExternalLink externalLink)
    throws JAXRException;
   public void addExternalLinks(Collection externalLinks)
    throws JAXRException;
```

```
    public void removeExternalLink(ExternalLink externalLink)
     throws JAXRException;
    public void removeExternalLinks(Collection externalLinks)
     throws JAXRException;
    public void setExternalLinks(Collection externalLinks)
     throws JAXRException;
    public Collection getExternalLinks() throws JAXRException;
    ...
}
```

A UDDI `Organization` object may refer to basically two types of `ExternalLink` objects: a required `"businessEntity"` link and any number of optional `"businessEntityExt"` links. A `"businessEntity"` `ExternalLink` is generated every time you update an information object in the UDDI registry. You cannot remove or modify this `ExternalLink`—only the UDDI registry can alter its value. You can however, add other `ExternalLink` objects, labeled `"businessEntityExt"`, which point to non-UDDI documents that you believe should be associated with your `Organization`. For example, you might define an `ExternalLink` that points to a PDF document that describes your business. It's likely, however, that in the future standard, `"businessEntityExt"` `ExternalLink` objects will be defined by standards bodies (WS-I, ebXML, and RosettaNet, for example).

The `ExternalLink` labeled `"businessEntity"`, which is managed automatically by the UDDI registry, will be the first element in the collection of external links. You output the name and URL values of `ExternalLink` objects associated with a particular organization with code like the following:

```
java.util.Iterator externalLinks =
  organization.getExternalLinks().iterator();
while(externalLinks.hasNext()){
    ExternalLink link = (ExternalLink)externalLinks.next();
    System.out.print("ExternalLink type=");
    System.out.print(link.getName().getValue());
    System.out.println(link.getExternalURI());
}
```

You can add a `"businessEntityExt"` external link to an organization by creating an `ExternalLink` object, then adding it to the collection of external links, as in the following snippet:

```
ExternalLink myLink = lifeCycleManager.createExternalLink(
    "http://www.Monson-Haefel.com/jwsbook/MonsonHaefelBooks.doc","");
organization.addExternalLink( myLink );
```

When this code is executed, an external link will automatically be added as a "businessEntityExt" type. The second parameter in the createExternalLink() method allows you to assign a description to the ExternalLink, but the underlying UDDI data structure does not support a description, so any value you place there will be ignored. You cannot remove, modify, or replace the ExternalLink labeled "businessEntity" because it is maintained by the UDDI registry—attempts to modify it will be ignored or generate an exception.

17.2.2.1 *The* ExternalLink *Information Object*

When used with UDDI, an Organization's ExternalLink object maps to the discoveryURL element of a businessEntity data structure (see Section 6.1.2). An instance of a UDDI discoveryURL element might look like this:

```
<discoveryURLs>
  <discoveryURL useType="buinessEntity">
   http://uddi.ibm.com/registry/uddiget?businessKey=01B1FA80…00629DC0A53
  </discoveryURL>
</discoveryURLs>
```

The ExternalLink interface defines methods for accessing and setting the values of the discoveryURL and useType attributes. The getName() method returns the value of the useType attribute, which will be either "businessEntity" or "businessEntityExt". The getName() and setName() methods are defined by ExternalLink's supertype, RegistryObject. Listing 17–6 shows the definition of the ExternalLink interface.

Listing 17–6

The javax.xml.registry.infomodel.ExternalLink *Interface*

```
package javax.xml.registry.infomodel;

public interface ExternalLink extends RegistryObject, URIValidator {
  public String getExternalURI() throws JAXRException;
  public void setExternalURI(java.lang.String uri) throws JAXRException;
  public java.util.Collection getLinkedObjects() throws JAXRException;
}
```

The ExternalLink interface also defines a getLinkedObjects() method, which is not supported by the underlying UDDI; accessing this method will result in a javax.xml.registry.InvalidRequestException.

17.2.3 `Name` and `Description`

In `JaxrExample_2` (Listing 17–3) you created an `Organization` with a name. Although you specified the name as a simple `String` type, under the covers the JAXR provider assigned the name a default language designator. If you are using the English-language version of a Java Virtual Machine, for example, then the default language designator assigned to the name will be `"en"`, for "English."

An `Organization` may have multiple names and descriptions in different languages. You access these language-specific names and descriptions using methods defined by `RegistryObject`, shown in the following snippet from Listing 17–1.

```
public interface RegistryObject extends ExtensibleObject  {
  ...
  //The name of this object.
  public InternationalString getName() throws JAXRException;
  public void setName(InternationalString name) throws JAXRException;

  //The text description for this object.
  public InternationalString getDescription() throws JAXRException;
  public void setDescription(InternationalString description)
   throws JAXRException;
  ...
```

In a UDDI registry, these accessor methods allow you to modify the `business Entity`'s name and `description` elements (see Sections 6.1.3 and 6.1.4).

The `InternationalString` type, which is the parameter or return type of the methods that operate on names and descriptions, can represent several different language-specific text values. For example, you might provide descriptions for an `Organization` in French, Spanish, and English—all of these descriptions would be represented by a single `InternationalString` object, which is accessed by calling the `getDescription()` method.

17.2.3.1 The `InternationalString` *Interface*

JAXR models language-specific name and description properties using the `InternationalString` type, which associates each string of text with a specific `java.util.Locale` object. Listing 17–7 shows the definition of the `InternationalString` type.

Listing 17–7

The `javax.xml.registry.infomodel.InternationalString` *Interface*

```
package javax.xml.registry.infomodel;

import javax.xml.registry.*;
```

```
import java.util.*;

public interface InternationalString {
  //Get|Set the String value for the Virtual Machine's default Locale.
  public String getValue() throws JAXRException;
  public void setValue(String value) throws JAXRException;

  //Get|Set the String value for the specified Locale.
  public String getValue(Locale locale) throws JAXRException;
  public void setValue(Locale locale, String value)
   throws JAXRException;

  //Manage the collection of LocalizedString values.
  public Collection getLocalizedStrings() throws JAXRException;
  public void addLocalizedString(LocalizedString localizedString)
    throws JAXRException;
  public void addLocalizedStrings(Collection localizedStrings)
    throws JAXRException;
  public void removeLocalizedString(LocalizedString localizedString)
    throws JAXRException;
  public void removeLocalizedStrings(Collection localizedStrings)
    throws JAXRException;
  public LocalizedString getLocalizedString(Locale locale,
                                            String charsetName)
    throws JAXRException;

}
```

Language-specific text values are represented by `LocalizedString` objects. An `InternationalString` contains a `Collection` of zero or more `LocalizedString` objects.

17.2.3.2 The `LocalizedString` *Interface*

Each name or description in an `InternationalString` object is enclosed in a `LocalizedString` object, a wrapper that associates a `java.util.Locale` object with a `String` value. An instance of `java.util.Locale` represents a geographic, cultural, or political region (for example, the French-speaking area of Canada, or Simplified Chinese). The `LocalizedString` interface is defined in Listing 17–8.

Listing 17–8

The `javax.xml.registry.infomodel.LocalizedString` *Interface*

```
package javax.xml.registry.infomodel;
import javax.xml.registry.*;
```

```
import java.util.*;

public interface LocalizedString {
  public static final String DEFAULT_CHARSET_NAME = "UTF-8";

  // Get or Set the canonical name for the charset for this object.
  public String getCharsetName() throws JAXRException;
  public void setCharsetName(String charsetName) throws JAXRException;

  // Get or Set the Locale for this object.
  public getLocale() throws JAXRException;
  public void setLocale(Locale locale) throws JAXRException;

  // Get or Set the String value for this object.
  public String getValue() throws JAXRException;
  public void setValue(String value) throws JAXRException;
}
```

The character set used in UDDI is UTF-8. The `value` property is the actual `String` value of the `LocalizedString` object, and the `Locale` provides its linguistic context.

17.2.3.3 *Working with* `InternationalString` *Objects*

You create an `InternationalString` using a `LifeCycleManager` object. Listing 17–9 shows how to create an `InternationalString` object with descriptions in English, French, and Spanish. It also shows how to set an `InternationalString` object as the description of an `Organization` object.

Listing 17–9

Creating an `InternationalString` *Object*

```
LocalizedString  english = lifeCycleManager.createLocalizedString(
                                      Locale.ENGLISH,
                                     "Technical book wholesaler");
LocalizedString  french = lifeCycleManager.createLocalizedString(
                                      Locale.FRENCH,
                                     "Un grossiste technique de livre");
LocalizedString  spanish = lifeCycleManager.createLocalizedString(
                                      new Locale("es", ""),
                                     "Un mayorista técnico del libro");
InternationalString descript =
  lifeCycleManager.createInternationalString();
```

```
descript.addLocalizedString(english);
descript.addLocalizedString(french);
descript.addLocalizedString(spanish);

organization.setDescription(descript);
```

The `java.util.Locale` type declares constant language and country codes for some languages and countries, but not all. Notice that the English and French descriptions were created using the `Locale.ENGLISH` and `Locale.FRENCH` constants, while the Spanish description required that a new `Locale` object be created using a two-letter language code. The codes for languages and countries are based on the legal values of the `xml:lang` attribute.[5] In Listing 17–9 we did not specify a country code for the Spanish description, only a language code. You are allowed to omit a country designator by simply making the second parameter of the `Locale` constructor an empty string (`""`).

The `Locale` object associated with each `LocalizedString` provides an easy mechanism for accessing only those names or descriptions relevant to you. For example, you can access the English-language version of an organization's description as in the following code snippet.

```
InternationalString descriptions = organization.getDescription();
LocalizedString englishString =
   descriptions.getLocalizedString(java.util.Locale.ENGLISH , "UTF-8");
if(englishString != null){
   String englishDescription = englishString.getValue();
}
```

If the `InternationalString` does not contain a `LocalizedString` value that matches the `Locale` specified, the `getLocalizedString()` method will return a `null`. UDDI `description` elements are required to have a language identifier, but `name` elements are not. As a result, `name` elements frequently don't have a language identifier, so even if the name is in English it might not be tagged as such. The method in Listing 17–10 will print out all the `LocalizedString` objects contained by an `InternationalString`.

Listing 17–10

Accessing All of the `LocalizedStrings` *Contained by an* `InternationalString`

```
public static void printInternationalString(InternationalString interString)
throws JAXRException{
```

[5] Legal values are specified in the IETF standard RFC 1766 and its successors (recently, RFC 3066), which are based in part on ISO 639:1988.

```
    Iterator names = interString.getLocalizedStrings().iterator();
    while(names.hasNext()){
        LocalizedString name = (LocalizedString)names.next();
        System.out.println(name.getValue());
    }
}
```

17.2.4 `User`

An organization may have zero or more `java.xml.registry.infomodel.User` objects, which represent people that can be contacted by postal mail, phone, or e-mail. These people might provide technical support, sales information, administrative services, or any other service an organization wants to make accessible. In a UDDI registry, the collection of `User` objects is represented by a `contacts` element (see Section 6.1.5). The definition of the `User` type is shown in Listing 17–11.

Listing 17–11

The `javax.xml.registry.infomodel.User` *Interface*

```
package javax.xml.registry.infomodel;
import java.net.*;
import javax.xml.registry.*;
import java.util.*;

public interface User extends RegistryObject {
    // Gets the Organization that this User is affiliated with.
    Organization getOrganization() throws JAXRException;

    // Get|Set the name of this User.
    public PersonName getPersonName() throws JAXRException;
    public void setPersonName(PersonName personName)
     throws JAXRException;

    // Get|Set the postal address for this User.
    public Collection getPostalAddresses() throws JAXRException;
    public void setPostalAddresses(Collection addresses)
     throws JAXRException;

    // Get|Set telephone numbers of the specified type.
    public Collection getTelephoneNumbers(String phoneType)
      throws JAXRException;
    public void setTelephoneNumbers(Collection phoneNumbers)
      throws JAXRException;
```

```
    // Get|Set the e-mail addresses for this User.
    public Collection getEmailAddresses() throws JAXRException;
    public void setEmailAddresses(Collection emailAddresses)
      throws JAXRException;

    // Get|Set the type for this User.
    public String getType() throws JAXRException;
    public void setType(String type) throws JAXRException;
}
```

Unfortunately, the `User` type doesn't map exactly to a UDDI `contact` element. As a matter of fact, there are a couple of Level 0 methods in `User` that do not work with UDDI. In addition, there is a significant misalignment between the `PostalAddress` JAXR type and the UDDI `address` element contained by the `contact` element. While these incongruities can be inconvenient, the JAXR specification does provide guidance for working around these differences.

In Listing 17–12, `JaxrExample_3` creates a new `Organization` and assigns it a `User` object that represents the technical-support contact for your Web services.

Listing 17–12

Assigning a `User` *Object to an* `Organization`

```
package com.jwsbook.jaxr;
import javax.xml.registry.ConnectionFactory;
import javax.xml.registry.Connection;
import javax.xml.registry.RegistryService;
import javax.xml.registry.BusinessLifeCycleManager;
import javax.xml.registry.infomodel.Organization;
import javax.xml.registry.infomodel.User;
import javax.xml.registry.infomodel.PersonName;
import javax.xml.registry.infomodel.EmailAddress;
import javax.xml.registry.infomodel.TelephoneNumber;
import javax.xml.registry.infomodel.PostalAddress;
import javax.xml.registry.infomodel.InternationalString;
import javax.xml.registry.infomodel.LocalizedString;
import javax.xml.registry.infomodel.Slot;
import javax.xml.registry.JAXRException;
import javax.xml.registry.BulkResponse;
import javax.xml.registry.JAXRResponse;
import java.util.Iterator;
import java.net.PasswordAuthentication;
import java.util.Properties;
import java.util.Set;
```

```
import java.util.Collection;
import java.util.HashSet;
import java.util.Locale;

public class JaxrExample_3 {
  public static void main(String [] args) throws JAXRException {
     // Extract parameters.
     String companyName = args[0];
     String userName = args[1];
     String password = args[2];

     // Access the BusinessLifeCycle object.
     Connection connection = connectToRegistry(userName,password);
     RegistryService registry = connection.getRegistryService();
     BusinessLifeCycleManager lifeCycleMngr =
                              registry.getBusinessLifeCycleManager();

     // Create an Organization object and assign it a name.
     Organization myOrganization =
                  lifeCycleMngr.createOrganization(companyName);

     // Create a new User object and add it to the Organization.
     User contact = lifeCycleMngr.createUser();
     myOrganization.addUser(contact);

     // Set the User's name.
     PersonName contactName = lifeCycleMngr.createPersonName(
                                                 "Stanley Kubrick");
     contact.setPersonName(contactName);

     // Set the English and French descriptions of the User.
     LocalizedString  english = lifeCycleMngr.createLocalizedString(
                                  Locale.ENGLISH,
                                 "Web Services Technical Support");
     LocalizedString  french = lifeCycleMngr.createLocalizedString(
                                  Locale.FRENCH,
                                 "Web Services le Soutien de Technial");
     InternationalString descript =
       lifeCycleMngr.createInternationalString();
     descript.addLocalizedString(english);
     descript.addLocalizedString(french);
     contact.setDescription(descript);
```

```
        // Set the User's e-mail addresses.
        EmailAddress email = lifeCycleMngr.createEmailAddress(
                             "Stanley.Kubrick@"+companyName+".com");
        Collection emails = new HashSet();
        emails.add(email);
        contact.setEmailAddresses(emails);

        // Set the User's telephone numbers.
        TelephoneNumber phone = lifeCycleMngr.createTelephoneNumber();
        phone.setNumber("01-555-222-4000");
        phone.setType("Voice");
        Collection phones = new HashSet();
        phones.add(phone);
        contact.setTelephoneNumbers(phones);

        // Set the User's postal address.
        PostalAddress address = lifeCycleMngr.createPostalAddress(
                                        "2001","Odyssey Ave.",
                                        "Galaxy","CA","USA","91223",
                                        "TechSupport");
        Collection addresses = new HashSet();
        addresses.add(address);
        contact.setPostalAddresses(addresses);

        // Save the Organization to the UDDI directory.
        Set organizationSet = new HashSet();
        organizationSet.add(myOrganization);
        BulkResponse response =
          lifeCycleMngr.saveOrganizations(organizationSet);

        // Check for registry exceptions.
        doExceptions(response);

        // Close connection.
        connection.close();
    }
    public static void doExceptions(BulkResponse rspns)
    throws JAXRException {
     /* The code for this method is omitted for brevity. See
     JaxrExample_2 (Listing 17-3) for a complete listing of this method.*/
    }
    public static Connection connectToRegistry(String userName,
                                               String password)
```

```
    throws JAXRException {
     /* The code for this method is omitted for brevity. See
     JaxrExample_2 (Listing 17-3) for a complete listing of this method.*/
    }
}
```

If you haven't done so already, I suggest you go to IBM's UDDI test Web site, sign in, and delete the organization you created in `JaxrExample_2` before running `JaxrExample_3`, to help keep the test registry as clean as possible. To run `JaxrExample_3` from a command window, execute a command in the following format:

```
[prompt] java com.jwsbook.jaxr.JaxrExample_3 organizationName userName password
```

Make sure that the organization name doesn't include spaces, because the Java VM interprets a space as a parameter separator.

If all goes well, you will find the `Organization` and contact information you created in the IBM test registry.

If you're already logged in to the IBM test registry, the company may not show up on the default Publishing page until you log out and log back in.

`JaxrExample_3` creates an `Organization` and a `User` information object. After the `User` object is added to the `Organization`, its attributes for person name, e-mail, telephone, and postal address are set. Finally the `Organization` is saved to the UDDI registry. `JaxrExample_3` may look complicated, but it's not. We'll examine each of the steps involved in creating and configuring a `User` object in the next few sections.

17.2.4.1 Creating a New `User` *Object*

The `BusinessLifeCycleManager` is used to create a `User` object, by invoking its `createUser()` method as in the following snippet from `JaxrExample_3` (Listing 17–12).

```
// Create a new User object and add it to the Organization.
User contact = lifeCycleMngr.createUser();
myOrganization.addUser(contact);
```

Initially the `User` object is a blank slate without any data, but once it's created we can use its accessor methods to add a person's name, e-mail addresses, telephone numbers, and postal address. A `User` object cannot be saved in a UDDI directory by itself; it must be added to an `Organization` object. The last line in the previous snippet does so by calling the `addUser()` method. An `Organization` may have many `Users` but one of them will be identified as the **Primary Contact.** UDDI doesn't actually support this concept; it's only an artificial label assigned by JAXR to the first contact element in the list of contact elements owned by the corresponding businessEntity data structure. Instead of calling addUser(), you could have invoked the setPrimaryContact() method as in the following example.

```
// Create a new User object and add it to Organization.
User contact = lifeCycleMngr.createUser();
myOrganization.setPrimaryContact(contact);
```

Only one User should be designated the Primary Contact, so if you have more than one contact person, it's better to add them with addUser() than with set PrimaryContext()—which could displace a User object previously designated the Primary Contact.

17.2.4.2 Setting a Person's Name

Every contact person should have a name. A person's name is not usually subject to translation in other languages—my name is always Richard Monson-Haefel no matter which language you are speaking—so the personName property of the User type doesn't support the concept of multiple language-specific names. This parallels the UDDI personName element in UDDI; it doesn't declare an xml:lang designator.

Because the User type's name property isn't specific to any language, it's very easy to create. You just call the BusinessLifeCycleManager.createPersonName() method, as shown in the following snippet from JaxrExample_3 (Listing 17–12).

```
// Set the User's name.
PersonName contactName = lifeCycleMngr.createPersonName(
                                          "Stanley Kubrick");
contact.setPersonName(contactName);
```

The PersonName type defines methods for accessing the first, middle, and last names of the contact as well as the combined full name. The UDDI personName element is a single field that does not break down into first, middle, and last names—there is only the full name. As a result, only the getFullName() method of the PersonName can be called when using a UDDI registry; the other methods (get FirstName(), setFirstName(), getLastName(), setLastName(), getMiddle Name(), and setMiddleName()) will throw a javax.xml.registry.Unsupported CapabilityException. You can access the name of a contact person as in this snippet.

```
String fullName = contactName.getFullName();
```

17.2.4.3 Adding Descriptions

A contact may have one or more language-specific descriptions, which are created using the InternationalString type discussed earlier, in Section 17.2.3. In

JaxrExample_3 (Listing 17–12) two descriptions—one in French and the other in English—are added to the User object.

```
// Set the English and French descriptions of the User.
LocalizedString  english = lifeCycleMngr.createLocalizedString(
                              Locale.ENGLISH,
                             "Web Services Technical Support");
LocalizedString  french = lifeCycleMngr.createLocalizedString(
                              Locale.FRENCH,
                             "Web Services le Soutien de Technial");
InternationalString descript =
   lifeCycleMngr.createInternationalString();
descript.addLocalizedString(english);
descript.addLocalizedString(french);
contact.setDescription(descript);
```

17.2.4.4 Adding E-Mail Addresses

A contact person may have one or more e-mail addresses, which are treated as a collection even if there is only one address. The following snippet from JaxrExample_3 (Listing 17–12) shows how to create an EmailAddress object and add it to the User object. Notice that the EmailAddress object must be placed into a java.util.Collection object to be added to the User.

```
// Set the User's e-mail addresses.
EmailAddress email = lifeCycleMngr.createEmailAddress(
                         "Stanley.Kubrick@"+companyName+".com");
Collection emails = new HashSet();
emails.add(email);
contact.setEmailAddresses(emails);
```

Having to create a Collection object when you have only one e-mail address is needlessly awkward. The API would be well served if it included an addEmailAddress() method. JAXR uses this Collection-only method idiom for accessing many of the information-model types.

The EmailAddress interface has a very simple definition, as shown in Listing 17–13.

Listing 17–13

The javax.xml.registry.infomodel.EmailAddress *Interface*

```
package javax.xml.registry.infomodel;
import javax.xml.registry.*;
```

```
public interface EmailAddress {
   // Get|Set the e-mail address for this object.
   public String getAddress() throws JAXRException;
   public void setAddress(String address) throws JAXRException;

   // Get|Set the type of e-mail address.
   public String getType() throws JAXRException;
   public void setType(String type) throws JAXRException;
}
```

The `address` property is the actual `String` value of the e-mail address. The `type` property maps to the `useType` attribute in the UDDI `email` element type. The proper values for the `type` property are not specified, but it could designate the purpose of the e-mail address (for example, "Technical Support" or "Sales"). The `type` property isn't required for e-mail addresses, so leaving it blank is fine.

17.2.4.5 Adding Phone Numbers

A contact person may have multiple phone numbers, each of which is represented by a `TelephoneNumber` object. Like `EmailAddress` objects, the `TelephoneNumber` objects are accessed by way of a `java.util.Collection`—you cannot add or remove an individual `TelephoneNumber` directly. The following snippet from `JaxrExample_3` (Listing 17–12) shows how to create a `TelephoneNumber` and add it to a `User` object.

```
// Set the User's telephone numbers.
TelephoneNumber phone = lifeCycleMngr.createTelephoneNumber();
phone.setNumber("01-555-222-4000");
phone.setType("Voice");
Collection phones = new HashSet();
phones.add(phone);
contact.setTelephoneNumbers(phones);
```

The `TelephoneNumber` interface, shown in Listing 17–14, actually defines several methods for accessing subparts of a phone number: country code, area code, number, and extension. In UDDI, however, a phone number is represented by the `phone` element, which is a simple `xsd:string` type with a `useType` attribute—it's not broken down into subparts—so most of the accessors in `TelephoneNumber` are not applicable to UDDI. The only accessors that do work are the `getNumber()` and `setNumber()` methods, which expect or return the `String` value of the entire telephone number. You can also use the `getType()` and `setType()` methods to get and set the `useType` of the phone number (voice, fax, or mobile, for example). There are no standardized values for `useType`; any string value can be used.

Listing 17–14

The `javax.xml.registry.infomodel.TelephoneNumber` *Interface*

```
package javax.xml.registry.infomodel;
import javax.xml.registry.*;

public interface TelephoneNumber {

    // Get|Set the entire telephone number.
    public String getNumber() throws JAXRException;
    public void setNumber(String number) throws JAXRException;

    // Get|Set the type of telephone number: "voice", "fax", etc.
    public String getType() throws JAXRException;
    public void setType(String type) throws JAXRException;

    // These methods are Level 1 and cannot be used with UDDI:
    public String getCountryCode() throws JAXRException;
    public String getAreaCode() throws JAXRException;
    public String getExtension() throws JAXRException;
    public String getUrl() throws JAXRException;
    public void setCountryCode(String countryCode) throws JAXRException;
    public void setAreaCode(String areaCode) throws JAXRException;
    public void setExtension(String extension) throws JAXRException;
    public void setUrl(String url) throws JAXRException;
}
```

17.2.4.6 Adding a Postal Address

A contact person may have multiple postal addresses, which are maintained in a collection, just as e-mail and telephone numbers are. In the JAXR information model, the `javax.xml.registry.infomodel.PostalAddress` type represents a postal address. The following snippet from `JaxrExample_3` (Listing 17–12) shows how to create and add a `PostalAddress` object to a `User`.

```
// Set the User's postal address.
PostalAddress address = lifeCycleMngr.createPostalAddress(
                                      "2001","Odyssey Ave.",
                                      "Galaxy","CA","USA","91223",
                                      "TechSupport");
Collection addresses = new HashSet();
addresses.add(address);
contact.setPostalAddresses(addresses);
```

The PostalAddress type assumes that an address has six address-specific properties: street number, street, city, state or province, country, and postal code. This is a fairly standard structure for addresses, but UDDI provides no native support for it. In UDDI an address is a simple list of addressLine elements, which are based on an extension of the xsd:string type. When JaxrExample_3 saves in the UDDI registry the PostalAddress object it created, each of the address properties (streetNumber, street, etc.) is placed on its own line, so that in UDDI it's structured as follows:

```
<contacts>
  <contact useType="TechSupport" >
    <personName>Stanley Kubrick</personName>
    ...
    <address>
      <addressLine>2001</addressLine>
      <addressLine>Odyssey Ave.</addressLine>
      <addressLine>Galaxy</addressLine>
      <addressLine>CA</addressLine>
      <addressLine>USA</addressLine>
      <addressLine>91223</addressLine>
    </address>
  </contact>
</contacts>
```

This format, where each address element is on its own line, is not the normal convention for U.S. addresses. Usually the street number and street are on the first line, the city, state, and zip code are on the second line, and the country name is on the third line. Other countries use their own formats. It would be better if the address information were stored as in the following listing:

```
<contacts>
  <contact useType="TechSupport" >
    <description xml:lang="en">Web Service Tech. Support</description>
    <personName>Stanley Kubrick</personName>
    ...
    <address>
      <addressLine>2001 Odyssey Ave.</addressLine>
      <addressLine>Galaxy, CA 91223</addressLine>
      <addressLine>USA</addressLine>
    </address>
  </contact>
</contacts>
```

There is a misalignment between the JAXR view of an address and the UDDI view. JAXR's `PostalAddress` assumes a certain structure, while UDDI's `address` does not. When you save a `PostalAddress` object, each property will appear in a different `addressLine` element. This arrangement makes the address kind of difficult to read. The workaround is to use the `createObject()` method and `Slot` objects, as in Listing 17–15.

Listing 17–15

Creating a Postal Address with `Slot` *Objects*

```
// Create an addressLines Slot.
Slot addressLines  = (Slot)
   blm.createObject(LifeCycleManager.SLOT);
addressLines.setName("addressLines");

// Create and add address lines to the Slot.
Collection addressValues = new ArrayList();
addressValues.add("2001 Odyssey Ave.");
addressValues.add("Galacy, CA 91223");
addressValues.add("USA");

addressLines.setValues(addressValues);
addressLines.setSlotType(null);

// Create an empty PostalAddress.
PostalAddress address = (PostalAddress)
   blm.createObject(LifeCycleManager.POSTAL_ADDRESS);

// Add the Slot to the PostalAddress.
address.addSlot(addressLines);
```

The `Slot` objects are mapped directly to the UDDI `addressLine` elements. The use of the `Slot` type and its enabling interface, `ExtensibleObject`, are covered in more detail later.

UDDI has a concept called a `tModel`, which stands for "technical model" or "type model" (see Section 6.3), which allows you to assign a schema to certain data structures, including the UDDI `address` element. You can assign an entire `address` to a specific `tModel`, then identify each address line as adhering to a specific element of that `tModel`. The schema described by the `tModel` defines how an address of a certain type (for example, U.S., Canadian, or Japanese) should be structured. Oddly enough, no one has defined a standard set of address `tModels` for UDDI, which means that developers will be using their own `tModel` schemas to define an address or no `tModel` at all.

17.2.5 Classification

The `RegistryObject` defines six methods for setting, getting, adding, and removing one or more `Classification` objects. The following snippet shows all of the `Classification` accessor methods defined by `RegistryObject` in Listing 17–1.

```
public interface RegistryObject extends ExtensibleObject  {
   ...
   //The collection of Classifications for this object.
   public void setClassifications(Collection classifications)
    throws JAXRException;
   public Collection getClassifications() throws JAXRException;
   public void addClassification(Classification classification)
    throws JAXRException;
   public void addClassifications(Collection classifications)
    throws JAXRException;
   public void removeClassification(Classification classification)
    throws JAXRException;
   public void removeClassifications(Collection classifications)
    throws JAXRException;
   ...
```

17.2.5.1 The Standard UDDI Classifications

Biologists classify living things by the structure of their bodies into a **taxonomy,** a hierarchy of categories: kingdom, phylum, class, order, family, genus, and species. In registry systems entries can also be classified with some type of taxonomy or system of categorization. There are three standard classification systems used in UDDI to categorize industries, products and services, and geographic locations. These categorizations can be associated with organizations and other JAXR types, to make finding particular kinds of businesses easier. You can, for example, search for all the organizations that are wholesalers, or manufacturers of toys, or mining companies, or accounting firms. There are many different types of taxonomies that can be used today, but UDDI specifically requires support for three of them:

1. **NAICS** (North American Industry Classification System) classifies businesses in Canada, the United States, and Mexico according to business type (Wholesaler, Health Care, and so on).
2. **UNSPSC** (Universal Standard Products and Services Classification) provides a global classification system for products and services (books, toys, and so on).
3. **ISO 3166** is a geographic locator system that identifies both the country and region (city, state, principality, and so on) in which a business is located (for example: US-MN = United States, Minnesota; FR-A = France, Alsace).

More detailed definitions of these systems can be found in Section 6.1.8.

One or more of the standard classifications can be added to certain UDDI types, including `Organization`, `Service`, and `Concept`. `JaxrExample_4` (Listing 17–16) demonstrates how standard classifications can be added to the `Organization` you generated in `JaxrExample_3` (Listing 17–12).

Listing 17–16

Adding Classifications to an `Organization`

```
package com.jwsbook.jaxr;
import javax.xml.registry.ConnectionFactory;
import javax.xml.registry.Connection;
import javax.xml.registry.RegistryService;
import javax.xml.registry.LifeCycleManager;
import javax.xml.registry.BusinessLifeCycleManager;
import javax.xml.registry.BusinessQueryManager;
import javax.xml.registry.infomodel.ClassificationScheme;
import javax.xml.registry.infomodel.Classification;
import javax.xml.registry.infomodel.Organization;
import javax.xml.registry.BulkResponse;
import javax.xml.registry.JAXRResponse;
import javax.xml.registry.JAXRException;
import java.net.PasswordAuthentication;
import java.util.Properties;
import java.util.Set;
import java.util.Collection;
import java.util.HashSet;
import java.util.Iterator;


public class JaxrExample_4 {
  public static void main(String [] args) throws JAXRException {
    // Extract parameters.
    String companyKey = args[0];
    String userName = args[1];
    String password = args[2];

    // Access BusinessLifeCycleManager and BusinessQueryManager object.
    Connection connection = connectToRegistry(userName,password);
    RegistryService registry = connection.getRegistryService();
    BusinessLifeCycleManager lifeCycleMngr =
                             registry.getBusinessLifeCycleManager();
    BusinessQueryManager queryMngr = registry.getBusinessQueryManager();
```

```
// Find my Organization by its Key.
Organization myOrganization = (Organization)
   queryMngr.getRegistryObject(companyKey.trim(),
                              LifeCycleManager.ORGANIZATION);

// Create a Classification object for a NAICS value.
ClassificationScheme naics_Scheme =
  queryMngr.findClassificationSchemeByName(null, "ntis-gov:naics");
Classification naics_BookWhslrClass =
  lifeCycleMngr.createClassification(naics_Scheme,
                                  "Book Wholesaler", "42292");

// Create a Classification object for a UNSPSC value.
ClassificationScheme unspsc_Scheme =
  queryMngr.findClassificationSchemeByName(null,
                                       "unspsc-org:unspsc");
Classification unspsc_TextBookClass =
   lifeCycleMngr.createClassification(unspsc_Scheme,
                                   "TextBook", "55.10.15.09");

// Create a Classification object for an ISO 3166 value.
ClassificationScheme iso3166_Scheme =
   queryMngr.findClassificationSchemeByName(null,
                                  "uddi-org:iso-ch:3166:1999");
Classification iso3166_MinnesotaClass =
   lifeCycleMngr.createClassification(iso3166_Scheme,
                                   "Minnesota, USA", "US-CA");


// Add Classifications to my Organization.
Collection classifications = new HashSet();
classifications.add(naics_BookWhslrClass);
classifications.add(unspsc_TextBookClass);
classifications.add(iso3166_MinnesotaClass);
myOrganization.addClassifications(classifications);

// Save the Organization to the UDDI directory.
Set organizationSet = new HashSet();
organizationSet.add(myOrganization);
BulkResponse response =
  lifeCycleMngr.saveOrganizations(organizationSet);

// Check for registry exceptions.
```

```
        doExceptions(response);

        // Close connection.
        connection.close();
    }
    public static void doExceptions(BulkResponse rspns)
    throws JAXRException {
     /* The code for this method is omitted for brevity. See
     JaxrExample_2 (Listing 17-3) for a complete listing of this method.*/
    }
    public static Connection connectToRegistry(String userName,
                                               String password)
    throws JAXRException {
     /* The code for this method is omitted for brevity. See
     JaxrExample_2 (Listing 17-3) for a complete listing of this method.*/
    }

}
```

To run this example, you'll need the UUID key of the `Organization` you created using `JaxrExample_3`. You should be able to log into IBM's UDDI test Web site and find it. Go to the detail page for your `Organization` (click on its name) and copy the key value (a key has 32 characters separated into five blocks by hyphens).

To run `JaxrExample_4` from a command window, execute a command in the following format:

```
[prompt] java com.jwsbook.jaxr.JaxrExample_4 orgKey userName password
```

Make sure that the key value is exactly the same as was displayed in your browser.

`JaxrExample_4` locates the `Organization` you created in `JaxrExample_3`, adds three classification codes to the `Organization`, and saves it in the UDDI registry. The following sections examine the process of creating and adding classifications to an `Organization`, and briefly address the use of the `BusinessQueryManager`.

17.2.5.1.1 The `BusinessQueryManager` Object

This section provides a very brief overview of how `JaxrExample_4` uses the `BusinessQueryManager`. A detailed discussion of this object can be found in Chapter 19: The JAXR Inquiry and Publishing APIs.

You obtain the `BusinessQueryManager` object from the `RegistryService` the same way you get a `BusinessLifeCycleManager`. The following snippet from `JaxrExample_4` (Listing 17–16) shows how to obtain a reference to the `BusinessQueryManager` for a UDDI registry.

```
// Access the BusinessLifeCycleManager and BusinessQueryManager objects.
Connection connection = connectToRegistry(userName,password);
RegistryService registry = connection.getRegistryService();
BusinessLifeCycleManager lifeCycleMngr =
                         registry.getBusinessLifeCycleManager();
BusinessQueryManager queryMngr = registry.getBusinessQueryManager();
```

The `BusinessQueryManager` provides a Web service interface to the UDDI Inquiry API, which all UDDI registries are required to support. You can use the `BusinessQueryManager` to find existing `Organization`, `Association`, `Service`, `ServiceBinding`, `ClassificationScheme`, and `Concept` objects in a UDDI registry. Searches can be based on the object's UUID key, name, and other criteria. In `JaxrExample_4` (Listing 17–16) we locate the business we created in `JaxrExample_3` (Listing 17–12) by its UUID key, as shown in the following snippet:

```
// Find my Organization by its Key.
Organization myOrganization = (Organization)
   queryMngr.getRegistryObject(companyKey.trim(),
                               LifeCycleManager.ORGANIZATION);
```

The `getRegistryObject()` method will find any data structure in the UDDI registry by its key and type. The `getRegistryObject()` is actually defined by the `BusinessQueryManager`'s supertype, the `QueryManager`.

You can also use any of several `BusinessQueryManager.findXXX()` methods to locate UDDI data structures by their names as well as other criteria. The following snippet from Listing 17–16 shows how `JaxrExample_4` uses the `BusinessQueryManager` to locate a `ClassificationScheme` by name.

```
// Create a Classification object for a NAICS value.
ClassificationScheme naics_Scheme =
   queryMngr.findClassificationSchemeByName(null, "ntis-gov:naics");
```

17.2.5.1.2 Adding Standard UDDI Classifications to an `Organization`

Adding one or more of the standard classifications to your `Organization` will help other people find it and identify the type of business you're in. `JaxrExample_4` (Listing 17–16) adds to your `Organization` three standard classifications from the NAICS, UNSPSC, and ISO 3166 systems.

Adding a standard classification requires that you first look up the classification scheme. Each of the standard classifications has a fixed name (as well as a UUID) that is the same across all UDDI registries. Because all UDDI operators are required to support, at a minimum, the same three classification systems, and under the same names, you'll always know how to find them. The names and UUIDs of the three standard classification systems are as follows:

NAICS

Name

`ntis-gov:naics:1997`

UUID

`uuid:C0B9FE13-179F-413D-8A5B-5004DB8E5BB2`

UNSPSC

Name

`unspsc-org:unspsc`

UUID

`uuid:CD153257-086A-4237-B336-6BDCBDCC6634`

ISO 3166

Name

`uddi-org:iso-ch:3166:1999`

UUID

`uuid:4E49A8D6-D5A2-4FC2-93A0-0411D8D19E88`

The SAP UBR operator site incorrectly gives ISO 3166 the name `uddi-org :iso-ch:3166-1999` ***(with a hyphen in place of the colon as the last separator)—probably because UDDI.org changed the name when the final specification was published.***

Using the fixed names, we can look up the `ClassificationScheme` for each of the standard classifications and create a `Classification` object based on that scheme. The following code snippet from `JaxrExample_4` (Listing 17–16) shows how.

```
// Create a Classification object for a NAICS value.
ClassificationScheme naics_Scheme =
   queryMngr.findClassificationSchemeByName(null, "ntis-gov:naics");
Classification naics_BookWhslrClass =
   lifeCycleMngr.createClassification(naics_Scheme,
                                      "Book Wholesaler", "42292");
// Create a Classification object for a UNSPSC value.
ClassificationScheme unspsc_Scheme =
   queryMngr.findClassificationSchemeByName(null, "unspsc-org:unspsc");
Classification unspsc_TextBookClass =
   lifeCycleMngr.createClassification(unspsc_Scheme,
                                      "TextBook", "55.10.15.09");
// Create a Classification object for an ISO 3166 value.
ClassificationScheme iso3166_Scheme =
   queryMngr.findClassificationSchemeByName(null,
                                            "uddi-org:iso-ch:3166:1999");
Classification iso3166_MinnesotaClass =
   lifeCycleMngr.createClassification(iso3166_Scheme,
                                      "Minnesota, USA", "US-CA");
```

The Classification object represents some code value in a specific ClassificationScheme. For example, in the NAICS classification system, the code "42292" represents a "Book Wholesaler". To create a Classification object that represents that code, you first have to look up the NAICS Classification Scheme object, then use it to create the desired Classification object as in the following snippet from Listing 17–16.

```
// Create a Classification object for a NAICS value.
ClassificationScheme naics_Scheme =
   queryMngr.findClassificationSchemeByName(null, "ntis-gov:naics");
Classification naics_BookWhslrClass =
   lifeCycleMngr.createClassification(naics_Scheme,
                                      "Book Wholesaler", "42292");
```

NAICS, UNSPSC, and ISO 3166 are all **checked** classifications, which means that the UDDI registry must validate the values you submit as correct for that schema. In other words, if you submit a code that isn't part of the scheme indicated, the UDDI registry will refuse to accept it and will generate a SOAP fault message. That message will be relayed to your JAXR application as a javax.xml.registry.SaveException, which is a subtype of the JAXRException.

The JAXR specification requires that all JAXR providers for UDDI provide some way to configure taxonomies for the provider, thus allowing clients to use the JAXR API to browse values within configured taxonomies. In addition, JAXR allows clients to configure custom taxonomies. JAXR also does client-side validation of configured taxonomies. Consult your JAXR provider's documentation for details on configuring taxonomies.

In addition to the three standard classifications, UDDI registries can choose to support their own classification systems. For example, the IBM UBR supports a classification system called WAND that's not supported by the other UBR operators. WAND is an on-line classification system with over 65,000 codes for various products and services (and that number is increasing rapidly). The following snippet shows how to locate the WAND ClassificationScheme and create a Classification object that represents the WAND product code for technical books.

```
// Create a Classification object for a WAND value.
ClassificationScheme wand_Scheme =
   queryMngr.findClassificationSchemeByName(null, "wand-com:WAND-Code");
Classification wand_TextBookClass =
   lifeCycleMngr.createClassification(wand_Scheme,
                                      "Technical Books", "3283989");
```

Private and marketplace UDDI registries frequently define their own classification schemes that are better suited for a particular organization or market. These custom classification systems can be quite extensive and numerous. UDDI experts believe that the classification systems are what makes UDDI so powerful.

17.2.5.2 *The* `Classification` *Interface*

The `Classification` interface, which represents a categorization of something, represents a `keyedReference` element contained by a UDDI `categoryBag` element (see Section 6.1.8).

The `Classification` interface defines methods for accessing the taxonomy value (`ClassificationScheme` or `Concept`) as well as the object being classified (for example, an `Organization`). Listing 17–17 is the definition of the `Classification` interface.

Listing 17–17

The `javax.xml.registry.infomodel.Classification` *Interface*

```
package javax.xml.registry.infomodel;
import javax.xml.registry.*;

public interface Classification extends RegistryObject {

  // Get|Set the Concept that is classifying the object.
  public Concept getConcept() throws JAXRException;
  public void setConcept(Concept concept) throws JAXRException;

  // Get|Set the ClassificationScheme used to classify the object.
  public ClassificationScheme getClassificationScheme()
   throws JAXRException;
  public void setClassificationScheme(ClassificationScheme
                              classificationScheme)
   throws JAXRException;

  // Get|Set the taxonomy value (the code) for this Classification.
  public String getValue() throws JAXRException;
  public void setValue(String value) throws JAXRException;

  // Get|Set the Object that is being classified.
  public RegistryObject getClassifiedObject() throws JAXRException;
  public void setClassifiedObject(RegistryObject classifiedObject)
   throws JAXRException;
```

```
    // Return true if this is an external classification.
    public boolean isExternal() throws JAXRException;
}
```

The categorization taxonomy value, which is the code that identifies the category for a specific classification system, is obtained via the `getValue()` method. The description of this code is obtained by calling the `getName()` method of the `Classification` interface's supertype, `RegistryObject`.

Although JAXR supports both internal and external classifications, UDDI itself supports only external classifications. **Internal classifications** are associated with a `Concept`, while **external classifications** are associated with a `ClassificationScheme`—the two types are mutually exclusive. JAXR requires that vendors support internal classifications for NAICS, UNSPSC, and ISO 3166. This is an important value-added feature of JAXR that is not duplicated in other UDDI client APIs.

17.2.5.3 *The* `ClassificationScheme` *Interface*

The `ClassificationScheme` interface represents the `tModel` referred to by a `keyedReference` element contained by a UDDI `categoryBag` or `identifierBag` element (see Sections 6.1.8 and 6.1.7).

The `ClassificationScheme` represents the taxonomy or system of categorization used by a `Classification` object. It is the root of a classification system. For example a NAICS `Classification` object (for example, `"Book Wholesaler"`), will refer to the NAICS `ClassificationScheme` object. Figure 17–2 illustrates the relationship between a `ClassificationScheme` and its `Classification` objects.

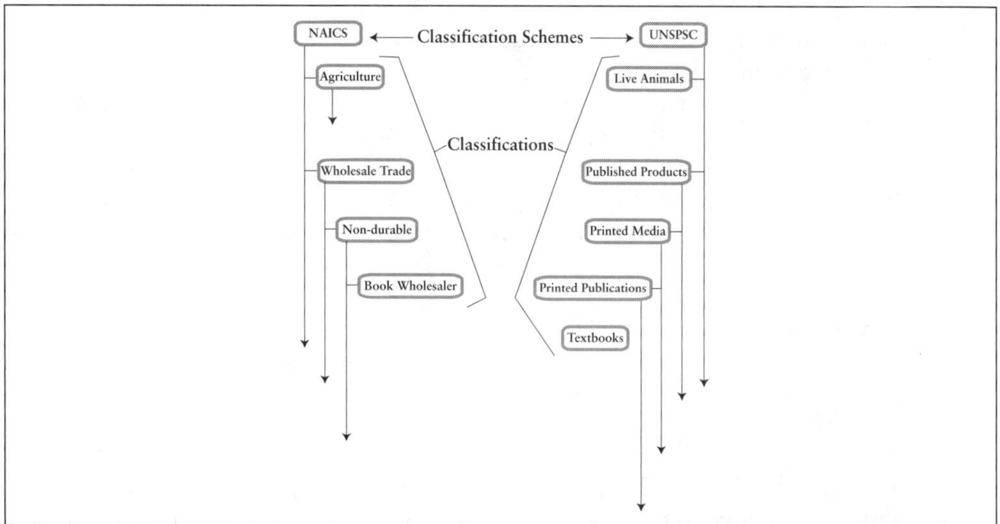

Figure 17–2 Hierarchies of `ClassificationSchemes` and `Classifications`

It's the `ClassificationScheme` that gives a `Classification` object its context. In other words, if you don't know what taxonomy a `Classification` is based on, then the code and description provided by the `Classification` have no context and therefore no meaning. For example, the following shows a classification code and description:

- Classification Code = `"1128605"`
- Classification Description = `"Book Wholesaler"`

Can you tell what classification system these come from? Probably not. That's the point behind the `ClassificationScheme` object: It gives you context. In the above case, the code and description belong to the WAND system. The `ClassificationScheme` interface is defined in Listing 17–18 (Level 1 methods and static fields are omitted).

Listing 17–18

The `javax.xml.registry.infomodel.ClassificationScheme` *Interface*

```
package javax.xml.registry.infomodel;
import javax.xml.registry.*;
import java.util.*;

public interface ClassificationScheme extends RegistryEntry {

  // Manage child Concepts.
  public void addChildConcept(Concept concept) throws JAXRException;
  public void addChildConcepts(Collection concepts)
   throws JAXRException;
  public void removeChildConcept(Concept concept) throws JAXRException;
  public void removeChildConcepts(Collection concepts)
   throws JAXRException;
  public int getChildConceptCount() throws JAXRException;
  public Collection getChildrenConcepts() throws JAXRException;
  public Collection getDescendantConcepts() throws JAXRException;

  // Determine whether this ClassificationScheme is an external one.
  public boolean isExternal() throws JAXRException;

}
```

Internal classifications have a taxonomy structure you can peruse with the `Concept` methods. JAXR requires that vendors provide a full internal taxonomy for NAICS, UNSPSC, and ISO 3166. You can browse these taxonomies and discover specific taxonomy values. This value-added feature is not duplicated by other UDDI client

APIs, and is very helpful when building UDDI browsers. Taxonomy browsing is covered later.

17.2.5.4 Reading `Classification` *and* `ClassificationScheme` *Objects*

In most cases the standard categorizations (NAICS, UNSPSC, and ISO 3166) are added to `Organization` objects, rather than to `Service` or `Concept` objects. Listing 17–19 shows how to read the categorizations of an `Organization` object and display them.

Listing 17–19

Accessing the `Classification` *Objects Associated with an* `Organization`

```
Iterator categories = myOrganization.getClassifications().iterator();
while(categories.hasNext()){
   Classification classif = (Classification)categories.next();
   ClassificationScheme scheme = classif.getClassificationScheme();
   printInternationalString(scheme.getName());
   System.out.println("  Classification Value = "+classif.getValue());
   System.out.print("  Classification Name = ");
   printInternationalString(classif.getName());
   System.out.println();
}
...
public static void printInternationalString(InternationalString interString)
throws JAXRException{
  Iterator names = interString.getLocalizedStrings().iterator();
  while(names.hasNext()){
     LocalizedString name = (LocalizedString)names.next();
     System.out.println(name.getValue());
  }
}
```

The code in Listing 17–19 can be run against any organization. For the `Organization` you classified in `JaxrExample_4` (Listing 17–16), the output would be as shown in Listing 17–20.

Listing 17–20

Output from the Code in Listing 17–19

```
unspsc-org:unspsc
  Classification Value = 55.10.15.09
  Classification Name = TextBook

iso-ch:3166:1999
```

```
  Classification Value = US-CA
  Classification Name = Minnesota, USA

ntis-gov:naics:1997
  Classification Value = 42292
  Classification Name = Book Wholesaler
```

At this writing, the IBM test registry appears to have a bug that lists the UNSPSC scheme name as `unspsc-org:unspsc:3-1`, ***even though you specifically created a classification using the name*** `unspsc-org:unspsc`, ***which represents UNSPSC version 7.3. Don't be surprised if the UNSPSC name is reported with the*** `3-1` ***suffix. With luck, this bug will be fixed by the time this book is published.***

17.2.6 External Identifiers

When you add a new `Organization` object to a UDDI registry, the registry will automatically generate a UUID key and assign it to the new `Organization` object. The UUID serves as the unique identifier for the object within the UDDI context, but there are other identifiers outside of UDDI that an `Organization` can have, some created by governments (such as U.S. Federal Tax IDs), some by private organizations. You can assign as many external identifiers to an `Organization` (as well as some other JAXR types) as you want. UDDI officially recognizes and supports two identification systems:

1. The **D-U-N-S** identification system is maintained by Dun & Bradstreet (D&B), which tracks the credit histories of 75 million companies in 214 countries. Every company listed by D&B has a unique identifier.
2. The **Thomas Register Supplier Identifier Code** system is an on-line registry for products produced by over 189,000 U.S. and Canadian manufacturing companies.

More detailed definitions of these systems can be found in Section 6.1.7.

You can get your company a D-U-N-S number, if it doesn't have one already, for free, but to get a Thomas Register identifier your company must be an American manufacturer or perform manufacturing services (machining, welding, packaging, and so on)—and pay a fee. Most companies have a D-U-N-S number, so we'll use that system in an example. `JaxrExample_5` in Listing 17–21 adds a D-U-N-S number to your `Organization` object.

Listing 17–21

Adding an `ExternalIdentifier` *to an* `Organization`

```
package com.jwsbook.jaxr;
import javax.xml.registry.ConnectionFactory;
import javax.xml.registry.Connection;
```

```
import javax.xml.registry.RegistryService;
import javax.xml.registry.LifeCycleManager;
import javax.xml.registry.BusinessLifeCycleManager;
import javax.xml.registry.BusinessQueryManager;
import javax.xml.registry.infomodel.ClassificationScheme;
import javax.xml.registry.infomodel.ExternalIdentifier;
import javax.xml.registry.infomodel.Organization;
import javax.xml.registry.JAXRException;
import javax.xml.registry.BulkResponse;
import javax.xml.registry.JAXRResponse;
import java.util.Iterator;
import java.net.PasswordAuthentication;
import java.util.Properties;
import java.util.Set;
import java.util.Collection;
import java.util.HashSet;


public class JaxrExample_5 {
  public static void main(String [] args) throws JAXRException {
    // Extract parameters.
    String companyKey = args[0];
    String userName = args[1];
    String password = args[2];

    // Access BusinessLifeCycleManager and BusinessQueryManager objects.
    Connection connection = connectToRegistry(userName,password);
    RegistryService registry = connection.getRegistryService();
    BusinessLifeCycleManager lifeCycleMngr =
                             registry.getBusinessLifeCycleManager();
    BusinessQueryManager queryMngr = registry.getBusinessQueryManager();

    // Find my Organization by its Key.
    Organization myOrganization = (Organization)
       queryMngr.getRegistryObject(companyKey.trim(),
                                   LifeCycleManager.ORGANIZATION);
    String orgName = myOrganization.getName().getValue();

    // Create a D-U-N-S identifier.
    ClassificationScheme duns_Scheme =
      queryMngr.findClassificationSchemeByName(null, "dnb-com:D-U-N-S");
    ExternalIdentifier dunsNumber =
      lifeCycleMngr.createExternalIdentifier(duns_Scheme,
                                         orgName, "038924499");
```

```
    // Add it to my Organization as an external identifier.
    myOrganization.addExternalIdentifier(dunsNumber);

    // Save the Organization in the UDDI directory.
    Set organizationSet = new HashSet();
    organizationSet.add(myOrganization);
    BulkResponse response =
                 lifeCycleMngr.saveOrganizations(organizationSet);

    // Check for registry exceptions.
    doExceptions(response);

    // Close connection.
    connection.close();
  }
  public static void doExceptions(BulkResponse rspns)
  throws JAXRException {
   /* The code for this method is omitted for brevity. See
   JaxrExample_2 (Listing 17-3) for a complete listing of this method.*/
  }
  public static Connection connectToRegistry(String userName,
                                             String password)
  throws JAXRException {
   /* The code for this method is omitted for brevity. See
   JaxrExample_2 (Listing 17-3) for a complete listing of this method.*/
  }
}
```

To run this example, you'll need the UUID key of the `Organization` you created in `JaxrExample_3` (Listing 17–12). You should be able to log into IBM's UDDI test Web site to find this key. To run `JaxrExample_5` from a command window, execute a command in the following format:

```
[prompt] java com.jwsbook.jaxr.JaxrExample_5 orgKey userName password
```

`JaxrExample_5` locates the `Organization` created in `JaxrExample_3` (Listing 17–16) and adds a D-U-N-S identification number to the `Organization`. The identifier used in this example is made up. If you want to find out the D-U-N-S number for your business (or be assigned a new one) browse D&B's Web site (www.dnb.com). The following sections examine the process of creating and adding `ExternalIdentifier` objects to an `Organization`.

You won't be able to see the D-U-N-S number you assigned your organization because IBM's UDDI Web service doesn't show identifiers at this time—an odd omission. Later in the book, however, you'll see some code that allows you to read the `ExternalIdentifier` *values for any* `Organization` *using JAXR.*

17.2.6.1 Managing External Identifiers

You can create a new `ExternalIdentifier` object using one of two overloaded `LifeCycleManager.createExternalIdentifier()` methods. `JaxrExample_5` (Listing 17–21) used the simpler of these two methods:

```
// Create a D-U-N-S identifier.
ClassificationScheme duns_Scheme =
    queryMngr.findClassificationSchemeByName(null, "dnb-com:D-U-N-S");
ExternalIdentifier dunsNumber =
   lifeCycleMngr.createExternalIdentifier(duns_Scheme,
                                          orgName, "01-010-1010");
```

The `createExternalIdentifier()` method used in `JaxrExample_5` takes as arguments a `ClassificationScheme` and the name and value of the `ExternalIdentifier`. The other `createExternalIdentifier()` method is the same, except that it uses an `InternationalString` for the name, so that you can submit a name with a specific language identifier. The `LifeCycleManager` interface defines the two methods as shown in Listing 17–22.

Listing 17–22

The `createExternalIdentifier()` *Methods of the* `LifeCycleManager` *Interface*

```
package javax.xml.registry;
import javax.xml.registry.infomodel.*;

public Interface LifeCycleManager {
  ...
  public ExternalIdentifier createExternalIdentifier(
                            ClassificationScheme identificationScheme,
                            String name, String value)
   throws JAXRException;
  public ExternalIdentifier createExternalIdentifier(
                            ClassificationScheme identificationScheme,
                            InternationalString name, String value)
   throws JAXRException;
   ...
}
```

In practice the method that takes an InternationalString is not very useful with UDDI because UDDI defines identifiers as keyedReference types, which do not allow for multiple language-specific names; only one name, with no language identifier, is allowed (see Section 6.1.7).

In addition to the Organization type, the ClassificationScheme and Concept types can have external identifiers. In most cases, however, it's the Organization objects that are assigned a D-U-N-S or Thomas Register identifier. RegistryObject, which is the supertype of Organization, ClassificationScheme, and Concept, defines the methods used to manage ExternalIdentifiers. The following expanded snippet from Listing 17–1 shows the six ExternalIdentifier methods defined by the RegistryObject interface.

```
public interface RegistryObject extends ExtensibleObject  {
  ...
  //The collection of ExternalIdentifiers for this object.
  public void setExternalIdentifiers(Collection externalIdentifiers)
   throws JAXRException;
  public Collection getExternalIdentifiers() throws JAXRException;
  public void addExternalIdentifier(ExternalIdentifier
                                    externalIdentifier)
   throws JAXRException;
  public void addExternalIdentifiers(Collection externalIdentifiers)
   throws JAXRException;
  public void removeExternalIdentifier(ExternalIdentifier
                                       externalIdentifier)
   throws JAXRException;
  public void removeExternalIdentifiers(Collection externalIdentifiers)
   throws JAXRException;
   ...
}
```

JaxrExample_5 (Listing 17–21) uses the addExternalIdentifier() method to add the D-U-N-S number to the Organization object, as shown in the following snippet.

```
// Add it to my Organization as an external identifier.
myOrganization.addExternalIdentifier(dunsNumber);
```

17.2.6.2 The ExternalIdentifier *Interface*

The ExternalIdentifier interface represents a keyedReference element in a UDDI IdentifierBag element (see Section 6.1.7).

The ExternalIdentifier interface defines methods for accessing its ClassificationScheme, which represents the taxonomy used (D-U-N-S, Thomas

Register, or other), the identifier value, description, and the object it's identifying (for example, an `Organization`). Listing 17–23 shows the definition of the `ExternalIdentifier` interface.

Listing 17–23

The `javax.xml.registry.infomodel.ExternalIdentifier` *Interface*

```
package javax.xml.registry.infomodel;
import javax.xml.registry.*;

public interface ExternalIdentifier extends RegistryObject {

  // Get the parent RegistryObject for this ExternalIdentifier.
  RegistryObject getRegistryObject() throws JAXRException;

  // Get|Set the value of an ExternalIdentifier.
  public String getValue() throws JAXRExcetion;
  public void setValue(String value) throws JAXRException;

  // Get the ClassificationScheme used as the identification scheme.
  public ClassificationScheme getIdentificationScheme()
    throws JAXRException;
  public void setIdentificationScheme(ClassificationScheme
                                          identifierScheme)
    throws JAXRException;
}
```

The identifier value, which is a unique value within a specific identification system, is obtained via the `getValue()` method. The description of this value, which is usually `"D-U-N-S"` or something like that, is obtained by calling the `getName()` method defined by the `RegistryObject` supertype.

The `ExternalIdentifier` belongs to a specific taxonomy, a system of identification, which is represented by a `ClassificationScheme` object. The `ClassificationScheme` object maps to a UDDI `tModel` in the registry, which describes the identification system.

The `ClassificationScheme` was covered in detail earlier in this chapter, when we discussed the `Classification` object (Section 17.2.5). You can go back and review that section if you need to. It addresses the `ClassificationScheme` as it relates to both of the `Classification` and `ExternalIdentifier` objects.

17.2.7 Services

The `Organization` interface defines a few methods for accessing, adding, and removing `Service` objects. A `Service` object represents a logical grouping of Web services, and an `Organization` may have one or more of them. The following snippet from Listing 17–4 shows the `Organization` methods used to manage `Service` objects.

```
package javax.xml.registry.infomodel;
import javax.xml.registry.*;
import java.util.*;

public interface Organization extends RegistryObject {
    ...
    // Service methods.
    public void addService(Service service) throws JAXRException;
    public void addServices(Collection services) throws JAXRException;
    public void removeService(Service service) throws JAXRException;
    public void removeServices(Collection services) throws JAXRException;
    public Collection getServices() throws JAXRException;
}
```

The `Service` type and others are covered in more detail in Chapter 18: The JAXR Technical Objects.

17.3 Wrapping Up

JAXR was actually built using the naming and operational concepts found in the ebXML registry specifications, and later mapped to UDDI. The result actually works pretty well because ebXML has a very general data model, but it can be distracting because many of the methods (all Level 1) simply don't work with UDDI. That said, for UDDI novices the JAXR infomodel is easier to navigate and use than other, more UDDI-centric APIs. You can learn JAXR without having to know much about the UDDI data structures and operations—which is arguably good and bad.

It's difficult to predict the fate of ebXML registries. It seems like all the major Web service vendors are flocking to UDDI, and only a few are supporting ebXML, but this may be a skewed perspective. The ebXML stack of technologies is endorsed and partly funded by the United Nations, and it's possible it could become a popular standard for countries other than the United States. This kind of technology split would be similar to the one that took place with EDI (Electronic Data Interchange) at the end of the last century—U.S. companies ended up supporting an EDI standard called X12, while the rest of the world settled on the UN/EDIFACT EDI standard championed by the United Nations.

Chapter 18

The JAXR Technical Objects

Chapter 17 introduced you to the JAXR API and explained the business-related infomodel types (Organization, User, PostalAddress, and so on), as well as other types, such as Classification, ExternalIdentifier, InternationalString, and ExternalLink.

This section completes the survey of the JAXR Information Model with coverage of the infomodel types that describe the Web services offered by organizations. I refer to these types as technical objects, but that distinction is an invention for this book; it's not a distinction made elsewhere. The assumption is that you've already read Chapter 17. If you have not, you should do so before reading this chapter, because the dependency and coupling between these chapters is quite strong.

18.1 The Service and ServiceBinding Information Objects

The JAXR Service interface represents the UDDI businessService data structure, which you can use to group one or more Web services together. Organizations that have many different Web services may group those services under different Service objects according to their purpose, or their Classification, or other criteria. A Service represents a logical service accessible in multiple modes (options, protocols, access points, and so on). Each ServiceBinding represents a different mode of access to a Service. In the context of this book, a ServiceBinding represents a Web service that conforms with the WS-I Basic Profile 1.0. A ServiceBinding object corresponds to the bindingTemplate data structure in

UDDI, which identifies the electronic address of a Web service and optionally refers to a set of specifications that describe that service. The UDDI `businessService` and `bindingTemplate` data structures were covered in detail in Section 6.2.

In Listing 18–1 `JaxrExample_6` creates very simple `Service` and `Service Binding` objects that represent the URL of an organization's Web site. You'll be using the same `Organization` object that you created in `JaxrExample_3` (Listing 17–12).

Listing 18–1

Adding a Simple `ServiceBinding` *to an* `Organization`

```
package com.jwsbook.jaxr;
import javax.xml.registry.ConnectionFactory;
import javax.xml.registry.Connection;
import javax.xml.registry.RegistryService;
import javax.xml.registry.LifeCycleManager;
import javax.xml.registry.BusinessLifeCycleManager;
import javax.xml.registry.BusinessQueryManager;
import javax.xml.registry.infomodel.Organization;
import javax.xml.registry.infomodel.Service;
import javax.xml.registry.infomodel.ServiceBinding;
import javax.xml.registry.infomodel.InternationalString;
import javax.xml.registry.JAXRException;
import javax.xml.registry.BulkResponse;
import javax.xml.registry.JAXRResponse;
import java.util.Iterator;
import java.net.PasswordAuthentication;
import java.util.Properties;
import java.util.Set;
import java.util.Collection;
import java.util.HashSet;
import java.util.Iterator;

public class JaxrExample_6{
  public static void main(String [] args) throws JAXRException {
    // Extract parameters.
    String companyKey = args[0];
    String userName = args[1];
    String password = args[2];

    // Access BusinessLifeCycleManager and BusinessQueryManager objects.
    Connection connection = connectToRegistry(userName,password);
```

```
    RegistryService registry = connection.getRegistryService();
    BusinessLifeCycleManager lifeCycleMngr =
                            registry.getBusinessLifeCycleManager();
    BusinessQueryManager queryMngr = registry.getBusinessQueryManager();

    // Find my Organization by its Key.
    Organization myOrganization = (Organization)
       queryMngr.getRegistryObject(companyKey.trim(),
                                  LifeCycleManager.ORGANIZATION);
    String orgName = myOrganization.getName().getValue();

    // Create and add a new Service to my Organization.
    Service service = lifeCycleMngr.createService(orgName+" Web Site");
    InternationalString desc = lifeCycleMngr.createInternationalString(
                              "The main HTML Web site for "+orgName);
    service.setDescription(desc);
    myOrganization.addService(service);

    // Create, add, and configure a new ServiceBinding.
    ServiceBinding binding = lifeCycleMngr.createServiceBinding();
    service.addServiceBinding(binding);
    binding.setValidateURI(false);
    binding.setAccessURI("http://www."+orgName+".com/index.html");

    // Save the Organization in the UDDI directory.
    Set organizationSet = new HashSet();
    organizationSet.add(myOrganization);
    BulkResponse response =
                lifeCycleMngr.saveOrganizations(organizationSet);

    // Check for registry exceptions.
    doExceptions(response);

    // Close the connection.
    connection.close();
  }
  public static void doExceptions(BulkResponse rspns)
  throws JAXRException {
   /* The code for this method is omitted for brevity. See
      JaxrExample_2 (Listing 17-3) for a
      complete listing of this method.*/
  }
  public static Connection connectToRegistry(String userName,
```

```
                                    String password)
    throws JAXRException {
     /* The code for this method is omitted for brevity. See
        JaxrExample_2 (Listing 17-3) for a
        complete listing of this method.*/
    }
}
```

To run this example, you'll need the UUID key of the `Organization` you created in `JaxrExample_3`. You should be able to log into IBM's UDDI test Web site to find this key. To run `JaxrExample_6` from a command window, execute a command in the following format:

```
[prompt] java com.jwsbook.jaxr.JaxrExample_6 orgKey userName password
```

`JaxrExample_6` adds the technical information for accessing the main Web site of your fictitious `Organization`. Later in this chapter you will learn how to add a `ServiceBinding` that describes a SOAP-based Web service, but for now we'll focus on a simpler service, a Web site.

18.1.1 Creating a New `Service` Object

The following snippet from Listing 16–4 shows the `LifeCycleManager` interface methods used to create `Service` objects—recall that you learned in Section 16.3.2 that `LifeCycleManager` is the supertype of the `BusinessLifeCycleManager` interface.

```
package javax.xml.registry;
import javax.xml.registry.infomodel.*;

public Interface LifeCycleManager {
  ...
  public Service createService(InternationalString name)
   throws JAXRException;

  public Service createService(String name)
   throws JAXRExcption;
  ...
}
```

A `Service`, like an `Organization`, can have multiple language-specific names. The overloading of the `createService()` method that expects an `International String` allows you to declare one or more language-specific names for the `Service` object. The overloading of `createService()` that expects an ordinary `String` will use the default Locale (obtained with a call to Locale.getDefault()) to determine the language identity of the name. So if your Locale is "English", xml: lang="en" will automatically be assigned to the Service object's name when it's saved in the registry.

The following code snippet from JaxrExample_6 (Listing 18–1) shows a Service object being created. This Service object represents the company's main HTML Web site, which can be accessed using a common Web browser.

```
// Create and add a new Service to my Organization.
Service service = lifeCycleMngr.createService(orgName+" Web Site");
InternationalString desc = lifeCycleMngr.createInternationalString(
                           "The main HTML Web site for "+orgName);
service.setDescription(desc);
myOrganization.addService(service);
```

You can access, add, and remove Service objects relating to an Organization object using methods defined by the Organization interface. These methods were introduced at the end of Section 17.2.7, but are shown again in the following code snippet, for your convenience.

```
package javax.xml.registry.infomodel;
import javax.xml.registry.*;
import java.util.*;

public interface Organization extends RegistryObject {
    ...
  // Service methods.
  publicvoid addService(Service service) throws JAXRException;
  publicvoid addServices(Collection services) throws JAXRException;
  publicvoid removeService(Service service) throws JAXRException;
  publicvoid removeServices(Collection services) throws JAXRException;
  publicCollection getServices() throws JAXRException;
    ...
}
```

18.1.2 Creating a New ServiceBinding Object

As shown in the following snippet from Listing 16–4, the LifeCycleManager defines one method for creating a ServiceBinding, createServiceBinding().

```
package javax.xml.registry;
import javax.xml.registry.infomodel.*;

public Interface LifeCycleManager {
```

```
    ...
    public ServiceBinding createServiceBinding() throws JAXRException
    ...
}
```

The ServiceBinding object does not have a name, but it will almost always have an accessURI, which is the electronic address of the service. The following snippet from JaxrExample_6 (Listing 18–1) shows a ServiceBinding being created, added to a service, and then configured with an access URI.

```
// Create, add, and configure a new ServiceBinding.
ServiceBinding binding = lifeCycleMngr.createServiceBinding();
service.addServiceBinding(binding);
binding.setValidateURI(false);
binding.setAccessURI("http://www."+orgName+".com/index.html");
```

In this case the access URI is the URL of an HTML Web page. If you were defining a Web service, it would be the URL of the Web service.

When a ServiceBinding is saved in the UDDI registry, the registry will verify that the accessURI is a valid URL—assuming it is a URL. Because you are probably making up an organization for this example, the method call setValidateURI (false) overrides this behavior. If you comment that line out of your code, and the URL you specified doesn't exist, the program will throw an exception indicating that the URL is invalid. This is an important added value of JAXR. Invalid URLs represent a significant problem in UDDI, and JAXR's ability to detect them on the client side, before they are saved in a UDDI registry, is important to ensuring the validity of data published to UDDI registries.

18.1.3 The Service Interface

There is not a lot to the Service interface. It simply provides accessors to a collection of ServiceBinding objects, each of which represents a different Web service. A Service has a name, a description, and a reference to its owning Organization, and can be associated with one or more Classification objects. Listing 18–2 shows the definition of the JAXR Service interface.

Listing 18–2

The javax.xml.registry.infomodel.Service *Interface*

```
package javax.xml.registry.infomodel;
import javax.xml.registry.*;
import java.util.*;

public interface Service extends RegistryEntry {
```

```
    // Get|Set the Organization that provides this service.
    public Organization getProvidingOrganization() throws JAXRException;
    public void setProvidingOrganization(Organization
                                              providingOrganization)
     throws JAXRException;

    // Manage the collection of ServiceBindings.
    public Collection getServiceBindings() throws JAXRException;
    public void addServiceBinding(ServiceBinding serviceBinding)
     throws JAXRException;
    public void addServiceBindings(Collection serviceBindings)
     throws JAXRException;
    public void removeServiceBinding(ServiceBinding serviceBinding)
     throws JAXRException;
    public void removeServiceBindings(Collection serviceBindings)
     throws JAXRException;
}
```

The `Service` interface defines five methods for accessing, adding, and removing `ServiceBinding` objects contained by a `Service` object. These methods are pretty straightforward; they act on a collection of `ServiceBinding` objects maintained by the `Service` object.

A `Service` can have multiple language-specific names and descriptions just as an `Organization` object can (see Section 17.2.3). You use the `getName()` and `getDescription()` methods that `Service` inherited from `RegistryObject` to access the `Service`'s `name` and `description` properties. You can give a `Service` any name you like, but you should choose a name that accurately describes the kind of Web services it contains.

You can access a `Service` object's UUID key, which was assigned by the UDDI registry when it was created, using the `RegistryObject.getKey()` method (see Section 17.1.1). You can also access the `Organization` object that owns the `Service` via the `getProvidingOrganization()` method.

A `Service` object can be associated with `Classification` objects, just as an `Organization` can. You add `Classification` objects to a `Service` using the `Classification` management methods defined by the `RegistryObject` interface (see Section 17.2.5).

18.1.4 The `ServiceBinding` Interface

`ServiceBinding` declares the electronic address of the Web service and associates one or more `SpecificationLink` objects with the Web service. Listing 18–3 shows the interface definition of the `ServiceBinding` type.

Listing 18–3

The `javax.xml.registry.infomodel.ServiceBinding` *Interface*

```
package javax.xml.registry.infomodel;
import javax.xml.registry.*;
import java.util.*;

public interface ServiceBinding extends RegistryObject, URIValidator {

  // Get|Set the URL of this ServiceBinding.
  public String getAccessURI() throws JAXRException;
  public void setAccessURI(String uri) throws JAXRException;

  // Get|Set a redirection ServiceBinding.
  public ServiceBinding getTargetBinding() throws JAXRException;
  public void setTargetBinding(ServiceBinding binding)
   throws JAXRException;

  // Get the parent Service that contains this ServiceBinding.
  public Service getService() throws JAXRException;

  // Manage the collection of SpecificationLink objects.
  public void addSpecificationLink(SpecificationLink specificationLink)
   throws JAXRException;
  public void addSpecificationLinks(Collection specificationLinks)
   throws JAXRException;
  public void removeSpecificationLink(SpecificationLink
                                       specificationLink)
   throws JAXRException;
  public void removeSpecificationLinks(Collection specificationLinks)
   throws JAXRException;
  public Collection getSpecificationLinks() throws JAXRException;

}
```

The `accessURI` property, manipulated using `getAccessURI()` and `setAccessURI()`, corresponds to the `accessPoint` element in the UDDI `bindingTemplate` data structure (see Section 6.2.2.1). An `accessURI` can have a `useType`, which is `http` by default. You can change the `useType` to one of six other predefined values: `mailto` (e-mail), `https`, `ftp`, `fax`, `phone`, or `other`. Working with predefined enumerated attributes, like `useType`, is covered in Section 18.5.

The `getTargetBinding()` and `setTargetBinding()` methods allow you to refer to a `ServiceBinding` owned by another organization. The `targetBinding` corresponds to the `hostingRedirector` element of the UDDI `bindingTemplate` (see Section 6.2.2.2). The BP explicitly prohibits the use of the `redirectionHost` field in UDDI, so you will not need to use its JAXR representation, `targetBinding`, either.

A `ServiceBinding` may have one or more `SpecificationLink` objects, which are maintained in a `Collection`. The `ServiceBinding` type provides several methods for accessing, adding, and removing `SpecificationLink` objects. The `SpecificationLink` type is covered in more detail a little later, in Section 18.3.

18.2 The `Concept` Information Object

In UDDI the `tModel` data structure can be used to describe the technical specifications of a Web service. A technical `tModel` (also called a "`tModel` fingerprint") can refer to a WSDL document, an XML schema document, or some other specification. In the case of J2EE Web services, a technical `tModel` usually refers to a WSDL document that describes the Web service.

In JAXR the `Concept` object represents a technical `tModel`. A `concept` object is created independently of an `Organization` and referred to by one or more Web services. This is especially useful when a technical `tModel` refers to an industry-standard WSDL document. For example, the wholesale book industry might create a standard Web service, with a standard WSDL document, for requesting quotes of book prices from a specific company. All of the the organization's members that supported this Web service would refer to the same WSDL document.

While sharing a `tModel` can be useful, most organizations will create their own `tModels` for a specific custom Web service. Creating a `tModel` is fairly easy. In Listing 18–4, `JaxrExample_7` creates a `Concept` object that represents a technical `tModel`, and saves it in the UDDI registry.

Listing 18–4

Creating and Saving a New Specification `Concept` *Object*

```
package com.jwsbook.jaxr;
import javax.xml.registry.ConnectionFactory;
import javax.xml.registry.Connection;
import javax.xml.registry.RegistryService;
import javax.xml.registry.BusinessLifeCycleManager;
import javax.xml.registry.BusinessQueryManager;
import javax.xml.registry.infomodel.Concept;
import javax.xml.registry.infomodel.Classification;
import javax.xml.registry.infomodel.ClassificationScheme;
```

```
import javax.xml.registry.infomodel.ExternalLink;
import javax.xml.registry.infomodel.InternationalString;
import javax.xml.registry.infomodel.Key;
import javax.xml.registry.JAXRException;
import javax.xml.registry.BulkResponse;
import javax.xml.registry.JAXRResponse;
import java.util.Iterator;
import java.net.PasswordAuthentication;
import java.util.Properties;
import java.util.Set;
import java.util.HashSet;

public class JaxrExample_7{
  public static void main(String [] args) throws JAXRException {
    // Extract parameters.
    String domainName = args[0];
    String userName = args[1];
    String password = args[2];

    // Access BusinessLifeCycleManager and BusinessQueryManager objects.
    Connection connection = connectToRegistry(userName,password);
    RegistryService registry = connection.getRegistryService();
    BusinessLifeCycleManager lifeCycleMngr =
                           registry.getBusinessLifeCycleManager();
    BusinessQueryManager queryMngr =
                           registry.getBusinessQueryManager();

    // Create the WSDL Concept object.
    Concept wsdlConcept = lifeCycleMngr.createConcept(null,"","");

    // Set the Concept name.
    InternationalString conceptName =
      lifeCycleMngr.createInternationalString(domainName+":BookQuote");
    wsdlConcept.setName(conceptName);

    // Set the URL to WSDL binding.
    ExternalLink overviewDoc = lifeCycleMngr.createExternalLink(
      "http://www."+domainName+"/jwsbook/BookQuote.wsdl"+
        "#xmlns(wsdl=http://schemas.xmlsoap.org/wsdl/) "+
        "xpointer(/wsdl:definitions/wsdl:portType["+
        "@name=\"BookQuoteBinding\"])",
      "The WSDL <binding> for this Web service");

    overviewDoc.setValidateURI(false);
    wsdlConcept.addExternalLink(overviewDoc);
```

```
    // Add the wsdlSpec Classification to the WSDL Concept.
    ClassificationScheme uddi_types =
      queryMngr.findClassificationSchemeByName(null, "uddi-org:types");
    Classification wsdlSpec_Class = lifeCycleMngr.createClassification(
      uddi_types,"WSDL Document","wsdlSpec");
    wsdlConcept.addClassification(wsdlSpec_Class);

    // Add the WS-I Conformance Classification to the WSDL Concept.
    ClassificationScheme wsI_types =
     queryMngr.findClassificationSchemeByName(
        null,
        "ws-i-org:conformsTo:2002_12");
    Classification wsIconform_Class =
     lifeCycleMngr.createClassification(
        wsI_types,
        "Conforms to WS-I Basic Profile 1.0",
        "http://ws-i.org/profiles/basic/1.0");
    wsdlConcept.addClassification(wsIconform_Class);

    // Save the Concept object.
    Set conceptSet = new HashSet();
    conceptSet.add(wsdlConcept);
    BulkResponse response = lifeCycleMngr.saveConcepts(conceptSet);

    // Check for registry exceptions.
    doExceptions(response);

    // Close connection.
    connection.close();
  }
  public static void doExceptions(BulkResponse rspns)
  throws JAXRException {
   /* The code for this method is omitted for brevity. See
      JaxrExample_2 (Listing 17-3) for a
      complete listing of this method.*/
  }
  public static Connection connectToRegistry(String userName,
                                            String password)
  throws JAXRException {
   /* The code for this method is omitted for brevity. See
      JaxrExample_2 (Listing 17-3) for a
      complete listing of this method.*/
  }
}
```

To run this example, you'll provide a domain name as the first parameter, followed by your user name and password. To run `JaxrExample_7` from a command window, execute a command in the following format:

```
[prompt] java com.jwsbook.jaxr.JaxrExample_7 domainName userName password
```

The domain name should be a valid domain with a proper suffix (.com, .org, or .net, for instance). Although `JaxrExample_7` *turns validation off, you may still get a validation error, because there's a bug in the JAXR RI. You have two options if validation cannot be turned off: You can upload a document to the URL specified, OR use the domain name "monson-haefel.com" in your example. I have placed a valid WSDL document at the URL "http://www.monson-haefel.com/jwsbook /Book Quote.wsdl" for your convenience.*

You can verify that the `Concept` was added by going to the IBM UDDI test registry and logging in. The new `tModel` should be listed on the publishing page under `tModels`. If you can't find it, try a `tModel` search using the name `"domain Name:BookQuote"`.

18.2.1 Creating a New `Concept`

To create a new `Concept` you have to manufacture an instance, set its `name` and `overviewDoc` properties, classify it as a `wsdlSpec` and WS-I conformant, and save it in the registry.

18.2.1.1 Create a `Concept` *Instance*

You create a `Concept` using either of two `createConcept()` methods defined in the `LifeCycleManager`. Here we'll use the method that takes a `RegistryObject`, a name, and a value as its parameters. In `JaxrExample_7` (Listing 18–4) we provide null or empty string values for the parameters, as in this snippet.

```
// Create the WSDL Concept object.
Concept wsdlConcept = lifeCycleMngr.createConcept(null,"","");
```

The `Concept` object can represent many things, including WSDL `tModels` or taxonomy values. The parameters used in the `createConcept()` methods generally apply to taxonomy values, and are not relevant to a WSDL `tModel`, so they are not given meaningful values in this example.

18.2.1.2 Set the `Concept` *Name*

After the `Concept` object instance is created, you need to set the name of the `Concept`. A `Concept` name can be any `InternationalString`, but a nice convention is to prefix the name with the name of the organization and a colon. In `JaxrExample_7` (Listing 18–4), the domain name "monson-haefel.com" is used as the prefix. The following snippet from `JaxrExample_7` (Listing 18–4) sets the `Concept` name to `"monson-haefel.com:BookQuote"`.

```
// Set the Concept name.
InternationalString conceptName =
  lifeCycleMngr.createInternationalString(domainName+":BookQuote");
wsdlConcept.setName(conceptName);
```

You must use an `InternationalString` object to set the name of the `Concept` object, but be aware that in UDDI the `Concept` object can have only one name. In other words, you cannot set more than one language-specific name for a `Concept` that maps to a UDDI `tModel`—the name can, however, be language-qualified. You can learn more about the `InternationalString` type in Section 17.2.3.

18.2.1.3 Set the `Overview` *Document*

After creating the `Concept` object, you can set the `ExternalLink` (see Section 17.2.2) to point to a specification or resource that describes the `Concept`. In the case of a `Concept` that represents a WSDL `binding`, the `ExternalLink` will point to an actual `binding` element in a WSDL document somewhere on the Internet. In `Jaxr Example_7` (Listing 18–4), the `ExternalLink` points to a fictitious WSDL `binding` hosted by the domain you specified.

```
// Set the URL to WSDL binding.
ExternalLink overviewDoc = lifeCycleMngr.createExternalLink(
  "http://www."+domainName+"/jwsbook/BookQuote.wsdl"+
    "#xmlns(wsdl=http://schemas.xmlsoap.org/wsdl/) "+
    "xpointer(/wsdl:definitions/wsdl:portType["+
    "@name=\"BookQuoteBinding\"])",
  "The WSDL <binding> for this Web service");

overviewDoc.setValidateURI(false);
wsdlConcept.addExternalLink(overviewDoc);
```

The `ExternalLink` of a `Concept` object corresponds to the `overviewDoc` element of a UDDI `tModel` (see Section 6.3.5.2). This element will contain a URL and an optional description. The Basic Profile requires that the `overviewDoc` element use the XPointer reference system to identify a specific `binding` in a specific WSDL document. XPointer is a powerful XML reference technology, which is outside the scope of this book.[1] You don't need to understand XPointer to use it in your WSDL `tModels`, however; all you have to do is fill in the proper URL and the

[1] World Wide Web Consortium, "XPointer xpointer() Scheme," W3C Working Draft 19. Available at http://www.w3.org/TR/2002/WD-xptr-xpointer-20020710/

name of the WSDL binding element you are referring to. See Section 6.3.1 to learn how to use a simple XPointer template with your overviewURL elements.

When the Concept object is saved in the UDDI registry, the JAXR provider will automatically validate the URL by checking to see if the named document is accessible. If not, it will throw a JAXRException. You can turn validation off, as JaxrExample_7 does, by calling setValidationURI(false) on the ExternalLink object, before saving the Concept in the UDDI registry.

18.2.1.4 Assign the wsdlSpec *Classification*

When you create a new Concept object, you should assign it a type from the UDDI types taxonomy, which is formally named uddi-org:types, and must be supported by all UDDI registries. All UDDI tModels belong to one of the categories of the uddi-org:types taxonomy, which can be thought of as the "supertaxonomy" for tModels. The following list shows all the categories. You can find detailed definitions of them in Section 6.3.3.

tModel	namespace	postalAddress	specification
soapSpec	protocol	signatureComponent	checked
identifier	categorization	relationship	xmlSpec
wsdlSpec	transport	unvalidatable	unchecked

In JaxrExample_7 (Listing 18–4) the uddi-org:types category "wsdlSpec" is assigned to the Concept after it is created, as in this snippet.

```
// Add the wsdlSpec Classification to the WSDL Concept.
ClassificationScheme uddi_types =
  queryMngr.findClassificationSchemeByName(null, "uddi-org:types");
Classification wsdlSpec_Class = lifeCycleMngr.createClassification(
  uddi_types,"WSDL Document","wsdlSpec");
wsdlConcept.addClassification(wsdlSpec_Class);
```

By categorizing the Concept as a "wsdlSpec" type, you make it easier for others to discover your organization when searching by tModel type. The BP requires that tModels representing Web services be categorized using the "wsdlSpec" UDDI type.

18.2.1.5 Assign the WS-I Conformance Claim

As explained in Section 6.6: WS-I Conformance Claims, the Basic Profile 1.0 defines a categorization that asserts that a WSDL tModel is compliant with the BP. This conformance categorization is assigned to the WSDL tModel by JaxrExample_7 (Listing 18–4) as follows:

```
// Add the WS-I Conformance Classification to the WSDL Concept.
ClassificationScheme wsI_types =
 queryMngr.findClassificationSchemeByName(
```

```
        null,
        "ws-i-org:conformsTo:2002_12");
    Classification wsIconform_Class = lifeCycleMngr.createClassification(
        wsI_types,
        "Conforms to WS-I Basic Profile 1.0",
        "http://ws-i.org/profiles/basic/1.0");
    wsdlConcept.addClassification(wsIconform_Class);
```

Assigning the WS-I Conformance claim to a WSDL concept is required in order to document conformance to the BP and aid searches for conformant Web services.

18.2.1.6 Save the `Concept` *Object*

The `Concept` object will not be saved as a `tModel` in the UDDI registry unless you use the `BusinessLifeCycleManager.saveConcepts()` method. The following snippet from `JaxrExample_7` (Listing 18–4) does exactly that:

```
// Save the Concept object.
Set conceptSet = new HashSet();
conceptSet.add(wsdlConcept);
BulkResponse response = lifeCycleMngr.saveConcepts(conceptSet);
```

18.2.2 The `Concept` Interface

The `Concept` interface provides many methods used in taxonomy browsing, which is actually not supported by UDDI. JAXR, however, requires that providers support browsing for the NAICS, UNSPSC, and ISO 3166 taxonomies. In other words, given a specific taxonomy you can navigate through all of its valid values using the methods defined in the `Concept` interface. Listing 18–5 shows the definition of the `Concept` interface.

Listing 18–5

The `javax.xml.registry.infomodel.Concept` *Interface*

```
package javax.xml.registry.infomodel;
import java.util.*;
import javax.xml.registry.*;

public interface Concept extends RegistryObject {
  // Get the taxonomy value of this Concept.
  public String getValue() throws JAXRException;
  public void setValue(String value) throws JAXRException;

  // Taxonomy browsing methods.
  public Collection getDescendantConcepts() throws JAXRException;
  public Collection getChildrenConcepts() throws JAXRException;
  public int getChildConceptCount() throws JAXRException;
```

```
    public void removeChildConcepts(Collection concepts)
     throws JAXRException;
    public void removeChildConcept(Concept concept) throws JAXRException;
    public void addChildConcepts(Collection concepts)
     throws JAXRException;
    public void addChildConcept(Concept concept) throws JAXRException;

    // Get the parent of the Concept.
    public RegistryObject getParent() throws JAXRException;
    public Concept getParentConcept()  throws JAXRException;
    public ClassificationScheme getClassificationScheme()
      throws JAXRException;

    // Get the canonical path representation for this Concept.
    public String getPath() throws JAXRException;
}
```

If the `Concept` object represents a WSDL `tModel`, then you cannot make use of the methods defined by the `Concept` interface; you must use the methods defined by its supertype, `RegistryObject`, for reasons I'll explain in a little bit. If, however, the `Concept` object represents a taxonomy value, then all its methods may be of use to you.

18.2.2.1 `Concept` *Methods and Taxonomy Browsing*

JAXR defines two types of taxonomies, internal and external. An **internal taxonomy** is one that is maintained by the JAXR provider and can be browsed using the `Concept` methods as an object graph. JAXR requires that all JAXR providers (vendors) include internal taxonomies for NAICS, UNSPSC, and ISO 3166. As a consequence, the JAXR provider you use in your client code will maintain an object graph representing all of the values in each of these taxonomies. This arrangement makes it fairly easy to create client-side browsers. For example, Listing 18–6 is an example of a very simple taxonomy browser.

Listing 18–6

Browsing an Internal Taxonomy Using Methods Defined by the `Concept` *Interface*

```
package com.jwsbook.jaxr;
import javax.xml.registry.ConnectionFactory;
import javax.xml.registry.Connection;
import javax.xml.registry.RegistryService;
import javax.xml.registry.BusinessQueryManager;
import javax.xml.registry.infomodel.Concept;
import javax.xml.registry.infomodel.ClassificationScheme;
```

```
import javax.xml.registry.JAXRException;
import java.util.Iterator;
import java.util.Collection;
import java.util.Properties;

public class TaxonomyBrowser {
  public static void main(String [] args)
  throws JAXRException, java.io.IOException {
    // Access BusinessLifeCycleManager and BusinessQueryManager objects.
    Connection connection = connectToRegistry();
    RegistryService registry = connection.getRegistryService();
    BusinessQueryManager queryMngr =
                              registry.getBusinessQueryManager();

    String taxonomyName = args[0];

    // Find the ClassificationScheme.
    ClassificationScheme taxonomy =
      queryMngr.findClassificationSchemeByName(null, taxonomyName);

    // Get first-level children.
    Collection children = taxonomy.getChildrenConcepts();

    // List all descendants.
    list(3,children);

    // Close the connection.
    connection.close();
  }
  /* This method is recursive. It lists all the children of a Concept.*/
  public static void list(int indent, Collection children)
  throws JAXRException{
    Iterator concepts = children.iterator();
    while(concepts.hasNext()){
      Concept concept = (Concept)concepts.next();
      for(int i = 0; i < indent;i++)System.out.print(" ");
      System.out.println(concept.getValue()+
                       " "+concept.getName().getValue());
      list(indent+3,concept.getChildrenConcepts());
    }
  }
  public static Connection connectToRegistry() throws JAXRException {
     // Create a ConnectionFactroy.
```

```
        ConnectionFactory factory = ConnectionFactory.newInstance();
        // Configure the ConnectionFactory.
        Properties props = new Properties();
        props.setProperty("javax.xml.registry.queryManagerURL",
                          "http://uddi.ibm.com/testregistry/inquiryapi");
        factory.setProperties(props);
        // Connect to UDDI test registry.
        Connection connection = factory.createConnection();
        return connection;
    }
}
```

To run this example, you must use one of the valid internal taxonomy names:

- `ntis-gov:naics:1997`
- `unspsc-org:unspsc`
- `uddi-org:iso-ch:3166-1999`

To run `TaxonomyBrowser` from a command window, execute a command in the following format:

```
[prompt] java com.jwsbook.jaxr.TaxonomyBrowser taxonomyName
```

The NAICS taxonomy (`ntis-gov:naics:1997`) ***is probably the best one to try. The UNSPSC taxonomy*** (`unspsc-org:unspsc`) ***contains thousands of values and takes a while to run. A bug may prevent the ISO 3166 taxonomy*** (`uddi-org:iso-ch:3166-1999`) ***from working properly if you're using the JAXR reference implementation.***

The first thing that `TaxonomyBrowser` does after connecting is to locate the `ClassificationScheme` that is associated with the taxonomy name you provided. The `ClassificationScheme` objects for NAICS, UNSPSC, and ISO 3166 must be accessible from an internal cache maintained by the JAXR provider.

```
// Find the ClassificationScheme.
ClassificationScheme taxonomy =
  queryMngr.findClassificationSchemeByName(null, taxonomyName);
```

Once the proper `ClassificationScheme` is located, we ask for its immediate children. These will be the taxonomy values that are at the first level in the taxonomy.

```
// Get first-level children.
Collection children = taxonomy.getChildrenConcepts();
```

Armed with the first-level `Concept` objects, we can recursively list their taxonomy values and names, and the values and names of their children, and of their children's children, and so on, until all the descendants of the taxonomy have been listed.

```
// List all descendants.
list(3,children);
```

An **external taxonomy** is one that is maintained by the UDDI registry or some other source, and cannot be browsed using JAXR. One example is the WAND taxonomy used by the IBM UBR registry. You can browse the WAND taxonomy only by using the external WAND Web site, or the IBM UBR Web interface.

18.2.2.2 `RegistryObject` *Methods and WSDL* `Concepts`

In addition to the methods defined in the `Concept` interface, some of the methods it inherits from `RegistryObject` are also useful. The following snippet from the definition of the `RegistryObject` interface (Listing 17–1) shows which methods you can use with a `Concept` object.

```
package javax.xml.registry.infomodel;
import java.io.*;
import java.net.*;
import javax.xml.registry.*;
import java.util.*;

public interface RegistryObject extends ExtensibleObject  {

  // Get|Set the universally unique ID (UUID) for this object.
  public Key getKey() throws JAXRException;
  public void setKey(Key key) throws JAXRException;

  // Get|Set the name of this object.
  public InternationalString getName() throws JAXRException;
  public void setName(InternationalString name) throws JAXRException;

  // Get|Set the text description for this object.
  public InternationalString getDescription() throws JAXRException;
  public void setDescription(InternationalString description)
    throws JAXRException;

  // Get|Set the collection of Classifications for this object.
  public void setClassifications(Collection classifications)
    throws JAXRException;
  public Collection getClassifications() throws JAXRException;
```

```
    // Get|Set the collection of ExternalIdentifiers for this object.
    public void setExternalIdentifiers(Collection externalIdentifiers)
      throws JAXRException;
    public Collection getExternalIdentifiers() throws JAXRException;

    // Get|Add the collection of ExternalLinks for this object.
    public void addExternalLink(ExternalLink externalLink)
      throws JAXRException;
    public Collection getExternalLinks() throws JAXRException;

}
```

The `getKey()` and `setKey()` methods return the UUID of the underlying `tModel`. The UUIDs for `tModels` are unique in that they always start with a `uddi` prefix, but otherwise they're the same as keys for `businessEntity`, `businessService`, and other UDDI structures (see Section 17.1.1).

The `getName()` and `setName()` methods provide access to the name of the `Concept` in the form of an `InternationalString` object. A `Concept` can have only one name (a `LocalizedString` value), but it may be language-specific. The `setDescription()` and `getDescription()` methods get or set the description of the `Concept`. A `Concept` may have multiple language-specific descriptions represented by an `InternationalString` object (see Section 17.2.3).

A `Concept` may be associated with `Classification` and `ExternalIdentifier` objects. The `Classification` and `ExternalIdentifier` types are discussed in more detail in Sections 17.2.5 and 17.2.6.

> ***The Basic Profile requires that a technical*** `tModel` ***for a WSDL document be classified as*** `wsdlSpec` ***and*** `ws-i-org:conformsTo:2002_12`.[BP]

The `ExternalLink` methods allow you to access the UDDI `overviewDoc` elements associated with the underlying `tModel`. A `Concept` may have many `ExternalLink` objects, but will usually have only one.

18.3 The `SpecificationLink` Information Object

You can associate a `Concept` object with your `ServiceBinding` using a `SpecificationLink`. A `ServiceBinding` may contain references to one or more `SpecificationLink` objects, which are maintained in a `Collection`. A `SpecificationLink` represents the UDDI `tModelInstanceInfo` and `tModel instance Details` elements of the `bindingTemplate` (see Section 6.2.2.3).

18.3.1 Using `SpecificationLink` Objects

In Listing 18–7, `JaxrExample_8` locates existing `Organization` and `Concept` objects and then links them together using new `Service`, `ServiceBinding`, and `SpecificationLink` objects.

Listing 18–7

Linking a `Concept` *to a* `ServiceBinding`

```
package com.jwsbook.jaxr;
import javax.xml.registry.ConnectionFactory;
import javax.xml.registry.Connection;
import javax.xml.registry.RegistryService;
import javax.xml.registry.LifeCycleManager;
import javax.xml.registry.BusinessLifeCycleManager;
import javax.xml.registry.BusinessQueryManager;
import javax.xml.registry.infomodel.Organization;
import javax.xml.registry.infomodel.Service;
import javax.xml.registry.infomodel.ServiceBinding;
import javax.xml.registry.infomodel.Concept;
import javax.xml.registry.infomodel.SpecificationLink;
import javax.xml.registry.infomodel.ExternalLink;
import javax.xml.registry.infomodel.InternationalString;
import javax.xml.registry.infomodel.Key;
import javax.xml.registry.JAXRResponse;
import javax.xml.registry.BulkResponse;
import javax.xml.registry.JAXRException;
import java.net.PasswordAuthentication;
import java.util.Properties;
import java.util.Set;
import java.util.Collection;
import java.util.HashSet;
import java.util.Iterator;


public class JaxrExample_8{
  public static void main(String [] args) throws JAXRException {
    // Extract parameters.
    String companyKey = args[0];
    String tModelKey = args[1];
    String userName = args[2];
    String password = args[3];
```

```
// Access BusinessLifeCycleManager and BusinessQueryManager objects.
Connection connection = connectToRegistry(userName,password);
RegistryService registry = connection.getRegistryService();
BusinessLifeCycleManager lifeCycleMngr =
                        registry.getBusinessLifeCycleManager();
BusinessQueryManager queryMngr = registry.getBusinessQueryManager();

// Find my Organization by its Key.
Organization myOrganization = (Organization)
   queryMngr.getRegistryObject(companyKey.trim(),
                               LifeCycleManager.ORGANIZATION);

String orgName = myOrganization.getName().getValue();

// Create and add a new Service to my Organization.
Service service = lifeCycleMngr.createService("BookQuoteService");
InternationalString desc = lifeCycleMngr.createInternationalString(
                   "This Web service provides "+orgName+
                   "'s current prices of Books");
service.setDescription(desc);
myOrganization.addService(service);

// Create, add, and configure a new ServiceBinding.
ServiceBinding binding = lifeCycleMngr.createServiceBinding();
service.addServiceBinding(binding);
binding.setValidateURI(false);
binding.setAccessURI("http://www."+orgName+".com/BookQuote");

// Create a SpecificationLink and add it to the ServiceBinding.
SpecificationLink specLink =
                 lifeCycleMngr.createSpecificationLink();
binding.addSpecificationLink(specLink);

// Locate and set the Concept for the SpecificationLink.
Concept wsdlConcept = (Concept)
        queryMngr.getRegistryObject(tModelKey.trim(),
                                    LifeCycleManager.CONCEPT);
specLink.setSpecificationObject(wsdlConcept);

// Save the Organization in the UDDI directory.
Set organizationSet = new HashSet();
organizationSet.add(myOrganization);
BulkResponse response =
```

```
                lifeCycleMngr.saveOrganizations(organizationSet);

        // Check for registry exceptions.
        doExceptions(response);

        // Close the connection.
        connection.close();
    }
    public static void doExceptions(BulkResponse rspns)
    throws JAXRException {
     /* The code for this method is omitted for brevity. See
        JaxrExample_2 (Listing 17-3) for a
        complete listing of this method.*/
    }
    public static Connection connectToRegistry(String userName,
                                               String password)
    throws JAXRException {
     /* The code for this method is omitted for brevity. See
        JaxrExample_2 (Listing 17-3) for a
        complete listing of this method.*/
    }
}
```

To run this example, you'll need the UUID key of the `Organization` you created using `JaxrExample_3` (Listing 17–12) and the `Concept` you created in `JaxrExample_7` (Listing 18–4). You should be able to log into IBM's UDDI test Web site and find the `businessEntity` and `tModel` associated with these `Organization` and `Concept` objects. To run `JaxrExample_8` from a command window, execute a command in the following format:

```
[prompt] java com.jwsbook.jaxr.JaxrExample_8 orgKey conceptKey userName password
```

18.3.1.1 *Create a* `Service` *and a* `ServiceBinding`

To associate a `Concept` with an `Organization`, you need to create a `Service` and a `ServiceBinding` as in the following snippet from `JaxrExample_8` (Listing 18–7).

```
// Create and add a new Service to my Organization.
Service service = lifeCycleMngr.createService("BookQuoteService");
InternationalString desc = lifeCycleMngr.createInternationalString(
                           "This Web service provides "+orgName+
                           "'s current prices of Books");
service.setDescription(desc);
myOrganization.addService(service);
```

```
// Create, add, and configure a new ServiceBinding.
ServiceBinding binding = lifeCycleMngr.createServiceBinding();
service.addServiceBinding(binding);
binding.setValidateURI(false);
binding.setAccessURI("http://www."+orgName+".com/BookQuote");
```

You learned in Sections 18.1 and 18.2 that a `Service` represents a logical grouping of electronic services. Each `Service` may contain many `ServiceBinding` objects, which assign an `accessURI` to a Web service and, optionally, associate one or more `Concept` objects with it.

18.3.1.2 Create a `SpecificationLink`

You create `SpecificationLinks` the same way as you do other infomodel objects, using the `LifeCycleManager` methods. Specifically you invoke the `create SpecificationLink()` method, of which there is only one version, with no parameters. Once a `SpecificationLink` is created, you can add it to the `ServiceBinding` and set it to refer to the `Concept` that represents the WSDL document. The following snippet from `JaxrExample_8` (Listing 18–7) illustrates:

```
// Create a SpecificationLink and add it to the ServiceBinding.
SpecificationLink specLink = lifeCycleMngr.createSpecificationLink();
binding.addSpecificationLink(specLink);

// Locate and set the Concept for the SpecificationLink.
Concept wsdlConcept = (Concept)
  queryMngr.getRegistryObject(tModelKey.trim(),
                              LifeCycleManager.CONCEPT);
specLink.setSpecificationObject(wsdlConcept);
```

You locate the `Concept` object the same way you found the `Organization` object, by its UUID key, using the `QueryManager`. Once you have a reference to the `Concept` object, you can associate it with the `SpecificationLink` by invoking the `setSpecificationObject()` method.

The `Concept` object must be created and saved independent of the `Organization`, `Service`, `ServiceBinding`, and `SpecificationLink`. That's because a `SpecificationLink` can be saved only if it refers to an existing `tModel` UUID key. Saving that `Organization` object at the end of `JaxrExample_8`, however, will result in the storage of all the new infomodel objects: `Service`, `ServiceBinding`, and `SpecificationLink`, as in this snippet from Listing 18–7.

```
// Save the Organization in the UDDI directory.
Set organizationSet = new HashSet();
organizationSet.add(myOrganization);
```

```
BulkResponse response =
            lifeCycleMngr.saveOrganizations(organizationSet);
```

18.3.2 The SpecificationLink Interface

The SpecificationLink interface defines methods for accessing the Concept object as well as declaring usage parameters. Listing 18–8 shows the definition of the SpecificationLink interface.

Listing 18–8

The javax.xml.registry.infomodel.SpecificationLink *Interface*

```
package javax.xml.registry.infomodel;
import javax.xml.registry.*;
import java.util.*;

public interface SpecificationLink extends RegistryObject {

  // Get|Set the Concept for this link.
  public RegistryObject getSpecificationObject() throws JAXRException;
  public void setSpecificationObject(RegistryObject obj)
   throws JAXRException;

  // Get|Set the description of the usage parameters.
  public InternationalString getUsageDescription() throws JAXRException;
  public void setUsageDescription(InternationalString usageDescription)
   throws JAXRException;

  // Get|Set any usage parameters.
  public Collection getUsageParameters() throws JAXRException;
  public void setUsageParameters(Collection usageParameters)
   throws JAXRException;

  // Get the parent ServiceBinding for this SpecificationLink.
  public ServiceBinding getServiceBinding() throws JAXRException;
}
```

The SpecificationLink object provides access to the Concept it refers to via the getSpecificationObject() and setSpecificationObject() methods.

The getUsageParameters() and setUsageParameters() methods provide access to technical properties that augment the information provided by the Concept object. The usageParameters in JAXR map to the instanceDetails element in the UDDI bindingTemplate data structure. It's unclear whether or not the instanceDetails element can be used in BP-conformant Web services, so you should probably avoid employing it in such services, and therefore avoid as well invoking `getUsageParameters()`, `setUsageParameters()`, `getUsageDescription()`, and `setUsageDescription()`, so there's no reason to discuss these methods here.

18.4 The `Association` Information Object

You can assert that your organization has a relationship with some other organization by creating an `Association` object. The `Association` object represents a categorized relationship between two `Organization` objects and corresponds to the UDDI `publisherAssertion` data structure (see Section 6.4).

Although `createAssociation()` is a general-purpose method in the JAXR API, when working with UDDI it is used only to assert a relationship between `businessEntity` data types—`Organization` objects.

18.4.1 Creating an `Association`

Creating an `Association` between two `Organization` objects is fairly easy. All you need to do is obtain a reference to each `Organization`, create an `Association`, and save the `Association` in the UDDI registry. `JaxrExample_9` (Listing 18–9) illustrates how to create an `Association` between two `Organization` objects.

Listing 18–9

Creating an `Association` *between Two* `Organizations`

```
package com.jwsbook.jaxr;
import javax.xml.registry.ConnectionFactory;
import javax.xml.registry.Connection;
import javax.xml.registry.RegistryService;
import javax.xml.registry.LifeCycleManager;
import javax.xml.registry.BusinessLifeCycleManager;
import javax.xml.registry.BusinessQueryManager;
import javax.xml.registry.infomodel.Association;
import javax.xml.registry.infomodel.Organization;
import javax.xml.registry.infomodel.Concept;
import javax.xml.registry.infomodel.Key;
import javax.xml.registry.JAXRException;
import javax.xml.registry.BulkResponse;
import javax.xml.registry.JAXRResponse;
import java.net.PasswordAuthentication;
import java.util.Properties;
import java.util.Set;
```

```
import java.util.Collection;
import java.util.HashSet;
import java.util.Iterator;

public class JaxrExample_9{
  public static void main(String [] args) throws JAXRException {
  // Extract parameters.
  String sourceOrgKey = args[0];
  String targetOrgKey = args[1];
  String userName = args[2];
  String password = args[3];

  // Access the BusinessLifeCycleManager and BusinessQueryManager.
  Connection connection = connectToRegistry(userName,password);
  RegistryService registry = connection.getRegistryService();
  BusinessLifeCycleManager lifeCycleMngr =
                         registry.getBusinessLifeCycleManager();
  BusinessQueryManager queryMngr = registry.getBusinessQueryManager();

  // Find my Organization by its Key.
  Organization sourceOrg = (Organization)
     queryMngr.getRegistryObject(sourceOrgKey.trim(),
                              LifeCycleManager.ORGANIZATION);

  // Find the other Organization by its Key.
  Organization targetOrg = (Organization)
     queryMngr.getRegistryObject(targetOrgKey.trim(),
                              LifeCycleManager.ORGANIZATION);
  // Find the AssociationType Concept object.
  Concept associationType  =
     queryMngr.findConceptByPath("/AssociationType/RelatedTo");

  // Create an Association object and add it to my Organization.
  Association association =
     lifeCycleMngr.createAssociation(targetOrg, associationType);
  sourceOrg.addAssociation(association);

  // Save the Association in the UDDI directory.
  Set assocSet = new HashSet();
  assocSet.add(association);
  BulkResponse response = lifeCycleMngr.saveAssociations(assocSet,true);

  // Check for registry exceptions.
  doExceptions(response);
```

```
    // Close the connection.
    connection.close();
    }
    public static void doExceptions(BulkResponse rspns)
    throws JAXRException {
     /* The code for this method is omitted for brevity. See
        JaxrExample_2 (Listing 17-3) for a
        complete listing of this method.*/
    }
    public static Connection connectToRegistry(String userName,
                                               String password)
    throws JAXRException {
     /* The code for this method is omitted for brevity. See
        JaxrExample_2 (Listing 17-3) for a
        complete listing of this method.*/
    }
}
```

To run this example, you'll need the UUID key of the `Organization` you created using `JaxrExample_3` (Listing 17–12). You'll also need to create a new `Organization` object with a different name. Run `JaxrExample_3` again to create another `Organization` (see Section 17.2.4). When the new `Organization` is created, get its UUID key from the IBM test registry.

Once you have the keys for both `Organization` objects, you are ready to run `Jaxr Example_9`, with a command in the format below, assuming that you are using a command window. Use the key for the `Organization` you've been developing all along as the `sourceOrgKey` and the key to the `Organization` you just created as the `targetOrgKey`.

```
[prompt] java com.jwsbook.jaxr.JaxrExample_9 sourceOrgKey
targetOrgKey userName password
```

18.4.1.1 Find the `Concept` *Object Representing the Association Type*

To create a new `Association` you need a `Concept` object that represents the **association type,** which represents the nature of the relationship between two organizations. JAXR implementations are required to support several different association types, which are predefined `Concept` objects that can be accessed by a simple path name. In `JaxrExample_9` (Listing 18–9), as shown in the following snippet, we are using the `RelatedTo` `Concept`, which belongs to the `AssociationType` scheme.

```
// Find the AssociationType Concept object.
Concept associationType  =
   queryMngr.findConceptByPath("/AssociationType/RelatedTo");
```

The association type is a predefined enumeration (see Section 18.5). Predefined enumeration types are built directly into the JAXR API and are accessed via specified path values (`"/AssocationType/RelatedTo"`, for example).

The `AssociationType ClassificationScheme` defines several relationship types, but only a few of them are relevant to `Organization`-to-`Organization` associations. The paths for predefined `Concepts` that can be used for `Association` objects in UDDI are described here:

- `"/AssociationType/RelatedTo"` represents a UDDI **peer-to-peer** relationship between two `Organizations` like a manufacturer and a supplier, or a retailer and a wholesaler.
- `"/AssociationType/HasChild"` represents a UDDI **parent-child** relationship in which the source organization owns the target organization. For example, the source is a company and the target is one of the company's divisions.
- `"/AssociationType/EquivalentTo"` represents a UDDI **identity** relationship, in which the source and target are actually the same entity. This might be used if a company has more than one name and lists itself under both in different entries in the UDDI directory.
- `"/AssociationType/HasMember"` has no corresponding type in UDDI. It represents the relationship between an industry organization and its member companies.
- `"/AssociationType/HasParent"` has no corresponding type in UDDI. It represents the relationship in which the source is owned by the target organization.

Neither UDDI nor JAXR requires that you use these association types; actually you can define any type of association `Concept` object you want. You may want to use the UDDI standard relationship types (peer-peer, parent-child, and identity), though, because these are standard and well known. That said, creating your own association type is fairly easy. The following code snippet shows how you can create your own association-type `Concept` and use it to add a new `Association` object to a registry.

```
// Create and save a new association-type Concept object.
Concept associationType  = lifeCycleMngr.createConcept(null,
                                             "uddi-org:types",
                                             "relationship");

InternationalString conceptName  =
     lifeCycleMngr.createInternationalString("supplier-buyer");
associationType.setName(conceptName);
Collection conceptSet = new HashSet();
conceptSet.add(associationType);
lifeCycleMngr.saveConcepts(conceptSet);
```

In this case, the relationship defined is between a supplier and a buyer of some product (for example, books). The code creates an association type—in UDDI-speak, a relationship type. If necessary you can create a whole taxonomy of relationship types for a particular organization or industry. This is standard fare in private and marketplace UDDI registries. Section 18.2.1 covers the creation of new `Concept` objects in more detail.

18.4.1.2 Create an `Association` *Instance*

Once you have a reference to an association-type `Concept`, you can create a new `Association` instance using the `LifeCycleManager` as shown in this snippet from `JaxrExample_9` (Listing 18–9).

```
// Create an Association object and add it to my Organization.
Association association =
    lifeCycleMngr.createAssociation(targetOrg, associationType);
sourceOrg.addAssociation(association);
```

The first argument of the `createAssociation()` method is the target `Organization` object. The second is the `Concept` object that defines the type of association. Both are required to create an `Association` you can save. To identify the other organization, you don't supply a reference to it to the `Association` object; instead you add the `Association` object to the source `Organization` object, using the method `addAssociation()`, which is defined by the `Registry Object` supertype.

18.4.1.3 Save the `Association`

To place the `Association` object in the UDDI registry, you have to save it directly. Simply saving the `Organization` object won't work. You have to invoke `LifeCycleManager.saveAssociations()` explicitly, as in the following snippet from `JaxrExample_9` (Listing 18–9).

```
// Save the Association in the UDDI directory.
Set assocSet = new HashSet();
assocSet.add(association);
BulkResponse response = lifeCycleMngr.saveAssociations(assocSet,true);
```

Although you must save the `Association` object, it's not necessary to save the `Organization` object too. In UDDI the `publisherAssertion`, which corresponds to the JAXR `Association` object, is independent of the `businessEntity` entries it represents. The `publisherAssertion` maintains a reference to the `businessEntity` entries, but the `businessEntity` entries do not have references to any `publisherAssertion` entries. Adding the `Association` to the `Organization` object simply sets the target Organization reference on the Association; it doesn't actually add the Association data to the Organization.

18.5 Predefined Enumerations

Some of the JAXR infomodel types can be assigned a designator that describes their usage. For example, you can designate a TelephoneNumber object as "home phone," "beeper," "fax," and so on. As a convenience, the JAXR specification requires that vendors support a set of **predefined enumeration types** that represent these designators. If you read the preceding section, on the Association type, then you've already seen a predefined enumeration used, when you set the relationship-type Concept on the Association object. The following shows a snippet from JaxrExample_9 (Listing 18–9) that uses the BusinessQueryManager to look up a predefined enumerated Concept object.

```
// Find the AssociationType Concept object.
Concept associationType  =
    queryMngr.findConceptByPath("/AssociationType/RelatedTo");

// Create an Association object and add it to my Organization.
Association association =
    lifeCycleMngr.createAssociation(targetOrg, associationType);
```

Each predefined enumeration type in JAXR is organized into a hierarchy, where a ClassificationScheme represents the base scheme for several different Concept objects. You can find an instance of any predefined Concept object by invoking BusinessQueryManager.findConceptByPath(). The path value used with this method takes the form "/*ClassificationSchemeName*/*ConceptName*". There are two predefined enumeration sets that are of interest when working with a UDDI registry: AssociationType and URLType. These are covered in the following two sections.

JAXR also defines other enumeration sets—ObjectType, PhoneType, and Postal AddressType—but these are not as useful with UDDI registries and are not covered. For more information about these other enumeration types consult the JAXR 1.0 specification.

18.5.1 The AssociationType Enumeration

Section 18.4 provided a detailed example of how the AssociationType enumeration is found and set on an Association object. There are several different AssociationType concepts, but only a few that make sense when associating two Organization objects. These are listed in Table 18–1.

Table 18–1 Mapping the Predefined AssocationType Values to UDDI Relationship Types

Concept Name	Concept Path	UDDI Equivalent
RelatedTo	/AssociationType/RelatedTo	peer-peer
HasChild	/AssociationType/HasChild	parent-child
EquivalentTo	/AssociationType/EquivalentTo	identity
HasMember	/AssociationType/HasMember	UDDI Equivalent
HasParent	/AssociationType/HasParent	peer-peer

The AssociationType of an Association object corresponds to the keyed Reference element of the UDDI publisherAssertion, which is covered in detail in Section 6.4.

18.5.2 The URLType Enumeration

The ExternalLink object of a ServiceBinding has a useType, which indicates the type of protocol used by the accessURI property specified for the Web service (see Section 18.1.2 for details on the accessURI). In UDDI the URLType corresponds to the useType attribute of the accessPoint element of the binding Template (see Section 6.2.2.1). JAXR defines a URLType enumeration that corresponds to the standard UDDI useType enumeration, as shown in Table 18–2.

By default the URLType is "http", but you can change it to one of the other enumerated types using code like the following.

```
ServiceBinding binding = // get service binding
// Set useType to https
Concept useType = queryMngr.findConceptByPath("/URLType/HTTPS");
Classification useType_https = lifeCycleMngr.createClassification(useType);
binding.addClassification(useType_https);
```

Table 18–2 The Predefined URLType Mapping to UDDI useTypes

Concept Name	Concept Path	UDDI Equivalent
SMTP	/URLType/SMTP	mailto
HTTP	/URLType/HTTP	http
HTTPS	/URLType/HTTPS	https
		ftp[a]
FAX	/URLType/FAX	fax
PHONE	/URLType/PHONE	phone
OTHER	/URLType/OTHER	other

[a] JAXR doesn't support the "ftp" useType. It's an oversight, a bug that will probably be fixed in a future version.

18.5.3 The ExtensibleObject and Slot Interfaces

ExtensibleObject is the supertype of the RegistryObject interface. It defines methods for manipulating Slot objects. A Slot object represents arbitrary meta-data that can be attached to any infomodel object that implements the javax.xml.registry.infomodel.ExtensibleObject interface. Listing 18–10 shows the ExtensibleObject interface.

Listing 18–10

The javax.xml.registry.infomodel.ExtensibleObject *Interface*

```
package javax.xml.registry.infomodel;
import java.util.*;
import javax.xml.registry.*;

public interface ExtensibleObject {

  // Add a Slot(s) to this object.
  public void addSlot(Slot slot) throws JAXRException;
  public void addSlots(Collection slots) throws JAXRException;

  // Remove a Slot(s) from this object. A Slot is identified by name.
  public void removeSlot(String slotName) throws JAXRException;
  public void removeSlots(Collection slotNames) throws JAXRException;

  // Get the Slot(s) specified by slotName.
  public Slot getSlot(String slotName) throws JAXRException;
  public Collection getSlots() throws JAXRException;
}
```

Each Slot object assigned to a RegistryObject object has a name and a Collection of values associated with that name. UDDI doesn't actually support the concept of arbitrary meta-data, but JAXR does take advantage of the Slot metaphor whenever it encounters difficulty mapping to UDDI. The PostalAddress is a perfect example of JAXR and UDDI not lining up very well, yet the Slot semantics enable JAXR to map the Slot type directly to the UDDI addressLines element. Other examples are the Concept and ClassificationScheme, which use Slot objects for the authorizedName and operator attributes normally associated with UDDI tModels—these Slot objects are read-only. Listing 18–11 shows the Slot interface definition.

Listing 18–11

The `javax.xml.registry.infomodel.Slot` *Interface*

```
package javax.xml.registry.infomodel;
import java.util.*;
import javax.xml.registry.*;

public interface Slot {
   // Predefined Slot names used for UDDI providers.
   public static final String SORT_CODE_SLOT = "sortCode";
   public static final String ADDRESS_LINES_SLOT = "addressLines";

   public static final String AUTHORIZED_NAME_SLOT = "authorizedName";
   public static final String OPERATOR_SLOT = "operator";

   // Get|Set the name for this Slot.
   public String getName() throws JAXRException;
   public void setName(String name) throws JAXRException;

   // Get|Set the values for this Slot.
   public Collection getValues() throws JAXRException;
   public void setValues(Collection values) throws JAXRException;

   // Get|Set the slotType for this Slot.
   public String getSlotType() throws JAXRException;
   public void setSlotType(String slotType) throws JAXRException;
}
```

The static final fields are used with UDDI registry. The `getSlotType()` and `setSlot Type()` methods are for assigning an arbitrary (possibly MIME) type to a `Slot`. This property is not used with UDDI.

18.6 Wrapping Up

The JAXR information model, unlike some other UDDI APIs, hides a lot of the UDDI SOAP operations in the information model. For example, when you navigate from one infomodel object to the next, the JAXR provider can execute SOAP operations automatically to retrieve the information you need—which is easier, from an application developer's perspective, than explicitly looking up every data structure. JAXR also allows you to save a graph of infomodel objects at one time. For example, calling the `saveOrganizations()` method will automatically save the `Services` and

`ServiceBindings` associated with the `Organization`. Because JAXR uses a business-object model, rather than a SOAP API model, navigation of a UDDI registry tends to be easier.

Although JAXR is probably easier for novices, for those individuals who prefer to "think in" UDDI, other APIs like UDDI4J or Systinet's WASP UDDI API may be more attractive. These UDDI-oriented APIs basically map the UDDI data structures and operations directly to Java classes and methods—but remember that JAXR is the only standard J2EE UDDI API.

Chapter 19

The JAXR Inquiry and Publishing APIs

In Part III: UDDI you learned about the UDDI Inquiry and Publishing APIs, two sets of SOAP operations designed for searching for and saving data in a UDDI registry. The JAXR API hides many of the Inquiry and Publishing operations behind compact and expressive Java code. For example, if you navigate from an `Organization` to its WSDL `Concept`, the underlying JAXR implementation may send several inquiry messages to the UDDI registry without your knowing—or needing to know. The JAXR implementation creates and sends the SOAP messages automatically, to construct a complete information model so that the registry is easier for you to peruse.[1]

The two major sections of this chapter show the mappings between the JAXR API and the UDDI Inquiry and Publishing APIs.

19.1 Mapping JAXR to the UDDI Inquiry API

The UDDI Inquiry API has basically two types of SOAP operations, `find_XXX` and `get_XXX`. Although the `find_XXX` operations map fairly directly to methods defined by the `BusinessQueryManager`, many of the `get_XXX` operations defined by the UDDI Inquiry API are implicit to navigating the infomodel objects. For example, when you call the `Organization.getServices()` method, the JAXR implementation executes a `get_services` SOAP operation under the covers. This transparency

[1] It's not specified whether the query messages are done all at once, or lazily, as needed. I suspect the latter in most cases, but JAXR is not an API in which performance is really important, so I'm not sure it matters which strategy is used.

is convenient, because it allows you to peruse the JAXR infomodel naturally, without having to execute a `get_XXX` SOAP operation explicitly every time you want to navigate to a new infomodel type.

The `BusinessQueryManager` interface defines several `findXXX()` methods that correspond closely to the find operations in the UDDI Inquiry API, which Chapter 7 discusses in detail. Table 19–1 shows you the `BusinessQueryManager.findXXX()` methods and their corresponding UDDI Inquiry SOAP operations.

The `findCallerAssociations()` method actually maps to two Publishing API operations, `get_publisherAssertions` and `get_assertionStatusReport`, but they are more like Inquiry operations so I've included them here. The only difference between `findCallerAssociations()` and the other `findXXX()` methods is that it is executed against the Publishing URL and thus requires authentication.

Each of the JAXR `findXXX()` methods includes one or more parameters on which the search is based, and most of them return a `BulkResponse` object (described in Section 16.4), which contains the results of the search. The `findOrganizations()` method is a prototypical example of the `findXXX()` methods in general. Most of the others use a subset of the same criteria used by `findOrganizations()`, which is defined in Listing 19–1.

Table 19–1 Mapping `BusinessQueryManager.findXXX()` Methods to the UDDI Inquiry API

`BusinessQueryManager` **Method**	**UDDI Operation**	**Description**
`findOrganizations`	`find_business`	Finds matching `businessEntity` entries.
`findAssociations`	`find_relatedBusiness`	Finds matching `publisherAssertion` entries.
`findCallerAssociations`	`get_publisherAssertions` `get_assertionStatus Report`	Finds caller's matching `publisherAssertion` entries.
`findServices`	`find_service`	Finds matching `businessService` entries.
`findServiceBindings`	`find_binding`	Finds matching `bindingTemplate` entries
`findClassificationSchemes`	`find_tModel`	Finds matching `tModel` entries.
`findClassificationScheme ByName`	`find_tModel`	Finds `tModel` entry with matching name.
`findConcepts`	`find_tModel`	Finds matching `tModel` entries.
`findConceptByPath`	`find_tModel`	Finds `tModel` entry with matching name.

Listing 19–1

The `BusinessQueryManager.findOrganizations()` *Method*

```
package javax.xml.registry;
import java.util.*;
import javax.xml.registry.infomodel.*;

public interface BusinessQueryManager extends QueryManager {

   // Finds all Organization objects that match criteria.
   public BulkResponse findOrganizations(Collection findQualifiers,
                                          Collection namePatterns,
                                          Collection classifications,
                                          Collection specifications,
                                          Collection externalIdentifiers,
                                          Collection externalLinks)
   throws JAXRException;
   ...
}
```

Each of the parameters of this method is discussed in detail in the next section, but a quick example of how a `findXXX()` method is used will give you some context for learning about them. In Listing 19–2, `JaxrExample_10` executes a `findOrganizations()` method call to locate all the `Organization` objects whose names start with the characters specified in the first argument.

Listing 19–2

Using the `findOrganizations()` *Method*

```
package jwsed1.part6_jaxr;
import javax.xml.registry.ConnectionFactory;
import javax.xml.registry.Connection;
import javax.xml.registry.RegistryService;
import javax.xml.registry.BusinessQueryManager;
import javax.xml.registry.infomodel.Organization;
import javax.xml.registry.JAXRException;
import javax.xml.registry.BulkResponse;
import javax.xml.registry.JAXRResponse;
import java.net.PasswordAuthentication;
import java.util.Properties;
import java.util.Set;
import java.util.Collection;
import java.util.HashSet;
```

```
import java.util.Iterator;

public class JaxrExample_10{
  public static void main(String [] args) throws JAXRException {
    // Extract parameters.
    String namePattern = args[0];
    String userName    = args[1];
    String password    = args[2];

    // Access the BusinessQueryManager object.
    Connection connection = connectToRegistry();
    RegistryService registry = connection.getRegistryService();
    BusinessQueryManager queryMngr = registry.getBusinessQueryManager();

    // Create name-pattern search criteria.
    Collection namePatterns = new HashSet();
    namePatterns.add(namePattern);

    // Find Organizations that meet search criteria.
    BulkResponse response = queryMngr.findOrganizations(null, namePatterns,
                                                  null,null,null,null);
    // Output results of query.
    Iterator results = response.getCollection().iterator();
    while(results.hasNext()){
       Organization org = (Organization)results.next();
       String orgName = org.getName().getValue();
       System.out.println(orgName);
    }

    // Check for registry exceptions.
    doExceptions(response);

    // Close the connection.
    connection.close();
  }
  public static void doExceptions(BulkResponse rspns)
  throws JAXRException {
   /* The code for this method is omitted for brevity. See
      JaxrExample_2 (Listing 17-3) for a
      complete listing of this method.*/
  }
  public static Connection connectToRegistry()
  throws JAXRException {
    // Create a ConnectionFactory.
```

```
        ConnectionFactory factory = ConnectionFactory.newInstance();

        // Configure the ConnectionFactory.
        Properties props = new Properties();
        props.setProperty("javax.xml.registry.queryManagerURL",
                          "http://uddi.ibm.com/testregistry/inquiryapi");
        factory.setProperties(props);

        // Connect to UDDI test registry.
        Connection connection = factory.createConnection();
        return connection;
    }
}
```

To run this program, you need to choose an `Organization` name, or a fragment of a name, for the first argument of the program. To run `JaxrExample_10` from a command window, execute a command in the following format:

```
[prompt] java jwsed1.part6_jaxr.JaxrExample_10 orgName userName password
```

Make sure that the organization name or fragment doesn't include spaces, because the Java VM interprets a space as a parameter separator.

If you want to get lots of output from the IBM test registry, try the name fragment `IBM`, running `JaxrExample_10` as follows:

```
[prompt] java jwsed1.part6_jaxr.JaxrExample_10 IBM userName password
```

If there is no error, you'll get a fairly long list of `Organization` names that start with "IBM."

`JaxrExample_10` executes a fairly simple search for all `Organization` objects whose names start with the characters the user specifies. Its first step is to get a reference to the `BusinessQueryManager`, which requires that it connect to the UDDI registry and obtain a `RegistryServer` reference as shown in the following snippet from Listing 19–2.

```
// Access the BusinessQueryManager object.
Connection connection = connectToRegistry();
RegistryService registry = connection.getRegistryService();
BusinessQueryManager queryMngr = registry.getBusinessQueryManager();
```

Although authentication is required when using the Publishing API, you are not usually required to authenticate when using the Inquiry API. For example, the UBR allows anyone to use its Inquiry services. In Listing 19–2 the call to `connectToRegistry()` was modified so that the client does not authenticate. The `connectToRegistry()` method simply connects to the Inquiry access point anonymously.

Once you have a reference to the `BusinessQueryManager`, you have the access you need to make queries, but before you can execute a `findXXX()` method you'll need to create one or more **criteria objects.** `JaxrExample_10` uses only one criterion—a name pattern—which is constructed just before executing the `findOrganizations()` method, as in the following snippet from Listing 19–2.

```
// Create name-pattern search criteria.
Collection namePatterns = new HashSet();
namePatterns.add(namePattern);
```

With the search criteria in hand, you are ready to execute the `findOrganizations()` method. Although this method declares several criteria, you don't have to create criteria objects for all of the parameters—you can pass a `null` value into any parameters you're not using. You must, however, pass in at least one criteria object, or the method will throw a `JAXRException`. The following shows the invocation of the `findOrganizations()` method from `JaxrExample_10` (Listing 19–2).

```
// Find Organization that meet search criteria.
BulkResponse response = queryMngr.findOrganizations(null, namePatterns,
                                                    null,null,null,null);
```

Most of the `findXXX()` methods return a `BulkResponse` object (see Section 16.4). This will contain the results of the query in a `Collection` object, which is accessed by calling the `getCollection()` method. The actual contents of the `Collection` will depend on which `findXXX()` method you invoked. The `findOrganizations()` method returns a `BulkResponse` with a `Collection` of zero or more `Organization` objects.

19.1.1 Using Search Criteria

The next few sections provide a more detailed explanation of the search criteria employed by the various `findXXX()` methods. Not all `findXXX()` methods use all the criteria types, but all them use a subset of the criteria discussed in the following sections.

Each `findXXX()` method declares one or more criteria parameters. You can use several criteria in a single find, but each find operation in the examples uses only one criteria type, so we can discuss each type in isolation.

19.1.1.1 The `namePattern` *Criteria*

Many of the `findXXX()` methods can perform name searches. For example, the following code snippet will search for all the `Organization` objects whose name begins with "Titan" or "Addison."

```
// Create name-pattern search criteria.
Collection namePatterns = new HashSet();
```

```
namePatterns.add("Titan");
namePatterns.add("Addison");

// Find Organizations that meet search criteria.
BulkResponse response = queryMngr.findOrganizations(null, namePatterns,
                                                    null,null,null,null);
```

Name-pattern search criteria normally take the form of a `Collection` of `Strings` or `LocalizedStrings`. You use the latter if you want to search for name patterns in specific languages. By default, a name search is an ORed search. In the above example the results will contain all the `Organization` objects whose name starts with either "Titan" or "Addison." Name searches are, by default, case-sensitive.

You can use a wild-card character (`%`) in `namePattern` searches. By default, a wild card is assumed to be at the end of each name. A search for "Titan," for example, might return entries named "Titan Books," "Titan Industries, Inc.," and "Titanium Mining Corporation." You can specify one or more wild-card characters explicitly, which overrides the default behavior. For example, a `namePattern` search on the value "Am%com" might return entries like "Amazon.com" and "American Qualicom."

The following `BusinessQueryManager` methods declare a `namePattern` search parameter.

- `findOrganizations()`
- `findServices()`
- `findClassificationSchemes()`
- `findConcepts()`

The `namePattern` search parameter corresponds to the UDDI `name` search element, which is discussed in Section 7.2.1.1.2.

19.1.1.2 *The* `classifications` *Criteria*

You can search for `Organization`, `Service`, `ServiceBinding`, `ClassificationScheme`, and `Concept` objects using the `classifications` criteria. The following snippet shows how this might be done with the `findOrganizations()` method.

```
// Create a NAICS Classification.
ClassificationScheme naics_Scheme =
   queryMngr.findClassificationSchemeByName(null, "ntis-gov:naics");
Classification naics_BookWhslrClass =
   lifeCycleMngr.createClassification(naics_Scheme,
                                      "Book Wholesaler", "42292");
// Create a UNSPSC Classification.
ClassificationScheme unspsc_Scheme =
   queryMngr.findClassificationSchemeByName(null, "unspsc-org:unspsc");
```

```
Classification unspsc_TextBookClass =
   lifeCycleMngr.createClassification(unspsc_Scheme,
                                  "TextBook", "55.10.15.09");

// Place Classification criteria into a Collection.
Collection classifications = new HashSet();
classifications.add(naics_BookWhslrClass);
classifications.add(unspsc_TextBookClass);

// Find Organization by search criteria.
BulkResponse response = queryMngr.findOrganizations(null, null,
                                                    classifications,
                                                    null,null,null);
```

To search by `Classification`, you have to instantiate the `Classification` class, which means you first have to find its `ClassificationScheme`, and then create a `Classification` instance.

When multiple `Classification` objects are used in the criteria, the search will be conducted as an AND search. In the preceding snippet, the results will contain only those `Organization` objects that refer to both NAICS "Book Wholesaler" and UNSPSC "TextBook" `Classification` objects.

The following `BusinessQueryManager` methods declare a `classifications` search parameter.

- `findOrganizations()`
- `findServices()`
- `findServiceBindings()`
- `findClassificationSchemes()`
- `findConcepts()`

The `classifications` search parameter corresponds to the UDDI `categoryBag` search element, which is discussed in Section 7.2.1.1.1.

19.1.1.3 The `externalIdentifiers` *Criteria*

You can search for `Organization` and `Concept` objects using the `externalIdentifiers` criteria. The following snippet shows an example using `findOrganizations()`.

```
// Create a D-U-N-S ExternalIdentifier.
ClassificationScheme duns_Scheme =
    queryMngr.findClassificationSchemeByName(null, "dnb-com:D-U-N-S");
ExternalIdentifier dunsNumber =
   lifeCycleMngr.createExternalIdentifier(duns_Scheme,
                               "Monson-Haefel, Inc.", "038924499");
```

```
// Place ExternalIdentifier criteria into a Collection.
Collection identifiers = new HashSet();
identifiers.add(dunsNumber);

// Find Organizations that meet search criteria.
BulkResponse response = queryMngr.findOrganizations(null, null, null,
                                        null, identifiers, null);
```

To search using `externalIdentifiers`, you have to create one or more `ExternalIdentifier` objects, which means you first have to find the proper `ClassificationScheme` objects, and then create the `ExternalIdentifier` instances using the desired values.

When multiple `ExternalIdentifier` objects are used in the criteria, the search will be conducted as an AND search, which means it will return only the `Organization` objects that declare all of the identifiers specified. It's possible to find more than one matching `Organization`, because some `Organization` objects represent units within a larger organization that is identified by a single external identifier.

The following `BusinessQueryManager` methods declare an `external Identifiers` search parameter.

- `findOrganizations()`
- `findConcepts()`

The `externalIdentifiers` search parameter corresponds to the UDDI `identifierBag` search element, which is discussed in Section 7.2.1.1.1.

19.1.1.4 The `specifications` *Criteria*

You can search for `Organization`, `Service`, and `ServiceBinding` objects using the `specifications` criteria. The `specifications` criteria take the form of a `Collection` of `Concept` objects that represent `tModels`. The following snippet shows how a call to `findOrganizations()` might use `specifications`.

```
// Find the Concept object for a specific tModel.
Concept bookQuote_concept = (Concept)queryMngr.getRegistryObject(
              "UUID:2E802060-3CF2-11D7-9590-000629DC0A53",
              LifeCycleManager.CONCEPT);


// Place the Concept into a Collection object.
Collection specifications = new HashSet();
specifications.add(bookQuote_concept);
```

```
// Find Organizations that meet search criteria.
BulkResponse response = queryMngr.findOrganizations(null, null, null,
                                                    specifications,
                                                    null, null);
```

This code will return all the `Organization` objects that declare a Web service that uses a specific `Concept` object. To succeed, it must first get a reference to the desired `Concept` from the UDDI registry by invoking the `getRegistryObject()` method, which is defined by the `QueryManager` supertype. Once it has the necessary reference, it searches for all `Organization` objects that support the `Concept`.

A search by `specifications` criteria is conducted as an AND search. If multiple `Concept` objects are used in the `specifications` criteria, only those `Organizations`, `Services`, or `ServiceBindings` that refer to all of those `Concept` objects will be returned.

This type of query can be useful if you are looking for `Organization`, `Service`, or `ServiceBinding` objects that support a common `tModel`. For example, suppose all book wholesalers support the BookQuote Web service using the same `tModel`. If you want a list of all the organizations that support this `tModel`, you'll use `specifications` criteria.

The following `BusinessQueryManager` methods declare a `specifications` search parameter.

- `findOrganizations()`
- `findServices()`
- `findServiceBindings()`

The `specifications` search parameter corresponds to the UDDI `tModelBag` search element, which is discussed in Section 7.2.1.1.3.

19.1.1.5 The `externalLinks` *Criteria*

You can also search for `Organization` objects using the `externalLinks` criteria. The following snippet shows how you might use the `findConcepts()` method to locate `Concept` objects with certain external links:

```
// Create ExternalLink criteria.
String url = "http://sometypeofURL.com/somefile";
ExternalLink link = lifeCycleMngr.createExternalLink(url, "");

// Place the criteria in a Collection object.
Collection externalLinks = new HashSet();
externalLinks.add(link);

// Find Organizations that meet search criteria.
BulkResponse response = queryMngr.findOrganizations(null, null,
```

```
                                        null,null,null,
                                        externalLinks);
```

The ExternalLink you are searching for is a UDDI discoveryURL element of a businessEntity data structure. It's not necessary to set the description parameter when creating the ExternalLink; the search is based on the URL attribute of the ExternalLink, not the description. When multiple ExternalLink objects are used in the criteria parameter, the search will be conducted as an AND search; only those Organization objects that contain all of the ExternalLink objects specified will match.

The findOrganizations() method of the BusinessQueryManager interface is the only one you can use with the externalLinks criteria. You can't search for external links with the findConcepts() and findClassificationSchemes() methods, even though each declares an externalLinks parameter, because the underlying UDDI Inquiry API doesn't support searching for Classification Schemes or Concepts (both tModels in UDDI) by their externalLink objects.

The externalLinks search parameter corresponds to the UDDI discovery URLs element in the find_business operation discussed in Section 7.2.1.2.2.

19.1.1.6 *The* findQualifiers *Criteria*

The findQualifiers criteria allow you to modify the default behavior of a findXXX() method. You can use them to specify ordering of results, the Boolean evaluation of other criteria, and wild-card searches on names. The following snippet demonstrates how you can modify the behavior of the findOrganizations() method with findQualifiers criteria.

```
// Create a NAICS and UNSPSC Classification Collection.
Classification naics_BookWhslrClass =
   lifeCycleMngr.createClassification(naics_Scheme,
                                   "Book Wholesaler", "42292");
Classification unspsc_TextBookClass =
   lifeCycleMngr.createClassification(unspsc_Scheme,
                                  "TextBook", "55.10.15.09");
Collection classifications = new HashSet();
classifications.add(naics_BookWhslrClass);
classifications.add(unspsc_TextBookClass);

// Create a Collection of FindQualifiers.
Collection findQualifiers = new HashSet();
findQualifiers.add(FindQualifier.OR_ALL_KEYS);
findQualifiers.add(FindQualifier.SORT_BY_NAME_DESC);
```

```
// Find Organizations that meet search criteria.
BulkResponse response = queryMngr.findOrganizations(findQualifiers, null,
                                                    classifications,
                                                    null,null,null);
```

The `javax.xml.registry.FindQualifier` type declares about a dozen qualifiers that can be used in `findXXX()` method calls.This snippet uses two of them: `OR_ALL_KEYS` and `SORT_BY_NAME_DESC`. The `OR_ALL_KEYS` qualifier changes all the criteria to perform ORed comparisons. This qualifier has a significant impact on this query, because comparisions based on `classifications` criteria are normally ANDed, which means that only organizations that contain both `Classification` objects will match. Using `OR_ALL_KEYS` overrides this default behavior so that any `Organization` that declares either `Classification` will be a match. Your results will tend to be larger. The `SORT_BY_NAME_DESC` find qualifier dictates that the results returned must be sorted by `Organization` name in descending alphabetic order. By default, results are sorted in ascending order.

Table 19–2 lists and describes all of the `FindQualifier` constants and the `findXXX()` methods that can use them. These constants map one-to-one to the UDDI `findQualifiers` listed in Table 7–1 in Section 7.2.1.1.4.

Table 19–2 `FindQualifier` Constants and the `findXXX()` Methods That Can Use Them

Qualifier	Description	Applicable `findXXX()` Methods

`EXACT_NAME_MATCH`	Signifies that lexical-order—that is, leftmost in left-to-right languages —name-match behavior should be overridden. When this behavior is specified, only entries that exactly match the entry passed in the name argument will be returned.	`findOrganizations()`
		`findServices()`
		`findConcepts()`
		`findClassification Scheme()`

`CASE_SENSITIVE_MATCH`	Signifies that the default case-insensitive behavior of a name match should be overridden. When this behavior is specified, case is relevant in the search results and only entries that match the case of the value passed in the name argument will be returned.	`findOrganizations()`
		`findServices()`
		`findConcepts()`
		`findClassification Scheme()`

Table 19–2 Continued

Qualifier	Description	Applicable findXXX() Methods
SORT_BY_NAME_ASC	Signifies that the result returned by a findXXX() call should be sorted on the name field in ascending alphabetic sort order. When there is more than one name field, the sort uses the first of them. This sort is applied prior to any truncation of result sets. Only applicable on queries that return a name in the topmost detail level of the result set. If no conflicting sort qualifier is specified, this is the default sort order for inquiries that return name values at this topmost detail level.	findOrganizations() findAssociations() findServices() findConcepts() findClassificationScheme()
SORT_BY_NAME_DESC	Signifies that the result returned by a findXXX() call should be sorted on the name field in descending alphabetic sort order. When there is more than one name field, the sort uses the first of them. This sort is applied prior to any truncation of result sets. Only applicable on queries that return a name element in the topmost detail level of the result set. This is the reverse of the default sort order for this kind of result.	findOrganizations() findAssociations() findServices() findConcepts() findClassificationScheme()
SORT_BY_DATE_ASC	Signifies that the result returned by a findXXX() call should be sorted based on the date last updated, in ascending chronological sort order (earliest returns first). If no conflicting sort qualifier is specified, this is the default sort order for all result sets.	findServiceBindings() findOrganizations() findAssociations() findServices() findConcepts()
SORT_BY_DATE_DESC	Signifies that the result returned by a findXXX() call should be sorted based on the date last updated, in descending chronological sort order (most recent change returns first). Sort qualifiers involving date are secondary in precedence to the SORT_BY_NAME qualifier. This causes SORT_BY_NAME values to be sorted within name by date, newest to oldest.	findServiceBindings() findOrganizations() findAssociations() findServices() findConcepts() findClassificationScheme()

Table 19–2 `FindQualifier` Constants and the `findXXX()` Methods That Can Use Them (Continued)

Qualifier	Description	Applicable `findXXX()` Methods
`OR_LIKE_KEYS`	When an infomodel object has multiple `Classification` or `External Identifier` objects, the objects associated with the same `Classification Scheme` are ORed together. Allows one to say "any of these four values associated with this `Classification Scheme`, and either of these two values associated with that `Classification Scheme`."	`findOrganizations()` `findServices()` `findConcepts()` `findClassification Scheme()`
`OR_ALL_KEYS`	Changes the behavior for `specifications` and `classifications` criteria to OR keys rather than ANDing them. Negates any AND treatment as well as the effect of `OR_LIKE_KEYS`.	`findServiceBindings()` `findOrganizations()` `findServices()` `findConcepts()` `findClassification Scheme()`
`COMBINE _CLASSIFICATIONS`	Used only in the `find Organizations()` message. Makes the `Classification` objects for the full `Organization` element behave as though all `Classification` objects found at the `Organization` level and in all contained or referenced `Service` objects were combined. Searching by `classifications` critiera will yield a positive match on a registered business if any of the `Classification` objects contained within the full `Organization` element (including the `Classification` objects within contained or referenced `Service` objects) contains the filter criteria.	`findOrganizations()`
`SERVICE_SUBSET`	Used only in the `findOrganizations()` method, and only in conjunction with passed `classifications` criteria. Causes the search to use only the `Classification` objects from contained or referenced `Services`. Ignores any `Classification` object set directly on `Service` object's `Organization`.	`findOrganizations()`

Table 19–2 Continued

Qualifier	Description	Applicable findXXX() Methods
AND_ALL_KEYS	Changes the behavior for externalIdentifiers to AND keys rather than ORing them.	findOrganizations() findConcepts() findClassificationScheme()

19.1.2 The findXXX() Methods

Each of the findXXX() methods is used to locate a different type of infomodel object in a UDDI registry. The following sections describe the BusinessQueryManager.findXXX() methods in detail.

19.1.2.1 The findAssociations() *Method*

The findAssociations() method returns a Collection of Association objects that match the criteria specified. It is defined as follows:

```
public BulkResponse findAssociations(Collection findQualifiers,
                                     String sourceObjectId,
                                     String targetObjectId,
                                     Collection associationTypes)
  throws JAXRException;
```

The sourceObjectId and the targetObjectId parameters are the UUID values of the source and target Organization objects. The associationTypes parameter is a Collection of Concept objects that represent the type of association (RelatedTo, HasChild, and so on). The associationTypes are ORed: An association need have only one of the Concepts specified to be a match. The following shows how you might use findAssociations().

```
// Find the AssociationType Concept object and add it to a Collection.
Concept relatedTo_Type  =
   queryMngr.findConceptByPath("/AssociationType/RelatedTo");
Collection associationTypes = new HashSet();
associationTypes.add(relatedTo_Type);

BulkResponse response = queryMngr.findAssociations(null,
                               "9C508570-393D-11D7-9F18-000629DC0A53",
                               null,associationTypes);
```

You need to provide only two of the three parameters expected, `sourceObjectId`, `targetObjectId`, and `associationTypes`; supply a `null` for the one you don't specify. For example, the code above requests all the `Association` objects for a specific source `Organization` and any target `Organization`, in which the relationship type is `RelatedTo` (peer-to-peer, in UDDI terms). Locating and using a predefined association type is covered in detail in Section 18.5.1.

This method ANDs all non-null parameters. If no parameters are specified, no `Associations` are returned.

19.1.2.2 *The* `findCallerAssociations()` *Method*

The `findCallerAssociations()` method returns a `Collection` of `Association` objects, relative to the caller, that match the criteria specified. Here, "the caller" is the authenticated client. Only those associations created using the caller's credentials (login) are returned by the `findCallerAssociations()` method, which is defined as follows:

```
public BulkResponse findCallerAssociations(Collection findQualifiers,
                                           Boolean confirmedByCaller,
                                           Boolean confirmedByOtherParty,
                                           Collection associationTypes)
```

In order for this method to work, the caller must have authenticated with the UDDI registry. Only those associations owned by the authenticated caller and matching the criteria specified will be returned. This method ANDs all non-null parameters. If no parameters are specified, no `Associations` are returned.

The following snippet shows an example of how the `findCallerAssociations()` might be invoked:

```
BulkResponse response =
    queryMngr.findCallerAssociations(null,Boolean.TRUE,Boolean.FALSE,null);
```

This call will return a `Collection` of `Association` objects that you have confirmed, but have not been confirmed by the other party. If you reverse these two parameters, supplying `true` for `confirmedByOtherParty` and `false` for `confirmedByCaller`, the returned collection will contain `Association` objects that have been asserted against your `Organization` object, but that you have not yet confirmed.

The `associationTypes` parameter is a `Collection` of `Concept` objects that represent the type of association (`RelatedTo`, `HasChild`, and so on). The `associationTypes` are ORed, so an association need have only one of the `Concepts` specified to be a match. Locating and using a predefined association type are covered in detail in Section 18.5.1.

19.1.2.3 *The* `findOrganizations()` *Method*

The `findOrganizations()` method returns a `Collection` of `Organization` objects that match the criteria specified. It is defined as follows:

```
public BulkResponse findOrganizations(Collection findQualifiers,
                                      Collection namePatterns,
                                      Collection classifications,
                                      Collection specifications,
                                      Collection externalIdentifiers,
                                      Collection externalLinks    )
  throws JAXRException;
```

This method ANDs all non-null parameters. If no parameters are specified, no `Organization` objects are returned.

19.1.2.4 *The* `findServices()` *Method*

The `findServices()` method returns a `Collection` of `Service` objects that match the criteria specified. It is defined as follows:

```
public BulkResponse findServices(Key orgKey,
                                 Collection findQualifiers,
                                 Collection namePatterns,
                                 Collection classifications,
                                 Collection specifications)
  throws JAXRException;
```

This method ANDs all non-null parameters. If no parameters are specified, no `Service` objects are returned. This method requires that you supply an `Organization` UUID key, so that the search is specific to services owned or referred to by a single `Organization`. The following snippet shows how to use this method.

```
// Create an organization Key object.
Key key = lifeCycleMngr.createKey("9C508570-393D-11D7-9F18-000629DC0A53");

// Create name-pattern search criteria.
Collection namePatterns = new HashSet();
namePatterns.add("TextBook");

// Find Organization by search criteria.
BulkResponse response = queryMngr.findServices(key, null, namePatterns,
                                               null,null);
```

19.1.2.5 The `findServiceBindings()` *Method*

The `findServiceBindings()` method returns a `Collection` of `ServiceBinding` objects that match the criteria specified. It is defined as follows:

```
public BulkResponse findServiceBindings(Key serviceKey,
                                        Collection findQualifiers,
                                        Collection classifications,
                                        Collection specifications)
  throws JAXRException;
```

This method ANDs all non-null parameters. If no parameters are specified, no `ServiceBinding` objects are returned. This method requires that you supply a `Service` UUID key, so that the search is specific to `ServiceBinding` objects owned by a single `Service`.

19.1.2.6 The `findClassificationSchemes()` *Method*

The `findClassificationSchemes()` method returns a `Collection` of `ClassificationScheme` objects that match the criteria specified. It is defined as follows:

```
public BulkResponse findClassificationSchemes(Collection findQualifiers,
                                              Collection namePatterns,
                                              Collection classifications,
                                              Collection externalLinks)
  throws JAXRException;
```

This method ANDs all non-null parameters. If no parameters are specified, no `ClassificationScheme` objects are returned.

19.1.2.7 The `findClassificationSchemeByName()` *Method*

The `findClassificationSchemeByName()` method returns a single `ClassificationScheme` object that matches the criteria specified. It is defined as follows:

```
public ClassificationScheme findClassificationSchemeByName
                                              (Collection findQualifiers,
                                              String namePattern)
  throws JAXRException;
```

If more than one `ClassificationScheme` matches, then a `javax.xml.registry.InvalidRequestException` is thrown. If no `ClassificationScheme` matches the criteria, the method returns `null`.

19.1.2.8 The `findConcepts()` *Method*

The `findConcepts()` method returns a `Collection` of `Concept` objects that match the criteria specified. It is defined as follows:

```
public BulkResponse findConcepts(Collection findQualifiers,
                                 Collection namePatterns,
                                 Collection classifications,
                                 Collection externalIdentifiers,
                                 Collection externalLinks)
  throws JAXRException;
```

This method ANDs all non-null parameters. If no parameters are specified, no `Concept` objects are returned.

19.1.2.9 The `findConceptByPath()` *Method*

This method can be used only with predefined enumeration types supported by JAXR—in UDDI there is no concept of a `tModel` path. It is defined as follows:

```
public Concept findConceptByPath(String path) throws JAXRException;
```

Predefined enumeration types and paths are covered in Section 18.5.

19.2 Mapping JAXR to the UDDI Publishing API

The UDDI specification includes a Publishing API that is used to save, modify, and remove data from the registry. Nearly all of the SOAP operations defined by the UDDI Publishing API (discussed at length in Chapter 8) map to similarly named methods in the `BusinessLifeCycleManager` interface, as you can see in Table 19–3.

Every one of these methods returns a `BulkResponse` object that contains a `Collection` of values related to the type of operation performed. In most cases, the objects returned in the `Collection` are `javax.xml.registry.infomodel.Key` objects, the UUID keys of the objects that were added, updated, or deleted. The `BulkResponse` type is covered in more detail in Section 16.4.

In many cases you don't need to save an infomodel object to the UDDI registry explicitly. If one object is contained by another, saving the containing object will often automatically save the contained object. For example, if you create a new `Organization` and add a `Service` and `ServiceBinding` to it, you can save all three just by invoking `saveOrganizations()` using the `Organization` object—its children (the `Service` and `ServiceBinding` objects) will be saved too. The same is not true of new and updated `Concept` and `ClassificationScheme` objects. These must be saved explicitly before any other infomodel object can refer to them.

Table 19–3 Mapping `BusinessLifeCycleManager` Methods to the UDDI Publishing API[2]

`BusinessLifeCycleManager` Method	UDDI Operation	Description
`saveAssociations()` `confirmAssociation()`	`add_publisherAssertions`	Adds a new `publisherAssertion` or confirms a relationship declared by a `publisherAssertion`.
`deleteServiceBindings()`	`delete_binding`	Removes one or more `templateBinding` entries.
`deleteOrganizations()`	`delete_business`	Removes one or more `businessEntity` entries.
`deleteAssociations()`	`delete_publisherAssertions`	Removes one or more `publisherAssertion` entries.
`deleteServices()`	`delete_service`	Removes one or more `businessService` entries.
`deleteClassification Schemes()` `deleteConcepts()`	`delete_tModel`	In UDDI `delete_tModel` does not delete the `tModel`. It simply hides it from `find_tModel` calls. The `QueryManager.get RegistryObject` calls will still return the deleted `tModel` after a `deleteConcepts` or `deleteClassification Schemes` call.
`saveServiceBindings()`	`save_binding`	Adds or modifies one or more `bindingTemplate` entries.
`saveOrganizations()`	`save_business`	Adds or modifies one or more `businessEntity` entries.
`saveServices()`	`save_service`	Adds or modifies one or more `businessService` entries.
`saveClassificationSchemes()` `saveConcepts()`	`save_tModel`	Adds or modifies one or more `tModel` entries.
`saveAssociations()`	`set_publisherAssertions`	Modifies one or more existing `publisherAssertion` entries.

[2] The descriptions used in this table come directly from the JAXR 1.0 Specification, Appendix D.2.

19.3 Wrapping Up

The search capabilities in UDDI can be very powerful, but they depend almost entirely on the quality of the data being searched. In the free and public UDDI Business Registry, the quality of data varies. There are considerable differences in how organizations register Web services, and how they use identifiers and categorizations. Standards like the WS-I Basic Profile 1.0 help a great deal, but the real power is in the taxonomies used for categorization. Private UDDI registries tend to be better at standardizing how data is published and categorized in UDDI. Of course, this is not a reflection on JAXR, which is a nice API for accessing UDDI registries. Like many data access tools, however, JAXR's usefulness depends in large part on the quality of data it's accessing; garbage in, garbage out.

Part VI

JAXP

The J2EE Web Services APIs you have learned about in this book (JAX-RPC, SAAJ, and JAXR) will automatically handle most, if not all, of the XML processing needed to implement Web services in J2EE. At some point, however, you may find yourself in a situation where you want to write Java programs that work directly with XML documents. In such cases the standard J2EE API you can use is the **Java API for XML Processing (JAXP)**, version 1.2.

This part of the book provides a primer on JAXP 1.2 as it relates to using SAX2 and DOM 2, but JAXP is an enormous topic and far too complex to cover completely in this book (it would have required another 300 pages!). Instead, this part of the book provides you with an introduction to JAXP, and to SAX2 and DOM 2 parsers. It's enough to get you started using JAXP, but for an in-depth study of JAXP you should read a book dedicated to the subject. You should get a copy of *Processing XML with Java* by Elliotte Rusty Harold (Addison-Wesley, 2002), which provides complete coverage of JAXP, SAX, DOM, and other Java parser technologies and is, in my opinion, the best book on Java and XML available today.

In This Part

Chapter 20
SAX2

The **Simple API for XML (SAX)** uses an event-based architecture for processing XML documents, similar to the event-based architecture employed by Swing, the Java GUI API. To use SAX, you create a class that implements one of the SAX **listener interfaces** (there are three of them), and register an instance of that class with a SAX parser at runtime. A SAX parser reads an XML document from a data stream sequentially, from beginning to end. As it reads the stream, the SAX parser sends events to the listener object that you registered. In other words, the parser invokes callback methods on the listener object as it encounters different parts of the XML document. For example, at the start of the XML document the parser invokes the listener's `startDocument()` method, when it reads the start tag of an element it invokes the listener's `startElement()` method, and when it reads the end tag of an element it invokes the listener's `endElement()` method. Figure 20–1 shows some of the events, in order, that a SAX parser would generate while reading a simple XML document, in this case a SOAP message.

SAX came out of a grassroots movement on the xml-dev mailing list. Originally designed as a common abstraction for several different XML parsers, SAX has since become a de facto standard and the core Java processing API for parsers. SAX has always been an open and free standard that anyone can implement without concern for patents, trademarks, or licensing.[1] This chapter concentrates on SAX2, which is the version supported by JAXP 1.2.

[1] Elliotte Rusty Harold, *Processing XML with Java*, Boston: Addison-Wesley, 2003, p. 260.

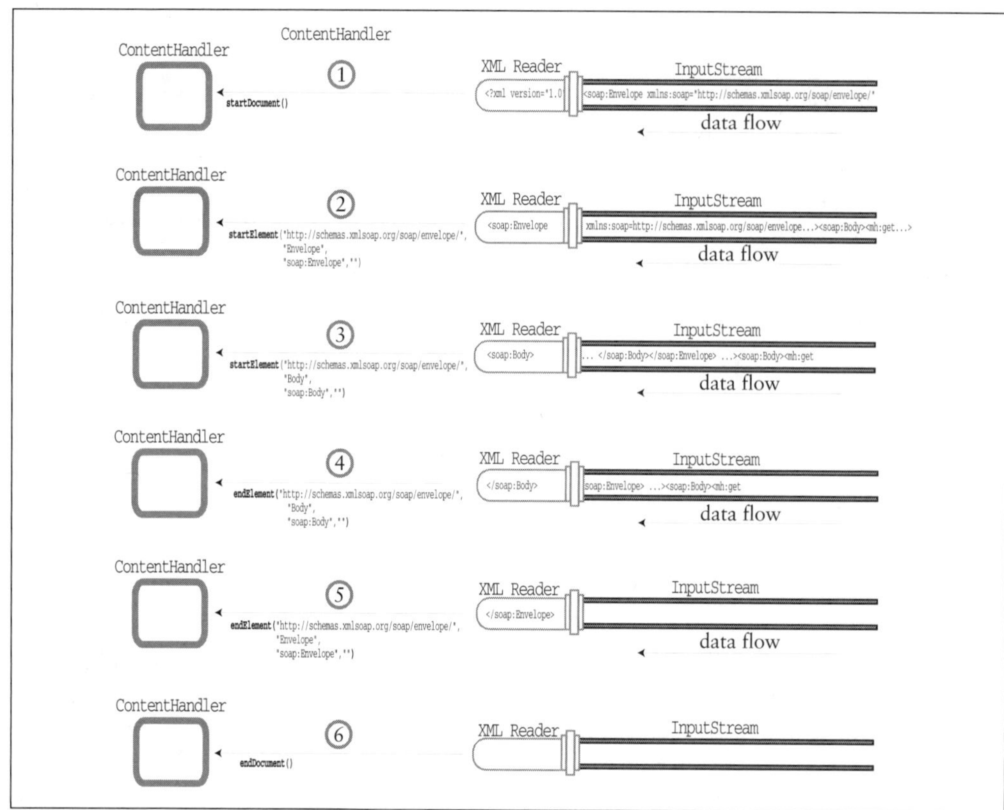

Figure 20–1 How SAX Parses an XML Document from a Stream

20.1 Parsing with SAX: `XMLReaderFactory` and `XMLReader`

Initially, SAX parsers differed in how they were instantiated and fed a document, which impaired portability; changing parsers would require changes in code. To overcome these problems, SAX2 provides two classes that are parser-agnostic: `org.xml.sax.helpers.XMLReaderFactory` and `org.xml.sax.XMLReader`. In Listing 20–1, `JaxpExample_1` shows a simple SAX program that uses these two classes to parse an XML document.

Listing 20–1

A Simple SAX Program

```
package com.jwsbook.jaxp;
import org.xml.sax.helpers.XMLReaderFactory;
```

```
import org.xml.sax.XMLReader;
import org.xml.sax.SAXException;
import java.io.IOException;

public class JaxpExample_1 {
  public static void main(String [] args) throws SAXException, IOException{
    String fileName = args[0];

    XMLReader parser = XMLReaderFactory.createXMLReader();
    parser.parse(fileName);

    System.out.println("No problems parsing the document");
  }
}
```

For the purposes of this chapter we'll be processing the SOAP request message that is used in the BookQuote Web service, and shown in Listing 20–2. You may want to dog-ear this page, because we'll refer to Listing 20–2 many times throughout this chapter.

Listing 20–2

A `BookQuote` *SOAP Request Message*

```
<?xml version="1.0" encoding="UTF-8"?>
<soap:Envelope
 xmlns:soap="http://schemas.xmlsoap.org/soap/envelope/"
 xmlns:xsi="http://www.w3.org/2001/XMLSchema-instance"
 xmlns:xsd="http://www.w3.org/2001/XMLSchema"
 xmlns:mh="http://www.Monson-Haefel.com/jwsbook/BookQuote">
   <soap:Body>
      <mh:getBookPrice>
          <isbn xsi:type="xsd:string">0321146182</isbn>
      </mh:getBookPrice>
   </soap:Body>
</soap:Envelope>
```

We don't need to declare the `xsi:type` ***attribute in the SOAP message, because the type can be derived from the XML schema declared in a WSDL document. This attribute is included here to demonstrate the support SAX2 provides for XML namespaces.***

Before you can run `JaxpExample_1`, you may need to set the `org.xml.sax.driver` system property, which tells JAXP exactly which SAX2 implementation you're using in your application. You can set the driver system property programmatically using the `java.lang.System` class, or in your operating environment, or on the command line when you execute the program. Avoid setting the system property programmatically unless you can obtain the property from a configurable source, like the JNDI ENC or a servlet initialization property. If you hard-code configuration of the system property using the `System` class, you create code that is not portable across JAXP providers. The following snippet shows the command you can use to set the driver system property when executing `JaxpExample_1`.

```
[prompt] java -Dorg.xml.sax.driver=org.apache.xerces.parsers.SAXParser
com.jwsbook.jaxp.JaxpExample_1 soapmsg.xml
```

If you see "No problems parsing the document," you will know that the program executed successfully.

20.2 The `ContentHandler` and `DefaultHandler` Interfaces

The primary listener interface in SAX2 is the `ContentHandler`, which defines 11 methods, each of which corresponds to some part of an XML document, such as an element, namespace declaration, document location, piece of text, white space, processing instruction, or DTD (Document Type Definition) entity. The `ContentHandler` interface is defined as shown in Listing 20–3.

Listing 20–3

The `org.xml.sax.ContentHandler` *Interface*

```
package org.xml.sax;

public interface ContentHandler {

  public void startDocument() throws SAXException;
  public void endDocument() throws SAXException;
  public void setDocumentLocator(Locator locator);
  public void startElement(String namespaceURI, String localName,
                           String qName, Attributes atts)
    throws SAXException;
  public void endElement(String namespaceURI, String localName,
                         String qName)
    throws SAXException;
  public void startPrefixMapping(String prefix, String uri)
    throws SAXException;
  public void endPrefixMapping(String prefix)
    throws SAXException;
  public void characters(char[] text, int start, int length)
```

```
    throws SAXException;
  public void ignorableWhitespace(char[] text, int start,
    int length) throws SAXException;
  public void processingInstruction(String target, String data)
    throws SAXException;
  public void skippedEntity(String name)
    throws SAXException;
}
```

In most cases, you'll need to implement only a subset of these methods. To make life easier, SAX2 provides an adapter class, `org.xml.sax.helpers.DefaultHandler`, which implements `ContentHandler` with empty methods. You can extend `DefaultHandler`, overriding only the event methods you want to implement, and ignore the rest. For example, Listing 20–4 shows a very simple content handler that implements just one method, `startElement()`.

Listing 20–4

Printing Out the Names of All the Elements in a Parsed Document

```
package com.jwsbook.jaxp;
import org.xml.sax.Attributes;
import org.xml.sax.SAXException;

public class SimpleHandler extends org.xml.sax.helpers.DefaultHandler {

  public void startElement(String namespaceURI, String localName,
                           String qName, Attributes atts){

    System.out.println(localName);

  }
}
```

Every time the SAX parser encounters the start tag of a new element, it will invoke this class's `startElement()` method. `SimpleHandler` simply prints out each element's local name, the tag name without the prefix. `JaxpExample_2` (Listing 20–5) shows you how to configure a parser to use `SimpleHandler`.

Listing 20–5

Configuring and Using a Simple Content Handler

```
package com.jwsbook.jaxp;
import org.xml.sax.ContentHandler;
```

```
import org.xml.sax.helpers.XMLReaderFactory;
import org.xml.sax.XMLReader;
import org.xml.sax.SAXException;
import java.io.IOException;

public class JaxpExample_2  {

  public static void main(String [] args) throws SAXException, IOException{
    String fileName = args[0];

    XMLReader parser = XMLReaderFactory.createXMLReader();
    ContentHandler contentHandler = new SimpleHandler();
    parser.setContentHandler( contentHandler);
    parser.parse(fileName);
  }
}
```

You can run `JaxpExample_2` on any XML document. The following shows `SimpleHandler`'s output if you parsed the SOAP request message in Listing 20–2.

```
[prompt] java -Dorg.xml.sax.driver=org.apache.xerces.parsers.SAXParser
com.jwsbook.jaxp.JaxpExample_2 soapmsg.xml

Envelope
Body
getBookPrice
isbn
```

Just as the parser invoked `SimpleHandler`'s `startElement()` each time it encountered a start tag, it will invoke other methods you implement in more elaborate handlers as it encounters other XML constructs in a document. The rest of this section covers most of the `ContentHandler` methods you are likely to use when processing documents in a BP-conformant Web service. Because the BP doesn't support processing instructions and DTD entities, events for these constructs will not be covered.

`JaxpExample_3` (Listing 20–6) is a general-purpose SAX application that can be configured at the command line to use any type of `ContentHandler`. This application is used throughout the rest of this chapter, so you may want to mark this page for later reference.

Listing 20–6

A General-Purpose SAX Application for Testing `ContentHandler` *Types*

```
package com.jwsbook.jaxp;
import org.xml.sax.ContentHandler;
```

```
import org.xml.sax.helpers.XMLReaderFactory;
import org.xml.sax.XMLReader;
import org.xml.sax.SAXException;
import java.io.IOException;

public class JaxpExample_3  {

  public static void main(String [] args)
  throws SAXException, IOException, Exception{
    String contentHanderClassName = args[0];
    String fileName = args[1];

    ContentHandler contentHandler = (ContentHandler)
     Class.forName(contentHanderClassName).newInstance();

    XMLReader parser = XMLReaderFactory.createXMLReader();
    parser.setContentHandler( contentHandler);
    parser.setFeature("http://xml.org/sax/features/namespace-prefixes",
true);
    parser.parse(fileName);
  }
}
```

Given the fully qualified name of a content handler, `JaxpExample_3` will load and instantiate the content handler class, then pass the instance to the parser. As a demonstration, you can run `JaxpExample_3` using `SimpleHandler` (Listing 20–4) as follows:

```
[prompt] java -Dorg.xml.sax.driver=org.apache.xerces.parsers.SAXParser
com.jwsbook.jaxp.JaxpExample_3 com.jwsbook.jaxp.SimpleHandler soapmsg.xml
```

The first parameter to `JaxpExample_3` is the class name of the content handler, and the second is the file name of the XML document to be parsed. When you run `JaxpExample_3` using `SimpleHandler`, the output will be just as before:

```
Envelope
Body
getBookPrice
isbn
```

`JaxpExample_3` turns on the `namespace-prefixes` property, which ensures that the parser will report XML namespace assignments and prefixes—this property may not be turned on by default.

```
parser.setFeature("http://xml.org/sax/features/namespace-prefixes", true);
```

20.2.1 The `startDocument()` and `endDocument()` Methods

The `startDocument()` and `endDocument()` methods mark the beginning and end of the processing for a specific XML document. These methods are generally used to initiate and clean up data cached by the content handler. For example, the `ElementCountHandler` in Listing 20–7 uses the `startDocument()` and `endDocument()` methods to count the number of elements in an XML document.

Listing 20–7

Using `startDocument()` *and* `endDocument()` *to Count Elements*

```
package com.jwsbook.jaxp;
import org.xml.sax.Attributes;

public class ElementCountHandler extends org.xml.sax.helpers.DefaultHandler {
  private int count = 0;
  public void startDocument(){
    count = 0;
  }
  public void startElement(String namespaceURI, String localName,
                          String qName, Attributes atts) {
    count++;
  }
  public void endDocument(){
    System.out.println("There are "+count+" elements in this document");
  }
}
```

The `startDocument()` method initializes `count`, `startElement()` increments it, and `endDocument()` displays its final value. The ability to perform processing before and after the document is parsed is useful when you are reusing the same content handler instance to process multiple XML documents. The `startDocument()` method allows you to re-initialize the data cached by the content handler, and the `endDocument()` method allows you to process the cached data after the parser has finished processing the XML document.

The following shows the command to run `JaxpExample_3` (Listing 20–6) using the `ElementCountHandler` on the SOAP document in Listing 20–2, and the output.

```
[prompt] java -Dorg.xml.sax.driver=org.apache.xerces.parsers.SAXParser
com.jwsbook.jaxp.JaxpExample_3 com.jwsbook.jaxp.ElementCountHandler
soapmsg.xml
There are 4 elements in this document
```

20.2.2 The `startElement()` and `endElement()` Methods

The parser invokes the `startElement()` and `endElement()` methods when it encounters the start and end tags (`<tag-name>` and `</tag-name>`) that mark the boundaries of elements in an XML document, in the order it finds them in the input stream. For example, in Listing 20–8, `ElementHandler` outputs the names of all the start and end tags in an XML document.

Listing 20–8

Using `startElement()` and `endElement()` to Output Start and End Tags

```
package com.jwsbook.jaxp;
import org.xml.sax.Attributes;

public class ElementHandler extends org.xml.sax.helpers.DefaultHandler {
  public void startElement(String namespaceURI, String localName,
                           String qName, Attributes atts) {
     System.out.println("<"+qName+">");
  }
  public void endElement(String namespaceURI, String localName,
                         String qName){
     System.out.println("</"+qName+">");
  }
}
```

To run `JaxpExample_3` (Listing 20–6) using `ElementHandler` to process the SOAP document in Listing 20–2, execute this command:

```
[prompt] java -Dorg.xml.sax.driver=org.apache.xerces.parsers.SAXParser com
.jwsbook.jaxp.JaxpExample_3 com.jwsbook.jaxp.ElementHandler soapmsg.xml
```

The output:

```
<soap:Envelope>
<soap:Body>
<mh:getBookPrice>
<isbn>
</isbn>
</mh:getBookPrice>
</soap:Body>
</soap:Envelope>
```

When it encounters a start tag, the parser invokes `startElement()`; when it encounters an end tag, it invokes `endElement()`; when it encounters an empty element (`tag-name/`), it invokes both methods, in sequence.

To keep track of the current element you can implement a cache using a local variable. For example, `ElementHandler2` (Listing 20–9) uses a variable named `indent` to output the XML document tag names with proper indentation.

Listing 20–9

Using `startElement()` *and* `endElement()` *to Output Start and End Tags, Indented*

```
package com.jwsbook.jaxp;
import org.xml.sax.Attributes;

public class ElementHandler2 extends org.xml.sax.helpers.DefaultHandler {
  private int indent = 0;
  public void startElement(String namespaceURI, String localName,
                           String qName, Attributes atts) {
     for(int i=0; i<indent;i++){
       System.out.print("   ");
     }
     System.out.println("<"+qName+">");
     indent++;
  }
  public void endElement(String namespaceURI, String localName,
                           String qName){
     indent--;
     for(int i=0; i<indent;i++){
       System.out.print("   ");
     }
     System.out.println("</"+qName+">");
  }
}
```

The following shows the command to run `JaxpExample_3` (Listing 20–6) using `ElementHandler2` on the SOAP document in Listing 20–2, and the output.

```
[prompt] java -Dorg.xml.sax.driver=org.apache.xerces.parsers.SAXParser
com.jwsbook.jaxp.JaxpExample_3 com.jwsbook.jaxp.ElementHandler2 soapmsg.xml

<soap:Envelope>
  <soap:Body>
    <mh:getBookPrice>
```

```
      <isbn>
      </isbn>
    </mh:getBookPrice>
  </soap:Body>
</soap:Envelope>
```

The indent variable helps startElement() and endElement() stay in sync in their indentation of the elements. This is a very simple example of how the startElement() and endElement() methods must coordinate their work to operate on elements as a whole.

The startElement() and endElement() methods define the same three parameters related to the name in the start and end tags: namespaceURI, localName, and qName, as shown in the following snippet from Listing 20–3.

```
public interface ContentHandler {
  ...
  public void startElement(String namespaceURI, String localName,
                           String qName, Attributes atts)
   throws SAXException;
  public void endElement(String namespaceURI, String localName,
                         String qName)
   throws SAXException;
  ...
}
```

- namespaceURI is the URI of the namespace to which the element belongs. For example, the namespace of the soap:Envelope element in Listing 20–2 is "http://schemas.xmlsoap.org/soap/envelope/".
- localName is the name of the elment without the prefix. For example, Listing 20–2 has four elements, whose localName values are Envelope, Body, getBookPrice, and isbn.
- qName is the fully qualified name of the element—that is, the prefix plus the localName. Examples from 20–2 include soap:Envelope, soap:Body, mh:getBookPrice, and isbn.

In addition to these parameters, the startElement() method declares the atts parameter, which contains the attributes declared for that element—recall that XML attributes are always declared in the start tag of an element, never in the end tag.

Attributes are accessed through an interface called, oddly enough, Attributes. Listing 20–10 shows the definition of this interface.

Listing 20–10

The `org.xml.sax.Attributes` *Interface*

```
package org.xml.sax;

public interface Attributes {
  public int    getLength ();
  public int    getIndex(String uri, String localPart);
  public int    getIndex(String qName);
  public String getLocalName(int index);
  public String getQName(int index);
  public String getURI(int index);
  public String getValue(String uri, String localName);
  public String getValue(String qName);
  public String getValue(int index);

  public String getType(String uri, String localName);
  public String getType(String qName);
  public String getType(int index);
}
```

The `Attributes` interface allows you to access an element's attributes by index (position), qualified name, or XML namespace and local name. The order of the attributes in the index is arbitrary; it may or may not be the same as the order in which the attributes were declared in the XML document. `AttributesHandler` in Listing 20–11 prints out the name of any element that has attributes, and the qualified names and values of those attributes.

Listing 20–11

Using `startElement()` *to Output Elements and Their Attributes*

```
package com.jwsbook.jaxp;
import org.xml.sax.Attributes;

public class AttributesHandler extends org.xml.sax.helpers.DefaultHandler {
  public void startElement(String namespaceURI, String localName,
                           String qName, Attributes atts) {
    int length = atts.getLength();
    if(length > 0){
      System.out.println("Element <"+qName+"> has the following attributes");
      for(int i = 0; i < length; i++){
        System.out.println("    "+atts.getQName(i)+" = "+atts.getValue(i));
      }
```

```
    }
  }
}
```

The `AttributesHandler` checks each element to see whether it has any attributes. If it does, the handler prints out its qualified name and the value of each attribute it declares. The following shows the command to run `JaxpExample_3` (Listing 20–6) using `AttributesHandler` on the SOAP document in Listing 20–2, and the output.

```
[prompt] java -Dorg.xml.sax.driver=org.apache.xerces.parsers.SAXParser
com.jwsbook.jaxp.JaxpExample_3 com.jwsbook.jaxp.AttributesHandler
soapmsg.xml

Element <soap:Envelope> has the following attributes
   xmlns:soap = http://schemas.xmlsoap.org/soap/envelope/
   xmlns:xsi = http://www.w3.org/2001/XMLSchema-instance
   xmlns:xsd = http://www.w3.org/2001/XMLSchema
   xmlns:mh = http://www.Monson-Haefel.com/jwsbook/BookQuote
Element <isbn> has the following attributes
   xsi:type = xsd:string
```

`AttributesHandler` prints out the qualified names (qNames) and values of attributes. You can also access the XML namespace assigned to the attribute (if namespaces are used) and the attribute type. The type reported by the `Attributes` interface is based on DTDs, not the W3C XML Schema Language. The type reported will always be `CDATA`—the default type if a DTD is not available—because BP-conformant Web services don't use DTDs. In a nutshell, this method is not going to be useful to you when developing BP-conformant Web services. You should be able to derive the type programmatically, however, from the XML namespace and the local name of the attribute, using the XML schema associated with the document you're processing.

20.2.3 The `startPrefixMapping()` and `endPrefixMapping()` Methods

Although the XML namespace of an element is available in the `namespaceURI` parameter of the `startElement()` and `endElement()` methods, and the XML namespace of an attribute is available in the `Attributes` parameter of `startElement()`, the XML namespaces of attribute and element *values* are not provided by these callback methods. Instead you must use the `startPrefixMapping()` and `endPrefixMapping()` methods to determine the XML namespace of a particular value.

When processing Web service documents such as SOAP messages and WSDL documents, it's very common to use XML namespaces for typing values. For example, the `xsi:type` attribute usually refers to a qualified value, such as `"xsd:string"`.

You can see this usage in the SOAP message in Listing 20–2, but you'll also see it in the `faultcode` element of a SOAP fault message (see Section 4.6.1), and in the `type` attribute used in WSDL elements such as `portType`, `binding`, `service`, and `port` (see Sections 5.3, 5.5, and 5.6).

`PrefixHandler`, in Listing 20–12, tracks the XML namespace declarations so that they can be used to determine the value types declared by the `xsi:type` attribute.

Listing 20–12

Using `startPrefixMapping()` *to Output the XML Namespaces of Values*

```
package com.jwsbook.jaxp;
import org.xml.sax.Attributes;
import java.util.HashMap;

public class PrefixHandler extends org.xml.sax.helpers.DefaultHandler {
  String XSI_NS = "http://www.w3.org/2001/XMLSchema-instance";
  HashMap prefixMap = new HashMap();

  public void startPrefixMapping(String prefix, String uri){
     prefixMap.put(prefix,uri);
  }
  public void startElement(String namespaceURI, String localName,
                           String qName, Attributes atts) {
     int length = atts.getLength();
     String attValue = atts.getValue(XSI_NS, "type");
     if(attValue != null){
       String prefix = attValue.substring(0, attValue.indexOf(":"));
       String uri = (String)prefixMap.get(prefix.trim());
       if(uri!=null){
          System.out.println("xsi:type = '"+attValue+
          "' xmlns:"+prefix+"='"+uri+"'");
       }
     }
  }
  public void endPrefixMapping(String prefix){
    prefixMap.remove(prefix);
  }
}
```

It's important to remember that the parser invokes `startPrefixMapping()` just before it invokes `startElement()` for each start tag, and that it invokes `endPrefixMapping()` immediately after it calls `endElement()` for any end tag.

The startPrefixMapping() method in the PrefixHandler stores XML namespace declarations in a HashMap. The startElement() method checks every start tag to see if it includes declaration of an xsi:type attribute. If it does, then startElement() extracts the value of the attribute and maps its prefix to one of the namespaces in the HashMap cache. The endPrefixMapping() method simply removes the cached XML namespace declaration from the HashMap.

The following shows the command to run JaxpExample_3 (Listing 20–6) using PrefixHandler on the SOAP document in Listing 20–2, and the output.

```
[prompt] java -Dorg.xml.sax.driver=org.apache.xerces.parsers.SAXParser
com.jwsbook.jaxp.JaxpExample_3 com.jwsbook.jaxp.PrefixHandler soapmsg.xml

xsi:type = 'xsd:string' xmlns:xsd='http://www.w3.org/2001/XMLSchema'
```

Although the PrefixHandler in Listing 20–12 works for the SOAP message, it's not a very robust implementation, because it can't deal effectively with XML documents that redefine the value of a prefix. For example, an XML document might reassign a prefix to a different URI in a child element. In this event, the previous mapping is simply lost; it's overwritten. To address this problem and to make life a little easier for SAX developers, SAX2 defines a helper class, org.xml.sax.helpers NamespaceSupport, which acts as a stack for XML namespace declarations. The NamespaceSupport class is outside the scope of this JAXP primer, but you can find out more about it in the SAX2 Javadoc, and in E. R. Harold's *Processing XML with Java*.

20.2.4 The characters() Method

In general, the parser invokes the characters() method when it encounters an element that contains text. This method may be called once, in which case it passes all the text contained by the element, or more than once, in which case it delivers the text in two or more blocks. The latter case is odd, and a nuisance, but it does arise sometimes, as a result of parser limitations. For example, the Crimson parser has a limit of about 8K of text. If the text contained by an element is longer than 8K, the Crimson parser will invoke characters() on the content handler multiple times, until all the text is processed.[2] To allow for multiple characters() invocations for one logical piece of text, you have to use some type of cache that can accumulate text fragments and concatenate them. For example, the CharactersHandler in Listing 20–13 uses a StringBuffer to accumulate text fragments, then outputs the result in the endElement() method. The reason this technique works is simple: Invocations of characters() are always nested between calls to startElement() and endElement(), so an uninterrupted series of calls to characters() can only be related to a single block of text within an element.

[2] Elliotte Rusty Harold, *Processing XML with Java*, Boston: Addison-Wesley, 2003, p. 284.

Listing 20–13

Using the `characters()` *Method to Accumulate Text*

```
package com.jwsbook.jaxp;
import org.xml.sax.Attributes;
import java.util.Stack;

public class CharactersHandler extends org.xml.sax.helpers.DefaultHandler {
  Stack stack = new Stack();

  public void startElement(String namespaceURI, String localName,
                           String qName, Attributes atts){
    StringBuffer buffy = new StringBuffer();
    stack.push(buffy);

  }
  public void characters(char[] chars, int start, int length){
     StringBuffer buffy = (StringBuffer)stack.peek();
     buffy.append(chars,start,length);
  }
  public void endElement(String namespaceURI, String localName,
                           String qName){
    StringBuffer buffy = (StringBuffer)stack.pop();

    System.out.println("The <"+qName+"> contains the following text:"+
                    "\""+buffy+"\"");
  }
}
```

Each time `CharactersHandler` is notified of a new start tag, `startElement()` pushes a new `StringBuffer` onto a `Stack` variable. If the `characters()` method is called, it will be for the element whose start tag was just processed by `start Element()`, so the `StringBuffer` for that element will be at the top of the stack. The `characters()` method peeks at the `StringBuffer` at the top of the stack and appends text to it. When `endElement()` is called, the `StringBuffer` for that element is popped off the stack and its contents are printed to the screen.

The following shows the command to run `JaxpExample_3` (Listing 20–6), using `CharactersHandler` on the SOAP document in Listing 20–2, and the resulting output.

```
[prompt] java -Dorg.xml.sax.driver=org.apache.xerces.parsers.SAXParser
com.jwsbook.jaxp.JaxpExample_3 com.jwsbook.jaxp.CharactersHandler
soapmsg.xml

The <isbn> contains the following text:"0321146182"
```

```
The <mh:getBookPrice> contains the following text:"

       "
The <soap:Body> contains the following text:"

    "
The <soap:Envelope> contains the following text:"

"
```

The `characters()` method returned the value of the `isbn` element, but it also returned all the white space (spaces, tabs, and such) contained by the other elements. Why did it do this? Without a DTD or schema to validate the document against, the parser can't distinguish between superfluous white space and meaningful white space. By default it assumes that all the elements contain mixed content, and that all text, including white space, is significant. Validation with the W3C XML schema is covered in Section 20.3.

20.2.5 Other `ContentHandler` Methods

In addition to the methods covered so far, the `ContentHandler` interface defines a few other methods that are useful in advanced circumstances, or when working with DTDs.

- `setDocumentLocator()` is called before `startDocument()`. It provides the content handler with a reference to a `Locator` object, which any method can use to determine the exact position of the parser in the document, measured in terms of rows and columns. This object can be useful for debugging code or reporting errors.
- `ignorableWhiteSpace()` is called when the parser encounters white space between elements in the document. It's used in advanced scenarios where white space needs to be managed—you'll probably never need to use this method.
- `processingInstruction()` is called when the parser encounters a processing instruction in the XML document. Because the Basic Profile prohibits the use of processing instructions, you are unlikely to use this callback method in your Web services.
- `skippedEntity()` is invoked by the parser when it encounters "skipped entities." Because entities are related to DTDs, which are not used in BP-conformant Web services, we'll skip them too.

20.2.6 Other SAX2 Listener Interfaces

In addition to `ContentHandler`, SAX2 defines a few other listener interfaces that you can register with a parser. The `DefaultHandler` discussed in the last section implements some of these, as well as the `ContentHandler` interface.

You use the `org.xml.sax.DTDHandler` and `org.xml.sax.EntityResolver` interfaces when you are parsing documents that are associated with a DTD.

SAX uses the `org.xml.sax.ErrorHandler` to notify the application that an error occurred while parsing the XML document. The methods defined by the `ErrorHandler` are the only mechanism for discovering these types of errors explicitly; the parser will not throw exceptions, it will call the `ErrorHandler` methods. The `ErrorHandler` interface is defined as in Listing 20–14.

Listing 20–14

The `org.xml.sax.ErrorHandler` *Interface*

```
package org.xml.sax;

public interface ErrorHandler {
  public void error(SAXParseException exception)  throws SAXException;

  public void fatalError(SAXParseException exception)  throws SAXException;

  public void warning(SAXParseException exception) throws SAXException;
}
```

The XML 1.0 Recommendation defines two types of errors the parser can generate while processing an XML document: errors and fatal errors. Errors should not end processing of the document. They report on things that are not fatal, such as validity errors (non-conformance with a DTD or W3C XML schema). Fatal errors, on the other hand, are errors that should stop the parser from continuing to parse the document. Fatal errors might signify encoding problems or more likely that a document is not well formed (that a start tag is missing an end tag, or some other syntax error perhaps). In general, a parser is not required to continue processing a document following a fatal error. These two errors are reported via the `error()` and `fatalError()` methods.

The `ErrorHandler` interface defines a third method for errors not addressed by the XML 1.0 Recommendation: The `warning()` method is used for all parser errors that are not categorized as XML 1.0 errors or fatal errors.

In a production implementation you have to decide how to react to warnings, errors, and fatal errors in a way that is appropriate to your application. In most cases you are going to want to throw an exception if a `fatalError()` method is called. If the `error()` method is called, you may or may not throw an exception, depending on how important validity is to your application. Because errors the parser reports with the `warning()` method don't cause the parser to stop processing, your content handler should not throw an exception.

20.3 Validating with W3C XML Schema

The SAX2 programming model is designed for validation using DTDs, but not using XML schemas. SAX2 is simple and adaptable, though, so many parsers provide custom configuration options that allow you to validate an XML document against a W3C XML schema.

In Listing 20–15 `JaxpExample_4`, which is based on `JaxpExample_3`, declares that the Xerces parser should use XML schema validation, and that it should load the schema from a local source, rather than from the location provided by an `xsi:schemaLocation` attribute. It accomplishes these purposes using Xerces-specific features and properties.

Listing 20–15

Using Vendor-Specific Features and Properties with SAX

```
package com.jwsbook.jaxp;
import org.xml.sax.ContentHandler;
import org.xml.sax.helpers.XMLReaderFactory;
import org.xml.sax.XMLReader;
import org.xml.sax.SAXException;
import java.io.IOException;

public class JaxpExample_4  {

  public static void main(String [] args)
    throws SAXException, IOException, Exception{
    String contentHanderClassName = args[0];
    String fileName = args[1];

    ContentHandler contentHandler = (ContentHandler)
     Class.forName(contentHanderClassName).newInstance();

    XMLReader parser = XMLReaderFactory.createXMLReader();
    parser.setContentHandler( contentHandler);
    parser.setFeature("http://xml.org/sax/features/namespace-prefixes", true);

    // Xerces-specific features and properties
    parser.setFeature(
     "http://apache.org/xml/features/validation/schema",true);

    parser.setProperty(
     "http://apache.org/xml/properties/schema/external-schemaLocation",
```

```
        "http://schemas.xmlsoap.org/soap/envelope/ SOAP-1_1.xsd "+
        "http://www.Monson-Haefel.com/jwsbook/BookQuote bookquote.xsd");

      parser.parse(fileName);
    }
}
```

In JaxpExample_4, setFeature() activates or deactivates a specific piece of functionality, in this case validation by XML schema. As an alternative you could use a more rigorous and processing-intensive XML schema validation by calling the setFeature() method as follows:

```
parser.setFeature(
  "http://apache.org/xml/features/validation/schema-full-checking",true);
```

The setProperty() call configures some aspect of a feature. In JaxpExample_4 it tells the parser to use specific files for XML schema validation. When you use the external-schemaLocation property, the parser will ignore xsi:schemaLocation attributes in favor of the XML schemas identified in the setProperty() call. Because a SOAP message doesn't usually include an xsi:schemaLocation attribute, using an external-schemaLocation property when validating SOAP messages makes sense—but validation of SOAP messages is not necessary in many cases when you're using JAX-RPC, because the marshalling from XML to JavaBeans components will detect many validity errors.

Each parser will offer its own custom features and properties in addition to the standard features and properties defined by SAX2. Using parser-specific features and properties reduces the portability of your code, so if you must use them, try to load them from a configuration file.

20.4 Wrapping Up

SAX2 parsers tend to be very fast compared to DOM parsers and also tend to have much smaller memory footprints, because they don't attempt to build an in-memory tree of an XML document. However, SAX2 also tends to be more difficult for people to learn—at least people used to object-oriented development. Unlike DOM 2, which uses an object model, SAX2 is event-based, which means you see the document as it's read, but cannot peruse it once it's parsed—unless you cache it, in which case you might as well use DOM.

As a primer, this chapter had as its mission to familiarize you with the basics of SAX2. There is a lot more to SAX2 than the material covered in this chapter. As I said in the introduction to Part VI, I recommend that you pick up a copy of *Processing XML with Java* by Elliotte Rusty Harold for a thorough treatment of this topic and others, like DOM, JDOM, and TrAX.

Chapter 21
DOM 2

Document **Object Model (DOM)** is a set of interfaces and classes used to model XML documents as a tree of objects called **nodes.** The DOM interfaces and classes represent XML documents, elements, attributes, text values, and pretty much all the other constructs from the XML 1.0 language. You use the DOM programming API to examine existing XML documents, or to create new ones.

When an implementation of DOM parses an XML document, it reads the XML text from some source (a file, network stream, or database, for example), then builds an object graph, called a **tree,** that mirrors the structure of the XML document. Figure 21–1 shows the mapping between a DOM tree and an XML document based on the Address Markup Language used in Chapter 2.

Every element in the XML document is represented by a corresponding instance of the DOM `Element` type. Each of the other XML artifacts has a corresponding DOM type; attributes map to the type `Attr`, comments to `Comment`, text to `Text`, CDATA sections to `CDATASection`, and so on. Their common supertype is the `org.w3c.dom.Node` interface. Figure 21–2 shows a class diagram of `Node` and its subtypes (grayed types are not discussed in this chapter).

When a DOM parser processes an XML document successfully, it returns an `org.w3c.dom.Document` object, which represents an XML document instance. The `Document` object provides access to the root `Element`, which in turn provides access to all the `Elements`, `Text`, `Comments` and other parts of the XML document.

DOM is not Java-specific. It was created by the World Wide Web Consortium in a language-neutral specification that has been implemented in several programming

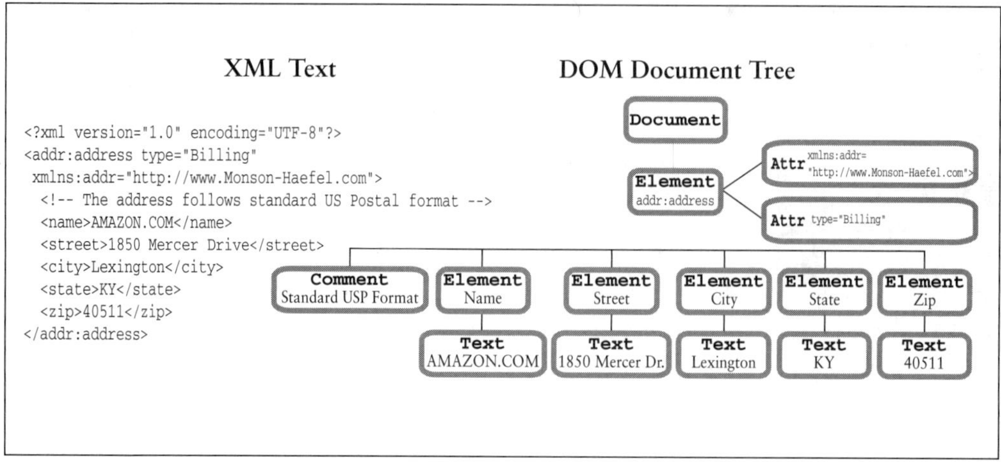

Figure 21–1 Mapping between XML and DOM

languages, including Perl, Python, C++, JavaScript, and Java. There are three versions of DOM, called Level 1, Level 2, and Level 3. JAXP 1.2 uses DOM 2, so it's the subject of this chapter. DOM 3, the next version, was still in development at the time the J2EE 1.4 and JAXP 1.2 specifications were released.

Several different organizations provide Java implementations of DOM 2, including Sun, Apache, and Oracle. Each of these DOM 2 providers implement the same package of interfaces, based on definitions provided by W3C. What differentiates one DOM 2 provider from the next is configurability, support for optional features, speed, memory footprint, and the method the parser uses to read documents.

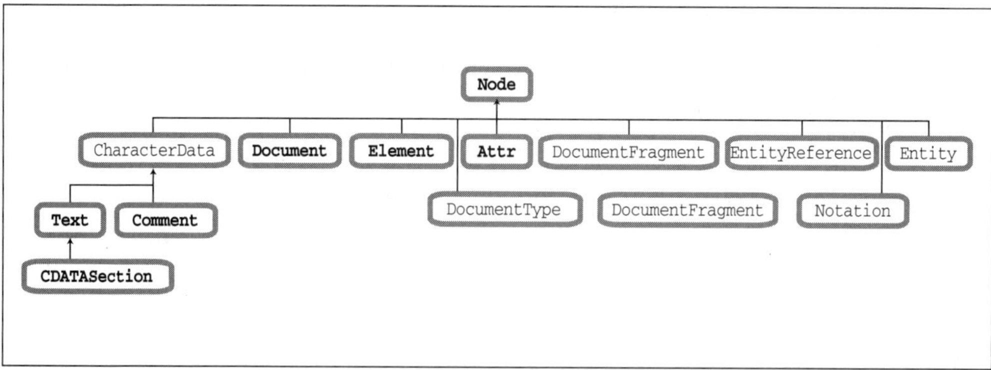

Figure 21–2 The `Node` Class and Its Subtypes

21.1 Parsing with DOM: `DocumentBuilderFactory` and `DocumentBuilder`

Although DOM 2 defines a standard object model for XML documents, it doesn't define a standard way of instantiating a parser and parsing a document, which could affect the portability of your code. If you are using the Apache DOM parser (Xerces) and decide to switch to the Sun parser (Crimson), you'll have to change the code that instantiates the parser and supplies it an XML document. JAXP largely eliminates this portability problem by providing a single programming API for creating parsers and supplying them XML documents. JAXP defines two classes that are used to bootstrap a DOM 2 parser: `javax.xml.parsers.DocumentBuilderFactory` and `javax.xml.parsers.DocumentBuilder`. These two types provide vendor-agnostic abstractions for accessing DOM parsers and supplying them with XML documents to be parsed.

To create a DOM tree from an existing XML document, all you need is a file name, or some type of input stream to the XML document. For example, Listing 21–1 shows how to use JAXP to create a DOM tree from an XML document stored in a file.

Listing 21–1

Creating a DOM Tree from an XML File

```
package com.jwsbook.jaxp;
import javax.xml.parsers.DocumentBuilderFactory;
import javax.xml.parsers.DocumentBuilder;
import org.w3c.dom.Document;
import java.io.FileInputStream;
import com.jwsbook.jaxp.DomOutputter;

public class JaxpExample_5 {
  public static void main(String[] args) throws Exception {

    String filePath = args[0];
    FileInputStream fileStream = new FileInputStream(filePath);

    DocumentBuilderFactory factory = DocumentBuilderFactory.newInstance();
    DocumentBuilder parser = factory.newDocumentBuilder();
    Document xmlDoc = parser.parse(fileStream);

    DomOutputter.write(xmlDoc, System.out);
  }
}
```

DocumentBuilderFactory is a factory for creating DOM parsers. You instantiate the factory class by calling its newInstance() method, then use the factory instance to create an instance of DocumentBuilder, which represents a DOM parser. When you invoke the DocumentBuilderFactory.newInstance() method, the JAXP runtime will follow a predefined routine for finding the proper parser. Basically, it will first check environment properties, then the Java runtime directory, then all the JAR files in the classpath. If it doesn't find a parser in any of these locations, it instantiates the default parser provided by the JAXP vendor. In most cases you are probably going to be satisfied with the default parser.

The DomOutputter class is a simple hack I created to print the contents of a Document object to a stream. DOM doesn't provide very good facilities for outputting XML content, so I used this class to keep the examples simple. In a nutshell it uses TrAX (Transformation API for XML) to output the contents of a Document to a stream.

The following is a command you can use to execute JaxpExample_5, and its output. In this case we are processing the XML document you'll see soon, in Listing 21–2.

```
[prompt] java com.jwsbook.jaxp.JaxpExample_5 address21-2.xml

<?xml version="1.0" encoding="UTF-8"?>
<addr:address type="Billing" xmlns:addr="http://www.Monson-Haefel.com">
  <!-- The address follows standard U.S. postal format -->
  <name>AMAZON.COM</name>
  <street>1850 Mercer Drive</street>
  <city>Macon</city>
  <state>KY</state>
  <zip>40511</zip>
</addr:address>
```

21.2 Nodes

You've already learned that DOM represents an XML document as a tree of nodes, and that nodes represent attributes, elements, comments, processing instructions, CDATA sections, text, and other XML artifacts. As a tree, the DOM representation of an XML document is fairly easy to peruse and manipulate. For example, we can use JAXP and DOM to access an address XML document like the one shown in Listing 21–2.

Listing 21–2

An Address Document

```
<?xml version="1.0" encoding="UTF-8"?>
<addr:address type="Billing"
```

```
 xmlns:addr="http://www.Monson-Haefel.com">
  <!-- The address follows standard U.S. postal format -->
  <name>AMAZON.COM</name>
  <street>1850 Mercer Drive</street>
  <city>Macon</city>
  <state>KY</state>
  <zip>40511</zip>
</addr:address>
```

> ***In general, using unqualified local names for elements (in this case,*** `name`, `street`, `city`, `state`, ***and*** `zip`) ***is discouraged. It's best if all elements are namespace-qualified: They should either belong to a default namespace or be prefixed with a namespace identifier, like*** `addr` ***in this example. The XML document in Listing 21–2 uses unqualified local names to illustrate how*** `Node`***s represent qualified versus unqualified local elements.***

In Listing 21–3, `JaxpExample_6` reads the XML document shown in Listing 21–2 from the file and prints out the names and contents of the elements as simple text.

Listing 21–3

Printing Out Element Names and Values

```
package com.jwsbook.jaxp;
import javax.xml.parsers.DocumentBuilderFactory;
import javax.xml.parsers.DocumentBuilder;
import org.w3c.dom.Document;
import org.w3c.dom.Node;
import org.w3c.dom.NodeList;

public class JaxpExample_6 {
  public static void main(String[] args) throws Exception {
    String filePath = args[0];
    // Create an instance of a DOM parser.
    DocumentBuilderFactory factory = DocumentBuilderFactory.newInstance();
    DocumentBuilder parser = factory.newDocumentBuilder();

    // Provide the parser with the file path and parse into a Document.
    Document xmlAddressDoc = parser.parse(filePath);

    // Obtain the root element of the document and output its name.
    Node rootElement = xmlAddressDoc.getDocumentElement();
    System.out.println(rootElement.getNodeName());
```

```
    // Output the elements contained by the root element.
    NodeList nodeList = rootElement.getChildNodes();
    for(int i=0;i < nodeList.getLength();i++){
      Node node= nodeList.item(i);
      if(node.getNodeType() == Node.ELEMENT_NODE){
        String tagName = node.getNodeName();
        System.out.println(" "+tagName);
        NodeList nodeList2 = node.getChildNodes();
        for(int j=0; j < nodeList2.getLength();j++){
          Node text = nodeList2.item(j);
          System.out.println("  "+text.getNodeValue());
        }
      }
    }
  }
}
```

JaxpExample_6 uses the JAXP API to access an XML document in a file and pass it to the DOM parser. Once the DOM parser has returned a Document object representing the XML document, JaxpExample_6 walks through it, printing out the names of elements and their values. The command to run JaxpExample_6 for the address document (Listing 21–2) and the resulting output are as follows:

```
[prompt] java com.jwsbook.jaxp.JaxpExample_6 address21-2.xml

addr:address
 name
  AMAZON.COM
 street
  1850 Mercer Drive
 city
  Macon
 state
  KY
 zip
  40511
```

JaxpExample_6 makes heavy use of the org.w3c.dom.Node interface, which defines a bevy of methods that can be used while navigating, reading, and updating a DOM tree. Listing 21–4 shows the definition of the Node interface.

Listing 21–4

The `org.w3c.dom.Node` *Interface*

```
package org.w3c.dom;

public interface Node {
  // Constants
  public static final short ATTRIBUTE_NODE;
  public static final short CDATA_SECTION_NODE;
  public static final short COMMENT_NODE;
  public static final short DOCUMENT_FRAGMENT_NODE;
  public static final short DOCUMENT_NODE;
  public static final short DOCUMENT_TYPE_NODE;
  public static final short ELEMENT_NODE;
  public static final short ENTITY_NODE;
  public static final short ENTITY_REFERENCE_NODE;
  public static final short NOTATION_NODE;
  public static final short PROCESSING_INSTRUCTION_NODE;
  public static final short TEXT_NODE;

  // Type-dependent properties
  public short    getNodeType();
  public String   getNodeName();
  public String   getNodeValue() throws DOMException;
  public void     setNodeValue(String nodeValue)
   throws DOMException;

  // The XML names of this node
  public String   getLocalName();
  public String   getNamespaceURI();
  public String   getPrefix();
  public void     setPrefix(String prefix) throws DOMException;

  // The attributes of this node
  public boolean      hasAttributes();
  public NamedNodeMap getAttributes();

  // The document to which this node belongs
  public Document     getOwnerDocument();

  // The parent, children, and sibling navigation methods
  public Node         getParentNode();
  public boolean      hasChildNodes();
  public Node         getFirstChild();
  public Node         getLastChild();
```

```
    public NodeList      getChildNodes();
    public Node          getPreviousSibling();
    public Node          getNextSibling();

    // The child-management methods
    public Node appendChild(Node newChild) throws DOMException;
    public Node replaceChild(Node newChild,  Node oldChild)
     throws DOMException;
    public Node removeChild(Node oldChild) throws DOMException;
    public Node insertBefore(Node newChild, Node refChild)
     throws DOMException;

    // Other methods
    public Node cloneNode(boolean deep);
    public void normalize();
    public boolean isSupported(String feature, String version);
}
```

In many cases, the methods defined by `Node` provide enough functionality that you don't need the specialized operations provided by its subtypes. For example, most of the processing done in `JaxpExample_6` (Listing 21–3) uses only `Node` references and methods. The `Node` methods do not exhibit the same behavior for all node types, however; when invoking some of the them, you need to know what type of node you are working on. For example, when you invoke `getNodeValue()` on an `Element` object, it returns a `null` value; but when you invoke it on a `Text` object, it returns the `String` value of the text.

The next few sections examine key `Node` methods and how they behave depending on the `Node` type.

21.2.1 Type-Dependent Properties

`Node` defines four methods that behave very differently depending on the type of `Node` being accessed: `getNodeType()`, `getNodeName()`, `getNodeValue()`, and `setNodeValue()`.

The `getNodeType()` method returns a `short` value equal to one of the constants defined by the `Node` interface. Each constant represents one of 12 different `Node` subtypes. Table 21–1 shows the mapping between the subtypes and the constants.

The first seven constants, in bold, are the ones you are most likely to encounter while working with XML documents in J2EE Web Services. You won't see the last five types often, because they apply to processing instructions and Document Type Definitions, which are not used in BP-conformant Web services. You'll use `getNodeType()` to determine the type of `Node` so you can cast it to the proper interface, or filter for specific types of nodes. For example, the following snippet from `JaxpExample_6` (Listing 21–3) searches for the `Element` nodes.

Table 21–1 Node Constants and Interface Types

Constants Defined by `org.w3c.dom.Node`	Interface Names from the `org.w3c.dom` Package
DOCUMENT_NODE	**Document**
ELEMENT_NODE	**Element**
TEXT_NODE	**Text**
ATTRIBUTE_NODE	**Attr**
COMMENT_NODE	**Comment**
DOCUMENT_FRAGMENT_NODE	**DocumentFragment**
CDATA_SECTION_NODE	**CDATASection**
PROCESSING_INSTRUCTION_NODE	ProcessingInstruction
DOCUMENT_TYPE_NODE	DocumentType
ENTITY_REFERENCE_NODE	EntityReference
ENTITY_NODE	Entity
NOTATION_NODE	Notation

```
...
for(int i=0;i < nodeList.getLength();i++){
  Node node= nodeList.item(i);
  if(node.getNodeType() == Node.ELEMENT_NODE){
    String tagName = node.getNodeName();
    System.out.println(" "+tagName);
    NodeList nodeList2 = node.getChildNodes();
    for(int j=0; j < nodeList2.getLength();j++){
      Node text = nodeList2.item(j);
      System.out.println("  "+text.getNodeValue());
    }
  }
}
...
```

This code checks all the children of the root node to find the ones with a type value of ELEMENT_NODE, and displays their tag names and text values.

The `Node.getNodeName()` and `Node.getNodeValue()` methods return different kinds of values depending on the node type being accessed. Table 21–2, which is based on a table defined in the JAXP API, shows the kinds of values processed by the `getNodeName()`, `getNodeValue()`, and `setNodeValue()` methods of each `Node` type.

Table 21–2 Kinds of Values Processed by Subtype-Specific Node Methods

Node Subtype	getNodeName()	getNodeValue() and setNodeValue()
Attr	name of attribute	value of attribute
CDATASection	"#cdata-section"	content of CDATA section
Comment	"#comment"	content of comment
Document	"#document"	null
DocumentFragment	"#document-fragment"	null
DocumentType	name of root element	null
Element	name of element (includes prefix)	null
Entity	name of entity	null
EntityReference	name of entity referred to	null
Notation	name of notation	null
ProcessingInstruction	target	entire content, excluding the target
Text	"#text"	content of text node

The getNodeName() values that begin with a pound sign (#) are fixed; all instances of that type return exactly the same String value. For example, if you invoke the getNodeName() method on a dozen different Comment objects, they will all return the value "#comment".

21.2.2 XML Name Methods

Only the Element and Attr types are assigned XML names, which may be qualified XML names (QNames). The Node interface defines four methods that operate on the local name (getLocalName()), XML namespace URI (getNamespaceURI()), and name prefixes (getPrefix() and setPrefix()) assigned to elements and attributes. JaxpExample_7, in Listing 21–5, uses these methods to print out all the element names in an XML document.

Listing 21–5

Accessing Element QNames

```
package com.jwsbook.jaxp;
import javax.xml.parsers.DocumentBuilderFactory;
import javax.xml.parsers.DocumentBuilder;
import org.w3c.dom.Document;
import org.w3c.dom.Element;
```

```
import org.w3c.dom.Node;
import org.w3c.dom.NodeList;

public class JaxpExample_7 {
  public static void main(String[] args) throws Exception {
    String filePath = args[0];
    // Create an instance of a DOM parser and get the Document object.
    DocumentBuilderFactory factory = DocumentBuilderFactory.newInstance();
    factory.setNamespaceAware(true);
    DocumentBuilder parser = factory.newDocumentBuilder();
    Document xmlAddressDoc = parser.parse(filePath);

    // Obtain the root element of the document and output its names.
    Element rootElement = xmlAddressDoc.getDocumentElement();
    printElementNames(rootElement);

    // Output the names of elements contained by the root element.
    NodeList nodeList = rootElement.getChildNodes();
    for(int i=0;i < nodeList.getLength();i++){
      Node childNode = nodeList.item(i);
      if(childNode.getNodeType() == Node.ELEMENT_NODE){
        printElementNames(childNode);
      }
    }
  }
  // Print out the local name, QName, and namespace URI of an element.
  public static void printElementNames(Node element){
    String prefix = element.getPrefix();
    if(prefix!=null){
      System.out.print(prefix+":");
    }
    String localName = element.getLocalName();
    System.out.print(localName);
    String uri = element.getNamespaceURI();
    if(uri!=null){
      System.out.print(" xmlns:"+prefix+"="+uri);
    }
    System.out.println();
  }
}
```

If you run `JaxpExample_7` against the address XML document shown in Listing 21–2, the command and its output will look as follows:

```
[prompt] java com.jwsbook.jaxp.JaxpExample_7 address21-2.xml

addr:address xmlns:addr=http://www.Monson-Haefel.com
name
street
city
state
zip
```

Notice in the following snippet from `JaxpExample_7` that the program calls the `DocumentBuilderFactory`'s `setNamespaceAware()` method and passes it a `true` argument. If this method is not invoked with a `true` value explicitly, there is no guarantee that the DOM parser will recognize XML namespace declarations or prefixes.

```
public class JaxpExample_7 {
  public static void main(String[] args) throws Exception {
    String filePath = args[0];
    DocumentBuilderFactory factory = DocumentBuilderFactory.newInstance();
    factory.setNamespaceAware(true);
    DocumentBuilder parser = factory.newDocumentBuilder();
```

21.2.3 Attribute Methods

The `Node` interface defines two methods for accessing attributes. The `hasAttributes()` method simply returns `true` if the node has attributes. Because only elements can have attributes, only `Element` objects may return `true`; all other `Node` types will automatically return `false`. The `getAttributes()` method returns a map of a specific `Element` object's attributes, along with their values. The method returns `null` if it's invoked on anything but an `Element`. In general, you should make sure that `hasAttributes()` returns `true` before invoking `getAttributes()`. `Jaxp Example_8` (Listing 21–6) illustrates how to use these two methods. It reads an XML document and prints out all the attribute values.

Listing 21–6

Outputting All the Attributes in an XML Document

```
package com.jwsbook.jaxp;
import javax.xml.parsers.DocumentBuilderFactory;
import javax.xml.parsers.DocumentBuilder;
import org.w3c.dom.Document;
import org.w3c.dom.Node;
import org.w3c.dom.Attr;
import org.w3c.dom.NodeList;
import org.w3c.dom.NamedNodeMap;
```

```
public class JaxpExample_8 {
  public static void main(String[] args) throws Exception {
    String filePath = args[0];
    // Create an instance of a DOM parser and get the Document object.
    DocumentBuilderFactory factory = DocumentBuilderFactory.newInstance();
    factory.setNamespaceAware(true);
    DocumentBuilder parser = factory.newDocumentBuilder();
    Document xmlAddressDoc = parser.parse(filePath);

    // Output the attributes of the root element and its child elements.
    Node rootElement = xmlAddressDoc.getDocumentElement();
    printAttributes(rootElement);
  }
  // Print out the attributes of a node. This method is recursive.
  public static void printAttributes(Node node){
    if(node.hasAttributes()){
      NamedNodeMap attrMap = node.getAttributes();
      for(int i=0;i<attrMap.getLength();i++){
        Attr attribute = (Attr)attrMap.item(i);
        System.out.println(attribute.getName()+"="+attribute.getValue());
      }
    }
    if(node.getNodeType() == Node.ELEMENT_NODE){
      NodeList nodeList = node.getChildNodes();
      for(int i=0;i < nodeList.getLength();i++){
        Node childNode = nodeList.item(i);
        printAttributes(childNode);
      }
    }
  }
}
```

If you ran `JaxpExample_8` against the XML address document in Listing 21–2, the command and its output would be the following:

```
[prompt] java com.jwsbook.jaxp.JaxpExample_8 address21-2.xml

type=Billing
xmlns:addr=http://www.Monson-Haefel.com
```

Notice that both the attribute and the XML namespace are printed out. DOM considers the XML namespace an attribute.

21.2.4 The Owner Document

The getOwnerDocument() method returns a reference to the Document object to which the Node belongs. It's important to understand that Nodes are owned by specific Documents, and that you cannot take a Node from one Document and add it to another—even if you remove it from the source Document. This prohibition comes as a surprise to most developers, and the reasoning for it is not entirely clear, but the following snippet would cause an exception to be thrown.

```
Document sourceDoc = sourceNode.getOwnerDocument();
SourceDoc.removeChild(sourceNode);

Document targetDoc = targetNode.getOwnerDocument();
// The next method call will throw an exception.
targetDoc.replaceChild(sourceNode,targetNode);
```

Although you cannot move Nodes between Documents, Document.importNode() method allows you to create a copy of a Node, and then assign to a different Document. The importNode() method is discussed in Section 21.4.

21.2.5 Navigating a Node Tree

You've seen that DOM manifests an XML document's hierarchical structure, in which elements may contain other elements, text, attributes, and other XML artifacts, as a tree of Node objects. A Node may contain other Nodes (children), and it may be contained by some other Node (a parent). You can navigate up and down a DOM tree using Node's navigation methods, which are shown in the following snippet from Listing 21–4.

```
// The parent, children, and sibling navigation methods
public Node          getParentNode();
public boolean       hasChildNodes();
public Node          getFirstChild();
public Node          getLastChild();
public NodeList      getChildNodes();
public Node          getPreviousSibling();
public Node          getNextSibling();
```

Most Nodes have a **parent.** Only Documents do not. The parent of an Element may be another Element or, in the case of the root element, a Document. The parent of an Attr is always an Element, as are the parents of Text, Comment, and CDATASection nodes.[1] You can navigate to the parent of a Node by invoking its getParent() method.

[1] This discussion will ignore ProcessInstruction, Entity, EntityReference, Notation, and DocumentType nodes because they are not used in BP-conformant Web services.

Most Node types can also have **siblings,** other Nodes that have the same parent. The siblings of an Element may be other Elements, Comments, or Text (if the parent Element contains mixed content). The siblings of Text nodes may be other Text nodes, or Element nodes. Even if the parent Element does not contain mixed content, it may contain multiple Text nodes, because some parsers distribute a single logical string of text into several sibling Text nodes—for example, when its size exceeds some limit. The siblings of Attr type Nodes are always other Attrs. The Document and the root Element node never have siblings. You can navigate to the preceding sibling by calling getPreviousSibling(), or to the next sibling by calling getNextSibling().

Document and Element types may contain **children.** The child of a Document is always an Element, which you can reach with getDocumentElement(). The children of an Element may be other Elements, Text, CDATASections, or Comments. You can reach the children of an Element using getChildNodes(), getLastChild(), and getFirstChild().

To illustrate the relationships between Node types, Listing 21–7 shows a simple XML document, which is followed by a table of Node relationships.

Listing 21–7

An Address Document

```
<?xml version="1.0" encoding="UTF-8"?>
<addr:address type="Business" use="Billing"
 xmlns:addr="http://www.Monson-Haefel.com">
  <!-- comment -->
  <name>AMAZON.COM</name>
  <street>1850 Mercer Drive</street>
  <city>Macon</city>
  <state>KY</state>
  <zip>40511</zip>
</addr:address>
```

If this document were **normalized**—if all the superfluous white space was removed—then the navigation methods would produce values like the ones in Table 21–3 (which contains only a sampling of nodes from Listing 21–7).

If the XML document is not normalized, however—if it includes spaces, tabs, carriage returns, and so on—the values returned by the navigation methods are very different, as you can see in Table 21–4.

As you can see, there's quite a difference. Most often, the first and last children of a parent are text nodes (represented by the token "#text") that contain trivial white space, as are many of the Element node's siblings. In fact, it can be a bit irritating navigating through so much white space, but that is the nature of DOM. Everything in an XML document is represented by a Node, include arbitrary white space. When you're processing non-normalized documents with DOM, you just have to be aware that white space will represent a significant number of `Nodes` in the `Document` tree.

Table 21–3 Relationships between Nodes for a Normalized Version of Listing 21–7

Node	**getParent Node()**	**getChild Nodes()**	**getFirst Child()**	**getLast Child()**	**getPrevious Sibling()**	**getNext Sibling()**
Element: addr :address	#document	#comment name street city state zip	#comment	zip	null	null
Element: name	addr :address	"Macon"	"Macon"	"Macon"	#comment	street
<!-- comment -->	addr :address	null	null	null	null	name

Table 21–4 Relationships between Nodes for a Non-normalized Version of Listing 21–7

Node	**getParent Node()**	**getChild Nodes()**	**getFirst Child()**	**getLast Child()**	**getPrevious Sibling()**	**getNext Sibling()**
Element: addr: address	#document	#text #comment #text name #text street #text city #text state #text zip #text	#text	#text	null	null
Element: name	addr :address	#text "Macon" #text	#text	#text	#text	#text
<!-- comment -->	addr :address	null	null	null	#text	#text

21.2.6 Methods for Child Management

The `Node` interface defines a set of methods for adding, removing, and replacing nodes in a DOM tree. These are discussed in detail in Section 21.3: Building a DOM Document.

21.2.7 Other Methods

The `Node` interface also defines three utility methods that don't fall into any particular category, yet do provide important funtionality. This snippet from Listing 21–4 shows the definitions of these methods.

```
// Other methods
public Node cloneNode(boolean deep);
public void normalize();
public boolean isSupported(String feature, String version);
```

The `cloneNode()` method, as its name suggests, makes a copy of the `Node` on which the method is invoked. The copy may be shallow or deep, depending on the value of the `boolean` parameter. A deep copy will make an exact copy of the `Node`, its attributes (if it's an `Element`), and all of its children. The only thing that isn't copied is the reference to the parent `Node`. The clone is associated with the same `Document` object as the original, but it's not assigned as a child to any other `Node` on the tree. That omission can be remedied simply by adding the clone to the tree using one of the child management methods.

The `normalize()` method removes all of the superfluous white space (spaces, tabs, carriage returns, and so on) from the node, reducing it to a leaner yet semantically equivalent version of itself. Invoking the `normalize()` method should consolidate adjacent `Text` nodes and delete superfluous white space. This method is especially helpful when using DOM with XPointer operations, which depend on succinct tree structures to operate properly.

The `isSupported()` method tests to see whether a `Node` supports a specific parsing feature, such as XML schema, DTDs, or XML namespaces. Some features are standard to JAXP, while others are provider-specific.

21.3 Building a DOM Document

Using JAXP, it's fairly easy to construct an in-memory DOM representation of an XML document. For example, you can use DOM to construct a simple SOAP 1.1 message, complete with elements, namespaces, and attributes, like the one in Listing 21–8.

Listing 21–8

A Simple SOAP Request Message

```
<?xml version="1.0" encoding="UTF-8"?>
<soap:Envelope
 xmlns:soap="http://schemas.xmlsoap.org/soap/envelope/"
 xmlns:xsi="http://www.w3.org/2001/XMLSchema-instance"
 xmlns:xsd="http://www.w3.org/2001/XMLSchema"
 xmlns:mh="http://www.Monson-Haefel.com/jwsbook/BookQuote">
   <soap:Body>
      <mh:getBookPrice>
          <isbn xsi:type="xsd:string">0321146182</isbn>
      </mh:getBookPrice>
   </soap:Body>
</soap:Envelope>
```

This SOAP message includes an `xsi:type` attribute, which indicates the type of values used in the `isbn` element. The `xsi:type` attribute isn't actually needed, provided that the SOAP message is properly defined by a WSDL document, but its use is not strictly prohibited by the Basic Profile. It's used in this example only to illustrate how attributes are added to a document using DOM. `JaxpExample_9` in Listing 21–9 is a Java program that uses JAXP and DOM 2 to construct an in-memory representation of the message.

Listing 21–9

Building a Simple XML Document Using JAXP and DOM

```
package com.jwsbook.jaxp;
import javax.xml.parsers.DocumentBuilderFactory;
import javax.xml.parsers.DocumentBuilder;
import org.w3c.dom.DOMImplementation;
import org.w3c.dom.Document;
import org.w3c.dom.Element;
import org.w3c.dom.Attr;
import org.w3c.dom.Text;

public class JaxpExample_9 {
  // XML namespace constants
  public final static String SOAP_NS =
   "http://schemas.xmlsoap.org/soap/envelope/";
  public final static String MH_NS =
   "http://www.Monson-Haefel.com/jwsbook/BookQuote";
  public final static String XSD_NS =
```

```
        "http://www.w3c.org/2001/XMLSchema";
    public final static String XSI_NS =
        "http://www.w3c.org/2001/XMLSchema-instance";

    public static void main(String[] args) throws Exception {

        // Create a new Document object representing a SOAP Envelope.
        DocumentBuilderFactory factory = DocumentBuilderFactory.newInstance();
        factory.setNamespaceAware(true);
        DocumentBuilder builder = factory.newDocumentBuilder();
        DOMImplementation domImpl = builder.getDOMImplementation();
        Document xmlDoc = domImpl.createDocument(
          SOAP_NS,"soap:Envelope",null);

        // Add namespace declarations to the root element.
        Element root = xmlDoc.getDocumentElement();
        root.setAttribute("xmlns:soap",SOAP_NS);
        root.setAttribute("xmlns:mh",MH_NS);
        root.setAttribute("xmlns:xsd", XSD_NS);
        root.setAttribute("xmlns:xsi", XSI_NS);

        // Add the Body element.
        Element body = xmlDoc.createElementNS(SOAP_NS,"soap:Body");
        root.appendChild(body);

        // Add the getBookPrice and isbn elements.
        Element getBookPrice = xmlDoc.createElementNS(
         MH_NS, "mh:getBookPrice");
        body.appendChild(getBookPrice);

        Element isbn = xmlDoc.createElementNS(MH_NS, "isbn");
        body.appendChild(isbn);

        // Add the xsi:type attribute to the isbn element.
        Attr typeAttr = xmlDoc.createAttributeNS(XSI_NS, "xsi:type");
        typeAttr.setValue("xsd:string");
        isbn.setAttributeNodeNS(typeAttr);

        // Add the text contained by the isbn element.
        Text text = xmlDoc.createTextNode("0321146182");
        body.appendChild(text);

        DomOutputter.write(xmlDoc,System.out);
    }
}
```

The DOMImplementation object, obtained from the DocumentBuilder, provides you with a factory for creating a Document object. It allows you to prime the new Document with the qualified name and XML namespace of the root Element.

```
DocumentBuilder builder = factory.newDocumentBuilder();
DOMImplementation domImpl = builder.getDOMImplementation();
Document xmlDoc = domImpl.createDocument(
  SOAP_NS,"soap:Envelope",null);
```

The first parameter we pass to the createDocument() method is the String value of the XML namespace assigned to the root element. If there is no namespace, you can simply pass in a null value. In this case we want the standard SOAP 1.1 namespace. The second parameter to createDocument() is the qualified name (prefix:local-name) of the root element. In SOAP 1.1 the soap:Envelope element is the root. The last parameter is a DocumentType type object, which represents a Document Type Definition. DTDs aren't used in BP-compliant Web services, so we pass a null here.

> ***You can also create a*** Document ***using the*** DocumentBuilder.newDocument() ***method, but this approach is a little more difficult and actually creates an XML document that is, initially, malformed.***[2]

Once the Document object is created, we can access the root Element, which represents the soap:Envelope element.

```
Element root = xmlDoc.getDocumentElement();
```

With the root Element in hand, we can begin adding the other elements. In this case we will be adding to the root Element an Element that represents the soap:Body element. To add a child Element to the root, or any other Element, you need to create the child Element first, then append it to its parent. JaxpExample_9 performs this simple procedure when it adds the soap:Body, mh:getBookPrice, and isbn elements.

```
Element body = xmlDoc.createElementNS(SOAP_NS,"soap:Body");
root.appendChild(body);

Element getBookPrice = xmlDoc.createElementNS(
 MH_NS, "mh:getBookPrice");
body.appendChild(getBookPrice);
```

[2] Elliotte Rusty Harold, *Processing XML with Java,* Boston: Addison-Wesley, 2003, p. 497.

```
Element isbn = xmlDoc.createElementNS(MH_NS, "isbn");
body.appendChild(isbn);
```

Its easy to assign an `Attr` to an `Element` (remember, `Attrs` can be assigned only to `Elements`). `JaxpExample_9` adds the `xsi:type` attribute to the `isbn` element thus:

```
Attr typeAttr = xmlDoc.createAttributeNS(XSI_NS, "xsi:type");
typeAttr.setValue("xsd:string");
isbn.setAttributeNodeNS(typeAttr);
```

Like `Elements`, `Attrs` can be created with an assigned XML namespace—in this case the `XMLSchema-instance` namespace. The value of the attribute is set by invoking `setValue()`. The `Attr` itself is assigned to the `soap:isbn Element` by calling `Element.setAttributeNodeNS()`. There are a variety of `setAttribute XXX()` methods; some are XML namespace-aware and others are not. You can assign more than one attribute to an element using the `setAttributeXXX()` methods, but you cannot use the same attribute name more than once in an `Element`.

`JaxpExample_9` adds a `Text` node to the `soap:isbn Element` in the accepted way: by invoking `appendChild()`.

```
Text text = xmlDoc.createTextNode("0321146182");
body.appendChild(text);
```

`JaxpExample_9` finishes up by having `DomOutputter` write the `Document` object to `System.out`. The command line and output should look something like the following:

```
[prompt] java com.jwsbook.jaxp.JaxpExample_9

<?xml version="1.0" encoding="UTF-8"?>
<soap:Envelope xmlns:soap="http://schemas.xmlsoap.org/soap/envelope/"
xmlns:mh="http://www.Monson-Haefel.com/jwsbook/Boo
kQuote" xmlns:xsd="http://www.w3c.org/2001/XMLSchema"
xmlns:xsi="http://www.w3c.org/2001/XMLSchema-instance"><soap:Body>
<mh:getBookPrice/><isbn
xsi:type="xsd:string"/>0321146182</soap:Body></soap:Envelope>
```

Although the output above is normalized, it is semantically equivalent to the original, in Listing 21–8.

In addition to the `Element`, `Attr`, and `Text` types, you can also create and add `Comment`, `CDATASection`, and other `Node` types to a `Document`. For example, `JaxpExample_10` in Listing 21–10 creates a simple XML document and assigns a `Comment` and `CDATASection` to it.

Listing 21–10

Building a DOM Tree with `Comments` *and* `CDATASections`

```
package com.jwsbook.jaxp;
import javax.xml.parsers.DocumentBuilderFactory;
import javax.xml.parsers.DocumentBuilder;
import org.w3c.dom.DOMImplementation;
import org.w3c.dom.Document;
import org.w3c.dom.Element;
import org.w3c.dom.Text;
import org.w3c.dom.CDATASection;
import org.w3c.dom.Comment;
import java.io.FileReader;
import java.io.StringWriter;
import com.jwsbook.jaxp.DomOutputter;

public class JaxpExample_10 {
  public static void main(String[] args) throws Exception {
    String filePath = args[0];

    // Create a new Document object with a root element named example.
    DocumentBuilderFactory factory = DocumentBuilderFactory.newInstance();
    DocumentBuilder builder = factory.newDocumentBuilder();
    DOMImplementation domImpl = builder.getDOMImplementation();
    Document xmlDoc = domImpl.createDocument(null,"example",null);
    Element root = xmlDoc.getDocumentElement();

    // Add a label element to the root.
    Element label = xmlDoc.createElement("label");
    Text text = xmlDoc.createTextNode("Listing 21-9");
    label.appendChild(text);
    root.appendChild(label);

    // Create a code element.
    Element code = xmlDoc.createElement("code");

    // Read an XML file and cache it in a String.
    FileReader fis = new FileReader(filePath);
    StringWriter sw = new StringWriter();
    for(int character = fis.read(); character!=-1; character = fis.read()){
      sw.write(character);
```

```
    }
    String soapMsg = sw.toString();

    // Create a new CDATASection with the XML document as its content.
    CDATASection cdata = xmlDoc.createCDATASection(soapMsg);
    code.appendChild(cdata);
    root.appendChild(code);

    // Add a comment to the Document, before the code element.
    Comment comment = xmlDoc.createComment(
     "This is a SOAP message inside a CDATA section");
    root.insertBefore(comment,code);

    DomOutputter.write(xmlDoc,System.out);
  }
}
```

If you run `JaxpExample_10` on the SOAP message in Listing 21–8, the command and output will look as follows—except that white space has been added for readability:

```
[prompt] java com.jwsbook.jaxp.JaxpExample_10 soapmsg.xml

<?xml version="1.0" encoding="UTF-8"?>
<example>
  <label>Listing 21-9</label>
  <!--This is a SOAP message inside a CDATA section-->
  <code><![CDATA[
    <?xml version="1.0" encoding="UTF-8"?>
    <soap:Envelope
     xmlns:soap="http://schemas.xmlsoap.org/soap/envelope/"
     xmlns:xsi="http://www.w3.org/2001/XMLSchema-instance"
     xmlns:xsd="http://www.w3.org/2001/XMLSchema"
     xmlns:mh="http://www.Monson-Haefel.com/jwsbook/BookQuote">
      <soap:Body>
        <mh:getBookPrice>
          <isbn xsi:type="xsd:string">0321146182</isbn>
        </mh:getBookPrice>
      </soap:Body>
    </soap:Envelope>
    ]]>
  </code>
</example>
```

JaxpExample_10 creates a Document object, and a root element named example. Notice that the root element is not namespace-qualified. In fact, none of the Elements created by JaxpExample_10 are namespace-qualified. This illustrates the difference between using the methods that have an NS suffix, meaning they are namespace-aware, and the methods that do not.

```
DOMImplementation domImpl = builder.getDOMImplementation();
Document xmlDoc = domImpl.createDocument(null,"example",null);
Element root = xmlDoc.getDocumentElement();
```

JaxpExample_10 creates a CDATASection that contains a SOAP message. The SOAP message is read from a file and written to a StringWriter, which is then used to obtain the String value of the SOAP message. Although the SOAP message is an XML document, the DOM parser will not check that it's well-formed or valid; it will be treated as opaque text—which is the whole purpose of the CDATA-section construct in XML (see Section 2.1.2.5).

```
Element code = xmlDoc.createElement("code");


FileReader fis = new FileReader(filePath);
StringWriter sw = new StringWriter();
for(int character = fis.read(); character!=-1; character = fis.read()){
  sw.write(character);
}
String soapMsg = sw.toString();

CDATASection cdata = xmlDoc.createCDATASection(soapMsg);
code.appendChild(cdata);
root.appendChild(code);
```

JaxpExample_10 also adds a Comment to the Document. Creating a Comment is pretty straightforward: You just pass to the method the text you want in the comment. What is particularly interesting about this example is that it uses the insert Before() method rather than appendChild():

```
Comment comment = xmlDoc.createComment(
 "This is a SOAP message inside a CDATA section");
root.insertBefore(comment,code);
```

The Node interface defines four methods for adding, removing, and replacing Nodes in a Document, as shown in the following snippet from Listing 21–4, the definition of the Node interface.

```
package org.w3c.dom;

public interface Node {
  ...
  // The child management methods
  public Node appendChild(Node newChild) throws DOMException;
  public Node replaceChild(Node newChild,  Node oldChild)
   throws DOMException;
  public Node removeChild(Node oldChild) throws DOMException;
  public Node insertBefore(Node newChild, Node refChild)
   throws DOMException;
  ...
}
```

The appendChild() method, used in all of the examples before this one, adds a Node to the end of the list of children of a parent Node. In contrast, insertBefore() places the new Node in the list of children just before the designated sibling. Jaxp Example_10 makes the Comment a child of the example Element by inserting it before the code Element.

The removeChild() method removes the designated Node from the tree, and replaceNode() replaces one Node with another. It's important to understand that removed and replaced Nodes cannot subsequently be assigned to some other Document object. They're not visible in the tree, but they're still owned by the same Document.

21.4 Copying Nodes

In some cases you may want to copy a Node from one Document to another. This may be necessary if you need to transfer a portion of an XML document from one source to another. For example, you may want to copy the billing address information in an XML Purchase Order document to an XML Invoicing document. Another reason for copying Nodes is reuse. If you have a Node of any kind that you use over and over, you may want to cache that Node in memory and make copies of it as needed.

In DOM 2, you can never truly move a Node from one Document to another, because DOM 2 specifies that the Document object that manufactures a Node owns that Node. So, if you want to use an existing Node in a different document you have to copy it. More accurately, you have to import the Node into the new Document, by invoking the Document.importNode() method. The following snippet shows this method's definition in the org.w3c.dom.Document interface.

```
public interface Document extends Node {
  ...
```

```
  public Node importNode(Node importedNode, boolean deep)
   throws DOMException;
  ...
}
```

Importing a Node consists of copying the data from an existing Node to a new Node that is associated with the Document on which you're invoking importNode(). For example, JaxpExample_11 in Listing 21–11 creates a source Document and copies one of its elements to a target Document.

Listing 21–11

Copying Nodes

```
package com.jwsbook.jaxp;
import javax.xml.parsers.DocumentBuilderFactory;
import javax.xml.parsers.DocumentBuilder;
import org.w3c.dom.DOMImplementation;
import org.w3c.dom.Document;
import org.w3c.dom.Element;
import org.w3c.dom.Node;
import org.xml.sax.SAXException;
import java.io.IOException;
import com.jwsbook.jaxp.DomOutputter;

public class JaxpExample_11 {
  public static void main(String[] args) throws Exception {
    // Get a DOMImplementation object.
    DocumentBuilderFactory factory = DocumentBuilderFactory.newInstance();
    DocumentBuilder builder = factory.newDocumentBuilder();
    DOMImplementation domImpl = builder.getDOMImplementation();

    // Create a source document with a sourceElement with some text.
    Document sourceDoc = domImpl.createDocument(null,"source",null);
    Element sourceElement = sourceDoc.createElement("sourceElement");
    sourceElement.appendChild(sourceDoc.createTextNode("This is a test"));
    sourceDoc.getDocumentElement().appendChild(sourceElement);

    // Create the target document and import the sourceElement element.
    Document targetDoc =
      domImpl.createDocument(null,"target", null);
    Element targetElement = (Element)
      targetDoc.importNode(sourceElement,  true);
    targetDoc.getDocumentElement().appendChild(targetElement);
```

```
        System.out.println("**SOURCE DOCUMENT**");
        DomOutputter.write(sourceDoc,System.out);

        System.out.println("\n\n**TARGET DOCUMENT**");
        DomOutputter.write(targetDoc,System.out);
    }
}
```

In `JaxpExample_11` the `sourceElement` element is created by the source `Document` (`sourceDoc`) and appended to the root element of that document. The `sourceElement` is subsequently imported into the target `Document` (`targetDoc`). The `importNode()` operation copies the `sourceElement` and assigns the copy to the target `Document`. After the `sourceElement` copy is imported, it's appended to the root node. The output from the following command to run `JaxpExample_11` shows that there are identical `sourceElements` in both the source `Document` and the target `Document` (white space added for readability).

```
[prompt] java com.jwsbook.jaxp.JaxpExample_11

**SOURCE DOCUMENT**
<?xml version="1.0" encoding="UTF-8"?>
<source>
  <sourceElement>This is a test</sourceElement>
</source>

**TARGET DOCUMENT**
<?xml version="1.0" encoding="UTF-8"?>
<target>
  <sourceElement>This is a test</sourceElement>
</target>
```

21.5 Wrapping Up

DOM 2 has proven to be a decent tool for processing XML with Java. It provides a complete image of an XML document and is fairly easy to work with, once you've studied it. That said, there are a couple of Java APIs that provide more "Java-friendly" interfaces for working with XML documents. One is JDOM (Java Document Object Model). JDOM is not an official part of the J2EE platform, so it's not covered in this book; but people seem to like it, so it may be worth checking out. a JDOM tree is not a DOM tree, however, so it cannot be used in conjunction with SAAJ 1.2.

DOM 2 is a low-level tool that allows you to get into the details of XML processing. In many cases you may not need to use DOM, or any other XML parser directly, because SAAJ and JAX-RPC tend to hide most of the XML processing nicely. DOM can be very useful when working with Document/Literal SOAP messaging, however. In particular, you can take advantage of it in the JAX-RPC 1.2 message handlers to help process SOAP header blocks—SAAJ by itself is sometimes too limited semantically.

The primary disadvantage of DOM is that it must parse the entire document before you can access any part of it in a DOM tree, which can degrade performance, especially when processing large volumes of documents, such as in message routing. DOM's principal advantage is that it provides an object-oriented view of an XML document. For most developers, this perspective makes DOM more readily comprehensible, and generally easier to work with. In addition, having a complete image of an XML document can be very useful when perusing or modifying it.

Part VII

Deployment

Up to this point this book has postponed discussion of deployment so that you could focus on the programming model rather than on deployment procedures. Deployment descriptors (which are XML documents) are pretty complicated, and they make little sense until you've learned to use the programming model. In fact, it's likely that you won't need to know anything about deployment descriptors at all, if such details are hidden behind your J2EE vendor's configuration tools. Rather than oblige you to work with the raw XML of the deployment descriptors, some vendors offer a nice GUI interface for setting things like properties, transaction attributes, resource connections, and so on.

That said, it's important for this book to include coverage of the deployment descriptors for those who need to edit them directly. This part of the book will explain how J2EE components are deployed in general, as well as how the normal deployment files are augmented by Web service-specific deployment files.

In This Part

Chapter 22

J2EE Deployment

22.1 Overview of the J2EE Deployment Process

After you develop a J2EE component (EJB, servlet, JSP, or JSE), you have to deploy it into your J2EE application server to get it working. The deployment process is conceptually the same from one J2EE platform to the next, but the tools used can vary radically among products. For example, most BEA WebLogic developers use command-line tools to deploy J2EE components, while IBM WebSphere developers tend to use WebSphere's GUI deployment tools. Although your skills as a J2EE developer are portable across vendors' products, the skills you acquire using their deployment tools are not. They are too vendor-specific.

That said, J2EE does define a portable mechanism for packaging J2EE components and describing their properties and runtime attributes. This mechanism is based on the **Java ARchive (JAR)** file format and XML configuration files called **deployment descriptors.** This JAR-based deployment process is not a slam dunk. In most cases, you'll still need to do some vendor-specific configuration, but it does enhance the portability of J2EE components by standardizing the way they are packaged and described. This standardization ensures that J2EE-compliant components from any source, in-house or third-party, will be recognized, and easily inspected and deployed by any J2EE application server. For example, if you buy a specialized servlet from Company X and it's packaged properly, you can deploy it into your J2EE application server from Company Y immediately, using the server's deployment tools.

A JAR file packages the class files and XML deployment descriptor of a J2EE component into a single file, which can be easily transferred or stored on a disk. When you deploy the component, the J2EE application server's deployment tool inspects the JAR file, reads the deployment descriptor, extracts the class files and other files (properties, images, and so on), and then instantiates and launches the component into the server. During this deployment process, you are usually given an opportunity to tune the runtime attributes of the J2EE component to meet your specific needs. This tuning is analogous to setting the background color, font, and other attributes on a visual widget, but instead of controlling visual attributes you're controlling non-visual enterprise attributes like security restrictions, transactional behavior, instance pooling, and threading. The deployment process is how a J2EE component goes from development into production. The following list enumerates the general steps involved in the deployment process.

1. A developer writes the Java classes and XML deployment descriptor for a J2EE component.
2. The developer packages the class files and deployment descriptor for the J2EE component in a JAR file.
3. The developer distributes the JAR file to anyone who needs it, colleague or customer.
4. The administrator who runs a J2EE application server receives the JAR file from the developer.
5. The administrator puts the JAR on a local drive, then loads it into the server's deployment tool.
6. The administrator modifies runtime attributes and tunes the J2EE component for the company's production environment.
7. The administrator launches the J2EE component into the application server.

Although the file format used to package J2EE components is based on the JAR specification, the directory structure and the type of deployment descriptor used for Web components (servlets, JSPs, and JSEs) are different from those for Enterprise JavaBeans. A JAR file that contains Web components is called a **Web ARchive (WAR) file.** A JAR file that contains Enterprise JavaBeans is called an **EJB JAR file.**

> ***Another type of JAR file is a** Resource ARchive (RAR)**, which contains J2EE connectors. A J2EE connector might be a JDBC driver, a JMS provider, a JDO provider, or an API that connects to a proprietary resource like SAP, PeopleSoft, CICS, or IMS. Although J2EE connectors are not actually J2EE components, they do have their own JAR file format and deployment descriptors, and follow the same general deployment process as traditional J2EE components like servlets, JSPs, and EJBs.***

A J2EE application is a complete business solution, which may use Web components, EJBs, and J2EE connectors. A J2EE application may be packaged in an **Enter-**

prise ARchive (EAR) file.** An EAR file contains a general XML deployment descriptor for the entire application, as well as all the J2EE components and connectors, packaged into their own EJB JAR, WAR, and RAR files.

JSEs are packaged into a WAR file, because the JSE is, as you learned in Chapter 10, built on top of the servlet programming model. The EJB endpoint is packaged into an EJB JAR file, because an EJB endpoint is an Enterprise JavaBean that happens to process SOAP messages. How JSEs and EJB endpoints are deployed is a rather tangled and complicated story, the telling of which starts with the next section.

22.2 J2EE Web Services Deployment

There is a very old riddle that goes: "Which came first? The chicken or the egg?" A similar riddle is asked in Web services: "Which comes first? The WSDL or the implementation?" Your answer to this question depends in large part on personal preferences and circumstances. Some people believe you should always create a WSDL document first and derive the Web service implementation from that, because that is the best way to create a language-neutral interoperable service. Others believe it's better to create the implementation first and generate a WSDL document from that, because it's simply easier and more intuitive. In practice, both approaches are acceptable and both are used regularly, so J2EE Web Services embraces both. This flexibility makes things somewhat complicated, because you have to create an infrastructure for deploying Web services that may start as a WSDL document, or as a JSE or an EJB endpoint.

The JAX-RPC specification requires that every JSE or EJB endpoint have a corresponding WSDL document that provides a platform-independent definition of the J2EE endpoint. This requirement helps ensure that J2EE endpoints are accessible to Web service clients from any platform (.NET, Perl, and others), not just J2EE applications. If you start with a J2EE component (JSE or EJB endpoint), you will use it to generate a WSDL document. If, however, you start with a WSDL document, you will use it to generate an endpoint interface and possibly a partial implementation class. The next three sections address both approaches. This material will also provide you with some context for learning about other aspects of J2EE Web service deployment.

22.2.1 Starting with a J2EE Endpoint

In Chapters 10 and 11 you created a JSE and an EJB endpoint respectively. Deployment was not covered in those chapters, but in both it was implied that you were starting with a J2EE component from which you'd derive the WSDL document and other deployment artifacts. The advantage of starting with a J2EE component is that you get to work in a familiar venue—namely, Java programming. You can develop the JAX-RPC endpoint interface and the implementation without having to worry so much about interoperability with other platforms. The idea is to write the Web service in Java, then derive a platform-independent WSDL document from the Java code. For Java developers this tends to be the easiest way to start developing Web services.

After you develop a J2EE component, you use its endpoint interface to generate a portion of the WSDL document. JAX-RPC provides very specific guidelines on how you should derive a WSDL document from an endpoint interface. It defines exactly how methods are mapped to `portType` elements, and how parameters are mapped to `message` and `part` elements. Consider, for example, the endpoint interface in Listing 22–1.

Listing 22–1

The `BookQuote` *Endpoint Interface*

```
public interface BookQuote extends java.rmi.Remote {
    public float getBookPrice(String isbn)
    throws java.rmi.RemoteException, InvalidIsbnException;
}
```

A JAX-RPC compiler would likely generate a WSDL document like Listing 22–2.

Listing 22–2

A WSDL Document Generated from the Endpoint Interface

```
<?xml version="1.0" encoding="UTF-8"?>
<definitions name="BookQuote"
   targetNamespace="http://www.Monson-Haefel.com/jwsbook/BookQuote"
   xmlns:mh="http://www.Monson-Haefel.com/jwsbook/BookQuote"
   xmlns="http://schemas.xmlsoap.org/wsdl/"
   xmlns:xsd="http://www.w3.org/2001/XMLSchema"
   xmlns:soap="http://schemas.xmlsoap.org/wsdl/soap/">

   <message name="getBookPriceRequest">
       <part name="isbn" type="xsd:string"/>
   </message>
   <message name="getBookPriceResponse">
       <part name="result" type="xsd:float"/>
   </message>
   <message name="InvalidIsbnException">
       <part name="message" type="xsd:string"/>
   </message>
   <portType name="BookQuote">
       <operation name="getBookPrice" parameterOrder="isbn">
          <input message="mh:getBookPriceRequest"/>
```

```
            <output message="mh:getBookPriceResponse"/>
            <fault name="InvalidIsbnException"
                   message="mh:InvalidIsbnException"/>
        </operation>
    </portType>
</definitions>
```

The JAX-RPC specification is very precise about the mapping from Java to WSDL. For example, it requires that each WSDL `operation` match a method in the endpoint interface. It also tells us that the input parameters and return types of methods are mapped to WSDL `part` elements. While the Java-to-WSDL mapping is very specific, it's impossible to create a complete WSDL document from the endpoint interface alone. Did you notice that the previous WSDL listing is missing the `binding` and `service` elements? The definitions of these elements cannot be derived from the endpoint interface, because the elements describe implementation-specific details. For example, the `binding` element tells us which protocol and messaging mode are to be used, and the `service` element identifies the URL of the Web service endpoint. It's impossible to derive this kind of information from the Java endpoint interface, so it must be provided separately, as, for example, in Listing 22–3.

Listing 22–3

WSDL `binding` *and* `service` *Elements*

```
<?xml version="1.0" encoding="UTF-8"?>
<definitions name="BookQuote" …
  …
  <binding name="BookQuoteBinding" type="mh:BookQuote">
    <soap:binding transport="http://schemas.xmlsoap.org/soap/http"
                  style="rpc"/>
    <operation name="getBookPrice">
      <soap:operation soapAction=""/>
      <input>
        <soap:body use="literal"
        namespace="http://www.Monson-Haefel.com/jwsbook/BookQuote"/>
      </input>
      <output>
        <soap:body use="literal"
        namespace="http://www.Monson-Haefel.com/jwsbook/BookQuote"/>
      </output>
      <fault name="InvalidIsbnException">
        <soap:fault name="InvalidIsbnException" use="literal" />
```

```
        </fault>
      </operation>
    </binding>
    <service name="BookQuoteService">
      <port name="BookQuotePort" binding="mh:BookQuoteBinding">
        <soap:address location="REPLACE_WITH_ACTUAL_URL"/>
      </port>
    </service>
</definitions>
```

The endpoint interface, along with binding information, can also be used to generate static JAX-RPC stubs, which can be used by Java clients to access the Web service. The stubs generated by a toolkit must adhere to the JAX-RPC specification for generated stubs, which is covered in Section 12.1.

Once you have the endpoint interface, its implementation, a corresponding WSDL document, and a special deployment descriptor called the `webservices.xml`, you are ready to deploy the J2EE endpoint into the J2EE container system. The exact steps used to deploy a J2EE endpoint are different for each vendor. In general, all vendors will host a JSE in a servlet container and an EJB endpoint in an EJB container.

22.2.2 Starting with WSDL

The central goal in Web services is interoperability between platforms, so there is a growing interest in taking a platform-agnostic approach to developing Web services, by starting with a WSDL document. When a WSDL document is designed independent of implementation, it tends to be more neutral in the XML types and idioms used to describe the Web service. In other words, generating a WSDL document from a Web service implementation will, in general, create a WSDL document that has a platform-specific flavor. For example, the WSDL document generated in the previous section was based on a Java interface definition that uses Java idioms and conventions for method names, parameter modes, exception handling, and so on. You can see this "Java bias" by taking another look at the `message` and `portType` definitions of the WSDL document in Listing 22–2.

```
<message name="getBookPriceRequest">
    <part name="isbn" type="xsd:string"/>
</message>
<message name="getBookPriceResponse">
    <part name="result" type="xsd:float"/>
</message>
<message name="InvalidIsbnException">
    <part name="message" type="xsd:string"/>
</message>
<portType name="BookQuote">
```

```
    <operation name="getBookPrice" parameterOrder="isbn">
      <input message="mh:getBookPriceRequest"/>
      <output message="mh:getBookPriceResponse"/>
      <fault name="InvalidIsbnException" message="mh:InvalidIsbnException" />
    </operation>
</portType>
```

This definition uses several naming conventions that are familiar to Java developers but alien to programmers who work in other fields. For example, the `operation` is named `getBookPrice`, which is a perfectly natural operation name to a Java developer, but is not at all conventional in C#, where a method name always begins with a capital letter—for example, `GetBookPrice`. This is a seemingly small distinction for a Java developer, but a rather annoying one for a C# developer. Another example is the naming of the fault message. In JAX-RPC, WSDL faults map to Java exceptions, so it's natural to give the fault name an `Exception` suffix, but C++ programmers use errors, not exceptions, so it's more natural for them to map a WSDL fault to an error code.

Another example of the influence of programming language on WSDL is the modes of parameters used. Java natively supports only IN parameters and methods that return only a single value, so we tend to design Java interfaces with several parameters and a single return type. By contrast, in programming languages like C++ and C#, the use of INOUT and OUT parameters (see Section 15.3: Holders) is commonplace, and the avoidance of these parameter modes in Java is alien to people who work in C++ and C#.

By starting with a WSDL document instead of a service implementation, you have an opportunity to leave the baggage of a specific programming language behind and embrace a more neutral Web service perspective.

For example, if we started with a WSDL document for the BookQuote Web service, we might define the `message` and `portType` as in Listing 22–4.

Listing 22–4

A Language-Agnostic WSDL Definition

```
<message name="BookPriceRequest">
    <part name="isbn" type="xsd:string"/>
</message>
<message name="BookPriceResponse">
    <part name="price" type="xsd:float"/>
</message>
<message name="InvalidIsbnFault">
    <part name="message" type="xsd:string"/>
</message>
<portType name="BookQuote">
```

```
    <operation name="GetBookPrice" parameterOrder="isbn">
       <input message="mh:BookPriceRequest"/>
       <output message="mh:BookPriceResponse"/>
       <fault name="InvalidIsbnFault" message="mh:InvalidIsbnFault" />
    </operation>
</portType>
```

If you hand these `portType` and `message` definitions to a JAX-RPC compiler, it's likely to generate an endpoint interface that looks like Listing 22–5.

Listing 22–5

The Endpont Interface Generated from the WSDL in Listing 22–4

```
public interface BookQuote extends java.rmi.Remote {
    public float GetBookPrice(String isbn)
    throws java.rmi.RemoteException, InvalidIsbnFault;
}
```

This interface definition doesn't exactly follow the Java conventions for method and exception naming, but it's not so bizarre that it can't be understood and used.

Assuming you have specified a complete WSDL document, including the `binding`, `service`, and `port` elements, you have most of the information you need to generate the code that will marshal SOAP messages to endpoint invocations. In other words, you won't need a vendor-specific mechanism for specifying the binding and service aspects of the J2EE endpoint. Depending on the vendor, the JAX-RPC compiler may also generate an implementation class for your endpoint interface. It might generate a JSE implementation class or an EJB class that declares the endpoint methods with empty implementations. This outcome is convenient; all you need to do is implement the endpoint methods, rather than develop the implementation class from scratch.

There are, however, still a few more deployment descriptors that need to be added to the J2EE endpoint before it can be deployed: a JAX-RPC mapping file, a `webservices.xml` file, and a J2EE deployment descriptor.

22.2.3 JAX-RPC Mapping Files

In addition to a J2EE endpoint and a WSDL file, the Web service must include a **JAX-RPC mapping file.** The JAX-RPC mapping file is responsible for synchronizing endpoint and service interfaces with a WSDL document. Basically it maps endpoint interfaces, methods, and parameters to WSDL `portType`, `operation`, and `message` definitions. It also maps a JAX-RPC service interface to a particular WSDL `service` definition.

There are a couple reasons you need a JAX-RPC mapping file. First, it associates a J2EE endpoint with an exact WSDL `port` definition. Remember that a WSDL document can define several different `port` and `binding` definitions that may share a common `portType`. Without a JAX-RPC mapping file it can be difficult to determine which WSDL `port` a J2EE endpoint is associated with. Second, a JAX-RPC mapping file can help to mitigate the "chicken and egg" problem with regard to WSDL and J2EE endpoints. A JAX-RPC mapping file allows you to use naming conventions in the WSDL file that are different from those of the corresponding J2EE endpoint. The native Java class, method, and exception names can be mapped to platform-agnostic WSDL names. For example, your endpoint interface can define an `InvalidIsbnException` that the JAX-RPC mapping file maps to a corresponding WSDL `message` named `InvalidIsbnFault`. Similarly, it can map a `getBookPrice()` method to a WSDL `operation` named `GetBookPrice`. JAX-RPC mapping files are discussed in detail in Chapter 24.

22.2.4 Deployment Descriptors for J2EE Components

JSEs are packaged in a WAR file along with a `web.xml` deployment descriptor, which defines all kinds of deployment properties related to security, threading, resources, and other runtime concerns. The `web.xml` deployment descriptor is used with servlets and JSPs, but has been adapted for use with JSE. Similarly, an EJB endpoint, which is a stateless session bean, is packaged in an EJB JAR file and described, in part, by an `ejb-jar.xml` deployment descriptor commonly used for EJB components.

Remember that J2EE endpoints are basically J2EE components that have been adapted to serve as Web services. A JSE is actually embedded into a servlet, and benefits from all the runtime and configuration options that a servlet enjoys. Similarly, an EJB endpoint is actually a stateless session bean and can do basically anything that any other stateless session bean can do. Rather than re-invent the wheel by creating new deployment descriptors for JSE and EJB endpoints, the J2EE community decided to use existing ones.

Accordingly, a JSE must be packaged in a WAR file with a `web.xml` deployment descriptor, just like a servlet or JSP. An EJB endpoint must be packaged in an EJB JAR file and include an `ejb-jar.xml` deployment descriptor, just like a regular EJB.

22.3 Deploying JSEs

Once you've developed the endpoint interface and implementation class for your JSE, you package it in a WAR file and deploy it into your J2EE application server. The following sections provide an overview of the JSE deployment process and detailed coverage of WAR packaging and the `web.xml` deployment descriptors.

22.3.1 Packaging JSEs in a WAR File

A WAR is just a JAR, except it has `.war` as the extension instead of `.jar`. WAR files, like JAR files, follow the zlib compression standards, which define algorithms for compressing and decompressing files, and packaging them in a single file. If you have ever used WinZip or any other ZIP program, then you've used zlib. In fact, you can create and open WAR and JAR files using WinZip and other zlib-based products. A WAR file usually contains compressed files that are organized into directories. Understanding that you can organize the contents of a WAR file into directories that are relative to the WAR file's root directory is important to understanding the rest of this section.

WAR files are used exclusively with Web components (servlets, JSPs, and JSEs) and must follow a specified directory structure. This structure dictates where the deployment descriptors, servlets, JSPs, JSEs, HTML pages, and images and other supporting files should be located in the WAR file. Basically, the directory structure must have a root and at least two subdirectories named `META-INF` and `WEB-INF`. In addition, you may include arbitrary subdirectories for images, HTML pages, etc. For example, an `index.html` page is customarily located in the root directory, while JPEG and GIF files may be contained in an `images` subdirectory, sound files in an `audio` subdirectory, and so on (see Figure 22–1).

A WAR file defines a **Web application**, which is composed of servlets, JSPs, Web pages, and/or JSEs, all of which share a common set of resources, configuration properties, and an XML deployment descriptor. When a Web application is deployed, it's associated with a URL, so that the contents of the root directory and subdirectories of the WAR are mapped to that URL. For example, if the Web application were associated with the URL `http://www.Monson-Haefel.com/jwsbook/`, then the contents of the `images` subdirectory would be available at `http://www.Monson-Haefel.com/jwsbook/images/`. Similarly, if the WAR's root directory contained an `index.html` file, its URL would be `http://www.Monson-Haefel.com/jwsbook/index.html`.

Although the contents of the root and its subdirectories are accessible as URLs (once they're deployed), the contents of the `META-INF` and `WEB-INF` subdirectories are *not* publicly accessible—they may be accessed only by the container system and the Web components themselves. The `META-INF` directory contains meta-data about the JAR file and is generated automatically when you create the JAR file. The `WEB-INF` subdirectory is the most important directory for JSE deployments. It contains the deployment descriptors and the JSE endpoint and implementation class files, as well as any other classes or libraries that your JSE code depends on. Specifically, deployment descriptors are located directly in `WEB-INF` itself, while the Java classes and supporting libraries (usually other JAR files) are located in the `WEB-INF/classes` and `WEB-INF/lib` subdirectories. Figure 22–1 depicts the locations of files in a WAR file. The gray areas are directories and file types that are optional for JSEs, the black areas are required.

Although the `web.xml` and `webservices.xml` deployment descriptors must be placed directly in the `WEB-INF` subdirectory, as in Figure 22–1, the WSDL documents, in this case `bookquote.wsdl`, are placed in the `WEB-INF/wsdl` subdirectory. In Figure 22–1 the BookQuote application's WSDL document is placed in the

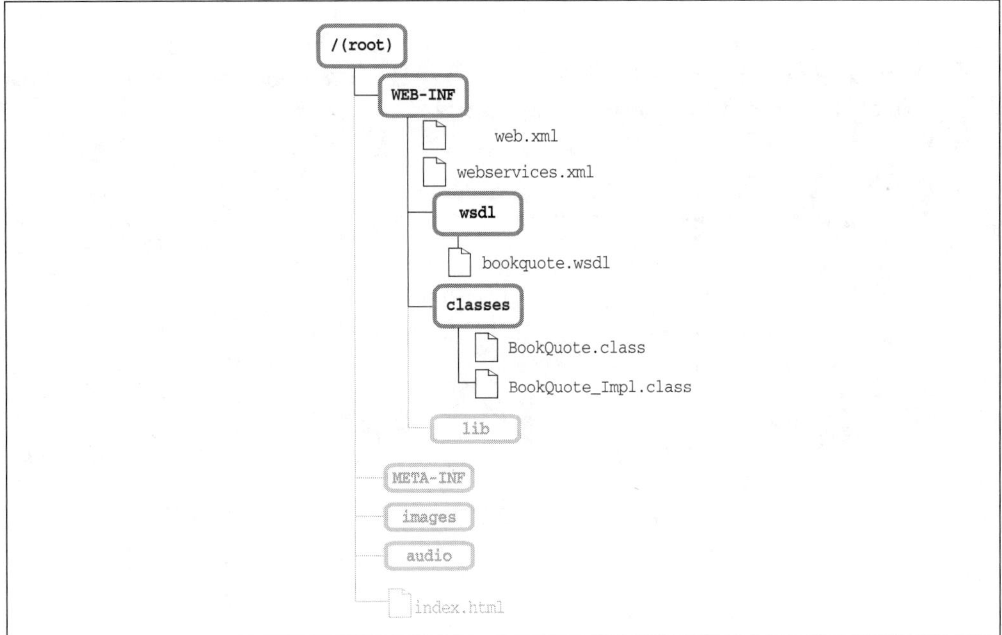

Figure 22–1 The WAR Directory Structure

`wsdl` directory under the `WEB-INF` directory. At runtime, the `wsdl` directory can be accessible to Web service clients directly. For example, you could access the `bookquote.wsdl` at `http://www.Monson-Haefel.com/jwsbook/wsdl/bookquote.wsdl`. In addition, WSDL and XSD documents imported by `bookquote.wsdl` must be stored in the `/META-INF/wsdl` directory, or its subdirectory, if they are imported using relative references—as opposed to explicit URLs.

When you're deploying Web services, you are mostly concerned with the `WEB-INF` and its wsdl subdirectory, and not with HTML pages, images, and other resources, because Web browsers do not usually access JSEs. They're typically accessed by client applications rather than people, and therefore do not generally provide HTML pages, images, and other visual artifacts. There are exceptions: You might want to document your Web service in HTML pages, or package JSEs with other servlets and JSPs.

22.3.2 The `web.xml` File

The usual role of a servlet deployment descriptor—always named `web.xml`—is to describe the runtime attributes of a servlet or JSP component. Because JSEs are actually embedded in a servlet at runtime, however, the servlet deployment descriptor—the `web.xml` file—has been co-opted to describe a JSE deployment. Actually, you can deploy servlets, JSPs, and JSEs all in the same WAR file, with the same `web.xml` file, but in this chapter we will be deploying a JSE by itself. The simplest `web.xml` file for deployment of the BookQuote JSE in J2EE 1.4, which is based on the Java Servlet 2.4 specification, looks like Listing 22–6.

Listing 22–6

A Simple `web.xml` *File*

```
<?xml version='1.0' encoding='UTF-8'?>
<web-app xmlns="http://java.sun.com/xml/ns/j2ee"
    xmlns:xsi="http://www.w3.org/2001/XMLSchema-instance"
    xsi:schemaLocation="http://java.sun.com/xml/ns/j2ee
                        http://java.sun.com/xml/ns/j2ee/web-app_2_4.xsd"
    version="2.4">

    <servlet>
        <servlet-name>BookQuoteJSE</servlet-name>
        <servlet-class>com.jwsbook.jaxprc.BookQuote_Impl</servlet-class>
    </servlet>
</web-app>
```

This `web.xml` file declares the `BookQuote_Impl` class in the `servlet-class` element. Normally, the `servlet-class` element describes a type of custom servlet, so using it for a JSE is a misnomer if there ever was one. `BookQuote_Impl` is not a servlet at all, so why declare it as such? The reason is simple: Declaring the JSE as the `servlet-class` is a way of supporting JSEs without having to change the existing format of the `web.xml` deployment descriptor.

The Web services deployment descriptor, `webservices.xml`, tells the container which "servlets" in the `web.xml` are actually JSEs. It does this by identifying a JSE and then referring to the servlet name that appears in the `web.xml` file. For example, the `webservices.xml` file in Listing 22–7 identifies the servlet named `"BookQuoteJSE"` in the `web.xml` file as a JSE, and tells the container where its WSDL file is located in the WAR, along with other information.

Listing 22–7

Identifying a JSE in a `web.xml` *File*

```
<webservices …>
   <webservice-description>
       <webservice-description-name>BookQuote</webservice-description-name>
       <wsdl-file>/WEB-INF/wsdl/bookquote.wsdl</wsdl-file>
       <jaxrpc-mapping-file>/WEB-INF/bookquote.map</jaxrpc-mapping-file>
       <port-component>
```

```
            <port-component-name>BookQuoteJSE</port-component-name>
            <wsdl-port>
                <!-- the fully qualified name of the WSDL port goes here -->
            </wsdl-port>
            <service-endpoint-interface>com.jwsbook.jaxprc.BookQuote
            </service-endpoint-interface>
            <service-impl-bean>
               <servlet-link>BookQuoteJSE</servlet-link>
            </service-impl-bean>
        </port-component>
    </webservice-description>
</webservices>
```

The `webservices.xml` file provides information about the JSE that is not provided by the `web.xml` deployment descriptor. The same `webservices.xml` file is used for both JSEs and EJBs, so rather than repeat a description of the elements several times in this chapter, the `webservices.xml` file is covered in detail in Chapter 23: Web Service Descriptors.

22.3.2.1 Configuring the `ServletContext`

Because the JSE is embedded in a servlet at runtime, it can take advantage of many of the configuration capabilities of `web.xml`. For example, Section 10.2.3.2.3 explains that the JSE has access to the `ServletContext` interface at runtime. This interface provides, among other things, access to initialization properties, which can be very useful to your JSE. The `web.xml` file can configure the initialization properties using the `context-param` elements, as shown in Listing 22–8.

Listing 22–8

A `web.xml` *File with Initialization Properties*

```
<?xml version='1.0' encoding='UTF-8'?>
<web-app xmlns="http://java.sun.com/xml/ns/j2ee"
    xmlns:xsi="http://www.w3.org/2001/XMLSchema-instance"
    xsi:schemaLocation="http://java.sun.com/xml/ns/j2ee
                        http://java.sun.com/xml/ns/j2ee/web-app_2_4.xsd"
    version="2.4">

    <context-param>
        <param-name>Webmaster</param-name>
        <param-value>webmaster@mycorp.com</param-value>
    </context-param>
    <servlet>
        <servlet-name>BookQuoteJSE</servlet-name>
```

```
        <servlet-class>com.jwsbook.jaxprc.BookQuote_Impl</servlet-class>
    </servlet>
</web-app>
```

The JSE should be able to access the initialization parameters set by the `context-param` element at any time by invoking the `ServletContext.getInitParameter()` method. See Section 10.2.3.2.3 for details on how to use the `ServletContext` interface.

22.3.2.2 Configuring the JNDI ENC

You also use `web.xml` to set the JNDI ENC entries used by the JSE. For example, Listing 22–9 shows a configuration for accessing a JDBC driver, an environment variable, and a local EJB reference using the JNDI ENC (access to these resources via the JNDI ENC is covered in Section 10.2.2).

Listing 22–9

Configuring the JNDI ENC in a `web.xml` *File*

```
<?xml version='1.0' encoding='UTF-8'?>
<web-app xmlns="http://java.sun.com/xml/ns/j2ee"
    xmlns:xsi="http://www.w3.org/2001/XMLSchema-instance"
    xsi:schemaLocation="http://java.sun.com/xml/ns/j2ee
                        http://java.sun.com/xml/ns/j2ee/web-app_2_4.xsd"
    version="2.4">

    <servlet>
        <servlet-name>BookQuoteJSE</servlet-name>
        <servlet-class>com.jwsbook.jaxprc.BookQuote_Impl</servlet-class>
    </servlet>
    <resource-ref>
        <res-ref-name>jdbc/BookDatabase</res-ref-name>
        <res-type>javax.sql.DataSource</res-type>
        <res-auth>Container</res-auth>
    </resource-ref>
    <env-entry>
        <env-entry-name>max_value</env-entry-name>
        <env-entry-type>java.lang.Double</env-entry-type>
        <env-entry-value>3929.22</env-entry-value>
    </env-entry>
    <ejb-local-ref>
        <ejb-ref-name>/ejb/BookHomeLocal</ejb-ref-name>
        <ejb-ref-type>Entity</ejb-ref-type>
        <local-home>com.companyz.BookHomeLocal</local-home>
        <local>com.companyz.BookLocal</local>
```

```
            <ejb-link>BookEJB</ejb-link>
        </ejb-local-ref>
    </web-app>
```


22.3.2.3 *Configuring Other Aspects of a JSE*

In addition to setting up access to the initial parameters and the JNDI ENC, you can configure a variety of other aspects of the JSE's deployment, using configuration elements normally associated with servlets and JSPs. Detailed coverage of these configuration elements is outside the scope of this book, but Table 22–1 provides a list of elements and their meaning. For a complete understanding of servlet configuration, I suggest you consult the Java Servlet 2.4 specification, which can be downloaded from Sun Microsystems' Java Servlet home page, http://java.sun.com/products/servlet/index.html.

Table 22–1 Configuration Elements

Configuration Element	Use or Meaning

`<filter>`
  `<filter-name>SecurityFilter</filter-name>`
  `<filter-class>com.xyz.SecurityFilter`
  `</filter-class>`
`</filter>`
	You can configure filters that can pre-process a servlet request and post-process a servlet response. A filter is similar in purpose to a JAX-RPC handler, except it operates on the raw data stream rather than a SAAJ `SOAPMessage` object. A filter class implements the `javax.servlet.Filter` interface.
	
	It's possible to use filter objects in conjunction with handlers or instead of handlers to provide more control over the entire incoming and outgoing data stream, including HTTP headers.

`<listener>`
  `<listener-class>com.xyz.SessionListener`
  `</listener-class>`
`</listener>`
	Servlet listeners are custom classes that are notified of state changes in `ServletContext` and `HttpSession` objects. `ServletContext` listeners are used to monitor and manage state and resources associated with servlets, while `HttpSession` listeners are used to monitor and manage state and resources associated with client sessions.

`<servlet-mapping>`
  `<servlet-name>BookQuoteJSE</servlet-name>`
  `<url-pattern>/BookQuote</url-pattern>`
`</servlet-mapping>`
	A `servlet-mapping` element assigns a JSE to handle requests for a specific URL. Unlike servlets and JSPs, JSEs are *not* allowed to use wild-card characters—the URL specified must be an exact URL. In addition, there may be only one URL specified for a JSE.
	
	When a JSE is deployed, the deployment tool will use this element to set the endpoint address of the JSE in the `port` element of the WSDL file.

Table 22–1 Configuration Elements (Continued)

Configuration Element	Use or Meaning
<session-config> <session-timeout>60</session-timeout> </session-config>	This element dictates the time, in minutes, that a client session will last before it times out. This is the period of inactivity, so as long as the client accesses the JSE before N minutes elapses, its session won't time out. A value of zero or less indicates that the session should never time out.
<security-constraint> <web-resource-collection> <web-resource-name>BookQuote </web-resource-name> <url-pattern>/BookQuote/*</url-pattern> <http-method>POST</http-method> </web-resource-collection> <auth-constraint> <role-name>employee</role-name> <role-name>client</role-name> </auth-constraint> <user-data-constraint> <transport-guarantee>CONFIDENTIAL </transport-guarantee> </user-data-constraint> </security-constraint>	The security-constraint allows you to declare who can access which resources (servlets, JSPs, and JSEs) based on the URL of the request and, optionally, the type of HTTP request (GET or POST). The URL and HTTP request type are set in the web-resource-collection element, while the names of parties authorized to access the resource are set in the auth -constraint element. The security names used in auth-constraint map to the security-role element, which is a logical identity that must be mapped to real security identities (individuals or groups) in the target environment at deployment time. Optionally, an asterisk (*) can be used to indicate that everyone has access. The user-data-constraint allows you to configure the confidentiality and integrity of HTTP messages exchanged with a client. In most cases, a value of CONFIDENTIAL or INTEGRAL indicates the use of SSL (Secure Sockets Layer), while a value of NONE indicates that SSL is not used.[a]
<login-config> <auth-method>BASIC</auth-method> <realm-name>Monson-Haefel</realm-name> </login-config>	The login-config element indicates the type of authentication used and the security realm that the client is to be authenticated in. The auth-method element may have one of four values (BASIC, CLIENT-CERT, DIGEST, or FORM), but only two of them must be supported for Web services: BASIC, which corresponds to HTTP Basic Authentication and

[a] CONFIDENTIAL actually means that some type of security technology that ensures confidentiality of the communication is required. This may be TSL or some other mechanism, but in most cases vendors use SSL. INTEGRAL means that the message must use some type of integrity mechanism such as XML Digital Signature, or SSL/TSL or the like.

Table 22–1 Continued

Configuration Element	Use or Meaning
	`CLIENT-CERT`, which corresponds to Symmetric HTTP. These types of authentication are explained in more detail in Section 10.2.3.2.1. The value of the `realm-name` element may correspond to a security-policy domain, or some other mechanism. Its exact meaning depends on the J2EE vendor and the target environment.

`<servlet>`
  `<servlet-name>BookQuoteJSE</servlet-name>`
  `<servlet-class>`
    `com.jwsbook.jaxprc.BookQuote_Impl`
  `</servlet-class>`
  `<init-param>`
    `<param-name>limit</param-name>`
    `<param-value>1000</param-value>`
  `</init-param>`
`</servlet>`
	The `init-param` elements, which are nested under the `servlet` element, are similar to the `context-param` elements, in that they provide initialization information to an individual servlet.
	
	There is no way for a JSE to access values configured in the `init-param` elements, however, so they are essentially useless to you as a Web service developer. Use the `context-param` elements discussed in Section 22.3.2.1; they set context-wide initialization parameters that can be accessed via the `ServletContext`.

`<servlet>`
  `<servlet-name>BookQuoteJSE</servlet-name>`
  `<servlet-class>`
    `com.jwsbook.jaxprc.BookQuote_Impl`
  `</servlet-class>`
  `<load-on-startup>5</load-on-startup>`
`</servlet>`
	The `load-on-startup` element, which is nested in the `servlet` element, indicates when the servlet container should load the JSE for receiving incoming messages. The value of this element must be a positive or negative integer. If it's negative, or if the element is omitted, the servlet container will not load the JSE until the first request for it is received. This option can conserve resources for infrequently used JSEs or other resources.
	
	If the value of the `load-on-startup` element is a positive integer, it is loaded immediately, which avoids a slow response to the first request. The servlet container loads all Web components (servlets, JSPs, and JSEs) in the order of their `load-on-startup` element values. The lower the value, the sooner a component is loaded. Web components with a `load-on-startup` value of 1, for example, are loaded before resources with a `load-on -startup` value of 10.

Table 22–1 Configuration Elements (Continued)

Configuration Element	Use or Meaning

`<servlet>`
`<servlet-name>BookQuoteJSE</servlet-name>`
`<servlet-class>`
`com.jwsbook.jaxprc.BookQuote_Impl`
`</servlet-class>`
`<run-as>`
`<role-name>MHApplication</role-name>`
`<run-as>`
`</servlet>`
	The `run-as` element, which is nested in the `servlet` element, determines the logical security identity under which the JSE will execute while processing requests. When the JSE accesses resources (JDBC, JMS, and so on) or EJBs, it propagates this identity as its own, for authentication and authorization purposes. The `run-as` element contains exactly one `role-name` element, whose value is a logical security name, which must be mapped to a real security identity in the target environment at deployment time.

`<servlet>`
`<servlet-name>BookQuoteJSE</servlet-name>`
`<servlet-class>`
`com.jwsbook.jaxprc.BookQuote_Impl`
`</servlet-class>`
`<security-role-ref>`
`<role-name>MNGR</role-name>`
`<role-link>manager</role-link>`
`</security-role-ref>`
`</servlet>`
	The `security-role-ref` element, which is nested in the `servlet` element, can be used to test the principal identity of a client accessing the Web component (servlet, JSP, or JSE). This element is used with the `HttpServlet Request` object and is normally not available to the JSE, unless you are implementing a servlet filter.

22.4 Deploying EJB Endpoints

22.4.1 Declarative Transaction Attributes

The biggest advantage of using an EJB endpoint is the automatic management of transactions. At deployment time you can choose how Web service methods support transactions. For example, you can choose to have a new transaction started every time the `getBookPrice()` method is called on the BookQuote EJB. As you learned in Section 11.1: An Enterprise JavaBeans Primer, the EJB container will start the new transaction just before it invokes the `getBookPrice()` method on the `Book QuoteBean` instance, and then commit the transaction immediately after the method returns. In this way, the transaction scope is delimited by the start and end of the method's execution automatically, eliminating the need for you to begin and commit transactions manually using the Java Transaction API.

Table 22–2 EJB Transaction Atrributes

Transaction Attribute	Description
`RequiresNew`	Begins a new transaction every time the method is invoked.
`Requires`	Begins a new transaction or propagates an existing transaction.
`Supports`	Propagates existing transactions, but will not start new transactions.
`NotSupported`	Will not start a new transaction, nor will it propagate existing transactions.
`Never`	Will not start a new transaction. Exception thrown if caller is transactional.
`Mandatory`	This attribute is not supported by EJB endpoints.

There are several different transaction attributes you can choose from when configuring the transactional behavior of an EJB endpoint method. Table 22–2 lists the transaction attributes and their behavior.

Each of the transaction attributes addresses the transactional behavior in terms of propagating transactions. For example, `RequiresNew` never propagates a transaction; it always starts a new transaction. Compare this to `NotSupported`, which will neither propagate the calling client's transaction nor start a new one. Although transaction propagation is important in EJB-to-EJB interactions—when one EJB calls a method on another EJB—it's less important when a SOAP client calls a method on an EJB endpoint. There is no widely accepted protocol for propagating transactions between SOAP senders and receivers, and no standard way for a SOAP client to propagate its transaction to an EJB endpoint. For this reason, you will usually choose `RequiresNew` or `Requires`, both of which start a new transaction when a method is invoked. If you find you do not need transactions at all, and are considering using `Supports`, `Never`, or `NotSupported`, then you may want to consider using a JSE instead. They are easier to develop, and can usually access any resource and perform the same tasks that EJB endpoints can. Of course if you are re-deploying an existing stateless session bean as an EJB endpoint, then using a JSE is not an option.

The `Mandatory` transaction attribute is the only one not supported by EJB endpoints. It requires that the client propagate a transaction to the EJB endpoint, and as you just learned, there is no standard way to do that.

There are actually a couple of Web service transaction standards competing for mind-share today: WS-Transactions has been developed by Microsoft, IBM, and BEA. BTP (Business Transaction Protocol) has been developed by the OASIS global consortium.

The transaction attributes assigned to EJB methods are set in the assembly section of the `ejb-jar.xml` deployment descriptor. As an example, the transaction attribute of the `getBookQuote()` method of the BookQuote EJB could be set to `Requires New` as in Listing 22–10.

Listing 22–10

Specifying Transaction Attributes in an `ejb-jar.xml` *File*

```
<ejb-jar ...>
  ...
  <container-transaction>
      <method>
          <ejb-name>BookQuoteEJB</ejb-name>
          <method-name>getBookPrice</method-name>
      </method>
      <trans-attribute>RequiresNew</trans-attribute>
  </container-transaction>
  ...
</ejb-jar>
```

22.4.2 Declarative Security Attributes

Just as you can declare transaction attributes at a method level, you can also declare security authorization at a method level. Specifically, you can declare in the deployment descriptor of an EJB endpoint which security roles can access which endpoint methods. For example, you could declare that retail customers and Monson-Haefel's own salespeople can access the `getBookPrice()` method, while wholesalers and others cannot. The roles allowed to access specific methods are declared in the `ejb-jar.xml` much as transaction attributes are, as shown in Listing 22–11 from the BookQuote EJB's deployment descriptor.

Listing 22–11

Specifying Security Attributes in an `ejb-jar.xml` *File*

```
<ejb-jar ...>
  ...
    <method-permission>
          <role-name>RetailCustomer</role-name>
          <role-name>MHSalesperson</role-name>
          <method>
              <ejb-name>BookQuoteEJB</ejb-name>
              <method-name>getBookPrice</method-name>
          </method>
    </method-permission>
  ...
</ejb-jar>
```

Any role not specified in the `method-permission` element will not be allowed to call the `getBookPrice()` method on the BookQuote EJB. Different methods can have different permissions so that some clients can invoke some methods, but not others. The implication of defining method permissions is that you are using some form of authentication and session tracking as described in Sections 10.2.3.2.1 and 10.2.3.2.2. If you're not, then you need to set up the method permissions so that they are *unchecked*, which means that anyone can access the EJB endpoint methods. Listing 22–12 shows how you would declare that no methods of the BookQuote EJB (you'll have to imagine there is more than one) have security authorization checks.

Listing 22–12

Using the `unchecked` *Element*

```
<ejb-jar ...>
  ...
    <method-permission>
        <unchecked/>
        <method>
            <ejb-name>BookQuoteEJB</ejb-name>
            <method-name>*</method-name>
        </method>
    </method-permission>
  ...
</ejb-jar>
```

The `unchecked` element signifies that no security-role authorization check is necessary; that is, any client, even anonymous ones, can invoke the method specified. The asterisk in the `method-name` element is a wild card that indicates that the method permission applies to all methods of the specified EJB endpoint.

In many cases you will not be authenticating SOAP clients before handling their requests, so you'll want to use the `unchecked` method permission. If you don't specify any method permission for an EJB endpoint method, no one will be allowed to access that method at all. Using the wild-card character (`*`) ensures that all methods have some type of security permission specified. In general, method permissions that specify specific method names in their `method-name` elements will override any wild-card assignment made by other `method-permission` elements.

In addition to specifying the roles that can access an EJB endpoint method, you can also specify the security identity under which the EJB endpoint will attempt to access other enterprise beans and resources. When one EJB calls another, or when an EJB accesses a resource like a JDBC connection, the EJB container will automatically authorize the calling EJB using its **`run-as` security identity**. The `run-as` security identity is the `java.security.Principal` object that the EJB endpoint presents when it attempts to access other EJBs or resources.

In some cases, the EJB endpoint will simply propagate the security identity of the caller. For example, if an authenticated SOAP client calls the BookQuote EJB, the

BookQuote EJB may use that caller's `Principal` to access the JDBC connection it uses to fetch wholesale prices from the database. It's also possible to specify that the EJB will execute under its own security identity, without regard to the security identity of the SOAP client. This approach can be beneficial for a couple of reasons: First, the SOAP client may not be authenticated, in which case there is no security identity to propagate. Second, you may want to limit access to resources and other enterprise beans to a specific security identity, and assign that identity to the EJB endpoint. Doing so makes it easier to manage access to resources and EJBs because you have fewer security identities to manage.

You specify the `run-as` security identity for an EJB endpoint in the `ejb-jar.xml` deployment descriptor, as shown in Listing 22–13, taken from the BookQuote EJB's deployment descriptor.

Listing 22–13

The `run-as` *Security Element*

```
<ejb-jar ...>
    <enterprise-beans>
        <entity>
            <ejb-name>BookQuoteEJB</ejb-name>
            ...
            <security-identity>
                <run-as>
                    <role-name>Administrator</role-name>
                </run-as>
            </security-identity>
            ...
        </entity>
    </enterprise-beans>
    ...
</ejb-jar>
```

This code indicates that no matter who the EJB endpoint's client is, the EJB endpoint will run under the `Administrator` principal and will use that security identity to access other EJBs and resources. If you wanted to specify instead that the EJB endpoint always propagates the security identity of the caller, you would write the `security-identity` element as in Listing 22–14.

Listing 22–14

Using the `user-caller-identity` *Element*

```
<ejb-jar ...>
    <enterprise-beans>
```

```
        <entity>
            <ejb-name>BookQuoteEJB</ejb-name>
            ...
            <security-identity>
                <user-caller-identity/>
            </security-identity>
            ...
        </entity>
    </enterprise-beans>
    ...
</ejb-jar>
```

22.5 Service References

You learned in Chapter 12 that all J2EE components use JAX-RPC generated stubs, dynamic proxies, or the DII to access Web service endpoints. JAX-RPC client APIs are accessed via the JNDI ENC, as in the following snippet.

```
InitialContext jndiContext = new InitialContext();
BookQuoteService service = (BookQuoteService)
      jndiContext.lookup("java:comp/env/service/BookQuoteService");
BookQuote BookQuote_stub = service.getBookQuotePort();
float price = BookQuote_stub.getBookPrice(isbn);
```

All J2EE components that access a Web service using JAX-RPC must declare the Web service reference using a `service-ref` element. The `service-ref` element appears in the deployment descriptor of the J2EE component. Listing 22–15 shows the use of the `service-ref` element in the deployment descriptor of an EJB or EJB endpoint.

Listing 22–15

The `service-ref` *Element in an* `ejb-jar.xml` *File*

```
<?xml version='1.0' encoding='UTF-8'?>
<ejb-jar xmlns="http://java.sun.com/xml/ns/j2ee"
   xmlns:xsi="http://www.w3.org/2001/XMLSchema-instance"
   xmlns:mh="http://www.Monson-Haefel.org/jwsbook/BookQuote"
   xsi:schemaLocation="http://java.sun.com/xml/ns/j2ee
                       http://java.sun.com/xml/ns/j2ee/ejb-jar_2_1.xsd"
   version="2.1">
  <enterprise-beans>
    <entity>
      <ejb-name>HypotheticalEJB</ejb-name>
```

```
      ...
      <service-ref>
        <service-ref-name>service/BookQuoteService</service-ref-name>
        <service-interface>com.jwsbook.jaxrpc.BookQuoteService
        </service-interface>
        <wsdl-file>META-INF/wsdl/BookQuote.wsdl
        </wsdl-file>
        <jaxrpc-mapping-file>META-INF/mapping.xml</jaxrpc-mapping-file>
        <service-qname>mh:BookQuoteService</service-qname>
      </service-ref>
      ...
    </entity>
  </enterprise-beans>
  ...
</ejb-jar>
```

The same `service-ref` element can be declared in the `web.xml` deployment descriptor of a servlet, JSP, or JSE as shown in Listing 22–16.

Listing 22–16

The `service-ref` *Element in a* `web.xml` *File*

```
<?xml version='1.0' encoding='UTF-8'?>
<web-app xmlns="http://java.sun.com/xml/ns/j2ee"
    xmlns:xsi="http://www.w3.org/2001/XMLSchema-instance"
    xmlns:mh="http://www.Monson-Haefel.org/jwsbook/BookQuote"
    xsi:schemaLocation="http://java.sun.com/xml/ns/j2ee
                        http://java.sun.com/xml/ns/j2ee/web-app_2_4.xsd"
    version="2.4">
  <servlet>
    <servlet-name>HypotheticalServlet</servlet-name>
    <servlet-class>com.jwsbook.jaxrpc.HypotheticalServlet</servlet-class>
  </servlet>
  ...
  <service-ref>
    <service-ref-name>service/BookQuoteService</service-ref-name>
    <service-interface>com.jwsbook.jaxrpc.BookQuoteService
    </service-interface>
    <wsdl-file>WEB-INF/wsdl/BookQuote.wsdl</wsdl-file>
    <jaxrpc-mapping-file>WEB-INF/mapping.xml</jaxrpc-mapping-file>
    <service-qname>mh:BookQuoteService</service-qname>
  </service-ref>
  ...
</web-app>
```

Although the location of the service-ref element depends on whether you are using an EJB or Web component, the structure of the element is the same. The purpose of the service-ref is to describe a specific Web service in detail so that the J2EE container can provide a reference to a JAX-RPC service object, which is used to access that Web service at runtime. A service-ref element can be used to access a Web service endpoint using one of the JAX-RPC client APIs. The details of using these APIs are covered in Chapter 12, but details about the service-ref element are presented here.

A service-ref element contains both mandatory and optional elements, which help describe a Web service. Listing 22–17 shows a service-ref with the mandatory elements in bold.

Listing 22–17

Mandatory Elements in a service-ref *Element*

```
<service-ref>
  xmlns:mh="http://www.Monson-Haefel.org/jwsbook/BookQuote/"BookQuote">
  <service-ref-name>service/BookQuoteService</service-ref-name>
  <service-interface>com.jwsbook.jaxrpc.BookQuoteService</service-interface>
  <wsdl-file>WEB-INF/wsdl/bookquote.wsdl</wsdl-file>
  <jaxrpc-mapping-file>WEB-INF/mapping.xml</jaxrpc-mapping-file>
  <service-qname>mh:BookQuoteService</service-qname>
  <port-component-ref>
    <service-endpoint-interface>com.jwsbook.jaxrpc.BookQuote
    </service-endpoint-interface>
    <port-component-link>BookQuoteJSE</port-component-link>
  </port-component-ref>
  <handler>
    <handler-name>MessageID</handler-name>
    <handler-class>com.jwsbook.jaxrpc.sec06.MessageIDHandler</handler-class>
    <soap-header>mi:message-id</soap-header>
    <soap-role>http://www.Monson-Haefel.com/logger</soap-role>
    <port-name>BookQuotePort</port-name>
  </handler>
</service-ref>
```

The rest of this section will examine each of the service-ref elements in detail.

22.5.1 The service-ref-name Element

The service-ref-name element declares the JNDI ENC lookup name that a J2EE component will use to obtain a JAX-RPC service reference at runtime. For example, Listing 22–17 declared the lookup name as follows:

```
<service-ref>
  <service-ref-name>service/BookQuoteService</service-ref-name>
  <service-interface>com.jwsbook.jaxrpc.BookQuoteService</service-interface>
  ...
</service-ref>
```

At runtime the J2EE component must use this JNDI name to obtain a JAX-RPC service reference as in the following code snippet.

```
InitialContext jndiContext = new InitialContext();
BookQuoteService service = (BookQuoteService)
      jndiContext.lookup("java:comp/env/service/BookQuoteService");
BookQuote BookQuote_stub = service.getBookQuotePort();
float price = BookQuote_stub.getBookPrice( isbn );
```

The value of the `service-ref-name` is always relative to the `java:comp/env/` namespace, which is the required context of the JNDI ENC. The value used in the `service-ref-name` can be any valid JNDI ENC name,[1] but the convention is to use the `service` subcontext, along with a descriptive service name.

22.5.2 The `service-interface` Element

The `service-interface` element provides the fully qualified class name of the JAX-RPC service interface that the JNDI ENC should return. When using JAX-RPC generated stubs, the service interface used is usually the one generated at deployment time. For example, Listing 22–18 shows the service interface you generated for the BookQuote Web service in Chapter 12.

Listing 22–18

A Service Interface Definition

```
package com.jwsbook.jaxrpc;

public interface BookQuoteService extends javax.xml.rpc.Service{
    public BookQuote getBookQuotePort()
    throws javax.xml.rpc.ServiceException;
}
```

This is the interface identified by the `service-interface` element seen in the following snippet from Listing 22–17.

[1] A valid JNDI ENC name is basically a set of names, without spaces or special characters, separated by forward slashes. The slashes separate JNDI namespace contexts, which are hierarchical, like directories in a file system.

```
<service-ref>
  <service-ref-name>service/BookQuoteService</service-ref-name>
  <service-interface>com.jwsbook.jaxrpc.BookQuoteService</service-interface>
  ...
</service-ref>
```

At runtime an implementation of this interface will be returned to the J2EE component via the JNDI ENC.

```
InitialContext jndiContext = new InitialContext();
BookQuoteService service = (BookQuoteService)
      jndiContext.lookup("java:comp/env/service/BookQuoteService");
BookQuote BookQuote_stub = service.getBookQuotePort();
float price = BookQuote_stub.getBookPrice( isbn );
```

If, however, the J2EE client uses JAX-RPC dynamic proxies or the DII, the interface named by the `service-interface` element will probably be the general-purpose interface, `javax.xml.rpc.Service`, which is defined by the JAX-RPC API. Listing 22–19 illustrates.

Listing 22–19

A General-Purpose Service Interface Declaration

```
<service-ref>
  <service-ref-name>service/GeneralService</service-ref-name>
  <service-interface>javax.xml.rpc.Service</service-interface>
  ...
</service-ref>
```

At runtime an implementation of this general-purpose interface is returned to the J2EE component via the JNDI ENC, as shown in the following snippet.

```
// A J2EE component using the DII
InitialContext jndiContext = new InitialContext();
javax.xml.rpc.Service service = (javax.xml.rpc.Service)
jndiContext.lookup("java:comp/env/service/GeneralService");
...
Call call = service.createCall(portName,operationName);
```

22.5.3 The `wsdl-file` and `service-qname` Elements

The `wsdl-file` element identifies the WSDL document that describes the Web service endpoint you are referring to. The `service-qname` identifies the specific WSDL service you are accessing. The following snippet from Listing 22–17 shows the relationship between these elements within a service-ref element.

```
<service-ref
 xmlns:mh="http://www.Monson-Haefel.org/jwsbook/BookQuote/BookQuote">
  <service-ref-name>service/BookQuoteService</service-ref-name>
  <service-interface>com.jwsbook.jaxrpc.BookQuoteService</service-interface>
  <wsdl-file>/WEB-INF/wsdl/bookquote.wsdl</wsdl-file>
  <jaxrpc-mapping-file>WEB-INF/mapping.xml</jaxrpc-mapping-file>
  <service-qname>mh:BookQuoteService</service-qname>
  ...
</service-ref>
```

The wsdl-file element identifies the exact location of the WSDL document in the component's archive file. In this case it's a file named bookquote.wsdl located in the WEB-INF/wsdl/ directory of the WAR file. The WSDL file must be located in the same JAR or WAR as the J2EE component; you can't point to a WSDL document in some other archive file even if it's in the same EAR (Enterprise ARchive) file.

The service-qname element provides the fully qualified name of the WSDL service it refers to. For example, the service-ref element shown in recent examples refers to the mh:BookQuoteService in the BookQuote.wsdl file. This service definition is shown in Listing 22–20.

Listing 22–20

The service *Element in a WSDL Document*

```
<?xml version="1.0" encoding="UTF-8"?>
<definitions xmlns="http://schemas.xmlsoap.org/wsdl/"
    xmlns:xsd="http://www.w3.org/2001/XMLSchema"
    xmlns:soap="http://schemas.xmlsoap.org/wsdl/soap/"
    xmlns:mh="http://www.Monson-Haefel.com/jwsbook/BookQuote"
    targetNamespace="http://www.Monson-Haefel.com/jwsbook/BookQuote">
  ...
  <service name="BookQuoteService">
    <port name="BookQuotePort" binding="mh:BookQuoteSoapBinding">
      <soap:address
       location="http://www.Monson-Haefel.com/jwsbook/BookQuoteService"/>
    </port>
  </service>
</definitions>
```

The service-qname element points to a single WSDL service definition in the WSDL file identified by the wsdl-file element. The deployment tool needs to know the exact WSDL service definition so it can generate the skeleton code used to marshal SOAP messages to and from the Web service endpoint. Remember that a WSDL `service` definition declares `port` elements, each of which is associated with a `binding` element, and the `binding` definition determines the messaging mode (RPC/Literal or Document/Literal) and the protocol (usually HTTP 1.1) used by the Web service endpoint.

22.5.4 The `jaxrpc-mapping-file` Element

The `jaxrpc-mapping-file` element declares the location of the JAX-RPC mapping file. This file defines the XML-to-Java mapping between the WSDL file and the arguments used with the JAX-RPC API. JAX-RPC mapping is covered in more detail in Chapter 24. The following snippet from Listing 22–17 highlights this element.

```
<service-ref>
  <service-ref-name>service/BookQuoteService</service-ref-name>
  <service-interface>com.jwsbook.jaxrpc.BookQuoteService</service-interface>
  <wsdl-file>/WEB-INF/bookquote.wsdl</wsdl-file>
  <jaxrpc-mapping-file>WEB-INF/mapping.xml</jaxrpc-mapping-file>
  ...
</service-ref>
```

22.5.5 The `port-component-ref` Element

The `port-component-ref` element is declared when the J2EE client will be using the `Service.getPort(Class)` method to obtain a JAX-RPC reference. The following snippet illustrates how that method is used.

```
InitialContext jndiContext = new InitialContext();
javax.xml.rpc.Service service = (javax.xml.rpc.Service)
jndiContext.lookup("java:comp/env/service/Service");
BookQuote BookQuote_proxy = (BookQuote)
          service.getPort(com.jwsbook.jaxrpc.BookQuote.class);
```

The `port-component-ref` element maps an endpoint interface type to a specific `service-ref` element, so that the JAX-RPC runtime knows which `service-ref` to use for a specific class name. It's important to emphasize that the `port-component-ref` element is necessary only when you're using the `Service.getPort(Class)` method—as you might when using dynamic proxies. The use of this element is illustrated in Listing 22–21.

Listing 22–21

The `port-component-ref` *Element*

```
<service-ref>
  <service-ref-name>service/BookQuoteService</service-ref-name>
```

```
  <service-interface>com.jwsbook.jaxrpc.BookQuoteService</service-interface>
  <wsdl-file>/WEB-INF/wsdl/bookquote.wsdl</wsdl-file>
  <jaxrpc-mapping-file>WEB-INF/mapping.xml</jaxrpc-mapping-file>
  <service-qname>mh:BookQuoteService</service-qname>
  <port-component-ref>
    <service-endpoint-interface>com.jwsbook.jaxrpc.BookQuote
    </service-endpoint-interface>
  </port-component-ref>
  ...
</service-ref>
```

Although JAX-RPC is usually used to access Web service endpoints on other platforms, occasionally a J2EE component may need to access a J2EE Web service (JSE or EJB endpoint) that is deployed in the same J2EE application (the same EAR file). In this case you can declare a `port-component-link` element, which links the JAX-RPC service reference directly to a J2EE endpoint. The following snippet from Listing 22–17 highlights this element.

```
<service-ref>
  <service-ref-name>service/BookQuoteService</service-ref-name>
  <service-interface>com.jwsbook.jaxrpc.BookQuoteService</service-interface>
  <wsdl-file>/WEB-INF/wsdl/bookquote.wsdl</wsdl-file>
  <jaxrpc-mapping-file>WEB-INF/mapping.xml</jaxrpc-mapping-file>
  <service-qname>mh:BookQuoteService</service-qname>
  <port-component-ref>
    <service-endpoint-interface>com.jwsbook.jaxrpc.BookQuote
    </service-endpoint-interface>
    <port-component-link>BookQuoteJSE</port-component-link>
  </port-component-ref>
  ...
</service-ref>
```

Again, `port-component-ref` is used only when a J2EE component will be invoking the `Service.getPort(Class)` element, and accessing a port component in the same J2EE application. This example assumes that the J2EE endpoint is located in the same archive as the deployment descriptor that declares the `service-ref`, but it's possible that it is located in a different archive. For example, if the port component were an EJB endpoint located in an EJB JAR in the same EAR, you would use a more qualified path in `port-component-link`, as in Listing 22–22.

Listing 22–22

Referring to a Port Component in a Separate EJB JAR File

```
<service-ref>
  <service-ref-name>service/BookQuoteService</service-ref-name>
```

```
    <service-interface>com.jwsbook.jaxrpc.BookQuoteService</service-interface>
    <wsdl-file>/WEB-INF/wsdl/bookquote.wsdl</wsdl-file>
    <jaxrpc-mapping-file>WEB-INF/mapping.xml</jaxrpc-mapping-file>
    <service-qname>mh:BookQuoteService</service-qname>
    <port-component-ref>
      <service-endpoint-interface>com.jwsbook.jaxrpc.BookQuote
      </service-endpoint-interface>
      <port-component-link>../ejb/BookQuote.jar#BookQuoteJSE
      </port-component-link>
    </port-component-ref>
    ...
</service-ref>
```

The part of the path before the pound symbol (#) specifies the path to the EJB JAR file within the EAR file. This path is relative to the location of the archive file that contains this `service-ref` element. The value after the pound symbol provides the unique component name within the `ejb-jar.xml` deployment descriptor of that EJB JAR file.

22.5.6 The Display Elements

The `service-ref` element may optionally declare a set of descriptive elements (`description`, `display-name`, `small-icon`, and `large-icon`) for display in visual deployment tools.

22.5.7 The `handler` Element

Chapter 14: Message Handlers gave you a brief introduction to the `handler` element so that we could discuss the order of handler processing. In addition, the `handler` element used in the `webservices.xml` file is discussed in detail in Section 23.6. The `handler` element used in the `service-ref` element is basically the same as the one used in the `webservices.xml` file, except that it's oriented to SOAP senders instead of SOAP receivers. As a result this section tends to repeat a lot of the material discussed in Section 23.6, but with the viewpoint of a J2EE component using a Web service reference, rather than a J2EE endpoint.

The message handlers employed by service references filter outgoing and incoming messages. They provide clients with a mechanism to access and modify SOAP messages just before they are sent across the network to the Web service. They also allow clients to modify reply messages received from Web services before the J2EE component gets the reply. Message handlers can be configured in the `service-ref` element as a chain of handlers, which will process request and reply messages in the order that the handlers are declared.

For example, the J2EE 1.4 `service-ref` element in Listing 22–23 declares two message handlers, the `MessageID` and the `ClientSecurityHandler`.

Listing 22–23

Declaring Message Handlers in the `service-ref` *Element*

```
<service-ref>
  <service-ref-name>service/BookQuoteService</service-ref-name>
  <service-interface>com.jwsbook.jaxrpc.BookQuoteService</service-interface>
  ...
  <handler>
    <handler-name>MessageID</handler-name>
    <handler-class>com.jwsbook.jaxrpc.sec09.MessageIDHandler</handler-class>
    <soap-header>mi:message-id</soap-header>
    <port-name>BookQuotePort</port-name>
  </handler>
  <handler>
    <handler-name>ClientSecurityHandler</handler-name>
    <handler-class>com.jwsbook.jaxrpc.sec09.ClientSecurityHandler
    </handler-class>
    <init-param>
      <param-name>KeyAlgorithm</param-name>
      <param-value>DSA</param-value>
    </init-param>
    <init-param>
      <param-name>KeySize</param-name>
      <param-value>512</param-value>
    </init-param>
    <init-param>
      <param-name>SignatureAlgorithm</param-name>
      <param-value>SHA1</param-value>
    </init-param>
    <soap-header>ds:Signature</soap-header>
    <soap-role>Security</soap-role>
    <port-name>BookQuotePort</port-name>
  </handler>
</service-ref>
```

22.5.7.1 The `handler-name` *Element*

The value of the `handler-name` element must be unique within a module (archive file), which means it must be unique across all deployment descriptors in the component's archive file. It's not clear how the value of the `handler-name` element is used. No API gives the developer access to it, so it appears to be useful only to the JAX-RPC runtime system. At any rate, the `handler-name` element does provide a unique identifier for a configured handler.

22.5.7.2 *The* `handler-class` *Element*

The `handler-class` element identifies the class that implements the handler. The handler class must implement the `javax.xml.rpc.handler.Handler` interface, as described in Chapter 14: Message Handlers.

22.5.7.3 *The* `init-param` *Elements*

The `init-param` elements are optional. They describe the initialization parameters that can be passed to the message handler at the begining of its life cycle. The parameters described by `init-param` are accessed collectively via the `java.util.Map` object returned by `HandlerInfo.getHandlerConfig()` method.

Listing 22–24 shows a set of `init-param` elements for the `ClientSecurityHandler`, which uses the Java Security Architecture to generate XML digital-signature header blocks.

Listing 22–24

The `init-param` *Elements of a Message Handler*

```
<handler xmlns:ds="http://schemas.xmlsoap.org/soap/security/2000-12">
   <handler-name>ClientSecurityHandler</handler-name>
   <handler-class>com.jwsbook.jaxrpc.ServerSecurityHandler</handler-class>
   <init-param>
       <param-name>KeyAlgorithm</param-name>
       <param-value>DSA</param-value>
   </init-param>
   <init-param>
       <param-name>KeySize</param-name>
       <param-value>512</param-value>
   </init-param>
   <init-param>
       <param-name>SignatureAlgorithm</param-name>
       <param-value>SHA1</param-value>
   </init-param>
   <soap-header>ds:Signature</soap-header>
   <soap-role>Security</soap-role>
   <port-name>BookQuotePort</port-name>
</handler>
```

The `ClientSecurityHandler` will use this information to set up a `KeyPair` and `Signature` object used to sign SOAP messages and construct XML digital-signature header blocks. The API for accessing message-handler parameters is discussed in detail in Section 14.3: The Handler Runtime Environment.

22.5.7.4 The soap-header *Elements*

A handler element may contain one or more soap-header elements, each of which declares the XML qualified names of the SOAP header blocks that the handler is supposed to process. For example, the ClientSecurityHandler handler has a value of ds:Signature as shown in Listing 22–25.

Listing 22–25

The soap-header *Element*

```
<handler xmlns:ds="http://schemas.xmlsoap.org/soap/security/2000-12" >
   <handler-name>ClientSecurityHandler</handler-name>
   <handler-class>com.jwsbook.jaxrpc.ServerSecurityHandler</handler-class>
   <init-param>
       <param-name>KeyAlgorithm</param-name>
       <param-value>DSA</param-value>
   </init-param>
   <init-param>
       <param-name>KeySize</param-name>
       <param-value>512</param-value>
   </init-param>
   <init-param>
       <param-name>SignatureAlgorithm</param-name>
       <param-value>SHA1</param-value>
   </init-param>
   <soap-header>ds:Signature</soap-header>
   <soap-role>Security</soap-role>
   <port-name>BookQuotePort</port-name>
</handler>
```

The JAX-RPC runtime uses the qualified name of the header block, as specified by the soap-header element, to identify header blocks in the reply message that should be processed by the handler chain. Whether or not a header block is supposed to be processed by the handler chain also depends on the values of the soap-role elements, which are discussed next.

22.5.7.5 The soap-role *Elements*

The soap-role elements identify roles that the handler assumes when processing header blocks. Only when the soap-role values are coupled with the soap -header elements do we know exactly which header blocks in SOAP reply messages a particular handler will process. The ClientSecurityHandler specifies its role as Security in Listing 22–26.

Listing 22–26

The `soap-role` *Element*

```
<handler
  xmlns:sec="http://schemas.xmlsoap.org/soap/security/2000-12" >
   <handler-name>ClientSecurityHandler</handler-name>
   <handler-class>com.jwsbook.jaxrpc.ServerSecurityHandler</handler-class>
   <init-param>
       <param-name>KeyAlgorithm</param-name>
       <param-value>DSA</param-value>
   </init-param>
   ...
   <soap-header>sec:Signature</soap-header>
   <soap-role>Security</soap-role>
   <port-name>BookQuotePort</port-name>
</handler>
```

Remember that the SOAP message will indicate the roles that are supposed to process each header block. If the `actor` attribute is specified, then only nodes that play the designated role may process the header block. If the `actor` attribute is not specified, only the ultimate receiver may process the header block. These rules were discussed in detail in Chapter 4: SOAP. Listing 22–27 shows an example of a SOAP reply message whose `sec:Signature` header blocks should be processed by the `ClientSecurityHandler` handler described in the preceding listing.

Listing 22–27

A SOAP Message with a `sec:Signature` *Header Block*

```
<soap:Envelope
 xmlns:soap="http://schemas.xmlsoap.org/soap/envelope/"
 xmlns:mh="http://www.Monson-Haefel.com/jwsbook/BookQuote"
 xmlns:sec="http://schemas.xmlsoap.org/soap/security/2000-12" >
  <soap:Header>
      <sec:Signature actor="Security">
           <!-- digital-security elements go here -->
      </sec:Signature>
   </soap:Header>
   <soap:Body>
      <mh:getBookPrice >
          <mh:price>29.95</mh:price>
      </mh:getBookPrice>
   </soap:Body>
</soap:Envelope>
```

The `ClientSecurityHandler` is responsible for processing the digital-security header block because the SOAP reply message declares the correct header-block name (`sec:Signature`) and, just as important, the correct role (`Security`).

22.5.7.6 *The* `port-name` *Element*

A JAX-RPC service can support multiple Web service ports, but a message handler is associated with only one WSDL `port`. The `port-name` element identifies the exact WSDL `port` definition that the message handler is associated with. Only messages that are sent or received from the Web service that implements that WSDL `port` definition will use that handler. For example, previous examples identified the WSDL `port` as `mh:BookQuotePort`. That WSDL `port` is defined in the `bookquote.wsdl` document, as in Listing 22–28.

Listing 22–28

The WSDL `port` *Element*

```
<?xml version="1.0" encoding="UTF-8"?>
<definitions xmlns="http://schemas.xmlsoap.org/wsdl/"
    xmlns:xsd="http://www.w3.org/2001/XMLSchema"
    xmlns:soap="http://schemas.xmlsoap.org/wsdl/soap/"
    xmlns:mh="http://www.Monson-Haefel.com/jwsbook/BookQuote"
    targetNamespace="http://www.Monson-Haefel.com/jwsbook/BookQuote">
  ...
  <service name="BookQuoteService">
    <port name="BookQuotePort" binding="mh:BookQuoteSoapBinding">
      <soap:address
       location="http://www.Monson-Haefel.com/jwsbook/BookQuoteService"/>
    </port>
  </service>
</definitions>
```

22.5.7.7 *Proper Processing by Handlers*

When a J2EE component uses JAX-RPC to send a SOAP request message, the handlers declared in the `service-ref` element will process the message before it is sent across the network to the Web service endpoint. When processing a SOAP request message for a J2EE client, the handlers are expected to add header blocks to the SOAP message. For example, the `MessageIDHandler` will add a unique `message-id` header, and the `ClientSecurityHandler` will add a `Signature` header block to the SOAP request. The same message handlers that add header blocks to outgoing request messages can also be used to process header blocks of incoming reply messages.

When the J2EE component receives a SOAP reply message, the JAX-RPC runtime will query the entire handler chain to see if any of its handlers process headers in the reply. If so, the handlers will process the message in the reverse of the order that they are declared in the `service-ref` element. Each message handler in the chain gets access to the entire SOAP message, not just the header block it's responsible for.

> ***Although message handlers should process only the header blocks they're identified with, there is nothing stopping them from processing other parts of the SOAP message as well.***

If a SOAP reply message contains a header block with the `mustUnderstand` attribute set to `true`, then there must be a message handler associated with the name and role of that header block. If not, the JAX-RPC runtime will throw an exception to the client.

22.5.7.8 The Handler Display Elements

It's not shown in the previous examples, but a `handler` element may contain certain display-oriented elements, as shown in Listing 22–29.

Listing 22–29

Display-Oriented Elements

```
<handler>
   <description>
      The MessageID handler adds to every outgoing message
      a unique id that is used primarily for debugging and auditing.
   </description>
   <display-name>Message ID</display-name>
   <small-icon>images/handlers/sm_messageid.gif</small-icon>
   <large-icon>images/handlers/lg_messageid.jpg</large-icon>
   <handler-name>MessageID</handler-name>
   <handler-class>com.jwsbook.jaxrpc.MessageIDHandler</handler-class>
   <soap-header>mi:message-id</soap-header>
</handler>
```

GUI deployment tools in graphical trees and other widgets use the information provided by the display elements (shown in bold). The locations of the icons are relative to the archive file in which the `service-ref` element is declared. These types of display elements are self-explanatory and common to most configurable components in J2EE, and will not be discussed further.

22.6 Wrapping Up

To say that deployment descriptors for Web services are complicated is a gross understatement. They are ridiculously complex, and a major source of headaches when done by hand. If your J2EE vendor gives you the capability to generate the deployment descriptors automatically, take advantage of it.

Chapter 23

Web Service Descriptors

J2EE Web Services requires that you include a Web service deployment descriptor named `webservices.xml` with any archive file that contains a JSE or EJB endpoint. You place `webservices.xml` in the `META-INF` directory of the EJB JAR file for EJB endpoints, and in the `WEB-INF` directory of a WAR file for JSEs. See Chapter 22 for details on packaging `webservices.xml` in a WAR file or EJB JAR file. Listing 23–1 shows the `webservices.xml` file for the BookQuote Web service.

Listing 23–1

The `webservices.xml` *File for the BookQuote Web Service*

```
<webservices
   xmlns="http://java.sun.com/xml/ns/j2ee"
   xmlns:xsi="http://www.w3.org/2001/XMLSchema-instance"
   xmlns:mh="http://www.Monson-Haefel.org/jwsbook/BookQuote/BookQuote"
   xsi:schemaLocation="http://java.sun.com/xml/ns/j2ee
                http://www.ibm.com/webservices/xsd/j2ee_web_services_1_1.xsd"
   version="1.1">

      <webservice-description>
         <webservice-description-name>BookQuote</webservice-description-name>
         <wsdl-file>/WEB-INF/wsdl/bookquote.wsdl</wsdl-file>
         <jaxrpc-mapping-file>/WEB-INF/bookquote.map</jaxrpc-mapping-file>
         <port-component>
            <port-component-name>BookQuoteJSE</port-component-name>
```

```
            <wsdl-port>mh:BookQuotePort</wsdl-port>
            <service-endpoint-interface>com.jwsbook.jaxrpc.BookQuote
            </service-endpoint-interface>
            <service-impl-bean>
               <servlet-link>BookQuoteJSE</servlet-link>
            </service-impl-bean>
         </port-component>
      </webservice-description>
</webservices>
```

The root element of the `webservices.xml` file is the `webservices` element, which may declare a set of descriptive elements (`description`, `display-name`, `small-icon`, `large-icon`) for display in visual deployment tools. More important is the requirement that the `webservices` element declare one or more `webservice-description` elements.

The `webservice-description` element describes a collection of JSEs or EJB endpoints that use the same WSDL file. In other words, there must be a separate `webservice-description` element for each WSDL file in an archive file. For example, if you package two different JSEs in the same WAR file, each with its own WSDL document, you will use a different `webservice-description` element to describe each JSE.

The function of the `webservice-description` element is to bind J2EE endpoints to their WSDL `port` definition, implementation deployment descriptor, JAX-RPC mapping file, and endpoint interface. Identifying the links between a J2EE endpoint and these other constituents is necessary to deploy a Web service in J2EE. The rest of this chapter explains the relationship of all these artifacts to the J2EE endpoint and why they are needed.

23.1 The `wsdl-file` and `wsdl-port` Elements

The `wsdl-file` element identifies the location of a WSDL document relative to the `META-INF/wsdl` directory of the WAR or EJB JAR file. The `port-component`, in turn, maps a specific JSE or EJB endpoint to a specific `port` element in that WSDL document. The content of Listing 23–1 is displayed again here, with the `wsdl-file` and `port-component` elements shown in bold.

```
<webservices
   xmlns="http://java.sun.com/xml/ns/j2ee"
   xmlns:xsi="http://www.w3.org/2001/XMLSchema-instance"
   xmlns:mh="http://www.Monson-Haefel.org/jwsbook/BookQuote/BookQuote"
   xsi:schemaLocation="http://java.sun.com/xml/ns/j2ee
              http://www.ibm.com/webservices/xsd/j2ee_web_services_1_1.xsd"
   version="1.1">
```

```
    <webservice-description>
      <webservice-description-name>BookQuote</webservice-description-name>
      <wsdl-file>/WEB-INF/wsdl/bookquote.wsdl</wsdl-file>
      <jaxrpc-mapping-file>/WEB-INF/bookquote.map</jaxrpc-mapping-file>
      <port-component>
        <port-component-name>BookQuoteJSE</port-component-name>
        <wsdl-port>mh:BookQuotePort</wsdl-port>
        <service-endpoint-interface>com.jwsbook.jaxrpc.BookQuote
        </service-endpoint-interface>
        <service-impl-bean>
          <servlet-link>BookQuoteJSE</servlet-link>
        </service-impl-bean>
      </port-component>
    </webservice-description>
</webservices>
```

The `wsdl-file` element identifies the exact location of the WSDL document in the J2EE endpoint's archive file. In this case it's a file named `bookquote.wsdl`, located in the `WEB-INF/wsdl` directory of the WAR file. The WSDL file must be located in the same EJB JAR or WAR as the `webservices.xml` file; you can't point to a WSDL document in some other archive file even if it's in the same EAR (Enterprise ARchive) file. Relative to the WSDL file specified by the `wsdl-file` element, the `wsdl-port` element provides the qualified name of the exact WSDL `port` that corresponds to the J2EE endpoint. The preceding snippet shows the `wsdl-port` element in bold. For example, the `BookQuoteJSE` J2EE endpoint is mapped to the `mh:BookQuote Port` port in the `bookquote.wsdl` file. Listing 23–2 shows a snippet of the WSDL document for the BookQuote Web service.

Listing 23–2

The `port` *Definition in the BookQuote WSDL Document*

```
<?xml version="1.0" encoding="UTF-8"?>
<definitions xmlns="http://schemas.xmlsoap.org/wsdl/"
    xmlns:xsd="http://www.w3.org/2001/XMLSchema"
    xmlns:soap="http://schemas.xmlsoap.org/wsdl/soap/"
    xmlns:mh="http://www.Monson-Haefel.com/jwsbook/BookQuote"
    targetNamespace="http://www.Monson-Haefel.com/jwsbook/BookQuote">

  ...

  <service name="BookQuoteService">
    <port name="BookQuotePort" binding="mh:BookQuoteSoapBinding">
      <soap:address
       location="http://www.Monson-Haefel.com/jwsbook/BookQuoteService"/>
```

```
    </port>
  </service>
</definitions>
```

The J2EE deployment tool needs to know where the WSDL file for each J2EE endpoint is located, so it can copy the endpoint to some public repository such as a URL or UDDI registry. Sometimes the WSDL file is published to a UDDI directory, sometimes to some URL that is based on the endpoint address of the Web service itself (for example, http://www.Monson-Haefel.com/jwsbook/wsdl/bookquote.wsdl/""), sometimes to both.

The `wsdl-port` points to a single WSDL `port` definition in the WSDL file identified by the `wsdl-file` element. The deployment tool needs to know the exact WSDL `port` definition so it can generate the skeleton code used to marshal SOAP messages into method calls on the J2EE endpoint. Remember that the WSDL `port` definition is associated with a `binding`, and that the `binding` definition determines the messaging mode (RPC/Literal or Document/Literal) as well as the protocol (usually HTTP 1.1) that the J2EE endpoint will use.

For JSEs the WSDL `port` definition and its corresponding `binding` are used to generate the JAX-RPC servlet that will host the JSE (see Section 10.2.1). For EJB endpoints the `port` and `binding` definitions are used to generate skeleton code used by the EJB container to marshal incoming SOAP messages into method calls that can be dispatched to the proper stateless bean instance (see Section 11.2).

The exact SOAP-to-EJB marshalling architecture varies from one vendor to the next, but in many cases a servlet that's similar to a JAX-RPC servlet is used to marshal SOAP message calls into calls on the EJB.

The WSDL `port` definition may also declare the SOAP address of the J2EE endpoint, but the deployment tool is not required to use this address. The deployer can choose to use this address, or overwrite it with some other URL, or, for JSEs, base the location on the `servlet-mapping` element in the `web.xml` file (see Section 22.3.2.3).

23.2 The `port-component-name` Element

The `port-component-name` element provides a name to identify a particular JSE or EJB endpoint. This name must be unique within the `webservices.xml` file. Deployment tools display it to identify the J2EE endpoint, and the JAX-RPC mapping file uses it to correlate a mapping with a specific J2EE endpoint.

```
<webservices
   xmlns="http://java.sun.com/xml/ns/j2ee"
   xmlns:xsi="http://www.w3.org/2001/XMLSchema-instance"
```

```
    xmlns:mh="http://www.Monson-Haefel.org/jwsbook/BookQuote/BookQuote"
    xsi:schemaLocation="http://java.sun.com/xml/ns/j2ee
                http://www.ibm.com/webservices/xsd/j2ee_web_services_1_1.
                xsd"
    version="1.1">
    <webservice-description>
        <webservice-description-name>BookQuote</webservice-description-name>
        <wsdl-file>/WEB-INF/wsdl/bookquote.wsdl</wsdl-file>
        <jaxrpc-mapping-file>/WEB-INF/bookquote.map</jaxrpc-mapping-file>
        <port-component>
            <port-component-name>BookQuoteJSE</port-component-name>
            ...
```

There are no standards for J2EE endpoint names. In this book J2EE endpoint names consist of the endpoint interface name and a suffix, either `JSE` or `EJB`. For example, the BookQuote JSE has the port name `BookQuoteJSE`, and the BookQuote EJB uses the name `BookQuoteEJB`. You can use any naming scheme you like.

23.3 The `service-endpoint-interface` Element

The `web.xml` deployment descriptor used by a JSE does not provide an element for declaring the type of the endpoint interface, so you must declare a fully qualified name for it in `webservices.xml`—specifically, in the `service-endpoint-interface`, as shown in bold in the following recapitulation of Listing 23–1.

```
<webservices
    xmlns="http://java.sun.com/xml/ns/j2ee"
    xmlns:xsi="http://www.w3.org/2001/XMLSchema-instance"
    xmlns:mh="http://www.Monson-Haefel.org/jwsbook/BookQuote/BookQuote"
    xsi:schemaLocation="http://java.sun.com/xml/ns/j2ee
            http://www.ibm.com/webservices/xsd/j2ee_web_services_1_1.xsd"
    version="1.1">
    <webservice-description>
        <webservice-description-name>BookQuote</webservice-description-name>
        <wsdl-file>/WEB-INF/wsdl/bookquote.wsdl</wsdl-file>
        <jaxrpc-mapping-file>/WEB-INF/bookquote.map</jaxrpc-mapping-file>
        <port-component>
            <port-component-name>BookQuoteJSE</port-component-name>
            <wsdl-port>mh:BookQuotePort</wsdl-port>
            <service-endpoint-interface>com.jwsbook.jaxrpc.BookQuote
            </service-endpoint-interface>
```

```
            <service-impl-bean>
                <servlet-link>BookQuoteJSE</servlet-link>
            </service-impl-bean>
        </port-component>
    </webservice-description>
</webservices>
```

You must also declare the interface type for EJB endpoints, but be aware that this type must be the same as the type declared by the `service-endpoint` element in the `ejb-jar.xml` file. The fact that you have to duplicate the declaration of the endpoint interface for EJB endpoints is unfortunate, but necessary to support backward-compatibility with J2EE 1.3 Web Services.

23.4 The `service-impl-bean` Element

The `service-impl-bean` element tells the deployment tool which implementation definition is associated with the J2EE endpoint. Specifically, for a JSE it points to a specific `servlet` definition in the `web.xml` file, and for an EJB endpoint it points to a `session-bean` definition in the `ejb-jar.xml` file. The link must point to an implementation definition in the archive file that contains the related `webservices.xml` file.

For a JSE the link is declared in a `servlet-link` element, as in Listing 23–3.

Listing 23–3

The `webservices.xml` *File for the BookQuote JSE*

```
<webservices
   xmlns="http://java.sun.com/xml/ns/j2ee"
   xmlns:xsi="http://www.w3.org/2001/XMLSchema-instance"
   xmlns:mh="http://www.Monson-Haefel.org/jwsbook/BookQuote/BookQuote"
   xsi:schemaLocation="http://java.sun.com/xml/ns/j2ee
              http://www.ibm.com/webservices/xsd/j2ee_web_services_1_1.xsd"
   version="1.1">
   <webservice-description>
       <webservice-description-name>BookQuote</webservice-description-name>
       <wsdl-file>/WEB-INF/wsdl/bookquote.wsdl</wsdl-file>
       <jaxrpc-mapping-file>/WEB-INF/bookquote.map</jaxrpc-mapping-file>
       <port-component>
          <port-component-name>BookQuoteJSE</port-component-name>
          <wsdl-port>mh:BookQuotePort</wsdl-port>
          <service-endpoint-interface>com.jwsbook.jaxrpc.BookQuote
```

```
            </service-endpoint-interface>
            <service-impl-bean>
               <servlet-link>BookQuoteJSE</servlet-link>
            </service-impl-bean>
         </port-component>
      </webservice-description>
</webservices>
```

The value of the `servlet-link` element must match the value of a `servlet-name` element in the local `web.xml` file, shown in Listing 23–4.

Listing 23–4

The `web.xml` *File for the BookQuote JSE*

```
<?xml version='1.0' encoding='UTF-8'?>
<web-app …>
    <servlet>
        <servlet-name>BookQuoteJSE</servlet-name>
        <servlet-class>com.jwsbook.jaxrpc.BookQuote_Impl</servlet-class>
    </servlet>
</web-app>
```

For an EJB endpoint the link is declared using an `ejb-link` element, as shown in the Listing 23–5.

Listing 23–5

The `webservices.xml` *File for the BookQuote EJB*

```
<webservices
   xmlns="http://java.sun.com/xml/ns/j2ee"
   xmlns:xsi="http://www.w3.org/2001/XMLSchema-instance"
   xmlns:mh="http://www.Monson-Haefel.org/jwsbook/BookQuote/BookQuote"
   xsi:schemaLocation="http://java.sun.com/xml/ns/j2ee
            http://www.ibm.com/webservices/xsd/j2ee_web_services_1_1.xsd"
   version="1.1">
   <webservice-description>
       <webservice-description-name>BookQuote</webservice-description-name>
       <wsdl-file>/WEB-INF/wsdl/bookquote.wsdl</wsdl-file>
       <jaxrpc-mapping-file>/WEB-INF/bookquote.map</jaxrpc-mapping-file>
       <port-component>
          <port-component-name>BookQuoteEJB</port-component-name>
          <wsdl-port>mh:BookQuotePort</wsdl-port>
```

```
            <service-endpoint-interface>com.jwsbook.jaxrpc.BookQuote
            </service-endpoint-interface>
            <service-impl-bean>
               <ejb-link>BookQuoteEJB</ejb-link>
            </service-impl-bean>
         </port-component>
      </webservice-description>
</webservices>
```

The value of the ejb-link element must match the value of an ejb-name element in the local ejb-jar.xml file, shown in Listing 23–6.

Listing 23–6

The ejb-jar.xml *File for the BookQuote EJB*

```
<ejb-jar ...>
    <enterprise-beans>
        <session>
            <ejb-name>BookQuoteEJB</ejb-name>
            <ejb-class>com.jwsbook.jaxrpc.BookQuoteBean</ejb-class>
            <session-type>Stateless</session-type>
            ...
        </session>
    </enterprise-beans>
    ...
</ejb-jar>
```

23.5 The jaxrpc-mapping-file Element

The jaxrpc-mapping-file element declares the location of the JAX-RPC mapping file, which defines the mapping between the WSDL file and the J2EE endpoint. JAX-RPC mapping files are covered in detail in Chapter 25.

```
<webservices
   xmlns="http://java.sun.com/xml/ns/j2ee"
   xmlns:xsi="http://www.w3.org/2001/XMLSchema-instance"
   xmlns:mh="http://www.Monson-Haefel.org/jwsbook/BookQuote/BookQuote"
   xsi:schemaLocation="http://java.sun.com/xml/ns/j2ee
             http://www.ibm.com/webservices/xsd/j2ee_web_services_1_1.xsd"
   version="1.1">
   <webservice-description>
```

```
        <webservice-description-name>BookQuote</webservice-description-name>
        <wsdl-file>/WEB-INF/wsdl/bookquote.wsdl</wsdl-file>
        <jaxrpc-mapping-file>/WEB-INF/wsdl/bookquote.map</jaxrpc-mapping-file>
        ...

    </webservice-description>
</webservices>
```

23.6 The handler Element

Message handlers filter messages sent and received by J2EE endpoints. They provide you with a mechanism to read and modify SOAP messages before and after the endpoint does its work. In the webservices.xml file you can configure a chain of message handlers, which will process incoming messages in the order they are declared, and outgoing messages in the opposite order. (To learn more about message handlers, see Chapter 14.)

For example, the J2EE 1.4 webservices.xml file shown in Listing 23–7 declares two message handlers, the Logger and the ServerSecurityHandler.

Listing 23–7

A webservices.xml *File That Declared Two Message Handlers*

```
<webservices
   xmlns="http://java.sun.com/xml/ns/j2ee"
   xmlns:xsi="http://www.w3.org/2001/XMLSchema-instance"
   xmlns:mh="http://www.Monson-Haefel.org/jwsbook/BookQuote/BookQuote"
   xmlns:ds="http://schemas.xmlsoap.org/soap/security/2000-12"
   xmlns:proc="http://www.Monson-Haefel.com/jwsbook/processed-by"
   xsi:schemaLocation="http://java.sun.com/xml/ns/j2ee
              http://www.ibm.com/webservices/xsd/j2ee_web_services_1_1.xsd"
   version="1.1">

  <webservice-description>
    <webservice-description-name>BookQuote</webservice-description-name>
    ...
    <port-component>
      <port-component-name>BookQuoteJSE</port-component-name>
      ...
      <handler>
        <handler-name>Logger</handler-name>
        <handler-class>com.jwsbook.jaxrpc.sec06.LoggerHandler</handler-class>
```

```
        <soap-header>mi:message-id</soap-header>
        <soap-header>proc:processed-by</soap-header>
        <soap-role>http://www.Monson-Haefel.com/logger</soap-role>
        <soap-role>http://schemas.xmlsoap.org/soap/actor/next</soap-role>
      </handler>
      <handler>
        <handler-name>ServerSecurityHandler</handler-name>
        <handler-class>com.jwsbook.jaxrpc.sec06.ServerSecurityHandler
        </handler-class>
        <init-param>
          <param-name>KeyAlgorithm</param-name>
          <param-value>DSA</param-value>
        </init-param>
        <init-param>
          <param-name>KeySize</param-name>
          <param-value>512</param-value>
        </init-param>
        <init-param>
          <param-name>SignatureAlgorithm</param-name>
          <param-value>SHA1</param-value>
        </init-param>
        <soap-header>ds:Signature</soap-header>
      </handler>
    </port-component>
  </webservice-description>
</webservices>
```

23.6.1 The `handler-name` Element

The value of each `handler-name` element must be unique within the `webservices.xml` file that contains it. It's not clear how the value of the `handler-name` element is used. No API gives the developer access to it, but it appears to be useful to the J2EE container system itself. At any rate the `handler-name` element provides a unique identifier for a configured handler.

23.6.2 The `handler-class` Element

This element identifies the class that implements the handler. The handler class must implement the `javax.xml.rpc.handler.Handler` interface as described in Chapter 14.

23.6.3 The `init-param` Elements

The `init-param` elements are optional, and describe the initialization parameters that can be passed to the message handler at the beginning of its life cycle. At runtime the parameters can be obtained from the java.util.Map object returned by the HandlerInfo.getHandlerConfig() method.

The following snippet shows a set of init-param elements for the ServerSecurityHandler, which uses the Java Security Architecture to generate XML-digital-signature header blocks.

```
<handler>
   <handler-name>ServerSecurityHandler</handler-name>
   <handler-class>com.jwsbook.jaxrpc.ServerSecurityHandler</handler-class>
   <init-param>
       <param-name>KeyAlgorithm</param-name>
       <param-value>DSA</param-value>
   </init-param>
   <init-param>
       <param-name>KeySize</param-name>
       <param-value>512</param-value>
   </init-param>
   <init-param>
       <param-name>SignatureAlgorithm</param-name>
       <param-value>SHA1</param-value>
   </init-param>
   <soap-header>
        http://schemas.xmlsoap.org/soap/security/2000-12
        Signature
   </soap-header>
 </handler>
```

The ServerSecurityHandler uses this information to set up KeyPair and Signature objects it will use to validate signed SOAP messages and to construct XML digital-signature header blocks for replies. The programming API for accessing message-handler parameters is discussed in more detail in Section 14.3: The Handler Runtime Environment.

23.6.4 The soap-header Elements

A handler element may contain one or more soap-header elements, which declare the fully qualified names of the SOAP header blocks that the handler is supposed to process.

In the BookQuote example, the Logger handler declares two soap-header elements that designate the two types of header blocks it will process, as you can see in the following snippet.

```
<webservices
  xmlns="http://java.sun.com/xml/ns/j2ee"
  xmlns:xsi="http://www.w3.org/2001/XMLSchema-instance"
  xmlns:mh="http://www.Monson-Haefel.org/jwsbook/BookQuote/BookQuote"
  xmlns:ds="http://schemas.xmlsoap.org/soap/security/2000-12"
  xmlns:proc="http://www.Monson-Haefel.com/jwsbook/processed-by"
  xsi:schemaLocation="http://java.sun.com/xml/ns/j2ee
              http://www.ibm.com/webservices/xsd/j2ee_web_services_1_1.xsd"
  version="1.1">
 <webservice-description>
  <webservice-description-name>BookQuote</webservice-description-name>
  ...
  <port-component>
   <port-component-name>BookQuoteJSE</port-component-name>
   ...
   <handler>
    <handler-name>Logger</handler-name>
    <handler-class>com.jwsbook.jaxrpc.sec06.LoggerHandler</handler-class>
    <soap-header>mi:message-id</soap-header>
    <soap-header>proc:processed-by</soap-header>
    <soap-role>http://www.Monson-Haefel.com/logger</soap-role>
    <soap-role>http://schemas.xmlsoap.org/soap/actor/next</soap-role>
   </handler>
```

The JAX-RPC runtime uses the qualified name of the header block, as identified by the soap-header element, to identify header blocks that handlers *may* process. Whether a header block should be processed by a particular handler also depends on the values of the soap-role elements, discussed next.

23.6.5 The soap-role Elements

The soap-role element identifies roles that the handler assumes when processing header blocks. Only when the soap-role values are coupled with the soap-header elements do we know exactly which header blocks the handler processes.

```
<handler>
  <handler-name>Logger</handler-name>
  <handler-class>com.jwsbook.jaxrpc.sec06.LoggerHandler</handler-class>
  <soap-header>mi:message-id</soap-header>
  <soap-header>proc:processed-by</soap-header>
  <soap-role>http://www.Monson-Haefel.com/logger</soap-role>
  <soap-role>http://schemas.xmlsoap.org/soap/actor/next</soap-role>
</handler>
```

Remember that the SOAP message will indicate the roles that are supposed to process each header block. If the actor attribute is specified, then only nodes that play the designated role may process the header block. If actor is not specified, then only the ultimate receiver may process the header block. These rules were discussed in more detail in Chapter 4: SOAP. The following listing shows an example of a SOAP message whose processed-by and message-id header blocks would be processed by the Logger handler.

```
<soap:Envelope
 xmlns:soap="http://schemas.xmlsoap.org/soap/envelope/"
 xmlns:mh="http://www.Monson-Haefel.com/jwsbook/BookQuote"
 xmlns:mi="http://www.Monson-Haefel.com/jwsbook/message-id"
 xmlns:proc="http://www.Monson-Haefel.com/jwsbook/processed-by">
   <soap:Header>
      <mi:message-id soap:actor="http://www.Monson-Haefel.com/logger">
           deabc782dbbd11bf:29e357:f1ad93fdbf:-8000
      </mi:message-id>
      <proc:processed-by
         soap:actor="http://schemas.xmlsoap.org/soap/actor/next" >
         <node>
            <time-in-millis>1013694684723</time-in-millis>
            <identity>http://www.client.com/JaxRpcExample_7</identity>
         </node>
      </proc:processed-by>
   </soap:Header>
   <soap:Body>
      <mh:getBookPrice >
          <mh:isbn>1565928695</mh:isbn>
      </mh:getBookPrice>
   </soap:Body>
</soap:Envelope>
```

The Logger handler will process both of these header blocks because they declare the correct header-block names (processed-by and message-id) and, just as important, the correct roles (http://www.Monson-Haefel.com/logger and http://schemas.xmlsoap.org/soap/actor/next).

23.6.6 Proper Processing by Handlers

When an incoming SOAP message arrives from the client, the JAX-RPC runtime will query the entire handler chain to determine whether there are handlers to process the SOAP headers. If there are, then all the handlers in the chain will process the message, in the order they are declared in the webservices.xml file. Each has access to the entire SOAP message, not just the header blocks it's responsible for, but a message handler should process only the header blocks identified by its `soap-header` and `soap-role` elements.

If an incoming SOAP message contains a header block with the `mustUnderstand` attribute set to `true`, then there must be a message handler associated with the name and role of the header block. If not, the JAX-RPC runtime will generate a SOAP fault message, in accordance with a standard SOAP processing rule that's described in detail in Section 4.6: SOAP Faults.

23.6.7 The Display Elements

A `handler` element may contain certain display-oriented elements, as shown in the following example.

```
<handler>
   <description>
      The Logger message handler is used to log incoming messages by their
      message-id header. The log entries are written to the database using
      JDBC.
   </description>
   <display-name>SOAP Logger</display-name>
   <small-icon>images/handlers/smlogger.gif</small-icon>
   <large-icon>images/handlers/lglogger.jpg</large-icon>
   <handler-name>Logger</handler-name>
   <handler-class>com.jwsbook.jaxrpc.sec06.LoggerHandler</handler-class>
   <soap-header>mi:message-id</soap-header>
   <soap-header>proc:processed-by</soap-header>
   <soap-role>http://www.Monson-Haefel.com/logger</soap-role>
   <soap-role>http://schemas.xmlsoap.org/soap/actor/next</soap-role>
</handler>
```

GUI deployment tools in graphical trees and other widgets use the information provided by the display elements (shown in bold). The locations of the icons are relative to the archive file in which the `webservices.xml` file is located. These types of display elements are self-explanatory and common to most configurable components in J2EE, and will not be discussed further.

23.7 Wrapping Up

Deployment descriptors really add a lot of complexity to the process of deploying a Web service in J2EE. It's my opinion that J2EE would benefit if the Web services deployment descriptors were incorporated into the component deployment descriptors, rather than using a separate `webservices.xml` file. In addition, it would be good to reduce the number of things that need to be configured by allowing the deployment process to assume some default values.

As I mentioned at the end of Chapter 22, it's likely that you will not need to look at or modify the XML deployment descriptors directly. Instead your J2EE vendor should generate them automatically, based on configuration you do using a deployment tool. Occasionally, however, you are going to need to get into the deployment files and manually tweak them, in which case understanding all the elements and their meaning will be very important.

Chapter 24

JAX-RPC Mapping Files

JAX-RPC mapping files help a JAX-RPC compiler understand the relationships between WSDL documents and the Java interfaces that represent Web service endpoints. In many cases the mapping between WSDL and Java is pretty straightforward, but certain aspects of that mapping may require clarification, and that is the job of the JAX-RPC mapping file. A mapping file is required whenever you use JAX-RPC for either a J2EE endpoint (JSE or EJB endpoint) or a J2EE Web service client. There is a one-to-one relationship between WSDL documents and JAX-RPC mapping files. For every WSDL document, there must be exactly one JAX-RPC mapping file.

There is no standard file name for the JAX-RPC mapping file; you can choose any name you want. In this book the convention is to name it after the WSDL document it applies to. For example, if the WSDL document used for the BookQuote Web service is named `bookquote.wsdl`, the corresponding JAX-RPC mapping file will be named `bookquote_mapping.xml`.

JAX-RPC mapping files come in two forms. A **lightweight** mapping file is short and simple; it only declares the package mapping. A **heavyweight** mapping file is verbose and complete; it covers every aspect of the WSDL-to-Java mapping.

At the time this was written a lightweight mapping required the use of RPC/Encoded messaging. Since this mode of messaging is not BP conformant, you will create a heavyweight mapping when you deploy a BP conformant Web service. However, a lightweight mapping is a subset of a heavyweight mapping so it's discussed first.

24.1 Conditions for a Lightweight JAX-RPC Mapping File

The Web Services for J2EE specifications establish an all-or-nothing trigger that determines whether the JAX-RPC mapping file will be heavyweight or lightweight. If the WSDL document meets certain conditions, then a lightweight mapping will suffice, but if any of the conditions aren't met, you must provide a heavyweight mapping file. Perhaps the most important criteria for a lightweight mapping is the use of RPC/Encoded messaging.

You may use a lightweight JAX-RPC mapping file if your WSDL document meets the following conditions:

- The `binding` definition uses the RPC messaging style (`style="rpc"`) and SOAP 1.1 Encoding (`encodingStyle="http://schemas.xmlsoap.org/soap/encoding/"`) for all parts of all input, output, and fault messages.
- There is only one `service` element, which contains one `port` element.
- The `service`, `binding`, `portType`, and all custom XML types, simple and complex, must have unique names.
- Header blocks and header faults cannot be specified in the `binding` definition; the `parts` attribute of input and output elements may be omitted, but if it's declared, it must list all parts.
- Each `operation` in a `portType` definition must have a unique name, and must include exactly one `input` element, zero or one `output` element, and zero or more `fault` elements.
- An `operation` in a `portType` definition may omit the `parameterOrder` attribute, but if it's declared, it must specify all parts from the input message in the order they are originally declared in the corresponding `message` definition.
- A fault `message` definition must have one part named `"message"` of type `"xsd:string"`.
- The input `message` definition may declare zero or more `part` elements, but the output `message` definition must declare zero or one `part` element.
- Every `part` definition is defined with a `name` attribute and a `type` attribute; the `element` attribute is not used. The `type` attribute may be one of the following:
  - An XML schema built-in type (listed in Section 15.2.1).
  - An XML schema-based complex type that uses either the `xsd:sequence` or `xsd:all` compositor and can be mapped to Java beans (as explained in Section 15.2.2).
  - A WSDL restricted SOAP encoded array (described in Section 15.2.3). The `wsdl:arrayType` must not be another array type.

24.2 A Lightweight Example

The basic BookQuote WSDL document used throughout this book meets all of the conditions for use of a lightweight mapping file. It's shown in Listing 24–1.

Listing 24–1

A WSDL Document That Supports Lightweight Mapping

```
<?xml version="1.0" encoding="UTF-8"?>
<definitions name="BookQuote"
 targetNamespace="http://www.Monson-Haefel.com/jwsbook/BookQuote"
 xmlns:mh="http://www.Monson-Haefel.com/jwsbook/BookQuote"
 xmlns="http://schemas.xmlsoap.org/wsdl/"
 xmlns:xsd="http://www.w3.org/2001/XMLSchema"
 xmlns:soap="http://schemas.xmlsoap.org/wsdl/soap/">

  <message name="BookQuote_getBookPrice">
    <part name="isbn" type="xsd:string"/>
  </message>
  <message name="BookQuote_getBookPriceResponse">
    <part name="result" type="xsd:float"/>
  </message>
  <message name="InvalidIsbnFault" >
    <part name="message" type="xsd:string"/>
  </message>
  <portType name="BookQuote">
    <operation name="getBookPrice">
      <input message="mh:BookQuote_getBookPrice"/>
      <output message="mh:BookQuote_getBookPriceResponse"/>
      <fault name="InvalidIsbnFault" message="mh:InvalidIsbnFault" />
    </operation>
  </portType>
  <binding name="BookQuoteBinding" type="mh:BookQuote">
    <soap:binding transport="http://schemas.xmlsoap.org/soap/http"
                  style="rpc"/>
    <operation name="getBookPrice">
      <soap:operation soapAction=""/>
      <input>
        <soap:body use="literal"
        namespace="http://www.Monson-Haefel.com/jwsbook/BookQuote/BookQuote"/>
      </input>
      <output>
        <soap:body use="literal"
        namespace="http://www.Monson-Haefel.com/jwsbook/BookQuote/BookQuote"/>
      </output>
      <fault name="InvalidIsbnFault" >
        <soap:fault name="InvalidIsbnFault" use="literal" />
      </fault>
    </operation>
```

```
  </binding>
  <service name="BookQuoteService">
    <port name="BookQuotePort" binding="mh:BookQuoteBinding">
      <soap:address
       location="http://www.Monson-Haefel.com/jwsbook/BookQuoteService"/>
    </port>
  </service>
</definitions>
```

When a WSDL document meets all the conditions for a lightweight JAX-RPC as this one does, the mapping between it and JAX-RPC interfaces and stubs is pretty straightfoward, and follows the rules covered in Chapter 15: Mapping Java to WSDL and XML. One detail of that mapping cannot be automatically derived, however: the package name. A lightweight mapping file is required, because we have to specify the package declared by endpoint interfaces, service interfaces, JavaBeans components, JAX-RPC stubs, and other products generated by the JAX-RPC compiler.

Given the BookQuote WSDL document in Listing 24–1, a JAX-RPC compiler will generate the endpoint interface in Listing 24–2.

Listing 24–2

The Endpoint Interface Generated from the Conforming WSDL

```
public interface BookQuote extends java.rmi.Remote {
    public float getBookPrice(String isbn)
    throws java.rmi.RemoteException, InvalidIsbnFault;
}
```

This definition is missing only one thing, the package declaration. You specify the package to which the endpoint interface belongs in the `package-mapping` element of a lightweight mapping file, as in Listing 24–3.

Listing 24–3

A Lightweight JAX-RPC Mapping File

```
<?xml version='1.0' encoding='UTF-8' ?>
<java-wsdl-mapping
  xmlns="http://java.sun.com/xml/ns/j2ee"
  xmlns:xsi="http://www.w3.org/2001/XMLSchema-instance"
  xsi:schemaLocation="http://java.sun.com/xml/ns/j2ee
          http://www.ibm.com/webservices/xsd/j2ee_jaxrpc_mapping_1_1.xsd"
  version="1.1">
  <package-mapping>
    <package-type>com.jwsbook.jaxrpc</package-type>
    <namespaceURI>
```

```
      http://www.Monson-Haefel.com/jwsbook/BookQuote
    </namespaceURI>
  </package-mapping>
</java-wsdl-mapping>
```

Based on this file, the JAX-RPC compiler would generate the endpoint interface as a member of the `com.jwsbook.jaxrpc` package, as shown in Listing 24–4.

Listing 24–4

The Endpoint Interface Generated from the Lightweight Mapping File

```
package com.jwsbook.jaxrpc;

public interface BookQuote extends java.rmi.Remote {
    public float getBookPrice(String isbn)
    throws java.rmi.RemoteException, InvalidIsbnFault;
}
```

The `InvalidIsbnFault` exception class, the service interface, its implementation, and the endpoint stub would all be generated with the same package name.

In a lightweight JAX-RPC mapping file, all you need to declare is the `package-mapping` element. The JAX-RPC mapping file is stored in the J2EE component's archive file, usually in the same directory as the WSDL document it pertains to.

24.3 A Heavyweight Example

When any of the conditions for a lightweight mapping file are violated, you must provide a complete JAX-RPC mapping file that details the mapping between

- XML complex types and Java beans
- Fault messages and exception classes
- The WSDL `portType` definition and the endpoint interface
- The WSDL `service` definition and the service interface

A lightweight mapping requires the use of RPC/Encoded messaging, which is not BP conformant. Consider as an example the WSDL document in Listing 24–5, which violates the conditions for lightweight mapping at a number of points, shown in bold.

Listing 24–5

A WSDL Document That Fails to Support Lightweight Mapping

```
<?xml version="1.0" encoding="UTF-8"?>
<definitions name="BookQuote"
 targetNamespace="http://www.Monson-Haefel.com/jwsbook/BookQuote"
```

```
  xmlns:mh="http://www.Monson-Haefel.com/jwsbook/BookQuote"
  xmlns="http://schemas.xmlsoap.org/wsdl/"
  xmlns:xsd="http://www.w3.org/2001/XMLSchema"
  xmlns:soap="http://schemas.xmlsoap.org/wsdl/soap/">

 <message name="BookQuote_getBookPrice">
   <part name="isbn" type="xsd:string"/>
 </message>
 <message name="BookQuote_getBookPriceResponse">
   <part name="result" type="xsd:float"/>
 </message>
 <message name="InvalidIsbnFault" >
   <part name="message" type="xsd:string"/>
 </message>
 <portType name="BookQuote">
   <operation name="getBookPrice">
     <input message="mh:BookQuote_getBookPrice"/>
     <output message="mh:BookQuote_getBookPriceResponse"/>
     <fault name="InvalidIsbnFault" message="mh:InvalidIsbnFault" />
   </operation>
 </portType>
 <binding name="BookQuoteBinding" type="mh:BookQuote">
   <soap:binding transport="http://schemas.xmlsoap.org/soap/http"
                 style="document"/>
    <operation name="getBookPrice">
     <soap:operation soapAction=""/>
     <input>
       <soap:body use="literal" />
     </input>
     <output>
       <soap:body use="literal" />
     </output>
     <fault name="InvalidIsbnFault">
       <soap:fault name="InvalidIsbnFault" use="literal" />
     </fault>
   </operation>
 </binding>
 <service name="BookQuoteService">
   <port name="BookQuotePort" binding="mh:BookQuoteBinding">
     <soap:address
      location="http://www.Monson-Haefel.com/jwsbook/BookQuoteService"/>
   </port>
 </service>
</definitions>
```

This WSDL definition for the BookQuote Web service is identical to the conforming definition in Listing 24–1, except for two important differences. The binding specifies `document` message style and `literal` encoding. For lightweight mapping a WSDL document must specify the RPC messaging style and SOAP 1.1 Encoding.

There is nothing inherently wrong with specifying Document/Literal messaging. It simply doesn't meet the criteria for lightweight mapping, and forces us to create a complete JAX-RPC mapping file for this version of the BookQuote Web service, like the one in Listing 24–6.

Listing 24–6

A Heavyweight JAX-RPC Mapping File

```
<?xml version='1.0' encoding='UTF-8' ?>
<java-wsdl-mapping
  xmlns="http://java.sun.com/xml/ns/j2ee"
  xmlns:mh="http://www.Monson-Haefel.com/jwsbook/BookQuote"
  xmlns:xsi="http://www.w3.org/2001/XMLSchema-instance"
  xmlns:xsd="http://www.w3.org/2001/XMLSchema"
  xsi:schemaLocation="http://java.sun.com/xml/ns/j2ee
           http://www.ibm.com/webservices/xsd/j2ee_jaxrpc_mapping_1_1.xsd"
  version="1.1">

  <package-mapping>
    <package-type>com.jwsbook.jaxrpc</package-type>
    <namespaceURI>
      http://www.Monson-Haefel.com/jwsbook/PurchaseOrder</namespaceURI>
  </package-mapping>
  <exception-mapping>
    <exception-type>com.jwsbook.jaxrpc.InvalidIsbnException</exception-type>
    <wsdl-message>mh:InvalidIsbnFault</wsdl-message>
  </exception-mapping>
  <service-interface-mapping>
    <service-interface>com.jwsbook.jaxrpc.BookQuoteService</service-interface>
    <wsdl-service-name>mh:BookQuoteService</wsdl-service-name>
    <port-mapping>
      <port-name>mh:BookQuotePort</port-name>
      <java-port-name>BookQuotePort</java-port-name>
    </port-mapping>
  </service-interface-mapping>
  <service-endpoint-interface-mapping>
    <service-endpoint-interface>com.jwsbook.jaxrpc.BookQuote
    </service-endpoint-interface>
    <wsdl-port-type>mh:BookQuote</wsdl-port-type>
    <wsdl-binding>mh:BookQuoteBinding</wsdl-binding>
```

```
    <service-endpoint-method-mapping>
      <java-method-name>getBookPrice</java-method-name>
      <wsdl-operation>mh:getBookPrice</wsdl-operation>
      <method-param-parts-mapping>
        <param-position>0</param-position>
        <param-type>java.lang.String</param-type>
        <wsdl-message-mapping>
          <wsdl-message>mh:BookQuote_getBookPriceRequest
          </wsdl-message>
          <wsdl-message-part-name>isbn</wsdl-message-part-name>
          <parameter-mode>IN</parameter-mode>
        </wsdl-message-mapping>
      </method-param-parts-mapping>
      <wsdl-return-value-mapping>
        <method-return-value>float</method-return-value>
        <wsdl-message>mh:BookQuote_getBookPriceResponse</wsdl-message>
        <wsdl-message-part-name>result</wsdl-message-part-name>
      </wsdl-return-value-mapping>
    </service-endpoint-method-mapping>
  </service-endpoint-interface-mapping>
</java-wsdl-mapping>
```

Like any deployment descriptor file, a complete JAX-RPC mapping file can be a bit intimidating the first time you see it. Don't let it concern you. The next section will discuss each of the mapping elements in detail, including some not included in this listing.

In many cases, even a heavyweight mapping file is complemented by the standard rules for mapping WSDL and XML to Java. These rules fill gaps you leave in the JAX-RPC mapping file, but an explicit declaration in the mapping file always overrides any of the standard mapping rules, discussed in Chapter 15.

24.4 Anatomy of a Mapping File

A mapping file can get to be pretty large. Some vendors may choose to support less verbose mapping files, that specify only the WSDL definitions that don't conform to the criteria for lightweight mapping. This "abbreviated mapping" can really reduce the amount of mapping information you must provide, but beware: It is not standardized, so abbreviated mapping files may not be portable across vendors. To ensure portability you should make your mapping as complete as you can.

I'll discuss individual elements in separate sections. Each should be a useful reference by itself, independent of other sections. In addition, sections do not depend on any one WSDL definition, but use a variety of WSDL documents to illustrate how each mapping element is used in practice.

It's important to remember that there is a one-to-one relationship between a JAX-RPC mapping file and a WSDL document, and that they must be packaged together in the same J2EE component archive file. The following snippet provides a rough skeleton of a JAX-RPC mapping file, showing only the primary elements. Use this skeleton to help understand the context in which the various mapping elements are declared.

```
<java-wsdl-mapping...>
  <package-mapping/>
  <java-xml-type-mapping/>
  <exception-mapping/>
  <service-interface-mapping/>
  <service-endpoint-interface-mapping>
      ...
      <service-endpoint-method-mapping/>
  </service-endpoint-interface-mapping>
</java-wsdl-mapping>
```

24.4.1 The `java-wsdl-mapping` Element

The `java-wsdl-mapping` element is the root of the JAX-RPC mapping file. It must be declared, and it will contain all other mapping elements. Listing 24–7 shows the root element of a JAX-RPC mapping file.

Listing 24–7

A `java-wsdl-mapping` *Element*

```
<?xml version='1.0' encoding='UTF-8' ?>
<java-wsdl-mapping
  xmlns="http://java.sun.com/xml/ns/j2ee"
  xmlns:mh="http://www.Monson-Haefel.com/jwsbook/BookQuote"
  xmlns:xsi="http://www.w3.org/2001/XMLSchema-instance"
  xmlns:xsd="http://www.w3.org/2001/XMLSchema"
  xsi:schemaLocation="http://java.sun.com/xml/ns/j2ee
            http://www.ibm.com/webservices/xsd/j2ee_jaxrpc_mapping_1_1.xsd"
  version="1.1">
  ...
</java-wsdl-mapping>
```

24.4.2 The `package-mapping` Element

As I said in Section 24.2, the `package-mapping` element may be the only child of the root element required, if the WSDL document conforms to the criteria for light-weight mapping.

When you use generated stubs and dynamic proxies, a JAX-RPC compiler will use the `package-mapping` element to generate Java class and interface definitions for a variety of types defined in the WSDL document.

- An endpoint interface for the WSDL `portType` element
- An endpoint stub that implements the endpoint interface (when you're using JAX-RPC generated stubs)
- A service interface for the WSDL `service` element
- A service implementation for the service interface (when you're using JAX-RPC generated stubs)
- A bean or plain Java class for each complex or simple type declared in the `types` element
- Holder types for INOUT and OUT parameters of `operation` elements

Each of these classes and interfaces needs to be placed in one Java package or another—the `package-mapping` element dictates which. A package mapping looks like this:

```
<java-wsdl-mapping ...>
  <package-mapping>
    <package-type>com.jwsbook.jaxrpc</package-type>
    <namespaceURI>http://www.Monson-Haefel.com/jwsbook/BookQuote
    </namespaceURI>
  </package-mapping>
</java-wsdl-mapping>
```

The value of the `package-type` element is the name of the Java package and can be anything that fits standard Java naming rules. The value of `namespaceURI` is the XML namespace that should be mapped to the Java package name. In most cases the XML namespace you are mapping is the target namespace of the corresponding WSDL document, as in this snippet:

```
<?xml version="1.0" encoding="UTF-8"?>
<definitions name="BookQuote"
 targetNamespace="http://www.Monson-Haefel.com/jwsbook/BookQuote"
 xmlns:mh="http://www.Monson-Haefel.com/jwsbook/BookQuote"
 xmlns="http://schemas.xmlsoap.org/wsdl/"
 xmlns:xsd="http://www.w3.org/2001/XMLSchema"
 xmlns:soap="http://schemas.xmlsoap.org/wsdl/soap/">
 ...
</definitions>
```

If the WSDL document uses more than one namespace for generated types, you must declare a separate `package-mapping` element for each XML namespace. For example, the WSDL document in Listing 24–8 uses two namespaces, one for the target namespace of WSDL definitions and the other for XML schema types defined in the `types` element.

Listing 24–8

A WSDL Document That Requires Multiple `package-mapping` *Elements*

```
<?xml version='1.0' encoding='UTF-8' ?>
<definitions xmlns="http://schemas.xmlsoap.org/wsdl/"
  xmlns:mh="http://www.Monson-Haefel.com/jwsbook/PurchaseOrder"
  targetNamespace="http://www.Monson-Haefel.com/jwsbook/PurchaseOrder"
  xmlns:soap="http://schemas.xmlsoap.org.wsdl/soap/"
  xmlns:xsd="http://www.w3.org/2000/10/XMLSchema"
  xmlns:po="http://www.Monson-Haefel.com/jwsbook/PO" >
 <types>
  <schema xmlns="http://www.w3.org/2001/XMLSchema"
      targetNamespace="http://www.Monson-Haefel.com/PO">
   <element name="purchaseOrder" type="po:PurchaseOrder"/>
   <complexType name="PurchaseOrder">
    <sequence>
     <element name="accountName" type="xsd:string"/>
     <element name="accountNumber" type="xsd:short"/>
     <element name="shipAddress" type="po:USAddress"/>
     <element name="billAddress" type="po:USAddress"/>
    </sequence>
    <attribute name="orderDate" type="xsd:date"/>
   </complexType>
   <complexType name="USAddress">
    <sequence>
     <element name="name" type="xsd:string"/>
     <element name="street" type="xsd:string"/>
     <element name="city" type="xsd:string"/>
     <element name="state" type="xsd:string"/>
     <element name="zip" type="xsd:string"/>
    </sequence>
   </complexType>
  </schema>
 </types>
 <message name="PurchaseOrderMessage">
  <part name="body" element="po:purchaseOrder"/>
 </message>
 <portType name="PurchaseOrder">
  <operation name="submitPurchaseOrder">
```

```
      <input message="mh:PurchaseOrderMessage"/>
    </operation>
  </portType>
  ...
</definitions>
```

In this case the XML namespace used for the WSDL definitions (`message`, `portType`, `binding`, `service`, and `port`) is different from the XML namespace used to define the XML schema types (`PurchaseOrder` and `USAddress`). Because the JAX-RPC compiler will create interfaces and classes for types from both namespaces, the mapping file must have a `package-mapping` element for each namespace, as shown in Listing 24–9.

Listing 24–9

A JAX-RPC Mapping File with Multiple `package-mapping` *Elements*

```
<java-wsdl-mapping ...>
  <package-mapping>
    <package-type>com.jwsbook.jaxrpc</package-type>
    <namespaceURI>http://www.Monson-Haefel.com/jwsbook/PurchaseOrder
    </namespaceURI>
  </package-mapping>
  <package-mapping>
    <package-type>com.jwsbook.jaxrpc.types</package-type>
    <namespaceURI>http://www.Monson-Haefel.com/jwsbook/PO</namespaceURI>
  </package-mapping>
</java-wsdl-mapping>
```

In this example the two XML namespaces are mapped to two different Java packages, but they don't have to be. You could map both namespaces to the same Java package, which is often more convenient.

24.4.3 The `java-xml-type-mapping` Element

The `java-xml-type-mapping` element is necessary when you are using complex or simple types, whether defined in the `types` element or imported from another XML document—with one exception. This element is not necessary if you're using standard XML schema built-in types with standard mapping to Java, as outlined in Section 15.2: Mapping XML Schema to Java. This element associates XML schema types with Java types.

As an example, let's say you want to map the WSDL document for the PurchaseOrder Web service to a JAX-RPC generated stub. This Web service uses One-Way Document/Literal messaging, and its `message` and `portType` elements are defined as in Listing 24–10.

Listing 24–10

A WSDL Document with `java-xml-type-mapping` *Elements*

```
<?xml version='1.0' encoding='UTF-8' ?>
<definitions xmlns="http://schemas.xmlsoap.org/wsdl/"
    xmlns:po="http://www.Monson-Haefel.com/1ed/PurchaseOrder"
    xmlns:soap="http://schemas.xmlsoap.org.wsdl/soap/"
    xmlns:xsd="http://www.w3.org/2000/10/XMLSchema"
    xmlns:mh="http://www.Monson-Haefel.com/jwsbook/PurchaseOrder"
    targetNamespace="http://www.Monson-Haefel.com/jwsbook/PurchaseOrder">
  <types>
    <schema xmlns="http://www.w3.org/2001/XMLSchema"
      targetNamespace="http://www.Monson-Haefel.com/1ed/PurchaseOrder">
      <element name="purchaseOrder" type="po:PurchaseOrder"/>
      <complexType name="PurchaseOrder">
        <sequence>
          <element name="AcctName" type="xsd:string"/>
          <element name="ShipAddr" type="po:USAddress"/>
          <element name="ISBN" type="xsd:string" maxOccurs="unbounded"/>
        </sequence>
      </complexType>
      <complexType name="USAddress">
        <sequence>
          <element name="Street" type="xsd:string"/>
          <element name="City" type="xsd:string"/>
          <element name="State" type="xsd:string"/>
          <element name="Zip" type="xsd:string"/>
        </sequence>
      </complexType>
    </schema>
  </types>
  <message name="PurchaseOrderMessage">
    <part name="body" element="po:purchaseOrder"/>
  </message>
  <portType name="PurchaseOrder">
    <operation name="submitPurchaseOrder">
      <input message="mh:PurchaseOrderMessage"/>
    </operation>
  </portType>
  …
</definitions>
```

In this case the mapping file will need a `java-xml-type-mapping` element for each complex type, one for `PurchaseOrder` and one for `USAddress`. The snippet in Listing 24–11 illustrates the mapping.

Listing 24–11

XML Schema Types Mapped to Java Types

```
<java-to-xml-mapping>
   <class-type>com.jwsbook.jaxrpc.PurchaseOrder</class-type>
   <root-type-qname>po:PurchaseOrder</root-type-qname>
   <qname-scope>element</qname-scope>
   <variable-mapping>
      <java-variable-name>accountName</java-variable-name>
      <xml-element-name>AcctName</xml-element-name>
   </variable-mapping>
   <variable-mapping>
      <java-variable-name>shipAddress</java-variable-name>
      <xml-element-name>ShipAddr</xml-element-name>
   </variable-mapping>
   <variable-mapping>
      <java-variable-name>isbn</java-variable-name>
      <xml-element-name>ISBN</xml-element-name>
   </variable-mapping>
</java-to-xml-mapping>

<java-to-xml-mapping>
<class-type>com.jwsbook.jaxrpc.USAddress</class-type>
   <root-type-qname>po:USAddress</root-type-qname>
   <qname-scope>complexType</qname-scope>
   <variable-mapping>
      <java-variable-name>street</java-variable-name>
      <xml-element-name>Street</xml-element-name>
   </variable-mapping>
   <variable-mapping>
      <java-variable-name>city</java-variable-name>
      <xml-element-name>City</xml-element-name>
   </variable-mapping>
   <variable-mapping>
      <java-variable-name>state</java-variable-name>
      <xml-element-name>State</xml-element-name>
   </variable-mapping>
   <variable-mapping>
      <java-variable-name>zip</java-variable-name>
```

```
        <xml-element-name>Zip</xml-element-name>
    </variable-mapping>
</java-to-xml-mapping>
```

24.4.4 The `exception-mapping` Element

An `exception-mapping` element maps a WSDL fault message to a Java exception class.

For example, the WSDL document in Listing 24–12 declares two fault messages that can be generated for the BookQuote Web service.

Listing 24–12

A WSDL Document That Declares Fault Messages

```
<definitions name="BookQuote"
    targetNamespace="http://www.Monson-Haefel.com/jwsbook/BookQuote"
    xmlns:mh="http://www.Monson-Haefel.com/jwsbook/BookQuote"
    xmlns="http://schemas.xmlsoap.org/wsdl/"
    xmlns:xsd="http://www.w3.org/2001/XMLSchema"
    xmlns:soap="http://schemas.xmlsoap.org/wsdl/soap/">
  ...
  <message name="InvalidIsbnFault" >
    <part name="message" type="xsd:string"/>
  </message>
  <message name="SecurityFault" >
    <part name="message" type="xsd:string"/>
  </message>
  <portType name="BookQuote">
    <operation name="getBookPrice">
      <input message="mh:BookQuote_getBookPrice"/>
      <output message="mh:BookQuote_getBookPriceResponse"/>
      <fault name="InvalidIsbnFault" message="mh:InvalidIsbnFault" />
      <fault name="InvalidIsbnFault" message="mh:SecurityFault" />
    </operation>
  </portType>
  ...
</definitions>
```

Based on this definition, two `exception-mapping` elements should be declared as in Listing 24–13.

Listing 24–13

Fault Messages Mapped to Java Exception Types

```
<java-xml-mapping ...
   xmlns:mh="http://www.Monson-Haefel.com/jwsbook/BookQuote"... >

   <package-mapping/>
   <exception-mapping>
      <exception-type>com.jwsbook.jaxrpc.InvalidIsbnException</exception-type>
      <wsdl-message>mh:InvalidIsbnFault</wsdl-message>
   </exception-mapping>
   <exception-mapping>
      <exception-type>com.jwsbook.jaxrpc.SecurityException</exception-type>
      <wsdl-message>mh:SecurityFault</wsdl-message>
   </exception-mapping>
   ...
</java-xml-mapping>
```

Notice that the class name of the exception ends with `Exception` rather than `Fault`. This ability to rename the exceptions to be more Java-friendly is a nice advantage of using the `exception-mapping` element, and might be one reason for defining a heavyweight mapping file even if it's not required.

As you know, a WSDL fault message can define only a single `part` element. In the preceding example, the WSDL fault messages contained a single XML schema built-in type (`xsd:string`), which makes for a fairly straightforward mapping. When a fault declares a `part` that refers to an XML schema complex type, however, you can specify in the mapping file an additional element, `constructor-parameter-order`, which dictates the order of parameters in the constructor of the exception class. This element can help the compiler create an exception class that relies on a complex type like the one in the following snippet.

```
<types>
  <xsd:schema
   targetNamespace="http://www.Monson-Haefel.com/jwsbook/BookQuote">
    <xsd:complexType name="InvalidIsbnType">
       <xsd:sequence>
         <xsd:element name="offending-value" type="xsd:string"/>
         <xsd:element name="conformance-rules" type="xsd:string"/>
       </xsd:sequence>
    </xsd:complexType>
  </xsd:schema>
</types>
...
```

```
<message name="getBookPriceFault">
  <part name="fault" type="mh:InvalidIsbnType" />
</message>
```

The `exception-mapping` element can specify which element of `InvalidIsbnType` is to be the first parameter passed to the exception's constructor and which is to be second, as here.

```
<java-xml-mapping …
   xmlns:mh="http://www.Monson-Haefel.com/jwsbook/BookQuote"… >
   <package-mapping/>
   <exception-mapping>
      <exception-type>com.jwsbook.jaxrpc.InvalidIsbnException</exception-type>
      <wsdl-message>mh:InvalidIsbnFault</wsdl-message>
      <constructor-parameter-order>
         <element-name>conformance-rules</element-name>
         <element-name>offending-value</element-name>
      </constructor-parameter-order>
   </exception-mapping>
   …
</java-xml-mapping>
```

The JAX-RPC compiler would create a constructor for the corresponding Java exception class with a constructor as follows.

```
public InvalidIsbnException(String conformanceRules,
                            String offendingValue);
```

24.4.5 The `service-interface-mapping` Element

The `service-interface-mapping` element maps a WSDL `service` definition to a custom JAX-RPC service interface type. It also specifies the names and types of the `get`*`PortName`*`()` methods, which return references to generated endpoint stubs at runtime. To illustrate I'll use a WSDL document that defines two different ports, one that uses RPC/Encoded messaging and another that uses Document/Literal messaging, as in Listing 24–14.

Listing 24–14

A WSDL Document That Supports Two Messaging Modes

```
<?xml version="1.0" encoding="UTF-8"?>
<definitions name="BookQuote"
    targetNamespace="http://www.Monson-Haefel.com/jwsbook/BookQuote"
    xmlns:mh="http://www.Monson-Haefel.com/jwsbook/BookQuote"  …>
```

```
<portType name="BookQuote">
  <operation name="getBookPrice">
    <input message="mh:BookQuote_getBookPrice"/>
    <output message="mh:BookQuote_getBookPriceResponse"/>
  </operation>
</portType>
<binding name="BookQuoteBinding_docLit" type="mh:BookQuote">
  <soap:binding transport="http://schemas.xmlsoap.org/soap/http"
              style="document"/>
   <operation name="getBookPrice">
    <soap:operation soapAction=""/>
    <input>
      <soap:body use="literal" />
    </input>
    <output>
      <soap:body use="literal" />
    </output>
  </operation>
</binding>
<binding name="BookQuoteBinding_rpcEnc" type="mh:BookQuote">
  <soap:binding transport="http://schemas.xmlsoap.org/soap/http"
              style="rpc"/>
  <operation name="getBookPrice">
    <soap:operation soapAction=""/>
    <input>
      <soap:body
        encodingStyle="http://schemas.xmlsoap.org/soap/encoding/"
        use="encoded"
        namespace=
          "http://www.Monson-Haefel.com/jwsbook/BookQuote/BookQuote"/>
    </input>
    <output>
      <soap:body
        encodingStyle="http://schemas.xmlsoap.org/soap/encoding/"
        use="encoded"
        namespace=
          "http://www.Monson-Haefel.com/jwsbook/BookQuote/BookQuote"/>
    </output>
  </operation>
</binding>
<service name="BookQuoteService">
  <port name="BookQuotePort_docLit" binding="mh:BookQuoteBinding_docLit">
    <soap:address
```

```
    location=
      "http://www.Monson-Haefel.com/jwsbook/doclit/BookQuoteService"/>
  </port>
  <port name="BookQuotePort_rpcEnc" binding="mh:BookQuoteBinding_rpcEnc ">
    <soap:address
    location=
      "http://www.Monson-Haefel.com/jwsbook/rpcenc/BookQuoteService"/>
  </port>
 </service>
</definitions>
```

The WSDL document defines a single service definition, BookQuoteService, that declares two separate port elements. The first, BookQuotePort_docLit, defines a Web service that uses the BookQuote portType with a Document/Literal binding. The second, BookQuotePort_rpcEnc, defines a Web service that also uses the BookQuote portType but an RPC/Encoded binding. This would be done to give the Web service's clients a choice of messaging modes.

Using a service-interface-mapping element, we can map the BookQuoteService to a JAX-RPC service interface that contains two get*PortName*() methods, one for each WSDL port definition, as in Listing 24–15.

Listing 24–15

Mapping the Two Messaging Modes to Java

```
<java-wsdl-mapping
  xmlns="http://java.sun.com/xml/ns/j2ee"
  xmlns:mh="http://www.Monson-Haefel.com/jwsbook/BookQuote" ...>
  <package-mapping/>
  <java-xml-type-mapping/>
  <service-interface-mapping>
    <service-interface>com.jwsbook.jaxrpc.BookQuoteService</service-interface>
    <wsdl-service-name>mh:BookQuoteService</wsdl-service-name>
    <port-mapping>
      <port-name>mh:BookQuotePort_docLit</port-name>
      <java-port-name>DocLitPort</java-port-name>
    </port-mapping>
    <port-mapping>
      <port-name>mh:BookQuotePort_rpcEnc</port-name>
      <java-port-name>RpcEncPort</java-port-name>
    </port-mapping>
  </service-interface-mapping>
  ...
</java-wsdl-mapping>
```

The `service-interface` element simply declares the fully qualified class name of the Java interface that will represent the WSDL `service` definition. The package name of the service interface should match the package name declared in the `package-mapping` element.

The `port-mapping` elements assign a name that will be used for each WSDL `port` in the `getPortName()` methods. The `port-name` element provides the fully qualified XML name of the `port` definition, and `java-port-name` provides the `port-name` part of the `getPortName()` method signature. Listing 24–16 shows how this mapping is manifested in a Java service interface definition.

Listing 24–16

The Service Interface That Supports Two Messaging Modes

```
package com.jwsbook.jaxrpc;

public interface BookQuoteService extends javax.xml.rpc.Service {

    public BookQuote getDocListPort();
    public BookQuote getRpcEncPort();

}
```

You can use any name you want for the `java-port-name` element, but it's a good practice to use something descriptive.

24.4.6 The `service-endpoint-interface-mapping` Element

The `service-endpoint-interface-mapping` element maps a JAX-RPC endpoint interface to a specific set of WSDL `portType` and `binding` definitions. This element helps the JAX-RPC compiler generate the proper endpoint stub and endpoint interfaces. It also details how WSDL `operation` and `message part` definitions map to endpoint methods.

As an example, we can take the RPC/Literal WSDL definition for the BookQuote Web service, shown in Listing 24–17, and map it using the `service-endpoint-interface-mapping`.

Listing 24–17

A WSDL Document That Defines a Service Endpoint Interface

```
<definitions name="BookQuote"
    targetNamespace="http://www.Monson-Haefel.com/jwsbook/BookQuote"
    xmlns:mh="http://www.Monson-Haefel.com/jwsbook/BookQuote"
    xmlns="http://schemas.xmlsoap.org/wsdl/"
    xmlns:xsd="http://www.w3.org/2001/XMLSchema"
```

```
    xmlns:soap="http://schemas.xmlsoap.org/wsdl/soap/">
  <portType name="BookQuote">
    <operation name="getBookPrice">
      <input message="mh:BookQuote_getBookPrice"/>
      <output message="mh:BookQuote_getBookPriceResponse"/>
      <fault name="InvalidIsbnFault" message="mh:InvalidIsbnFault" />
    </operation>
  </portType>
  <binding name="BookQuoteBinding" type="mh:BookQuote">
    <soap:binding transport="http://schemas.xmlsoap.org/soap/http"
                  style="rpc"/>
    <operation name="getBookPrice">
      <soap:operation soapAction=""/>
      <input>
        <soap:body
        use="literal"
        namespace="http://www.Monson-Haefel.com/jwsbook/BookQuote/BookQuote"/>
      </input>
      <output>
        <soap:body
        use="literal"
        namespace="http://www.Monson-Haefel.com/jwsbook/BookQuote"/>
      </output>
      <fault name="mh:InvalidIsbnFault">
        <soap:fault
        use="literal"
      </fault>
    </operation>
  </binding>
  ...
</definitions>
```

The `service-endpoint-interface-mapping` element for this WSDL `portType` and `binding` pair would look like Listing 24–18.

Listing 24–18

Mapping the Service Endpoint Interface to Java

```
<?xml version='1.0' encoding='UTF-8' ?>
<java-wsdl-mapping
  xmlns="http://java.sun.com/xml/ns/j2ee"
  xmlns:mh="http://www.Monson-Haefel.com/jwsbook/BookQuote"...>
```

```
  <package-mapping/>
  <java-xml-type-mapping/>
  <exception-mapping/>
  <service-interface-mapping/>
  <service-endpoint-interface-mapping>
    <service-endpoint-interface>com.jwsbook.jaxrpc.BookQuote
    </service-endpoint-interface>
    <wsdl-port-type>mh:BookQuote</wsdl-port-type>
    <wsdl-binding>mh:BookQuoteBinding</wsdl-binding>
    <service-endpoint-method-mapping>
      <!-- method mapping goes here -->
    </service-endpoint-method-mapping>
  </service-endpoint-interface-mapping>
</java-wsdl-mapping>
```

The `service-endpoint-interface` element declares the fully qualified Java class name of the endpoint interface that the compiler should generate.

The `wsdl-port-type` and `wsdl-binding` elements define the fully qualified XML names of the WSDL `portType` definition and the `binding` definition associated with the endpoint interface, respectively.

The `service-endpoint-method-mapping` element is fairly complex. It's responsible for mapping a WSDL `operation` and its message `part` definitions to a specific method signature in the endpoint interface. For example, suppose the WSDL `message` and `portType` definitions for the BookQuote Web service looked like these:

```
<message name="BookQuote_getBookPrice">
  <part name="isbn" type="xsd:string"/>
</message>
<message name="BookQuote_getBookPriceResponse">
  <part name="result" type="xsd:float"/>
</message>
<message name="InvalidIsbnFault" >
  <part name="message" type="xsd:string"/>
</message>
<portType name="BookQuote">
  <operation name="getBookPrice">
    <input message="mh:BookQuote_getBookPrice"/>
    <output message="mh:BookQuote_getBookPriceResponse"/>
    <fault name="InvalidIsbnFault" message="mh:InvalidIsbnFault" />
  </operation>
</portType>
```

Then the service-endpoint-method-mapping element in the mapping file would look like this:

```
<service-endpoint-interface-mapping>
  <service-endpoint-interface>com.jwsbook.jaxrpc.BookQuote
  </service-endpoint-interface>
  <wsdl-port-type>mh:BookQuote</wsdl-port-type>
  <wsdl-binding>mh:BookQuoteBinding</wsdl-binding>
  <service-endpoint-method-mapping>
    <java-method-name>getBookPrice</java-method-name>
    <wsdl-operation>mh:getBookPrice</wsdl-operation>
    <method-param-parts-mapping>
      <param-position>0</param-position>
      <param-type>java.lang.String</param-type>
      <wsdl-message-mapping>
        <wsdl-message>mh:BookQuote_getBookPriceRequest</wsdl-message>
        <wsdl-message-part-name>isbn</wsdl-message-part-name>
        <parameter-mode>IN</parameter-mode>
      </wsdl-message-mapping>
    </method-param-parts-mapping>
    <wsdl-return-value-mapping>
      <method-return-value>float</method-return-value>
      <wsdl-message>mh:BookQuote_getBookPriceResponse</wsdl-message>
      <wsdl-message-part-name>result</wsdl-message-part-name>
    </wsdl-return-value-mapping>
  </service-endpoint-method-mapping>
</service-endpoint-interface-mapping>
```

The service-endpoint-method-mapping element has four important child elements: java-method-name, wsdl-operation, method-param-parts-mapping, and wsdl-return-value-mapping.

The java-method-name element simply declares the Java method name for a specific WSDL operation, and the wsdl-operation element provides the fully qualified XML name of the WSDL operation being mapped.

A method-param-parts-mapping element is declared for every part definition defined by the input message of the WSDL operation. The getBookPrice WSDL operation's input message has only one part, so we need only one method-param-parts-mapping element, as shown in the following snippet.

```
<method-param-parts-mapping>
  <param-position>0</param-position>
  <param-type>java.lang.String</param-type>
  <wsdl-message-mapping>
```

```
    <wsdl-message>mh:BookQuote_getBookPriceRequest</wsdl-message>
    <wsdl-message-part-name>isbn</wsdl-message-part-name>
    <parameter-mode>IN</parameter-mode>
  </wsdl-message-mapping>
</method-param-parts-mapping>
```

The `param-position` element specifies the position that the Java parameter will have in the method signature (positions numbered from zero). The `param-type` declares the Java type of the parameter; in this case we're mapping the simple XML schema built-in type `xsd:string` to the Java type `java.lang.String`. If the `part` were a complex type, then you would map a Java class name to that complex type in the `java-xml-type-mapping` element, at the beginning of the mapping file.

The `wsdl-message-mapping` element pinpoints the WSDL `message` and `part` definition that's being mapped, declaring the fully qualified XML name of the `message` definition, while the `wsdl-message-part-name` declares the name of the `part`.

The `parameter-mode` element indicates whether the parameter is an IN, INOUT, or OUT parameter. Any INOUT and OUT parameters will be mapped to JAX-RPC holder types that wrap around the Java types defined by the `param-type` elements, in accordance with the rules discussed in Section 15.3: Holders.

The `wsdl-return-value-mapping` element is similar to the `method-param-parts-mapping` element. There are two differences: It can be declared only once for each operation because a Java method can have only one return value, and its parameter mode is assumed to be OUT. Compare and contrast `wsdl-return-value-mapping` with `method-param-parts-mapping` in the following snippet.

```
<service-endpoint-method-mapping>
  <java-method-name>getBookPrice</java-method-name>
  <wsdl-operation>mh:getBookPrice</wsdl-operation>
  <method-param-parts-mapping>
    <param-position>0</param-position>
    <param-type>java.lang.String</param-type>
    <wsdl-message-mapping>
      <wsdl-message>mh:BookQuote_getBookPriceRequest</wsdl-message>
      <wsdl-message-part-name>isbn</wsdl-message-part-name>
      <parameter-mode>IN</parameter-mode>
    </wsdl-message-mapping>
  </method-param-parts-mapping>
  <wsdl-return-value-mapping>
    <method-return-value>float</method-return-value>
    <wsdl-message>mh:BookQuote_getBookPriceResponse</wsdl-message>
    <wsdl-message-part-name>result</wsdl-message-part-name>
  </wsdl-return-value-mapping>
</service-endpoint-method-mapping>
```

The service-endpoint-method-mapping element can be especially useful when WSDL operation definitions don't map naturally to Java methods. For example, a portType can quite legally define two operations that have the same name and the same input messages but different output messages, but the Java programming language doesn't allow the equivalent method overloading. Two methods can't have the same name and different return types unless they also have different parameters. In the following snippet, the WSDL definition defines two getBookPrice operations, one whose output is an xsd:float and another whose output is an xsd:string.

```
<message name="IsbnRequest">
  <part name="isbn" type="xsd:string"/>
</message>
<message name="FloatResponse">
  <part name="result" type="xsd:float"/>
</message>
<message name="StringResponse" >
  <part name="result" type="xsd:string"/>
</message>
<portType name="BookQuote">
  <operation name="getBookPrice">
    <input message="mh:IsbnRequest"/>
    <output message="mh:FloatResponse"/>
  </operation>
  <operation name="getBookPrice">
    <input message="mh:IsbnRequest"/>
    <output message="mh:StringResponse"/>
  </operation>
</portType>
```

If the JAX-RPC compiler mapped this directly to a Java endpoint, it would create an illegal interface definition, in which methods are overloaded by return type.

```
public interface BookQuote extends java.rmi.Remote {

    public float getBookPrice(String isbn):
    public String getBookPrice(String isbn); // Illegal overloading
}
```

To avoid this conflict, you can provide different names for the two Java methods in the service-endpoint-method-mapping element, as in the following snippet.

```
<service-endpoint-method-mapping>
  <java-method-name>getBookPriceFloat</java-method-name>
  <wsdl-operation>mh:getBookPrice</wsdl-operation>
  <method-param-parts-mapping>
    <param-position>0</param-position>
    <param-type>java.lang.String</param-type>
    <wsdl-message-mapping>
      <wsdl-message>mh:IsbnRequest</wsdl-message>
      <wsdl-message-part-name>isbn</wsdl-message-part-name>
      <parameter-mode>IN</parameter-mode>
    </wsdl-message-mapping>
  </method-param-parts-mapping>
  <wsdl-return-value-mapping>
    <method-return-value>float</method-return-value>
    <wsdl-message>mh:FloatResponse</wsdl-message>
    <wsdl-message-part-name>result</wsdl-message-part-name>
  </wsdl-return-value-mapping>
</service-endpoint-method-mapping>
<service-endpoint-method-mapping>
  <java-method-name>getBookPriceString</java-method-name>
  <wsdl-operation>mh:getBookPrice</wsdl-operation>
  <method-param-parts-mapping>
    <param-position>0</param-position>
    <param-type>java.lang.String</param-type>
    <wsdl-message-mapping>
      <wsdl-message>mh:IsbnRequest</wsdl-message>
      <wsdl-message-part-name>isbn</wsdl-message-part-name>
      <parameter-mode>IN</parameter-mode>
    </wsdl-message-mapping>
  </method-param-parts-mapping>
  <wsdl-return-value-mapping>
    <method-return-value>java.lang.String</method-return-value>
    <wsdl-message>mh:StringResponse</wsdl-message>
    <wsdl-message-part-name>result</wsdl-message-part-name>
  </wsdl-return-value-mapping>
</service-endpoint-method-mapping>
```

Given the above mapping, the compiler will generate methods named `getBookPriceFloat()` and `getBookPriceString()`, and dodge the overloading problem.

24.5 Wrapping Up

Although the JAX-RPC mapping file can be very useful in some situations, for the most part it's just a lot of work with little payoff. The all-or-nothingness of the lightweight versus heavyweight mapping files is not good. As I indicated at the end of Chapter 23, developers should be able to make a lot of assumptions, and to focus on configuring only the exceptions to those assumptions. Requiring the developer to write a heavyweight mapping file if only one of the rules is broken is unnecessary. You should be able to declare only those attributes that don't comply with the rules for lightweight mapping.

If it isn't obvious by now, I'm not a big fan of the XML deployment descriptors used in J2EE, and those used in Web services in particular. They are far too complicated and fragile. It's my understanding that J2EE 1.5 will let you make more assumptions about values, and allow you to declare exceptions in the code as metadata rather than in XML files, which would be a big improvement over the current requirements.

Appendices

The appendices cover technologies that don't conform to the WS-I Basic Profile 1.0, and a few subjects that are somewhat tangential to the general topic of J2EE Web Services. This part of the book is by no means required reading, but it does provide you with some resources for further exploration.

In the Appendices

Appendix A
XML DTDs

A DTD (Document Type Definition) provides a detailed description of a particular XML markup language and can be used by XML parsers to verify that XML instances conform to that markup language. For example, the Address Markup Language we created in Chapter 2 can have its own DTD. When a validating parser reads an Address Markup instance, it can use the Address Markup DTD to verify that the instance contains the correct elements and attributes in the right organization.

Web services use the W3C XML Schema Language, not DTDs, so understanding DTDs is not critical to reading this book. You can read this appendix to help round out your understanding of XML, but it's not necessary.

A DTD may be included directly in an XML document instance, but it is usually a separate document. An XML document instance points to its DTD using a document type declaration, which is a special type of tag that says, "This is the DTD that's used to validate my contents, and here is where it's located." A document type declaration for an instance of the Address Markup Language might look as shown in Listing A–1 (it's conventional to name a DTD file with the suffix `.dtd`).

Listing A–1

Using a Document Type Declaration

```
<?xml version="1.0" encoding="UTF-8" standalone="yes" ?>
<!DOCTYPE addresses SYSTEM "address.dtd">
<addresses>
   <address category="friend">
```

```
        <name>Bill Frankenfiller</name>
        <street>3243 West 1st Ave.</street>
        <city>Madison</city>
        <state>WI</state>
        <zip>53591</zip>
    </address>
    <address category="business">
        <name>Amazon.com</name>
        <street>1516 2nd Ave</street>
        <city>Seattle</city>
        <state>WA</state>
        <zip>90952</zip>
    </address>
</addresses>
```

When an XML document declares a document type declaration, a **validating parser** (a parser that supports validation using DTDs) reads the DTD and uses it to check the XML document. If the XML document doesn't conform to the DTD, it's said to be invalid and the parser should generate an error message.

The Document Type Definition has its own grammar, which is different from XML. A DTD for Address Book Markup might look like Listing A–2.

Listing A–2

The Address DTD

```
<?xml version="1.0" encoding="UTF-8"?>
<!ELEMENT addresses (address*) >
<!ELEMENT address (street+, city?, state?, zip)>
<!ELEMENT street (#PCDATA) >
<!ELEMENT city (#PCDATA) >
<!ELEMENT state (#PCDATA) >
<!ELEMENT zip (#PCDATA) >
<!ATTLIST address category CDATA #REQUIRED >
```

The Address DTD tells us exactly which elements may be used in an Address Book instance document. It also dictates the order of elements, how elements are nested, and the attributes each element may have. A DTD describes the structure of an XML document.

A DTD declares the contents of an element to be text, other elements, or both. An element that contains only text is declared as containing `PCDATA`, which basically means, "any Unicode character that is not a special XML symbol." Special XML symbols (<, &, and so on) must be escaped. The Address DTD in Listing A–2 declares four elements that contain only text (and not other elements):

```
<!ELEMENT street (#PCDATA) >
<!ELEMENT city (#PCDATA) >
<!ELEMENT state (#PCDATA) >
<!ELEMENT zip (#PCDATA) >
```

Elements can be nested in other elements. For example, the `street`, `city`, `state`, and `zip` elements appear in the `address` element. Nested elements are called **child elements, children,** or **descendants** of the address element. The element that contains the children is called the **parent.**

```
<!ELEMENT address (street+, city?, state?, zip)>
```

The children listed inside the parentheses of the parent should occur in XML documents that claim to conform to this DTD in exactly the order shown. For example, listing the `street` after the `city` in an instance document would be invalid.

DTDs can also specify the cardinality of an element's children, using three special symbols: `*`, `+`, and `?`.

The asterisk indicates that a child may occur zero or more times. This is used in the `addresses` element declaration. The asterisk signifies that an `addresses` root element may contain zero or more `address` elements, just one `address`, or many.

```
<!ELEMENT addresses (address*) >
```

The plus sign indicates that a child occurs one or more times. The Address Book DTD uses this symbol for the `street` within the `address` element declaration. It indicates that the `address` element must have at least one `street`, and may have more.

```
<!ELEMENT address (street+, city?, state?, zip)>
```

The question mark indicates that the child element is optional, that it may occur once or not at all. The question mark is used with the `city` and `state`, because these elements are not necessary if the correct zip code is used in the `zip` element (a zip code can be used to determine the city and state of a residence).

```
<!ELEMENT address (street+, city?, state?, zip)>
```

Finally, the absence of any cardinality symbol signifies that the element must occur exactly once. This is the case with the `zip` element. which must be present, and only once.

```
<!ELEMENT address (street+, city?, state?, zip)>
```

The children of element declarations may be XOR (exclusive OR), which means that either element may be present but not both. The XOR symbol in DTDs is the vertical bar (|). Children may also be grouped using parentheses, which allows them to be treated as a single child. Listing A–3 shows a new version of our Address DTD that uses grouping and XOR symbols.

Listing A–3

An Enhanced Address DTD

```
<?xml version="1.0" encoding="UTF-8"?>
<!ELEMENT addresses (address*) >
<!ELEMENT address (street+, ((city, state, zip) | zip) )>
<!ELEMENT street (#PCDATA) >
<!ELEMENT city (#PCDATA) >
<!ELEMENT state (#PCDATA) >
<!ELEMENT zip (#PCDATA) >
<!ATTLIST address category CDATA #REQUIRED >
```

The `address` element declaration specifies that either `city`, `state`, and `zip` elements must be present *or* just the `zip` element. Notice that no cardinality symbol is applied to the entire grouping, meaning that whichever combination is used, either `city`, `state`, and `zip`, or just `zip`, it may occur only once.

The following snippet shows an Address Book instance with two valid addresses that conform to the Address DTD in Listing A–3.

```
<?xml version="1.0" encoding="UTF-8" standalone="yes" ?>
<!DOCTYPE addresses SYSTEM "address.dtd">
<addresses>
    <address category="friend">
        <name>Bill Frankenfiller</name>
        <street>3243 West 1st Ave.</street>
        <zip>53591</zip>
    </address>
    <address category="business">
        <name>Amazon.com</name>
        <street>1516 2nd Ave</street>
        <city>Seattle</city>
        <state>WA</state>
        <zip>90952</zip>
    </address>
</addresses>
```

Notice that the first address uses only a `zip` and the second uses a `city`, `state`, and `zip`. Both are valid. An address containing only the `city` and `state`, or a `zip` with a `city` but no `state` would be invalid.

A DTD can also declare attributes. An attribute declares which element the attribute is associated with as well as the name of the attribute, whether it is required or optional, or whether it has a default value. The category attribute used by the address element is declared as follows.

```
<!ATTLIST address category CDATA #REQUIRED >
```

Here, the category attribute is associated with the address element. The associated element is the first argument after ATTLIST, and the name of the attribute is the second. The type of data, CDATA, is third; then the argument is declared as #REQUIRED, which means it must be present. If it's #IMPLIED, it can be omitted. If it's #FIXED, it's always equal to a value specified. If it's none of these three, it's optional and may have a default value. The following shows the category attribute declaration with a default of "business".

```
<!ATTLIST address category CDATA "business" >
```

An attribute with a CDATA type may contain Unicode text, even special symbols, but must be delimited by single or double quotes. There are other types of attributes, including "tokenized" and "enumerated" types, but the CDATA type is the most common and is the only one covered here.

DTDs have a number of limitations, the most important of which is that they do not support the use of XML namespaces and they do not tell us much about the contents of text data. For example, there is no way in a DTD to specify that the zip is composed of only digits and not letters. Similarly, there is no way to restrict the value of the state element to an enumeration of two-letter state codes. In a nutshell, DTDs allow us to validate the organization of an XML document but not the data itself, which is why the W3C XML Schema Language, which supports both XML namespaces and strong typing, is preferred to DTDs.

Appendix B

XML Schema Regular Expressions

A regular expression is a kind of mini programming language used for text pattern matching. Regular expressions have been around for a long time and are supported by many different tools and programming languages, including Java, Perl, Python, sed, awk, procmail, grep, vi, and emacs, to name a few.[1] Although the exact syntax used for regular expressions varies from one technology to the next, the fundamentals are the same.[2]

In XML schemas, regular expressions are used with the **pattern facet** to restrict the values allowed for a derived simple type. Regular expressions tell us which characters can be used for a simple type value.

For example, we can decide that a phone number should contain only digits. To enforce this constraint, we can create a new simple type called `Phone`, which can be used by any complex type (for example, `Address`). The following type definition illustrates.

```
<simpleType name="Phone">
  <restriction base="string">
    <pattern value="[0-9]*"/>
  </restriction>
</simpleType>
```

The regular expression `[0-9]*` has two parts: a set of allowed characters and a **quantifier.** The set of allowed characters is shown as a range inside the square brackets, `[0-9]`, and tells us that only the digit characters 0 through 9 are allowed. The

[1] As of JDK 1.4, Java supports regular expressions via the new Regex core package (`java.util.regex`).

[2] *Mastering Regular Expressions* by Jeffrey Friedl (O'Reilly & Associates) provides a detailed and comprehensive coverage of regular expressions.

Table B–1 Allowed Character Sets

Regular Expression	Description	Valid Examples
`[0-9]*`	Zero or more of any digit	`''  '5'  '30283023820293'`
`[6-8]*`	Zero or more of any combination of 6, 7, and 8	`''  '6'  '8'  '876666787768'`
`[a-z]*`	Zero or more of any letter between lowercase a and z	`''  'e'  'aibksopekc'`
`[W-Z]*`	Zero or more of any letter between uppercase W and Z	`''  'X'  'WZZZYXWWXX'`
`[abc]*`	Zero or more combinations of a, b, and c	`''  'a'  'ca'  'ccabaabbcbaabc'`
`[x-zB]*`	Zero or more combinations of characters x, y, z, and B	`''  'y'  'B'  'xByzzzBBxxBz'`
`[a-zA-Z0-9]*`	Zero or more combinations of any letter a–z, A–Z, and any digit	`''  'X'  '8h'  '9t747FGksk03'`
`R*`	Zero or more R characters	`''  'R'  'RRRRRRRRR'`
`f*`	Zero or more f characters	`''  'f'  'ffffffffff'`

second part of the regular expression, the quantifier, uses the asterisk (also known as a Kleene star) to indicate that any of the allowed characters may occur zero or more times. The quantifier applies to only the set of characters or character that immediately precedes it.

B.1 Character Sets

An allowed character set can be expressed as a range using the square brackets, as a single character, such as x or b, or using a special **meta-character.** Table B–1 shows various character sets used with the asterisk quantifier.

A circumflex ^ can be used to negate any set of characters within a set of square brackets. For example, `[^6-9]` means "any character other than the digits 6 through 9," and `[^x]` means "any character other than x."

B.2 Quantifiers

The asterisk indicates that the preceding character or set of characters occurs zero or more times. Another quantifier is the plus sign, which signifies that the preceding character set occurs at least once and maybe more. The question mark is used to indicate that a character set is optional; it may occur zero times or once. The absence of any quantifier indicates that the character or set of characters must occur exactly once.

Table B–2 Using Quantifiers

Regular Expression	Description	Valid Examples
`b`	`b` must occur exactly once	`'b'`
`b*`	`b` may occur zero or more times	`''` `'b'` `'bbbbbbb'`
`b+`	`b` must occur one or more times	`'b'` `'bbb'` `'bbbbb'`
`b{2}`	`b` must occur exactly 2 times	`'bb'`
`b{3,5}`	`b` must occur 3, 4, or 5 times	`'bbb'` `'bbbb'` `'bbbbb'`
`b{2,}`	`b` must occur 2 or more times	`'bb'` `'bbbbbb'` `'bbbbbbbbb'`
`b?`	`b` may occur zero times or one time	`''` `'b'`

You can use curly braces to express the minimum and maximum number of times a character can occur, in an expression of the form `{minimum,maximum}`. For example, `{1,2}` means that the preceding character set may occur once or twice; `{2}` means the character set must occur exactly two times; `{2,}` means that the preceding character must occur two or more times. You can use parentheses `()` to indicate that part of a larger expression is optional—for example, the last four digits of a nine-digit zip code. The use of quantifiers is shown in Table B–2.

B.3 Other Meta-characters

The quantifiers are part of a larger set of **meta-characters,** symbols that have special meaning in regular expressions. In addition to pairs of brackets and braces, and the quantifiers, regular expressions use the period, backslash, and vertical bar meta-characters as summarized in Table B–3. Frequently, meta-characters serve as shorthand for commonly used character sets; for example, `\d` ("any digit") is equivalent to `[0-9]`.

Table B–3 Other Meta-characters

Regular Expression	Description	Valid Examples
`.`	Any character	`'b'` `'8'` `'B'`
`\d`	Any digit	`'4'` `'6'` `'0'`
`\D`	Any non-digit character	`'t'` `'Y'` `'b'`
`\w`	A single "word character": any character that is not a punctuation mark, a separator, white space, or other	`'a'` `'bed'` `'Monson-Haefel'`
`\s`	Any white-space character: space, tab, newline, and so on	`'\s'` `'\t'` `'\n'`
`a|b`	Either `a` or `b`	`'a'` `'b'`

You can use quantifiers with the period, backslash, and vertical bar just as you use them with character sets. For example, `\d{4}` means "any four digits" and `\D+` means "one or more non-digits."

Any time you want to use a quantifier or other meta-character as a regular character, you just need to precede it with a backslash as an escape. For example, if a period is a valid character and is not intended to stand for "any character," you can include it in a character set by using the `\.` escape sequence. Any character that occurs inside square brackets is automatically assumed to be an ordinary character and doesn't need to be escaped. For example, the regular expression `[.+]` indicates that the period and plus sign are valid characters.

> ***Regular expressions in XML schema are similar to regular expressions used in Perl, but there are some important differences, one of which is the absence of** line anchors. **In XML schema, the expressions are matched against entire lexical representations (the value of the element or attribute token) rather than a line or paragraph, so XML schema's regular expressions do not use the meta-characters `^` and `$` to anchor the pattern to the beginning or end of a string.***

B.4 Real-World Examples

Following are some real-world regular expressions used to define commonly used simple types in XML schemas.

B.4.1 ISBN (International Standard Book Number)

Rules:

- The first nine characters must be digits.
- The last character may be a digit or the letter `X` (case is not important).

Regular Expression: `[0-9]{9}[0-9Xx]`

Valid Examples: `'0596002262'`, `'157231687X'`

An Example in Context:

```
<simpleType name="ISBN">
   <restriction base="string">
      <pattern value="[0-9]{9}[0-9Xx]" />
   </restriction>
</simpleType>
```

B.4.2 United States Zip Code

Rules:

- The code must consist of five digits, optionally followed by a hyphen and four more digits.

Regular Expression: `[0-9]{5}(-[0-9]{4})?`

Valid Examples: `'55419'`, `'90101-3982'`

An Example in Context:

```
<simpleType name="USZipCode">
   <restriction base="string">
      <pattern value="[0-9]{5}(-[0-9]{4})?" />
   </restriction>
</simpleType>
```

B.4.3 United States Phone Number

Rules:

- A phone number must be seven or ten digits.
- A local phone number must have seven digits. The last four digits are separated from the first three by a hyphen.
- A national long distance number must have ten digits. An area code of three digits is separated from a prefix of three digits, separated from a suffix of four digits. A hyphen is used for both separations.

Regular Expression: `([0-9]{3}-)?[0-9]{3}-[0-9]{4}`

Valid Examples: `'888-255-2525'`, `'233-2332'`

An Example in Context:

```
<simpleType name="USPhone">
   <restriction base="string">
      <pattern value="([0-9]{3}-)?[0-9]{3}-[0-9]{4}" />
   </restriction>
</simpleType>
```

B.4.4 United Kingdom Postal Code

Rules:

- The total length must be six, seven, or eight characters, and a gap (space character) *must* be included.
- The "inward code," the part to the right of the gap, must always be three characters.
- The first character of the inward code must be a digit.
- The second and third characters of the inward code must be alphabetic.
- The "outward code," the part to the left of the gap, may be two, three, or four characters.
- The first character of the outward code must be alphabetic.

Regular Expression: `[A=Z][A=Z0-9]{1,3}\s\d[A=Z]{2})?`

Valid Examples: `'DT4 0QR'`, `'W1 9BY'`, `'EC2A 4DL'`

An Example in Context:

```
<simpleType name="UKPostalCode">
   <restriction base="string">
      <pattern value="[A-Z][A-Z0-9]{1,3}\s\d[A-Z]{2}" />
   </restriction>
</simpleType>
```

Appendix C

Base64 Encoding

Base64 encoding was originally described in 1993 in the Internet Engineering Task Force's RPC 1421, a specification for e-mail encryption and authentication. Since that time, Base64 has been employed in a number of protocols and technologies, including MIME and XML. Base64 is a simple encoding algorithm, used to convert binary data into blocks of ASCII characters. It is useful in technologies that are text-based, such as SMTP (e-mail) and XML.

The "64" in Base64's name comes from its use of 64 ASCII characters to represent all possible byte values.[1] Base64 uses a special conversion table to assign one of 64 ASCII characters to every six bits of a byte stream. In other words, a binary stream is sliced up into six-bit segments and each segment is mapped to an ASCII character. The ASCII character with a value of 64 (the equals sign) is used for padding at the end of the stream. Table C–1 shows the mapping between the decimal value of a six-bit segment and its corresponding ASCII character.

The algorithm to convert a stream of binary data into a stream of Base64 ASCII characters is simple and elegant. You simply take a block of 24 bits, divide it into four segments of six bits each, and convert the four segments into their corresponding ASCII characters from Table C–1. Figure C–1 illustrates how three bytes of data (24 bits) are converted into four ASCII characters.

By repeating this process for each block of 24 bits, you can encode an entire stream of binary data into ASCII text.

[1] Decimal is sometimes called base-10, hexadecimal is base-16, and binary (zeros and ones) is base-2. The base size is determined by the number of different characters used to represent a digit. Decimal uses 10 characters (0–9), so it's base-10. Binary uses only two characters, 0 and 1, so it's base-2.

Table C–1 The Base64 Conversion Table

Value	Encoding	Value	Encoding	Value	Encoding	Value	Encoding	Value	Encoding
0	A	13	N	26	a	39	n	52	0
1	B	14	O	27	b	40	o	53	1
2	C	15	P	28	c	41	p	54	2
3	D	16	Q	29	d	42	q	55	3
4	E	17	R	30	e	43	r	56	4
5	F	18	S	31	f	44	s	57	5
6	G	19	T	32	g	45	t	58	6
7	H	20	U	33	h	46	u	59	7
8	I	21	V	34	i	47	v	60	8
9	J	22	W	35	j	48	w	61	9
10	K	23	X	36	k	49	x	62	+
11	L	24	Y	37	l	50	y	63	/
12	M	25	Z	38	m	51	z	64	=

If the total number of bits in the stream is not divisible by 24, you simply pad the remainder with zero bits to a value divisible by six, then append padding characters until you have four characters. For example, if a byte stream has 500 bytes, you divide it into 166 blocks of 24 bits each (500 × 8 = 4,000 bits. 4,000/24 = 166 blocks), and a remainder of two bytes (166 × 8 = 498 bytes. 500 – 498 = 2 bytes, or 16 bits). You add two zero bits to pad the 16 bits to 18, then divide these into three six-bit

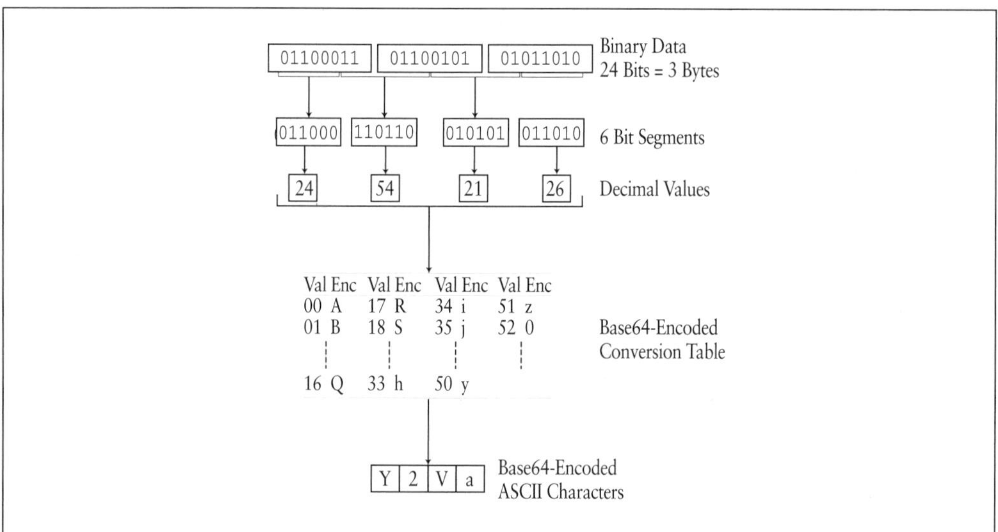

Figure C–1 Converting Binary to Base64

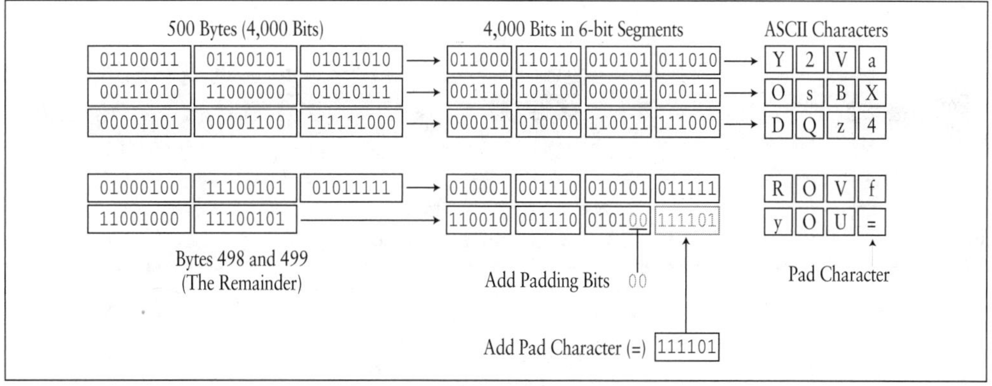

Figure C–2 Adding Padding to a Base64-Encoded Stream

segments. To get the fourth segment, simply append an equal sign for padding. Figure C–2 depicts this example.

To decode a Base64 stream, you simply reverse the process. First, remove the padding character(s) and bits. Next, convert the ASCII characters to their decimal equivalents using Table C–1. Then, convert the decimal values to a stream of six-bit segments. This stream will be equal, bit-for-bit, to the original byte stream.

> ***You can determine the number of padding bits from the number of padding characters. If there are two equal signs for padding, the original stream had a remainder of one byte (eight bits) and required four padding bits (all zeros) and two padding characters to equal 24 bits (8 + 4 + 6 + 6). If there is only one padding character, the original stream had a remainder of two bytes (16 bits) and required two padding bits and one padding character to equal 24 bits (8 + 8 + 2 + 6). If there are no padding characters, the original stream had no remainder; the original byte stream had a bit count exactly divisible by 24.***

You can use Base64 in an XML document to encode a binary stream into ASCII characters. XML schema provides a `base64` simple type, which can be used in a `type` definition just like any other simple type. MIME uses Base64 to encode binary data like GIF images and PDF files into text for e-mail. MIME is also used in SOAP Messages with Attachments to convert binary data to text so that it can be carried in SOAP messages.

Base64 is a very simple and powerful algorithm, but it has one big drawback: It bloats the size of the original binary stream by 33 percent. Every three bytes of binary data (24 bits) is converted into four ASCII characters, each of which uses eight bits in transmission; thus four bytes of character data go over the network for every three bytes of data in the original stream. There is an additional small increase in size if padding is added. Figure C–3 illustrates this bloating.

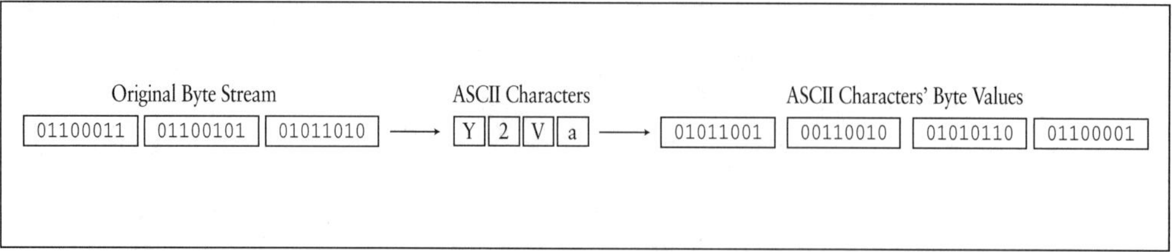

Figure C–3 Byte-Stream Bloat Caused by Base64 Encoding

Appendix D
SOAP RPC/Encoded

Any encoding style can be used with SOAP 1.1, but the SOAP 1.1 Note offers a "standard" encoding style, called **SOAP Encoding,** which is what most SOAP toolkits support. SOAP Encoding generally is used with the RPC messaging style, in which case it's called RPC/Encoded messaging. RPC/Encoded messaging is not supported by the WS-I Basic Profile 1.0 (BP), because it is a major source of interoperability problems. Instead, the BP supports the RPC/Literal and Document/Literal messaging modes. It's likely that you will encounter legacy Web service endpoints that use RPC/Encoded messaging mode. In such cases, this appendix will serve as a useful reference for you.

RPC/Encoded messaging defines rules for serializing programming-language structures into XML. In other words, it explains how SOAP toolkits should map arguments in a programming language into a SOAP message. SOAP is language-neutral. RPC/Encoded messaging was designed to be flexible enough to accommodate most modern programming languages by defining types that are portable, so that data can be exchanged between different platforms. For example, SOAP Encoding makes it possible for you to invoke a Web service implemented in Java from an application written in Perl, by defining rules that allow data to be mapped from Perl to XML and from XML to Java.

This appendix describes the structure of SOAP messages based on RPC/Encoded messaging, the messaging mode that many stub-based SOAP toolkits still support. Understanding the mechanics of RPC/Encoded messaging is not critical to using stub-based toolkits, because most toolkits hide the details of encoding behind the stub; but in general, it's best to have an idea of how RPC/Encoded messaging works if you need to interoperate with Web services based on it. This appendix ends with a discussion of the differences between RPC/Encoded messaging and XML schema, and why they differ.

D.1 The `soap:encodingStyle` Attribute

Before we can create a SOAP message using RPC messaging style, we have to know what encoding style is being used. The encoding style of a SOAP message is indicated using the `soap:encodingStyle` attribute, which is part of the SOAP namespace. It can be any value, as long as the sender and receiver both understand it. When standard SOAP Encoding is used (as is often the case with RPC-style messaging), the attribute value will be `"http://schemas.xmlsoap.org/soap/encoding/"`, as in Listing D–1.

Listing D–1

An RPC/Encoded SOAP Request Message

```
<soap:Envelope
 xmlns:soap="http://schemas.xmlsoap.org/soap/envelope/"
 xmlns:xsi="http://www.w3.org/2001/XMLSchema-instance"
 xmlns:mh="http://www.Monson-Haefel.com/jwsbook/BookPrice"
 soap:encodingStyle="http://schemas.xmlsoap.org/soap/encoding/" >
   <Body>
      <mh:getBookPrice>
        <isbn xsi:type="string">0321146182</isbn>
      </mh:getBookPrice>
   </Body>
</soap:Envelope>
```

This attribute can be declared anywhere, but it's commonly declared in the `Envelope` or an immediate child of the `Body` element. This appendix does both.

D.2 The Operation Structs

RPC-style messaging, regardless of the encoding style, requires that the `Body` of the SOAP message have only one immediate child element. That child element identifies the Web service operation that is being invoked, and is called the **operation struct.** For example, the SOAP message for the `getBookQuote` operation might look like Listing D–2.

Listing D–2

An RPC/Encoded Operation Struct

```
<soap:Envelope
 xmlns:soap="http://schemas.xmlsoap.org/soap/envelope/"
 xmlns:xsi='http://www.w3.org/2001/XMLSchema-instance'
 xmlns:mh="http://www.Monson-Haefel.com/jwsbook/BookPrice"
 soap:encodingStyle="http://schemas.xmlsoap.org/soap/encoding/">
   <Body>
      <mh:getBookPrice>
          <isbn xsi:type="string">0321146182</isbn>
      </mh:getBookPrice>
   </Body>
</soap:Envelope>
```

Identifying the operation immediately under the `Body` element makes it pretty easy for the Web service to map the SOAP message to the correct Web service component when it receives a message. The child element is called the *operation struct* because, like a struct in C or C++, it defines a set of named arguments, which are represented as elements. Each element in the operation struct maps to a parameter of the Web service operation (method call).

Obviously, procedure and method calls will often have multiple parameters that can be represented in RPC/Encoded messaging using multiple elements in the operation struct. Each element in an operation struct is called an *accessor*. For example, the Web service might support a slightly more complex operation called the `getBulkBookPrice`, which has two arguments: the ISBN number of the book and a quantity that allows the caller to query for bulk discounts on a particular book (see Listing D–3).

Listing D–3

RPC/Encoded Messaging with a Complex Type Accessor

```
<soap:Envelope
 xmlns:soap="http://schemas.xmlsoap.org/soap/envelope/"
 xmlns:xsi="http://www.w3.org/2001/XMLSchema-instance"
 xmlns:mh="http://www.Monson-Haefel.com/jwsbook/BookPrice"
 soap:encodingStyle="http://schemas.xmlsoap.org/soap/encoding/">
   <Body>
      <mh:getBookPrice>
          <isbn xsi:type="string">0321146182</isbn>
          <quantity xsi:type="int">100</quantity>
      </mh:getBulkBookPrice>
   </Body>
</soap:Envelope>
```

Technically, the names of the accessors in an operation struct of a SOAP message can be anything. In the preceding example, the accessor names could match the argument names in a remote interface, but such matching isn't required by the specification. The SOAP specification (specifically, Section 5) doesn't dictate the mapping between SOAP program arguments and accessors—that's up to the SOAP toolkit. JAX-RPC (Java API for XML-based RPC) happens to specify a one-to-one mapping between the method argument names and the accessor names of the operation struct, but this is only a convention of JAX-RPC (and some other toolkits) and is not a standard. Some SOAP toolkits use arbitrary names. For example, the GLUE SOAP toolkit uses array-like position names (`arg0`, `arg1`, ... `argN`) for accessors, as in Listing D–4.

Listing D–4

RPC/Encoded Messaging with Arbitrary Accessor Names

```
<soap:Envelope
 xmlns:soap="http://schemas.xmlsoap.org/soap/envelope/"
 xmlns:xsi="http://www.w3.org/2001/XMLSchema-instance"
 xmlns:mh="http://www.Monson-Haefel.com/jwsbook/BookPrice" >
   <Body>
      <mh:getBookPrice
       soap:encodingStyle="http://schemas.xmlsoap.org/soap/encoding/">
          <arg0 xsi:type="string">0321146182</arg0>
          <arg1 xsi:type="int">100</arg1>
      </mh:getBulkBookPrice>
   </Body>
</soap:Envelope>
```

Notice that the elements reflect the arguments' types, but not their names, which are determined by the conventions of the SOAP toolkit used. You might think that this would cause interoperability problems: If JAX-RPC uses the struct style and GLUE uses the array style (`arg0`, `arg1`, ... `argN`), how can a GLUE client talk to a JAX-RPC Web service, or vice versa? The answer is WSDL (Web Services Description Language).

SOAP messages are usually constructed according to a WSDL document. The WSDL document describes the operations supported by a Web service, including the operation parameter names. Stub-based SOAP toolkits generate client stubs that exchange SOAP messages according to the WSDL document and not their own conventions. If a GLUE SOAP client, for example, wants to talk to a JAX-RPC-based Web service, it uses JAX-RPC-style operation structs as described by that Web service's WSDL document.

In the examples used throughout this book, the operation element, the immediate child element of the `Body` element, is namespace-qualified. This qualification is actually not required. You don't need to namespace-qualify the operation element and its subelements, but doing so allows you to distinguish elements of the operation structure from standard SOAP elements.

D.3 Simple Types

RPC/Encoded uses the XML schema simple types in the definitions of structures and arrays. You might have noticed that each of the arguments in the `BulkBookQuote` SOAP method explicitly declares its type using XML schema simple types, as shown in bold in Listing D–5.

Listing D–5

RPC/Encoded XSI Type Declarations

```
<soap:Envelope
 xmlns:soap="http://schemas.xmlsoap.org/soap/envelope/"
 xmlns:xsi="http://www.w3.org/2001/XMLSchema-instance"
 xmlns:mh="http://www.Monson-Haefel.com/jwsbook/BookPrice" >
   <Body>
      <mh:getBookPrice
       soap:encodingStyle="http://schemas.xmlsoap.org/soap/encoding/">
          <isbn xsi:type="string">0321146182</isbn>
          <quantity xsi:type="int">100</quantity>
      </mh:getBulkBookPrice>
   </Body>
</soap:Envelope>
```

The use of XML Schema-Instance simple types allows simple values to be portable, validated, and matched with corresponding types of the Web service component or object. XML schema simple types were adopted by RPC/Encoded messaging because that part of the XML schema specification was stable at the time SOAP 1.1 was completed. As you'll see in the next section, complex types in SOAP do not conform with complex types in XML schema.

SOAP Encoding also defines a set of global elements that correspond to XML simple types. For example, `string`, `int`, `double`, `dateTime`, and other elements defined in the namespace of SOAP Encoding are based on the XML simple types. These simple type elements can be used in RPC/Encoded messages as shown later, in Sections D.5: Array Types and D6: References.

D.4 Complex Types

RPC/Encoded allows you to use complex types as parameters and describes how complex types should be mapped to elements in the SOAP `Body`. For example, the BookQuote Web service might include an operation called `getBulkBookPriceWithShipping()`, which gives the bulk price but also adds in the shipping costs for a specified address. The method signature in Java would look as in Listing D–6.

Listing D–6

A Java Interface Definition for the BookQuote Web Service

```
public interface BookQuote extends javax.rmi.Remote {
   public float getBookPrice(String isbn)
     throws RemoteException, InvalidIsbnException;
   public float getBulkBookPrice(String isbn, int quantity)
     throws RemoteException, InvalidIsbnException;
   public float getBulkBookPriceWithShipping(String isbn, int quantity,
                                              Address addr)
     throws RemoteException, InvalidIsbnException;
}
```

The `Address` type is a Java serializable class, which is defined as follows.

```
public class Address implements java.io.Serializable {

   public String name;
   public String street;
   public String city;
   public String state;
   public String zip;

   // accessors and constructor follow
}
```

When the `getBulkBookPriceWithShipping()` method is invoked, all the arguments, including the `Address` object, are encoded into the SOAP `Body`, as in Listing D–7.

Listing D–7

RPC/Encoded Messaging with Multiple Parameters

```
<soap:Envelope
 xmlns:soap="http://schemas.xmlsoap.org/soap/envelope/"
```

```
 xmlns:xsi="http://www.w3.org/2001/XMLSchema-instance"
 xmlns:mh="http://www.Monson-Haefel.com/jwsbook/BookPrice">
   <Body>
      <mh:getBookPrice
       soap:encodingStyle="http://schemas.xmlsoap.org/soap/encoding/">
         <isbn xsi:type="string">0321146182</isbn>
         <quantity xsi:type="int">100</quantity>
         <addr>
            <name xsi:type="string">Amazon.com</name>
            <street xsi:type="string">1516 2nd Ave</street>
            <city xsi:type="string">Seattle</city>
            <state xsi:type="string">WA</state>
            <zip xsi:type="string">90952</name>
         </addr>
      </mh:getBulkBookPrice>
   </Body>
</soap:Envelope>
```

Notice that each field in the Address class has a corresponding accessor in the addr element. The addr element is named after the method argument, whereas each of its accessors are named and typed according to the fields of the Address class. This matching is not required by the specification but is a convention supported by JAX-RPC.

Although simple-type arguments in RPC/Encoded messaging are based on the XML Schema-Instance simple types, complex types like addr are not typed—a departure from most object-oriented languages, which define named types for both simple and complex data. In RPC/Encoded messaging, complex data structures do not have explicit, named types. This weak type system is one the drawbacks of RPC/Encoded messaging. The fact that a complex data object does not have an explicit type definition makes validating its structure difficult, and eliminates the possibility of complex-type inheritance. These limitations are one of the reasons that developers prefer RPC/Literal and Document/Literal to the RPC/Encoded mode.

D.5 Array Types

In addition to complex types, RPC/Encoded messaging defines the Array type. The Array type provides a standard representation for arrays—a feature not offered by XML schema. The standardized representation of arrays in XML is one of the reasons some developers favor RPC/Encoded messaging.

The BookQuote Web service might define a method that provides the prices for several books at once, instead of a single book, as in Listing D–8—eliminating the need for multiple invocations when prices for more than one book are needed.

Listing D–8

A Java Interface Definition for the BookQuote Web Service

```
public interface BookQuote extends javax.rmi.Remote {
   public float getBookPrice(String isbn)
     throws RemoteException, InvalidIsbnException;
   public float getBulkBookPrice(String isbn, int quantity)
     throws RemoteException, InvalidIsbnException;
   public float getBulkBookPriceWithShipping(String isbn, int quantity,
                                              Address addr)
     throws RemoteException, InvalidIsbnException;
   public [] float getBookPrice(String [] isbns)
     throws RemoteException, InvalidIsbnException;
}
```

A SOAP message request for the `getBookPrice()` method might look like Listing D–9.

Listing D–9

RPC/Encoded Messaging Using the `Array` Type Attribute

```
<soap:Envelope
 xmlns:soap="http://schemas.xmlsoap.org/soap/envelope/"
 xmlns:xsd="http://www.w3.org/2001/XMLSchema"
 xmlns:xsi='http://www.w3.org/2001/XMLSchema-Instance'
 xmlns:enc="http://schemas.xmlsoap.org/soap/encoding/"
 xmlns:mh="http://www.Monson-Haefel.com/jwsbook/BookPrice" >
   <Body>
      <mh:getBookPrice
       soap:encodingStyle="http://schemas.xmlsoap.org/soap/encoding/">
          <isbns xsi:type="enc:Array" enc:arrayType="xsd:string[4]">
             <isbn xsi:type="xsd:string">0596002262</isbn>
             <isbn xsi:type="xsd:string">0596000685</isbn>
             <isbn xsi:type="xsd:string">1558604154</isbn>
             <isbn xsi:type="xsd:string">0132017997</isbn>
          </isbns>
      </mh:getBulkBookPrice>
   </Body>
</soap:Envelope>
```

This is only one of several possible representations of the same array using SOAP. RPC/Encoded messaging defines an `Array` element, as well as elements corresponding to many of the simple types defined by XML schema. For example, RPC/Encoded messaging defines `int` and `string` elements. Listing D–10 shows the same SOAP message, but this time it uses the RPC/Encoded `Array` and simple type elements.

Listing D–10

RPC/Encoded Messaging Using the `Array` Type Attribute

```
<soap:Envelope
 xmlns:soap="http://schemas.xmlsoap.org/soap/envelope/"
 xmlns:xsd='http://www.w3.org/2001/XMLSchema'
 xmlns:enc="http://schemas.xmlsoap.org/soap/encoding/"
 xmlns:mh="http://www.Monson-Haefel.com/jwsbook/BookPrice" >
   <Body>
      <mh:getBookPrice
       soap:encodingStyle="http://schemas.xmlsoap.org/soap/encoding/">
         <enc:Array enc:arrayType="xsd:string[4]">
            <enc:string>0596002262</enc:string>
            <enc:string>0596000685</enc:string>
            <enc:string>1558604154</enc:string>
            <enc:string>0132017997</enc:string>
         </enc:Array>
      </mh:getBulkBookPrice>
   </Body>
</soap:Envelope>
```

You refer to an element of an array by its position or index rather than to a named field, as you do in the case of structs or objects. As a result, the names of the accessors for elements of an `Array` type are not important. Different SOAP toolkits use different accessor names, but when reading an `Array` value these are ignored anyway; only the ordinal positions of the elements are important.

The elements of a SOAP `Array` are polymorphic, which means they can contain any subtype of the array-element type. For example, an `Array` of `integers` can contain elements of type `integer` but may also contain elements of types `long`, `int`, `short`, and `byte`, because these other types are derived from `integer` in XML schema (see Listing D–11).

Listing D–11

RPC/Encoded Messaging Using a Polymorphic Array

```
<SomeArray xsi:type="enc:Array" enc:arrayType="xsd:integer[4]">
   <number>0596002262</number>
   <number xsi:type='int' >0596000685</number>
   <number xsi:type='short'>31930</number>
   <number xsi:type='byte'>132</number>
</SomeArray>
```

The Java programming language does not support polymorphism in its primitive array types, so this type of array would probably be mapped to an array type like `Object[]` or some `java.util.Collection` type, and the elements would be of wrapper types (`Integer`, `Short`, and `Byte`) instead of their primitive counterparts (`int`, `short`, and `byte`).

Arrays can also contain complex types and other arrays. Accessors that contain complex types or other arrays can be represented in line, as in Listing D–12, or using references, as discussed in the next section. The array in the following example is of type `ur-type`, which is the base type of all the other XML schema types. The `ur-type` is analogous to the `Object` type in Java.

Listing D–12

RPC/Encoded Messaging Using an Array of Complex Types and Other Arrays

```
<SomeArray xsi:type="enc:Array" enc:arrayType="xsi:ur-type">
   <item xsi:type='string'>0596002262</item>
   <item xsi:type='mh:USAddress' >
       <address>
          <name>Amazon.com</name>
          <street>1516 2nd Ave</street>
          <city>Seattle</city>
          <state>WA</state>
          <zip>90952</zip>
       </address>
   </item>
   <item xsi:type='enc:Array'>
      <enc:Array enc:arrayType='int' enc:arraySize='3'>
          <number>541</number>
          <number>3833452</number>
          </number>20382</number>
      <enc:Array>
   </item>
</SomeArray>
```

When arrays are elements of some other array, as in the preceding example, the result is not the same as a multi-dimensional array. The distinction is the same as in the Java programming language. In Java, an array of type `Object` may contain other arrays as elements. For example, the following code creates an `Object` array that contains two other arrays.

```
// create an array of arrays
int [] intArray = {22, 33, 44};
double [] doubleArray = {22.22, 33.33, 44.44};
```

```
Object [] objectArray = new Object[2];
ObjectArray[0] = intArray;
ObjectArray[1] = doubleArray;
```

This type of array is very different from a multi-dimensional array, which is a matrix of ordinal values. For example, the following code creates a multi-dimensional array that contains both `Integer` and `Double` values.

```
// create a multi-dimensional array
Object [][] objectArray = new Object[2,3];
objectArray[0,0] = new Integer(22);
objectArray[0,1] = new Integer(33);
objectArray[0,2] = new Integer(44);
objectArray[1,0] = new Double(22.22)
objectArray[1,1] = new Double(33.33);
objectArray[1,2] = new Double(44.44);
```

RPC/Encoded messaging mode makes the same distinction between arrays that contain other arrays and multi-dimensional arrays. When a multi-dimensional array is serialized into a SOAP message using RPC/Encoded messaging, the contents of the array are listed in order, incrementing the index of the lowest dimension first. For example, the multi-dimensional Java array in the previous snippet might be represented using RPC/Encoded messaging as in Listing D–13.

Listing D–13

An RPC/Encoded Multi-dimensional Array

```
<enc:Array enc:arrayType='xsi:ur-type' enc:arraySize='2,3'>
     <item xsi:type="string">22</item>
     <item xsi:type="string">33</item>
     <item xsi:type="string">44</item>
     <item xsi:type="string">22.22</item>
     <item xsi:type="string">33.33</item>
     <item xsi:type="string">44.44</item>
</enc:Array>
```

D.5.1 Array Size

The array size is indicated using a size qualifier following the type identification in the value of the `arrayType` attribute. This qualifier indicates the size of each dimension of the array. If the array has only one dimension, a single integer value is used, as in Listing D–14.

Listing D–14

A One-Dimensional Array

```
<isbns xsi:type="enc:Array" enc:arrayType="xsd:string[4]">
   <isbn xsi:type="xsd:string">0596002262</isbn>
   <isbn xsi:type="xsd:string">0596000685</isbn>
   <isbn xsi:type="xsd:string">1558604154</isbn>
   <isbn xsi:type="xsd:string">0132017997</isbn>
</isbns>
```

If the array has multiple dimensions, the size of each dimension is listed from the highest (leftmost) dimension to the lowest (rightmost) dimension, separated by commas, as in the following snippet.

```
<enc:Array enc:arrayType='xsi:ur-type' enc:arraySize='2,3'>
     <item xsi:type="string">22</item>
     <item xsi:type="string">33</item>
     <item xsi:type="string">44</item>
     <item xsi:type="string">22.22</item>
     <item xsi:type="string">33.33</item>
     <item xsi:type="string">44.44</item>
</enc:Array>
```

D.5.2 Other Features of Arrays

There are other ways in which arrays are manifested, including partially transmitted arrays, sparse arrays, and arrays of bytes. These are somewhat esoteric and are covered only in brief in this section.

Partially transmitted arrays allow very large arrays to be transmitted in multiple SOAP messages. For example, one SOAP message can contain the first part of a large array, while the next SOAP message contains the second part of the array. This feature is rarely used.

Sparse arrays allow arrays with lots of empty elements to be compressed, so that only the positions that contain values are transmitted. The relative index of each position is indicated so the sparse array can be reconstructed.

The byte array uses Base64 encoding to transmit binary data as ASCII text. It's not an array in the same sense as the SOAP Encoding `Array` type. It is just a data type of `base64` whose value is a character-encoded binary stream. For example, the following shows a byte array for an image.

```
<image xsi:type="enc:base64">
   aG93IG5vDyBicm73biBjb3cNCg==
</image>
```

Base64 encoding is covered in detail in Appendix C.

D.6 References

One of the principal advantages of RPC/Encoded messaging over RPC/Literal and Document/Literal messaging is the capability to use references. An object graph will sometimes have multiple references to the same instance of an object. As an example, we can imagine an object graph of book authors, as illustrated in Figure D–1.

Figure D–1 illustrates graphically the relationship between instances of three `Book` objects and two `Author` objects. In this case, all three `Book` instances refer to a single author, Richard Monson-Haefel. As a result, the three `Book` instances share a reference to the same `Author` instance. You can represent this multiplicity in RPC/Encoded messaging using the `href` and `id` attributes, as in Listing D–15.

Listing D–15

RPC/Encoded Messaging References

```
<books enc:arrayType="addBook:ArrayOfBooks[3]">
    <book>
        <title>J2EE Web Services</title>
        <authors enc:arrayType="addBook:ArrayOfAuthors[1]">
            <author href="#author_1" xsi:type="addBook:Author" />
        </authors>
    </book>
    <book>
        <title>Enterprise JavaBeans, 4th Edition</title>
        <authors enc:arrayType="addBook:ArrayOfAuthors[1]">
            <author href="#author_1" xsi:type="addBook:Author" />
```

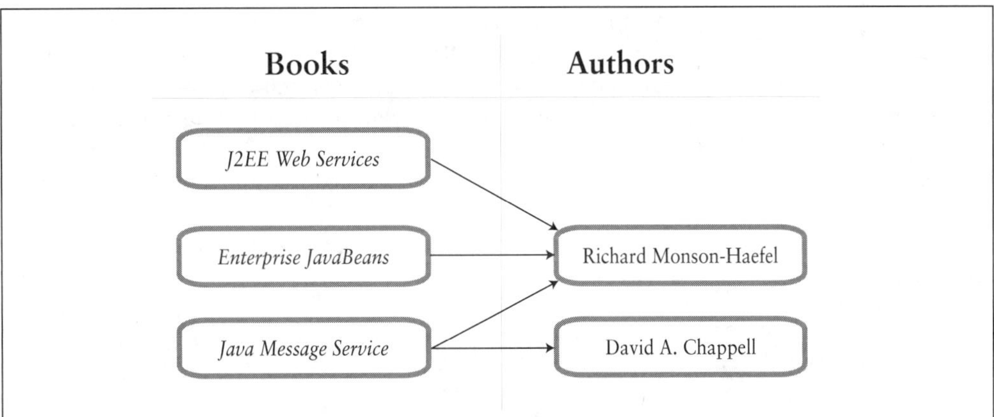

Figure D–1 Object Graph of Books and Their Authors

```
            </authors>
        </book>
        <book>
            <title>Java Message Service</title>
            <authors enc:arrayType="addBook:ArrayOfAuthors[2]">
                <author href="#author_1" xsi:type="addBook:Author" />
                <author xsi:type="addBook:Author" >
                    <fname>David</fname>
                    <mi>A</mi>
                    <lname>Chappell</lname>
                </author>
            </authors>
        </book>
    </books>
    <author id="#author_1" xsi:type="addBook:Author">
        <fname>Richard</fname>
        <mi>W</mi>
        <lname>Monson-Haefel</lname>
    </author>
```

The three books all share a reference to a single author element. When an element is not shared, it must be embedded. For example, in this example, the third book element contains a single reference to an element representing David A. Chappell, which is embedded and not referred to. An object graph may use local or remote references, depending on the value of the href attribute.[1]

If you have worked with HTML, the href attribute may look familiar. The value of the href attribute in RPC/Encoded messaging, like the href in HTML, can be an absolute, relative, or fragment address. In practice, the value of the href attribute is normally a fragment, which is a reference to an element in the same document.

You may run across the use of a full URL, one that points to an element of an XML document located at some remote Internet address, but don't hold your breath. This is rarely, if ever, done. The following is an example of a remote reference.

```
<mh:book>
  <title>J2EE Web Services</title>
  <author href='http://wwww.Monson-Haefel.com/jwsbook/authors.xml#author_1' />
<mh:book>
```

[1] In addition to the book *Java Message Service* (O'Reilly, 2000), David A. Chappell is also the co-author of the books *Java Web Services* (O'Reilly, 2002) and *Professional ebXML Foundations* (Wrox, 2001).

A local reference points to a shared element that is listed within the same SOAP message. The `href` value is usually prefixed with a pound sign (#), followed by an identifier. The identifier corresponds to the value of an `id` element. The value of an element `id` attribute must be unique; two elements cannot have the same `id` attribute value.

In addition to referring to complex types, the `href` attribute may refer to simple types that are reused in an object graph. Normally, this technique is applied only to string types. For example, Listing D–16 shows two different authors sharing the same first and last names, but having different middle initials.

Listing D–16

Referring to Simple Types

```
<book>
    <title>Java Message Service</title>
    <authors enc:arrayType="addBook:ArrayOfAuthors[2]">
        <author href="#author_1" xsi:type="addBook:Author" />
        <author xsi:type="addBook:Author" >
            <fname href="string_1" />
            <mi>A</mi>
            <lname href="string_2" />
        </author>
    </authors>
</book>
<book>
    <title>Understanding .NET</title>
    <authors enc:arraySize="2" enc:itemType="addBook:ArrayOfAuthors">
        <author href="#author_2" xsi:type="addBook:Author" />
    </authors>
</book>
...
<author id="#author_2" xsi:type="addBook:Author">
    <fname href="string_1" />
    <mi>F</mi>
    <lname href="string_2" />
</author>
<soap-encoding:string id="string_1">David</soap:encoding>
<soap-encoding:string id="string_2">Chappell</soap:encoding>
```

Whether encoded messages benefit from shared references to elements of simple types depends on how often a simple value is reused or how many characters are used for a simple type value. In many cases, it's probably more efficient simply to repeat the value rather than refer to it, but the better strategy to use depends on the SOAP toolkit.

D.7 Wrapping Up

It's important to understand that the first SOAP specification (SOAP 1.1) was completed before XML schema became a final recommendation. In fact, at the time that SOAP 1.1 was submitted as a Note to the W3C, XML schema was still in development. At that time, XML schema defined only simple types and not complex types. As a result, SOAP Encoding tends to overlap with the XML schema specification when it comes to defining complex types. This overlap creates a lot of confusion. If XML schema had been completed before SOAP 1.1, the SOAP Encoding might have been better aligned with the final XML schema recommendation.

Because SOAP 1.1 was in use for a while before XML schema, a lot of toolkits still support the SOAP RPC/Encoded mode of messaging. The general trend today, however, is to move away from RPC/Encoded messaging and toward the RPC/Literal and Document/Literal modes, because XML schema is perceived as offering a stronger type system and better interoperability.

Although Web service pundits tend to dismiss SOAP Encoding, the fact is that there are aspects of SOAP Encoding that are necessary in RPC programming and not available in XML schema. Specifically, SOAP Encoding supports object graphs with shared references, whereas XML schema doesn't support shared references. In addition, SOAP Encoding provides a common definition of an array, which is pervasive in programming languages but is not explicitly supported by XML schema. Still, RPC/Encoded messaging is not supported by the WS-I Basic Profile 1.0, so you should avoid SOAP Encoding if you can.

Appendix E
SOAP Messages with Attachments

A SOAP message is an XML document, which is essentially just text. Unicode characters are the only kind of data that can be exchanged using SOAP. This restriction is not a problem in most cases, because W3C's XML schema allows us to exchange a fairly rich set of typed data: `int`, `double`, `date`, and so on. In some cases, however, you may need to convey binary data in SOAP messages. For example, you may want to send a SOAP message that contains a JPEG image or a document that uses a proprietary format such as PDF. SOAP Messages with Attachments (SwA) provides a mechanism to "attach" binary data to a SOAP message without converting binary data to ASCII characters using Base64 encoding.

SwA is certainly one way to exchange binary data using SOAP, but it's not the only way. Microsoft, IBM, and others have offered a couple of different solutions, including DIME (Direct Internet Message Encapsulation) and WS-Attachments. The futures of DIME, SwA, and WS-Attachments are questionable, however. Each of these solutions defines a separate mechanism for associating SOAP messages with binary data. Some experts believe that the real solution lies in XML itself. Rather than use a second data packaging standard to associate binary data with SOAP messages, it's possible to place binary data directly into the SOAP message itself using Base64 or Hexadecimal encoding, or by using XInclude.[1]

Because SwA's future is uncertain, you should consider this appendix optional. Although the JAX-RPC (Java API for XML-based RPC) and SAAJ (SOAP with Attachments API for Java) APIs both support SwA, it is not endorsed or even mentioned

[1] World Wide Web Consortium, *XML Inclusions (Xinclude)*, Version 1.0, W3C Candidate Recommendation 17, September 2002, http://www.w3.org/TR/2002/CR-xinclude-20020917/.

by the WS-I Basic Profile 1.0 (BP). Because BP doesn't address SwA, or any other mechanism for associating binary data with SOAP messages, SwA and other non-conformant attachment mechanisms should be held suspect. The WS-I Basic Profile 1.1, which is still in development at the time of this writing, promises to extend support of the BP to include SwA—this is one of the primary reasons SwA is covered in this appendix. Support for SwA in J2EE 1.4 is also covered by Appendix F and G.

E.1 Understanding MIME

SwA is based on MIME (Multipurpose Internet Mail Extensions), which was originally designed in 1996 for the Internet e-mail protocol SMTP. MIME defines a way of embedding many different kinds of non-text data in an e-mail message. Although you may not be aware of it, you use MIME every time you send an e-mail with an attached file. When you send someone an e-mail with a PDF or a JPEG attached, your mail client embeds the file in the e-mail using the MIME data format (see Figure E–1). When you receive e-mail with a file attached, your e-mail client displays it as a link or icon that can be opened with a click of your mouse. In reality, the e-mail client is hiding the fact that the body of the e-mail message actually contains a lot of binary data, encoded in a special format, which would be illegible if displayed.

The Internet Engineering Task Force first standardized SMTP, the e-mail protocol of the Internet, under RFC 822 in 1982, back when ASCII text was the standard for

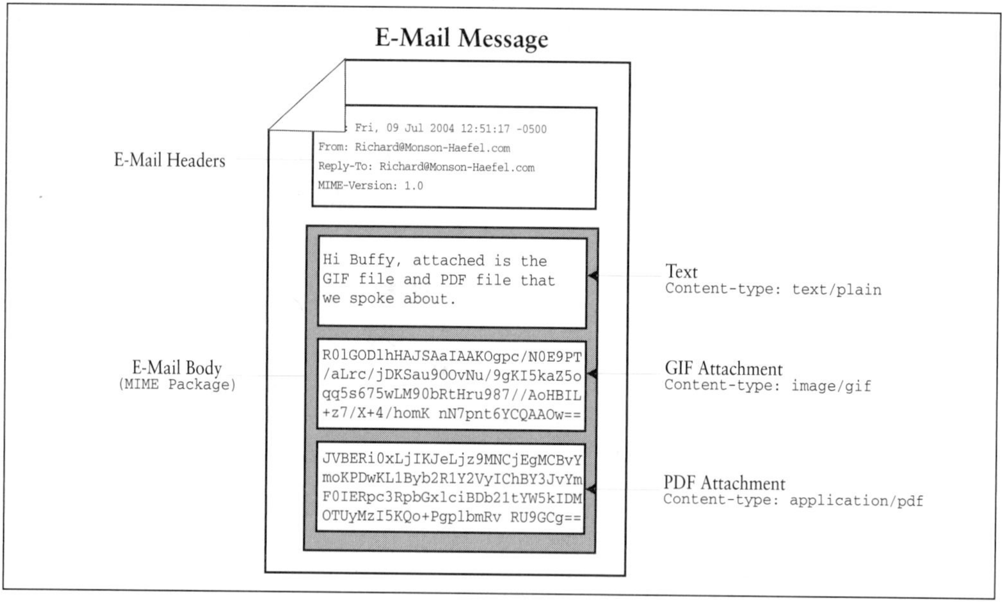
E-Mail Message
Fri, 09 Jul 2004 12:51:17 -0500
From: Richard@Monson-Haefel.com
Reply-To: Richard@Monson-Haefel.com
MIME-Version: 1.0
E-Mail Headers
Hi Buffy, attached is the
GIF file and PDF file that
we spoke about.
Text
Content-type: text/plain
R0lGODlhHAJSAaIAAKOgpc/N0E9PT
/aLrc/jDKSau9OOvNu/9gKI5kaZ5o
qq5s675wLM90bRtHru987//AoHBIL
+z7/X+4/homK nN7pnt6YCQAAOw==
E-Mail Body
(MIME Package)
GIF Attachment
Content-type: image/gif
JVBERi0xLjIKJeLjz9MNCjEgMCBvY
moKPDwKL1Byb2R1Y2VyIChBY3JvYm
F0IERpc3RpbGxlciBDb21tYW5kIDM
OTUyMzI5KQo+PgplbmRv RU9GCg==
PDF Attachment
Content-type: application/pdf

Figure E–1 An E-Mail with Attachments Using the MIME Message Format

character codes. As a result, any e-mail message, including the headers and the message body, is limited to seven-bit ASCII characters. In other words, SMTP doesn't support eight-bit binary data. MIME allows binary data to be embedded in the body of e-mail by converting it into ASCII text and placing it into a block called an **attachment** or **MIME part.** MIME also defines the headers that describe the data type of each attachment, as well the boundaries that separate one attachment from another. For example, the e-mail shown in Figure E–1 would look like Listing E–1 when viewed with a standard text editor. (Note that the entire Base64-encoded content of each attachment is not shown, because it would require several pages of what looked like random text that would provide no value.)

Listing E–1

E-Mail with MIME Attachments

```
Date: Fri, 09 Jul 2004 12:51:17 -0500
From: Richard@Monson-Haefel.com
Reply-To: Richard@Monson-Haefel.com
MIME-Version: 1.0
To: Buffy.Summers@upn.com
Subject: The book files
Content-Type: Multipart/Mixed;
 boundary="------------56C4BEFA835541B020058DF8"

This is a multi-part message in MIME format.
--------------56C4BEFA835541B020058DF8
Content-Type: text/plain; charset=us-ascii
Content-Transfer-Encoding: 7bit

Hi Buffy, attached is the GIF file and PDF file that we spoke about.

--------------56C4BEFA835541B020058DF8
Content-Type: image/gif;
 name="jwsed1_cover.gif"
Content-Transfer-Encoding: base64
Content-Disposition: inline;
 filename="book_cover.gif"

R0lGODlhHAJSAaIAAKOgpc/N0E9PTyAgIHJDknp5e0oNc////yH5BAAAAAAALAAAAAAcAlIBAAP
/aLrc/jDKSau9OOvNu/9gKI5kaZ5oqq5s675wLM90bRtHru987//AoHBILBqPyKRyyWw6n9CodE
qtWq8/BnbL7Xq/4LB4TC6bqdqzes1uu9/wuLyantvv+Lx
...
+z7/X+4CBgoOEhX1/homK nN7pnt6YCQAAOw==
--------------56C4BEFA835541B020058DF8
```

```
Content-Type: application/pdf;
 name="jwsed1_manuscript.pdf"
Content-Transfer-Encoding: base64
Content-Disposition: inline;
 filename="manuscript.pdf"
```


```
JVBERi0xLjIKJeLjz9MNCjEgMCBvYmoKPDwKL1Byb2R1Y2VyIChBY3JvYmF0IERpc3RpbGxl-
ciBDb21tYW5kIDMuMDEgZm9yIFNvbGFyaXMgMi4zIGFuZCBsYXRlciBcKFNQQVJDXCkpCi9UaXR
sZSAoanRzKQovQ3JlYXRvciAoRnJhbWVNYWtlciA1LjUuNi4...
OTkxMTI0MTUyMzI5KQo+PglbmRv RU9GCg==
```


```
--------------56C4BEFA835541B020058DF8--
```

The beginning of the e-mail contains the standard e-mail headers, including the identity of the MIME version used (1.0, the only one in use at this time).

```
Date: Fri, 09 Jul 2004 12:51:17 -0500
From: Richard@Monson-Haefel.com
Reply-To: Richard@Monson-Haefel.com
MIME-Version: 1.0
To: Buffy.Summers@upn.com
Content-Type: Multipart/Mixed;
  boundary="------------56C4BEFA835541B020058DF8"
```

`Content-Type` identifies the kind of MIME content; `Multipart/Mixed` tells us that the body of the e-mail is made up of multiple parts (attachments) of mixed types. The `boundary` header declares the set of characters that will be used to separate one attachment from another. In this message, every time you see the characters "------------56C4BEFA835541B020058DF8", you'll know that one MIME part (attachment) just ended and a new one is starting.

As is the usual case, the first MIME part of the example e-mail is the text message. Every MIME part starts with a special `Content-Type` header that identifies the type of data the part contains and the type of encoding used. In the first MIME part, the type of data is plain text (`Content-Type: text/plain`) and the encoding style is SMTP's traditional seven-bit encoding, which is ASCII text. MIME headers are always separated from the data they describe by an empty line.

```
--------------56C4BEFA835541B020058DF8
Content-Type: text/plain; charset=us-ascii
Content-Transfer-Encoding: 7bit

Hi Buffy, attached is the GIF file and PDF doc. we spoke about

--------------56C4BEFA835541B020058DF8
```

The next MIME part identifies the data type as a GIF image (`Content-Type: image/gif`) and the encoding style as Base64 (`Content-Transfer-Encoding: base64`). The name header simply identifies the name of the original file.

```
--------------56C4BEFA835541B020058DF8
Content-Type: image/gif;
 name="column-icon.gif"
Content-Transfer-Encoding: base64
Content-Disposition: inline;
 filename="book_cover.gif"

R01GODlhHAJSAaIAAKOgpc/N0E9PTyAgIHJDknp5e0oNc////yH5BAAAAAAALAAAAAAcAlIBAAP
/aLrc/jDKSau9OOvNu/9gKI5kaZ5oqq5s675wLM90bRtHru987//AoHBILBqPyKRyyWw6n9Cod
EqtWq8/BnbL7Xq/4LB4TC6bqdqzes1uu9/wuLyantvv+Lx
...
+z7/X+4CBgoOEhX1/homK nN7pnt6YCQAAOw==
--------------56C4BEFA835541B020058DF8
```

Base64 is an algorithm that converts binary data into ASCII text, so it can be carried by e-mail. The algorithm is very simple. First, it converts the binary data into six-bit segments. Next, it uses a translation table to convert each six-bit segment into one of the 64 ASCII characters that represent the values 0 through 63 (integers that can be represented by six bits). At the end, the binary data has been replaced by a string of ASCII characters. The process can be reversed later to convert the string of characters back to binary data. Appendix C provides a complete and detailed description of the Base64 encoding algorithm.

E.2 Using MIME with SOAP

Although MIME was originally developed for e-mail, it's not limited to that application. SOAP employs MIME for the same reason as e-mail: to transfer binary data. A SOAP message doesn't contain a MIME package, however. On the contrary, the SOAP message is actually part of the MIME package. As you learned in Chapter 4, SOAP is usually the payload of some other application protocol, usually HTTP. HTTP already supports the use of MIME packages, so SOAP Messages with Attachments wisely exploits the existing infrastructure for MIME and simply embeds the SOAP message as a MIME part, along with its related binary data. Figure E–2 is an example of a SOAP message with attachments embedded in an HTTP request message. Notice that the MIME package is the payload of the HTTP request, and that it contains both the SOAP message and its attachments.

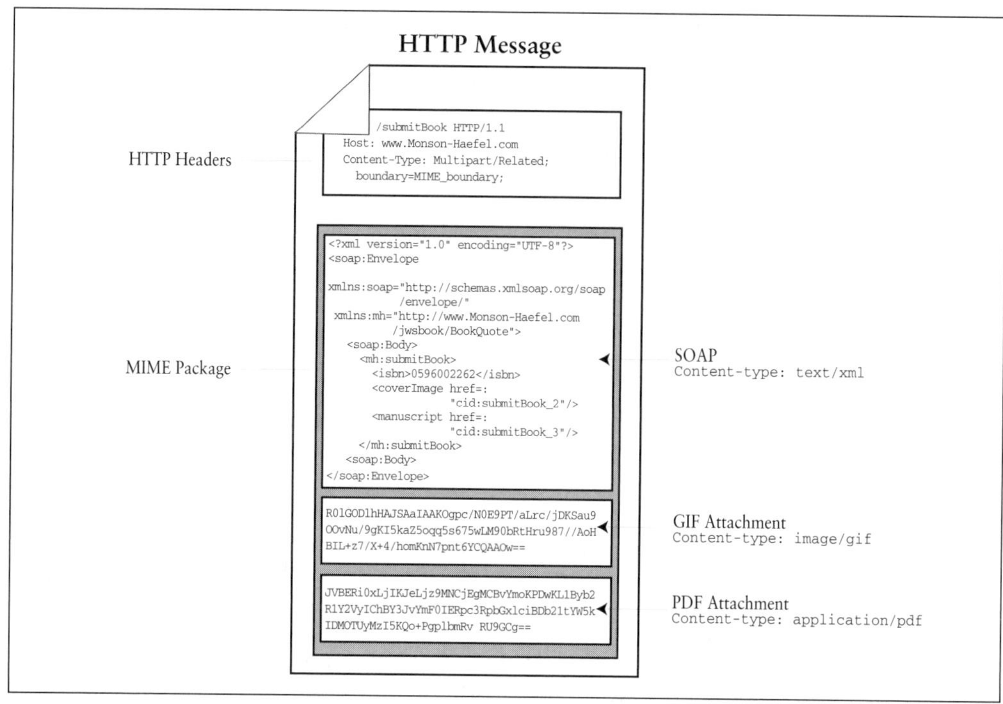

Figure E–2 A SOAP Message with Attachments

SOAP Messages with Attachments use the `Multipart/Related` content type, which is similar to the `Multipart/Mixed` content type in Listing E–1, with one important difference: `Multipart/Related` allows the root MIME part to refer to other MIME parts. This is a good solution for SOAP, because it allows a SOAP message, as an XML instance, to refer to non-XML (usually binary) data in the same payload. Listing E–2 is an example of a SOAP message with attachments embedded in an HTTP request.

Listing E–2

SOAP Message with Attachments Sent over HTTP

```
POST /submitBook HTTP/1.1
Host: www.Monson-Haefel.com
Content-Type: Multipart/Related; boundary=MIME_boundary; type=text/xml;
        start="<submitBook_1>"
Content-Length: XXXX

--MIME_boundary
Content-Type: text/xml; charset=UTF-8
```

```
Content-Transfer-Encoding: 8bit
Content-ID: <submitBook_1>

<?xml version="1.0" encoding="UTF-8"?>
<soap:Envelope
 xmlns:soap="http://schemas.xmlsoap.org/soap/envelope/"
 xmlns:mh="http://www.Monson-Haefel.com/jwsbook/BookQuote">
   <soap:Body>
     <mh:submitBook>
       <isbn>0596002262</isbn>
       <coverImage href=:"cid:submitBook_2"/>
       <manuscript href=:"cid:submitBook_3"/>
     </mh:submitBook>
   <soap:Body>
</soap:Envelope>

--MIME_boundary
Content-Type: image/gif
Content-Transfer-Encoding: binary
Content-ID: <submitBook_2>

R0lGODlhHAJSAaIAAKOgpc/N0E9PTyAgIHJDknp5e0oNc////yH5BAAAAAAALAAAAAAcAlIBAAP
/aLrc/jDKSau9OOvNu/9gKI5kaZ5oqq5s675wLM90bRtHru987//AoHBILBqPyKRyyWw6n9CoEq
tWq8/BnbL7Xq/4LB4TC6bqdqzes1uu9/wuLyantvv+Lx
...
+z7/X+4CBgoOEhX1/homK nN7pnt6YCQAAOw==
--MIME_boundary
Content-Type: application/pdf;
Content-Transfer-Encoding: binary
Content-ID: <submitBook_3>

JVBERi0xLjIKJeLjz9MNCjEgMCBvYmoKPDwKL1Byb2R1Y2VyIChBY3JvYmF0IERpc3RpbGxlciB
Db21tYW5kIDMuMDEgZm9yIFNvbGFyaXMgMi4zIGFuZCBsYXRlciBcKFNQQVJDXCkpCi9UaXRsZS
AoanRzKQovQ3JlYXRvciAoRnJhbWVNYWtlciA1LjUuNi4...
OTkxMTI0MTUyMzI5KQo+PgplbmRv RU9GCg==
--MIME_boundary--
```

Identifiers of the three parts of the MIME package, and references to the two attachments in the text part, are shown in bold. There are a couple of ways that `Multipart/Related` MIME messages can employ references: The example in Listing E–2 uses **content-ids (CIDs)**. Another approach makes use of `Content-Location` headers, but CIDs are recommended by the SOAP Messages with Attachments Note.

A CID is a unique ID that is assigned to a MIME part. Listing E–2 has three MIME parts, each of which has a `Content-ID` header with a unique identifier: the CID. When you use `Multipart/Related` MIME types, you must include one root

MIME part that is identified by the HTTP `Content-Type` header. The root is identified with the `start` parameter, as in the following snippet.

```
POST /submitBook HTTP/1.1
Host: www.monson-haefel.com
Content-Type: Multipart/Related; boundary=MIME_boundary; type=text/xml;
        start="<submitBook_1>"
Content-Length: XXXX
```

The `start` content-id always points to the MIME part that contains the SOAP message—the root MIME part. The GIF and PDF MIME parts, which are transferred as binary data, are also assigned content-ids, which the `Body` element of the SOAP message part refers to.

```
<?xml version="1.0" encoding="UTF-8"?>
<soap:Envelope
 xmlns:soap="http://schemas.xmlsoap.org/soap/envelope/"
 xmlns:mh="http://www.Monson-Haefel.com/jwsbook/BookQuote">
   <soap:Body>
     <mh:submitBook>
       <isbn>0596002262</isbn>
       <coverImage href=:"cid:submitBook_2"/>
       <manuscript href=:"cid:submitBook_3"/>
     </mh:submitBook>
   <soap:Body>
</soap:Envelope>
```

Different SOAP toolkits use different values for CIDs. A CID must start with the scheme identifier `cid:` followed by a set of characters. In the example, we use identifiers like `submitBook_n`, but in practice it's more likely that some random, unique value will be used (for example, `cid:20040709.125120`).

When the SubmitBook Web service receives the HTTP request in Listing E–2, it opens the MIME package and extracts the SOAP message. If the SOAP message is well formed and properly structured, the Web service then uses the content-id references to locate the MIME parts containing binary data, then decodes them and processes them.

E.3 Wrapping Up

In the beginning of this appendix, I mentioned that the future of SwA will probably be supported in the future by the WS-I Basic Profile 1.1. However, some experts argue that using Base64 or Hexadecimal encoding forbinary data is a simpler solution.

For example, Listing E–3 shows an example of an SwA message that uses Base64 encoding and is delivered using an HTTP request message.

Listing E–3

Embedding Binary Data in a SOAP Message Using Base64

```
POST 1ed/BookQuote HTTP/1.1
Host: www.Monson-Haefel.com
Content-Type: text/xml; charset="utf-8"
Content-Length: nnnn
SoapAction=""

<?xml version="1.0" encoding="UTF-8"?>
<soap:Envelope
 xmlns:soap="http://schemas.xmlsoap.org/soap/envelope/"
 xmlns:mh="http://www.Monson-Haefel.com/jwsbook/BookQuote">
  <soap:Body>
    <mh:getBookPrice>
      <isbn>0321146182</isbn>
      <coverImage mimeType="image/gif">
        R01GODlhHAJSAaIAAKOgpc/N0E9PTyAgIHJDknp5e0oNc////yHs1uu9/wu
        5BAAAAAAALAAAAAAcAlIBAAP/aLrc/jDKSau9OOvNu/9gKI5kaZ5oqq5s67
        5wLM90bRtHru987//AoHBILBqPyKRyyWw6n9CodEqtWq8/BnbL7Xq/4LB4T
        ...
        +z7/X+4CBgoOEhX1/homK nN7pnt6YCQAAOw==
      </coverImage>
      <manuscript mimeType="application/pdf">
        JVBERi0xLjIKJeLjz9MNCjEgMCBvYmoKPDwKL1Byb2R1Y2VyIChBY3JvYmF0I
        1tYW5kIDMuMDEgZm9yIFNvbGFyaXMgMi4zIGFuZCBsYXRlciBcKFNQQVJDXCk
        aXRsZSAoanRzKQovQ3J1YXRvciAoRnJhbWVNYWtlciA1LjUuNi4zIGFupCi9U
        ...
        OTkxMTI0MTUyMzI5KQo+PgplbmRv RU9GCg==
      </manuscript>
    </mh:getBookPrice>
  </soap:Body>
</soap:Envelope>
```

At this time, there is no standard for embedding binary data as Base64 or Hexadecimal text in a SOAP message, but it's probably needed. Although the XML schema of the SOAP application data in the `Body` element can tell us that it's Base64 or Hexadecimal, there is no standard way to indicate the type of binary data (for example, GIF, PDF, and so on) represented by the binary encoding. Listing E–3 uses the `mimeType` attribute, but this is something that was made up for this example; there is currently no standard.

Base64 and Hexadecimal encoding tend to inflate the size of the data being encoded. For example, Base64 encoding increases the size of the binary stream by approximately 30 percent. For some, this is difficult to swallow, especially when faced with the prospect of sending very large attachments. There are some in the Web services community who would like to see the XML recommendation enhanced to allow for binary data to be nested within the XML document, thereby eliminating the bloat normally associated with encoding.

Base64 encoding is covered in more detail in Appendix C. It is important, however, that you understand that the use of Base64 or Hexadecimal encoding for attachments within a SOAP message is not yet standardized, so using this technique creates serious interoperability problems.

Appendix F
SAAJ Attachments

In addition to the resources it gives you when building simple SOAP messages, SAAJ can help you build SOAP Messages with Attachments (SwA). Appendix E pointed out that SwA is not supported by the WS-I Basic Profile 1.0. Supported or not, SwA is a major piece of functionality in SAAJ, so it's covered by this book. Still, I recommend you use SwA only when your project requires you to.

SwA was covered in detail in Appendix E, but a review of the basic concepts here will be helpful. SwA uses the MIME message format to allow SOAP documents to refer to non-XML data, such as images, documents, digital signatures, and serialized objects. A **MIME message** (also called a **package**) is divided into parts, each of which is a block of raw data and MIME headers, separated by a line of unique boundary characters. An SwA message has a MIME type of `multipart/related`. The root part of an SwA MIME message is the actual SOAP message. Listing F–1 shows an example of an SwA message (the bulk of the raw data in each MIME part is omitted for brevity).

Listing F–1

A Sample SwA Message

```
------=_Part_0_8994558.1029754184304
Content-Type: text/xml
Content-Transfer-Encoding: 8bit
Content-Id: cid:submitBook_1@xyxcorp.com

<soap:Envelope
 xmlns:soap="http://schemas.xmlsoap.org/soap/envelope/">
   <soap:Body>
```

```
      <mh:submitBook xmlns:mh="http://www.Monson-Haefel.com/jwsbook/mh">
         <isbn>0596002262</isbn>
         <coverImage href="cid:submitBook_2@xyxcorp.com"/>
         <manuscript href="cid:submitBook_3@xyxcorp.com"/>
      </mh:submitBook>
   </soap:Body>
</soap:Envelope>
------=_Part_0_8994558.1029754184304
Content-Type: image/jpeg
Content-Transfer-Encoding: binary
Content-Id: submitBook_2@xyxcorp.com

ÿØÿà ÔJ+ñ á Ëïør‡ü C_'Ñû# á-_ ÿ +ëüŒ¿à¥^_—ÃÏø(qÛø§ìj( ò£â-ìmû@|X´ø_¨xËâwÃh_#~Ô-
...
°_ÁŸÙâ÷‰|;£kÚfo_sR_î»ñãVøÓñö _Æ¯qâgÔ‡ÄHÿ h© __ƒã rvNRË§&>N_|_é~_É·tÏÂ¸_,¥'Oë
------=_Part_0_8994558.1029754184304
Content-Type: application/pdf
Content-Transfer-Encoding: binary
Content-Id: submitBook3@xyxcorp.com

%PDF-1.3
...
%%EOF

------=_Part_0_8994558.1029754184304--
```

You learned in Chapter 13 that SAAJ is a SOAP API that models the structure of an SwA message. SAAJ treats all SOAP messages as SOAP messages with attachments. You can build a simple SOAP message without attachments, but you still need to use the SAAJ SwA programming model to do so. In this section we'll develop SwA messages with real attachments, but before we can start building SwA messages, you need to learn a little about the Java Activation Framework, which is central to SAAJ's support for SwA.

F.1 The Java Activation Framework

The Java Activation Framework (JAF) was finalized in 1998, back when Sun was primarily focused on Java's role as a GUI programming language. At that time JavaBeans was still in vogue, Swing was hot, servlets were new, and the J2EE platform didn't even exist. Back then Sun needed a standard discovery API for both file viewers and JavaMail, which provided the impetus for creating JAF. By "discovery" I mean a mechanism that can dynamically find the right components to handle data that's arbitrary, but typed. In particular, JAF was developed as a discovery API to enable GUI developers to discover viewers and editors for documents and image data dynamically.

If you have used a GUI file browser, a modern e-mail application, or a Web browser, then you have used a discovery mechanism. All of these applications allow you to view and edit a file or embedded data (such as a document or image) using programs associated with that type of data. For example, when you receive an e-mail with a PDF attachment, double-clicking on the attachment will, if you're like most people, launch Adobe Acrobat viewer. In most modern operating systems, double-clicking on an HTML file in a file browser will launch your default Web browser. That's discovery.

Discovery depends on a registry of some kind that can associate each file type with an appropriate application. Microsoft Windows, for example, allows you to associate file extensions (`.html`, `.doc`, `.gif`, and so on) with specific applications, which is how Windows Explorer knows what application to launch when you double-click on a file. Another example is an e-mail application like Microsoft's Outlook Express or Mozilla (open source Netscape), which maps MIME types to software applications. When you choose to view an e-mail attachment, the e-mail program examines the MIME content-type to find out which application to launch.

Simply put, JAF provides a framework for dynamically discovering visual widgets to handle (view, edit, print, and so on) any kind of data described by MIME headers. While JAF is focused on the GUI side of things, as a framework for dynamically discovering objects that can manipulate specific MIME types, it's useful for non-visual systems like SAAJ as well. In particular JAF can map Java types, like `java.awt.Image`, to special handlers that seamlessly convert them to streams of data. This mechanism is important in SOAP messaging because it allows SAAJ to convert Java objects (such as AWT images, DOM `Document` objects, and files) into raw data contained by SwA MIME parts, automatically. For example, using SAAJ, you can add an `Image` object to a SOAP message without having to convert the image to a stream of bytes first—JAF will take care of that for you, behind the scenes. The following code snippet illustrates.

```
MessageFactory mf = MessageFactory.newInstance();
SOAPMessage message = mf.createMessage();
java.awt.Image image = …; // get an image form somewhere
AttachmentPart jpegAttach =
              message.createAttachmentPart(image ,"image/jpeg");
```

While JAF makes it simple to add attachments to SAAJ messages, it's also full of pitfalls that can cause a lot of unexpected problems. The rest of this section will explain in detail how JAF accomplishes its magic so that you are aware of its strengths and weaknesses and can avoid some of the traps that less knowledgeable developers are sure to encounter when using attachments.

F.1.1 `DataHandler`

Central to the JAF framework is the `javax.activation.DataHandler` class, which is also the central figure in SAAJ facilities for creating and adding attachments to SOAP messages. Whenever an attachment is added to a SAAJ message, the attached object is invariably embedded in a `DataHandler` object. This may be hidden, occurring behind the scenes, as was the case in the first example, or it can be done explicitly, as in the following snippet.

```
AttachmentPart pdfAttach = message.createAttachmentPart();
FileDataSource file = new FileDataSource("manuscript.pdf");
DataHandler pdfDH = new DataHandler(file);
pdfAttach.setDataHandler(pdfDH);
```

The `DataHandler` class, in Listing F–2, can be instantiated to represent just about any kind of data: an image, a PDF document, a DOM `Document` object—whatever you like. The `DataHandler` provides methods for reading and writing data streams, accessing the MIME type of the data, and creating a Java object that represents the data in a stream.

Listing F–2

The `javax.activation.DataHandler` *Class (Abbreviated)*

```
package javax.activation;
import java.io.*;
...
public class DataHandler implements java.awt.datatransfer.Transferable {
  ...
  public java.io.InputStream  getInputStream()  ...
  public java.io.OutputStream getOutputStream() ...
  public void writeTo(java.io.OutputStream os) ...
  public String getContentType() ...
  public Object getContent() ...
  public DataSource getDataSource() ...
  ...
}
```

- The **`getInputStream()`** method provides access to the data contained by the `DataHandler` as an `InputStream`, which you can use to read the data.
- The **`getOutputStream()`** provides access to the data contained by the `Data Handler` via an `OutputStream`, which you can use to overwrite the data.
- The **`writeTo()`** method writes the data contained by the `DataHandler` to any output stream that you provide.
- The **`getContentType()`** method returns the MIME content-type, such as `image/jpeg`, `application/pdf`, or `text/xml`, of the data contained by the `DataHandler`.
- The **`getContent()`** method returns an object that represents the data contained by the `DataHandler`. If the data is an image, for example, it might return a `java.awt.Image` object.

- The **getDataSource()** method returns a `javax.activation.DataSource` object, which is discussed in detail later.

`DataHandler` also defines many other methods related to GUI operations that use the JAF `CommandInfo` object, which identifies viewers, editors, and printers, and transfers data to AWT components. These are not important to SAAJ, however, because it's not a GUI tool, and won't be covered in this overview of JAF.

`DataHandler` follows the Delegation pattern, providing a consistent interface to data available from many different sources and in many different formats. The term "Delegation" is taken from the lexicon of basic design patterns, and refers to an object that delegates some or all of its work to other objects.[1] When you invoke a method of a `DataHandler`, a completely different and hidden object may do the work. `DataHandler` defines three constructors, shown in Listing F–3. The type of object to which it delegates tasks depends largely on the constructor used.

Listing F–3

Constructors for the `javax.activation.DataHandler` *Class (Abbreviated)*

```
package javax.activation;

public class DataHandler ...

    public DataHandler(DataSource ds) ...
    public DataHandler(Object obj, String mimeType) ...
    public DataHandler(java.net.URL url) ...
    ...
}
```

When `DataHandler` is instantiated using the constructor that expects an `Object` and a `String` identifying a MIME type, it will dynamically discover and use a specialized content handler, which is an implementation of the class `javax.activation.DataContentHandler`. If it's instantiated with either of the other two constructors, the `DataHandler` will delegate to a subtype of the `javax.activation.DataSource` interface. The difference between these delegates is significant, so understanding their strengths and weaknesses is important. The next two sections describe the `DataContentHandler` class and the `DataSource` interface in detail.

F.1.2 DataContentHandler

An implementation of the `DataContentHandler` interface is used to convert a Java object into a stream of data, or vice versa. Each different combination of Java object

[1] Erich Gamma, et al. *Design Patterns: Elements of Reusable Object-Oriented Software.* Reading, MA: Addison-Wesley, 1995, p. 20.

type and data stream type has its own DataContentHandler type (called a DCH for short). For example, if you need to convert java.awt.Image objects into JPEG data streams, you configure your system to use a DCH designed specifically for that purpose. Similarly, DCHs can be used to convert a DOM Document object into a character stream, a serializable Java object into a Java standard serialized stream, and so on. The possibilities are limitless.

When DataHandler is instantiated using the DataHandler(Object obj, String mimeType) constructor, it will delegate exclusively to one specialized type of DCH. Which type depends on the MIME type associated with the DataHandler when it was created. In the following code snippet, the data contained by a DataHandler that handles the image/jpeg MIME type is written to a stream. In order for this to work, the DataHandler must discover and delegate to a DCH that can handle Image type objects and JPEG data.

```
java.awt.Image image = …; // get image from somewhere
DataHandler dataHandler = new DataHandler( image, "image/jpeg" );
FileOutputStream outStream = FileOutputStream( "image.jpg" );
dataHandler.writeTo( outStream );
```

The DataHandler discovers the type of DCH it will use from a registry called a mailcap file. (Vendors can implement registries in other ways, but mailcap is the default.) A mailcap file maps MIME types to DCHs and other components. The mailcap file format is defined by RFC 1524, which specifies a generic format for associating MIME content-types with specific applications.[2] RFC 1524 has been around since 1993—before the Java platform was released—but it's well understood and flexible, so it was adopted for use in JAF. Because JAF is a Java API, the only kinds of entries it can understand in a mailcap file are those that pertain to Java types, so JAF defines a standard naming system to identify JAF DCHs and other types of components in a mailcap file. For example, Listing F–4 shows two entries in a mailcap file that map DCHs provided by the SAAJ reference implementation to their respective MIME types.

Listing F–4

A mailcap *File*

```
image/jpeg; ; x-java-content-handler=
com.sun.xml.messaging.saaj.soap.JpegDataContentHandler

text/xml; ; x-java-content-handler=
com.sun.xml.messaging.saaj.soap.XmlDataContentHandler
```

[2] Borenstein and Bellcore, *RFC 1524: A User Agent Configuration Mechanism for Multimedia Mail Format Information* (1993). Available at http://www.ietf.org/rfc/rfc1524.txt.

Each entry in a mailcap file appears as a single line (this book is not wide enough to display a whole line), and each new line designates a new mapping. An entry starts with the MIME type, followed by name-value pairs associating an application with a command. JAF defines several standard commands, such as x-java-view, x-java-print, x-java-edit, and x-java-content-handler. We are concerned with the x-java-content-handler command here, and not the GUI-related commands for viewing, editing, and printing.

The JAF framework will use a mailcap file located anywhere in the classpath, and will usually be able to use the ones in the java.home/lib directory or in the "users home" directory. The best place to put the mailcap file is in the META-INF subdirectory of the JAR file that contains the DCH class files. If the DCH's JAR file is included in the classpath, the mailcap will be found and its entries registered with JAF. The mailcap file should always be named mailcap with no extension. You can have as many mailcap files as you wish.[3]

The default behavior is for DataHandler to use the MailcapCommandMap class to load mailcap files from the classpath. When trying to find a DCH, it builds a list of mailcap files, and checks them in the order found. For JAF 1.0.2 (where the behavior was extended slightly to find all mailcap files), the mailcap list order is:

1. user.home/mailcap
2. java.home/lib/mailcap
3. META-INF/mailcap
4. /META-INF/mailcap.default

When looking for a content-type, the DataHandler traverses this list in order, and uses the first mailcap file that has a mapping for the desired MIME type to create the DCH. When you're adding your own DCH to override the behavior of a DCH included with some other API, such as JavaMail, it's vital to understand where it will appear in the above order—especially with the classpath ordering of the META-INF/mailcap case. A problem occurs when JavaMail is in the classpath, for example, because it defines the following mappings:

```
text/plain;;    x-java-content-handler=com.sun.mail.handlers.text_plain
text/html;;     x-java-content-handler=com.sun.mail.handlers.text_html
text/xml;;      x-java-content-handler=com.sun.mail.handlers.text_xml
image/gif;;     x-java-content-handler=com.sun.mail.handlers.image_gif
image/jpeg;;    x-java-content-handler=com.sun.mail.handlers.image_jpeg
multipart/*;;   x-java-content-handler=com.sun.mail.handlers.multipart_mixed
```

Each of these MIME types also has a mapping in SAAJ/JAX-RPC. If you want to use the mailcap files that come with a specific SAAJ/JAX-RPC implementation, you have to make sure that they are found before the JavaMail mailcap files. This

[3] Each mailcap file must be in a different directory, because you can't store two files with the same name in a single directory.

is tricky business that can cause you some real headaches if `mailcap` files are not set up properly.

> ***Another approach to mapping MIME types to DCHs, which avoids the use of*** `mailcap` ***files, is to implement a custom*** `DataContentHandlerFactory`. ***There is a static reference to this type in the*** `DataHandler` ***class that is consulted before the*** `mailcap` ***files are checked, provided you set it programmatically. A big drawback of this approach is that the factory may be set only once in a VM process.***

Once the mapping is discovered and the DCH type appropriate to the MIME type is instantiated, the `DataHandler` delegates to the DCH object. For example, the code snippet below creates a `DataHandler` instantiated with a MIME type of `image/jpeg`, and the `writeTo()` call should trigger the instantiation of a `DataContentHandler` for that MIME type.

```
java.awt.Image image = … get image from somewhere
DataHandler dataHandler = new DataHandler( image, "image/jpeg");
FileOutputStream outStream = FileOutputStream( "image.jpg" );
dataHandler.writeTo( outStream );
```

For the `writeTo()` method to achieve that result, a DCH must exist that is mapped to the `image/jpeg` MIME type and is able to convert an `Image` object into a data stream. Figure F–1 illustrates the steps that a `DataHandler` will go through to locate and delegate to a DCH.

The first time a `DataHandler` needs to delegate to a DCH, it will request an instance of the proper DCH from the JAF framework. The JAF framework checks the

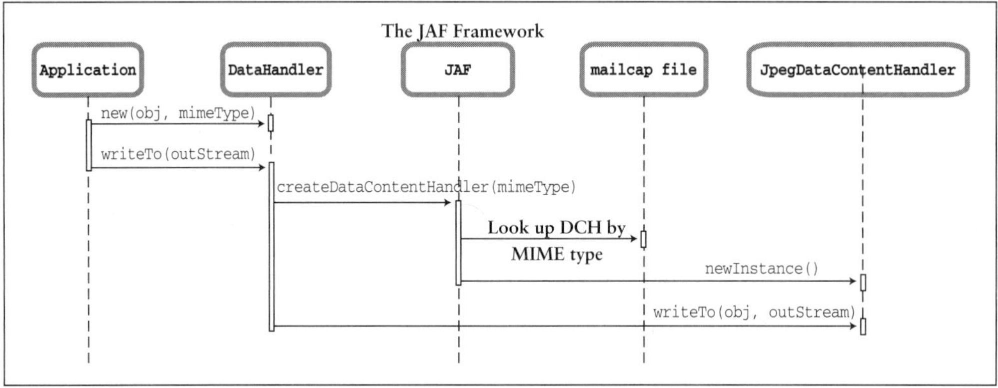

Figure F–1 Sequence Diagram of `DataHandler` Delegation to `DataContentHandler`

mailcap registry to see if a DCH type is registered for the DataHandler object's MIME type. If it finds such a DCH type, the JAF creates an instance of that type and returns it to the DataHandler, which will use the DCH as its delegate. If no DCH is associated with the MIME type, the JAF throws an exception. The DataHandler object will not attempt to find a DCH until it's actually necessary (lazily), which is why it doesn't throw an exception as soon as it's created with a MIME type that isn't mapped to a DCH.

An important thing to remember is that DCHs are limited to the types of Java objects they are programmed to handle. For example, the reference implementation of SAAJ, which is written by Sun Microsystems, has two DCHs for processing image data: GifDataContentHandler for the image/gif MIME type, and JpegDataContentHandler for the image/jpeg MIME type. Although JpegDataContentHandler works fine, the GifDataContentHandler is practically useless. It cannot convert any type of object (not even java.awt.Image) into a data stream. Of course, this DCH is part of the reference implementation, so it's not so bad that it's limited, but it's an excellent illustration of an important point: The types of Java objects you can attach to a SOAP message are limited by the types of DCHs you have available. In other words, you cannot arbitrarily attach Java objects to SAAJ messages. You have to be sure that there is a DCH mapped to that MIME type and that the DCH will be able to handle that type of Java object. This information can be obtained only by examining the mailcap files to discover which DCHs are registered, and then examining the documentation of the DCHs themselves to see what type of Java objects they support. This research takes time, but it can save you a lot of headaches.

If the MIME type or Java object you want to attach to SOAP messages is not supported, you can develop a new DCH and register it in a mailcap file. That may be a trivial effort or it may be a lot of work, depending on what you want to attach. Fortunately, DCHs are not your only option.

F.1.3 DataSource

In addition to the DataContentHandler type, JAF defines the interface type javax.activation.DataSource, which can be very useful when attaching data derived from some resource like a file or a Web server. When a DataHandler is created using a DataSource object, the DataHandler will not depend on the presence of a DCH to function properly—the DataSource will possess all the functionality necessary to perform the delegated operations. A DataHandler will use a DataSource instead of a DCH when it is constructed with a DataSource or URL parameter. The following recapituation of Listing F–3 highlights these two constructors.

```
package javax.activation;

public class DataHandler …
```

```
    public DataHandler(DataSource ds) ...
    public DataHandler(java.net.URL url) ...
    public DataHandler(java.lang.Object obj, java.lang.String mimeType) ...
...
}
```

> ***Careful—don't use a*** `DataSource` ***as the*** `obj` ***parameter in the constructor*** `DataHandler(java.lang.Object obj, java.lang.String mime Type)`***. The*** `DataHandler` ***will not recognize the*** `DataSource` ***and will attempt to delegate operations to a DCH—which will cause the Data Handler to throw an exception.***

The `DataSource` interface follows the Adapter design pattern.[4] It provides a single abstraction for any kind of data source. The `DataSource` interface defines methods for accessing an `InputStream`, an `OutputStream`, the MIME type, and the name of the underlying source of data. It's defined as shown in Listing F–5.

Listing F–5

The `javax.activation.DataSource` *Interface*

```
package javax.activation;
import java.io.InputStream;
import java.io.OutputStream
import java.io.IOException;

public interface DataSource {

    public String getName();
    public String getContentType();
    public InputStream getInputStream() throws IOException;
    public OutputStream getOutputStream() throws IOException;

}
```

You may have noticed that the methods defined in `DataSource` have the same signatures as some of the methods defined in `DataHandler`. When a `DataHandler` is created with a `DataSource` object, it will delegate to the `DataSource` the methods they have in common.

JAF defines two standard `DataSource` objects: `javax.activation.File DataSource` and `javax.activation.URLDataSource`. As its name suggests, `FileDataSource` provides access to a file using its `getInputStream()` and `getOutputStream()` methods, and allows you to read from and write to that file.

[4] Erich Gamma, et al. *Design Patterns: Elements of Reusable Object-Oriented Software.* Reading, MA: Addison-Wesley, 1995, p. 139.

Under the covers, the `FileDataSource` uses `java.io.FileInputStream` and `java.io.FileOutputStream` to read and write. The following snippet shows you how to create a `DataHandler` that will use a `FileDataSource`.

```
// Create a FileDataSource that represents a JPEG file
FileDataSource jpegSource = new FileDataSource("someimage.jpeg");

// Create a DataHandler that delegates to the FileDataSource
DataHandler dataHandler = new DataHandler( jpegSource );
```

The `URLDataSource` represents a file at some URL. Under the covers the `URLDataSource` uses a `java.net.HttpURLConnection` if the file is at some distant Internet address, or a `java.net.JarURLConnection` if the URL points to a local JAR file, or any other implementation of `URLConnection`. The `HttpURLConnection` employs the HTTP protocol to read and write files on an HTTP Web server. The `HttpURLConnection.getOutputStream()` method will throw an exception, so this method won't work if you are accessing a URL at a distant Web server—but it does work with JAR files. The following shows how to create a `DataHandler` that will use a `URLDataSource` object.

```
// Create a URL that points to a remote PDF document
URL url = new URL("http://www.Monson-Haefel.com/jwsbook/document.pdf")

// Create a DataHandler that delegates to the URLDataSource
URLDataSource dataSource = new URLDataSource( url );
DataHandler pdfHandler = new DataHandler( dataSource );
```

The URL constructor uses a `URLDataSource` under the covers, so it's the same as calling the `DataHandler` class's `DataSource` constructor with the `URLDataSource` parameter. The following code snippet also results in a `DataHandler` that will use a `URLDataSource`.

```
// Create a URL that points to a remote PDF document
URL url = new URL("http://www.Monson-Haefel.com/jwsbook/document.pdf")

// Create a DataHandler that delegates to the URLDataSource
DataHandler pdfHandler = new DataHandler( url );
```

Some `DataSource` implementations are designed to discover their MIME types dynamically. The `FileDataSource`, for example, discovers its MIME type using the MIME-type registry. The default MIME-type registry in JAF is the `mimetypes.`

default file, which is included in the JAF binary JAR file. You can augment this registry with your own mime.types file, which should be stored in the same kinds of locations you'd place mailcap files (see Section F.1.2). The mime.types and mimetypes.default files map file extensions to MIME types. Listing F–6 shows the mimetypes.default file that is included with JAF.

Listing F–6

The mimetypes.default *File*

```
text/html                  html htm HTML HTM
text/plain                 txt text TXT TEXT
image/gif                  gif GIF
image/ief                  ief
image/jpeg                 jpeg jpg jpe JPG
image/tiff                 tiff tif
image/x-xwindowdump        xwd
application/postscript     ai eps ps
application/rtf            rtf
application/x-tex          tex
application/x-texinfo      texinfo texi
application/x-troff        t                    tr roff
audio/basic                au
audio/midi                 midi mid
audio/x-aifc               aifc
audio/x-aiff               aif aiff
audio/x-mpeg               mpeg mpg
audio/x-wav                wav
video/mpeg                 mpeg mpg mpe
video/quicktime            qt mov
video/x-msvideo            avi
```

Because the mimetypes.default file is included in the standard JAF binary JAR file, all these MIME-type/file-extension mappings are available by default. Each line in the MIME-type registry represents a different MIME-type/file-extension mapping. If a given file extension doesn't have a matching MIME type, then the default MIME type application/octet-stream is used.

In the next section, you will learn how to apply what you have learned about JAF to the task of creating attachments in SAAJ. As you will quickly discover, having a good understanding of DataHandler, DataContentHandler, and DataSource types will be indispensable to creating SOAP Messages with Attachments using SAAJ.

F.2 SAAJ and JAF: `AttachmentPart`

Adding attachments to a SAAJ `SOAPMessage` object is done using an `AttachmentPart` object, which represents a MIME part—that is, an attachment in an SwA message. The `AttachmentPart` provides methods for manipulating the headers, as well as the raw data content of a MIME part. `AttachmentPart` objects are contained by the `SOAPMessage` and are siblings of the `SOAPPart` object, which models the root MIME part (the SOAP document) of the SwA message.

In Listing F–7, `SaajExample_F1` creates an SwA that has two attachments: a JPEG image and a PDF document. The SwA generated by `SaajExample_F1` is incomplete at this point. As the section progresses, I will fill in the missing pieces.

Listing F–7

Creating a Simple SwA Message with SAAJ

```
package com.jwsbook.saaj;
import javax.xml.soap.*;
import java.awt.Image;
import java.awt.Toolkit;
import java.io.FileOutputStream;
import javax.activation.FileDataSource;
import javax.activation.DataHandler;

public class SaajExample_F1 {
  public static void main(String [] args) throws Exception {
    // Create SOAPMessage
    MessageFactory mf = MessageFactory.newInstance();
    SOAPMessage message = mf.createMessage();

    // Attach java.awt.Image object to SOAP message.
    Image image = Toolkit.getDefaultToolkit().createImage("cover.jpg");
    AttachmentPart jpegAttach = message.createAttachmentPart();
    jpegAttach.setContent( image ,"image/jpeg");
    message.addAttachmentPart(jpegAttach);

    // Attach PDF FileDataSource to SOAP message
    FileDataSource file = new FileDataSource("manuscript.pdf");
    DataHandler pdfDH = new DataHandler(file);
    AttachmentPart pdfAttach = message.createAttachmentPart();
    pdfAttach.setDataHandler(pdfDH);
    message.addAttachmentPart(pdfAttach);

    // Write SOAPMessage to file
```

```
            FileOutputStream fos = new FileOutputStream("SaajExample_F1.out");
            message.writeTo(fos);
            fos.close();
        }
    }
```

Executing `SaajExample_F1` produces a file that contains the MIME message, including the default SOAP document as well as the JPEG and PDF MIME parts. An abbreviated version of the output file, `SaajExample_F1.out`, is shown in Listing F–8.

Listing F–8

The Output of `SaajExample_F1` *(Abbreviated)*

```
------=_Part_0_14746332.1029863145115
Content-Type: text/xml

<soap:Envelope
    xmlns:soap="http://schemas.xmlsoap.org/soap/envelope/">
    <soap:Header/>
    <soap:Body/>
</soap:Envelope>
------=_Part_0_14746332.1029863145115
Content-Type: image/jpeg

ÿØÿà ÔJ+ñ á Ëïør‡ü C_‘Ñû# á-_ ÿ +ëüŒ¿à¥^_—ÃÏø(qÛø§ìj( ò£â-ìmû@|X´ø_¨xËâwÃh_#~Ô-
...
°_ÁŸÙâ÷‰|;£kÚfo_sR_î»ñãVøÓñö _Æ¯qâgÔ‡ÄHÿ h© __ƒã rvNRË§&›N_|_é~_É·tÏÂ¸_,¥’Oë
------=_Part_0_14746332.1029863145115
Content-Type: application/octet-stream

%PDF-1.3
...
%%EOF

------=_Part_0_14746332.1029863145115--
```

If you compare this SwA message to the one at the beginning of this Appendix, you'll notice some things are missing, like the `Content-Transfer-Encoding` and `Content-Id` MIME headers. In addition, the SOAP document itself is devoid of any meaningful content; it's just a skeleton. Later we'll fix these problems, but for now we want to focus on how attachments are added to the `SOAPMessage` object.

To run `SaajExample_F1` and the rest of the examples in this book, you'll need to have a J2EE platform installed, the proper classpaths set up, and supporting Web services deployed.

F.2.1 Data Objects

SaajExample_F1 (Listing F–7) starts out by creating a SOAPMessage and then proceeds to add two attachments: a JPEG image and a PDF document. To create an attachment, you'll first need an object that represents the data you want to attach—we can refer to this object generically as the **data object.** The JPEG attachment uses an Image object, while the PDF attachment uses a FileDataSource as shown in this snippet from SaajExample_F1.

```
// Attach with java.awt.Image object to the SOAP message
Image image = Toolkit.getDefaultToolkit().createImage("cover.jpg");
...

// Attach with PDF FileDataSource to SOAP message
FileDataSource file = new FileDataSource("manuscript.pdf");
...
```

Image and FileDataSource are very different kinds of data objects, which illustrates the variety of types you can use to create attachments. As you will soon see, however, this variety depends largely on the types of DataContentHandler and DataSource available.

F.2.2 The createAttachmentPart() Method

You create an AttachmentPart using the SOAPMessage.createAttachmentPart() method. This method creates an empty, disconnected AttachmentPart with no data or MIME type. Once an empty AttachmentPart is created, its content must be set explicitly using either the setContent() or setDataHandler() method, as shown in this snippet from SaajExample_F1 (Listing F–7).

```
// Attach java.awt.Image object to SOAP message
Image image = Toolkit.getDefaultToolkit().createImage("cover.jpg");
AttachmentPart jpegAttach = message.createAttachmentPart();
jpegAttach.setContent( image ,"image/jpeg");
message.addAttachmentPart(jpegAttach);

// Attach PDF FileDataSource to SOAP message
FileDataSource file = new FileDataSource("manuscript.pdf");
DataHandler pdfDH = new DataHandler(file);
AttachmentPart pdfAttach = message.createAttachmentPart();
pdfAttach.setDataHandler(pdfDH);
message.addAttachmentPart(pdfAttach);
```

The SOAPMessage class also provides two more createAttachmentPart() methods, each of which consolidates the operations of creating the Attachment

Part and setting the data object in one operation. The following code snippet shows how these alternative createAttachmentPart() methods might have been used in SaajExample_F1.

```
// Attach java.awt.Image object to SOAP message
Image image = Toolkit.getDefaultToolkit().createImage("cover.jpg");
AttachmentPart jpegAttach = message.createAttachmentPart(image ,"image/jpeg");
message.addAttachmentPart(jpegAttach);

// Attach with PDF FileDataSource to SOAP message
FileDataSource file = new FileDataSource("manuscript.pdf");
DataHandler pdfDH = new DataHandler(file);
AttachmentPart pdfAttach = message.createAttachmentPart(pdfDH);
message.addAttachmentPart(pdfAttach);
```

F.2.3 The setContent() and setDataHandler() Methods

There are two methods for adding data objects and MIME types to an empty AttachmentPart. You can use the AttachmentPart.setContent() or the AttachmentPart.setDataHandler() method. SaajExample_F1 uses both methods, as illustrated in the following snippet from Listing F–7.

```
AttachmentPart jpegAttach = message.createAttachmentPart();
jpegAttach.setContent(image ,"image/jpeg");
...
AttachmentPart pdfAttach = message.createAttachmentPart();
DataHandler pdfDH = new DataHandler(file);
pdfAttach.setDataHandler(pdfDH);
```

The setDataHandler() and setContent() methods accomplish exactly the same result. Under the covers, the setContent() method actually creates a new DataHandler object and then calls its own setDataHandler() method. For example, Listing F–9 shows an implementation of AttachmentPart by a fictitious vendor, XYZ Corporation, that represents the most likely implementation of these methods by a vendor.

Listing F–9

A Hypothetical AttachmentPart *Implementation*

```
package com.xyz.saaj;

import javax.xml.soap.*;
import javax.activation.DataHandler;
```

```
/*
 This is a hypothetical example of a vendor's implementation of
 AttachmentPart.

 It illustrates that the most likely implementation of the setContent and
 getContent methods is to reuse the setDataHandler and getDataHandler methods.
*/
public class XyzAttachmentPart implements javax.xml.soap.AttachmentPart{

    DataHandler dataHandler;

    public DataHandler getDataHandler() throws SOAPException {
        return dataHandler;
    }

    public void setDataHandler(DataHandler dh)
    throws java.lang.IllegalArgumentException{
        dataHandler = dh;
    }

    public Object getContent() throws SOAPException {
        try{
            return this.getDataHandler().getContent();
        }catch (IOException ex){
            throw new SOAPException(ex);
        }
    }

    public void setContent(Object object, String mimeType)
    throws java.lang.IllegalArgumentException{
        DataHandler dh = new DataHandler(object, mimeType);
        this.setDataHandler(dh);
    }

    ...
}
```

As this example illustrates, both `setDataHandler()` and `setContent()` have corresponding get methods. `setContent()` and `getContent()` are more convenient to use in some cases because they don't require that you work directly with a `DataHandler` object. In most cases they save you a couple of lines of code. Of course, if your data is contained in a `DataSource` object, you'll have to use the `setDataHandler()` method because the `setContent()` method works only with simple data objects like `java.awt.Image`. Never pass a `DataSource` or `DataHandler` object into the `setContent()` method.

F.2.4 The `getContent()` Method

As you can see in Listing F–9, `AttachmentPart.getContent()` delegates its work to the underlying `DataHandler` object, which will attempt to delegate the call to a `DataContentHandler` object. If the `DataHandler` was constructed with a data object, then it will delegate to a DCH—provided it can find a match in the `mailcap` registry; if it can't locate a DCH, it will throw an exception. If the `DataHandler` was constructed with a `DataSource` object, it will first attempt to delegate the `getContent()` method to a DCH; if it can't find a DCH, it will return an `InputStream` obtained from the `DataSource`. Interestingly, the `DataHandler` always attempts to delegate to a DCH first, even if it was created using a `DataSource`.

This seemingly minor point is quite important. It illustrates the purpose of the `getContent()` method, which is to return a Java object that represents the attachment. The `InputStream` of the `DataSource` is returned only as a last resort. For example, if when using the SAAJ reference implementation you create an `AttachmentPart` using a `FileDataSource` based on a JPEG file, and then call `AttachmentPart.getContent()`, the method returns a `java.awt.image.BufferedImage` object (a subtype of `java.awt.Image`). Although the attachment is created with a `DataSource`, a DCH found in the `mailcap` file is used to generate a Java object for the JPEG data. The following snippet shows how the JPEG is added to an `AttachmentPart` as a `FileDataSource`, and subsequently accessed as an `Image` object.

```
FileDataSource file = new FileDataSource("cover.jpg");
DataHandler jpegDH = new DataHandler(file);
AttachmentPart jpegAttach = message.createAttachmentPart(jpegDH);
...
Image image = (Image)jpegAttach.getContent();
```

The type of object returned from a DCH will depend on how that DCH is coded, but SAAJ specifies a set of return types for five specific MIME types that must be supported by a JAX-RPC-compliant implantation of SAAJ. Because you are likely to use SAAJ in combination with JAX-RPC, this requirement is important. Your vendor may support additional MIME types; check your vendor's documentation for details. Table F–1 shows five MIME types and their corresponding Java types.

Appendix G provides a more detailed explanation of each of these mappings.

Notice that the `MimeMultipart` class is part of the JavaMail API, so JavaMail will be in the classpath, with its `mailcap` file—which could cause problems when you add your own `mailcap` file—as I described in Section F.1.2.

Table F–1 Minimum `AttachmentPart.getContent()` Return Types

MIME Type	`AttachmentPart.getContent()` Return Type
`text/plain`	`java.lang.String`
`text/xml or application/xml`	`javax.xml.transform.Source`
`image/jpeg`	`java.awt.Image`
`image/gif`	`java.awt.Image`
`multipart/*`	`javax.mail.internet.MimeMultipart`

In essence the type returned by `AttachmentPart.getContent()` depends on the DCHs that are installed. One consequence is that developing portable SAAJ applications may force you to register the same DCHs on every platform you expect your SAAJ application to run on. You can, however, expect compliant J2EE Web Services platforms to support, at the very least, the MIME-to-Java mappings shown in Table F–1.

F.2.5 The MIME Header Methods

`AttachmentPart` offers a number of methods for adding, finding, removing, and replacing the MIME headers associated with an attachment. Listing F–10 shows these methods as they're declared in the `AttachmentPart` class. Most of these methods are self-describing and are also well documented by the SAAJ API documentation, so I'll discuss only a few of them here.

Listing F–10

The `javax.xml.soap.AttachmentPart` *Class (Abbreviated)*

```
package javax.xml.soap;
import java.util.Iterator;
...
public abstract class AttachmentPart {

    // Commonly used MIME header methods
    public String getContentId() ...
    public void setContentId(String contentId)
      throws IllegalArgumentException ...

    public String getContentLocation()...
    public void setContentLocation(String contentLocation)
      throws IllegalArgumentException ...

    public String getContentType() ...
```

```
    public void setContentType(String contentType)
      throws IllegalArgumentException ...

    // Generic MIME header methods
    public abstract void addMimeHeader(String name,String value)
      throws IllegalArgumentException ...
    public abstract void setMimeHeader(String name,String value)
      throws IllegalArgumentException ...
    public abstract String[] getMimeHeader(String name) ...
    public abstract Iterator getAllMimeHeaders() ...
    public abstract Iterator getMatchingMimeHeaders(String[] names)...
    public abstract Iterator getNonMatchingMimeHeaders(String[] names) ...
    public abstract void removeAllMimeHeaders() ...
    public abstract void removeMimeHeader(String header) ...
    ...
}
```

Appendix E: SOAP Messages with Attachments explains that SwA employs the `Multipart /Related` MIME message style when packaging a SOAP document with its attachments. This means that it is the root MIME part, the SOAP document, that refers to the attachments in an SwA, using either `Content-Id` or `Content-Location` headers. As an example, let's take a closer look at the complete SwA message, shown in Listing F–11. The attachments are referred to by their `Content-Id` MIME headers, using `href` attributes in the SOAP document.

Listing F–11

A Sample SwA Message

```
------=_Part_0_8994558.1029754184304
Content-Type: text/xml
Content-Transfer-Encoding: 8bit
Content-Id: cid:submitBook_1@xyxcorp.com

<soap:Envelope
 xmlns:soap="http://schemas.xmlsoap.org/soap/envelope/">
   <soap:Body>
      <mh:submitBook xmlns:mh="http://www.Monson-Haefel.com/jwsbook/mh">
         <isbn>0596002262</isbn>
         <coverImage href="cid:submitBook_2@xyxcorp.com"/>
         <manuscript href="cid:submitBook_3@xyxcorp.com"/>
      </mh:submitBook>
   </soap:Body>
</soap:Envelope>
```

```
------=_Part_0_8994558.1029754184304
Content-Type: image/jpeg
Content-Transfer-Encoding: binary
Content-Id: submitBook_2@xyxcorp.com

ÿØÿà ÔJ+ñ á Ëïør‡ü C_'Ñû# á-_ ÿ +ëüŒ¿à¥^_—ÃÏø(qÛø§ìj( ò£âìmû@|X´ø_¨xËâwÃh_#~Ô-
…
º_ÁŸÙâ÷‰|;£kÚfo_sR_î»ñãVøÓñö _Æ¯qâgÔ‡ÄHÿ h© __ƒã rvNRË§&>N_|_é~_É·tÏÂ¸_,¥'Oë
------=_Part_0_8994558.1029754184304
Content-Type: application/pdf
Content-Transfer-Encoding: binary
Content-Id:submitBook3@xyxcorp.com

%PDF-1.3
…
%%EOF

------=_Part_0_8994558.1029754184304--
```

The SAAJ reference implementation doesn't create `Content-Id` headers automatically; you must add them manually. In addition, the developer can add other MIME headers, such as the `Content-Transfer-Encoding`, which tells us the format of the data (such as binary or base64). You can also change headers. For example, when `SaajExample_F1` (Listing F–7) generates its output, it sets the PDF attachment with a `Content-Type` of `"application/octet-stream"`, because no MIME type is associated with the `.pdf` extension in the `mimetypes.default` file. You can create a `mime.types` file with an entry for the `.pdf` extension, or you can change it manually, as `SaajExample_F2` does in Listing F–12, using one of the MIME header methods.

`SaajExample_F2` modifies `SaajExample_F1` by employing methods for setting the `Content-Id` and the `Content-Transfer-Encoding`, and modifying the `Content-Type` header of the PDF attachment. This example also adds a `SOAPPart` with a complete SOAP message that refers to the attachments by way of their `Content-Id` headers.

Listing F–12

Creating a Complete SwA Message

```java
package com.jwsbook.saaj;
import javax.xml.soap.*;
import java.awt.Image;
import java.awt.Toolkit;
import java.io.FileInputStream;
```

```
import java.io.FileOutputStream;
import javax.activation.FileDataSource;
import javax.activation.DataHandler;
import javax.xml.transform.stream.StreamSource;

public class SaajExample_F2 {
  public static void main(String [] args) throws Exception {
    // Create SOAPMessage
    MessageFactory mf = MessageFactory.newInstance();
    SOAPMessage message = mf.createMessage();

    // Create the SOAPPart
    createSOAPPart(message);

    // Attach with java.awt.Image object to the SOAP message
    Image image = Toolkit.getDefaultToolkit().createImage("cover.jpg");
    AttachmentPart jpegAttach =
                message.createAttachmentPart(image ,"image/jpeg");
    jpegAttach.addMimeHeader("Content-Transfer-Encoding","binary");
    jpegAttach.setContentId("submitBook_2@xyxcorp.com");
    message.addAttachmentPart(jpegAttach);

    // Attach with PDF FileDataSource to SOAP message
    FileDataSource file = new FileDataSource("manuscript.pdf");
    DataHandler pdfDH = new DataHandler(file);
    AttachmentPart pdfAttach = message.createAttachmentPart(pdfDH);
    pdfAttach.addMimeHeader("Content-Transfer-Encoding","binary");
    pdfAttach.setContentId("submitBook_3@xyxcorp.com");
    pdfAttach.setContentType("application/pdf");
    message.addAttachmentPart(pdfAttach);

    // Write SOAPMessage to file
    FileOutputStream fos = new FileOutputStream("SaajExample_F2.out");
    message.writeTo(fos);
    fos.close();
  }

  public static void createSOAPPart(SOAPMessage message)
  throws SOAPException, java.io.IOException {
      // implementation goes here
  }
}
```

The output of SaajExample_F2 will be similar to the output shown previously in Listing F–11.

Except for the implementation of the createSOAPPart() method, the example above is complete. The creation of the SOAPPart is very similar to that of the AttachmentPart. The next section will address the SOAPPart and show three different implementations of the createSOAPPart() method of SaajExample_F2.

F.3 The SOAPPart

A SOAPPart object represents the root MIME part of an SwA message, which is always a SOAP document. The SOAPPart class includes many of the same methods defined in AttachmentPart, but it doesn't implement the AttachmentPart interface, because the SOAPPart is more restrictive than the AttachmentPart. The SOAPPart is designed exclusively to handle SOAP documents (MIME type text/xml), and to provide a means for accessing the SOAPEnvelope and its children.

For example, in the AttachmentPart the setContent() and getContent() methods return the java.lang.Object type, so they can work with any kind of data object. The SOAPPart also defines setContent() and getContent() methods, but they set and get the javax.xml.transform.Source type instead. The Source type is the return type that JAX-RPC requires for the text/xml MIME type (see Table F–1), so it's the appropriate type for the SOAPPart object to set and get. Listing F–13 shows these method signatures in a partial listing of the SOAPPart class.

Listing F–13

The javax.xml.soap.SOAPPart *Class (Abbreviated)*

```
package javax.xml.soap;
import javax.xml.transform.Source;
...
public abstract class SOAPPart {

    public abstract void setContent(Source source)
      throws SOAPException ...

    public abstract Source getContent()
      throws SOAPException ...
    ...
}
```

SOAPPart is also more restrictive than the AttachmentPart with its Content-Type MIME header. Unlike the AttachmentPart, the SOAPPart doesn't define a setContentType() method, because this MIME header must be text/xml for a SOAP 1.1 document. Like AttachmentPart, SOAPPart does provide general-purpose MIME methods (that is, addMimeHeader(), setMimeHeader(), and removeMimeHeader()), but any attempt to change the Content-Type using one of these methods will result in an IllegalArgumentException.

For all its restrictions a SOAPPart does represent a MIME part, and as such it contains a content section (data) and MIME headers. You can populate the content section of a SOAPPart manually by creating a SOAPEnvelope, SOAPBody, and SOAP BodyElement, and so on. The SOAPMessage.getSOAPPart() method allows you to access the SOAP MIME part directly as shown in this snippet.

```
MessageFactory msgFactory = MessageFactory.newInstance();
SOAPMessage message = msgFactory.createMessage();
SOAPPart soap = message.getSOAPPart();
```

As an alternative, you can populate the content section with an existing SOAP document using a javax.xml.transform.Source type object, which is how SaajExample_F2 builds its SOAP message. It first reads a file containing a SOAP document using a StreamSource object (an implementation of Source) and then passes the StreamSource to the SOAPPart using the setContent() method. The following snippet is the implementation of the createSOAPPart() method, which was omitted from the previous listing of SaajExample_F2 (Listing F–12).

```
import java.io.FileInputStream;
import javax.xml.transform.stream.StreamSource;
...
public class SaajExample_F2 {
  ...
  public static void createSOAPPart(SOAPMessage message)
  throws SOAPException, java.io.IOException {
    SOAPPart soapPart = message.getSOAPPart();
    FileInputStream soapFile = new FileInputStream("soapwa.xml");
    StreamSource source = new StreamSource(soapFile);
    soapPart.setContent(source);
    soapPart.addMimeHeader("Content-Transfer-Encoding","8bit");
    soapPart.setContentId("submitBook_1@xyxcorp.com");
    soapFile.close();
  }
}
```

StreamSource is only one of three standard Source types (StreamSource, DOMSource, and SAXSource), that you can use to set the content of a SOAPPart. The Source type and its subtypes are members of the TrAX API, which is the standard Java API for XSLT.

F.3.1 XSLT

XSLT (Xtensible Stylesheet Language Transformation) is an XML technology that defines a grammar, called an XSLT stylesheet, and processing rules for mapping documents in one format to documents in some other format. For example, you might use XSLT to translate XML-RPC messages into SOAP, or DocBook into XHTML.[5] XSLT stylesheets rely heavily on another XML technology called XPath, which is a declarative language for describing elements in an XML document, something like SQL for XML (that's a loose analogy). The key point is that, using XSLT, you can convert one XML document into another XML document. While XSLT is very powerful and interesting in its own right, an in-depth discussion of it is outside the scope of this appendix. Fortunately, you can remain blissfully ignorant of XSLT without it hampering your use of SAAJ one bit.

F.3.2 TrAX

What we are interested in here are the `Source` types defined by TrAX (Transformation API for XML), which is the J2EE standard API for XSLT. TrAX is defined in the `javax.xml.transformation` package and its subpackages. One of the primary types defined by TrAX is `javax.xml.transform.Source`, which is not much more than an empty interface. The `Source` interface is used as an abstraction for an object that contains or has access to an XML document. In TrAX there are three standard implementations of the `Source` type:

1. `javax.xml.transform.stream.StreamSource`
2. `javax.xml.transform.dom.DOMSource`
3. `javax.xml.transform.sax.SAXSource`

The TrAX `Source` subtypes provide a convenient mechanism for embedding an XML SOAP document in a `SOAPPart`. It should be noted that the TrAX `Source` type doesn't provide any common methods for extracting the XML data from the `Source` object. Each implementation is completely different, which means the `SOAPPart` won't be able to handle arbitrary implementations of the `Source` type; it supports only the standard TrAX implementations: `StreamSource`, `DOMSource`, and `SAXSource`.

F.3.3 Using a `StreamSource`

You use a `StreamSource` when an XML document is accessible via some sort of data stream, specifically with `java.io.InputStream` and `java.io.Reader` types. `SaajExample_F2` uses a `FileInputStream`, a subtype of `InputStream`. It could just as easily have used the `FileReader` type, which is better at dealing with

[5] Elliotte Rusty Harold, *Processing XML with Java*. Boston: Addison-Wesley, 2002.

international character sets.[6] The following snippet shows how SaajExample_F2 could be implemented to use a FileReader instead of a FileInputStream.

```
import java.io.FileReader;
import javax.xml.transform.stream.StreamSource;
...
public static void createSOAPPart(SOAPMessage message)
throws SOAPException, java.io.IOException {
    SOAPPart soapPart = message.getSOAPPart();
    FileReader soapFile = new FileReader("soapwa.xml");
    StreamSource source = new StreamSource(soapFile);
    soapPart.setContent(source);
    soapPart.addMimeHeader("Content-Transfer-Encoding","8bit");
    soapPart.setContentId("submitBook_1@xyxcorp.com");
    soapFile.close();
}
```

Of course a file represents only one type of data stream; you can use StreamSource to read SOAP messages from network streams or JDBC or JMS or some other resource.

F.3.4 DOMSource

You use a DOMSource when the XML document is contained in a DOM Node object, specifically the org.w3c.dom.Node type, which is a part of the JAXP (Java API for XML Processing) family of technologies. If you work with DOM, a DOMSource is an excellent means to pass the SOAP document to the SOAPPart. In the following code snippet the createSOAPPart() method is modified to build a DOM Document (a subtype of Node) object from a file, then set the Document object as the content of the SOAPPart.

```
import javax.xml.transform.dom.DOMSource;
import org.w3c.dom.Document;
import javax.xml.parsers.DocumentBuilder;
import javax.xml.parsers.DocumentBuilderFactory;
...
public static void createSOAPPart(SOAPMessage message)
    throws SOAPException, java.io.IOException, org.xml.sax.SAXException,
        javax.xml.parsers.ParserConfigurationException {

    DocumentBuilderFactory factory = DocumentBuilderFactory.newInstance();
    DocumentBuilder builder = factory.newDocumentBuilder();
```

[6] Elliotte Rusty Harold, *Java I/O*. Beijing: O'Reilly & Associates, 1999.

```
    Document document = builder.parse("soapwa.xml");
    document.getChildNodes();
    DOMSource domSource = new DOMSource(document);

    SOAPPart soapPart = message.getSOAPPart();
    soapPart.setContent(domSource);
    soapPart.addMimeHeader("Content-Transfer-Encoding","8bit");
    soapPart.setContentId("submitBook_1@xyxcorp.com");
}
```

F.3.5 `SAXSource`

You can also fill the contents of a `SOAPPart` object from a SAX parser using a `SAXSource` as shown in the following snippet.

```
import javax.xml.transform.sax.SAXSource;
import org.xml.sax.InputSource;
import java.io.FileReader;
...
public static void createSOAPPart(SOAPMessage message)
throws SOAPException, java.io.IOException, org.xml.sax.SAXException {
    FileReader soapFile = new FileReader("soapwa.xml");
    InputSource stream = new InputSource(soapFile);
    SAXSource saxSource = new SAXSource(stream);

    SOAPPart soapPart = message.getSOAPPart();
    soapPart.setContent(saxSource);
    soapPart.addMimeHeader("Content-Transfer-Encoding","8bit");
    soapPart.setContentId("submitBook_1@xyxcorp.com");
}
```

F.4 The `SOAPEnvelope`

The `SOAPEnvelope` interface represents the root of the XML SOAP document. It includes methods for accessing or creating the `SOAPHeader` and `SOAPBody`. It also includes two methods for creating `Name` objects. Listing F–14 shows the complete definition of the `SOAPEnvelope` interface.

Listing F–14

The `javax.xml.soap.SOAPEnvelope` *Interface*

```
package javax.xml.soap;

public interface SOAPEnvelope extends SOAPElement {
```

```
    public SOAPBody getBody() throws SOAPException;
    public SOAPHeader getHeader() throws SOAPException;
    public SOAPBody addBody() throws SOAPException
    public SOAPHeader addHeader() throws SOAPException;
    public Name createName(String localName) throws SOAPException;
    public Name createName(String localName, String prefix, String uri)
    throws SOAPException;

}
```

SOAPEnvelope is a subtype of the SOAPElement interface, which is a subtype of the Node interface. The same is true of the other SAAJ types (SOAPBody, SOAPHeader, and so on) that represent elements of the SOAP document. The SOAPElement and Node interfaces are covered in Chapter 13.

F.4.1 The getHeader(), getBody(), addHeader(), and addBody() Methods

I noted in Chapter 13 that a new SOAPMessage already contains the framework of an XML SOAP document including the Envelope, Body, and Header elements. The getBody() and getHeader() methods of the SOAPEnvelope interface return SAAJ objects of type SOAPBody and SOAPHeader, which represent the empty Header and Body elements.

```
SOAPEnvelope envelope = soap.getEnvelope();
envelope.getHeader().detachNode();
...
SOAPBody body = envelope.getBody();
```

The call to getHeader() is chained to a detachNode() call, which effectively removes the Header element from the SOAP document—useful when header blocks are not used in the SOAP message. Calling the detachNode() method removes the empty Header element and creates a tighter SOAP document.

You can also add a new Body or Header element using the corresponding addBody() or addHeader() method, but you use them only if you have already removed the Body or Header element from the SOAP document; if you haven't, these methods will throw a SOAPException.

F.4.2 The createName() Method

The SOAPEnvelope also provides two factory methods for creating Name type objects. These behave the same as the createName() method defined in the SOAPFactory class discussed in Chapter 13. As you already know from Section 2.2: XML Namespaces, the name of an element or attribute dictates which XML namespace it belongs to. A Name object is simply an abstraction of an XML qualified name. For example, in Listing F–15 SaajExample_F3 shows how the SOAPEnvelope is used to create the getBookPrice and isbn elements in the GetBookQuote SOAP message.

Listing F–15

Creating and Using Name *Objects*

```
package com.jwsbook.saaj;
import javax.xml.soap.*;

public class SaajExample_F3 {
  public static void main(String [] args)
  throws SOAPException, java.io.IOException{

    MessageFactory msgFactory = MessageFactory.newInstance();
    SOAPMessage message = msgFactory.createMessage();
    SOAPPart part = message.getSOAPPart();
    SOAPEnvelope envelope = part.getEnvelope();

    Name getBookPrice_Name = envelope.createName("getBookPrice","mh",
                              "http://www.Monson-
Haefel.com/jwsbook/BookQuote");
    Name isbnName = envelope.createName("isbn");

    SOAPBody body = message.getBody();
    SOAPBodyElement getBookPrice_Element =
                    body.addBodyElement(getBookPrice_Name);
    getBookPrice_Element.addChildElement( isbnName );

    SaajOutputter.writeToScreen(message);
  }
}
```

F.5 Wrapping Up

Creating SwA messages is fairly easy with SAAJ, provided you have the right kinds of DCHs and DataSource objects. If you don't, then you'll need to change the types of attachments you use or find or develop DCHs or DataSource objects that fulfill your needs. Developing and registering a new DCH is not very complicated; all you do is implement the javax.activation.DataContentHandler interface, then register the implementation in a mailcap file. In many cases you may not need a DCH. For example, if you obtain data objects from files, you can use the `javax.activation.FileDataSource`, as `SaajExample_F1` and `SaajExample_F2` did with the PDF file, in Listings F–7 and F–12.

Although SAAJ can be used independently of JAX-RPC, in many cases they're used together. Use of SAAJ with JAX-RPC is covered in Chapter 14: Message Handlers.

Appendix G
JAX-RPC and SwA

Sending and receiving SOAP Messages with Attachments (SwA) using JAX-RPC is deceptively easy. I say "deceptively" because, like SAAJ, JAX-RPC depends on the Java Activation Framework (JAF) to handle the marshalling of attachments to and from SOAP messages, so sending and receiving attachments depends in large part on the types of `DataContentHandler` classes that your J2EE application server provides. This appendix will explain how JAX-RPC supports the SwA standard using JAF.

It's important to remember that the WS-I Basic Profile 1.0 does not endorse or support SwA—but you are likely to run into Web services that use SwA, which is why this appendix is here.

G.1 JAF Revisited: `DataContentHandler` and `DataSource` Types

Essentially there are two ways to support attachments in JAF: You can use `javax.activation.DataContentHandler` classes or `javax.activation.DataSource` classes. Each of these interfaces has its strengths and weaknesses. Generally `DataContentHandler` types are more convenient, because their operation is hidden, while the `DataSource` types are less user-friendly but easier to get working. The following provides a quick overview of the `DataContentHandler` and `DataSource` types and their strengths and weaknesses. For in-depth coverage of JAF, though, you should read Section F.1 of Appendix F: SAAJ Attachments.

Every subclass of `DataContentHandler` (that is, every DCH) is designed to convert a specific type of Java object to a stream, and a stream to a Java object, automatically. For example, you may have a DCH that can convert a `java.awt.Image` file into a JPEG or GIF encoded stream and vice versa. Using this type of DCH, you could easily convert an `Image` object into a stream of data to be carried as a MIME part in an SwA message, then on the receiving end use the same DCH to convert the stream of data in the MIME part back into an `Image` object. This bidirectional character makes DCHs very easy to use in many cases, because you can work with Java objects and not worry about data streams. The disadvantage of DCHs is that they are usually very limited in scope, with each one capable of converting a single type of object into a single type of data stream. In addition, J2EE application vendors often provide DCHs for just a few types. If you want to work with Java object types that do not have a corresponding DCH, you'll have to write your own DCH or find an alternative.

`DataSource` objects provide a nice alternative to DCHs. Unlike DCHs, `DataSource` objects deal only with streams of data. You use a `DataSource` to read a stream of data from some type of resource and write a stream of data to it. For example, JAF provides a `FileDataSource`, which allows the JAF framework to use a data stream to access and update data in a file. `DataSource` types tend to be more versatile because they focus on the stream rather than on a Java object type. Their disadvantage is that they are not as easy to work with, because you are dealing directly with a stream and not a Java object. If you read a JPEG file using a `FileDataSource`, you have to jump through some programmatic hoops to get an `Image` object out of it. Compare this effort to the convenience of DCHs, which convert data streams to objects and back again automatically.

G.2 A Simple Example

As usual, to generate a JAX-RPC stub we can use in an example, we'll need to start with a WSDL document. In WSDL, SOAP messages with attachments are described using the MIME and SOAP WSDL extensions, which are covered in Chapter 5: WSDL.

Monson-Haefel Books maintains a catalog of all the books that it distributes. Each catalog entry is indexed by the ISBN number and lists the title of the book, its wholesale price, a cover image, a short description, and so on. Publishers can submit new books to the catalog using a Web service. The Web service for submitting new books to the catalog is described by the WSDL document in Listing G–1.

Listing G–1

A WSDL Document That Defines MIME Attachments

```
<?xml version="1.0" encoding="UTF-8"?>
<definitions xmlns="http://schemas.xmlsoap.org/wsdl/"
    xmlns:wsdl="http://schemas.xmlsoap.org/wsdl/"
```

```
    xmlns:xsd="http://www.w3.org/2001/XMLSchema"
    xmlns:soap="http://schemas.xmlsoap.org/wsdl/soap/"
    xmlns:mime="http://schemas.xmlsoap.org/wsdl/mime/"
    xmlns:tns="http://www.Monson-Haefel.com/ed1/SubmitBook"
    targetNamespace="http://www.Monson-Haefel.com/ed1/SubmitBook">

  <message name="submission">
    <part name="title" type="xsd:string"/>
    <part name="price" type="xsd:float" />
    <part name="image" type="xsd:hexBinary"/>
  </message>
  <portType name="SubmitBook">
    <operation name="submit">
      <input message="tns:submission"/>
    </operation>
  </portType>
  <binding name="SubmitBookMimeBinding" type="tns:SubmitBook">
      <soap:binding style="document"
        transport="http://schemas.xmlsoap.org/soap/http"/>
      <operation name="submit">
        <soap:operation soapAction="" style="document"/>
        <input>
           <mime:multipartRelated>
               <mime:part>
                    <soap:body parts="title price" use="literal"
                         namespace=
                             "http://www.Monson-Haefel.com/ed1/SubmitBook"/>
               </mime:part>
               <mime:part>
                    <mime:content part="image" type="image/jpeg"/>
               </mime:part>
           </mime:multipartRelated>
        </input>
     </operation>
  </binding>
  <service name="SubmitBookService">
    <port name="SubmitBookPort" binding="tns:SubmitBookMimeBinding">
      <soap:address
       location="http://localhost:8080/1ed/SubmitBook"/>
    </port>
  </service>
</definitions>
```

This WSDL document defines One-Way, Document/Literal messaging with a MIME binding. (JAX-RPC also supports the use of MIME bindings with RPC/Encoded, and RPC/Literal messaging modes.) The MIME contents will have two parts: a SOAP part and a binary image part. Appendix E: SOAP Messages with Attachments explains that the first part of an SwA message is always a SOAP message. The MIME binding dictates which `part` definitions of the `input` message go with the SOAP message and which `part` definitions describe attachments. Specifically, the first `mime:part` element in a MIME binding usually contains a `soap:body` element, which lists the parts contained by the SOAP message. Any part not listed by the `soap:body` element is assumed to be a separate attachment (MIME part) and should be described in a subsequent `mime:part` element.

For example, the previous WSDL document lists the `title` and `price` parts in the `soap:body` element, but omits the `image` part. As shown in the following snippet from Listing G–1, the second `mime:part` definition defines the `image` part as an attachment of MIME type `image/jpeg`.

```
<mime:multipartRelated>
   <mime:part>
      <soap:body parts="title price" use="literal"
           namespace="http://www.Monson-Haefel.com/ed1/SubmitBook"/>
   </mime:part>
   <mime:part>
      <mime:content part="image" type="image/jpeg"/>
   </mime:part>
</mime:multipartRelated>
```

Based on this WSDL definition, a JAX-RPC compiler should generate an endpoint interface like the one in Listing G–2.

Listing G–2

The Endpoint Interface Generated from the WSDL Document in Listing G–1

```
public interface SubmitBook extends java.rmi.Remote {
  public void submit(String title, float price, java.awt.Image image)
   throws java.rmi.RemoteException;
}
```

The `SubmitBook` interface defines three parameters. The first two represent elements of the SOAP message, while the third represents the attachment. The JAX-RPC compiler automatically uses the `java.awt.Image` Java type to represent the image part because the `Image` type is normally associated with a MIME type of `image/jpeg`. The JAX-RPC specification requires that a JAX-RPC provider be able to map a MIME type of `image/jpeg` to the Java type `java.awt.Image`, among other standard mappings between MIME types and Java classes. These mappings are discussed in the next section.

The JAX-RPC compiler will also generate an endpoint stub. To use it, all you need to do is invoke the method with the proper parameters, as in Listing G–3, the `JaxRpcExample_G1` class.

Listing G–3

Using a Generated Stub with SOAP Attachments

```
package jwsed1.part5_jaxrpc;
import javax.naming.InitialContext;
import java.awt.Image;
import java.awt.Toolkit;

public class JaxRpcExample_G1 {
  public static void main(String [] args) throws Exception{
    InitialContext jndiContext = new InitialContext();

    SubmitBookService service = (SubmitBookService)
    jndiContext.lookup("java:comp/env/service/SubmitBookService");

    SubmitBook sb_stub = service.getSubmitBookPort();

    Image image = Toolkit.getDefaultToolkit().createImage("image.jpg");

    sb_stub.submit("J2EE Web Services", 29.99f, image);
  }
}
```

`JaxRpcExample_G1` creates the `Image` object from a JPEG file and passes it to the `SubmitBook.submit()` method just like any other parameter. At runtime the JAX-RPC endpoint stub will use JAF to convert the `Image` object into a JPEG encoded stream and place it in the attachment of the SwA message. The SwA message will look something like Listing G–4 (the HTTP POST message is included):

Listing G–4

The SwA Message Generated by `JaxRpcExample_8` *(Listing G–3)*

```
POST /1ed/SubmitBook HTTP/1.0
Content-Type: multipart/related; type="text/xml";
              start="<submitBook_1@xyxcorp.com>";
              boundary="-----------938302838kd203"
Host: Monson-Haefel.com
```

```
SOAPAction: ""
Content-Length: 41195


-----------938302838kd203
Content-Type: text/xml; charset=UTF-8
Content-Transfer-Encoding: 8bit
Content-Id: <submitBook_1@xyxcorp.com>

<?xml version="1.0" encoding="UTF-8"?>
<env:Envelope
  xmlns:env="http://schemas.xmlsoap.org/soap/envelope/"
  xmlns:xsd="http://www.w3.org/2001/XMLSchema"
  xmlns:xsi="http://www.w3.org/2001/XMLSchema-instance"
  xmlns:mh="http://www.Monson-Haefel.com/ed1/SubmitBook">
 <env:Body>
  <mh:submit>
   <title xsi:type="xsd:string">J2EE Web Services</title>
   <price xsi:type="xsd:float">24.95</price>
   <image href="cid:submitBook_2@xyxcorp.com"/>
  </mh:submit>
 </env:Body>
</env:Envelope>
-----------938302838kd203
Content-Type: image/jpeg
Content-Transfer-Encoding: binary
Content-Id: <submitBook_2@xyxcorp.com>

ÿØÿàa"ûZ)·ºËÙŒeC"Ú?R? …
-----------938302838kd203--
```

As you can see, JAX-RPC makes support for SwA messages pretty easy. You simply treat the attachment as a Java object and pass it to the method just like any other parameter. The next couple of sections will fill in some details regarding the use of JAX-RPC for SwA messages, specifically the standard mappings and the use of `DataHandler` and `DataSource` types with JAX-RPC.

G.3 Mapping MIME Types to Java

The JAX-RPC specification requires that JAX-RPC providers support the Java-to-MIME type mappings listed in Table G–1.

Table G–1 Required Mappings: Java to MIME

MIME Type	Java Type
image/gif	java.awt.Image
image/jpeg	java.awt.Image
text/plain	java.lang.String
multipart/*	javax.mail.internet.MimeMultipart
text/xml or application/xml	javax.xml.transform.Source

For each of the MIME types listed, the JAX-RPC endpoint stub must be able to convert the specified Java type into a properly encoded stream of data and back again. The JAX-RPC specification requires that the stub accomplish this conversion using the Java Activation Framework (JAF). Under the covers, the endpoint stub will use the Java object to create a new `DataHandler` object, then use the `DataHandler` to construct the MIME attachment part. Listing G–5 provides a rough illustration of how the `SubmitBook` endpoint stub might use JAF to map a method call into an SwA message.

Listing G–5

Inside a JAX-RPC Stub: Mapping Method Calls to SwA Messages

```
public class SubmitBook_Stub implements SubmitBook, javax.xml.rpc.Stub {
  ...
  public void submit(String title, float price, java.awt.Image image)
  throws java.rmi.RemoteException {
    ...
    DataHandler dataHandler = new DataHandler(image, "image/jpeg");

    stream.writeLn(boundryCharacters);
    stream.writeLn("Content-Type: "+dataHandler.getContentType());
    stream.writeLn("Content-Transfer-Encoding: binary");
    stream.writeLn("Content-Id: <submitBook_2@xyxcorp.com>");
    stream.writeLn();
    stream.write(dataHandler.getOutputStream());
    stream.writeLn(boundryCharacters);
    ...
  }
  ...
}
```

The `DataHandler` goes through the normal process of finding the DCH assigned to handle the `image/jpeg` MIME type (usually registered in a `mailcap` file), then uses that DCH to convert the object into a stream of data, which it then embeds into the attachment part of the MIME message. All of the required MIME-to-Java type mappings operate the same way, as will any other type mappings the J2EE vendor chooses to support. It should also be possible to add your own custom DCHs, to support types of attachments that your vendor does not.

The `image/gif` MIME type also maps to the `java.awt.Image` type, and the `text/plain` MIME type maps to `java.lang.String`. These MIME types are as easy to use as `image/jpeg` was in the `SubmitBook` example. The `multipart/*`, `text/xml`, and `application/xml` types are a little more complicated, however, and are discussed in detail in the following sections.

G.3.1 The `multipart/*` MIME Type

The `javax.mail.internet.MimeMultipart` class comes from the JavaMail API; it's used to support an arbitrary set of MIME parts. In other words, when the MIME type of a parameter is `multipart/*` (which means "any collection of MIME types") the JAX-RPC compiler will use `MimeMultipart` to represent the parameter in the endpoint interface. For example, the WSDL document in Listing G–6 includes a MIME binding of `multipart/*`.

Listing G–6

A WSDL Document That Defines a `multipart/*` *MIME Binding*

```
<message name="submission">
  <part name="title" type="xsd:string"/>
  <part name="price" type="xsd:float" />
  <part name="attachments" type="xsd:hexBinary"/>
</message>
<portType name="SubmitBook">
  <operation name="submit">
    <input message="tns:submission"/>
  </operation>
</portType>
<binding name="SubmitBookMimeBinding" type="tns:SubmitBook">
    <soap:binding style="document"
      transport="http://schemas.xmlsoap.org/soap/http"/>
    <operation name="submit">
      <soap:operation soapAction="" style="document"/>
      <input>
         <mime:multipartRelated>
             <mime:part>
                  <soap:body parts="title price" use="literal"
                       namespace=
```

```
                        "http://www.Monson-Haefel.com/ed1/SubmitBook"/>
            </mime:part>
            <mime:part>
                <mime:content part="attachments" type="multipart/*"/>
            </mime:part>
        </mime:multipartRelated>
    </input>
  </operation>
</binding>
```

The endpoint interface generated from this WSDL binding would look like Listing G–7.

Listing G–7

The Endpoint Interface Generated from the WSDL Document in Listing G–6

```
public interface SubmitBook extends java.rmi.Remote {
  public void submit(java.lang.String title, float price,
                     javax.mail.internet.MimeMultipart attachments)
   throws java.rmi.RemoteException;
}
```

Using the JavaMail `MimeMultipart` type is a little involved and will require you to study the `MimeMultipart` class and its friends in more depth than the scope of this book allows, but Listing G–8 should give you a general idea. It shows how you might construct a `MimeMultipart` object from a couple of different sources.

Listing G–8

Creating a `MimeMultipart` *Object*

```
// Create a MIME Part from a Java object
Image image = Toolkit.getDefaultToolkit().createImage("image.jpg");
MimeBodyPart imagePart = new MimeBodyPart();
imagePart.setContent(image,"image/jpeg");

// Create a MIME Part from an InputStream
FileInputStream xmlStream = new FileInputStream("document.xml");
MimeBodyPart pdfPart = new MimeBodyPart(xmlStream);

// Create MimeMultipart
MimeMultipart mimeMultipart = new MimeMultipart();
mimeMultipart.addBodyPart(imagePart);
mimeMultipart.addBodyPart(pdfPart);

sb_stub.submit("J2EE Web Services", 29.99f, mimeMultipart);
```

You can also create a MimeMultipart directly from a DataSource object, as in Listing G–9.

Listing G–9

Creating a MimeMultipart *Directly from a* FileDataSource

```
// Create a MimeMultipart from a DataSource
FileDataSource xmlSource = new FileDataSource("document.xml");
MimeMultipart mimeMultipart = new MimeMultipart(xmlSource);

sb_stub.submit("J2EE Web Services", 24.95f, mimeMultipart);
```

While using MimeMultipart when sending arbitrary attachments could be convenient, I found that JAX-RPC providers support this feature poorly. The JAX-RPC provider must provide a DCH that can convert the MimeMultipart object into one or more attachments, and if this basic functionality is not properly implemented it won't work. It's anticipated that vendors will work the bugs out, but be forewarned that this feature may not be properly supported.

G.3.2 The text/xml and application/xml MIME Types

A JAX-RPC provider may support either text/xml or application/xml MIME types for XML data. Some vendors may choose to support both. The two MIME types are very similar—both apply to XML documents—but they have different audiences. The text/xml type is generally reserved for XML documents that are readable by humans, and can be displayed as plain text. text/xml documents are limited to a simpler character set. The application/xml type is used for XML documents that are exchanged between software applications and are not generally read by humans.[1] Because Web services focus on the exchange of documents between applications, you would expect most JAX-RPC providers to support application/xml rather than text/xml, but in tests I discovered that vendors support either or both MIME types. If your documents use larger character sets like Unicode, you are better off using application/xml; but if you are sticking with the ASCII character set, then text/xml is fine. Consult your vendor's documentation to find out which of these types they support.

A WSDL document declares the XML MIME type just like any other type, as shown in Listing G–10.

[1] Internet Engineering Task Force, *RFC 3023: XML Media Types* (2001). Available at http://www.ietf.org/rfc/rfc3023.txt.

Listing G–10

A WSDL Document That Defines the Two XML MIME Bindings

```
<message name="submission">
  <part name="title" type="xsd:string"/>
  <part name="price" type="xsd:float" />
  <part name="xmlDoc" type="xsd:string"/>
</message>
<portType name="SubmitBook">
  <operation name="submit">
    <input message="tns:submission"/>
  </operation>
</portType>
<binding name="SubmitBookMimeBinding" type="tns:SubmitBook">
    <soap:binding style="document"
      transport="http://schemas.xmlsoap.org/soap/http"/>
    <operation name="submit">
      <soap:operation soapAction="" style="document"/>
      <input>
         <mime:multipartRelated>
             <mime:part>
                 <soap:body parts="title price" use="literal"
                       namespace=
                           "http://www.Monson-Haefel.com/ed1/SubmitBook"/>
             </mime:part>
             <mime:part>
                 <mime:content part="xmlDoc" type="text/xml"/>
                 <mime:content part="xmlDoc" type="application/xml"/>
                 <!-- Multiple MIME types are treated as alternatives -->
             </mime:part>
         </mime:multipartRelated>
      </input>
   </operation>
</binding>
```

When a JAX-RPC provider compiles this WSDL document, it will map the XML MIME type to the `javax.xml.transform.Source` interface, which is part of the Java Transformation API for XML (TrAX). A `Source` type object can represent certain sources of XML data. Listing G–11 shows the endpoint interface that is generated from the WSDL document you've just seen.

Listing G–11

The Endpoint Interface Generated from the WSDL Document in Listing G–10

```
public interface SubmitBook extends java.rmi.Remote {
    public void submit(String title, float price,
                       javax.xml.transform.Source xmlDoc)
    throws java.rmi.RemoteException;
}
```

Using TrAX to transfer XML documents as attachments is pretty easy. You have your choice of standard TrAX `Source` types, including `DOMSource`, `SAXSource`, and `StreamSource`, which you can create from `java.io.File`, `java.io.InputStream`, or `java.io.Reader` type objects.

In Listing G–12, `JaxRpcExample_G2` uses TrAX to read an XML document from a file, then passes it to the `SubmitBook.submit()` method as a `StreamSource` type object, along with the `title` and `price` parameters.

Listing G–12

Using a Generated Stub and XML Attachment

```
package jwsed1.part5_jaxrpc;
import javax.naming.InitialContext;
import javax.xml.transform.stream.StreamSource;
import javax.xml.transform.Source;
import java.io.File;

public class JaxRpcExample_G2 {
  public static void main(String [] args) throws Exception{
    InitialContext jndiContext = new InitialContext();

    SubmitBookService service = (SubmitBookService)
    jndiContext.lookup("java:comp/env/service/SubmitBookService");

    SubmitBook sb_stub = service.getSubmitBookPort();

    Source xmlDoc= new StreamSource(new File("document.xml"));

    sb_stub.submit("J2EE Web Services", 29.99f, xmlDoc);
  }
}
```

G.3.3 MIME Attachments as Return Types, and INOUT and OUT Parameters

The JAX-RPC MIME-to-Java mapping rules apply no matter what the parameter mode (IN, INOUT, or OUT). For example, if the output message specifies a single return value that is a MIME attachment, then that return value will map to one of the MIME types. In Listing G–13, the WSDL fragment declares the output parameter to be a MIME attachment.

Listing G–13

A WSDL Document That Declares a MIME Attachment as a Return Type

```
<message name="fooRequest">
  <part name="param1" type="xsd:string"/>
  <part name="param2" type="xsd:int" />
</message>
<message name="fooResponse">
  <part name="param3" type="xsd:hexBinary" />
</message>
<portType name="FooBar">
  <operation name="foo" >
    <input message="tns:fooRequest"/>
    <output message="tns:fooResponse"/>
  </operation>
</portType>
<binding name="FooBarSoapBinding" type="tns:FooBar">
  <soap:binding style="rpc"
        transport="http://schemas.xmlsoap.org/soap/http"/>
  <operation name="foo">
    <soap:operation soapAction="" style="rpc"/>
    <input>
       <soap:body use="encoded"
                  namespace="http://examples.org/ed1/FooBar"
                  encodingStyle="http://schemas.xmlsoap.org/soap/encoding/"/>
    </input>
    <output>
       <mime:multipartRelated>
           <mime:part>
               <mime:content part="param3" type="image/gif"/>
           </mime:part>
       </mime:multipartRelated>
    </output>
  </operation>
</binding>
```

The endpoint interface generated from this WSDL document is defined in Listing G–14.

Listing G–14

The Endpoint Interface Generated from the WSDL Document in Listing G–13

```
public interface FooBar extends java.rmi.Remote {
  public java.awt.Image foo(String param1, int param2)
   throws java.rmi.RemoteException;
}
```

INOUT and OUT parameters can also be MIME attachments. In such cases the JAX-RPC will generate a `Holder` type that contains the INOUT or OUT attachment parameter. In Listing G–15, the WSDL fragment declares two parameters, a standard IN parameter of type `int` and an INOUT parameter that's a MIME attachment.

Listing G–15

A WSDL Document That Defines a MIME Attachment as an INOUT Parameter

```
<message name="fooRequest">
  <part name="param1" type="xsd:int" />
  <part name="param2" type="xsd:hexBinary" />
</message>
<message name="fooResponse">
  <part name="param2" type="xsd:hexBinary" />
</message>
<portType name="FooBar">
  <operation name="foo" >
    <input message="tns:fooRequest"/>
    <output message="tns:fooResponse"/>
  </operation>
</portType>
<binding name="FooBarSoapBinding" type="tns:FooBar">
  <soap:binding style="rpc"
        transport="http://schemas.xmlsoap.org/soap/http"/>
  <operation name="foo">
    <soap:operation soapAction="" style="rpc"/>
    <input>
       <mime:multipartRelated>
          <mime:part>
            <soap:body parts="param1" use="encoded"
                namespace="http://examples.org/ed1/FooBar"
```

```
                encodingStyle="http://schemas.xmlsoap.org/soap/encoding/"/>
          </mime:part>
          <mime:part>
            <mime:content part="param2" type="image/gif"/>
          </mime:part>
       </mime:multipartRelated>
    </input>
    <output>
       <mime:multipartRelated>
           <mime:part>
               <mime:content part="param2" type="image/gif"/>
           </mime:part>
       </mime:multipartRelated>
    </output>
  </operation>
</binding>
```

The JAX-RPC compiler will map the image/gif attachment to the java.awt.Image type, but because it's an INOUT parameter, it will wrap that Image parameter in an ImageHolder as shown in Listing G–16.

Listing G–16

The Endpoint Interface Generated from the WSDL Document in Listing G–15

```
public interface FooBar extends java.rmi.Remote {
    public void foo(int param1, ImageHolder param2)
        throws java.rmi.RemoteException;
}
```

ImageHolder is not a standard holder type; it's generated by the JAX-RPC compiler. See Section 15.3.4.4: Generated Holder Types for details about how Holder types are generated.

G.4 Using DataHandler and DataSource Types

When the JAX-RPC endpoint converts types like java.awt.Image and javax.transform.Source objects into data streams, it relies on JAF and a set of DCHs that support these types. As I pointed out earlier, under the covers the stub first wraps the object in a javax.activation.DataHandler and then—following the JAF delegation model—converts the object into a data stream. It's also possible to use the DataHandler type as an explicit parameter in a JAX-RPC endpoint method. This approach allows you to handle arbitrary attachments, but more importantly it provides an inroad into using `DataSource` objects, which tend to be more flexible because they don't require the support of preconfigured DCHs.

For example, the WSDL document in Listing G–17 specifies a MIME type of `application/pdf`, which is not generally supported by JAX-RPC providers.

Listing G–17

A WSDL Document That Defines a PDF Attachment

```
<binding name="SubmitBookMimeBinding" type="tns:SubmitBook">
    <soap:binding style="document"
      transport="http://schemas.xmlsoap.org/soap/http"/>
    <operation name="submit">
      <soap:operation soapAction="" style="document"/>
      <input>
        <mime:multipartRelated>
            <mime:part>
                <soap:body parts="title price" use="literal"
                      namespace=
                          "http://www.Monson-Haefel.com/ed1/SubmitBook"/>
            </mime:part>
            <mime:part>
                <mime:content part="pdfDoc" type="application/pdf"/>
            </mime:part>
        </mime:multipartRelated>
      </input>
   </operation>
</binding>
```

You can handle this type of MIME binding with the explicit use of the `DataHandler` class as the attachment parameter, as shown in Listing G–18.

Listing G–18

The Endpoint Interface Generated from the WSDL Document in Listing G–17

```
public interface SubmitBook extends java.rmi.Remote {
    public void submit(java.lang.String title, float price,
                       javax.activation.DataHandler pdfDoc)

      throws java.rmi.RemoteException;
}
```

In this case, you could construct the `DataHandler` from a `DataSource`, as in Listing G–19. Using a `DataSource` with a `DataHandler` parameter type provides enough flexibility to handle a variety of attachments, not just those required by the JAX-RPC specification.

Listing G–19

Using DataSource *and* DataHandler *Objects for Unsupported MIME Types*

```
SubmitBookService ser = new SubmitBookServiceLocator();
SubmitBook port = ser.getSubmitBookPort();

FileDataSource pdfSource = new FileDataSource("document.pdf");
DataHandler handler = new DataHandler(pdfSource);

sb_stub.submit("J2EE Web Services", 24.95f, handler);
```

This approach is convenient, but the DataHandler parameters for arbitrary MIME types may not be supported by all vendors. There is a gap in the specification that doesn't cover how vendors are supposed to handle arbitrary MIME types, so if you use a MIME type that is not supported, the compiler might generate an endpoint with a DataHandler parameter—or it might fail. Consult your documentation to find out which behavior your vendor's JAX-RPC compiler will exhibit.

The best way to help your JAX-RPC compiler in mapping arbitrary MIME types to DataHandler parameters is to use a JAX-RPC mapping file, which is covered in detail in Chapter 24. A mapping file helps a JAX-RPC compiler understand the relationship between endpoint interfaces and WSDL documents, and enables you to deal with unusual mapping situations. The JAX-RPC mapping file is deployed with the Web service client or service (JSE or EJB endpoint), along with other deployment descriptors.

We can use a JAX-RPC mapping file to declare that a parameter of an endpoint method should be manifested as a DataHandler for an arbitrary MIME type. Listing G–20 shows a small part of a JAX-RPC mapping file for the SubmitBook Web service. The explicit mapping of the DataHandler parameter is shown in bold.

Listing G–20

Mapping a DataHandler *Parameter*

```
<?xml version='1.0' encoding='UTF-8' ?>
<java-wsdl-mapping
  ...
  <service-endpoint-method-mapping>
    <java-method-name>submit</java-method-name>
    <wsdl-operation>mh:submit</wsdl-operation>
    ...
    <method-param-parts-mapping>
```

```
        <param-position>2</param-position>
        <param-type>javax.activation.DataHandler</param-type>
        <wsdl-message-mapping>
          <wsdl-message>mh:submission
          </wsdl-message>
          <wsdl-message-part-name>pdfDoc</wsdl-message-part-name>
          <parameter-mode>IN</parameter-mode>
        </wsdl-message-mapping>
      </method-param-parts-mapping>
    </service-endpoint-method-mapping>
  </service-endpoint-interface-mapping>
</java-wsdl-mapping>
```

This snippet represents only about 20 percent of the complete JAX-RPC mapping file, which is far too complex to cover in this section, but it does show clearly that the parameter at position 2 (that is, the third parameter, starting from 0) is the `DataHandler` that maps to the WSDL `part` labeled `pdfDoc`.

G.5 Wrapping Up

JAX-RPC makes SwA very easy, provided your vendor properly supports the minimum MIME type mappings and allows you to add new DCH types. As was the case with SAAJ, depending on JAF for handling attachments is both a blessing and a possible cause for concern. JAF makes the mapping between Java objects and encoded data streams very easy, but it requires that your vendor either support the Java and MIME types with appropriate DCHs, or allow you to use a `DataSource` to marshal data streams into MIME attachments. Vendor support for JAF and SwA in general varies, so be sure to consult your vendor documentation and do a lot of testing before deciding to use JAX-RPC for handling attachments in production. If it works, JAX-RPC can make the handling of attachments easy and your development time productive, but if it doesn't, it can give you some serious headaches.

Appendix H
Using JAX-RPC DII without a WSDL Document

The WS-I Basic Profile 1.0 requires that Web service endpoints make a WSDL document available. When you deal with non-conformant Web services, however, you may not have access to a Web service's WSDL document, in which case neither the generated stub nor dynamic proxy programming models are going to be much good to you. They depend on the availability of a WSDL document—but DII does not. You can use DII to invoke Web service operations without a WSDL document, although you'll need to know details about the operation style, operation names, parameters, and so on. Basically, you have to provide a `Call` object with all the information that is normally specified in the WSDL document. In Listing H–1, `JaxRpcExample_H1` uses DII to invoke the BookQuote Web service without using the `BookQuote.wsdl` document as a guide.

Listing H–1

Using DII without a WSDL Document

```
package com.jwsbook.jaxrpc;
import javax.naming.InitialContext;
import javax.xml.rpc.Service;
import javax.xml.rpc.Call;
import javax.xml.rpc.ParameterMode;
import javax.xml.rpc.NamespaceConstants;
import javax.xml.rpc.encoding.XMLType;
import javax.xml.namespace.QName;
```

```
public class JaxRpcExample_H1 {
  public static void main(String [] args) throws Exception{
    String isbn = args[0];

    InitialContext jndiContext = new InitialContext();
    javax.xml.rpc.Service service = (javax.xml.rpc.Service)
         jndiContext.lookup("java:comp/env/service/Service");

    Call call = service.createCall();

    QName operationName =
     new QName("http://www.Monson-Haefel.com/jwsbook/BookQuote",
              "getBookPrice");
    call.setOperationName( operationName );

    call.addParameter("isbn", XMLType.XSD_STRING, ParameterMode.IN);

    call.setProperty(Call.OPERATION_STYLE_PROPERTY, "rpc");
    call.setProperty(Call.ENCODINGSTYLE_URI_PROPERTY,"");

    call.setReturnType( XMLType.XSD_FLOAT);

    call.setTargetEndpointAddress
        ("http://www.Monson-Haefel.com/jwsbook/BookQuote");

    Object [] inputParams = new Object[]{isbn};
    Float price = (Float)call.invoke(inputParams);

    System.out.println("The price is = "+price.floatValue());
  }
}
```

Actually, among JAX-RPC implementations there is varying range of assumed values for DII calls when there is no WSDL document. For example, the JAX-RPC reference implementation provided by Sun Microsystems requires that you explicitly set the encoding style property and the return value type, while Apache Axis does not. If you fail to set the encoding style property in Axis, it assumes SOAP 1.1 RPC/Encoded. Axis can also figure out the return type automatically if the reply SOAP message specifies the `type` attribute and uses one of the XML schema built-in types, such as `xsd:float`. Without testing, you won't know which properties and attributes a JAX-RPC implementation requires and which ones it can figure out for itself. For this reason, it's a good idea to specify all the properties and attributes you know, as JaxRpcExample_H1 does in Listing H–1, so that your DII code will be portable accross implementations.

The rest of this appendix walks through JaxRpcExample_H1 to explain the DII API calls in detail.

The first step to using DII in the absence of a WSDL document is to create a Call object using the no-argument version of the Service.createCall() method.

```
InitialContext jndiContext = new InitialContext();
javax.xml.rpc.Service service = (javax.xml.rpc.Service)
   jndiContext.lookup("java:comp/env/service/Service");
Call call = service.createCall();
```

Once we have the Call object (a blank slate at this point), we have to configure it to enable the JAX-RPC runtime to construct a SOAP message and send it to a Web service endpoint. The next few lines of code in JaxRpcExample_H1 set the operation name on the Call object.

```
Call call = service.createCall();
QName operationName =
 new QName("http://www.Monson-Haefel.com/jwsbook/BookQuote",
           "getBookPrice");
call.setOperationName( operationName );
```

Recall that the QName type represents an XML qualified name, with an XML namespace and a local name. By setting the operation name, we have given the Call object the information it needs to construct a SOAP message with a Body, and the immediate child element of the Body to identify the operation being invoked. For example, without further configuring the Call object, it would be capable of generating a SOAP message like the following:

```
<soap:Envelope
 xmlns:env="http://schemas.xmlsoap.org/soap/envelope/"
 xmlns:mh="http://www.Monson-Haefel.com/1ed/BookQuote" >
   <soap:Body>
      <mh:getBookPrice>

      </mh:getBookPrice>
   </soap:Body>
</soap:Envelope>
```

After identifying the operation name, JaxRpcExample_H1 identifies the parameter of the call. Obviously, this assumes that the message has parameters. In other words, the basic assumption is that we are using an RPC operation style.

```
call.setOperationName( operationName );
call.addParameter("isbn", XMLType.XSD_STRING, ParameterMode.IN);
```

There are two versions of the `addParameter()` method. The one used here takes three arguments: the name of the parameter, its type, and whether it's an IN, OUT, or INOUT parameter. The `ParameterMode` type has one purpose, to specify the mode of the parameter used in `Call.addParameter()`. The `getBookPrice` operation has only one parameter, `isbn`, an IN parameter of type `xsd:string`. The other `addParameter()` method includes a Java `Class` parameter that represents the Java type to which the XML schema type is mapped. Once the `addParameter()` method is invoked, the `Call` object knows the contents of the `operation` element in the SOAP message. It can now generate a SOAP message that looks something like the following:

```
<?xml version="1.0" encoding="UTF-8"?>
<soap:Envelope
 xmlns:soap="http://schemas.xmlsoap.org/soap/envelope/"
 xmlns:mh="http://www.Monson-Haefel.com/jwsbook/BookQuote">
   <soap:Body>
      <mh:getBookPrice>
          <isbn></isbn>
      </mh:getBookPrice>
   </soap:Body>
</soap:Envelope>
```

Most JAX-RPC implementations don't require you to set the parameters. They can use reflection to figure out the parameters when the `Call.invoke()` method is executed, because the `invoke()` method takes an array of argument values, and each argument has a class that can be identified using the `Object.getClass()` method. Provided that the argument types are primitives, primitive wrappers, or `Strings`, it's fairly easy for the `Call` object to figure out the parameter type.

There is a danger to doing so, however. Although the `Call` object can figure out the parameter type by reflection, it cannot figure out the name of the parameter element, so it uses an arbitrary name. Each JAX-RPC implementation uses its own convention for naming unspecified parameters. For example, Apache Axis uses a naming scheme of `arg0`, `arg1`, ... `argN`. If you use the `Call` object without specifying the names and types of parameters (and there is no WSDL document), Apache Axis will construct a SOAP message like the following.

```
<soapsoap:Envelope
 xmlns:soapenv="http://schemas.xmlsoap.org/soap/envelope/"
 xmlns:xsd="http://www.w3.org/2001/XMLSchema"
 xmlns:xsi="http://www.w3.org/2001/XMLSchema-instance">
  <soapsoap:Body>
```

```
    <ns1:getBookQuote
     xmlns:ns1="http://www.Monson-Haefel.com/jwsbook/BookQuote">
       <arg0></arg0>
    </ns1:getBookQuote>
  </soapsoap:Body>
</soapsoap:Envelope>
```

Unfortunately, not all Web services tolerate arbitrary names for parameters. In fact, the WS-I Basic Profile 1.0 requires that parameter names match, exactly, the names specified in a WSDL document. Of course, we are already assuming the absence of a WSDL document, which is non-conformant anyway. To minimize problems it's a good idea to use the `Call.addParameter()` method to set the parameter information even if the JAX-RPC implementation can figure out the parameter type automatically.

The next couple of lines from `JaxRpcExample_H1` set the operation style and encoding style used. According to the specification, both of these properties are optional. In other words a J2EE vendor is not required to support them. In reality, most JAX-RPC implementations will support these properties. They aren't always necessary, but in the interest of portability you should assume that all properties must be explicitly set.

```
call.addParameter("isbn", XMLType.XSD_STRING, ParameterMode.IN);
call.setProperty(Call.OPERATION_STYLE_PROPERTY, "rpc");
call.setProperty(Call.ENCODINGSTYLE_URI_PROPERTY,"");
```

Both of the invocations of `setProperty()` use standard constant values defined in the JAX-RPC API. Constants are defined in the `Call` interface, the `javax.xml.rpc.NamespaceConstants` class, and the `javax.xml.rpc.encoding.XMLType` class. A description of the constants is provided in Section 12.3.4: JAX-RPC Standard Properties and Constants. You do not have to use the constants defined by JAX-RPC, but they are convenient and help ensure that typos don't introduce bugs.

The only thing that is missing from the BookQuote SOAP request now is the actual value of the `isbn` element. This will be provided when the `Call.invoke()` method is executed. Before we can call that method, however, we need to set the return value's type and the Internet address of the Web service, without which the `Call` object will not know where to send the SOAP request, or how to process the response. The following line from `JaxRpcExample_H1` shows how to configure the return type.

```
call.setReturnType( XMLType.XSD_FLOAT );
```

Setting the return type lets the `Call` object know the type of value the SOAP reply message is expected to return. If a SOAP message also has OUT or INOUT parameters, these will be set using the `addParameter()` method discussed earlier. In this case there is only a return value of type xsd:float, which represents the wholesale price of the book. The SOAP reply message will look something like this:

```
<?xml version="1.0" encoding="UTF-8"?>
<soap:Envelope
 xmlns:soap="http://schemas.xmlsoap.org/soap/envelope/"
 xmlns:mh="http://www.Monson-Haefel.com/jwsbook/BookQuote">
   <soap:Body>
      <mh:getBookPrice>
          <result>29.99</result>
      </mh:getBookPrice>
   </soap:Body>
</soap:Envelope>
```

The Call object must make some assumptions to process the SOAP reply message. It assumes that the reply message uses the same operation and encoding style as the request, in this case RPC/Literal. It also assumes that the Body element will contain a structure that is appropriate for the messaging style. It doesn't need to know the names of these elements, because the structure is the same no matter what their names. In this case the operation element is getBookPriceResponse and the result element is result—but these elements could have any names as long as the structure is the same.

For the Call object to know where to send the SOAP message, you must set the Internet address of the Web service. When there is no WSDL document, you do so using the Call.setTargetEndpointAddress() method, as shown in the following snippet from JaxRpcExample_H1.

```
call.setReturnType( XMLType.XSD_FLOAT);
call.setTargetEndpointAddress(
    "http://www.Monson-Haefel.com/jwsbook/BookQuote");
```

Finally, the Call.invoke() method can be called. The invoke() method used in JaxRpcExample_H1 declares a single argument, an array of objects. Each element in the array is a parameter for the call. If you have used the Call.addParameter() methods, then you must include a value for each parameter that you set—you can use a null value for any parameter whose type allows it. If you have not called any add Parameter() methods, then it's still possible to pass it an array of values. I already mentioned that some JAX-RPC implementations use reflection and generate parameters with arbitrary names—a nice feature, but it can be problematic when the receiving Web service doesn't support arbitrary names. In JaxRpcExample_H1 there is only one parameter, isbn, which is placed in an Object array that is used in the invoke() method:

```
call.setTargetEndpointAddress(
     "http://www.Monson-Haefel.com/jwsbook/BookQuote");
Object [] inputParams = new Object[]{isbn};
Float price = (Float)call.invoke(inputParams);
```

The `invoke()` method returns a `Float` value, as this was the return type set earlier in the program. If the return type in the SOAP reply message is not `xsd:float`, a `JAXRPCException` will be thrown.

Bibliography

Web Services Specifications

Web Services Interoperability Organization:

Basic Profile 1.0a, Final Specification, August 8, 2003. http://www.ws-i.org/Profiles/Basic/2003-08/BasicProfile-1.0a.htm.

XML

World Wide Web Consortium:

Extensible Markup Language (XML) 1.0 (Second Edition), W3C Recommendation, October 6, 2000. http://www.w3.org/TR/REC-xml.

Namespaces in XML, W3C Recommendation, 1999. http://www.w3.org/TR/REC-xml-names/.

XML Schema Part 0: Primer, W3C Recommendation, May 2, 2001. http://www.w3.org/TR/xmlschema-0/.

XML Schema Part 1: Structures, W3C Recommendation, May 2, 2001. http://www.w3.org/TR/xmlschema-1/.

XML Schema Part 2: Datatypes, W3C Recommendation, May 2, 2001. http://www.w3.org/TR/xmlschema-2/.

XPointer xpointer() Scheme, Working Draft, December 19, 2002. http://www.w3.org/TR/xptr-xpointer/.

SOAP

World Wide Web Consortium:

Simple Object Access Protocol (SOAP) 1.1, W3C Note, May 8, 2000. http://www.w3.org/TR/SOAP/.

SOAP Messages with Attachments, W3C Note, December 11, 2000. http://www.w3.org/TR/SOAP-attachments.

SOAP Security Extensions: Digital Signature, W3C Note, February 2001. http://www.w3.org/TR/SOAP-dsig/.

WSDL

World Wide Web Consortium:

Web Services Description Language (WSDL) 1.1, W3C Note, March 15, 2001. http://www.w3.org/TR/wsdl/.

UDDI

Organization for the Advancement of Structured Information Standards:

Providing a Taxonomy for Use in UDDI version 2, 2002. http://www.oasis-open.org/committees/uddi-spec/doc/tn/uddi-spec-tc-tn-taxonomy-provider-v100-20010716.htm.

UDDI Version 2.04 API Specification, 2002. http://uddi.org/pubs/ProgrammersAPI-V2.04-Published-20020719.htm.

UDDI.org:

UDDI Core tModels: Taxonomy and Identifier Systems, 2001. http://www.uddi.org/taxonomies/Core_Taxonomy_OverviewDoc.htm.

J2EE 1.4 Specifications

Sun Microsystems, Inc.:

Enterprise JavaBeans, version 2.1, Proposed Final Draft 2, June 26, 2003. http://www.jcp.org/en/jsr/detail?id=153.

Java 2 Platform, Enterprise Edition, version 1.4, Proposed Final Draft 3, April 15, 2003.
http://www.jcp.org/en/jsr/detail?id=151.

Java Servlet, version 2.4, Proposed Final Draft 3, April 17, 2003.
http://www.jcp.org/en/jsr/detail?id=154.

Web Services

Sun Microsystems, Inc.:

Implementing Enterprise Web Services, version 1.1, Maintenance Draft Review 2, May 19, 2003.
http://www.jcp.org/en/jsr/detail?id=921.

Java API for XML-Based RPC, version 1.1, Maintenance Draft Review, April 21, 2003.
http://www.jcp.org/en/jsr/detail?id=101.

Java API for XML Processing, version 1.2, Final Release 2, September 10, 2002.
http://www.jcp.org/en/jsr/detail?id=63.

Java API for XML Registries, version 1.0, June 11, 2002.
http://www.jcp.org/en/jsr/detail?id=93.

SOAP with Attachments API for Java, version 1.2, Maintenance Draft Review, April 21, 2003.
http://www.jcp.org/en/jsr/detail?id=67

Miscellaneous Specifications

Institute of Electrical and Electronics Engineers:

IEEE Standard for Binary Floating-Point Arithmetic, 1990.
http://standards.ieee.org/reading/ieee/std_public/description/busarch/754-1985_desc.html.

ISO 639: Codes for the Representation of Names of Languages—Part 1: Alpha-2 code.
http://www.w3.org/WAI/ER/IG/ert/iso639.htm.

Internet Engineering Task Force:

RFC 1766: Tags for the Identification of Languages, 1994.
http://www.ietf.org/rfc/rfc1766.txt.

RFC 2045: Multipurpose Internet Mail Extensions (MIME) Part One: Format of Internet Message Bodies, 1996.
http://www.ietf.org/rfc/rfc2045.txt.

RFC 2459: Internet X.509 Public Key Infrastructure Certificate and CRL Profile, 1999.
http://www.ietf.org/rfc/rfc2459.txt.

Books

Chappell, David A., *Understanding .NET: A Tutorial and Analysis*. Boston: Addison-Wesley, 2002.

Harold, Elliotte Rusty, *Processing XML with Java™: A Guide to SAX, DOM, JDOM, JAXP, and TrAX*. Boston: Addison-Wesley, 2003.

Manes, Anne Thomas, *Web Services: A Manager's Guide*. Boston: Addison-Wesley, 2003.

Monson-Haefel, Richard, *Enterprise JavaBeans, 4th Edition*. Cambridge, MA: O'Reilly & Associates, 2004.

Credits

Reproductions of woodblock prints by Katsushika Hokusai (1760–1849) courtesy of The Minneapolis Institute of Arts, Bequest of Richard P. Gale.

Part I, page 15
Mishima Pass in Kai Province, c. 1829–1833

Part II, page 79
Under the Wave off Kanagawa, c. 1829–1833

Part III, page 163
Reflection in Lake Misaka, Kai Province, c. 1829–1833

Part IV, page 271
Umezawa Manor in Sagami Province, c. 1829–1833

Part V, page 475
Waterwheel at Onden, c. 1829–1833

Part VI, page 603
Shichiri-ga-hama in Suruga Province, c. 1829–1833

Part VII, page 653
Hakone Lake in Sagami Province, c. 1829–1833

Appendices, page 737
Enoshima in Sagami Province, c. 1829–1833

Index

B

C

D

G

H

I

J

K

L

N

O

P

Q

R

T

U

V

W

X

Z